Retail Management

BONWIT TELL

Woolworth

John Wanamaker

Jewel
Food Stores

MONTGOMERY

WARD

GIMBELS

JCPenney

Neiman-Marcus

Stouffer's

PET PAC

BF Goodrich

STE

Walgreens

Sea

Retail Management

Satisfaction of Consumer Needs
Second Edition

Raymond A. Marquardt/University of Wyoming

James C. Makens/University of Hawaii

Robert G. Roe/University of Wyoming

The Dryden Press/Hinsdale, Illinois

To our wives Alberta, Kay, and Suzanne
for their patience, understanding, and inspiration

The Dryden Press
Series in Marketing

Blackwell, Engel and Talarzyk
Contemporary Cases in Consumer Behavior

Block and Roering
Essentials of Consumer Behavior
Second Edition

Boone and Kurtz
Contemporary Marketing
Second Edition

Boone and Kurtz
Foundations of Marketing

Churchill
Marketing Research:
Methodological Foundations
Second Edition

Dunn and Barban
Advertising:
Its Role in Modern Marketing
Fourth Edition

Engel, Kollat and Blackwell
Cases in Consumer Behavior

Green
Analyzing Multivariate Data

Green and Rao
Applied Multidimensional Scaling:
A Comparison of
Approaches and Algorithms

Green and Wind
Multiattribute Decisions in Marketing:
A Measurement Approach

Johnson, House and McDaniel
Readings in Contemporary Marketing
Second Edition

Kollat, Blackwell and Robeson
Strategic Marketing

Kotler
Marketing Decision Making:
A Model Building Approach

Marquardt, Makens and Roe
Retail Management:
Satisfaction of Consumer Needs
Second Edition

Nicosia and Wind
Behavioral Models for Market Analysis:
Foundations for Marketing Action

Rosenbloom
Marketing Channels: A Management View

Scheuing
New Product Management

Schultz, Zaltman and Burger
Cases in Marketing Research

Talarzyk
Cases for Analysis in Marketing

Talarzyk
Contemporary Cases in Marketing
Second Edition

Terpstra
International Marketing
Second Edition

Young and Mondy
Personal Selling:
Function, Theory and Practice

Zaltman and Burger
Marketing Research:
Fundamentals and Dynamics

Zaltman, Pinson and Angelmar
Methatheory and Consumer Research

Preface

Retailing, as used in this book, refers to all business activities concerned with selling goods and services directly to ultimate consumers. The definition includes all forms of direct selling: direct-to-consumer sales made through store outlets, by house-to-house canvass, or by mail order, and the selling of services as well as goods. This last inclusion broadens the definition of retailing in an important sense, as the annual growth in consumer demand for services is expanding faster than the demand for many merchandise items.

A retailer cannot be limited by a narrow definition of a business. The firm's very existence depends upon its ability to satisfy consumer wants. This cannot always be accomplished if a retailer retains the traditional product-service offering. The rising level of competition offered by other retailers, increasing disposable personal income, increased consumer mobility, and the psychological need of consumers for individualized, personal service have made it imperative that retailers truly satisfy consumers' needs even to remain in the retailing business.

Clearly, the retailer must first determine what the consumer wants. Then the firm can use all the elements in the marketing mix (such as price, promotion, service, merchandise selection, and location) to satisfy these consumer needs. This is not an easy task. Retailers must use a great deal of ingenuity and creativity to meet the ever-changing needs of consumers.

Any change in merchandise selection, prices, promotion, location, or service involves the consideration of many alternatives. To further complicate matters, a change in any one element may affect all the other elements the retailer uses to sell merchandise. For example, changing from a high-price policy to a low-price policy will also affect the quality of merchandise carried, the merchandise assortment carried, the level of service provided, and the type of promotion used. Although a retailer may not be able to investigate every interrelationship in detail, management must be able to determine which interactions are significant and then investigate the consequences of these interactions.

This book discusses the continual process of choice in retailing. It provides the reader with more than a descriptive view of retailing by using marketing analysis to obtain the *why* and *how,* in addition to the *what,* of retailing. The retail manager is the decision maker who determines goals and objectives, defines problems needing attention, and generates and evaluates alternative courses of action. This view of the retailer should provide the reader with a broad, sound understanding of retailing fundamentals. Emphasis is placed on the development of a process to be used to think through and solve retail problems.

Retailing is influenced by many external factors besides consumer preferences. Our legal system prevents the retailer from having complete control over most of the elements of the marketing mix. Increased governmental regulation over pricing, advertising, and mergers illustrates a trend toward restrictions on retailers. This book examines some of the important current legislation that influences retailing, since in some areas restrictions may become so involved that firms can spend most of their time and effort in complying with the law. The area of business law may well become a functional, as well as theoretical, part of the firm's activities.

Audience

This book is written for several types of prospective readers. The person who investigates retailing because of vocational interest in it will find a comprehensive treatment of the fundamental retailing principles. The more casual reader, looking at the book to see what goes on in a retail store, will find a discussion of the actions that take place in the entire retailing system. Such readers will find that economic, social, and legal environments affect retailing greatly.

Some of the newer retail concepts derived from the fields of marketing, finance, economics, statistics, and the behavioral sciences have been integrated with the retailing basics. This has been done so that the reader benefits by the exposure to new ideas. Thus, the book contains material that will be useful to persons presently engaged in retailing and to those who will later begin retailing careers.

Organization

This book proceeds from the general to the specific. The general retailing environment is discussed in the first three chapters, which provide the foundation for retail decision making. They also emphasize the fact that retailing depends for its existence on consumers, who are influenced in their buying decisions by many factors. Chapter 1 presents an overview of the retail environment, including current retailing trends and some of the alternatives available to would-be retailers. Contributions that the fields of consumer behavior, management, and marketing make to retailing are discussed in Chapters 2 and 3.

Part 2 consists of four chapters that identify the retailing opportunities available through the use of proper procedures in product planning (Chapter 4), store location (Chapters 5 and 6), and store layout (Chapter 7). These three procedures require careful planning before the outlet is opened because they involve fairly long-term commitments. The merchandise assortment is probably determined first because it is usually dependent upon specialized managerial skills or particular market demands.

The most appropriate store location may then be selected so that the business will be assured a sufficient market volume to profitably support a retail outlet of the selected type. This is a critical and complex process. Store layout can next be determined so that it will provide physical and psychological support for the selected product line and the site.

Operation policies, practices, and controls are discussed in the four chapters of Part 3. Merchandise buying and handling and physical distribution decisions are presented in Chapter 8. Merchandise management is discussed in Chapter 9. Pricing is the subject of Chapter 10. Other topics included in this section are management of human resources (Chapter 11) and financial control (Chapter 12). This section deals with the organization of the work that will accomplish the firm's objectives. Successful store operation requires that a large number of tasks be performed by the store's personnel, who use their skills, and the firm's equipment and labor-saving techniques to reach the business's goals. Financial control is complex. It involves seeing that the performance of the firm conforms to the company plans, establishing desired standards of financial performance, providing for periodic information on whether the plan is being carried out, and taking appropriate action to bring ineffective activities back in line with the plan.

Part 4 contains a discussion of sales stimulation policies, such as advertising strategy (Chapter 13), promotion (Chapter 14), and personal selling and customer services (Chapter 15). Policies are required in these areas as they identify basic courses of action to guide the successful business. If the retailer fails to develop policies, the business manager is likely to become so occupied with routine operating details that major decisions are given insufficient consideration. Poor management, especially in the planning area, is a prime cause of business failure.

Part 5 consists of a one-chapter presentation of some of the peculiarities that retail service firms incur in their effort to serve customer needs at a profit.

The concluding two chapters are concerned with planning for the future and evaluating the effectiveness of the retailer's current activities. Chapter 17 contains a discussion of the planning and research efforts needed to prepare for changes that seem likely to occur the future. Chapter 18 attempts to pull all the concepts together in the form of a retailing audit. This chapter considers the retailing audit as something separate from and more comprehensive than other control efforts. This chapter provides an opportunity to review the major concepts in effective contemporary retailing that the book presents.

Each chapter begins with several learning goals and a list of key terms and concepts, and each chapter concludes with a summary and several short cases. The cases are designed to illustrate the principles developed in the chapter. A glossary of the more important terms in retailing is presented at the end of the book in Appendix A.

A great deal of change has occurred in the past few years, and we have attempted to reflect these changes in this second edition. Thus, the coverage in all of the chapters and the organization of the book have been altered somewhat to incorporate recent changes in the industry.

Acknowledgments

It is impossible to enumerate all the persons who contributed to the preparation of the book. Especially helpful criticisms and comments were made by Professor Henry Wichmann of the University of Wyoming, Steve Despain of Joy & Garaman, Inc., Patricia Penney and Kathy Turner of May D & F, Jay Seiner of Miller Stockman, Marl Shanahan of King Soopers Discount, and Professors Michael F. D'Amico of the University of Akron, Michael Farley of Del Mar College, John W. Lloyd of Monroe Community College, Suzanne McWhorter of North Texas State University, Will Moon of Lane Community College, Millard Pace of the University of Evansville, Carl J. Sonntag of Pikes Peak Community College, and Ray Tewell of American River College.

We are also very much indebted for the exceptional typing and organizational assistance of Lucille Roehrkasse.

Finally, we take pleasure in thanking our wives—Alberta, Kay, and Suzanne—for patience and assistance under sometimes chaotic conditions.

To all these people we are deeply grateful. Responsibility for any errors or omissions is certainly ours, but the book would not have been possible without the help of these people.

r.a.m.
j.c.m.
r.g.r.

Contents

Chapter 3   Understanding the Consumer   59

Part Two   Retailing Opportunities

Chapter 4   The Product and Product Planning   88

Chapter 5   Store Location Considerations   121

The Retail Audit   572   Chapter 18

Retail Management

Part One

General Retailing Environment

Chapter 1

An Overview of the Retail Environment

Learning Goals

1. To be aware of the size and significant characteristics of our nation's population.

2. To learn what functions retailing plays in an economic system.

3. To know how population demographics can be used to define a market and how retailers use the data to identify retail opportunities.

4. To understand the present state of retailing.

5. To be able to discuss how projected trends will affect specific segments of the retail industry.

Key Terms and Concepts

retailing	marketing functions	wheel of retailing concept
demographic characteristics	marketing specialists	accordion theory
life cycle	retail classification systems	retail life cycle

Chapter 1 examines the role that retailing plays in the American economic system. Specifically, the demographic characteristics of the American consumer will be presented in order to sketch the dimensions of the total aggregate retail demand. The present retail network will be examined as a part of the total marketing-distribution system. Significant retail institutions will be identified. The role each plays in retailing as well as current and future challenges to the industry will be assessed.

An Overview of the Retail Environment

Fundamental Considerations

Retailing, in our interdependent society, determines your daily survival. Each person has certain daily minimum requirements for food, shelter, and clothing. Additionally, other "necessities" must be provided if that person is to be productive. These fundamental facts are vividly brought to light during a natural or economic disaster. During the last decade, many individuals have taken action to decrease their dependence on "the system" and have returned to a rural setting to become more self-sufficient. However, their experience has shown that individuals are incapable of complete self-sufficiency and therefore must partly depend on others for certain goods and services.

The extraction or growth of raw materials and commodities, the orderly transformation of these commodities into useful goods and services, and the distribution of these need-satisfying elements to individuals must be accomplished in any society.

Definition of Retailing

Each nation has its own unique way of performing the vital functions of production and distribution of need-satisfying goods. In the United States the economic needs of the nation are met by a capitalistic system strongly influenced by government. Regardless of the philosophical orientation of the economic system, some institution must systematically act as the final bridge in the production-consumption system in order to have the right goods or services at the right place, when they are needed, in the appropriate quantity, quality, and assortment, and at an affordable price to meet the needs of the people.

Within this context, *retailing* may be defined as all of those activities performed by merchants in order to offer goods and services for sale to the ultimate consumer. Any goods purchased for incorporation into other goods and services or to be consumed by governmental agencies are considered wholesale sales. For example, if Ford Motor Company purchases Motorola car radios to be installed in vehicles as factory options, the price of that radio is included in the final retail price charged by the local Ford dealership. The original purchase would be considered by Motorola as a wholesale transaction with the Ford Motor Company. Conversely, if the local Ford dealership sells the same type of radio over the parts counter to an ultimate consumer, the transaction would be a retail sale.

This distinction between retail and wholesale transactions is vitally important for two reasons: (1) retail sales are subject to state sales and federal excise tax collections and (2) federal antimonopoly laws restrict wholesalers in their ability to give arbitrary discounts to retailers on goods for resale. This latter restriction becomes critical when a single firm acts as both a retailer and a wholesaler.

To illustrate this distinction, if an automobile parts house sells to both professional mechanics and "do-it-yourselfers," it must record the mechanics' purchases as wholesale sales for future Federal Trade Commission audits. The consumer purchases are recorded as retail sales on which state sales taxes are collected.

The retailing institution encompasses many different forms. The traditional distinctions usually begin with store and nonstore presentations. The store category can be further fragmented into stores offering products, those offering services, and those outlets combining both goods and services. Nonstore retailers include direct-to-consumer sales, house-to-house solicitation, mail order sales, and vending machine sales. Each retail presentation has its own unique approach to meeting the needs and wants of society's members.

Consumer Characteristics

In order to gain some appreciation and understanding of the enormity of the challenge that the retailing industry is daily called upon to meet, it is necessary to examine the total retail market in the United States.

Population data stating how many persons there are in a given place of a certain age, sex, or race are referred to as *demographic characteristics*. Additionally, such personal attributes as single, married, or divorced and employed or unemployed are included to give an aggregate view of the nation's human resource.

The concept of the human life cycle is vital to the understanding of consumer behavior. The term *life cycle* refers to identifiable stages through which an organism or organization goes from conception to demise. Human life cycles include birth-childhood, the teens, young adulthood, middle age, old age, and death. The same concept has been adapted to describe the product life cycle and retail store life cycle. The basic concept will be used throughout the book and forms a main thread of continuity for the discussion.

In the next few pages the text will sketch out the general portrait of the American population. Keep in mind that as each demographic characteristic is presented, an additional piece of information is available to define the market. The process will be similar to an artist creating a mosaic tile mural. If one stands very close to the wall, only bits of colored tile and mortar seams will be seen. The image is unclear, the picture is incomplete. However, if one steps back across the room, the entire mural comes into focus and the little colored chips blend into a complete segment of the greater design. Viewed individually the following data may present an incomplete picture, but by the end of the discussion the retail market picture will become more clear.

Population

As of June, 1976, 214.5 million persons were considered residents of the United States. Depending on the assumptions one accepts from the demographers, the population will continue to grow and reach the level of 245 to 287 million persons by the year 2000.[1] (Table 1–1)

Table 1–1 **United States Population Projections to 2050**

Year	Series I	Series II	Series III	Series II-X
1974	212	212	212	212
1980	226	223	220	220
1985	241	234	228	229
1990	258	245	236	237
1995	273	254	241	244
2000	287	262	245	249
2010	322	279	250	259
2020	362	294	252	267
2030	403	304	247	270
2040	449	312	238	271
2050	499	318	227	270

Includes Armed Forces abroad.

Source: U.S. Department of Commerce, Bureau of the Census, *Pocket Data Book, USA 1976* (Washington, D.C.: Government Printing Office, 1976), p. 41.

Note: Projections were prepared using the cohort-component method. Series I, II, and III assume slight improvement in mortality, annual net immigration of 400,000, and completed cohort fertility rates (average number of lifetime births per woman) that move toward the following levels: I—2.7, II—2.1, III—1.7. Series II and II-X assume the fertility will equal the "replacement rate."

Geographical Dispersion

The resident population is concentrated in the northeast and north central parts of the country. These combined areas contain about 50.3 percent of the total population.[2] However, the most populated state is California, with an estimated 21.2 million persons (Figure 1–1).[3] This is consistent with the general trend in population migration to the South and Southwest. Between 1970 and 1975 Florida and Arizona respectively experienced population increases of 23 and 25 percent. (Figure 1–1).[4] In the near future the energy- and resource-rich states of Colorado, Montana, and Wyoming are expected to experience significant population increases.

A significant portion of the population is leaving the central cities and moving to the suburbs and rural areas (Table 1–2).[5] Such migrations not only transfer absolute consumer needs to new locations, but also may cause significant shifts in the types of goods and services that are desired. Former central city apartment dwellers who purchase a new house in a suburban development might need a lawn mower and related lawn supplies for the first time. Conversely, if the now-vacant apartment is not rented by a person moving into the central city area, or if other people are not attracted to shop in the central business district (CBD), its retail opportunities are

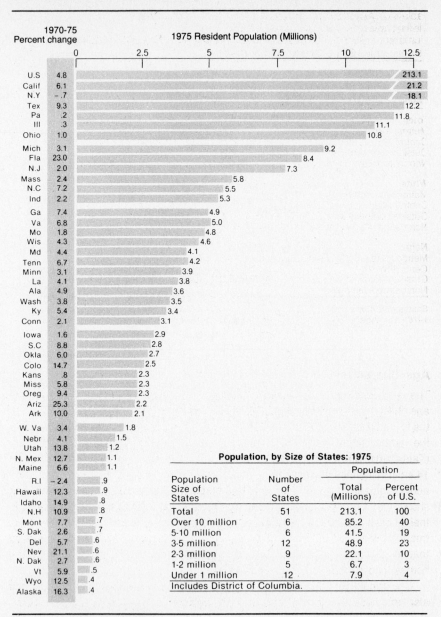

	1970-75 Percent change	1975 Resident Population (Millions)
U.S	4.8	213.1
Calif	6.1	21.2
N.Y	-.7	18.1
Tex	9.3	12.2
Pa	.2	11.8
Ill	.3	11.1
Ohio	1.0	10.8
Mich	3.1	9.2
Fla	23.0	8.4
N.J	2.0	7.3
Mass	2.4	5.8
N.C	7.2	5.5
Ind	2.2	5.3
Ga	7.4	4.9
Va	6.8	5.0
Mo	1.8	4.8
Wis	4.3	4.6
Md	4.4	4.1
Tenn	6.7	4.2
Minn	3.1	3.9
La	4.1	3.8
Ala	4.9	3.6
Wash	3.8	3.5
Ky	5.4	3.4
Conn	2.1	3.1
Iowa	1.6	2.9
S.C	8.8	2.8
Okla	6.0	2.7
Colo	14.7	2.5
Kans	.8	2.3
Miss	5.8	2.3
Oreg	9.4	2.3
Ariz	25.3	2.2
Ark	10.0	2.1
W. Va	3.4	1.8
Nebr	4.1	1.5
Utah	13.8	1.2
N. Mex	12.7	1.1
Maine	6.6	1.1
R.I	-2.4	.9
Hawaii	12.3	.9
Idaho	14.9	.8
N.H	10.9	.8
Mont	7.7	.7
S. Dak	2.6	.7
Del	5.7	.6
Nev	21.1	.6
N. Dak	2.7	.6
Vt	5.9	.5
Wyo	12.5	.4
Alaska	16.3	.4

Population, by Size of States: 1975

Population Size of States	Number of States	Population	
		Total (Millions)	Percent of U.S.
Total	51	213.1	100
Over 10 million	6	85.2	40
5-10 million	6	41.5	19
3-5 million	12	48.9	23
2-3 million	9	22.1	10
1-2 million	5	6.7	3
Under 1 million	12	7.9	4
Includes District of Columbia.			

Figure 1-1 **State Population**

Source: U.S. Department of Commerce, Bureau of the Census, *Pocket Data Book, USA 1976* (Washington, D.C.: Government Printing Office, 1976), p. 45.

diminished. CBDs everywhere are suffering the effects of fewer tax-paying residents, reduced tax bases, and increasing demands for public services. Realizing that active profitable retailing activities generate badly needed revenue, some cities, such as Boston, have had some success luring stores back by rebuilding downtown shopping malls and encouraging high-rise condominium construction.

Table 1–2 **Population, Standard
Metropolitan Statistical Areas (SMSA)**
Number in millions. Noninstitutional population; as of April. 243 SMSA's
as defined in 1970 Census publications.

| | Population | | | | Percent Change 1970-75 |
| | 1970 | | 1975 | | |
Residence and race	Total	Percent	Total	Percent	
Total	200	100.0	210	100.0	5.0
Metropolitan areas	137	68.6	143	68.0	4.1
Central cities	63	31.5	61	29.2	−2.7
Outside central cities	74	37.1	82	38.9	10.0
Nonmetropolitan areas	63	31.4	67	32.0	6.8
White	175	100.0	183	100.0	4.2
Metropolitan areas	119	67.9	122	66.8	2.5
Central cities	49	27.9	46	25.1	−6.4
Outside central cities	70	40.0	76	41.7	8.7
Nonmetropolitan areas	56	32.1	61	33.2	7.7
Negro	22	100.0	24	100.0	8.6
Metropolitan areas	16	74.1	18	75.6	10.7
Central cities	13	58.5	14	58.2	8.0
Outside central cities	3	15.6	4	17.3	20.9
Nonmetropolitan areas	6	25.9	6	24.4	2.4

Source: U.S. Department of Commerce, Bureau of the Census, *Pocket Data Book, USA
1976* (Washington, D.C.: Government Printing Office, 1976), p. 48.

Age Characteristics

The needs and wants of individuals change as they progress through life.[6] Thus, the
age characteristics of the population are of interest to retailers. The median age of
the United State population is about twenty-nine years and is rising slowly. In 1975
the largest single group (15.7 percent) was the five- to thirteen-year-old group
(Table 1–3).[7] In second place, the twenty-five- to thirty-four-year-old group made up
14.4 percent of the population. Third place honors were held by the young transitory
adults eighteen to twenty-four with 12.8 percent. A further examination of the data
shows that if one combines the two age groups that traditionally earn the most in
their chosen occupation (thirty-five to forty-four and forty-five to fifty-four), one finds
that this group accounts for 21.8 percent of the population. Retailers should realize
that people in this group often are investing most of their income in family education,
homes, and general health maintenance.

One should note that the various groups not only have varying needs today but
also that these needs will change over the next twenty years. In fact, there is some
evidence that the traditional life cycle model used for predicting consumer needs
may not apply to a growing segment of our single population.

Social Characteristics

The single, separated, widowed, and divorced (SSWD) segment of the population
has received considerable attention in the popular press. Approximately 15.5 million
persons live alone and account for 21 percent of the households in the nation, which
is a 17 percent increase over the last seven years.[8] During 1976, 1.3 million Ameri-

Table 1-3 **United States
Resident Population, by Age**

Age	Population (mil)				Percent			
	1950, Apr.	1960, Apr.	1970, Apr.	1975, July	1950, Apr.	1960, Apr.	1970, Apr.	1975, July
All ages	151.3	179.3	203.2	213.1	100.0	100.0	100.0	100.0
Under 5 years	16.2	20.3	17.2	15.9	10.7	11.3	8.4	7.5
5-13 years	22.3	32.7	36.7	33.5	14.7	18.2	18.1	15.7
14-17 years	3.5	11.2	15.9	16.9	5.6	6.2	7.8	7.9
18-24 years	15.8	15.6	23.7	27.4	10.4	8.7	11.7	12.8
25-34 years .	23.9	22.8	24.9	30.8	15.8	12.7	12.3	14.4
35-44 years	21.5	24.1	23.1	22.8	14.2	13.4	11.4	10.7
45-54 years	17.4	20.5	23.2	23.8	11.5	11.4	11.4	11.1
55-64 years	13.3	15.6	18.6	19.8	8.8	8.7	9.2	9.3
65-74 years	8.4	11.0	12.4	13.9	5.6	6.1	6.1	6.5
75 years and over	3.9	5.6	7.6	8.5	2.6	3.1	3.7	4.0
Median age—years ...	30.2	29.5	28.0	28.8	x	x	x	x

x Not applicable.

Source: U.S. Department of Commerce, Bureau of the Census, *Pocket Data Book, USA
1976* (Washington, D.C.: Government Printing Office, 1976), p. 50.

cans formed new households. A closer examination of the data reveals that 174,000 of these new households were formed by couples with or without children, while 549,000 were set up by individuals.[9] Single-parent families accounted for 577,000 new households. Thus, an additional 1 million single individuals in 1976 alone made the purchase decisions necessary to set up housekeeping. The significant size of this emerging market has forced home furnishing retailers to change their marketing practices in order to meet the tastes of this market.

This trend to single living is further augmented by higher divorce rates, later marriages, and an increasing gap between the life experiences of men and women.[10] The Census Bureau confidently predicts that one out of three persons between the ages of twenty-five and thirty-five will be divorced. Given this and other evidence, sociologist Frank Furstenberg noted that he sees a national trend toward individuals adopting "separate economic and psychological modules." He projects that traditional family living will only occupy the middle years of a person's life, while the balance will be spent in living alone or in "transitory arrangements."[11]

In the past women have statistically outlived men, and that trend continues today. Despite major strides in geriatric research, the wife of today can expect to outlive her husband by about eight years. As a result, approximately one third of the single households are occupied by widows.[12]

The significance of this SSWD trend goes beyond sheer numbers. This segment of the population represented a $115 billion market in 1976. Individuals living alone have distinctly different needs from the rest of the population. Today they often: (1) live in townhouses or condominiums, (2) buy 26 percent of the passenger cars, (3) purchase newly developed lines of mini-appliances as well as new single serving packaging forms of frozen foods, (4) buy fewer refrigerators and washer-dryers than the general consuming public and (5) spend about as much as married couples on restaurant dining.[13]

Changes are also occurring within the traditional family. An ever-increasing number of wives are working outside the home. Nearly half of the families in the United States are composed of two or more workers. Such families are greater potential customers for fast frozen dinners, microwave ovens, labor-saving appliances, and extended day-care services.

While individual life styles will vary, it is possible to estimate personal needs of each group. As the individual retailer begins to focus on a chosen market, detailed census information becomes extremely valuable in identifying profitable opportunities.

Additional information is available on factors such as income per capita by states, family income related to family characteristics, percent of households owning homes, cars, and appliances, and persons below the poverty level by region and by state. Projections of changes in consumer demographics to the year 1985 are contained in Exhibit 1–1. One of the fundamental decisions that every retail firm must make is what demographic information is appropriate to its situation and how the specific data should be interpreted. These analyses will be discussed more completely as they apply to various decision variables throughout the balance of the text.

In summary, one interpretation of the foregoing data is that total retail demand continues to increase but its component parts are undergoing shifting emphases. The population is moving to the southern, the southwestern, and the Rocky Mountain regions. Not only is there a migration toward the sunbelt states, but also the central business districts and central cores of the major cities are being abandoned by those economically able to flee to the suburbs and rural areas.

The social structure of the population would appear to be undergoing a significant change, both in terms of life style and in consumption patterns. The singles segment of the population is increasing, with attendant major changes in consumption patterns which the retail community must recognize and devise appropriate adjustments for. These and other changes in the demographic characteristics of our society promise a continued dynamic retail environment.

Retailing Characteristics

Role of Retailing in the U.S. Economy

The three basic types of economic activity in our economy are extracting and manufacturing, marketing, and consumption. Extractive activities are exemplified by mining, fishing, and agriculture. Manufacturing processes change the form of the physical or chemical composition of materials by assembling, processing, fabricating, and the like.

Marketing activities move and store merchandise so that it is available to the consumer and inform the prospective buyer of the attributes, capabilities, and usefulness of goods and services. Wholesalers and other middlemen assist the manufacturing and extractive institutions by making the latter's products and materials available to retailers at the time and in the place desired by the retailer. The retailer,

Exhibit 1-1 To 1985: Changing Demographics

Willard M. Salzer outlined the following key economic and demographic changes retailers will face in the years ahead:

Population

Population has been growing at an average annual rate of 1.7 million people since 1970. Based on the latest Census Bureau figures, population should grow by 234.1 million people in 1985, an average of 2.1 million increase per year.

Year	U.S. Population
1970	204.0 million
1976	215.1 million
1980 (proj.)	222.8 million
1985 (proj.)	234.1 million

Household Income

Average household after-tax income is presently estimated at $16,000 for 1976 and is expected to increase to $22,000 by 1980 and $29,000 by 1985.

Year	Average Income
1970	$10,818
1976	$16,049
1980 (proj.)	$21,988
1985 (proj.)	$29,425

Total Income

Total after-tax income has increased from $686 billion in 1970 to $1,186 billion in 1976. This should increase to $1,700 billion by 1980 and $2,500 billion by 1985.

Year	Total Income
1970	$685.9 billion
1976	$1,186.0 billion
1980 (proj.)	$1,657.0 billion
1985 (proj.)	$2,499.4 billion

Department Store Sales

Total U.S. department store sales have maintained a share of after-tax income since 1971 at a level of 5.7 to 5.8 percent.

Year	% of Total Income
1971	5.7
1972	5.8
1973	5.8
1974	5.7
1975	5.7
1976	5.8

In terms of dollars, total U.S. department store sales have increased from $16.8 billion in 1963 to $46.7 billion in 1972, and $68.2 billion for 1976. Department store sales could hit $142 billion by 1985, based upon keeping a 5.7 percent share of income:

Year	Dept. Store Sales
1963	$16.8 billion
1970	$38.6 billion
1972	$46.7 billion
1976	$68.2 billion
1980 (proj.)	$94.4. billion
1985 (proj.)	$142.5 billion
1980 ('76 dollars)	$81.3 billion
1985 ('76 dollars)	$101.8 billion

Age

The 20 to 34 years of age group is expected to continue to be the group showing the most growth. The 35 to 44 age group and the 0 to 4 group are expected to show increases from 1975 to 1980 compared with the 1970 to 1975 period when these groups showed declines.

Age Group Years	% of Change 1970-75	1975-80
20-34	+19%	+15%
35-44	-2	+11
0-4	-2	+11
55 & over	+8	+8
45-54	0	-5
5-19	-3	-6

Size of Households

The size of households is continuing its declining trend and the rate appears to be accelerating:

Year	Size	% of change preceding period
1960	3.33	
1964	3.33	—
1970	3.14	-1.0½
1975	2.94	-1.3
1976	2.89	-1.7

Type of Households

There has been a dramatic shift in the composition of households since 1970. The number of individual male households has grown by 61 percent. Female households, both individual and as head of family, have grown by approximately one-third, male head of family by 16 percent and husband-wife teams by only 5.7 percent.

Type of household	% of Change 1970-76
Individual male	61.2%
Female head of family	33.4
Individual female	30.2
Male head of family	16.0
Husband-wife	5.7
All households	14.9

Source: "Convention '77: Retailing in 1999," *Stores* (February, 1977): 36, 37. Reprinted from *Stores* Magazine; © National Retail Merchants Association, 1977.

in turn, must satisfy consumer needs by offering goods and services in the form and at the time and place desired by the consumer. The consumption activities use the output of extractive, manufacturing, and marketing activities to satisfy individual human desires.

The collective consumption activities of the population have demonstrated that the human desire for a state of well-being is insatiable. Thus, new and modified products are introduced each year by firm after firm in an attempt to meet these individual human needs. Figure 1-2 illustrates this process.

Retailing takes many forms in a never-ending attempt to create a more efficient distribution system than is currently available to meet differing consumer demands. Several factors necessitate a strong retail system.

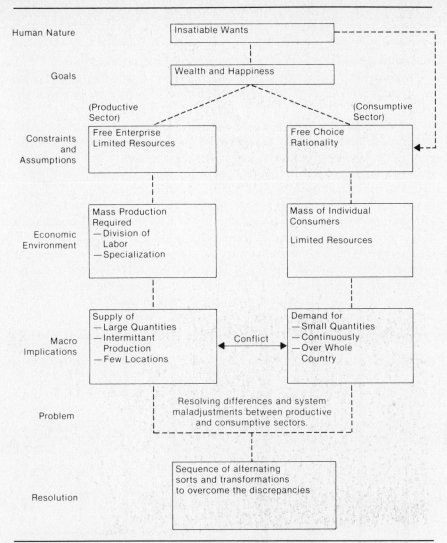

Figure 1-2 **Marketing in the United States: A Macro View**

Source: Reprinted with permission from John F. Grashof and Alan P. Kelman, *Introduction to Marco-Marketing* (Columbus, Ohio.: Grid, Inc., 1973), p. 75

First, the American economy relies on mass production and consumption to maintain its growth and development. Mass production leads to economies of scale which generate lower unit prices and permit more people to enjoy a higher standard of living. However, supply of and demand for goods vary seasonally and geographically. These dissimilarities generate the need for the performance of such *marketing functions* as transporting, accumulating, storing, financing, and reshipping goods in appropriate assortments and quantities to retailers. *Marketing specialists,* such as brokers and wholesalers, perform the required distribution activities, including arranging for transportation to bridge the gap between producer and retailer (Figure 1–2). From time to time, as innovations occur or consumer buying habits change, it becomes necessary to adapt the existing channels of distribution so that marketing middlemen can meet the needs of the consuming public more efficiently.

Retailers serve as the final link in this complicated process by providing the consumer with the opportunity to make transactions efficiently and at convenient times.

The retailer also performs a useful function by helping other marketing middlemen sort and transform goods, or break the large-volume shipments from specialized manufacturers and producers into smaller units that consumers can use most efficiently. The necessity for breaking of bulk is illustrated by the supermarket, which receives case lots of fresh produce but sells small quantities to meet individual consumers' needs. A typical sorting and transformation process is shown in Figure 1–3. The raw material may be sorted before manufacturing, transformed into a consumer product, and shipped to a wholesaler or retailer warehouse where it is stored until it is needed. When the store buyer orders various styles, sizes, and colors from the warehouse, they are shipped and displayed by the retailer so that the consumer will know of their availability and can purchase the merchandise in the desired form at the preferred place, and at a convenient time.

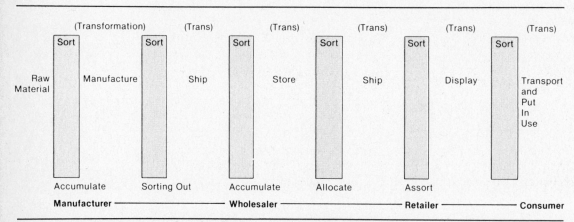

Figure 1–3 **Typical Resource-Creation Process: Sorts and Transformations**

Source: Reprinted with permission from John F. Grashof and Alan P. Kelman, *Introduction to Macro-Marketing,* (Columbus, Ohio: Grid, Inc. 1973), p. 77.

Retailers also function as an informational source for both the manufacturers and the consumers. Retailers, the mass media, and fellow consumers are the main sources of product and/or service information available to consumers. In many cases, cooperative advertising programs between a manufacturer and retailers are used to provide consumers with timely product information, such as the introduction of new, unique products and services. The trend toward consumerism has also placed more emphasis upon the presentation of factual information by retail salespeople and retail advertisements so that the customer can make a more informed choice. Another phase of the information transmittal process provided by retailers is the feedback of consumer preference and reactions to manufacturing firms, which is needed if production firms are to respond to changes in consumer tastes, needs and demands. Retailers and wholesalers communicate consumer information to manufacturers by their order levels, buyers' comments, refunds on inferior merchandise, and merchandise returns.

All marketing functions must be performed if the desired goods and services are to reach the consumer at a convenient place and time and in the quantities demanded by the consumer. Certainly, manufacturers can eliminate all middlemen, including retailers, by assuming the costs of storage, of breaking bulk, and of the risk of loss or product deterioration and sell directly to the consumer. This is called vertical integration and it occurs when the producer feels that the firm can perform the marketing functions more efficiently than they are being performed by the current middlemen. In certain cases the manufacturer becomes a retailer selling directly to consumers. One axiom of marketing is that no marketing function can be eliminated; the function can only be shifted forward or backward in the distribution channel.

Importance of Retailing in the U.S. Economy

The importance of retailing is evident from many perspectives. From an employment point of view, approximately 12.8 million individuals, or 16.6 percent of all American employees were employed by 1.9 million retail firms in 1972.[14] From a monetary point of view, retail outlets generated annual sales of over $584.4 billion in 1975.[15] In addition, retailing offers the qualitative advantage of obtaining independence by being one's own boss. Retailing is one of the few remaining business alternatives that require a relatively modest investment of private capital.

Structure of Retailing in the U.S. Economy

The structure of retailing also can be analyzed from several points of view, but space limitations confine our discussion to the classification systems used to describe retail stores and to legal forms of retail organizations.

Classification of Retail Stores

Four *retail classification systems* will be used to describe retailing from various viewpoints: the type of merchandise or service offered, the number of outlets owned or controlled by a single firm, the relative emphasis on prices, and the number and nature of surrounding stores.

By Merchandise Offered This classification groups retail establishments according to the types of merchandise offered for sale. Several classification systems are commonly used. The Bureau of Census uses the predominant type of merchandise offered by a store as its criterion, such as building materials, hardware, farm equipment dealers, general merchandise group stores (which include department stores, discount department stores, and variety stores), food stores, apparel and accessory stores, gasoline service stations, and nonstore retailers.[16] Trade associations recognize specific merchandise classifications such as the "National Automobile Dealers Association."

Alternately one might construct a continuum ranging from general store on one end to specialty store on the other end. A store with a wide offering of different types of products to meet a wide range of consumer needs would be classed as a general store. Many large-scale mass merchandisers, such as K mart, offer "one-stop shopping" that is reminiscent of the earlier general store. Admittedly, the variety of goods has been significantly expanded, but so have consumer needs. The largest single example of this strategy, the hypermarket, which combines a large supermarket and a discount store, is Meijers Thrifty Acres in Detroit or Oshawa in Canada.[17]

On the other end of the spectrum are specialty stores, which appeal with a narrow range of merchandise to a specific segment of the market. Thom McAn shoe stores, Mrs. Steven's candy shops, and travel agencies all exhibit a narrow line or assortment of merchandise and service. Their competitive advantage lies in their depth of assortment. They usually operate under the motto, "If we don't have it, or can't get it, you don't need it."

The nation has experienced a significant increase in the number of specialty stores such as the furniture warehouse, the home improvement center, and the catalog showroom. Department stores are retrenching in certain merchandise areas and no longer can be considered as full line, but are not quite specialized. In fact, they seem to be searching for a profitable identity somewhere in the clothing fashions. The consuming public seems to be in a state of change in its shopping habits and currently enjoys a large variety of stores and a wide selection of merchandise. Consumers seem to be shopping for everyday needs in general stores and expressing a desire for individuality by patronizing specialty shops.

By Service Offered In these days of relative consumer affluence the services that a retail firm offers may determine its survival. The American consumer appears to be willing to spend more disposable income on the purchase of services. Thus the product offered for sale today tends to be a product-service mixture that will yield satisfaction to the consumer.

In discount department stores the consumer expects little or no service beyond exchange privileges and credit. Conversely, in specialty stores such as a ski shop, potential customers expect to be greeted and professionally assisted in their purchase decisions. Thus the breadth of merchandise is generally inversely related to the amount of service provided. Department stores, having made a point of recognizing the differing needs of various consumer groups, provide both minimum-service bargain basements and boutique-like departments on upper floors. Some retail authorities question this split-personality strategy and conclude that the traditional department store form is passé.

By Number of Outlets under Common Ownership Another method of classifying retail activity is by the number of outlets owned by a retail organization. The term *chain store* is often used to designate a group of stores under common ownership. For the present purpose the use of the term will be limited to geographically dispersed, commonly owned units that number four or more. Common examples would be Safeway, Skaggs Drug, and K mart. Such stores have grown because of economies of scale that can be effected through more efficient advertising exposure and the centralized buying of goods. All units within the chain generally exhibit uniform architectural motif, pricing, and availability of credit. Such firms as J. C. Penney and Montgomery Ward attempt to centralize all their purchasing and credit operations so that consistent prices and credit policies are presented to customers everywhere in the nation. Regional grocery chains, such as King Soopers in Denver, will often attempt to accomplish similar objectives with regard to price, product assortment, and store decor.

Another aspect of classification by number of outlets is the branch or catalog store. In both cases, firms attempt to establish a presence in a suburban or rural community. They rely on central warehouse or main store stocks and expeditious merchandise interchange and delivery to meet the customer's need. This practice makes it unnecessary for each store to carry duplicate or complete assortments of merchandise, and it limits the amount of fixed overhead required in numerous buildings. Recent renewed consumer interest in catalog sales, if not discouraged by costly and ineffective delivery systems, may reduce the need for numerous outlets while still producing additional sales revenues.

By Relative Emphasis on Price A close relationship exists between classifying a store according to merchandise diversity and according to relative emphasis on price. There are no free services. Every activity performed by a retailer costs money that must be recouped either by charging directly for it or by distributing the cost over the entire merchandise line and raising prices to higher levels. Retail establishments that emphasize relatively lower prices either perform fewer customer services than competitors or use a variable markup strategy to achieve higher than normal markups on noncomparable or luxury items. The point is that retailers tend to differentiate themselves on the basis of initial markup on the merchandise they offer. Suffice it to say, retail organizations generally can be categorized by their relative emphasis on markups, which results in varying price lines and price images in the mind of the consumer.

By Nature of Neighborhood Lastly, it is possible to group retail establishments according to the number and nature of neighboring stores. Historically, retailers have gathered together at convenient points of travel. Early settlements were usually placed at the convergence of rivers, land trails, or transportation intersections. Today this same tendency can be observed in (a) central business districts, (b) regional shopping centers, (c) community shopping centers, (d) neighborhood shopping centers, and (e) free-standing units. The specific characteristics of each retailing cluster will be presented in Chapter 5.

Certain types of retail stores require more "aggregate convenience" than others to prosper and grow.[18] Here again the assortment of offered goods becomes important when viewed in the light of consumer shopping habits. For example, when consumers want to do comparative shopping for apparel, they may frequent a regional shopping center because the central business district, containing the "main" stores, no longer has complete assortments or depth of stock. Many small retailers prosper in close proximity to large "anchor" department or chain stores that serve as focal points for regional shopping malls. These shops attempt to intercept customers as they shop for unique, personalized apparel.

Similarly, it is quite common for neighborhood shopping center clusters to contain supermarkets, drug centers, hardware stores, and service stations because they complement each other's merchandise assortments and are convenient for customers. If properly located, merchandised, and managed, these complementary stores should succeed as a collective unit.

Legal Forms of Retail Establishments

Retail organizations may take one of three common legal forms: sole proprietorship, partnership, or incorporation.

Sole Proprietorship The single proprietorship continues to be the most popular form of legal organization in the nation (see Figure 1–4). The sole proprietorship, often equated with entrepreneurship, is the simplest form of business. In order to start a business, one simply finds an unmet need in the marketplace and attempts to provide goods and services to consumers. For example, an acquaintance of one of the authors was a successful house framer by trade. However, he was also a highly competent archer who had won many prizes and trophies. After several years of commuting to a large city to purchase equipment and supplies, he decided to open his own shop in the basement of his home. Fortunately, local zoning ordinances permitted limited commercial business in his neighborhood so he procured the necessary city licenses, established a line of credit at the bank, and wrote to suppliers for permission to become a franchised dealer and stock their products. The shop is only open at nights and on Saturday, but the business has been so successful that he has expanded his line to include canoes, which he stores in his garage. In the near future he must decide whether to continue to build houses and sell the business or leave his profession, open a full-time store in a separate location, and become a professional retailer. From this illustration it becomes clear that the qualifications for membership are minimal.

They consist of personal incentive, relatively small initial capital investment, and compliance with local licensing and ordinances. The owner-manager goes into business simply by opening the door. While the initiation dues are deceptively low, the attendant risks of failure are high.

Partnership (Creative Combination of Talents) Partnerships are created to overcome some of the inherent disadvantages in sole proprietorships. A partnership really represents an agreement of co-ownership, usually among individuals who have complementary business or production skills, some venture capital, confidence in the joint effort, and personal compatibility. While this form of legal organization would appear to be a near optimum arrangement, a partnership is not without potential problems.

Each partner can make a decision without necessarily consulting the other part-

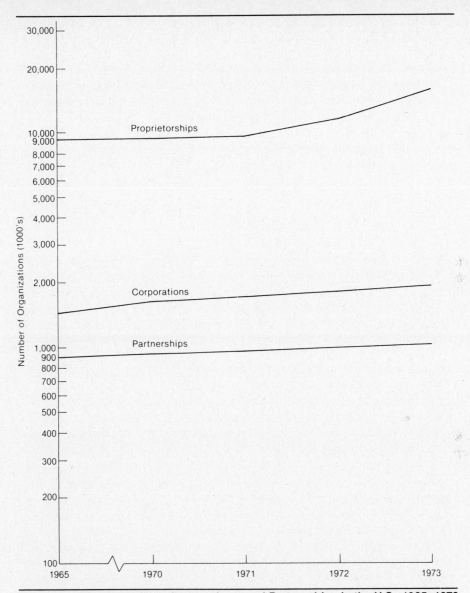

Figure 1–4 **Proprietorships, Corporations, and Partnerships in the U.S., 1965–1973**

Source: U.S. Internal Revenue Service.

ners and can commit the firm to contract obligations. If a partner decides to withdraw from the arrangement, the partnership ceases to exist (a partner's interest is non-transferable), and a new legal organization must be formed. Even though its access to capital and capacity to borrow are greater than in a proprietorship, the partnership still experiences limited financial capability. In short, there is a wide range of potential conflicts among the partners that may result in a short life for the firm. One should not conclude, however, that a partnership arrangement is unworkable but rather that a partnership provides a vehicle for a joint effort in certain appropriate situations.

Corporation (Legal Depersonalization of an Organization) When confronted with starting a new business venture, many individuals automatically think of the corporate form of organization, which is exceeded only by sole proprietorships in popularity. The corporate form provides these advantages:

1. Limited liability of stockholders if the stock is widely held and ownership and management are distinctly separated
2. Firm life limited only by managerial effectiveness and economic conditions
3. Virtually unlimited access to a wide range of talents and the abilities of specialists, including professional management
4. Technically better access to sources of equity capital and a wide variety of debt instruments that are attractive to lending institutions because of the potential permanence of the organization

The potential entrepreneur should be cautioned that while the seeming advantages of incorporation make this form of legal organization most attractive, it has its limitations. For the small business that is just beginning, incorporation is appropriate only when some potential investors have access to significant quantities of venture capital and are looking for capital appreciation through company growth and development rather than income from their investments.

Some novice entrepreneurs may try to limit their personal liability by incorporating as a closely held firm by naming members of the family or friends as corporate officers. The courts have decided that in fact ownership and management reside in the same person or group of persons and that the limited liability concept cannot act as a shield for their personal assets from loss through litigation or court order. In such situations any limited corporate liability protection becomes illusory for small retailers.

Other disadvantages of incorporation include (1) double taxation of profits, (2) greater state and federal regulation, (3) difficulty of maintaining personal control of the firm, due to the separation of ownership and management and the conflicting goals of operating management and stockholders, and (4) the general depersonalization of the organization. The appropriate time to use the corporate form would appear to be after the firm has successfully evolved into an ongoing business.

Factors Encouraging Expansion of Retail Institutions

Every prospective retail career specialist should have a general knowledge of how environmental influences affect the growth and development or the demise of retail institutions. While the retailer may not be able to control these influences, there may be an opportunity to influence certain outcomes that will assure the survival of the retail institution.

Population Trends

Without doubt, the most important variable in the success or failure of retail institutions in general is the absolute growth or decline in the population. Some retail authorities feel that women's desires for more personal freedom and autonomy helped spur the development and adoption of fast-food franchising. The harried mother, with her typical 2.5 children, under pressure to fulfill many different roles in her home, job, and community, welcomed the convenience of the limited-menu, fast-food service.

Population movements can have significant impact on retail institutions as well as individual stores. The mass movement of a major portion of affluent citizens to the suburbs has contributed to the demise of the central business district as a center for consumer shopping. Severe traffic congestion and increased street crime in most large cities have reduced the consumer traffic to individuals who could not afford to move out of the inner city and to office employees who spend part of their lunch hour in impulse buying.

Similarly, many small retailers who once thrived on the business generated by people who travel to and from central work areas along major arterials have gone broke. The shopping habits of the American family have been changed by the movement to the suburbs and by the high-speed expressways that connect downtown business centers and suburbia. Shopping centers are in, major arterial and intersection shopping clusters are out.

Transportation

The nation has experienced significant transportation changes within a single generation. We moved from the horse and buggy to limited car ownership and mass transportation provided by street cars and commuter trains. Then came the present situation of mass automobile ownership and jet air travel. Convenient and relatively cheap transportation by personal automobiles has assisted in the development of such retail institutions as the drive-ins, including convenience food merchandisers (such as 7-11 stores) and mass merchandisers of furniture and home furnishings (such as Levitz). Free-standing one-stop shopping centers (such as K mart and Target Stores) and the entire shopping center cluster also owe their development to mass automobile ownership. Rising automobile and fuel costs have cast some doubt on the future of isolated shopping facilities. As a result, the size and placement of these free-standing units are becoming critical.

Technological Development

The retail community has progressed very far from the days when business was conducted in multiple-purpose buildings with drop-cord incandescent lights. The introduction of elevators and escalators, pneumatic tube cash systems, glass-front display cases, open displays, computer-linked cash registers, and other physical changes have played a major role in changing the image of retail institutions. Currently, large retailers are adopting electronic transaction centers capable not only of handling the economic exchange but also of recording merchandise movements for inventory management, fashion trend analysis, consumer credit validation, and other valuable information for managerial decision making. The limited use of electronic funds transfer systems (EFTS) in some stores herald the long-anticipated (but yet to be realized) "cashless society."

Retailers' Traditionalism

Established retail institutions sometimes resist any change that might better meet the needs of the consumer if the changes also threaten a loss of patronage to their establishments. One might call such retailers "protectionists" or "micro-oriented merchandisers." Philosophically, the average retailer takes the present retail system as a given and attempts to fine-tune the system by maximizing internal efficiencies. However, such preoccupation with detail encourages nonretailers to innovate and carve out new structural niches for themselves. For example, why did the low-price restaurants not recognize and respond to the need for fast-service, limited-menu outlets? They were too busy serving food and competing with each other. Such conservative traditionalism serves as an invitation for the development of new forms of institutional competition by nontraditional, retail-oriented enterprises.

Environmental Factors

Much speculation has been advanced as to why and how retail institutions either fail or adapt and survive.

The concept of natural selection, or survival of the fittest, maintains that the retail institution that most effectively adapts to its environment is the one most likely to survive and grow. A firm must be able to adjust to changes in technology, competition, consumer demographics, economic conditions, and social and cultural attitudes on relatively short notice if it is going to survive in the competitive business world. Retail organizations must be flexible enough to make needed responses quickly.

The *wheel of retailing,* or life cycle, concept explains the evolution of retail institutions. The basic premise, developed by Professor Malcolm P. McNair, is that a new retail institution first appears with low-margin, low-price, and minimum-service offerings. As time passes, these establishments add more service and upgrade their facilities and offerings. These changes require higher margins and higher prices. The process continues until these firms eventually become high-cost, high-price retailers that are therefore vulnerable to the next innovator.

An *accordion theory* is frequently used by retailers to explain fluctuations in merchandise assortments. This theory describes the tendency for retail business to become dominated (in an alternating pattern) first by general stores, then by specialty stores, and again by general stores. This concept suggests that merchandise balance is yet another element that influences retail institutional change. A new institution would probably begin as a specialty store because of limited capital and managerial knowledge. Gradually, as it became more successful, it would tend to expand offerings until it eventually became a general store.

A common thread runs through these three explanations—inappropriate cost management. In each case, a new institution is launched with a limited selection that is deliberately chosen for a specific customer group that purchases on the basis of price. It is located in a simple facility, which results in lower overhead costs. Combined, all these factors permit the new retailer to offer relatively low-price products and services. If the firm is successful, it is emulated by other competitors, each trying to win a share of the relevant market segment.

If one assumes that, for all practical purposes, prices cannot be significantly lowered, then the emulators practice one-upmanship by adding "free services," broader assortments, credit, and even trading stamps to hold or increase their share of the market. As the services become institutionalized by this steady, incremental, spiral process, the affected retail institutions become "fat," traditional, and generally locked into a higher cost level of operation due to consumer expectations. In the meantime, prices have been gradually and selectively raised—and are usually publicly justified on the basis of increased manufacturing costs—until the very thing that gave the institution its start, low price, has been lost.

Astute marketers detect periodic consumer dissatisfaction with relatively high prices, particularly during periods of significant recession or inflation. They rush in with the original low-price concept, and the cycle repeats itself.

Some retailers justify adding frills by saying that as their target market's income is increased, they must trade-up or lose the market, because the consumers want to shed their "poor" image and buy products and services that carry more status. This may be an appropriate strategy for some merchandise, but it has been overused.

The *retail life cycle* concept represents an attempt to apply the product life cycle concept to the evolutionary changes that retail firms seem to exhibit.[19] The classic terms *innovation, accelerated development, maturity,* and *decline* are applied to identify specific, unique stages that retail firms usually encounter. The most useful application of this concept is found in Table 1–4 where the terms suggest appropriate management activities for each stage of life cycle development. As the text explores these managerial concerns in more detail in later chapters, one should refer back to this set of recommendations for further information on and validation of the construct.

The life cycle of certain retail institutions provides evidence that retail institution life cycles are becoming significantly shorter (Table 1–5). Thus, there should be considerable managerial attention devoted to staying flexible, to analyzing risks and profits, particularly the idea of utilizing second-use space for new retail ventures, to extending the maturity stage by attracting new market segments while retaining existing customers, and to emphasizing ongoing research.[20] Even though the future retail environment may become more turbulent, the adoption of these suggestions may mean the difference between survival and failure.

In summary, a detailed portrait of *any* customer-retailer market may be captured by using population demographic characteristics, retail institution classifications, and consumer behavioral research techniques.

Table 1-4 **Management activities in the life cycle**

Area	Area of Subject of Concern	Stage of Life Cycle Development			
		1 Innovation	2 Accelerated Development	3 Maturity	4 Decline
Market characteristics	Number of competitors	Very few	Moderate	Many direct competitors Moderate indirect competition	Moderate direct competition Many indirect competitors
	Rate of sales growth	Very rapid	Rapid	Moderate to slow	Slow or negative
	Level of profitability	Low to moderate	High	Moderate	Very low
	Duration of new innovations	3 to 5 years	5 to 6 years	Indefinite	Indefinite
Appropriate retailer actions	Investment/growth/ risk decisions	Investment minimization— high risks accepted	High levels of investment to sustain growth	Tightly controlled growth in untapped markets	Minimal capital expenditures and only when essential
	Central management concerns	Concept refinement through adjustment and experimentation	Establishing a preemptive market position	Excess capacity and "overstoring" Prolonging maturity and revising the retail concept	Engaging in a "run-out" strategy
	Use of management control techniques	Minimal	Moderate	Extensive	Moderate
	Most successful management style	Entrepreneurial	Centralized	"Professional"	Caretaker
Appropriate supplier actions	Channel strategy	Develop a preemptive market position	Hold market position	Maintain profitable sales	Avoid excessive costs
	Channel problems	Possible antagonism of other accounts	Possible antagonism of other accounts	Dealing with more scientific retailers	Servicing accounts at a profit
	Channel research	Identification of key innovations	Identification of other retailers adopting the innovation	Initial screening of new innovatation opportunities	Active search for new innovation opportunities
	Trade incentives	Direct financial support	Price concessions	New price incentives	None

Retailing Trends

The number of U.S. retail establishments has increased significantly since 1958. The fastest-growing segment is the multi-unit (chain and franchise) stores (Table 1–6). Between 1958 and 1972 their number increased by 59 percent. In contrast, the number of independent, single-unit retail outlets has continued to decline slightly

Table 1-5 **Life cycle characteristics of five retail institutions**

Institution	Approximate Date of Innovation	Approximate Date of Maximum Market Share	Approximate Years Required to Reach Maturity	Estimated Maximum Market Share	Estimated 1975 Market Share
Downtown department store	1860	1940	80	8.5%	1.1% of total retail sales
Variety story	1910	1955	45	16.5%	9.5% of general merchandise sales
Supermarket	1930	1965	35	70.0%	64.5% of grocery store sales
Discount department store	1950	1970	20	6.5%	5.7% of total retail sales
Home improvement center	1965	1980 (estimate)	15	35.0%	25.3% of hardware and building material sales

Sources: National Bureau of Economics Research, U.S. Department of Commerce, *Progressive Grocer, Discount Merchandiser,* National Retail Hardware Association, and Management Horizons, Inc.

As cited in: William R. Davidson, Albert D. Bates, and Stephen J. Bass, "The Retail Life Cycle," *Harvard Business Review* November–December 1976, p. 94. Copyright © 1976 by the President and Fellows of Harvard College; all rights reserved.

since 1958. This same trend toward multi-unit organizations is even evident in the figures for retail sales volume. Multi-unit retail organizations accounted for only 33.5 percent of total retail sales in 1958, but they now account for 44 percent (Table 1–6).

The overall increase in retail sales has taken some of the sting out of the increased competition that multi-unit organizations are giving independent, single-outlet operators. Retail sales have increased from $200 billion in 1958 to $459 billion in 1972 (Table 1–6). Thus, although single-unit retailers have been losing their share of the total business to multi-unit organizations, the total retail market has expanded so rapidly that the sales of single-unit outlets have increased from about $25 billion in 1965 to about $32 billion in 1975.[21] This pattern does not exist in all types of retailing. For example, multi-unit stores accounted for about 89 percent of all department store sales in 1974.[22]

A particularly disturbing phenomenon is the precipitous drop in the number of proprietors of unincorporated businesses between 1967 and 1972. Also, five hundred thousand, or fully 30 percent of these retailers left the retail trade. Previous variations have occurred over the years but this significant drop bears special mention (Table 1–6).

The trend in services continues to display an even faster rate of growth, both in number of firms and in sales, than it has in the past (Table 1–6). Sales have increased almost fourfold since 1958, while the number of firms has increased by over 62 percent. Unlike their retail trade counterparts, the proprietors of unincorporated service establishments continue to enjoy a net upward trend in their numbers. Between 1958 and 1972 the number of these firms has increased approximately 20 percent, bearing out the general conclusion that the American consumer is purchasing more services from more service firms.

Table 1-6 **U.S. Retail Trends**

Item	1958	1963	1967	1972
Retail Trade				
Total establishments (thousands)	1,795	1,708	1,763	1,913
Multi-unit organizations (thousands)	183	220	220	291
Total sales ($ billion)	200	244	310	459
By multi-units	33.5%	36.6%	39.8%	44.0%
Per capita	$1146	$1290	$1561	$2198
Payroll ($ billion)	22	28	36	55
Paid employees, Nov. 15 work week (thousands)	7,942	8,410	9,381[a]	11,211[a]
Proprietors of unincorporated businesses (thousands)	1,825	1,546	1,624	1,137
Selected Services				
Total establishments (thousands)	979	1,062	1,188	1,590
Receipts ($ billion)	33	45	61	113
Payroll ($ billion)	9	12	18	33
Paid employees, Nov. 15 work week (thousands)	2,904	3,262	3,841[A]	5,305[A]
Proprietors of unincorporated businesses (thousands)	996	1,017	1,082	1,193

A. Data for week including March 12.

Source: U.S. Department of Commerce, Bureau of the Census, *Pocket Data Book, USA 1976* (Washington, D.C.: Government Printing Office, 1975), p. 352.

Retail experts have mixed views about what lies ahead for the retailing industry and for specific segments of this vital activity. What does the future hold for consumers and the retailing industry?

Demographic Trends

Most retail experts expect the migration to the Southeast, Southwest, Far West, and Rocky Mountains to continue. They note that such climates promote the current life style based on youthfulness, physical fitness, and outdoor activities.[23]

When one looks at the age distribution for the next twenty years, it becomes apparent that the "baby boom" of the late 1940s will become the dominant age group thirty-five to forty-four in the 1980s.[24] As this wave of humanity has made its way through earlier age periods, its impact has been felt in large school enrollments, the creation of youth markets, and now the increasing rate of unemployment. As noted earlier, if this group's penchant for singleness continues, and all indications point in that direction, it will have a growing impact on the proper placement of retailers in the retailing system.

A related side effect of the single mode of living is the declining birth rate. After considerable public concern over the worldwide population explosion in the late 1960s, Americans seem to be doing their part by having approximately 1.9 children per woman of childbearing age, which means that at the moment the American population is not replacing itself with offspring. Most authorities anticipate that this low birthrate will continue at least until 1990 because of factors such as new cultural values, more women entering and staying in the labor force, cost of child rearing, and improved birth control technology.[25]

One could safely conclude that our nation is heading into an era of absolute population decline, fewer families, and increasing numbers of adults seeking employment in tight labor markets. These indicators, taken alone, do not bode well for the retailing industry. However, the single life style may moderate these prospects and generate new and profitable retail markets.

Cultural Values

Throughout the chapter many references have been made to singles and their life style. One should not assume that this is the only cultural change currently taking place. Environmental awareness enjoys an increasing popularity among the consuming public. This awareness has taken many forms, ranging from conservation of natural resources to active opposition to dam construction and strip mining. In short, there seems to be a "being awareness" that self-fulfillment may not lie in materialism, but rather that satisfaction lies more in the realm of "experiencing." If this ethic begins to gain converts, it will have a significant impact on the travel, recreation, and leasing industries. Some futurists are currently preaching "lease what is needed for the time it is needed, but don't own it." This serves the conservation ethic and acknowledges the realistic limitations of most personal incomes.

Additional clues that signal a major shift in values are provided by: collective action groups such as consumerism and women's liberation movements, the increasing restlessness of employees at all levels in organizations, and increasing concern over persistent high unemployment and increasing taxes. Everyone can cite personal examples of the effect of these factors in our society. Berry and Wilson make the point that these movements do not refute the value of gaining and using money per se; rather, these movements stress a reordering of our priorities and hence affect *how* we spend our money. Briefly stated, the emerging priorities stress that ". . . the quality of life is more important than the quantity of life; that human beings are more important than things."[26]

Economic Considerations

A creeping, deep-seated feeling of caution and uncertainty seems to be settling into the national psyche. The flamboyant days of high employment, low inflation, low-cost energy, consistent economic growth as indicated by an ever-rising gross national product, and high consumer and investor confidence will not automatically continue.

What lies ahead? Every crystal ball seems to cloud up beyond forecasts for the next six months. However, there seems to be some degree of consensus on several points. According to General Electric forecasts, the growth in disposable personal income (DPI) will slow from an average rate of 3.3 percent in the 1960s to about 3.1 percent between 1976 and 1982 and further slow to 2.4 percent between 1982 and 1990.[27]

The inflation rate, which affects the individual's disposable income, is expected to average 6 percent annually between 1976 and 1990. Higher inflation rates (in excess of 6 percent) are expected to occur in the areas of food, energy, housing, and transportation.[28] Even though an expected 41 percent of all households should have an after-tax income of $15,000 (in 1975-constant dollars) by the late 1900s, many experts question how much of this sum will be available for truly discretionary purchases.[29]

Where are all these projected inflationary pressures coming from? The simplest answer seems to be increasing raw material and labor costs. Retailing will continue to be especially vulnerable because it is by its very nature labor intensive. During the period between 1960 and 1975, retailing compensation and new store construction costs increased significantly faster than manufacturing costs reflected by the consumer electronics and appliances line in Figure 1–5.[30] These data become even more disturbing when one adds projected additional energy costs at all levels of economic activity.

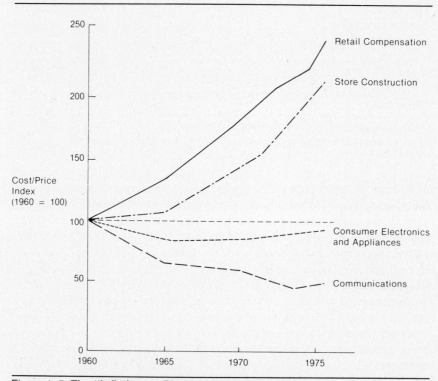

Figure 1–5 **The "Inflationary Disadvantage" of Retailing**

Source: Bureau of Labor Statistics as cited in Leonard L. Berry and Ian H. Wilson, "Retailing: The Next Ten Years," *Journal of Retailing* 53, No. 3 (Fall 1977): 14.

Compounding the confusion about the future of retailing is the projected availability and cost of capital during the balance of the twentieth century. According to one analysis conducted in 1975 by the Institute of Life Insurance Trend Analysis Program, there will be shortfalls in all forms of capital.[31] This problem carries particular concern for the retailing industry because, if the analysis in Table 1–7 is an indication of the future, retail firms achieving only 1.8 percent to 2.7 percent net profits after taxes and 4.2 percent to 6.5 percent return on assets will be in a poor position to attract or bargain for needed capital to finance their operations and for needed renovation and expansion.[32] All but one performance ratio, total assets to equity, have shown a pronounced deterioration between 1965 and 1974. Bates concludes, "The combination of increased investment demands and the decline in the quality of retail profits represents a quiet and largely unnoticed crisis in retailing."[33]

Table 1–7 **Composite Performance Ratios
for 111 Major Retailing Corporations, 1965–1974**

Ratio	1965	1966	1967	1968	1969	1970	1971	1972	1973	1974
Profit margin (after-tax)	2.7%	2.5%	2.5%	2.5%	2.4%	2.3%	2.4%	2.3%	2.3%	1.8%
Return on assets	6.5%	5.9%	5.9%	5.7%	5.5%	5.3%	5.6%	5.4%	5.4%	4.2%
Return on equity	12.9%	12.0%	12.1%	12.8%	12.9%	12.1%	12.3%	12.0%	12.4%	9.0%
Net sales to total assets	2.5	2.4	2.3	2.3	2.3	2.3	2.3	2.3	2.3	2.4
Total assets to equity	2.0	2.0	2.1	2.2	2.3	2.3	2.2	2.2	2.3	2.3
Current ratio	2.1	2.0	2.0	1.9	1.8	1.8	1.8	1.8	1.7	1.7
Quick ratio	1.1	1.0	1.0	1.0	.9	.9	.8	.8	.7	.7
Interest coverage ratio	11.7	8.3	8.2	8.1	6.6	5.7	6.9	6.8	5.7	3.9
Inventory turnover	6.0	5.9	5.9	5.7	5.6	5.7	5.5	5.4	5.2	5.5

Source: Investors Management Sciences, Inc., and author's calculations.

As cited in: Albert D. Bates, "The Troubled Future of Retailing," *Business Horizons* 19 (August 1976): 23.

Political Environment

During recent periods of stress a new radicalism has become more evident. Individuals no longer are willing to plead their special interest through traditional political channels. Now people with common causes are banding together into organized coalitions to petition the federal, state and local governments to pass legislation or to have the courts interpret current legislation to advance their cause. Unfortunately, because of a series of events, the American business community does not enjoy the widespread confidence among the populace it once did. Retailing is no exception.

Current interest in various forms of foreign trade restrictions should be of concern to retailers. All barriers to foreign trade, be they quotas, duties, or other restrictions, are designed to raise product prices so that domestic industries with higher cost structures will become competitive with foreign goods. Thus, the retailer's ability to offer a wide range of prices and qualities to meet different needs of consumers is significantly impaired. Such action carried to extreme leads to economic stagnation and depressions. This larger view is often overlooked as politicians attempt to meet the immediate, narrow interest of a vocal minority.

Continuing pressure for the civil rights of the citizenry is being observed and felt by all segments of the business community, including retailers. Legislative action regarding employment and credit granting and billing has been taken in recent years which creates an added burden both in absolute dollars and increased responsibilities for the retailer. Specific details will be considered elsewhere in other chapters, but one should note that there seems to be no end in sight for this kind of governmental intervention into the retail arena. Specific new areas of concern are ill defined but will be brought into sharper focus as the twentieth century winds toward a conclusion.

Technological Innovations

New advances in technology are expected to have an important effect on the retailing structure. Retail executives believe that in ten years better in-store use of computerized information will reverse the present trend for tactical decisions to be centralized in chain store operations (even though they accept a trend toward centralized buying).[34] Between 50 and 60 percent of the general merchandise purchasing is now handled through general buying facilities or cooperative central buying offices, and this figure is expected to rise to 75 percent by 1986.[35] A nationwide computerized credit and banking system is expected to be in operation by 1989.[36] Such a system will eliminate many customer service problems that result from a lack of coordination among the numerous retail credit cards and accounts. It will reduce operating expenses, but it may also reduce store loyalty.

Cable television is likely to revolutionize promotion and sales methods by the early 1990s, when 50 percent of American households are expected to have cable television.[37] It will be designed so that consumers may use it to order merchandise that has been displayed on their television set and pay for it through an electronic fund transfer tapped out on an in-home keyboard.

Future Trends

One could say that the next decade will be the era of transition. Recognized challenges are the forerunners of profitable opportunities. The trends are discernible despite the fog of uncertainty. Consumers want rewarding experiences and increasingly high quality of life, are increasingly aware of the dangers of unwise use of credit, and are moderating their expectations in light of an emerging conservation ethic with more emphasis on individuality.[38]

Some retail experts suggest that the key terms for retailer consideration will include *selectivity, reallocation, flexibility, renovation, and utilization.*[39] All these terms suggest that a retailer will be in an era of conservatism. Introspective efforts to improve sales productivity, that is, the generation of higher profit levels, will take high priority. One form these efforts will take will be a change in managerial thinking from "sales per square foot" (two dimensions) to "sales per cubic foot." The heretofore overlooked sales effectiveness of vertical displays will become critical to retailer profits. Along the same lines, increasing use of centralized distribution centers (automated warehouses) will permit existing retail stores to reduce the amount of cost-inefficient non-selling space required in each store. Inefficient stores, both in terms of sales generation and energy consumption, will either be closed or remodeled. If remodeling is not practical, many retailers will recycle vacant buildings for different retail purposes.[40]

Improved profitability will also result from discarding traditional merchandising conventions and developing new, appropriate strategies. Such "unthinkable" actions as dropping entire merchandise lines, moving out of large stores in declining regional shopping malls to smaller stores nearer the growing target market, reducing administrative-staff-to-selling-personnel ratios by centralizing operations, and using improved telecommunications to bridge the gaps will become commonplace.

Perhaps the best current examples of such radical actions are the department stores. May and McNair note, ". . . the department stores may be visualized as occupying a middle ground, hemmed in at the top by the prestige apparel chains; walled off on the bottom by the discounters, the superstores, and other self-service checkout establishments; and encroached upon at the sides by some of the newer types of specialty operations as well as the older national private brand merchandise chains."[41] Everywhere department store managements have dumped such merchandise lines as major appliances, records, and sporting goods. Newly vacated space is devoted to enlarging and emphasizing fashion merchandise that has been regrouped to create "image boutiques" which appeal to consumers in certain age and life-style groups. Some department stores, such as The Fashion Bar, have opened new competing specialty shops, such as the Stage, in the same shopping centers to attract the young, single, fashion-conscious female. Some speculate that this particular chain may abandon its department stores entirely and concentrate its efforts on effective merchandising in the proper retail position and locations with smaller, more efficient and profitable operations. Such a move would provide the flexibility needed during these turbulent times. Other current examples of similar retail position strategies include the Image, Limited Stores, Petrie Stores, and Miller-Wohl.[42]

Strategic Fundamentalism

Even detailed self-examination by retailers may not be enough to meet the challenges ahead.[43] Such fine tuning as the incorporation of home improvement centers or the diversification into catalog showrooms are, at best, short-term remedies. What is needed is a fundamental reconsideration of the target market to be served by the retail firm. How can this be done profitably in light of shorter retail life cycles, with less investment in construction, fixturing, and merchandise inventory, and with fewer employees? Perhaps warehouse retailing is a partial answer. Physically, facilities can be built quickly, at low cost, usually with exposed beam rafters rather than ceilings, bare cinder block walls, rough wood interiors that suggest a degree of temporariness. A true warehouse outlet is characterized by:

1. Large, low-cost physical facilities—a store size that is several times that of conventional outlets and built economically
2. Warehouse operations—the use of low-cost warehouse operating techniques
3. Warehouse merchandising—displaying merchandise in a vertical rather than horizontal format, and utilizing warehouse fixturing
4. Large, narrow inventory—maintaining a rather substantial inventory to satisfy large sales volume levels, but carrying only the leading items
5. Service reduction—a total elimination of every nonessential customer service
6. Price appeal—a reliance on price as a major consumer variable.[44]

Perhaps the most often cited example of this type of operation is the food warehouse. Goods are stacked on the floor in original cases, prices marked by customers using an ordinary grease pencil, and purchases sacked by individual customers in self-provided boxes and reused cloth or paper bags. Usually these outlets are located in recycled buildings near shopping centers and trade lower prices for lack of convenience.

Not all consumers seem quite ready to accept such harsh, abrupt changes in retailing. A growing chain of record stores, Peaches, seems to have captured the essence of warehouse retailing without the usual harsh appearance. The interior executes the Peaches theme by using specially manufactured peach crates for the display of records set on simple fixtures that are arranged in long parallel aisles. The limited services offered include the "widest, most complete selection in town," a few employees to direct customers looking for a particular record or tape, extended hours tailored to the young working class, and acceptance of credit cards. The only semblance of scrambled merchandising is found in their "crate" sales and sale of T-shirts bearing their distinctive logo. Perhaps similar adaptations of the warehouse concept will become commonplace in the future.

An alternative to warehouse retailing is the wider adoption of "rationalized retailing."[45] Simply stated, this approach relies on highly centralized management control and strict operating procedures that leave no detail to chance. Perhaps the most familiar example is Tandy's Radio Shack operation. Every store carries exactly the same assortment displayed on identical racks or wall fixtures in the same general location in each store. Such standardization permitted the firm to add 333 additional stores during 1975 alone.

Food Retailing Prospects

The food retailing industry has often shown the way to the future by introducing new marketing strategies and techniques. It continues its pioneering tradition with the introduction of the universal product code (UPC), electronic funds transfer (EFTS), and scrambled merchandising epitomized by superstores.

Other innovators have begun to experiment with selectively stocking generic foods such as catsup, canned vegetables, and puddings. Each package is labeled with minimum information, carries no brand name, and sells for substantially less than house brand equivalent items. Each of these latest innovations is an attempt to fight the constant cost control battle and win higher profit margins.

However, individual store survival will be tied much more in the future "... to the image it projects."[46] The successful retailers of the future must segment their market and focus so that they can react appropriately to consumers' age, income, social status, and life style. Such efforts may serve well to reduce the tendency to engage in nonprofitable price competition. Product mix, service, store design, and employee attitude toward customers will be used to achieve the unique image necessary to capture the localized market.[47]

Franchising's Future

Franchising has had a checkered reputation in the past. Today it is an accepted retailing institution. The "explosion" and "frontierism" of the 1960s are behind and the future looks promising for orderly growth and development. According to the United States Department of Commerce, franchised outlets showed their greatest growth to date between 1974 and 1976, expanding from 399,000 in 1974 to 458,000 in 1976, or a 14.7 percent increase in two years.[48] The industry, being primarily service oriented, has benefited from a general trend toward more consumer spending in this area. This trend is expected to continue and franchising's future looks bright. Significant legislative action such as full-disclosure and fair-practice acts pending in Congress may reduce the current friction between franchisors and franchise holders, particularly in the areas of providing complete and accurate information about the investment potential of any proposed location as well as operating and buy-back provisions. These governmental efforts toward regulation will be augmented by the rise of more associations of franchise holders, which will act as forums for the discussion of common problems and concerns that could lead to litigation on behalf of entire segments of the industry.

Franchising is alive and well but, like most adolescents, is suffering growing pains that will eventually result in a mature retail component. A more detailed discussion of the specific problems and practices will be discussed later.

In conclusion, it would appear that the entire retail industry and its consumer market is undergoing significant changes. Some of the more obvious future trends have been discussed. Clearly, not every new event or trend has been catalogued, which leaves a large portion of the future labeled "unknown." Perhaps the bottom line of the future for everyone, retailer and consumer, will be determined by the availability and affordability of energy. This common thread which runs throughout the fabric of our advanced postindustrial and interdependent society has the potential to invalidate even the most well-thought-out, documented forecast of the future. Adaptability to change has been the key to survival in the past and provides the best hope for the future.

Summary

In this chapter we have attempted to identify the significant retail institutions and to examine the future of the retail industry. We found that the general trend of retail growth is healthy.

Significant changes are taking place among the various retail institutions. Large, multi-unit organizations are growing at the most rapid rate. Catalog stores, discount stores, furniture warehouse retailers, supermarkets, drug store chains, franchises, and carefully managed specialty stores are expanding their sales volume. However, the number of small, independent retailers continues to decline.

These changes have resulted from environmental influences (such as increased incomes, population increases, movement to the suburbs, increased mobility, and technological changes) and the resulting managerial responses to these changes.

Products and services must continue to reach the consumer in the form and at the time and place that he or she desires. The retailing industry plays an important role in this process, but individual retailers will continue to be successful only if they are the most efficient means by which manufacturers and producers can reach the ultimate consumer.

Questions

1. Why is retailing vitally important in an interdependent society? What function(s) does retailing serve in meeting individual needs?

2. What are demographic characteristics? Why should a retailer be interested in them?

3. What are the retail implications of the population migration to the South, Southeast, Southwest, and the West Coast? Explain.

4. What actions might be taken to stem the movement out of metropolitan areas? Should retail organizations play any part in such efforts? Explain.

5. What economic impact is the SSWD group having in our society? How should the retail community respond to this group's needs?

6. What are four methods of classifying retail institutions? What are the advantages and disadvantages of using each method?

7. Distinguish between sole proprietorship, partnership, and corporate forms of retail establishments. Which form is the best for small retail businesses?

8. If the Life Insurance Trend Analysis Program's conclusion is accurate and there is a capital shortfall, what strategies can retailers take to deal with this situation?

9. What would be the impact on the retail community if gasoline reached a price of $1.50 per gallon in 1980? Would all retailers be affected equally?

10. How might retailers be affected by changing cultural values? Should retailers take an active part in shaping these cultural values?

11. What is meant by *strategic fundamentalism*? How is this phenomenon being manifested currently in the retailing industry?

12. If the consuming public accepts EFTS and UPC, what benefits will accrue to retailers and their customers? Explain.

13. How would you characterize the future for retailing during the next twenty years? Explain.

Footnotes

1. U.S. Department of Commerce, Bureau of the Census, *Pocket Data Book, USA 1976* (Washington, D.C.: Government Printing Office, 1976), p. 41.

2. Ibid., p. 43.

3. Ibid., p. 45.

4. Ibid., p. 46.

5. Ibid., p. 48.

6. William R. Davidson, Albert D. Bates, and Stephen J. Bass, "The Retail Life Cycle," *Harvard Business Review* 54, (November-December 1976): 89–96.

7. U.S. Department of Commerce, Bureau of the Census, *Pocket Data Book,* p. 50.

8. June Kronholz, "A Living-Alone Trend Affects Housing, Cars and Other Industries," *The Wall Street Journal,* 16 November 1977.

9. Ibid.

10. Ibid.

11. Ibid.

12. Ibid.

13. Ibid.

14. U.S. Department of Commerce, Bureau of the Census, *Pocket Data Book,* pp. 163, 353.

15. Ibid., p. 355.

16. U.S. Department of Commerce, Bureau of the Census, *1972 Census of Retail Trade, Area Statistics, United States, RC-72-A-52* (Washington, D.C.: Government Printing Office, 1975), p. 38.

17. Albert D. Bates, "Ahead—The Retrenchment Era," *Journal of Retailing* 53, (Fall 1977): 34.

18. Reavis Cox, "Consumer Convenience—Retail Structure of Cities," *Journal of Marketing* 23 (April 1959): 355–362.

19. Davidson et al., "The Retail Life Cycle," p. 92.

20. Ibid., p. 96.

21. U.S. Department of Commerce, Bureau of the Census, *Pocket Data Book,* p. 356.

22. Ibid., p. 355.

23. Leonard L. Berry and Ian H. Wilson, "Retailing: The Next Ten Years," *Journal of Retailing* 53 (Fall 1977): 6.

24. Ibid., p. 7.

25. Ibid.

26. Ibid., p. 10.

27. Ibid., p. 12.

28. Ibid.

29. Ibid.

30. Ibid., p. 14.

31. Institute of Life Insurance, "A Culture in Transformation: Toward a Different Societal Ethic?" *Trend Analysis Program Report #12,* Fall 1975, p. 17.

32. Albert D. Bates, "The Troubled Future of Retailing," *Business Horizons* 19 (August 1976): 23.

33. Ibid., p. 24.

34. *The Future of Retailing* (Bryn Mawr, Pa.: Robinson Associates, 1973), p. 14.

35. Ibid., p. 15.

36. Ibid.

37. Ibid., p. 14.

38. Berry and Wilson, "Retailing: The Next Ten Years," p. 19.

39. Ibid., p. 22.

40. Bates, "Ahead—The Retrenchment Era," pp. 29–46.

41. Eleanor G. May and Malcolm P. McNair, "Department Stores Face Stiff Challenges in Next Decade," *Journal of Retailing* 53 (Fall 1977): 56.

42. Ibid., p. 55.

43. Bates, "Ahead—The Retrenchment Era," p. 48.

44. Ibid., pp. 42–43.

45. Bates, "The Troubled Future of Retailing," p. 27.

46. Ibid.

47. Danny N. Bellenger, Thomas J. Stanley, and John W. Allen, "Food Retailing in the 1980s: Problems and Prospects," *Journal of Retailing* 53 (Fall 1977): 69.

48. Shelby D. Hunt, "Franchising: Promises, Problems, Prospects," *Journal of Retailing* 53 (Fall 1977): 79.

Chapter 2

Application of the Marketing Concept: Developing a Marketing Strategy for Retailing

1. To understand how the marketing concept may be applied to retailing.

2. To be able to discuss how a target market can be used to narrow the retail effort in order to increase the retail firm's profitability.

3. To learn the variables that can be manipulated by the retailer to create a unique product or service.

4. To understand the critical legislation that affects the retail firm's internal operations and relations with external clients.

Learning Goals

marketing concept	target market	promotion
marketing	product differentiation	retailing mix
integrated marketing	marketing mix	merchandising

Key Terms and Concepts

Chapter 1 demonstrated that retailing is the most important institution in the process of distributing goods and services in the American economy. Retailing represents the ultimate link in the channel of distribution, which involves complex production and marketing systems that have been created to meet consumer needs. This chapter is devoted to showing how the marketing process, the contribution of the marketing concept, and marketing mix combine to improve retailing efforts. Although the retail process has succeeded in assembling vast assortments of merchandise to meet client needs, it has not yet totally implemented a true marketing concept. The retail process, as practiced by a significant sector of the economy, is a relic of a past emphasis on production that is in need of innovation and change.

A brief review of economic history reveals that prior to the late 1950s the nation was operating on a limited production base, which caused a scarcity of consumer goods; that is, not enough goods and services were produced at low enough prices for mass consumption and mass consumer satisfaction. Particularly during the depression years of the 1930s, when there were few jobs and little money to buy the available goods, people were concerned with meeting their basic needs for food, clothing, and shelter. Some economic historians claim this was a period of surplus, but to the family without work it was a time of scarcity and economic hardship.

The brief period from 1946 to 1948 was marked by national emergency labor disputes and a transition from a wartime economy to a peacetime, consumer oriented production effort. As consumer goods began to flow into the marketplace, the liquid assets of the nation became available, and prices for scarce goods were bid higher. Just as supply began to catch up with pent-up demand, the Korean conflict again thrust the nation into a partial war effort, and consumer goods again became scarce. However, by the late 1950s the nation's manufacturing and distribution system satisfied consumer demand, and a subtle but profound change occurred in the nation's economic system. Manufacturers and marketers alike needed a new method of tapping the relative affluence of the consumers. A new, more appropriate concern for individual consumers was required to encourage consumption. The **marketing concept** was formulated to meet this challenge.

The Marketing Concept

The essence of this change in thinking is expressed in the definition of *marketing* as "the performance of business activities which direct the flow of goods and services from producer to consumer or user in order to satisfy customers and accomplish the company's objectives."[1] Instead of centering all the firm's efforts on inventing, producing, and selling a generalized product, the emphasis shifted to determining the consumer's needs and wants. Using these findings, the firm can then attempt to develop, produce, and make available the best product or service to meet perceived consumer needs.

When a firm adopts this philosophy, "the consumer is king." All company efforts are focused on having the right product at the right place, at the right time, at the right price, and in the right quantity to capture the consumer's dollars—profitably.

How does the marketing concept facilitate the meeting of consumer needs? The implementation of the concept is based on three major concerns: genuine consumer orientation, an integrated marketing approach, and the generation of customer satisfaction.[2]

Consumer orientation is implemented by the firm's (1) adopting a definition of the basic needs that it intends to serve, (2) identifying the target group(s) of customers it wants to serve, and (3) meeting the varying needs of its target group(s) by using a differentiated product/service offering.

Integrated marketing means that each department in the firm must recognize that its actions will have an effect upon the company's ability to attract and retain customers. Integrated marketing also means that the firm's entire effort can be coordinated to build a strong, positive, consistent image in the minds of consumers. To achieve such integration a marketer should carry out a market opportunity analysis (Figure 2–1). One might begin the analysis with an investigation of the projected Gross National Product, which is published by the government and includes all products, goods and services produced in the nation.

Secondly, an industry analysis, in this case the retail industry, might be undertaken to determine the size of the market and the extent and quality of services offered by industries competing for the consumer's discretionary income and to identify marketing opportunities for unmet consumer needs. Additional information can be gained by executing a competition and demand analysis. If the additional information from these research efforts validates the previously identified market opportunity, the retail firm must conduct a segmentation analysis to determine whether the group is large enough to make it profitable to develop and implement a retail offering. A detailed discussion of these analytical processes will be found in later chapters.

The third major concern of the marketing concept involves the recognition that the firm's long-run welfare is dependent upon the amount of customer satisfaction it is able to provide. A firm's sales force can periodically report relevant customer comments on the performance of the firm and its product/service offerings.

Sales personnel are helpful in supplementing research efforts to analyze consumer repeat purchase patterns, attitudes toward merchandise selection, store image, and other measures of customer satisfaction.

The firm can also conduct in-depth studies to analyze consumer repeat purchase patterns and to obtain other measures of consumer satisfaction. The spirit of appropriate customer concern seems to be captured by the following:

THE CUSTOMERS

A Customer is the most important person in any business.

A Customer is not dependent on us. We are dependent on him.

A Customer is a part of our business—not an outsider.

A Customer is not just a statistic. He is a flesh-and-blood human being with feelings and emotions, like ourselves.

A Customer does us a favor when he comes in. We are not doing him a favor by serving him.

A Customer is deserving of the most courteous and attentive treatment we can give him.

A Customer is the life-blood of this and every other business. Without him we would have to close our doors. Don't ever forget it.[3]

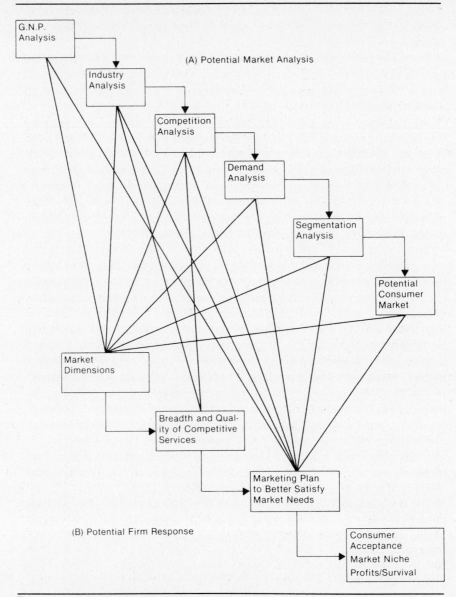

Figure 2-1 **Assessing a Marketing Opportunity**

The salesperson serves as the last vital link in the marketing chain. Customers often make long-term patronage decisions on the basis of limited encounters with retailers' sales personnel. The quality of the personal interaction often can be traced to profits or losses on year-end financial statements.

The marketing concept provides for the accomplishment of one of the company's objectives—profit. The concept of profit has always had its critics and champions.

Today, the consuming public must be made aware that profits are simply charges for services rendered. While one can argue and disagree on how profits should be generated and on what constitutes a reasonable profit, the retail firm cannot be expected to provide its services for free. Retailers invest their time, money, and talents to assume the risks associated with providing consumers with goods and services that best meet their needs. Marketing functions, such as buying, transporting, storing, risk bearing, financing, and providing market information can be shifted to others in any distribution system. Thus, if customers want to pay less, they must assume some portion of the marketing functions. For example, you might purchase a CB set in a discount store at a "discount." If anything goes wrong with the set, you must have it repaired either by sending it back to the factory (and being without the use of the set for six to eight weeks) or paying for the repairs locally. Any "savings" are achieved at the cost of assuming the marketer's risk-bearing function. If consumers expect to have product/price choices, they must be prepared to pay for both the product and the services rendered by the retailer.

Developing a Retail Strategy

Once the retail firm accepts the need for a marketing orientation, the next step is to consider the development of a competitive retail marketing strategy.[4]

The formation of a retail strategy consists of (1) the identification of target markets and their needs and (2) formulation of a retailing mix that satisfies the needs of the target market.[5]

Target Market:
Appropriate Consumer with Buying Power

A retailer's most fundamental task is to identify and satisfy a profitable **target market** (the group of consumers that the retailer is trying to satisfy). The wide diversity of consumers, all of them with unique and personal needs, combined with intense competition from other retailers for their patronage, makes it impossible for a single retailer to be "all things to all people." The effective retailer concentrates on satisfying a profitable set of needs held in common by a certain group of consumers within a reasonable geographic proximity. For a hardware store this usually means that its relevant market lies within a circle with a radius that represents fifteen minutes' driving time to the store. The distance will vary with the type of merchandise carried by the store, other competition, and other factors.

Consumers with unmet needs do not automatically become a profitable target market. Experience has amply demonstrated that financial limitations prevent individuals from satisfying all of their personal needs. Therefore, the retailer should concentrate on identifying consumers who have similar needs as well as the economic ability (money and credit) to purchase the need-satisfying goods or services. Thus, the retailer's target market defines a group of qualified buyers with inadequately satisfied needs.

Market Segmentation:
Characteristics of Qualified Buyers

Market segmentation is the practice of dividing the population into various sub-groups of people in such a manner that all of the people within each group have similar characteristics. Using this approach, consumers can be classified into sub-groups or segments on the basis of demographic characteristics such as sex, age, marital status, gross income, geographic location, and so on. Other, more compre-hensive classifications may be made on the basis of personal behavioral character-istics, such as social values or biases or prejudices that affect individual purchase decisions. Information derived from market segmentation provides the basis for a number of marketing decisions. For example, if your store specialized in young professional women's fashions, the store should be located in a shopping mall near apartments or condominiums which contain a high concentration of your target market. Also your hours of operation should be tailored to their free-time schedules.

Product Differentiation: A Unique Total Offering

Product differentiation is an image-creation process in which a product or service that is similar to other products or services is made to stand out in the consumer's mind. Often retailers lose sight of the fact that products alone do not yield customer satisfaction, and that products or services are means to an end. The consumer's mere possession of a product does not accomplish any goal in and of itself. The perceived usefulness that the product or service will provide in the hands of the owner is the reason the customer wants to acquire it. The retail firm must remember that its ultimate goal is customer need satisfaction, not just the sale of goods or services.

Such need satisfaction may be achieved in three ways. First, the product or service may, in the act of being consumed, serve some physical need, such as hot coffee on a cold day. Second, the possession or use of a product or service may serve to meet psychological needs—for example, a large diamond engagement ring. Last, a combination of physical and psychological needs may be met by the acquisition and use of products or services—perhaps a Honda Accord XL for a couple in suburban Chicago. In each case the retailer sold a physical product/service, but in reality also sold human need satisfaction.

Consumer satisfaction is affected by the concept of relative value derived over time. A consumer who has made a sizeable investment will be especially sensitive to any indications that the investment will or will not prove satisfying over a long period of time. The product may perform perfectly and reliably but yet not be perceived by the purchaser as meeting his or her needs. As a result, postpurchase dissatisfaction will be felt. For example, it is quite common for automobile purchas-ers to search for postpurchase support for their decision to buy a certain car. Often the complaints that are made during the immediate warranty period (ninety days) include "rattles in the dash," "poor mileage," and other general nonspecific dissatisfactions which may reflect psychological dissatisfaction. The quality of the follow-up service received during this postpurchase period is critical to long term, repeat business, word-of-mouth advertising, and ultimately to the firm's survival.

Branding may play a large part in a product's success and hence affect the retailer's degree of success. Branding becomes particularly important to retailers when national producers develop consumer confidence in their branded product to the point that a significant segment of the population will not accept a substitute. Such customer loyalty is often associated with products that are distributed through exclusive dealerships. For many years, the California Packing Company built and maintained such a strong reputation for quality that the retailer was able to charge premium prices for Del Monte foods. More recently, the Pendleton Woolen Mills have been successful in associating their Pendleton label with quality merchandise. Any apparel store in the West is assured of added prestige and profitable sales from customers who recognize and appreciate quality merchandise. Thus, whenever consumers cannot determine value/price/quality comparisons readily by inspection, branding may become a valuable part of product satisfaction for them.

In addition to the physical aspects of products, the retailer can differentiate the firm's product assortment for the chosen target market by varying the amount, kind, and quality of supporting services the firm provides. Such services may include the installation of major appliances, education in the use of certain products (such as microwave ovens), the repair of products, the delivery of goods (either free or for a minimum charge), gift wrapping, clothing alterations, return of merchandise privileges, and credit. Each of these services may enhance the attractiveness of a product or the patronage of an establishment because the combined product package provides better customer need satisfaction. Every added service cost must be covered by higher gross margins, be recoverable in increased volume at normal markups on the products, or as a last resort, be paid by direct charge. Accurate retailer perception of the target market's needs will determine the composition of the total product the firm can attempt to provide profitably.

Product differentiation may be achieved by artfully blending the four marketing variables of product, place, price, and promotion, into a *marketing mix*. Each of these variables can be combined in an almost infinite number of sets to generate a wide range of consumer need-satisfying products and services. The question for the retailer is how to combine these variables into a unique, dynamic package to meet the needs of the chosen target market better than any other current and potential competitor.

Product/Service Offering:
A Means to Consumer Satisfaction

The selection of product/service assortments to offer the consumer represents the toughest and least well-performed function in retailing. Retailers generally identify a target market, then search out the various goods being produced and purchase items that they feel will appeal to their customers. Generalizations are always dangerous, but frequently small retailers go to merchandise shows or markets semiannually and make buying decisions based solely on past personal experience and some vague, rough summary of sales records.

Through a combination of economies of scale, large concentrations of capital, and intensive and extensive consumer research through advertising agencies, the producers or manufacturers more or less dictate what products will be available in the retail marketplace. Retailing—the very institution that deals most directly with the consumer—has generally performed the preproduction consumer information-gathering and product-shaping functions very poorly. With some marked exceptions, many retailers view their role in product management as determining the location and arrangement of goods that are demanded by their patrons, who have been presold by mass media techniques.

Increasingly, large retail chains, such as J. C. Penney, Sears Roebuck and Company, and Safeway are having products manufactured or processed to their specifications to be sold under their own brand labels. Such product-shaping decisions are possible only through some degree of vertical integration or through the capture of large segments of the target market, which Sears has done with its Kenmore line of home appliances.

What product variables can be used to tailor products to a target market's need satisfaction? The physical product can vary in quality or workmanship, type and quality of materials used, or design and manufacture.

The concept of multiple usage seems to be assuming more importance in the products sold in retail markets today, particularly appliances. More and more radios, stereos, and television sets are being produced that use conventional alternating current or that may be powered by batteries. Small imported cars, such as Toyota, Datsun, and the Volkswagen Rabbit are being purchased for multiple uses, such as commuting and as general-purpose runabouts.

Similarly, products are being produced that have wide product adaptability to individual requirements. Such items as pocket calculators perform mathematical functions, calculate biorhythms, and provide the user with day, date, and time. Thus, a single product (calculators), based on micro-chip circuitry, serves a wide range of consumer needs.

Another aspect of product determination that may often be overlooked is the package in which a product is presented to the customer. With heavy emphasis on preselling merchandise by mass media and with self-service facilities, the package becomes the point-of-purchase sales agent. For example, the Remington Arms Company Incorporated is merchandising 675 .22 cartridges in a decorative limited edition metal cannister called the "Remington Five Pounder." Traditionally, the industry has packaged the product in convenient lots of fifty or one hundred in cardboard or plastic boxes. An accompanying advertising campaign stresses, "Just reach in and take a handful, as many as you want for a full day's shooting." Initial consumer response has been surprising, with initial stock sellouts widely reported by sporting goods dealers across the country.

A package may enhance or encourage the appropriate use of a product. The widespread prescription of birth control pills, for example, was delayed until a suitable package could be perfected that would assist the user in maintaining daily usage of the product. A whole range of products has been introduced into mass markets since the widespread adoption of "plastic bubble" packaging. Such packaging not only protects the merchandise but also permits the potential user to see the product without opening or destroying the package.

Another aspect of packaging is providing the appropriate quantity for convenience of purchase and consumption. For example, the Coors Brewing Company spent considerable sums of money on research to determine the average beer consumption by women at one sitting. The results indicated that women prefer smaller quantities at one sitting than men. Coors developed a 7-ounce aluminum can for the female market, and subsequently has enjoyed great success in tapping that market.

Similar decisions, made by manufacturers of hundreds of items, have allowed retailers to better satisfy consumer preferences. As a result, more pressure is placed on stores to offer a greater assortment of different quantities of goods. If the retailers agree, they encounter shelf-space limitations that may force them to reduce their merchandise assortment or ultimately move to a larger facility. This is just one example of the interrelatedness of the variables in the marketing mix. Just one change in a small basic decision has its effect throughout the operation.

Proper Product Placement: Location

The one market variable that cannot be duplicated is place. Only one store can occupy a prescribed space at one time. One example of an attempt to reduce the competitive impact of location was the placement of service stations on all four corners of an intersection of major arterial streets. Despite this attempt at place equalization, each corner had its own set of unique advantages and disadvantages, and now some stations are closed or are being recycled as convenience stores after past tenants found the critical location and competitive factors did not favor the stations' continued operation.

For all practical purposes, the place variable can be thought of as yielding convenience satisfaction for the customer. The degree of convenience is closely related to the type of product(s) currently needed by the customer to meet perceived wants. Entire retail businesses, such as the 7-11 Stores, have been based on merchandising a limited assortment of convenience merchandise in high-population densities and operating from 7 a.m. to 11 p.m. daily. The specific location of a retail establishment has been the subject of considerable research, and will be discussed at length in Chapters 5 and 6.

Store location is doubly important now, when greater consumer attention is being directed toward rising transportation costs and the constant threat of petroleum shortages. Some futurists predict a complete change of the American life style, which until now has been based on a high degree of mobility. At the moment, however, despite repeated efforts to lure the population to use mass transit systems, people refuse to give up their cars. It appears that the automobile will continue to provide a vital link between the consumer and the retailer for the foreseeable future.

The automobile can be a curse to a retailer if too many are driven on poorly designed highway systems, with resulting serious traffic jams and poor store access. Thus, it is important for any shopping center to have adequate entries and exits available to and from a spacious, amply lighted parking lot. This will encourage customers to shop in the center, thereby potentially increasing customer density or "traffic" for most resident stores.

With increased pressure on people to become involved in more activities, both business and leisure, time has become a scarce commodity and convenience a necessity. Thus, retail chains have followed migrating population to the suburbs to be near their market and to minimize customer travel and shopping time. In well-designed shopping centers, such major stores have generated customer traffic that has given the small retailer opportunities to capture impulse buyers. New shopping centers in prosperous subdivisions do not spell instant success for all retailers, but they do increase the concentration of consumers with wants to be met.

Recent Federal Trade Commission hearings and related court cases have brought to light the fact that some large department or chain stores, usually referred to as "anchor stores," have in the past attempted to dictate the terms and conditions of the competition they would allow in a specific shopping center. Such action has been declared illegal under the terms of the Clayton Act. Additionally, large retail chains can be prevented from purchasing other retail outlets that sell similar merchandise in the same geographical area if such action is interpreted as intention to reduce competition significantly. This restriction has been particularly important in the grocery industry over the last half century.

Place considerations should not be limited just to external or geographic alternatives. Interior design, or store layout, constitutes a vital consideration in conducting the ongoing business of the retail firm. A potential retail lessee may be offered a location in a shopping center that is quite attractive in terms of pedestrian traffic density but may find the interior space is unsuitable for the purpose. One national chain store accepted an anchor position at one end of a medium-size shopping center, only to find that there was no way of utilizing the irregularly shaped space. Departmental isolation and poor traffic circulation resulted in substantially lower sales than had been projected on the basis of the characteristics of the target market.

Another interior layout problem may result from the critical placement of supporting structural members or columns. Recent developments in cantilever roof construction in new shopping centers have alleviated this problem to some degree, but the potential store lessee should still consider the usability of the space being offered.

Customers' needs are relatively infinite, and the customers are constantly searching for new modes of need satisfaction. Thus, they shop "where the action is" or "where things are happening." Innovative retailers should periodically consider interior store rearrangement as well as frequent changes of merchandise displays to create customer interest. Store layout will be explored in depth in Chapter 7, but it is important to note that the placement of a department's merchandise and its systematic rearrangement can serve a vital function in generating customer interest. Such changes also serve an important supporting role in an effective interior promotion program.

Channels of Distribution: Tapping Differing Target Markets

Many firms use different brand names on identical products to reach different target markets. General Motors has done this for years in their automobile production and sales. Evinrude and Johnson outboard motors are made by the same firm but have different suggested retail prices and different advertising appeals. Remington chain saws are physically similar to Montgomery Ward chain saws, yet similar models sell at different prices through different channels with differing levels of supporting services, such as parts availability. Remington goes through wholesalers and retailers, while the Wards product is distributed direct from the manufacturer to the retail store or mail order desk.

The above examples demonstrate that distribution through differing channels can create a unique product. The services provided by channel members can transform similar physical products into distinct and separate products in the marketplace. Customer service, credit, return privileges, and convenient location of an outlet can make one product more attractive than another when viewed in the light of the total product concept.

Price: Relative Value

Most consumers are concerned with one question when it comes to price: "How much does it cost?" The usual clerical reply is some dollar figure, which doesn't answer the full implication of the question. What the consumer is actually requesting is information with which to make a comparative decision. The complex question in the mind of the consumer is, "Are the benefits promised by this product or service worth the expenditure relative to other possible purchase choices?" The actual total cost, in dollar terms, is not generally considered in isolation, as the original question would imply. The price question is just the top of a complex economic iceberg.

At this introductory point it would seem appropriate for students of retailing to note that the price variable is the least effective long-term competitive tool of the four Ps (product, place, price, promotion) available to the marketer. Any retailer can buy merchandise and "give it away" by reducing the price below that of the competition. Additionally, any competitor can duplicate any other competitor's price policy in the short run to attract or hold patronage. An excellent example of the marketing effectiveness of price competition among retailers is the self-service gasoline stations. Consumers have come to view gasoline as a homogeneous product delivered by indifferent attendants in service stations offering the same products, so price becomes the main decision criterion. National petroleum firms are converting many smaller units to self-service. As a result, in some communities it is difficult to find a full service station that can provide periodic and emergency maintenance for any car.

The classic presentation of price determination is usually based on such concepts of supply and demand. Retailers will supply goods and services only as long as they can recover their costs and make an acceptable return on their investment of time and money. This was graphically demonstrated during the late stages of Phase III wage and price controls in 1973. If the producers and retailers could not raise prices to obtain an acceptable profit, they quit making the product and scarcities resulted. Consumers, similarly, will buy the goods and services only when they have resources (money and credit) and are willing to trade their scarce resources for goods and services that provide greater need satisfaction than retaining money or a line of credit.

Mutual buyer-seller agreements in a free market establish the "price." But this is an ideal relationship and rarely explains retail pricing behavior accurately. Prices are actually set at "what the traffic will bear." (Chapter 8 will discuss at length the interactive variables of price determination.) Suffice it to say here that the typical small retailers go to the market and select merchandise that they think will be attractive to their customers. Retail buyers are quoted a list price by the suppliers (less any applicable quantity and cash discounts), add in freight and overhead costs, and add a markup of 30 to 50 percent so that they can "price line" the merchandise. Such items as shrinkage, theft, and markdowns are supposedly considered in the overhead costs.

In summary, price is a very relative concept that helps consumers establish their priorities and levels of acceptable need satisfaction. Many different price strategies are available to retailers, but ultimately they must decide which strategy best fits their firm's image and its ability to best meet the needs of the target market.

Promotion: Providing Market Knowledge

Promotion is an all-encompassing term for all the ways of telling the consumers what products and services are being offered to meet their needs. In addition, promotions may inform consumers of related product attributes, prices, and locations of goods and services, and may attempt to persuade the consumer to take purchase action. The promotion process is perhaps the most researched and yet least understood aspect of marketing.

Certain aspects of promotion, particularly advertising, have been—and are—under attack for creating or uncovering latent consumer needs that lead to wasteful uses of the nation's resources. Conversely, without advertising and other promotional processes consumers would not be aware of need-satisfying products unless they undertook a personal search of retail establishments. Most consumers have neither the time nor inclination for such activities. Complete discussions of the social benefits and liabilities of the use of promotion can be found elsewhere; the task here is to discuss promotion as a retailing competitive strategy.

Retailers can use the promotional process in a variety of ways, but it is useful to separate promotional efforts into two classes. The first category contains those communicative efforts that are directed at a broad general class or target market by impersonal means, through such mass media as magazines, newspapers, radio, television, billboards, car cards, handbills or circulars, point-of-purchase displays, window displays, and the like. A second type, personal promotional effort, is directed toward a single individual, as in personal selling in a store, via telephone, or door-to-door, or in-home presentations of encyclopedia collections.

Regardless of the type or combination of types of promotion a retailer may choose to use, it is vitally important that the firm use a "rifle" instead of a "shotgun" approach to get the most effective return on their promotional investment. One is best advised to focus on the promotional tasks to be performed, establish priorities for each task, select the most appropriate promotional tool, allocate adequate funds to do the job, and then implement the plan. A follow-through evaluation will help determine the effectiveness of the firm's promotional strategy. The firm can learn from past mistakes by keeping a daily diary of promotional efforts and those of competitors. One might even keep an annual scrapbook of advertisements, both the firm's and those of its relevant competition, and perform a sales analysis correlating promotional efforts and gross sales. Admittedly, one cannot say with absolute assurance that an advertisement resulted in X dollars of sales, but some inferences may be made and insights gained about one's future promotional efforts.

It is important here to point out the connections between the promotional tools. Retail advertising should be focused on generating traffic. This can be accomplished by providing information on seasonal, consumer-wanted products or by reducing prices on regular merchandise for limited periods. Other useful promotional techniques include the purchase of special merchandise to sell at a "lower price" or using "give away" contests or drawings for prizes or cash. The essential point of retail promotions is to get people to frequent the establishment so that they may be exposed to merchandise the retailer has acquired for their need satisfactions. Additionally, sales personnel are given an opportunity to encourage, persuade, and convince the potential customers that the firm's products best meet their needs. It should be noted that retail mass media promotions are aimed not only at retaining present patrons but also at attracting new customers. This latter function is particularly important when the selected target market includes young adults who display high geographic-economic mobility and a propensity to adopt new lifestyles.

Personal promotion in retailing is primarily limited to big-ticket or high-profit-margin items that require personal instruction, persuasion, or advice. Unfortunately, the "salesman" stereotype is not held in high regard by the general public because of past unpleasant experiences. Paradoxically, retail salespersons are both the lowest and the highest-paid employees in business. Many retail clerks earn minimum hourly wages, while life insurance salespersons make tens of thousands of dollars per year. The retail firm must decide, in light of its target market's need characteristics, what balance of mass media and personal selling will best inform and motivate its potential clientele to patronize its establishment.

Developing an Appropriate Marketing Mix

The selection of a unique set of relationships between price, product, place, and promotion results in a marketing mix that sets a given firm apart from the other competitors by creating a unique instrument of need satisfaction.

A retail store may compete on the basis of its unique combination of location, store layout, organization, promotion, pricing, service, merchandise assortment, and buying. In so doing, it creates its own *retailing mix*.[6] The integrated decisions reached in each of the competitive areas will collectively create the store image in the minds of the customers. Consumers consider patronizing that establishment which appears to be capable of most completely satisfying their needs. If the firm has anticipated the needs of the consumer in the past, a patronage motive or connective link has been made for associating need satisfaction with that particular store. Thus, an appropriate retail marketing mix creates a retail personality that will generate seller-buyer trust, loyalty, and good will.

In order to anticipate the target market's collective needs, a retail firm must engage in market planning and research. Each firm must segment its market and focus its efforts on a profitable but limited target market. However, even within this target market it may discover varying degrees of heterogeneity among its potential customers. While the major attribute of the target market will be the degree of common needs among these potential customers, selected individuals will have unique needs that the retail firm cannot afford to meet.

For example, suppose a woman's retail clothing boutique finds that it has two potential customers out of twenty possible customers that require a size 20 dress. The source supplies these dresses in a selected grouping and prices them by the dozen, with each dress retailing for $130. Should the boutique attempt to meet such customer needs? The answer, obviously, is no. The cost of inventory maintenance, the loss of alternative use of rack space and its associated costs, plus the ordinary fashion obsolescence of a single style, would make such a decision unprofitable. As a consequence, the women's dress shops are specializing in complete ensembles, including accessories, in petite, junior, women's, or extra large sizes. In short, each fashion boutique has defined its market precisely and attempts to market a "look" or "image" for its chosen clients.

Such decisions may appear clear-cut, but as the number of such customers increases or the various needs begin to be more commonly shared, the more difficult the decision becomes. This is the point where market planning really pays off. Instead of reacting to an individual and immediate customer demand and later regretting it, the effective retail firm delimits its market mix and *profitably adheres to it.*

However, such lack of response to market requests cannot be absolutely and blindly observed or the firm will not adapt to the changing market needs. Constant market awareness through research begins to pay dividends in return for its costs. Properly designed and implemented market research will alert a retail firm to long run as well as fad trends that must be recognized and merchandised if it is to be competitive and profitable.

Marketing Research: Defining the Environment

Marketing research, as it is generally applied, had its origin in the early 1900s when marketers began to apply the principles of scientific investigation to marketing unknowns. The application of the techniques of observing, formulating hypotheses, testing hypotheses, and predicting the future has led to considerable insight into a more effective functioning of the marketing system.[7] Such important areas of investigation have included (1) target market segmentation, (2) market forecasting and analysis, (3) market investment considerations, (4) customer behavior, (5) product development, (6) merchandising, (7) advertising, (8) pricing, (9) personal selling, and (10) physical distribution.[8]

This partial list of marketing research efforts gives some feeling of the complexity of the marketing process. While retailing is the terminal system of the marketing process, it contains micro examples of similar macro-marketing problems. The same techniques that are used to solve macro-marketing problems can be adapted and applied to similar retail situations. Territory decisions become location decisions; product development questions become assortment decisions, and so on.

Perhaps the most concentrated marketing research effort during the last decade has been focused on consumer behavior and is carried out primarily by advertising agencies and producer-sponsored university research. Generally, the retail industry has been reluctant to encourage or even permit experimentation in its stores. Actually, the store represents an ideal laboratory for the study of consumer purchase behavior, yet in order to do such research the investigator must simulate the environment. The retail industry should make more test stores available and should provide more active support of research to find out what the consumer needs are, rather than going to market and taking what the producers offer. Retailers should take a more active part in product development in order to better represent their customers.

Marketing Management: Effective Merchandising

The term *merchandising* means many things to different marketing practitioners. The American Marketing Association defines merchandising as the planning and supervision involved in marketing the particular merchandise or service at the places, times, prices, and in the quantities that best serve to realize the marketing objective of the business.[9] For the purpose of this text, we will consider merchandising to be the internal coordinative effort to meet the customers' needs. Admittedly, external environmental conditions, influenced by international trade conditions and agreements, domestic suppliers, competitors, economic conditions, governmental regulations, product development, and consumer demands, will affect the merchandising effort. However, it is important to stress that just as no single customer will determine consumer demand, no single product or department will determine, in isolation, the viability of a retail operation.

As noted earlier, the consumers have a mental image of a firm or its store, and this conditions their behavior. A retail operation is a composite blend of goods, services, prices, promotion, and personnel with certain personality characteristics. Merchandising ties these various qualities together to form a retail business. Differences in merchandising methods are not simply the result of outside factors affecting customer demand; they grow out of differences in the thinking of each store's management team and its degree of willingness to plan ahead in a systematic way.[10] That is, simply stated, the difference between a true merchandiser and a store owner.

The merchandiser fits complementary assortments of goods together in logically grouped categories in attractive store layouts. The prices provide quality satisfaction for the customer at a reasonable profit for the service provided, and the retailer anticipates customer needs of tomorrow. Store owners buy goods for people to buy today, based on their own personal choices and experience. Market management through merchandising is the route to retailing growth and survival.

Legislation Affecting Retailers

In their efforts to serve consumers the retailers are restricted by the existing legal environment which has developed in response to attitudes of the public as expressed through legislation and interpretive court decisions. The common thread has been that economic competition, as expressed by small competitors, must be preserved at all costs. Bigness is, apparently, increasingly becoming suspect.

Specifically, the Sherman Act of 1890 was intended to deal with monopoly practices that resulted in unlawful restraint of trade. This act set the stage for an era of trust-busting and a continued campaign against the concentration of economic power. The Clayton Act (1914) was passed in an attempt to specifically define certain acts that were then considered unlawful restraints of trade. The accompanying Federal Trade Commission Act set up the implementing machinery to handle the enforcement of the Sherman Act, the Clayton Act, and subsequent related legislation.

While these acts are used to regulate competition in the general economic arena, other attempts have been made to control retail competition. Small, independent retailers attempted, at the state level, to tax department stores out of existence. Only one state, Missouri, actually passed such a law, which was in effect from 1899 until 1909, when it was declared unconstitutional by the Supreme Court of Missouri, and was later repealed.[11]

During this same period an investigation of internal trade and commerce was conducted by the U.S. Industrial Commission, specifically examining the competitive effect of the mail-order system.

There can be no doubt that the establishment of the mail-order system tends to decrease sales of the local dealer, and that he has reason to view its growth with a certain degree of apprehension. . . . In so far as the mail-order system exists, however, it must exist because the people in the small towns can not be served so satisfactorily by their home stores as they can by the department stores in the large cities. The first consideration is doubtless the greatest good to the greatest number, and if customers find the mail-order system of advantage there is every reason for its continuance.[12]

Even though the commission laid to rest the attacks against the mail-order system, the anticompetition spirit was reborn in the 1920s by passage of chain store regulatory legislation in various states. The attack was mounted in the form of a graduated license fee based on the number of stores operated by the chain in the state. Some state legislatures even considered taxing the chain stores on the number of stores nationwide, but abandoned this proposal as unenforceable.

An examination of the history of retailing seems to indicate that whenever an innovative idea to reduce retail costs and prices is introduced, it is immediately subject to competitor litigation. While some states were busy attempting to curb chain store growth, other coordinated attacks were being directed at supermarkets. Local ordinances concerning zoning, public parking in front of the stores, special taxes, and license fees created impediments to the introduction of new forms of retail competition.

Such grass roots concern inevitably resulted in anticompetition legislation at the federal level in the form of the Robinson-Patman Act (1936), the Miller-Tydings Act (1937), and later the McGuire Act (1952).

In order to appreciate fully the impact of the various laws, it is necessary to consider the environment of the times when such legislation was passed. After eight years of severe economic depression, many small businessmen were fighting for their economic lives. The basic issue was the size of discounts, such as quantity discounts, promotion discounts, and the like, to be given to various retailers. From the evidence presented to Congress, it appeared that certain producers gave "extraordinary" discounts to large-volume purchasers or retailers, hence putting the small merchant at a competitive disadvantage. Much controversy still shrouds the Robinson-Patman Act, but it went far in the regulation of discounts offered to differentiated retailers.

Perhaps of most interest are the unfair practices acts or minimum markup laws now in effect in some thirty-two states. Technically, these laws require retailers to maintain a stated markup of 6 to 12 percent on invoiced cost, although retailers are permitted to lower such markups to meet competition or to close out discontinued or damaged goods. Most of these laws are not vigorously enforced, but they still remain a potential anticompetitive restriction on retailers.

Credit Legislation

Without doubt, the most costly and significant related legislation in recent years is encompassed by the Consumer Credit Protection Act of 1968, generally known as the Truth in Lending Act; the Fair Credit Reporting Act of 1970; and the Fair Credit Billing Act of 1975. In the past debtors have been placed in an inferior legal position to creditors. With this in mind, the Congress attempted to give the users of consumer credit some basic rights. For example, when credit customers seek credit by opening a new account they are given a detailed statement of the exact credit terms, written in ordinary language. The same information must be provided twice yearly either with the bill or through a separate mailing.

Additionally, each monthly bill must include the address and telephone number where complaints and inquiries may be lodged. Under the terms of this provision a customer has sixty days in which to make a complaint about an alleged billing error and the credit granting agency must acknowledge and reply within thirty days of receipt of the complaint. The credit agency must exercise reasonable efforts to resolve the difference and to resolve the final issue within ninety days after the receipt of the complaint.

Other sections of the act specify that the bills must be mailed at least fourteen days before finance charges may be assessed if there is a free period provision in the basic agreement, payments are to be credited to a customer's account the day they are received, and credit card firms cannot prohibit participating merchants from giving discounts for cash purchases up to five percent. One should note that the last provision does not require the retailer to give a cash discount; the legislation is only permissive without recourse.

Civil Rights Legislation

Another significant legislative action created the Civil Rights Act of 1964 as amended in 1972 with its Title VII provisions prohibiting illegal discrimination against persons on the basis of sex, race, religion, or country of national origin. While the act applies only to firms employing fifteen or more employees, every firm is judged to some extent by the community on its employment practices in general as well as on its adherence to the principles set forth in the act.

In keeping with the changing social awareness expressed in the Civil Rights Act of 1964 as amended in 1972, governmental interest was expressed concerning equal credit opportunity, particularly for minorities and women. In the past a woman heading a household had been discriminated against on the basis of a point scoring system that favored married males with steady employment. Particular problems were encountered by widows and divorced women who did not have separate credit histories based on their own ability to manage credit extensions. Often, even though they were good credit candidates, members of this group were denied any credit. Now, after the passage of the Equal Credit Opportunity Act, no creditor may inquire about the marital status of a person nor treat part-time income differently from full-time income. Rejected credit applicants now have the right to know why they were denied credit. Last, since November 1, 1976 any married credit account holder can ask that his or her credit record be kept separately from a spouse's record. This creates an added cost burden for the retailer, but society has mandated that this service is in the public interest and such records must be maintained by any credit grantor.

With the increasing centralization of retailing, more chains are operating in all fifty states. In order to obtain some uniformity in credit transactions with consumers, the National Conference of Commissioners on Uniform State Legislation developed the Uniform Consumer Credit Code, or "U3C," for consideration and adoption in all fifty states. One of the more interesting proposed provisions was the right of the consumer to cancel an installment credit agreement within three days as the result of a change of mind. The proposal has caused considerable debate and has yet to be adopted by many states.

Although not specifically directed at the creation or maintenance of a competitive environment for retailing, several other related pieces of federal legislation have had a considerable impact on retailers. Among these are the Wheeler-Lea Act (1938), dealing with truth in advertising; the Antimerger Act of 1950 (an amendment to the Clayton Act); and the Fair Labor Standards Act of 1938 (amended in 1977), which sets the current minimum wage of certain hourly employees (with attendant overtime provisions). Every time the minimum wage is raised, the added cost must be recouped in higher prices or lower profits. Current legislation provides for increases which are so sizable that some experts predict some marginal firms will be forced to close rather than pay the higher wages. Whether or not this will happen only the future can tell.

Employee Health and Safety

Significant changes in the practices of health and safety in retailing have occurred as a result of passage of the Occupational Safety and Health Act of 1970. Admittedly, not all retailers were equally affected, but the provisions of the act as well as questionable enforcement practices of the Department of Labor have put a particularly heavy burden on some retail service firms. While no one will deny the need for a clean, safe work place, some of the required changes in practices have bordered on the ridiculous. Currently steps are being taken to rationalize the implementation of the program so that the original spirit of the legislation might be realized.

Employee Retirement

The latest labor-related legislation to affect the retail industry is the Employee Retirement Income Security Act (ERISA) passed in 1975. The basic intent of the act was to establish guidelines for instituting and administering employee retirement funds or pensions so that the employees would be assured that when they retire the funds will be available to fulfill the contractual retirement agreement. Unfortunately, the act requires a great deal of financial responsibility and paperwork to be assumed by the firm, so that more firms have terminated their plans than have created new ones. The very firms that the act was directed toward have been unable to comply, and another employee fringe benefit has been lost to bureaucratic red tape.

Union-Management Relations

Organized labor has had a mixed record of selling union membership to the retail employees. However, where it has succeeded, the retail firm must observe all the provisions of the National Labor Relations Act of 1935 (Wagner Act), the Labor-Management Relations Act of 1947 (Taft-Hartley Act) as well as the precedent-setting rulings by the National Labor Relations Board and federal court decisions. Further in-depth consideration of these and other employer-employee matters will be examined in more detail in a later chapter.

Environmental Concerns

Recently the choice of packaging material has become a source of considerable consumer concern. While it is quite true that retailers usually do not participate in packaging decisions, their sales can be strongly affected by an ecologically aware public. Certain types of plastic containers, once created, are not biodegradable, nor can they be burned because they generate noxious fumes. Knowledgable persons will not purchase products that are dispensed in this type of container, forcing the retailer to take this into consideration when establishing the merchandising plan.

On the state level, Oregon has banned the sale of beverages in nonreturnable containers. As a result, all the drugstores, grocery stores, liquor dealers, convenience stores, and vending machine operators had to hire additional staff to handle the bottles, give up valuable space for storing them between collections, and tie up funds in bottle inventory. These added costs must be covered by higher prices for the products.

Other states are considering similar legislation. Such action may have a profound effect on the packaging of certain products, and the impact may even extend to the mode of display of these products in retail outlets. For example, if "bubble packaging" were to be outlawed, all the merchandise currently sold on hanging cards would have to be repackaged. Retailers would have to buy new display fixtures to replace the obsolete racks. Every retailer has a direct interest in future packaging decisions and legislation.

One could go on cataloguing the various legal areas of concern with suppliers (Uniform Commercial Code), stockholders (Federal Securities Act 1933, 1934, 1964, and the Securities Investor Act of 1970) and so forth to document that retailing, when practiced on a large scale, is a very complicated activity. The legal implications involve virtually every government agency, from the federal government down to local levels where retailers must secure licenses and permits to do business. Governmental intervention into the retailing industry has been and continues to be extensive and pervasive. However, to date the retail industry has adapted to the changing conditions and survives to serve the consuming public.

Summary

The marketing concept represents a fundamental reorientation in the U.S. economic system. The industrial revolution emphasized mass production of uniform goods at prices that a wide segment of the population could afford. An age of relative scarcity during the World War II years gave way to an age of relative affluence that demanded new methods of product and service distribution.

The marketing concept was born in the mid-1950s and continues to gain acceptance in enlightened business centers around the world. The marketing concept stresses consumer need satisfaction through the possession and use of goods and services. For example, instead of designing a car body based on aerodynamic characteristics or an automotive engineer's calculations, the Japanese automakers surveyed American consumer tastes and designed automobiles to sell in America. Their success speaks for itself.

Through the skillful blending of various combinations of product, place, promotion, and price, marketers everywhere are devising an almost infinite series of total need-satisfying packages to vie for the customer's dollar vote in the retail marketplace. Thus the retailer, the ultimate bridge between producer and consumer, bears the heavy burden of anticipating consumer needs and buying patterns and of transporting, financing, promoting, merchandising, and pricing goods and services. All of this is done in competition with other retailers in an attempt to serve consumers better, transforming them into repeat customers, thereby assuring the business of continued survival. The task of profitably meeting consumer needs has been made even more challenging with increased governmental intervention and regulation. Federal, state, and local laws increasingly reduce the retailer's sphere of free choice in the operation of the business.

Questions

1. Discuss the meaning of the marketing concept. Can you anticipate any future limits on the implementation of this concept?

2. How would you determine how far a retailer should go in satisfying consumer needs?

3. What factors determine whether a retailer has an effective marketing mix?

4. How does promotion serve consumers?

5. Why do retailers generally prefer nonprice competition in their long-run pricing plans?

6. What variables are at a retailer's disposal in deciding on a retailing mix? Using a systems approach, trace the effects on the organization of manipulating these variables. Consider both short- and long-run effects.

7. From your own experience and observations, cite some examples of product differentiation for various target markets.

8. Pick a consumer product that might be sold by a retailer and suggest a method of segmenting the market for that product.

9. How would you explain the development of anticompetition-curbing legislation such as the Robinson-Patman Act?

10. What is a full disclosure statement? What consumer benefits can you see in requiring a full disclosure statement? Do you think that this statement has made consumers more reluctant to make purchases on time?

11. What recourse does a consumer have if he or she is rejected for credit?

Footnotes

1. E. Jerome McCarthy, *Basic Marketing: A Managerial Approach* (Homewood, Ill.: Richard D. Irwin, 1971), p. 19.

2. Philip Kotler, *Marketing Management,* 2d ed. (Englewood Cliffs, N.J.: Prentice-Hall, 1972), p. 18.

3. Ray Geiger, ed., *Farmer's Almanac for 1976* (Lewiston, Maine: Almanac Publishing Company, 1975), vol. 159, p. 1.

4. Richard M. Bessom and Donald W. Jackson, Jr., "Service Retailing: A Strategic Marketing Approach," *Journal of Retailing* 51 (Summer 1975): 77.

5. William Lazer and Eugene J. Kelley, "The Retailing Mix: Planning and Management," *Journal of Retailing* 45 (Spring 1969): 34–41.

6. Ronald R. Gist, *Basic Retailing: Text and Cases* (New York: John Wiley & Sons, 1971), pp. 65–66.

7. McCarthy, *Basic Marketing*, p. 77.

8. Joseph C. Seibert, *Concepts of Marketing Management* (New York: Harper & Row, 1973), p. 364.

9. Ralph S. Alexander, ed., *Marketing Definitions: A Glossary of Marketing Terms* (Chicago: American Marketing Association, 1960), p. 17.

10. John W. Wingate, Elmer O. Schaller, and F. Leonard Miller, *Retail Merchandise Management* (Englewood Cliffs, N.J.: Prentice-Hall, 1972), p. 16.

11. *Laws of Missouri*, H.B. 384, passed at the session of the 39th Assembly, January 4, 1899 (Jefferson City: Tribune Printing Co., 1899), p. 72.

12. U.S. Industrial Commission, *Final Report of the Industrial Commission* (Washington, D.C.: Government Printing Office, 1902), 19: 548.

Case Study

Carbone's Meat Market

Joe Carbone Inc. is a cattle feeder who buys 650-pound feeder cattle from ranchers and fattens them in their feedlot to a weight of about 1050 pounds. The firm has recently established two of its own retail meat market outlets in two of the more affluent areas of a large midwestern city. They did this to bypass the middlemen generally involved in the meat marketing channel. The traditional channel usually involves the sale of fat cattle to a packing plant which may sell the processed meat to a wholesaler or directly to a supermarket, cafe, retail meat market, or other meat handling agencies.

Joe Carbone Inc. pays a slaughterhouse for its slaughtering services. The ungraded sides are then transported to a processor who is paid to process the meat into quarters. These quarters are then transported to the retail outlet where they are cut and prepared for sale.

Buying beef by the quarter has resulted in a considerable stocking problem; the ratio of high-volume cuts to low-volume cuts is difficult to optimize. The slaughterhouse delivers not only the quarters but also other meat which the firm does not really want. The firm is now negotiating a deal under which the slaughterhouse performs its services and keeps the by-products as its fee for the slaughter. The main problem continues to be the inability to obtain an optimum blend of the cuts demanded by consumers. Both of the firm's stores are located in affluent areas, so they are unable to sell all of their lower quality cuts. These cuts continue to accumulate in the store.

The beef they are selling is fabricated under government inspection, but it is not graded because grading costs between twelve to fifteen dollars a head, depending on the quantities that are inspected. The owners of the retail meat market believe that the selling of nongraded beef is not a problem in their sales because they believe their beef would be equivalent to Choice or Prime in grade if it were graded. Marketing methods that have been used by the firm are: self-service, open-shelf, bulk marketing of halves and quarters, and selling bulk family packs.

Only about 10 percent of the meat is now sold in bulk halves and quarters. The rest is sold in cuts but often sold in large quantities. Retail meat prices in these stores are comparable to those of other supermarkets. Carbone's has emphasized the price appeal by advertising the elimination of middlemen from the marketing channels in their promotional campaign. They are planning to open more stores under their direct control. They are also investigating franchising plans for operating other stores. More outlets are needed because they are not selling all of their beef to their own markets. Their intent is to increase profits by controlling the entire market channel and to sell all their beef through this particular channel.

Discussion Questions

1. Do you think Carbone's meat markets will be successful? Why or why not?

2. Evaluate Carbone's marketing mix. Recommend changes that could improve his marketing mix.

3. What do you think consumers consider when they buy meat? How well does Carbone's offering satisfy these needs?

Case Study

Gas Saver, Inc.

Jack Larsen has invented a simple device which can be attached to the carburetor of any motor driven vehicle to decrease the consumption of gasoline. The proper installation of the device must be performed by a skilled mechanic. However, it only takes about one hour for an experienced mechanic to install the device. The device can be produced, distributed, installed, and sold to the consumer for about $150.

Mr. Larsen knew that many phony gas savings devices have been peddled to the public. He realized that the consumer is not likely to believe fully his claims of reduced gas consumption. So he agreed to let the state highway department test the performance of his device in its cars under actual driving conditions. The device proved to be effective; the state highway department tests showed that the installation of the device increased gas mileage on its cars and pickup trucks by about 50 percent.

Mr. Larsen is thus faced with a real dilemma. His background is strong in the mechanical field, but he has no experience in the marketing field. The firm currently employs ten people and is able to produce about 500 devices per day.

Discussion Questions

1. Develop a list of the potential market segments that might be interested in Mr. Larsen's device.

2. Evaluate the annual sales potential for each segment described in your list.

3. Select the most appropriate market target for Mr. Larsen to reach with his initial marketing efforts. Remember, he has a small business with a limited supply of funds.

4. What kind of marketing channel do you recommend that Mr. Larsen use in his marketing efforts?

5. What type of promotional efforts do you think would be most effective?

Chapter 3

Understanding the Consumer

1. To learn how economics affects consumer purchase behavior.

2. To be able to discuss how social dimensions influence consumer buying decisions.

3. To understand how cognition, perception, motivation, and learning contribute to the decision-making process used by consumers.

4. To know how a retailer's attributes are evaluated by consumers.

5. To be aware of the effect that the consumer movement has had upon the retailing industry.

substitute items	family life cycle	self-actualization needs
complementary items	drives	cognition
nondiscretionary expenditure	cues	perception
discretionary expenditures	response	motivation
conspicuous consumption	reinforcement	learning
reference group	physiological needs	functional needs
social class	safety needs	nonfunctional needs
	social needs	consumerism
	esteem needs	

The first two chapters stressed the need for retail managers to study consumer behavior to obtain an understanding of consumer habits and motivations. An improved understanding of the reasons consumers behave as they do can enable management to predict changes in tastes, behavior, and attitudes. These predictions can be used to plan a retail strategy that will reach the consumer more effectively and more efficiently. Indeed, the success of the retailing effort depends upon an understanding of consumer behavior. The effectiveness of retail merchandise assortments, price and promotion policies, and the selection of store location(s) depends on how well management understands the needs, motivation, and habits of its potential customers.

This chapter is devoted to setting forth some basic explanations for consumer behavior. It is concerned with the question, "Why do consumers behave as they do? How do consumers learn? How can consumers' impressions and opinions be modified?" Many large retail managers no longer have the time to interact with many of their retail customers on a face-to-face basis; nevertheless, these managers must understand consumers in terms of the general concepts defining consumer behavior and by undertaking specific marketing research projects (such as those described in Chapter 17). Management can then use its understanding of consumer behavior as a basis for building a retail strategy that will better meet the needs of the consumer group(s) the outlet is attempting to serve.

General Approaches to Understanding Consumer Behavior

The study of consumer behavior will now be examined from four different standpoints. These standpoints reflect the economic, social, psychological and sociopsychological aspects of consumer behavior.

Unfortunately, none of these approaches offers a complete explanation of consumer behavior, but each approach provides a partial explanation of consumer behavior in the retail environment.

Economic Aspects of Consumer Behavior

The economic aspects of behavior involve those elements of consumer behavior that are influenced by income or purchasing power.

Maximizing Satisfaction

Traditional economic theory has focused on the belief that consumers act to maximize the satisfaction that they purchase with available monetary resources.[1]

Despite some limiting assumptions, this theory suggests several useful behavioral explanations of consumer buying behavior.

First—other things being equal—the lower the price of the merchandise, the higher the sales level on that product. For most items a price reduction increases the consumer's perception of the relative value of the item and thereby generates increased sales. This is a general rule, which does not apply to all people or all merchandise items. If some consumers buy a smaller quantity as a result of a price decrease, they may believe that the quality has deteriorated or that ownership of the item has less status value as a result of the price decrease. Some items (diamonds, jewelry, furs, boats, campers, and so forth) are used as status symbols and are displayed to gain and maintain esteem. Severe price reductions on these items may not stimulate sales but may merely reduce the value of the items in the minds of the consumer. In this case the consumer may not believe that the actual quality of the item has declined, but the display or status value has declined.

Price also appears to be directly related to the amount of searching that consumers do before they make a purchase. The searching activity includes store visits, exposure to promotions, discussions with knowledgeable people, and reading consumer publications. The direct relationship between the amount of searching done and the item's price simply implies that consumers spend more time evaluating expensive goods and services and less time evaluating inexpensive items. For example, about three-fourths of the clothing, fabrics, and small household soft goods are purchased in the first store that the consumer visits. However, the number of stores visited before a consumer makes a soft goods purchase increases with the price of the item and with merchandise involving fashion and style.[2]

A second implication of the economic model involves the interrelationship of merchandise items. Other things being equal, a lowering of the price on *substitute* (or similar) *items* will lower the sales of the item being observed. For example, a price reduction on the retailer's house brand of clock radios will probably cause an increase in the sales of that item but reduce the sales of the other brands of clock radios the store carries. Some items tend to generate sales for *complementary* items (companion merchandise), and the economic model predicts that lowering the price on one item will stimulate additional sales of its complementary products. For example, retailers may reduce the price and/or increase the promotion of a card table in the hope of stimulating the sales of card tables *and* folding chairs.

The third implication of the economic model is that higher real personal income tends to result in higher sales of goods and services. The amount of the increase, however, varies among specific items and services, and two basic consumer expenditure patterns have implications for retailers. These patterns are the nondiscretionary and the discretionary patterns of income allocation.

The *nondiscretionary expenditure* pattern concentrates upon the consumer's monetary outlays on contractual, necessary, and habitual expenditures.[3] Mortage payments, installment debt, and insurance premiums are examples of contractual expenditures for which the consumer's commitment cannot be changed unless he or she wishes to lose some or all of the value of the past payments. Necessary expenditures are those life-sustaining purchases that are made mostly for food, clothing, and medical care. Habitual expenditures are the purchases made so frequently that the consumer develops a regular purchasing plan to acquire them. Daily newspapers, cigarettes, and beer are examples of habitual outlays of a relatively low unit value.

Discretionary expenditures are made for those purchases in which the consumer is not motivated by a compelling need and is not generally governed by habit, and which entail some deliberation prior to purchase.[4] Many retailers depend upon discretionary consumer expenditures for their main source of business. Rising consumer income and increased consumer willingness to use credit has caused some retailers to concentrate on product and service offerings that capitalize on these trends.

Certainly the proportion of income spent for nondiscretionary goods and services tends to decrease as consumer income increases. Similarly, Engel's laws and the income elasticity concept can be used to identify those products and services that respond best to increases in consumer income. These concepts are explained and their use is illustrated in Chapter 5.

Thus, income determines one's ability to buy. For this reason many retailers define their target market to be consumers in the top half of the income distribution. This 50 percent of the people controls 75 percent of the total income and hence 75 percent of the buying power in the country. Thus, it is relatively inexpensive to only have to serve half the people in order to reach three-fourths of the total buying potential.

Income also affects the way people shop. For example, people with higher incomes and more education, children, and fashion consciousness are greater users of in-home shopping methods such as mail order, telephone, and buying from door-to-door salespeople.[5] Items that are easily standardized and identified are most likely to be purchased at home. But merchandise items such as clothing that must be offered in many different sizes, colors, styles, and so forth are less likely to be purchased in the home because they entail more risk of producing consumer disappointment.

Reacting to Expected Changes in Income

Another aspect of income that influences consumer behavior is expected changes in the consumer's income. Income expectations depend upon the percent of chance that the consumers attach to the likelihood that their incomes will change in the near future. Expectations also depend upon the amount consumers believe their income will increase or decrease in the near future. Finally, expectations depend upon whether consumers view the anticipated change in income as a permanent or a temporary change. Consumers who expect a temporary decrease in income usually do not immediately adapt their purchases to this reduced income level.

As income declines, expenditures decline, but at a much slower rate than the decline in income would suggest. On the other hand, unexpected income (which the consumers didn't believe they would receive in the near future) is usually spent fairly quickly. For example, 63 percent of a group of consumers who did not intend to buy a new car actually bought a new car soon after they received an unexpectedly large income.[6]

Social Aspects of Consumer Behavior

Social dimensions of consumer behavior are implicit in those consumer actions that are related either to demographic matters or to reference-group considerations. A demographic study of a population involves an analysis of the effect that age, social class, education, geographical density characteristics, occupation, marriage status, and sex have upon purchase behavior. The term "reference group" refers to any group of people that is capable of influencing the behavior of an individual.[7]

Demographic Characteristics

Demographic characteristics that are particularly critical to retailers are population size, geographical distribution of the population, and social class. Trends in these factors have been discussed in Chapters 1 and 2. The importance of demographic characteristics is reflected in retailers who have learned that they must serve consumers from a location that is conveniently reached by the consumer. For example, the suburban shopping centers are an outgrowth of population movements to the suburbs.

Not only is population increasing, but Americans have become a mobile people. About 20 percent change their address each year. About two-thirds of these moves involve a relocation in the same county.

Whenever people move they develop new store patronage habits. Thus, a retailer may continually lose 20 percent of the firm's customers each year. However, the firm also has the opportunity of gaining at least an equal percentage of the consumers who are new to the area. The astute retailer will determine what goods and services these new consumers want and then adjust the firm's offerings to meet these needs. Sometimes retailers find that the new consumers in the community are quite different from the previous consumers. For example, only young people from eighteen to twenty-two years old may be moving into the area to replace older families who are moving out of the area. If the magnitude of the shift is large, then the retailer will have to make radical changes in the firm's retailing mix. In this case the firm which was selling major home appliances may have to completely redefine its market and switch to handling more small appliances, stereos, and so forth that will better appeal to the new younger market. If the firm does not want to undergo such radical changes in the nature of its business, then it may eventually have to consider moving to a new location.

Social Role

A consumer's social position and the perceptions of his or her role in society also exert an influence upon retail buying habits. For example, isolated urban dwellers have been found to prefer making purchases in small stores because the small store provides them with personal contacts.[8]

Conspicuous consumption, or the purchase and use of goods and services primarily to raise prestige rather than to satisfy material needs, is designed to gain acceptance from the consumer's reference group. Thus the newly rich minority-group member may be in a market group that is especially likely to buy large diamonds or fashion clothing because they offer visual proof that the individual has arrived. It is important that retailers identify purchases made for purposes of conspicuous consumption, because their pricing, advertising, merchandise selection, and packaging can be used to appeal to this consumer motivation.

The desire to improve the quality of one's life and to enjoy some luxuries has led to the human desire to always want the "new and improved" or the best and most unusual merchandise and services. Retailers of durable goods have capitalized on these desires of conspicuous consumption by always trying to get the consumers to purchase the top-of-the-line merchandise because it offers more and better features than do the less expensive models. Other examples of conspicuous consumption are increased trends in: (1) the frequency of eating out at restaurants, (2) the demand for wines and gourmet foods, (3) attending live entertainment events (4) purchases of art, antiques, and precious minerals.

The individual's role in the family also has important implications for retailers. Some retailers' merchandising strategy may be oriented exclusively toward the actual buyer of the merchandise. Others may orient their merchandising toward the users of the item. For example, a supermarket's breakfast cereal assortment may reflect the preference of children rather than the preference of the adult buyer.

The where, when, what, and how-much-to-spend decisions are not always made by the same individual and in fact may be made jointly. The purchase of expensive goods or services (such as autos, major appliances, and housing) that affect a number of family members is usually made after very careful planning and the involvement of more than one group member. Most major joint purchases are heavily influenced by the person who knows the most about the items under consideration. For example, Table 3–1 indicates that the husband may have more influence than the wife on when an automobile should be purchased, where it should be purchased, and how much should be spent on it, but the color, model, and make may be decided by mutual agreement between husband and wife. Similarly, the wife may have more influence in determining the style, color, and fabric of furniture purchases, but the how-much-to-spend, when to buy, and where to buy decisions may be made jointly by husband and wife (Table 3–1).

It is important for retailers to realize who is buying and to identify the degree of influence the buyer is receiving from within or outside the family. If the influences can be identified, the firm's promotion and merchandise assortment can be shaped to appeal to both the buyer and the influencing *reference group* (the group of people that the individual aspires to belong to).

It is also important to realize that consumers may identify negatively with particular reference groups. That is, they avoid the unique behavioral traits of such a group.[9] Thus a store may have considerable difficulty appealing to two widely different consumer groups simply because members of each group perceive the store to be catering to the other group.

Social Class
Social class is another sociological consideration that has helped retailers better understand consumer behavior. All U.S. citizens do not have the same power and

Table 3-1 **Marital Roles in Selected Automobile and Furniture Purchase Decisions as Perceived by Wives and Husbands**

Who Decided:	Patterns of Influence (%) as Perceived by Wives			Patterns of Influence (%) as Perceived by Husbands		
	Husband Has More Influence than Wife	Husband and Wife Have Equal Influence	Wife Has More Influence than Husband	Husband Has More Influence than Wife	Husband and Wife Have Equal Influence	Wife Has More Influence than Husband
When to buy the automobile?	68	30	2	68	29	3
Where to buy the automobile?	59	39	2	62	35	3
How much to spend for the automobile?	62	34	4	62	37	1
What make of automobile to buy?	50	50	—	60	32	8
What model of automobile to buy?	47	52	1	41	50	9
What color of automobile to buy?	25	63	12	25	50	25
How much to spend for furniture?	17	63	20	22	47	31
When to buy the furniture?	18	52	30	16	45	39
Where to buy the furniture?	6	61	33	7	53	40
What furniture to buy?	4	52	44	3	33	64
What style of furniture to buy?	2	45	53	2	26	72
What color and fabric to select?	2	24	74	2	16	82

Note: Table is based on a survey to which 97 people responded.

Source: Harry L. Davis, "Dimensions of Marital Roles in Consumer Decision Making," *Journal of Marketing Research 7* (May 1970): 169, 170. Reprinted from Journal of Marketing Research published by the American Marketing Association.

prestige. They are engaged in different occupations that are not equally prestigious. They do not have similar possessions or value systems. Thus there is an informal ordering of individuals into relatively homogeneous groupings in terms of social status. A *social class* is a group of many people who are about equal to one another in prestige and community status. People within a social class regularly interact among members of their group and share the same general goals and philosophy of life.

Professor W. Lloyd Warner is largely responsible for the development of a description of social stratification that divides U.S. society into six social classes (which are described in Exhibit 3–1). The major contribution of the study of social classes to a retailer's understanding of consumer behavior is that it provides a useful tool with which to segment the market into meaningful consumer groups.

Shoppers in the various social classes seek out retail outlets that make them feel most comfortable and that cater to their particular class. The lower-status woman has been found to believe that if she enters high-status department stores, the clerks and the other customers will make her wait or will punish her in some other subtle way.[10] This belief causes lower-status people to avoid the upper-class stores. The result is retail institutions that convey a sense of different levels of social class and social prestige to their customers.

Such differences are more noticeable with some merchandise lines than others.

Exhibit 3–1 A Description of Warner's Six Commonly Used Social Classes

---

1—Upper-Upper or "Social Register" consists of locally prominent families, usually with at least second or third generation wealth. Basic Values: living graciously, upholding family reputation, reflecting the excellence of one's breeding, and displaying a sense of community responsibility. About ½ of 1% of the population.

2—Lower-Upper or "Nouveau Riche" consists of the more recently arrived and never-quite-accepted wealthy families. Goals: blend of Upper-Upper pursuit of gracious living and the Upper-Middle drive for success. About 1½% of the population.

3—Upper-Middle are moderately successful professional men and women, owners of medium-sized businesses, young people in their twenties and early thirties who are expected to arrive at the managerial level by their middle or late thirties. Motivations: success at a career, cultivating charm and polish. About 10% of the population.

4—Lower-Middle are mostly non-managerial office workers, small business owners, highly paid blue-collar families. Goals: respectability, and striving to live in well-maintained homes, neatly furnished in more-or-less "right" neighborhoods, and to do a good job at their work. They will save for a college education for their children. Top of the Average Man World. About 30%–35% of the population.

5—Upper-Lower or "Ordinary Working Class" consists of semi-skilled workers. Although many make high pay, they are not particularly interested in respectability. Goals: enjoying life and living well from day to day, to be at least modern, and to work hard enough to keep safely away from the slum level. About 40% of the population.

6—Lower-Lower are unskilled workers, unassimilated ethnics, and the sporadically employed. Outlooks: apathy, fatalism, "get your kicks whenever you can." About 15% of the population, but have less than half that of the purchasing power.

Source: Irving J. Shapiro, *Marketing Terms: Explanations, Definitions, and/or Aspects* (West Long Branch, N.J.: S-M-C Publishing Company, 1973), pp. 156–157. Reprinted by permission.

The middle-class shopper may patronize relatively low-status discount stores to buy large items (such as refrigerators, color television, washing machines, etc.) whose quality is "assured" by the brand name of a national manufacturer. The selection of the "right" store is much more important for items (such as clothing or furniture) whose style or taste is important to the consumer, because these items convey social awareness and values.[11]

Preferences for different types of retail outlets are also related to social class membership. The lower-level working class tends to prefer the neighborhood store because they fear being snubbed or ignored if they go outside the neighborhood to a downtown merchant or large shopping center. Middle-class housewives are more confident in their shopping ability and are more willing to seek out new stores and new shopping experiences. Lower-status consumers appear to prefer face-to-face contact with friendly local clerks whom they know and believe can be trusted to assist them in making purchase decisions. They also prefer to shop in stores that extend credit.

The difference in store choice by members of different social classes can be illustrated by consumer behavior in buying cosmetics. Upper middle-class women buy their cosmetics in department stores while lower-class women prefer to buy cosmetics in variety stores. Drug stores appear to be equally suitable to all classes.[12] When consumers from several different social strata buy in the same store, they are likely to purchase different items or to buy the same items for different reasons. For example, when the lower-class woman shops in a store patronized by middle-class women, she may be interested only in buying gifts for others and not in making purchases for herself.

The social class concept is also useful in selecting media that can be used to reach the various market segments, because corresponding differences occur in the exposure to media. The following quotation summarizes some of the differences in media reaction or behavior among classes.

> The different meanings of media have been explored in many studies. The media function in varied ways, and each also fits differentially into the lives of the social classes. There are (sometimes sharp) class preferences among the newspapers available in a community, in evaluating magazines, in selecting television shows, in listening to the radio, in how newspapers are read, in receipt and meaning of direct mail; and, in general, in the total volume of materials to which people are exposed and to which they attend in one or another of the media. Higher status people see more magazines, read more of the newspaper, and buy more newspapers. Lower class people tend to prefer the afternoon paper, middle class people tend to prefer the morning paper. Studies in recent years of television in fifteen major cities show that upper middle class people consistently prefer the NBC channel, while lower middles prefer the CBS; and these preferences are in keeping with the images of the networks and the characteristics of the social classes.[13]

Family Life Cycle

The *family life cycle* concept, which divides the population into different groups, with each group representing a different stage in life, is also used to segment markets and identify market targets. Expenditure patterns and purchase motivations change over a consumer's lifetime (Table 3–2 contains a general description of such changes). Market targets, revealed by the family life cycle concept and identified in Table 3–2, include clothing for the fashion-conscious singles. The young, married, no-children family is a good market for consumer durable goods. The change toward more youth-oriented products is apparent for the full-nest stages. The empty-nest stages are identified as good markets for luxury goods and services and other quality merchandise. Some of the families in the empty-nest stages are now moving to exclusive apartment buildings or condominiums that require little upkeep and are convenient to their places of work. This group of people represents a new market segment with new needs and purchase motivations. Alert retailers will respond to meet these needs and increase profits by recognizing this shift in consumer behavior.

Psychological Aspects of Consumer Behavior

Several psychological concepts make important contributions to the study of consumer behavior.[14]

Table 3-2   An Overview of the Family Life Cycle

Stage	Financial and Purchasing Characteristics				
Bachelor Stage: young, single, not living at home	Few financial burdens.	Fashion opinion leaders.	Recreation oriented.		Buy: basic kitchen equipment, basic furniture, cars, equipment for the mating game, vacations.
Newly Married Couples: young, no children	Better off financially than they will be in near future.	Highest purchase rate and highest average purchase of durables.			Buy: cars, refrigerators, stoves, sensible and durable furniture, vacations.
Full Nest I: youngest child under six	Liquid assets low.	Dissatisfied with financial position and amount of money saved.	Interested in new products.	Like advertised products. Home purchasing at peak.	Buy: washers, dryers, TV, baby food, chest rubs, cough medicine, vitamins, dolls, wagons, sleds, skates.
Full Nest II: youngest child six or over six	Financial position better.	Some wives work.		Less influenced by advertising. Buy larger sized packages, multiple-unit deals.	Buy: many foods, cleaning materials, bicycles, music lessons, pianos.
Full Nest III: older married couples with dependent children	Financial position still better.	More wives work.	Some children get jobs.	Hard to influence with advertising. High average purchase of durables.	Buy: new, more tasteful furniture, auto travel, non-necessary appliances, boats, dental services, magazines.

Stage	Financial and Purchasing Characteristics					
Empty Nest I: older married couples, no children at home, head of family employed	Most satisfied with financial position and money saved.	Make gifts and contributions.	Not interested in new products.	Interested in travel, recreation, self-education.	Home ownership at peak.	Buy: vacations, luxuries, home improvements.
Empty Nest II: older married couples, no children at home, head of family retired	Drastic cut in income.		Keep home.			Buy: medical appliances, medical care, products which aid health, sleep, and digestion.
Solitary Survivor: employed	Income still good, but likely to sell home.					
Solitary Survivor: retired	Drastic cut in income.		Special need for attention, affection, and security.		Same medical and product needs as other retired groups.	

Adapted from William D. Wells and George Gubar, "Life Cycle Concept in Marketing Research," *Journal of Marketing Research* 3 (November 1966): 362. Reprinted from *Journal of Marketing Research* published by the American Marketing Association.

Pavlovian Learning Model

The Pavlovian learning model, as it has been modified over the years, is based on the four concepts of *drive, cue, response,* and *reinforcement.*[15]

Drives are an individual's strong internal stimuli that impel the person to action. Drives, or needs, may be either physiological (hunger, thirst, cold, pain, and sex) or socially derived motives (cooperation, fear, and acquisitiveness), which are learned.

Cues are weaker stimuli in the individual and/or environment that influence the consumer's response. For example, a McDonald's hamburger advertisement can serve as a cue that stimulates the hunger drive in a child. The response will depend upon the advertisement cue and other cues, such as the time of day, the relative availability of other hunger-satisfying alternatives, and the like. A change in the relative intensity can frequently be more forceful than the absolute level of the cue. For example, a child who has only a small amount of money may be more motivated by a special price offer that is good for one day only than by the fact that the hamburger is usually low priced.

The *response* is the individual's reaction to all of the cues. The same relative arrangement of cues will not always produce the same response each time in the individual because the earlier experience may or may not have been rewarding. If the response generates a favorable experience, that response is strengthened or *reinforced* and the response will probably be repeated when and if the same arrangement of cues reappears.

The Pavlovian model does not adequately treat concepts such as perceptions, the subconscious, and interpersonal influence. It does, however, offer some useful insight into consumer behavior. It provides guidelines in developing advertising strategy by suggesting that a single exposure to an advertisement is too weak a cue to stimulate a strong, favorable response. Thus it is desirable to repeat advertisements because repetition reduces forgetting on the part of the consumer. The absence of a message would tend to result in a weakened learned response, according to the Pavlovian model.

In addition, repetitive advertising provides reinforcement as the consumer becomes selectively exposed to the advertisement after making the purchase. The Pavlovian model also indicates that copy strategy must arouse strong drives in the individual if it is to be effective as a cue. The strongest item- or service-related drives must be identified and presented with the right words, colors, and pictures to provide the strongest stimulus to these drives.

Maslow's Hierarchy of Motives

Maslow's hierarchy of motives offers a good perspective for a better understanding of consumer behavior. Maslow believed that a person is a perpetually wanting individual. As certain needs are satisfied, the next most important need tends to dominate the individual's conscious life.[16] Maslow considers *physiological needs* (hunger, sex, thirst, and so forth) to be the most basic type of needs. These must be satisfied before an individual can be concerned about other needs. When these physiological needs are satisfied, the buyer proceeds to the second-level needs, which are *safety needs.* Safety needs consist of the desire for security, protection, and order or routine. Consumers satisfy their safety needs by means of savings accounts, insurance, pension plans, refrigerators, home freezers, and the like.

After the physiological and safety needs are satisfied, individuals become concerned about *social needs* such as love needs, or the need for affection and belonging. To satisfy love needs, the individual strives to be accepted by the members of his family and to be an important person to them and to others who are close friends. The fourth need level, *esteem needs,* emerges as soon as the love needs are satisfied. The esteem needs are demands for reputation, self-respect, prestige, success, and achievement. Different status groups and symbols emerge as ways of satisfying this level of need satisfaction.

The fifth and last basic need is the desire to know, understand, organize, and construct a system of values that can be used to develop one's desire for self-fulfillment. These needs, called the *self-actualization needs,* consist of developing one's self to the fullest.

Maslow's theory is based on the concept that people have these five kinds of goals or needs. People are motivated to achieve various conditions that provide satisfaction for these needs. The needs are related in order of importance in such a way that the most powerful need will monopolize the conscious thought process of the individual, who will minimize the less pressing needs. When that need is satisfied, the next most powerful need emerges to dominate the individual's conscious reactions. Thus, a starving person (need 1) is not likely to be interested in whether he or she is breathing unpolluted air (need 2), or in how he or she is seen by others (need 3 or 4), or in a travel tour of Europe (need 5).

Socio-Psychological Aspects of Consumer Behavior

The socio-psychological concept of consumer behavior views behavior as the result of four factors: cognition, perception, motivation, and learning.[17]

Cognition

Cognition is a process individuals use to make sense out of what they see or perceive. It is the individual's total belief system, consisting of values, ideas, and attitudes. Cognitive processes assist people in their attempts to achieve their needs satisfactorily and to determine the direction to take in their attempts to attain satisfaction of the initiating need.

Perception

Perception is what individuals "see" as a result of complex patterns of stimulation filtered through their own unique cognitive processes. Perception reflects the person's past experience, present attitudes, and inclinations. For example, a customer entering a store "perceives" things that are not "seen." The person "sees" the physical items, such as the building, fixtures, merchandise, people, but the individual's perception is influenced by previous experience in shopping in the store, by conversations with friends, and the like. Thus, a person may perceive the outlet to be a warm, friendly place, conducive to shopping and lingering, if previous exposure has been pleasant.

No two people perceive a situation in exactly the same terms because people have different views of the world. Each person's view, or total belief system, is formed over time as a result of physiological abilities (eyesight, sense of smell, intelligence level, and so forth), psychological characteristics (personality and need-value systems), and the nature of past experiences.

The consumer's total belief system, or cognitive set, predisposes the person to receive and retain perceptions that he or she wants to see. Thus the consumer is a decision maker in the communications process. Consumers decide what messages to receive from their exposure to different kinds of media. They also decide what messages to perceive and retain on the basis of their attitudes, culture, and past experiences.

Risk is one element of perception that deserves further discussion. Any consumer action can produce consequences that cannot be anticipated by the consumer with 100 percent certainty.[18] Any purchase competes with alternative uses of the same money, and any purchase involves a risk that the product will not work properly, that the consumer's friends may not approve of the selection, that the service was performed improperly, and the like. *Perceived risk* may exist when the consumer is not able to define his or her buying goals and/or there are some unforeseeable consequences related to the quality of the product or service and the ability of the purchase to fulfill the consumer's psychological and social needs. Thus the consumer may perceive risk to be the result of one or more of the following factors:

1. *She may be uncertain as to what the buying goals are.* Would she rather have an outrageously expensive new dress or a new piece of furniture? If a dress, should it be the cocktail dress she has always wanted or a more functional wool suit?

2. *The consumer may be uncertain as to which purchase (product, brand, model, etc.) will best match or satisfy acceptance level of buying goals.* Should the suit be purchased at Lord and Taylor's or the local discount house? Will she really be more satisfied with a modern styling or a more conservative basic cut?

3. *The consumer may perceive possible adverse consequences if the purchase is made (or not made) and the result is a failure to satisfy her buying goals.* For example, she may suffer intense embarrassment if she buys her cocktail dress, and it is much too risqué at a party, or she looks fat, or it fits poorly.[19]

Consumer risk can be reduced by either decreasing the possible consequences or increasing the certainty of the possible outcome. Consumers read advertisements and *Consumer Reports,* examine merchandise, talk to friends, purchase items that have performed well for them in the past, buy advertised products, and buy at familiar stores to increase the certainty of the outcome of their purchases. Retailers can assist the consumer in reducing uncertainty by refusing to handle items that have not performed well for their customers. The rate of product returns and the frequency of consumer complaints will quickly identify these inferior-quality items that may have slipped through a buyer's careful selection process.

In addition, retailers can reduce consumer's perception of risk by providing a good warranty policy complemented by a good public relations policy in the consumer complaint or refunds and exchange departments. Retail advertising can also reduce consumer uncertainty by truthfully emphasizing the styling, function, and performance attributes of merchandise or service. Retail salespeople can reduce the consumer's perception of risk by assisting the individual in defining buying goals or identifying problem(s) and then providing the best available solution. Handling nationally advertised, familiar brand-name products also results in a reduction of the consumer's perceived risk.

Motivation

Motivation, the driving force behind consumer behavior, is aimed at attaining protection, satisfaction, and self-enhancement. Motives are the impulses or desires that initiate behavior. The major motives can be divided into physiological and psychological or social forces.

Maslow's hierarchy of needs, discussed previously, reveals that people first satisfy their physiological needs. The major motivating force is then channeled to satisfy the individual's next highest order need, according to Maslow's listing.

Retailing is a means by which consumers can reach their goals. In other words, retailing assists the consumer in satisfying the range of needs contained in Maslow's list. Maslow's ranking also indicates that a satisfied need is no longer an important consumer motive. Because most American consumers are able to satisfy their basic physiological desires, retailers should concentrate on strategies that satisfy consumers' social needs (love and belongingness), esteem needs, and self-actualization needs. Indeed, most consumers in American society appear to make discretionary purchases to satisfy social or esteem needs.[20] For example, advertising does not emphasize the nutritional content of food items but concentrates on social messages that illustrate how well various products will be enjoyed at parties, by friends, and so on.

Learning

Finally, the socio-psychological approach views behavior as depending upon learning, in addition to the cognition, perception, and motivation factors just discussed. *Learning* is the change in the individual's response tendencies due to the effects of his or her insight and experience.[21] The experience may be a previous visit made to a particular retail outlet, a promotional message sent by a retailer, or merely a suggestion made by a friend. The person's response may be a strong inclination to return to the store the next time he or she needs the merchandise and/or service it offers, a weak inclination to return, or a strong inclination to avoid the outlet if at all possible.

The learning process involves the four concepts discussed previously in the

Pavlovian learning model: drives, cues, responses, and reinforcement. In addition, learning involves the restructuring of the individual's attitudes and beliefs about the environment. A consumer's learned response is thus based on insight and past experiences. He or she has the capacity to solve problems by selecting the response that is most appropriate to the situation, without necessarily having previously encountered an identical situation. Some aspects of learning that affect buyer behavior are illustrated in the following observation.

The first time a man looks at an advertisement, he does not see it.

The second time he does not notice it.

The third time he is conscious of its existence.

The fourth time he faintly remembers having seen it before.

The fifth time he reads it.

The sixth time he turns up his nose at it.

The seventh time he reads it through and says, "Oh brother!"

The eighth time he says, "Here's that confounded thing again!"

The ninth time he wonders if it amounts to anything.

The tenth time he thinks he will ask his neighbor if he has tried it.

The eleventh time he wonders how the advertiser makes it pay.

The twelfth time he thinks perhaps it may be worth something.

The thirteenth time he thinks it must be a good thing.

The fourteenth time he remembers that he has wanted such a thing for a long time.

The fifteenth time he is tantalized because he cannot afford to buy it.

The sixteenth time he thinks he will buy it some day.

The seventeenth time he makes a memorandum of it.

The eighteenth time he swears at his poverty.

The nineteenth time he counts his money carefully.

The twentieth time he sees it, he buys the article.[22]

Generalizations about Consumer Behavior

Many of the concepts discussed above can be incorporated into the model of buyer behavior presented in Figure 3–1, which consists of four "fields." Subfield one includes the retailer's attributes, such as location, interior and exterior appearance, merchandise offering, price levels, and so forth, and the promotional message, such as advertising, personal selling, displays, consumer services. As the total attribute and promotional message reaches the consumer, it becomes an input into subfield two, which is the consumer's psychological attributes and inclinations. The total message is received and acted upon in light of the individual's psychological orientation, to form an attitude toward the retail outlet's total offering.

The consumer's decision to buy or not to buy is influenced mainly by the nature of the consumer's desires. The basic necessities (need for food, shelter, and health)

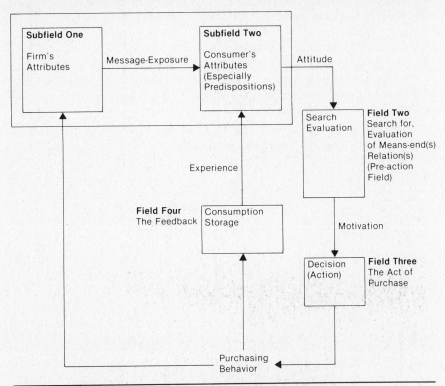

Figure 3–1 **Summary of the Nicosia Model of Buyer Behavior**
Source: Reprinted by permission of the author from Francesco M. Nicosia, *Consumer Decision Processes: Marketing and Advertising Implications* (Englewood Cliffs, N.J.: Prentice-Hall, 1966), p. 156.

are obtained by most consumers. The rise in the standard of living allows the consumer to satisfy new desires stimulated by the affluent society. This results in consumers experiencing both *functional needs* and *nonfunctional,* or psychological, *needs.* Functional needs are linked to the use of an item or service for its practical use. Consumers need fast transportation, so they buy an auto or motor bike.

However, consumers also evaluate their needs and wants from the standpoint of their environment and past experiences. Thus, factors such as education, social status, financial means, and so forth cause consumers to judge merchandise not only on its ability to satisfy their functional needs but also on its other image-generating qualities such as style, prestige, beauty, and uniqueness. The consumer's evaluation of these nonfunctional desires is linked to the social and psychological needs of creating a favorable impression, identifying with a group, and expressing one's personality.

Buying motivations arise from these consumer desires. Some of the essential buying motives are based on the wish for newness, exclusiveness, economy, dependability, and simplicity. The desire for newness is expressed by wanting to: (1) use the latest methods, (2) be associated with progress, and (3) follow the latest fashion or fad.

The desire for exclusiveness produces the wish to: (1) be different, (2) possess beautiful goods and services, (3) accumulate wealth, and (4) identify with one's reference group.

The appeal of economy provides the motive for wanting to: (1) obtain the best value for one's money, (2) buy at a reasonable price, and (3) save time.

Desiring dependability is the motive to: (1) feel safe, (2) be certain the choice is correct, (3) have warranties and guarantees, (4) have assurance that retailers will stand behind their merchandise and service.

Looking for simplicity is the motive for the consumer to: (1) do things in the easiest manner, (2) simplify work and consumption activities. This process is illustrated in Figure 3–2.

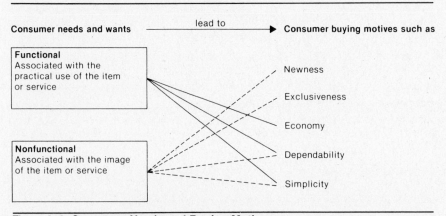

Figure 3-2 **Consumer Needs and Buying Motives**

Consumers may or may not be aware that their buying behavior is based on the motives presented in Figure 3–2. If they know why they do certain things, then they are said to be conscious of their buying motives. Sometimes, however, the reason that the consumer gives for pursuing a specific course of action may not be the only reason. In fact it may not even be the most important or the correct reason. But generally the conscious motives expressed by consumers for using a purchase pattern will provide either the most important reason or clues that will lead to the discovery of other important reasons for their behavior.

Frequently consumers know why they behave as they do, but they are reluctant to admit the reasons for their behavior. They do not want the retailer to know what really motivates them, and sometimes they do not know or even want to think of the real reason themselves. For example, a consumer may buy a big powerful auto because it satisfies the conscious and expressed motive to save driving time. But the real motive may be to draw attention and to be different. The motives that consumers do not perceive at all are called unconscious motives. These unconscious motives have a considerable influence on consumer behavior. The retailer must be constantly aware that if the firm pays attention to only what the consumer says, it will be ignoring the consumer's unconscious motives.

The consumer attitudes originating in subfield two then serve as the input for field two (Figure 3–1), which consists of the consumer's search and evaluation of an outlet's offerings and the total offerings of alternative outlets. The degree of prepurchase search depends upon many factors, as shown in Table 3–3. This table presents sixteen different determinants as developed by the expert(s) whose names appear within the parentheses. The statement *search varies directly* appears frequently in the exhibit. This means that if a consumer places a greater value on or includes a large number of items in a given determinant, the search effort will be proportionately greater (that is, will include evaluations of more alternative brands, styles, colors, advertisements, and outlets). If the search varies inversely, the greater numerical value for the determinant produces a proportionately less active search effort. For example, the prepurchase search is expected to be very active if the consumer uses a higher number of attributes as a basis to judge the product (determinant 2). But if the product is something purchased quite frequently, the search effort will be relatively inactive (determinant 4).

The output from field two may be a motivation to buy a particular product and/or service in that outlet. If so, the motivation is an input for field three because it transforms the motivation into purchasing action. The retail sales person is an especially important factor in instilling in the consumer the motivation needed to make the purchase. Finally, field four represents the feedback of the sales information to the retailer and the retention of the consequences of the purchase in the consumer's memory.

This model and our previous discussion indicate that consumers make rational efforts toward problem solving. Rational motives originate from a process of conscious deliberation and are aroused by appeals to reason. Buying motives generally belong to two groups—operational buying motives and sociopsychological buying motives.[23] Operational buying motives are directly related to the physical performance characteristics of the merchandise and service. Socio-psychological buying motives are more related to the consumer's social and psychological interpretation of the merchandise and/or service.

The consumer's efforts are considered to be rational if they fit his or her own goal-oriented behavior pattern. The consumer's needs—whatever they might be—lead to drives. As these drives to satisfy these needs are intensified, the consumer tends toward a state of tension or disequilibrium. Cues (the retailers' attributes and promotional efforts) provide the consumer with a means of differentiating between alternative retail merchandise/service offerings.

Part of the consumer's behavior is occupied with search activity, which may consist of straight data gathering or receiving information presented in the form of semi-entertainment. In either case, the consumer's behavior is rational in light of the goals he or she is seeking. If the search activity leads to a purchase, that need is at least temporarily satisfied and the original causes for behavior tend to be removed. The consumer learns from experience in searching for and evaluating alternative solutions to a problem and in making the purchase.

Some consumer purchase decisions are sufficiently repetitive and routine so that a definite purchase procedure is developed and is repeated until some strong change occurs in purchase motivation or by presentation of a strong cue by a

Table 3-3 **Suggested Determinants of Prepurchase Search**

Consumer Determinants	Predicted Effect on Prepurchase Search
1. Presence and configuration of preference map for the product (Bucklin)	Most search if no preference map; least if preference map exists indicating several equally preferred alternatives
2. Number of salient attributes used to judge the product (Kaish)	Search varies directly
3. Importance attributed to product category (Kaish; Kelly; Ratchford and Andreasen)	Search varies directly
4. Purchase frequency (Bucklin; Groeneveld; Kelly)	Search varies inversely
5. Personality and self-perception (Kelly)	Search varies directly with perception of self as deliberate decision maker
Decision Environment Determinants	
6. Availability of information (Ratchford and Andreasen)	Search varies directly
7. Depth of product assortment available (Kaish)	Search varies directly
8. Degree of differentiation among available alternatives (Kaish)	Search varies directly
9. Frequency of change in prices, styles, and product technology (Bucklin)	Search varies directly
Product Characteristic Determinants	
10. Price (Groeneveld; Kaish; Kelly)	Search varies directly
11. Size or physical bulk (Groeneveld)	Search varies directly
12. Length of life (Groeneveld)	Search varies directly
13. Relationship between observable physical product characteristics and performance differences (Kaish)	Search varies directly with observability of product differences
14. Subjectivity of evaluative criteria (Ratchford and Andreasen)	Search varies inversely with number of objective criteria
15. Social conspicuousness (Kelly)	Search varies directly
16. Complexity (number of attributes) (Ratchford and Andreasen)	Search varies directly

Source: Donald H. Granbois, "Shopping Behavior and Preferences" in *Selected Aspects of Consumer Behavior—A Summary from the Perspective of Different Disciplines* (Washington, D.C.: National Science Foundation, 1977), pp. 261-262.

retailer. A retailer's ability to change the consumer's purchase behavior for these types of purchases may be very slight. Convenience products, such as cigarettes, newspapers, headache remedies, or toothpaste, are examples of routinely purchased merchandise. Retailers of these types of merchandise generally sell via self-service, as retail salespeople are not needed except to indicate where the merchandise is located. Similar layouts and merchandise arrangement in all outlets of a chain allow the consumer to develop a constant shopping routine for these types of merchandise.

Other purchasing decisions are novel, complex, or important enough to the consumer to warrant renewed search and evaluation efforts. In this case, because consumers are more open-minded about the decision and want to receive information on several alternatives, they investigate merchandise and store attributes and match these images with their own self-images and life styles. (It should be emphasized that consumers' self-images—the impressions that they form of themselves—are likely to be a little different from the way they appear to other people. Consumers are striving to purchase goods or services that enhance, increase, or change their self-images. Their purchases are made so that they might see themselves as bolder, smarter, richer, more secure, and more socially acceptable.) To make these nonroutine purchase decisions, consumers are searching for detailed information on merchandise, services, and/or outlets. Retailers that provide such information will appeal favorably to them. In addition, because they have an open mind in these cases, they are more receptive to personal sales efforts that attempt to identify and solve their problems.

Field four in the buyer behavior model (the feedback process occurring after the purchase) contains some important implications for retailers. There is frequently a lack of harmony (dissonance) among the buyer's various cognitions about the product and/or service purchased and the missed alternatives. Dissonance occurs as a result of the consumer's having made a decision which the individual may doubt is the right choice.[24] The magnitude of postpurchase dissonance is believed to be an increasing function of the general importance of the decision to the consumer and of the relative attractiveness of the unpurchased alternatives.[25] Thus, postpurchase dissonance may be common among buyers of foreign travel tours, automobiles, major appliances, homes, and the like.

Consumer behavior that is influenced by dissonance may lead to sufficient guilt feelings that the purchase is returned, or it may simply lead the customer to achieve internal harmony by intensifying the search for additional information that will support the original decision. The retailer can reduce dissonance by emphasizing personal selling, by advertising, warranties, and return policies, and by not offering too many similar product choices. The personal selling, advertising, warranty, and return programs should be designed to thoroughly convince the customer of the worth of the store and its merchandise/service offering.

Customers who are presented with adequate information experience less dissonance, but the retail communications process must be truthful and consistent if consumer postpurchase dissonance is to be decreased. Consumers who receive conflicting information about an item will experience more dissonance, so the firm's advertising, sales, and warranty and return policies must be consistent, and each salesperson must be informed of their content. Retailers may want to consider showing or carrying fewer similar product choices, since the presentation of many close alternatives can lead to increased dissonance. Shoe salespersons, for example, may limit the number of shoes they present to the customer at any one time.

Effect of Consumerism on the Retailer

Consumerism is the activity of consumers to take measures to protect the general public from misrepresentation, poorly made merchandise, and bad service. Consumers of every income and educational level are currently more aware of their rights than ever before. But consumers in the higher income groups and those with better educational backgrounds are frequently the most dissatisfied with the actions of retailers. There is an increasing awareness on the part of consumers of their ability to alter any retail action that they perceive as being harmful or dishonest to consumers. Thus, one must conclude that consumerism is here to stay. It is a powerful political force that is influencing the enactment of numerous laws that regulate very specific activities of retailers.

The political influence of consumers is not really a new force. It is just gaining more publicity and increasingly obtaining more influence than ever before. This influence has resulted in the passing of many different acts which protect the consumer against health hazards, harmful selling practices, and physical harm. These acts become increasingly more specific and detailed as consumers become more vocal and better organized.

The increased number of consumer organizations has resulted in more effective pressure on the federal government to enforce disclosure of product knowledge about merchandise and retail selling practices. There is little doubt that these trends will continue.

How to Deal with Consumerism

The previous discussion and a daily monitoring of the news illustrate that retailers must seriously consider how consumers will react to every action the retailer makes.

The first fact that retailers must realize is that consumers are really the bosses of the marketplace. This is simply the application of the market concept discussed in Chapter 2. It is not a new concept; it has been used for years by most of the really successful retailers, such as Marshall Field in Chicago and Nieman-Marcus in Dallas. These retailers recognized who their customers were, gave them what they wanted, and treated them fairly. Other firms operated under the motto "let the buyer beware." This philosophy caused many a retail failure, especially after the merchandise presented in the marketplace became so technically complex that the consumer could not properly evaluate its contents, performance, safety, health hazards, and so forth.

Today customers are the retailer's boss. They have the mobility to patronize many different stores. They also have a tremendous legal influence. Thus, the second thing a retailer must do is to become aware of the various federal, state, and local laws that have been passed. By adhering to these laws a retailer can avoid offering goods and services that are not properly labeled or that have been pulled out of circulation and can avoid using illegal selling practices. The National Retail Merchants Association and many other trade associations are helpful in providing information on the legal status of various retail activities.

It is not enough to merely keep up with the latest legal developments. A retailer can suffer tremendous losses because of the publicity associated with the failure to pull an out-of-date item from the shelf. Thus, merchandise and selling activity must be continually monitored to be sure that they are legal and ethical.

Some retailers also obtain significant benefits from creating their own information system to keep up to date with changing consumer interests. These retailers may even create their own consumer panel, which advises the retailer if any of the retailer's activities appear to be unfair to consumer interests. The consumer panel also provides ideas for new actions that appeal to consumers in general. Other retailers read the consumer literature or join consumer groups to see what they are thinking.

The result of obtaining consumer reactions should be ideas that can be used in promoting the firm's merchandise and service. For example, some secondary source or consumer group may approve some of the merchandise that a retailer carries. These comments could be included in the retailer's promotional efforts. If the consumer groups and secondary sources downgrade some merchandise that the store carries, the merchandise should be investigated and, if the consumers' findings are true, a new line of merchandise should be secured.

Summary

Consumer behavior is subject to many influences. Consumers attempt to satisfy a variety of needs—physiological, safety, belonging, status, and self-actualization—with the financial resources available to them. There are different explanations of how they pursue these objectives.

The Nicosia buyer behavior model presented in Figure 3–1 is a summary explanation of the activities in the consumer's decision-making process. This model reflects the nearly boundless aspects of consumer behavior. Thus, the retail manager must be aware of the consumer's psychological attributes, his or her self-image, how he or she interprets the retailer's attributes and messages, the resulting consumer attitude, the way that the consumer approaches the search and evaluation process, the motivation that may result in a purchase, and even the post-purchase feeling of the customer.

Keeping abreast of changes in consumer attitudes and motivations is mandatory if a retailer is to develop effective merchandising strategies.

Retailers must realize that in today's market consumers are the bosses of the marketplace. Consumerism is a powerful political force that is influencing the enactment of numerous laws that regulate the activities of retailers.

Questions

1. Discuss how retailers have capitalized on conspicuous consumption. Why is it important to retailing?

2. Maslow's theory is based on the concept that people have five basic goals or needs. Discuss these five needs.

3. Many retailers define their target market as being consumers in the top half of the income distribution. Discuss how these retailers can reach three-fourths of the total buying population potential yet only have to serve 50 percent of the people.

4. Discuss why a current knowledge of consumer behavior is vital to retailers.

5. In what way are reference groups important to retailing?

6. Discuss the four central concepts of the Pavlovian learning theory as they apply to retailing.

7. Buying motivations arise from consumer wants. List five of the essential buying motives and discuss how each motive can be satisfied by a jewelry retailer.

8. Discuss how the family life cycle influences retailing.

9. How does real personal income affect the discretionary and nondiscretionary patterns of consumer spending?

10. Describe buyer risk and postpurchase dissonance. What techniques currently in use tend to reduce real and perceived buyer risk and postpurchase dissonance?

Footnotes

1. Philip Kotler, *Marketing Management Analysis Planning and Control,* 2d ed. (Englewood Cliffs, N.J.: Prentice-Hall, 1972), pp. 102–104.

2. Matilda Frankel, "What Do We Know about Consumer Behavior?" in *Selected Aspects of Consumer Behavior—A Summary from the Perspective of Different Disciplines* (Washington, D.C.: National Science Foundation, 1976), p. 12.

3. George Katona, *The Powerful Consumer: Psychological Studies of the American Economy* (New York: McGraw-Hill, 1960), pp. 14–15.

4. Ibid., pp. 11–12.

5. Ibid., p. 13.

6. Ibid., pp. 150–151.

7. T. M. Newcomb, *Social Psychology* (New York: Dryden Press, 1950), pp. 225–232.

8. Gregory Stone, "City Shoppers and Urban Identification," *American Journal of Sociology* 55 (July 1954): 36–45.

9. James E. Stafford, "Effects of Group Influence on Consumer Brand Preferences," *Journal of Marketing Research* 3 (February 1966): 69.

10. Pierre Martineau, "Social Classes and Spending Behavior," *Journal of Marketing* 23 (October 1958): 121–130.

11. Peter D. Bennett and Harold H. Kassarjian, *Consumer Behavior* (Englewood Cliffs, N.J.: Prentice-Hall, 1972), p. 119.

12. Sidney J. Levy, "Social Class and Consumer Behavior," in J. W. Newman, ed., *On Knowing the Consumer* (New York: John Wiley & Sons, 1966), p. 154.

13. Ibid., pp. 155–156.

14. Kotler, *Marketing Management Analysis Planning and Control,* pp. 104–108.

15. John Dollard and Neal E. Miller, *Personality and Psychotherapy* (New York: McGraw-Hill, 1950), Chap. 3.

16. A. H. Maslow, "A Theory of Human Motivation," *Psychological Review* 50 (1943): 370–396.

17. Rom J. Markin, Jr., *Retailing Management: A Systems Approach* (New York: Macmillan, 1971), pp. 152–157.

18. Raymond A. Bauer, "Consumer Behavior as Risk Taking," in Robert S. Hancock, ed.,

Dynamic Marketing for a Changing World (Chicago: American Marketing Association, 1960), pp. 389–398.

19. Adapted from Donald F. Cox, ed., *Risk Taking and Information Handling in Consumer Behavior* (Boston: Harvard University Division of Research, Graduate School of Business Administration, 1967), pp. 5–6.

20. Thomas S. Robertson, *Consumer Behavior* (Glenview, Ill.: Scott, Foresman, 1970), pp. 33–34.

21. James F. Engel, David T. Kollat, and Roger D. Blackwell, *Consumer Behavior* (New York: Holt, Rinehart and Winston, 1968), p. 140.

22. Thomas Smith, *Hints to Intended Advertisers* (London, 1885), quoted in Herbert E. Krugman, "An Application of Learning Theory to TV Copy Testing," *Public Opinion Quarterly* 26 (1962): 626–634.

23. John G. Udell, "A New Approach to Consumer Motivation," *Journal of Retailing* 40 (Winter 1964/65): 9.

24. Leon Festinger, *A Theory of Cognitive Dissonance* (Stanford, Calif.: Stanford University Press, 1957), p. 12.

25. Ibid., p. 262.

Case Study

Midwest Supermarkets, Inc.

Midwest Supermarkets, Inc. is a division of a major national retail chain. Midwest Supermarkets, Inc. has three supermarkets in a midwestern city with a population of 500,000. It competes with 60 other supermarkets and 210 smaller grocery stores for the consumer's food dollar.

The three Midwest stores were some of the first stores in the U.S. to use the Universal Product Code, hereafter referred to as UPC, and an Electronic Checkout System (ECS). The stores have never marked the prices on individual items. Instead, the item price is labelled on the shelf along with the unit price. The stores' checkout cashiers merely pass packages over a slotted panel in the checkout stands, exposing the printed UPC symbols contained on each item to the bar scanning devices. Scanners transmit the coded number to the in-store computer where it is matched with a similar number in memory. The price and product description are transmitted back to the cash register, which prints the data on a customer receipt and adds the price to the total at the same time that the price is flashed on a digital display panel. All this happens in the time it takes to move each item past the scanning window.

Because 50% of its operating costs are labor, Midwest looks to the automatic pricing of products at the checkout stand as a means of increasing labor productivity and thereby lowering costs, because each item does not have to be individually price marked.

Midwest recently conducted a research project which revealed that in general consumers have accepted the ongoing use of the UPC system. This conclusion is supported by the finding that 79 percent of the people who had shopped at the Midwest stores using the UPC system still shop at these stores and by the finding that only 15 percent of the Midwest shoppers have developed an attitude of distrust toward the Electronic Checkout System (ECS).

The study also revealed that the primary reason for this group's distrusting the use of the UPC checkout system is their basic distrust of computers rather than a basic distrust of grocery stores.

This study of consumer shopping attitudes revealed that 37 percent of the Midwest shoppers believe the prices should be marked on each item. Their primary reason for this belief is that shelf prices may be in error. The next major reasons cited by consumers for their disliking the absence of individual prices are that it is harder to compare prices and it makes budget shopping harder. Midwest does provide checkout slips that describe the item and its price, but the price is not revealed on the package. Consumers indicate they are inconvenienced by not being able to compare prices easily before they check out because they cannot carry a marked can or package from one area of the store to another.

Each Midwest store is saving about $2,750 per month by using the UPC system. About $750 of this monthly saving is directly attributable to not having to price mark each item. The remainder of the savings comes from: (1) faster and more accurate checkout, which saves about $1000 per month, (2) automatic reordering of stock items which saves about $250, (3) a labor reduction in balancing cash registers of about $400, (4) a reduction in the number of errors caused by the checker mismarking price in the favor of the customer which saves about $225 and (5) a reduction in having to make more purchases of conventional cash registers of $125. About one-half of this cost saving is being passed on to Midwest's consumers in the form of lower retail prices.

The management of Midwest does not want to lose the cost savings associated with the use of the UPC and ECS systems, but they are beginning to become concerned that consumers' attitudes are hurting their sales.

Discussion Questions

1. Do you believe that consumer attitudes are hurting Midwest's sales? Why or why not?

2. What can Midwest do to improve its position in the eyes of the consumer?

3. What is the legal status of not marking the price on each item?

4. Do you believe that Midwest should continue to use the UPC-ECS systems? Why and why not?

Case Study

Mid States Savings and Loan Association (A)

Mid States Savings and Loan Association is in the process of constructing a new ten-floor building that will house its facilities on the ground floor. Space on the other nine floors will be rented for business and professional offices. The building will cover the entire city block.

The site for the new building is in a crowded downtown area that does not provide much of an opportunity for parking. The new building will have parking facilities in the basement. However, the entrance curves under the building. This traffic pattern is not believed to present a problem except for older patrons who may be psychologically inclined to avoid the underground parking lot.

Mid States has savings deposits of $80 million in the current office facilities. These facilities are crowded and located two blocks away from the new site. The population in the service area is 70,000. There are two other savings and loan associations and seven commercial banks serving the area.

Ms. Mary Gibson, the director of market development for Mid States is concerned that the older customers, who account for a significant portion of the firm's savings deposits, will shun the new facility because of city traffic and the parking situation.

Discussion Questions

1. Do you think her fears are justified?

2. Should Ms. Gibson investigate a location for a drive-in branch facility in a non-downtown area?

3. What marketing alternatives does Ms. Gibson have besides locating a drive-in branch facility in another location?

4. What do you recommend that she do?

Part Two

Retailing Opportunities

Chapter 4

The Product
and Product Planning

Learning
Goals

1. To understand why a retailer must stock merchandise and services that satisfy the needs of the firm's target market consumers.

2. To be able to discuss the methods retailers use to arouse consumer interest in the firm's offerings.

3. To be aware of the current trends in franchising.

4. To be able to discuss the advantages and disadvantages of franchising.

Key Terms
and Concepts

total product
systems selling
generic product
want slip
vendors
shopping the
competition
shopping goods
specialty goods
convenience goods
width of merchandise
assortment

merchandise line
merchandise
assortment
depth of merchandise
assortment
consistency of
merchandise
assortment
inconsistent
merchandise
assortment
product life cycle
fashion cycle

fashion item
staple goods
compatability of
product lines
scrambled
merchandising
turnover
gross margin dollars
return on investment
net space
yield concept
franchising

A successful retail outlet must stock goods of a type and a price level that are consistent with the target consumer's needs and the store's location and image. The discussion in the present chapter will concentrate on the importance of stocking a product line that will meet the needs of the retailer's potential or actual customers. It will examine the major merchandise policy decisions faced by retailers—those relating to the question, "What products should we stock?" The first section presents some basic product concepts. The second section examines the merchandise assortment decision—the range, kind, and brands of products the retailer should stock. This second section also examines the product elimination decision.

Total Product Concept

The idea of a product seems to be simple and easily defined.

A product consists of more than the tangible, physical thing that is offered to consumers. The *total product* is the tangible item combined with the whole set of services that accompany it when it is sold to the consumer.[1] Total product sales can be accomplished by using either systems selling or suggestive selling.

The term *systems selling* is used to convey the idea of selling a total product. Additional elements contributing to customer satisfaction may include a formal, written guarantee and assistance in full utilization of the product or in its proper care and maintenance. When retailers fully appreciate the extended product concept, they profitably consider their potential customer's total consumption system. The consumption system describes the way a purchaser performs the total task of whatever it is that he or she is trying to accomplish when using the product.[2]

An illustration of total product sales using suggestive selling is an observed reaction to an announcement of stricter enforcement of a local ordinance requiring the use of metal garbage cans with lids. All retailers—except one—stocked many pairs of garbage cans and lids to sell to the consumers who would be "forced" to buy their product at a combined price of about five dollars. The astute exception stocked some matched garbage cans and lids, but recognized that the main consumer need was not for more cans but only for lids to cover their old garbage cans. He therefore stocked and sold lids separately (at about $1.19) to a volume market. Of course, this retailer did not make a fortune from the sale of lids, but, through suggestive selling, he sold chains to fasten the lids to the garbage cans so they could not be lost again. The profits derived from the combined sales were not large, but his recognition of this consumer need attracted several hundred new customers into his store for the first time.

This kind of creative merchandising can have a tremendous long-run impact upon business. Satisfied consumers who give word-of-mouth reference for a retailer can influence more consumers to shop at that store than any single expenditure in the mass media.

Total product selling can also treat an item as a *generic product*. The generic product is not the item itself but the essential benefit that the buyer expects to get from the product. Consumers will be looking for different benefits, depending upon their needs. The generic product idea implies that benefits, not product features, should guide the retailer's strategy.

The retailing of cosmetics can be used to illustrate the function of the generic product concept. In this case, the tangible product, the cosmetic, is in a strictly physical sense a product possessing a specified set of chemical and physical attributes. But the tangible product is not what the consumer is buying; she is buying beauty. Thus, retailing the generic product involves selling beauty—not lipstick or eye shadow—to provide the essential benefit expected by the potential customer. Once retailers recognize this, they begin to provide beauty counselors to assist women to become (or remain) beautiful by suggesting the purchase and use of certain cosmetics that would go well together and be tailored to suit individual needs.

Clothing retailers can use the same reasoning to sell color-coordinated ties, suits, shoes, and socks.

In summary, the total product concept involves using the whole product—tangible product, service, warranty, and psychological contributions—to coincide with the benefits that a group of potential consumers expects to receive from a product.

Merchandise Line Decisions

Current Customer Need Satisfaction

Customer needs are the most basic considerations in establishing a retailer's product line policy. Customers' preferences with regard to the price class of goods, quality, styles, colors, and the like determine if products will sell well or will not sell at all. In an economy where discretionary consumption is quite prevalent, the task of anticipating consumer preferences successfully is quite difficult. Information on consumer preferences can be obtained through research conducted within the company and from outside sources.

Data from Company Sources

An analysis of past sales records provides one of the best estimates of consumer preferences for all items, including those that are subject to changes in demand because of preference switches made on the basis of fashion, style, or whatever. Analysis of a retailer's past sales data, adjusted for seasonal fluctuations, indicates consumer preferences for size, color, style, quality, brand labels, and so forth. This information allows the retailer to identify those items that are most likely to be best sellers.

Returned goods and adjustment data also contain information pertinent to product line decisions. Frequent consumer complaints and/or frequent returns of an item indicate some fundamental weakness in that item's ability to give satisfaction under normal use conditions. Such negative feedback should be given more serious weight than it might at first appear to deserve because only a few of the dissatisfied customers will make the effort to complain and/or return merchandise. Severely dissatisfied consumers are also likely to classify all of the store's merchandise in the same category as the inferior items. This can lead to a switch in store patronage and cause the store to lose many previously loyal customers. Thus, products made of inferior material or with poor workmanship should be eliminated from the product line as soon as their inferior qualities are discovered.

A record of items requested by potential customers but not carried by the store is an excellent source of new product ideas. This record could be maintained on a form located near the cash register. The request record or *want slip* should be sufficiently detailed to include a description of the items desired, plus other consumer-provided information on color, size, style, price, and so forth (Exhibit 4–1). This type of form is frequently contained in a want book with perforated pages that can be easily torn out and sent to the merchandise buyers.

Exhibit 4–1 **Sample Want Slip Form**

WANT SLIP

Dept. _____

Please fill in the information listed
below and submit the completed want-slip
at the end of each day to your buyer.
Thank You.

ITEM: _____

_____

_____

_____

PRICE: _____

QUANTITY: _____

CLERK NUMBER: _____

DATE: _____

ACTION TAKEN: _____

_____

DATE: _____

Salespeople may be encouraged by certain incentives and regular supervision to suggest alternative merchandise that is currently in stock. If such substitutes are not acceptable, the originally requested item should be reported. Usually sales clerks are also able to make good suggestions on the types of products that should be stocked. Because salespeople have the most direct contact with customers, they are good sources of product ideas.

Careful consideration should be given to want slip information. Requests for fad and/or fashion items require an immediate, decisive response. The greatest risk is getting too much merchandise too late to capitalize on the item profitably. Fast twenty-four- to forty-eight hour delivery can spell success in these situations.

Customer inquiries for additional staple items require a different retailer response. The danger in meeting isolated, individual requests is accumulating slow-moving inventories and overstock. Most merchandise is packaged in multiple units that require special orders and entail delays. Unless the customer makes a significant deposit, he or she may be tempted to purchase elsewhere, leaving the merchant with excessive stock.

Remember, the retailer must be responsive to target market needs but cannot be "all things to all people."

Information from Outside Sources

Retailers can obtain estimates of consumer demand from the wholesalers, manufacturers, jobbers, and others who sell merchandise to the store. The accuracy of such estimates is dependent upon the amount of consumer research conducted by these sellers. Some *vendors* (as these sellers are commonly called) provide bulletins or computer reports that indicate past sales for items they are selling. Franchise vendors usually provide sales estimate data to their outlets to assist their client-partners in maximizing their profitability.

Retailers may observe the product lines offered by other retailers with the idea that successful outlets have already identified the items that are selling well. Such visits to other local stores and similar stores in other areas are made by retail management personnel, who may even purchase merchandise for the purpose of making a detailed comparison with their store's offerings. These visits also provide retailers with an estimate of the intensity of the competition they are likely to encounter on each item.

Many retailers are successful because they offer unique product lines. *Shopping the competition* (allowing store employees to make price and product comparisons in competitive outlets) is done by all types of retailers, but especially by small retailers who cannot afford more costly methods of demand estimation. These smaller retailers are more likely to be able to carry unique merchandise because they are not bound by established product line policies as are some large chain stores. The store visits are also used by retailers who are opening a new outlet in the area and lack past sales records for the target area.

Trade magazines, newspapers, and other publications also contain information on the items, styles, colors, and so forth that consumers appear to prefer or are likely to prefer in the near future.

Consumer surveys can be used by large retailers to provide preference information on fashion items. Such surveys could be conducted in person, by telephone, or by mailing questionnaires to the store's current or potential customers. The store's credit and customer records could serve as a mailing or telephone listing. These surveys should be designed and analyzed by knowledgeable persons who are familiar with proper survey procedures, since the use of improper survey techniques can lead to incorrect decisions.

Several "outside" agencies conduct customer surveys that provide retailers with information on consumer purchasing habits. The A. C. Nielsen Company and the R. L. Polk Company are sources of detailed consumer buying data. Newspapers such as the *Denver Post,* the *Chicago Tribune,* the *New York Times,* and many smaller newspapers also sponsor periodic research on consumer buying patterns.

Interest Arousal with Merchandise Assortment

Retail competition frequently involves the use of market segmentation based on merchandise assortment. Retailers use market segmentation by planning their merchandise assortment to meet the demands of some particular subgroup of consumers who have similar motivations. One of the first requirements for successful use of the market segmentation concept is to identify the consumer group or groups that appear to offer the best potential market. The retail merchandise assortment can then be altered to meet the needs and preferences of these target market groups.

Just as it is necessary to segment the market to improve retailing efficiency, it is also important to classify products according to the amount of time and effort spent by the average consumer in seeking to purchase the product (Table 4–1). The three broad categories of consumer goods are: (1) shopping goods, (2) specialty goods, and (3) convenience goods. The basic goal of retailing is consumer satisfaction. Thus, this classification of goods and services focuses on the consumer, not on the products themselves. Since the consumer is the focal point for the entire retailing program, retailers should use this classification of products concept when they make decisions not only on merchandise, but on all elements of the retailing mix.

Table 4–1 **Classification of Consumer Goods
Based on Degree of Consumer Prepurchase Planning**

| | Classification of Good | | |
	Convenience Goods	Shopping Goods	Specialty Goods
Degree of Prepurchase Planning Made by Consumer	Little	Some	Considerable
Degree of Brand Preference	Little	Makes brand comparison	Insists on specific brand
Amount of Shopping Effort Used by Consumer	Minimum	Moderate	Maximum

Stores selling *shopping goods* (goods the consumer usually purchases only after making several comparisons on quality, price, and style) usually make the most distinct segmentation appeals. The merchandise assortment in stores selling mainly shopping goods such as furniture, clothing, shoes, used automobiles, and major appliances may be selected to appeal to a specific market target, which may be the youth market, a specific ethnic group, an extremely high income group, and the like.

Shopping goods are products about which the consumer does not have thorough knowledge. The consumer shops for this information by making several trips to various stores where he or she compares one product with another. Because the price of shopping goods is relatively high and because the item may account for a relatively high percentage of the individual's budget, the consumer purchases shopping goods much less frequently than he or she purchases convenience goods.

Frequently the consumer buys shopping goods on the basis of the best price, delivery, and customer service available to them. Independent shopping goods retailers have become successful by offering delivery, repair, return, credit, installation, and other customer services along with the product. This combination is frequently preferred by consumers, since they like to have their products serviced by the retailer from whom they bought the item. For this reason shopping goods lend themselves to a franchising arrangement between a local retailer who can provide the service and a national company which can provide a well-known quality product.

Retailers of shopping goods usually try to locate near one another so that the consumers who want to go from one store to another to seek advice and information may do so with a minimum of effort.

Stores selling *specialty goods* (goods that are sufficiently unique or have a strong enough brand identification to entice a significant group of buyers to habitually make a special purchasing effort) can also benefit by developing a merchandise assortment to reach one or more market segments. Some retailers of photographic equipment, hi-fi components, sporting goods, and men's suits, for example, carry only exclusive, high-quality brands to cater to the very quality-conscious segment of the market.

There is generally a strong brand preference for specialty goods, and the consumer has a fairly complete knowledge of the product. The consumer tends to accept no substitute for this brand but continues to shop for the specific brand he or she prefers. Frequently, when he or she finds a retail store which offers this favorite brand, the consumer continues to patronize that store because the item can be purchased without using any extra effort to find the item elsewhere. It is important to note that it is the brand name which serves as the basis for the consumer selecting one outlet over other outlets. Generally there is only one retailer offering specialty goods in a given trading area during any one point in time. This gives the competitive advantage to the retailer who does not have to compete with other local stores on this particular brand. Thus, specialty stores too can also lend themselves to a franchise agreement between a local retailer and a supplier of a well-known branded product. Under such a contract, the retailer may be guaranteed the right to be the only outlet allowed to handle the specified brand in a certain geographic area.

Segmentation is used to a lesser extent by stores that primarily sell *convenience goods* (goods the consumer usually purchases with minimum effort at the most convenient and accessible place). Stores stocking only well-known branded merchandise appeal to a different market group than do stores that stock mostly unadvertised brand items or private brand items that are associated with the retailer or some wholesaler instead of with a nationally known manufacturer. Soap, personal care items, packaged food items, other staple items, and impulse goods are examples of convenience goods.

Retailers who sell convenience goods must place emphasis upon the proper location of their outlets. Convenience goods are purchased frequently, and usually the consumer has only a slight brand preference. Consumers of convenience goods generally spend only a minimum amount of effort on making their purchases. Thus they are likely to make most of their purchases of convenience goods at the nearest outlet that sells acceptable merchandise. Thus, the same brand of goods may be sold in many different retail outlets.

Advertising and promotional efforts on convenience goods will not be as likely to lure customers from long distances as similar efforts featuring shopping goods. Retailers who offer mostly shopping goods may therefore be better able to use promotional appeals to overcome a less than optimal location.

Types of Merchandise Assortment

The merchandise assortment decision involves three dimensions—width, depth, and consistency. The *width* or breadth of a merchandise assortment refers to the number of different merchandise lines a store may carry. *Merchandise line* refers to a group of products that are closely related because they satisfy a single class of needs, are used together, or are sold to the same consumer groups. A *merchandise assortment* is composed of a series of demand-related merchandise items that is unique and distinguishable as a separate entity. A supermarket's merchandise assortment typically consists of hundreds of merchandise lines (soft drinks, for example). However, a supermarket generally carries over 10,000 different merchandise items (such as Coke, merchandised in sixteen-ounce bottles in a carton consisting of eight bottles).

Stores offering many merchandise lines (supermarkets, for example) are said to offer a wide line of goods. Stores selling only one line, such as Shakey's Pizza, are said to offer a narrow, specialized line.

Merchandise assortments also differ in respect to their depth. *Depth of assortment* refers to the number of items offered within each merchandise line. A shallow assortment is an offering of several items within a product line. A deep assortment involves the stocking of many different items within a merchandise line.

The use of a deeper merchandise assortment generally results in a larger trading area for a given store (Figure 4–1). In addition, a higher percentage of the store's customers are satisfied since they do not have to go to another store to buy that type of merchandise. For example, the stocking of an adequate supply of many different brand names, each of which offers a good selection in color, style, and size, will please nearly all customers. However, it also results in a large investment in inventory. If the sales volume is not large enough to warrant this huge investment in inventory, then the firm's profits will be adversely affected. In addition, the store's limited selling space forces its management to either not stock many merchandise categories with a deep assortment or use only a few merchandise categories.

The *consistency of the merchandise assortment* (the degree of relationship of various merchandise lines in terms of consumer end use) is also an important aspect of merchandise assortment planning. Merchandise assortments that are very closely related in use are highly consistent. Liquor stores that sell only liquor and mix items offer a highly consistent merchandise assortment. An *inconsistent merchan-*

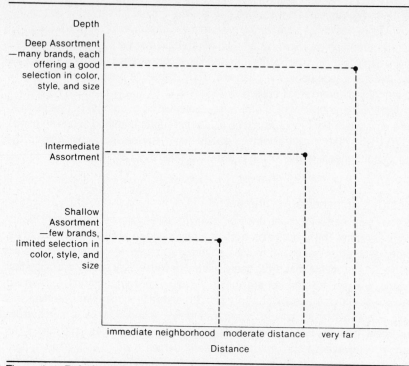

Figure 4–1 **Relationship between Depth of Merchandise Line and Distance Consumer Is Willing to Travel to Reach a Store**

dise assortment exists when the merchandise lines offered are not related to one another in terms of consumer usage. The proper grouping of related merchandise within departments, as well as logical arrangement in a store layout, enhances the possibility of additional impulse purchases by customers.

The appropriate assortment is affected by the estimate of the marketing opportunity and by the image the store wishes to project. A store that emphasizes "one-stop shopping" or "full-service merchandise" advertising themes is likely to offer complete merchandising assortments—wide merchandising lines with deep assortments of goods and services that complement one another. Other retailers, who find a small market segment to serve, usually offer more narrow merchandise lines and more shallow merchandise assortments because their offering is reduced to the most popular items that appeal to their target market.

For example, if a retail manager of such a store finds that three-fourths of his store's sales in a certain merchandise line originate from only four of the fifteen items carried, he is likely to decide that it is not worth the extra effort and expense to stock and maintain eleven extra items. On the other hand, a store that has a "one-stop shopping" or "full service" theme is more likely to carry all fifteen items because of its different management philosophy. Neither policy is incorrect, because merchandise assortments must be based on company goals and objectives and on consumer preferences.

Adding and Dropping Merchandise Lines

Retailers are continually besieged with offers of "new" merchandise. This merchandise may be considered new because it is an entirely new technological development or merely because it is a substitute "me-too" product (one that is similar to those already on the market) being offered for the first time by a particular manufacturer. This continuous stream of new product offerings and a rapid decline in the popularity of some current product offerings force retailers to develop systems that will assist them in identifying the products that should be discontinued. The same systems could be used in the selection of new merchandise lines. Some large firms have developed elaborate point systems, based on projected volume, gross margin, turnover, and so forth, which they effectively use to make their product line decisions.

Growth Potential The growth potential of the new merchandise line should be evaluated to determine how the proposed line compares to other lines in terms of expected performance. Some products' sales (those with high income elasticities, as outlined in Chapter 5) respond better to increases in consumer incomes than do other products (those with low income elasticities). Accelerated growth potential is indicated on merchandise lines having a high income elasticity (those products for which a relatively higher percentage of income is spent as consumers' incomes increase).

Radios, television sets, foreign travel, sporting goods, and toys have responded very favorably to the income increases that occurred between 1948 and 1965. Items that are associated with the rise of leisure time have recently experienced relatively significant growth. The most spectacular increase is in the purchase of products used in the pursuit of pleasure and relaxation. Items such as bowling balls, color television sets, camping vehicles, cameras, and boats are faring quite well in this boom.[3] Expenditures related to the use of these goods, such as traveling and vacationing, also are increasing rapidly.

Merchandise line growth is also affected by the age of the product line being considered. Products age and their sales decline over time. The product life cycle concept can be used to provide some insight and guidelines to assist the retailer in making merchandise assortment decisions. The term *product life cycle* suggests that products move through success stages of sales and profit conditions: introduction, growth, maturity, and decline. Figure 4–2 is a graph of a product life cycle.

Retailers frequently incur losses in the introduction phase of a product life cycle because many risks are associated with products in this stage. Generally the price is relatively high, and the item may be merchandised only by exclusive outlets. Sales volume is normally low. The low sales volume and the high degree of risk influence the retailer to carry only a relatively low level of inventory for the product positioned in the introduction phase.

The growth phase begins when sales start to rise rapidly. The retail merchandise assortment usually increases as more models, styles, colors, sizes, and so forth are manufactured to meet increased consumer demands. A buildup of larger retail inventories is needed to lessen the possibility of being out of stock.

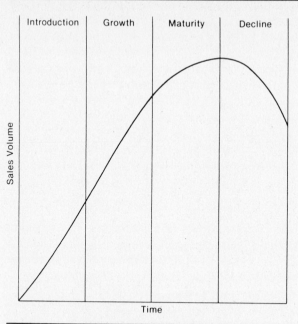

Figure 4-2 **Typical Product Life Cycle**

The rate of growth begins to decline at the start of the maturity phase. Sales continue to increase, but at a decreasing rate. Competition also begins to intensify as more me-too products are introduced. This causes a decline in prices, which requires a more careful balancing of retail inventories. Retailers may also attempt to capitalize on the product differentiation and packaging innovations offered by the leading suppliers during this maturity stage of the cycle.

Sales of merchandise start to turn downward at the beginning of the decline stage. The product is making continually smaller contributions to retail profit primarily because of lower sales volume. The retailer's responses made at this stage include the reexamination of required inventory levels and a decision on the appropriate time to close out the remaining product stock.

The *fashion cycle* concept is also important to retailing, since the fashion-minded consumer is a prime target market for the retail industry. *Fashion items* are associated with frequent changes in style, color, or design. The other merchandise term, *staple goods,* refers to standardized items that change slowly over time. The increasing emphasis on new products, colors, and unique designs is making it more difficult to distinguish staple goods from fashion goods. However, staple goods are the necessity items. As incomes increase, the relative importance of fashion goods increases.

The length of the fashion cycle is affected by the same factors that affect the product life cycle, and the same four stages can be defined. However, the fashion cycle can repeat itself continuously over a period of time for the same item or style, because the decline phase may be temporary. It is followed by an upswing and a new cycle. A successful fad product may also follow the typical product life cycle, but its sales usually rise faster, reach a peak (as opposed to a plateau), and then fall more abruptly (Figure 4–3).

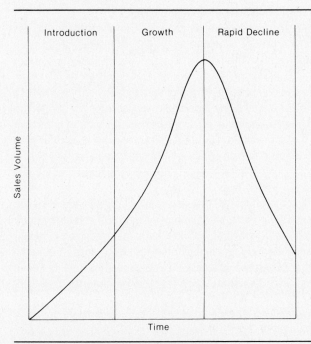

Figure 4–3 **Life Cycle for Fad Product**

As noted earlier, retail managers should consider the fashion cycle concept when they are planning their merchandise assortment. And certain types of stores are more appropriate than others for merchandising a given fashion through each of its four stages. If the store is to project its desired image, its management should balance the store's merchandise assortment of fashion items with its customers' shopping attitudes and practices.

Compatibility with Other Merchandise Lines The compatibility of product lines refers to the degree that either current or planned lines meet the needs of the market segments being served by the store. The trend toward *scrambled merchandising* (unrelated merchandise sold by the same store) may have decreased the relative importance of this compatibility consideration. However, merchandise lines must agree (in terms of quality, style, color, size, and so forth) with the preferences of the target market customers.

Some of the merchandise lines available to the store are simply consumer substitutes for one or more of the store's existing lines; that is, the consumers use several products for the same purpose. The products may be identical except for the brand name or color, or they may differ in some slight way. Stocking similar, or me-too, merchandise lines usually causes most sales to originate from the brand that is considered to be superior by the store's consumers. One brand begins to divert sales from the others.

Because a store's selling space is limited, each item's sales must be evaluated to determine if it is worth handling. In cases where one item is superior to other similar items, the inferior items may be pared from the offering.

In some instances, however, consumers do not consider one item to have a market superiority over other so-called substitute items. If this is the case, total store sales volume can increase because the consumer responds favorably to a wider merchandise selection.

Merchandise lines can also complement one another. Perfectly complementary items are usually sold together because the sale of one necessitates the sale of the other if the first item is to be used immediately. For example, the sale of a camera necessitates the sale of the appropriate film before the consumer is able to take pictures. The sale of a fishing pole can be combined with the sales of a reel, fishing line, and lures, because the customer ultimately will need to acquire these items before he or she can use the fishing pole.

Stocking complementary merchandise lines is usually desirable because the sale of one item can stimulate the unplanned purchase of several complementary or accessory items. Moreover, the customer is likely to be less sensitive to higher price tags on smaller complementary items, such as film, fishing lines, and lures. Ties, belts, and shoes that are color coordinated with a sport coat that has just been purchased are also examples of accessory items that can be merchandised successfully because of their complementarity to a larger item.

Other merchandise lines that are neither substitutes nor complements for existing merchandise lines should generate sufficient sales to be profitable by themselves. In other words, items that are unrelated to the rest of the merchandise assortment can increase store profits and remain in the merchandise line only if they make a positive contribution to overhead. If such products do not generate traffic for complementary, accessory, or substitute products, the stocking decision must be based solely on the items' own merits.

Competitive Conditions Competition is another consideration in the task of evaluating the worth of a new merchandise line. If a retail outlet can obtain an exclusive geographical right to carry an item, this agreement would minimize direct competition with other local retailers. Retailers may also prefer to handle a specific item if the estimated sales volume appears to justify its addition to their lines and if the manufacturer is going to spend a considerable amount of money promoting the item. It is a risky practice not to handle popular, well-promoted new items, because consumers will be drawn into stores by national advertising and it is difficult to tell these customers (who may be regular customers) that such an item is not carried by the store. They will probably go to a competitor to make that purchase. Once they enter a competitor's store, they may make price, merchandise, and service comparisons that may result in the loss of their patronage.

Profitability of Merchandise Lines Direct profitability is one of the most important considerations in merchandise planning. Evaluating the profitability of a proposed merchandise line generally involves the use of some estimated elements. Manufacturers may offer retailer clients test market results that estimate dollar sales based on store size or volume. The estimated unit sales can be multiplied by the gross margin percentage to obtain estimates of future total receipts. The expenses associated with the item can be subtracted from total receipts to obtain the item's contribution to overhead.

Retailing expenses vary from item to item, depending on how much time is required for their sale, the amount of service they require, the amount of money required to carry an inventory, and the amount of shelf or floor space required to stock the items. However, from the store management point of view, the profitability resulting from the addition or deletion of an item is the change in contribution to store profit resulting from the decision to stock or not stock the item.

The more conventional ways of determining an item's profitability involve a series of techniques such as calculating indices of turnover rates, gross margin dollars, return on investment, and dollar margins per linear or cubic foot of shelf space.

Turnover data is usually obtained by dividing total dollar sales volume by the average retail price value of inventory. *Gross margin dollars* refers to the dollar difference between per unit selling price (retail) and purchase price (wholesale). Both turnover and margin influence a good's profitability.

Return on investment is an important measure of effective capital utilization. It indicates profitability as a percentage of the amount of money invested in the store. It can be calculated using the following formula.

$$\text{ROI\%} = \frac{\text{Profits \$}}{\text{Tangible assets \$}} \times 100$$

Tangible assets include the value of the store building and equipment (counters, cash registers, and so forth), the amount of money owed the store on credit sales (accounts receivable), and the store's investment in inventory.

The *net space yield* concept is a more complete approach in determining product profit. It takes handling costs, space costs, and margins into account. The concept is based on the fact that the exposure area of a store (the area exposed to the shopper) must be used in the most productive way.

Under the net space yield concept, the space dimension is considered in exposure area terms because:

1. Different stores use different shelf depths. Exposure (facing) area is more likely to be uniform.

2. Exposure area can be studied from photographs and easily charted on graph paper.

3. Manufacturers can compute the necessary exposure area for their own products. All they need know is the number of facings required.

4. Store personnel think in terms of facing or exposure.

5. Companies using computers can determine exposure area by item and insure adequate shelf allocation from store to store.[4]

Table 4–2 shows the necessary measurements that must be completed so that space yield can be calculated for three merchandise categories. The handling cost per case is the cost of handling from warehouse through checkout. The amount of handling cost can be estimated by retail management, or it can be obtained by using secondary estimates available from retail trade associations such as those listed in Appendix 17A.

Table 4–2 **Illustrative Net Space Yield Calculations for Three Merchandise Categories**

(A) Handling Cost per Case (¢)	(B) Cases Sold	(C) Total Handling Cost $ Equals (A) × (B)	(D) Linear Display Feet	(E) Exposure Area Display (sq. ft.)	(F) Occupancy Cost $ Equals (10¢)×(E)	Merchandise Category	(G) Gross Margin (%)	(H) Weekly Dollar Sales	(I) Gross Margin Dollars Equals (G)×(H)	(J) Net Gain $ Equals (I) Minus (C+F)	(K) Net Space Yield $ Equals (J)/(E)
42	170	72	32	160	16	Vegetables	25	1000	250	162	1.01
24	112	27	18	90	9	Babyfood	13.2	360	47	11	0.12
37	95	35	30	150	15	Health and beauty aids	38	1000	380	330	2.20

Source: Paul J. Cifrino, "Cifrino's Space Yield Formula," *Chain Store Age*, November 1963, pp. 32-34. Reprinted by permission.

In the example in Table 4–2, the handling cost for vegetables is estimated to be 42 cents per case. This figure, multiplied by the number of cases sold per week, gives the total weekly handling cost. The linear display of vegetables is measured as 32 feet long and 5 feet high, so that the total exposure and display area in square feet is 160. The shelf depth is 1½ feet, so that the exposure area is 240 cubic feet. The "occupancy" cost for vegetables is estimated to be $16, based on a 10 cents per square foot occupancy cost. The occupancy cost is derived by adding the estimated annual cost for rent, utilities, and depreciation, and dividing the result by the square feet of exposure area in the store.

The gross margin percentage obtained by merchandising vegetables is 25 percent and weekly sales have averaged about $1,000, so the gross profit for vegetables is $250 (gross margin percentage × dollar sales). The net gain is the sum of the total handling cost and the occupancy cost, subtracted from the gross profit: $250 − ($16 + $72) = $162. To obtain the net space yield, the net gain is divided by exposure area display in square feet, giving a value of ($162 / 160 ft. = $1.01), the net profit yield per square foot in the area occupied by vegetables.

This procedure is repeated for all of the merchandise lines the store carries. In this example, baby food items contributed only 12 cents per square foot of exposure area—considerably less than the $1.01 yield on vegetables and the $2.20 on health and beauty items. Thus, the health and beauty line appears to be the most profitable. The high gross margin percentage (38%) obtained on the health and beauty line combined with a good weekly sales level ($1,000) to make this a very profitable line. Baby items, on the other hand, have a low gross margin percentage (13.2%), combined with low weekly sales ($360), to considerably reduce their profitability.

The net space yield concept provides the basis for the following recommendations:

1. Give profitable categories more display space.

2. Give them more desirable locations.

3. Prune variety in low-yield categories.

4. Enrich variety in high-yield categories. Retailers will want to consider doing something even more basic. They will want to set in motion a dialogue with suppliers to learn what can be done with low-yields. Together with suppliers, they will try among other things:

   a. To reduce handling costs.

   b. To reduce bulk wherever possible and urge redesign of hard-to-handle packages.

   c. To shed more light on the relative impact of couponing and deal promotions.[5]

Thus, in our three-category example, the health and beauty aid line could be expanded by adding more items that provide the consumer with more variety. The display space could also be increased for health and beauty items, and they should be given a desirable, high-traffic location in the store. If possible, some items might be pruned from the baby food category.

However, even a low profitability does not automatically indicate that those lines should be severely reduced or eliminated. Baby food is an essential product that will be purchased *somewhere* by a specific segment of the market. A severe reduction in item variety could easily result in a loss of sales for other items, or even store patronage. The more practical alternative would be to reduce the display space devoted to baby food and place this category in a less desirable location, which will raise the net space yield and redistribute customer traffic past impulse items.

Merchandise Lines Must Change over Time

Consumers' desires and needs change not only seasonally but also over long periods of five- to ten-year cycles. For example, the automobile preferences of Americans have changed over the last twenty years. The '60s began with great consumer interest in foreign and American compact cars, but gradually the consuming public expressed its preference for larger, better-equipped, full-size units. With the advent of pollution controls and fuel shortages, the current auto buyer is showing great interest in subcompact cars loaded with luxury accessories such as power steering, air conditioning, and so forth. It is even predicted that the true full-size auto will not again be available in the United States.

It should particularly be noted that even though a cycle has seemed to repeat itself, there have been subtle but profound changes in the merchandise offerings that reflect the needs and preferences of today's consumer. Every retailer must be aware of these attitudinal changes and make appropriate adjustments in merchandise offering.

Many of these attitudinal changes are traceable to the consumer's changing demographic characteristics. For example, the characteristics of variety store customers are shifting to a younger group. In 1963, 50 percent of all variety store customers were in the thirty-five- to forty-five-year-old group.[6] Current variety store shoppers are younger. The younger customers, particularly teenage girls, also have more money to spend. Teenage boys are also increasingly good customers. Other market segments that account for an increasing amount of the variety store sales are senior citizens, young married couples, and minority groups.

Changes of the magnitude indicated in the above examples illustrate the need for a continual reevaluation of the merchandise assortment to ensure that the store is stocking items that satisfy consumer demand.

Supermarkets have also had to change their offerings to better meet the needs of their customers. A declining birthrate, plus demographic changes such as more working women and the decline of the conventional family, has put the traditional supermarket in competition with fast-food restaurants and, to a lesser degree, with convenience stores for a share of the consumer's food budgets.

Americans now eat 18 percent of their meals away from home but spend 36 percent of their food dollars doing so. Sales of the nation's 27,400 convenience stores account for 5 percent of the consumer's food dollar and are increasing at an annual rate of about 20 percent. Some industry experts believe that the number of convenience food stores, which offer a limited line of groceries but stay open at odd hours, will soon outnumber the nation's 32,700 supermarkets.

Thus, supermarkets are placing more emphasis on nonfood items as a way of maintaining sales and profits. In some areas the overbuilt supermarket facilities, high grocery inventory, and increased competition from the fast-food and convenience outlets have caused the supermarket to not make any money on traditional food items.

The selling of nonfoods in supermarkets is nothing new, but the wide assortment of nonfood items currently offered by supermarkets is new. Many new supermarkets devote about one-third of their selling space to nonfood sections such as appliances (television sets, coffee makers, hair dryers, and so forth), hardware, housewares, and auto products. It is now getting to the point that in many areas the grocery business is just a drawing card for the general merchandise business.

Supermarkets are also beginning to meet the fast-food competition head on with expanded deli sections (some of which feature in-store seating and offer specialty items such as teriyaki rolls, barbecued chicken, and lox), in-store restaurants, and even cocktail lounges. Generally these deli and restaurant sections cater to the store's specific target market. For example, Ralph's Grocery Co. stores in the Los Angeles area offer their Oriental population special frozen shrimp and crab dishes which are flown in from Japan.

The extremely wide line of goods offered by these new, huge supermarkets is designed to compete directly with fast-food, convenience grocery and general merchandise stores. Management frequently believes that if the customer comes into the store wanting fifteen items but only finds twelve, he or she may not return. These managers believe that the curve outlined in Figure 4–4 represents the relationship between the number of merchandise lines stocked and the percentage of customers who will not return to the store because of an incomplete merchandise assortment. Supermarkets also use private label items (products which carry no association with a nationally advertised manufacturing company) to increase the selection.

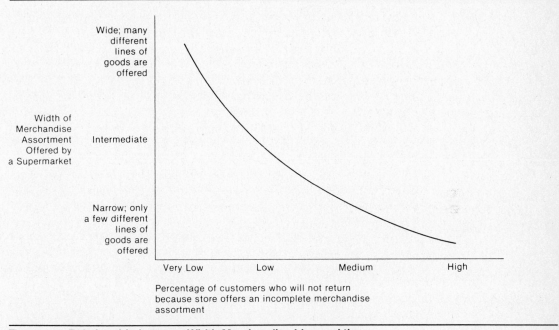

Figure 4-4 **Relationship between Width Merchandise Line and the Percentage of Nonreturning Customers**

Franchising

Franchising represents one instance when the merchandise line decision is usually accepted in its entirety or rejected. The current popularity of franchising warrants a detailed discussion of this important product decision. *Franchising* is a joint venture or cooperative agreement between an owner of a product/service and a dealer, a form of licensing by which the owner (the francishor of a product or service or method) obtains distribution at the retail level through retail distributors (franchisees). The product, service, or method to be marketed is usually identified by a brand name and associated trademarks, uniform symbols, standardized equipment, common storefronts, and stores that operate under a set of standardized policies and procedures. While the franchisee is usually given exclusive access to a relevant target market, the franchisor maintains some degree of control over the operational aspects of marketing the product or service.[7]

Franchise agreements exhibit a wide range of permissions, prohibitions, and statements of duties and responsibilities on the part of both the franchisor and the franchisee. In many cases the relationship extends beyond mere licensing, as is noted by the International Franchise Association when it defines franchising as "a continuing relationship in which the franchisor provides a licensee the privilege to do business, plus assistance in organizing, training, merchandising, and management in return for a consideration from the franchisee."[8]

Franchises are also making important contributions to the U.S. economy. Voluntary chain associations of independent retailers (usually sponsored by wholesalers) serve the vital functions of providing lower costs for goods through economies of scale for the retailer and assured outlets for the wholesalers' products. For example, in the food field the Independent Grocers' Alliance (IGA) will grant a franchise to a wholesaler, who in turn licenses member stores to participate in the collective group.

Other examples of wholesaler-sponsored retail franchise outlets are Western Auto Stores, Radio Shack, Coast-to-Coast Stores, and some small, relatively isolated Sears and Montgomery Ward mail-order catalog-retail stores.

Sometimes retailers come together and form a franchise cooperative by setting up a wholesale operation (or retail cooperative chain) for their mutual benefit. Such chains as Associated Grocers (AG) and Certified Grocers represent such franchising arrangements.

Some franchise agreements may take the form of franchised departments in discount centers, where the grocery operation, the shoe department, the optical department, and others are operated by independent retailers under terms of a franchise-lease agreement. The more popular, modern form of producer-sponsored franchise, however, usually covers the entire operation of a particular physical plant and/or service, such as Dairy Queen, Colonel Sanders Kentucky Fried Chicken, and Holiday Inns.

Basic Franchise Forms

Franchise agreements can be divided into two fundamental types—those that are based on territorial considerations and those concerned with operating aspects.[9]

A territorial franchise provides the franchisee with the exclusive right to develop the market potential in a given area, with the expectation that the individual or firm already possesses the necessary skill and resources to proceed on its own with the development of that area for that product or service, bound only by certain basic policies and understandings. Such territorial franchises may encompass a country, a state or region, a city, or a section of a community. Quite often such firms or individuals subfranchise their region and act as the resident management for the parent franchisor.

The more popular operating franchise agreement concentrates on attracting individuals who qualify for franchisee training and have access to sufficient investment or risk capital. In this case the franchisee receives training, guidance, and assistance from the parent franchisor in return for his or her own work and a share of the gross sales. Franchisors consider their fees as operating expenses of the franchisee and thus receive their remittance on gross sales whether the outlet is profitable or not. Some alternative variations frequently found in franchise agreements are presented in Table 4–3. A classification of different franchise business organizations and representative franchise firms for each category is contained in Table 4–4.

Table 4–3 **Variations in Franchise Agreements**

Variation in Agreement	Description of Arrangement in Franchise Agreement
1. Distributorship	Franchisee who is the distributor takes title to goods and redistributes goods to subfranchisees who sell goods to consumer.
2. Leasing	Franchisor leases buildings, equipment and/or land to franchisee.
3. Manufacturing	Franchisor gives franchisee the right to manufacture its product via the use of a specified process. Franchisee distributes product using franchisor's practices.
4. Licensing	Franchisor gives franchisee a license to use franchisor's trademarks and business practices. Franchisor may supply product or give franchisee a list of approved suppliers.
5. Service	Franchisor specifies methods that the franchisee can use to supply the service to consumers.
6. Co-ownership	Franchisor and franchisee share the investment and profits.
7. Co-management	Franchisor retains major part of investment and partner-manager shares profits on a basis of a predetermined percentage.

Historical Perspective on Franchising

Even though the current interest in the franchise industry and its expansion might lead one to believe that franchising is a twentieth-century innovation, historical evidence indicates that limited franchising was practiced in the early 1800s.[10] Modern franchising, as practiced today, really dates back to 1898, when it was introduced by General Motors. This pioneering effort was followed by Rexall (1902), Western Auto (1909), A & W Root Beer (1919), and Howard Johnson (1926), plus innumerable petroleum, soft-drink bottling, variety, grocery, drug, hardware, motel, and fast-food merchandisers through the intervening years.[11] The growth of the franchise industry has demonstrated considerable expansion in both the types of retail products and services offered and the absolute increase in sales.

Franchising Trends

Franchise sales of goods and services have increased from $156 billion in 1973 to $239 billion in 1977. Not only have sales increased, but so has the number of franchised businesses. In 1971 some 431,000 franchisors were engaged in a wide variety of business activities, and their number has continued to increase to at least 464,000 in 1977.[12]

While the spotlight of public attention has focused on the newer methods of franchising, the traditional forms (such as automobile dealers, service stations, and soft drink bottlers) still represent the backbone of the industry, with some 218,000 outlets generating an estimated $188 billion in sales in 1977. These traditional franchisees seem to have reached a maturity plateau and are decreasing in num-

Table 4-4 **Categories of Franchise Business Organizations with Representative Firms**

Classification	Representative Firms
Automotive Products/Services	AAMCO Automatic Transmissions, Inc. B.F. Goodrich Tire Company Western Auto
Auto/Trailer Rentals	Budget Rent-A-Car Corporation Hertz Corporation
Beauty Salons/Supplies	Edie Adams Cut & Curl
Business Aids/Services	H & R Block, Inc. Business Consultants of America
Campgrounds	Kampgrounds of America, Inc.
Clothing/Shoes	Just Pants Mode O'Day Company
Construction/Remodeling Materials/Services	Munford Do-it-Yourself Stores
Cosmetics/Toiletries	Color Me Beautiful Cosmetics
Drug Stores	Rexall Drug Company
Educational Products/Services	Evelyn Wood Reading Dynamics
Employment Services	Dunhill Personnel System, Inc.
Equipment/Rentals	United Rent-All, Inc.
Foods-Donuts	Dunkin-Donuts of America, Inc. Spudnuts, Inc.
Foods—Grocery/Specialty Stores	The Circle K Corporation Hickory Farms of Ohio, Inc. Baskin-Robins, Inc.
Foods—Pancake/Waffle/Pretzel	Village Inn Pancake House, Inc.

bers of outlets (especially gasoline stations), but they still serve a vital retail function and are obtaining an increased sales volume (Figure 4–5).

Franchising's hopes for future growth would seem to lie in the other areas of fast food, recreation, entertainment, service, travel, and so forth, all of which utilize the newer methods of retail merchandising. Gross sales from this sector alone amounted to $51 billion in 1977. This volume was obtained by 246,000 outlets.

Among the newer franchising fields the fastest growing sectors include business aids and services, equipment rentals, fast food operations, and recreation, entertainment, and travel. In 1977 sales increases in these franchise areas are expected to exceed 15 percent.

Between 1970 and 1976 receipts of franchised business service establishments more than doubled and reached an estimated $1.6 billion. In 1977 receipts were expected to exceed $2 billion, with the largest increases expected for printing and copying services (24 percent) and miscellaneous business services (24 percent). Strong gains in miscellaneous business service receipts and establishments reflect expansion of real estate franchises across the country. Under real estate franchise agreements, brokers receive guidance in office management and personnel train-

Table 4-4 Continued

Classification	Representative Firms
Foods—Restaurants/Drive-ins/Carry-outs	A & W International, Inc. Burger King Corporation McDonald's Corporation
General Merchandise Stores	Coast-to-Coast Stores Gamble-Skogmo, Inc.
Health Aids/Services	Health Clubs of America
Home Furnishings/Furnishings/Furniture—Retail/Repair/ Services	Amity, Inc.
Laundries, Dry Cleaning Services	Dutch Girl Continental Cleaners
Lawn and Garden Supplies/Services	Lawn Medic Inc.
Maintenance/Cleaning/Sanitation—Services/Supplies	Americlean National Service Corporation
Motels, Hotels	Days Inns of America, Inc. Holiday Inns, Inc.
Paint and Decorating Supplies	Mary Carter Industries, Inc.
Printing	Kwik-Kopy Corporation
Real Estate	Century 21 Real Estate Corporation
Recreation/Entertainment/Travel—Services/Supplies	Billie Jean King Tennis Centers, Inc.
Security Systems	Dictograph Security Systems
Soft Drinks	Bubble-Up Company
Swimming Pools	Sylvan Pools
Tools, Hardware	Snap-On Tools Corporation
Transit Service	Aero Mayflower Transit Company, Inc.
Vending	Ford Gum & Machine Co., Inc.
Water Conditioning	Culligan International Company

Source: Summarized from United States Department of Commerce, *Franchise Opportunities Handbook, 1977* (Washington, D.C.: Government Printing Office, 1977), pp. 75-86.

ing, benefits of bulk purchases of stationery, signs and forms, as well as access to financing, insurance and escrow services.

The biggest growth sector of the restaurant industry continues to be the franchised food business. Fast-food restaurant sales reached almost $14 billion in 1976, about 13 percent over 1975 levels. Sales are expected to increase more than 15 percent in 1977 and total more than $16 billion. There were an estimated 47,167 franchised food outlets in 1976, almost 4,200 more than a year earlier. Survey respondents expect that about 6,000 new fast-food outlets will be started in 1977.[13]

Some of the underlying reasons for this phenomenal increase in franchise growth are:

1. Technological advances—equipment and systems have been perfected that reduce product variability and provide uniform products/services. Also, certain products can more effectively be merchandised as a product group rather than in combination with other products. (Example: Amway, Avon, Tupperware, etc.)

2. Businessmen realize that national saturation of product/service potentially produces better profit returns, but the cost of creating and maintaining the neces-

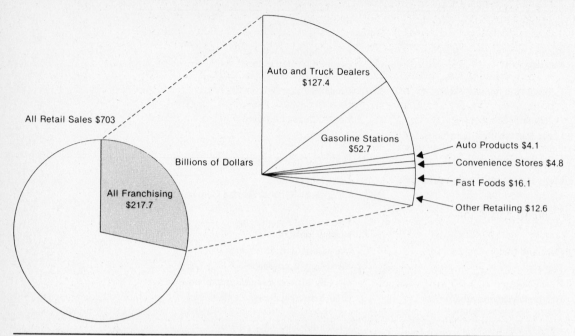

Figure 4-5 **Franchising Encompasses 31% of Retail Sales in 1977**

Source: U.S. Department of Commerce, *Franchising in the Economy 1975–77* (Washington, D.C.: Government Printing Office, 1976), p. 6.

sary nationwide network of outlets is prohibitive. Thus, through franchising they can tap the savings and credit capacity of small investors who may want to be "independent" but lack the proven product/service or the demonstrated managerial skill to pursue an entrepreneurial career. Such an arrangement assists the producer in reaching his goal while maintaining some degree of control over the distribution of his product/service.

3. The American Dream of independence through "owning your own business" supplies motivation for many people who actually work harder for themselves than for an employer. Such perceived "independence" is economically and psychologically rewarding to the franchisee while providing the franchisor with, perhaps, the best sales force available, provided of course that appropriate selection procedures are followed and adequate training and support are continually supplied.

4. Recent economic reverses have resulted in selective massive layoffs creating doubt in the minds of the affected employees about the future security "in working for someone else." Unfortunately, some unscrupulous franchise promoters have captalized on such fears and promised financial security for a relatively worthless franchise opportunity. Be that as it may, many professional and skilled employees have sought personal security on the perceived independence of becoming franchisees.

5. Urban "sprawl," or decentralization, has created a need for more small retail establishments, particularly those specializing in convenience goods and services which franchising is well adapted to market effectively.

6. Last, as our population has increased its geographical mobility, it has created some psychological uncertainty about meeting everyday, basic needs of food and shelter while traveling. Creative, modern franchising has met this need by providing a certain level of homogeneous quality in its product or service so a traveler (or newcomer to the community) can depend on, with some degree of certainty, these retail merchants to meet his needs. For seasoned travelers, this "sameness" of Holiday Inns or McDonald's, while reassuring for others, may be dissatisfying. Which target market do you wish to please? At the moment, gross sales figures would indicate the former represent the majority of the consuming public.[14]

Factors That Breed Franchise Success

Products and Services

Significant product characteristics that best lend themselves to distribution through franchising are:

1. The product is sufficiently distinctive and identifiable by brand or trademark, and consumer acceptance has reached a point where customers will search out the product when it is needed.

2. The product cannot be offered along with similar products and still have public acceptance, i.e., prepared foods, rug and upholstery cleaning services.

3. The product has unique qualities that require special handling or preparation for proper product consistency and satisfaction when sold to the consumer. (Example: Shakey's Pizzas, Coca-Cola, etc.)

4. The product-service requires installation, periodic service, and a stock of locally available parts such as automobile repair services.[15]

Franchisor-Franchisee Qualifications

Specific qualities that are desirable for potential franchisees are good health, outgoing personality, good credit and financial standing, sufficient educational level, stable and productive work experience, and the ability to manage people and operations.

A potential franchisor should be evaluated on the basis of knowledge of financial requirements, fairness, expected profitability, the training programs provided, the reputation and progressiveness of the firm, and consumers' demand for the product or service.

The six criteria that have been rated by both franchisors and francisees to be most important to franchise success are presented in Exhibit 4–2.

The Other Side of Franchising: Disadvantages

Without a doubt, one of the most discouraging influences on the growth of franchising has been the problem of "exclusive dealing arrangements" or "tying contracts," which are expressly prohibited by the Clayton Act. Franchisors argue, and with some justification, that such contracts can *potentially* result in cost savings to their

Exhibit 4-2 **Criteria for Determining Whether a Franchise Should Be Located in a Community**

(1) The community met a specific population size.
(2) There was an adequate supply of labor available.
(3) The income level in the community was the type to create an active market for the product.
(4) Property in a good site location was owned or could be acquired.
(5) There appeared to be little competition for the product in the area.
(6) A good franchisor (franchisee) was available in the community.

The franchisor and franchisee ranked the six criteria as to which they felt were the most important. The results were that they both agreed on a top three and bottom three but the order within the two areas was different.

Source: Ronald F. Bush, Ronald L. Tatham, and Joseph F. Hair, Jr., "Community Location Decisions by Franchisors: A Comparative Analysis," *Journal of Retailing* 52 (Spring 1976): 33–42. Reprinted by permission.

franchisees due to bulk purchases and resulting quantity discounts. Second, and particularly in the fast-food segment of the industry, in order to maintain consistent product quality throughout a wide geographic area a franchisor should be able to control the quality of the raw material and supply inputs by supplying all these items and assuring their proper use through frequent visits to the various locations.[16]

From the franchisee point of view, such an argument represents a two-edged sword. If indeed the franchisor really had the best interest of the franchisee at heart and attempted to maximize the gross profits through such suggested economies of scale, then such practices should be encouraged. However, in most situations under such tying contractual arrangements, the franchisor negotiates the price of the raw materials and supplies with outside vendors, adds its expenses of handling and distribution, plus a profit margin for its "managerial" activities, and then charges the entire cost to "its" franchisees. In short, the franchisees represent a captive market that the franchisor can monopolize. The franchisor is free to charge virtually any price for the basic ingredients that the franchisee must have in order to operate. From a macro point of view, such exclusive agreements would preclude local competition for the franchisee's purchases, which is anticompetitive. This issue, particularly in fast-food franchise arrangements, has yet to be clearly resolved.[17]

Despite the legal uncertainty of the practice of franchisors furnishing franchisees with supplies, sales of supplies by franchisors to franchisees amounted to a $4.5 billion business in 1977 (Table 4–5).

Another problem pertains to the right of the franchisor to repurchase the franchise after the franchisee has made the outlet successful. Many franchise agreements have guaranteed-repurchase clauses, permitting the franchisor to repurchase the outlet after some period of time, say two to five years. At first glance, potential franchisees might view such a provision as being to their benefit if they should want to sell out or the business turns out to be less profitable than anticipated. Actually, the guarantee is exercisable only by the franchisor, at its option, which will be exercised only if the guaranteed price is less than the value of the going business.

Most startup and buildup headaches are borne by the franchisee. The person who can raise the considerable capital (see Table 4–6) needed to start a franchise

Table 4-5 **Sales of Supplies by Franchisors to Franchisees, 1977**

Franchisees by Industry	Amount Spent with Franchisors (millions of dollars)
Shoe stores, apparel shops, furniture, gift shops	$1605
Auto accessory stores, repair services, car washes, tire stores	1807
Convenience stores	351
Fast-food restaurants (hamburgers, chicken, pizza, ice cream, donuts)	619
Includes: Food ingredients $224 Supplies (paper) 94 Merchandise (nonfood) 24	
Rental services, laundry & dry cleaning services	29
Travel facilities (hotels, motels, etc.)	38
Copying services, income tax preparation, employment services	3

Source: U.S. Department of Commerce, *Franchising in the Economy, 1975–1977* (Washington, D.C.: Government Printing Office, 1976), p. 32.

can get sick and tired of that business and sell it back to the company. Thus, many stores are really owned by the franchisor and not the person running his or her own business. In some industries, for example automobile and truck dealers, automobile products and services, construction, home improvement, maintenance and cleaning services, fast-food restaurants, hotels and motels, campgrounds, and rental services, the franchisor has managed to own the high sales volume outlets while letting the franchisee own the lower sales volume outlets (Table 4–7).

Another problem is the maintenance of exclusivity in the geographical area. Many franchisees have found that their "exclusive territories" shrink in size or are carved up by the franchisor so as to increase the level of product or service saturation. The franchisor will not suffer, because it still reaps its collective share of the gross sales, but the franchisees may find their markets too small to sustain the needed profit levels for their personal independence.

A serious problem that seems to be a major point of contention in most modern franchise relationships is the matter of initial and continuing managerial training and assistance. Many potential franchisees have little or no business or managerial experience. (If they had such abilities and capital, they would have their own retail operations.) While most franchise agreements provide for some initial managerial training, they do not guarantee success, or, for that matter, make any statement about the quality of the training or continuing assistance. If the franchisor is primarily interested in making money by charging a sizable fee for setting up franchise outlets and using the franchisees' capital and borrowing ability, little or no assistance may be expected after the "grand opening." Alternatively, a change in the franchisor ownership or top management may result in a deemphasis on training and development. In any event, the potential franchisee should be aware of these and other pitfalls before becoming an "instant entrepreneur."

One type of franchise to avoid is the multilevel (or pyramid) plan. This form of

Table 4-6 **Total Investment and Start-up Cash**
Required for a Franchise-Owned Retail or Service Business 1975[A]
(Thousands of Dollars)

Kinds of Franchised Business[B]	Total Investment	Start-up Cash Required
Automotive products and services	43	20
Business aids and services		
Accounting, credit, collection agencies and general business systems	15	8
Employment services	20	15
Printing and copying services	39	15
Tax preparation services	2	2
Miscellaneous business services	15	8
Construction, home improvement, maintenance, and cleaning services	20	10
Convenience stores	55	10
Educational products and services	30	15
Fast-food restaurants (all types)	80	20
Hotels and motels	600	100
Campgrounds	225	50
Laundry and dry cleaning services	55	15
Recreation, entertainment, and travel	50	15
Rental services (auto-truck)	80	50
Rental services (equipment)	35	10
Retailing (non-food)	40	20
Retailing (food other than convenience stores)	50	20
Miscellaneous	25	12

A. Investment and start-up cash represent median averages reported by respondents.

B. Does not include automobile and truck dealers, gasoline service stations, and soft drink bottlers, for which data were not collected.

Source: U.S. Department of Commerce, *Franchising in the Economy 1975–77* (Washington, D.C.: Government Printing Office, 1976), p. 43.

franchising has come under considerable attack by consumer groups and legal authorities.

The multilevel plan was used in the retailing of products and services. This plan called for many levels of investors to buy in at a certain level in the corporate pyramid. An individual could buy in at one of the upper positions such as a distributor and then in turn sell positions such as an area sales position to others.

Under the multilevel plan the franchise fee paid by each entrant might be split among those in levels above him or her. Each entrant was also usually required to purchase a certain amount of merchandise.

At first this might not seem to be different from the pyramid type of organization within any large corporation.

One difference is that the pyramid organization within most established firms represents positions which are earned rather than purchased. Moreover, the individuals in those positions are commonly paid a salary by the corporation.

In the case of the multilevel plan, a position in the pyramid or territory was

Table 4-7 **Average Annual Sales per Establishment 1977**
(Thousands of Dollars)

| Kinds of Franchised Business | 1977[A] | | |
	Total	Company Owned	Franchisee Owned
Total—All Franchising	515	414	539
Automobile and Truck Dealers	3,998	26,763	3,781
Automotive Products and Services	120	397	86
Business Aids and Services	69	80	67
Accounting, Credit, Collection Agencies and General Business Services	46	105	45
Employment Services	205	377	165
Printing and Copying Services	69	91	68
Tax Preparation Services	23	26	21
Miscellaneous Business Services	69	198	67
Construction, Home Improvement, Maintenance and Cleaning Services	60	178	58
Convenience Stores	306	282	344
Educational Products and Services	108	78	118
Fast Food Restaurants (All Types)	303	363	280
Gasoline Service Stations	287	287	287
Hotels and Motels	888	1,477	747
Campgrounds	66	356	61
Laundry and Dry Cleaning Services	70	111	68
Recreation, Entertainment and Travel	54	348	49
Rental Services (Auto-Truck)	242	537	128
Rental Services (Equipment)	118	412	97
Retailing (Non-Food)	249	317	228
Retailing (Food Other Than Convenience Stores)	134	672	106
Soft Drink Bottlers	3,678	3,579	3,682
Miscellaneous	184	393	167

A. Estimated by respondents.

Source: U.S. Department of Commerce, *Franchising in the Economy 1975–77*, (Washington, D.C.: Government Printing Office, 1976), p. 36.

purchased. Those purchasing the position may or may not have any experience or ability to perform the task.

In many cases, it was found that the company that had established the multilevel plan was primarily interested in selling entrance-fee franchises rather than merchandise or service.[18]

By 1975 ten states had passed full disclosure laws dealing with franchises. These laws are aimed at controlling the unfair practices in the granting or selling of franchises. These laws state that the franchisor must give the prospective franchisee a sufficient amount of unbiased information to help him or her make wise investment decisions. All franchisors (except large ones) must register a prospectus which must contain the following: the background of the franchisor; a recent financial statement; the franchisor's control policy concerning fees, royalties, and supplies; contract termination policy; terms of the financial arrangements; substantiation of any profit projections; disclosure relating to the using of names of public figures; the number of franchises operating; and the territory protection provided. The franchisor must show the prospective franchisee a copy of the prospectus before anything can be signed. This applies to all franchisors including the large ones.[19]

These laws have led to a reduction of misleading information being given to franchisees. The laws have also led to small franchisors being squeezed out of states with these laws because of the large amount of money required to file the prospectus. Thus, franchising is being watched very closely at the current time.

The Future of Franchising

The future of franchising seems bright and promising. It is generally agreed that the modern forms of franchising have grown and continue to grow in number and sales volume at a remarkable rate. Some segments of the industry have yet to experience the "shake out" of marginal product/service ideas and selling firms that will inevitably occur as this form of franchising matures. Cyclical economic events may take their toll as rising prices make consumers more aware of the costs of specialized services and prepared foods. The same effect may result during a significant economic slowdown, when every consumer's pennies count.

Another conditioning element in the prediction of franchise growth is the pending legislative backlash, particularly against pyramid types of franchises. "Franchise fair dealing" legislation has been introduced in Massachusetts, New York, California, Texas, and Colorado. This same concern was embodied in Senator Harrison A. Williams' Senate bill (The Franchise Full Disclosure Act of 1970) and similar federal legislative proposals.[20] Such nationwide concern is not unexpected in light of a 1966 study that revealed that 38 percent of the franchisor respondents had been involved in legal disputes with their franchisees.[21]

Successful franchisee recruitment and the establishment of appropriate (continuing) franchisor-franchisee relationships are vital if the franchising industry is to enjoy continued public confidence and support. Individuals who contemplate participating in the franchising field should be fully aware that this is not a short cut to retail success, but it may provide an opportunity for entrepreneurs to partially realize their dreams of independence and success.

Summary

Retailers' merchandise/service offerings must meet the needs of their target market consumers. They should analyze the way potential customers use the merchandise in order to offer a goods/service mix that reflects customer demand. This can be accomplished by evaluating the offering in terms of the benefits desired by the consumer, which may go well beyond the tangible products themselves. Thus the offering should provide assistance to the consumer in using the item, maintenance and repair service, and warranties. Delivery and credit also should be provided, but only if the consumers want and are willing to pay for these extended versions of the product. The merchandise assortment must provide the quality, style, color, size, and variety that the target consumer groups demand. A deeper merchandise assortment can increase the distance that consumers are willing to travel to reach the outlet.

Store shelf and floor space limit the width and depth of the merchandise assortment an outlet can offer. Outlets that sell shopping and specialty goods may benefit by using their limited selling space to concentrate on meeting the needs of a single, narrowly defined target group. Stores that sell convenience goods generally define their target market in broader terms, to include numerous market segments.

Each merchandise line should be evaluated on the basis of its current sales, growth potential, compatibility with other merchandise offered, profitability per unit of selling space, and its availability in competitive stores. The profitability criterion indicates that the more profitable merchandise lines should be given relatively more display space in the more desirable locations. This will allow retailers to enrich the variety of their offering in the higher profit categories.

Finally, franchising represents a rather unusual product decision because in many cases the retailer is under contract to sell only products associated with a particular franchise. Persons considering the purchase of a franchise outlet should make a thorough investigation of contract terms, market potential, cost structure, and pay-back period before they make any commitment. Failures occur in franchise outlets despite the current increase in the number of franchise outlets in operation. The franchise concept perhaps exemplifies the ultimate in a total product designed for a narrowly defined market.

Questions

1. What is meant by a wide line of goods? A narrow line? A deep line? A shallow line? Cite real or hypothetical examples of each.

2. Discuss the concept "consistency of merchandise assortment." In what types of retailing would you expect the assortment to be consistent?

3. Discuss the concept of complementary goods and cite examples of such goods. Discuss and cite examples of substitute goods. What are the retailing implications of these concepts?

4. A company has a $100,000 inventory and sales of $10,000 per month.

   a. Find the turnover.

   b. If inventory is increased by 20 percent and turnover remains constant, what is the new sales volume?

   c. Assuming the same turnover rate, what margin is required if management decides it must have a 20 percent return on investment?

d. If management finds that it must maintain a 5 percent margin on a certain product line and turnover is 50, what is the ROI for this product line? What would you recommend to management in this situation?

5. Why is net space yield considered to be the most reliable measure of product line profitability?

6. Define *franchising.* Why do you think franchising might reduce the retail failure rate?

7. What are the basic forms of franchise agreements? What types of establishments would be amenable to each?

8. Discuss the reasons for the recent rate of growth in franchising.

9. Using a total systems approach, how would you design a franchise system to maximize the probability of long run success?

10. What characteristics would you look for in a franchisor if you were considering the franchise business as a career or investment? If you were the franchisor, what characteristics would be important in the franchisee?

Footnotes

1. Philip Kotler, *Marketing Management: Analysis, Planning and Control,* 2d ed. (Englewood Cliffs, N.J.: Prentice-Hall, 1972), pp. 424–425.

2. Harper W. Boyd, Jr., and Sidney J. Levy, "New Dimensions in Consumer Analysis," *Harvard Business Review* 41 (November-December 1963): 129–140.

3. "Leisure Boom: Biggest Ever and Still Growing," *Business Week,* 17 April 1972, pp. 42–45.

4. Paul J. Cifrino, "Cifrino's Space Yield Formula," *Chain Store Age,* November 1963, pp. 32–34.

5. Ibid.

6. "Variety Store Shopper Is Changing," *Marketing Insights,* 18 March 1968, p. 16.

7. U.S. Department of Commerce, Bureau of Domestic Commerce, *Franchise Company Data: For Equal Opportunity in Business,* (Washington, D.C.: Government Printing Office, December 1970), p. xi.

8. Ibid.

9. Harry Kursh, *The Franchise Boom,* rev. ed., (Englewood Cliffs, N.J.: Prentice-Hall, 1968), pp. 30–40.

10. Ibid., p. 5.

11. Aaron M. Rothenberg, "A Fresh Look at Franchising," *Journal of Marketing* 31 (July 1967): 52–53.

12. U.S. Department of Commerce, *Franchise Company Data,* p. xi.

13. U.S. Department of Commerce, *Franchising in the Economy 1975–77* (Washington, D.C.: Government Printing Office, 1977), p. 4.

14. Jack M. Starling, "Franchising," *Business Studies,* Fall 1970, pp. 10–16.

15. Robert J. Mockler and Harrison Easop, "Guidelines for More Effective Planning and Management of Franchise Systems," Research Paper 42, Bureau of Business and Economic Research, Georgia State College, Atlanta, May 1968, pp. 14–16.

16. Red Rock Bottlers Inc. v. Red Rock Cola Company, 195 F.2d 406 (CA-5, 1952).

17. Sigel v. Chicken Delight, CCH 73, 703 (CA-9, September 1971); Cartrade Inc. v. Ford Dealer's Advertising Association et al., CCH 73, 760 (CA-9, August 1971); England v. Chrysler Corporation, CCH 73, 668 (D.C. N. Cal., August 1971).

18. National Better Business Bureau Inc., Health and Safety Div., August 1969 newsletter, 230 Park Ave., N.Y.

19. Shelby D. Hunt and John R. Nevin, "Full Disclosure Laws in Franchising: An Empirical Investigation," *Journal of Marketing* 40 (April 1976): 53–62.

20. Starling, "Franchising," p. 14.

21. J. A. H. Curry et al., *Partners for Profit: A Study of Franchising* (New York: American Management Association, 1966), p. 107.

Case Study

First Floor Manager

Ms. Debra Robbins is the assistant manager of a local outlet which is affiliated with one of the five largest retailers in the United States. She is responsible for the performance of the entire first floor of the two story building which houses the chain's outlets in a midwestern town that has a population of 25,000 in its trading area. The income level of the consumers in this trading area is slightly higher than the U.S. average. About 70 percent of the workers are white collar employees with the remainder working in blue collar types of employment.

Although sales and profits have been satisfactory for this outlet, Ms. Robbins is concerned that the first floor space consisting of 9,000 square feet of selling space is not being used in the most efficient manner. The current allocation of space, sales, percent gross margin, percent handling costs, and the average inventory value for each merchandise category is:

Merchandise Category	Square Feet of Space Used by Each Category	1978 Sales Volume	Gross Margin Percentage	Handling Cost as a Percentage of Retail Sales	Average Inventory Value in Retail Prices
Women's Clothing	3000	$339,000	40	9	327,000
Men's Clothing	2250	248,000	32	7	275,000
Children's Clothing	1000	86,000	36	5	18,000
Shoes	650	98,000	39	8	109,000
Sporting Goods	2100	95,000	30	6	23,000
	9000	$866,000			

Annual rental cost for the first floor is $8 per square foot of selling space.

The competition for the first floor merchandise is two mail catalog outlets (one of which is housed in the basement of the same building and is operated by the same national chain), one small department store, nine women's shops, five men's stores, one children's store, seven shoe stores, two sporting goods stores and three discount stores which sell all of the lines carried on the first floor.

Discussion Questions

1. Evaluate the merchandise offering of the first floor.

2. Calculate the return on investment in inventory for each merchandise category.

3. Calculate the net space yield for each merchandise category.

4. Make recommendations on what Ms. Robbins should do based upon your findings for questions 2 and 3 and your knowledge of retailing.

Case Study

Ann's Dream

Ann is interested in entering the retailing business. She has investigated the various retailers located in a city with a trading area of 65,000. The population is comparable to the average U.S. community in respect to income and social class. She has discovered that there are no decorator shops specializing in bathroom and bedroom decorations. The current competition consists of a J. C. Penney outlet, several gift shops, and a small department store. Each of the outlets offers only a few bath and bedroom items.

Ann would like to open a shop which carries a wide merchandise assortment containing most items that are used in decorating the bathroom or bedroom.

Discussion Questions

1. Is Ann considering merchandise lines that are compatible? Explain.

2. Develop an appropriate merchandise assortment for Ann.

3. Are the items included in your list staple items or fashion items?

4. Who should Ann's target market be?

5. How large an outlet will Ann need to meet her customer's needs and still operate at a profitable level?

6. Do you think Ann will be able to develop a successful outlet?

Chapter 5

Store Location Considerations

1. To understand why a retail outlet's success depends upon how many of its target market people reside in the trading area.

2. To be able to discuss the methods retailers use to evaluate a town or city as a possible location site.

3. To understand the characteristics of the different types of retail locations: free-standing, business-associated, and planned shopping centers.

4. To be able to list the advantages and disadvantages of locating in a shopping center.

general trading area
buying power index
understored
overstored
index of retail
saturation

free-standing site
business-associated
site
planned shopping center
neighborhood shopping
centers

community shopping
centers
regional shopping
centers
lead tenants
tenant mix

121

A retailer's merchandise may be easily duplicated. Promotions can be imitated. Prices can be matched. But through a good location the retailer achieves a unique advantage. Once the site has been selected and secured, the space cannot be occupied by a competitive retailer. This chapter examines the factors that retailers should consider when choosing a general trade area in which they may locate an outlet. The process for selecting a specific site within the general trade area is discussed in Chapter 6.

Location has an influence upon all the other elements which the retailer uses to attract customers. In a poor location a retailer will have to spend additional effort persuading people to seek out the store. This may simply mean that more will be spent on advertising and promotion. However, added drawing power might also be obtained by lowering prices or increasing service—all of which costs money. Thus, a good location can save future expenditures that might otherwise be needed to attract customers to the store.

Most site evaluation work consists of a careful investigation of a location for a new store. However, changes in consumer behavior may make a once suitable site suddenly unprofitable. For example, the deterioration of a neighborhood or the opening of a new freeway often causes a change in consumer demand that calls for a site (or at least a consumer target) reevaluation. Therefore, present sites must be continually reevaluated.

A particularly crucial location decision arises every time a retailer signs a new lease. By signing a lease he or she commits the store to continue operations from the same location for a specific period, ranging from six months to twenty-five years. It is advisable to analyze the current location every year or two with the same care as if a new store location decision were being made.

These periodic analyses allow the retailer to spot current or potential deficiencies in market saturation and thereby anticipate the need to change the location to meet changing consumer demands. Although the following discussion is conducted in terms of a new store, the factors involved are also applicable to the appraisal of an established store.

General Trading Area Evaluation

An evaluation of the *general trading area* (the entire city or county in which the outlet may be located) is needed before the specific site is selected. Often, however, this evaluation of the city or trading area is omitted because the retailer believes that it is convenient to locate in a certain area. This can be a tragic mistake, as competitive or environmental conditions may cause the business to fail even if the best site is chosen. Thus, the evaluation must be objective and include an analysis of the general trading area as well as the specific site. The profit potential in different areas can be compared. The retailer can then choose the opportunity that appears to offer the best profit potential. The factors to consider when evaluating a community as a possible retail location are presented in Table 5–1.

Table 5-1 **Factors to Consider in Selecting a General Trade Area**

People Living in or Coming into Trade Area	Community Environment	Business Growth
Population	Legislative restrictions	Present industries
Trend in population	Taxes	Proposed new industries
Income or purchasing power	Competition	Area promotions
Distribution of income	Advertising media available	
Stability of income	Transportation facilities	
Trend of income	Banking and credit facilities	
Purchasing habits	Insurance rates	
Life-style	Protection from fire,	
Social class	theft and the elements	
Age	Rental cost	
Race	Availability of	
Nationality	employees	
Religion		

Selection of a City or Town

Population

The number of people in the general trading area and the age distribution of this population determine the number of potential customers of retail stores of a particular type. Generally, the purchase rate of most retail products responds favorably to population increases.

The average population served by retailers has increased by 29 percent during the 1948–1972 period as annual sales volumes have increased (Table 5–2). However, the total number of retail establishments increased only 8 percent from 1948 to 1972. These trends would indicate that a retailer would want to locate in areas where the average population served per store was (or will be) above the national average population served per store as reported in Table 5–2.

City and town population data are available from the U.S. Census Bureau. Detailed demographic data are collected every ten years and are available by state, county, and city in the *County and City Data Book: A Statistical Abstract Supplement.* This supplement is published by the U.S. Department of Commerce every five years. *The Editor & Publisher Market Guide* and *Sales and Marketing Management* also provide annual population estimates by town and county. An example of the type of data provided is presented in Table 5–3. If current secondary population data are not available, the number of new residential electrical connections has been found to provide reliable estimates of an area's population growth. The last known number of people per household for the area (generally obtainable from census data) can be multiplied by the number of new residential electrical connections to provide an estimate of population growth.

The data provided by most sources do not account for seasonal shifts in population. Some trading areas gain people during the summer and lose them during the

Table 5–2 Comparison of Sales Factors for Selected Retail Outlets in 1948 and 1972

Type of Retail Outlet	Number of Stores (in Thousands)		Sales (in Millions $)		Average Population Served per Store[A]		Average Annual Sales Per Store[B]	
	1948	1972	1948	1972	1948	1972	1948	1972
Retail trade, total	1,773	1,912	130,521	459,040	82	106	74	240
Hardware stores	35	26	2,494	3,957	4,213	7,727	72	150
Department stores (including Mail-order sales)	3	8	10,645	51,084	56,125	26,391	4,125	6,634
Variety stores	20	22	2,507	7,344	7,229	9,322	124	337
Grocery stores	378	194	24,774	93,327	386	1,046	125	480
Gasoline service stations	188	227	6,483	33,655	776	897	34	149
Total apparel and accessory stores	115	129	9,803	24,741	1,268	1,572	85	191
Eating and drinking places	347	360	10,683	36,868	422	565	31	103
Drug and proprietary stores	56	51	4,013	15,599	2,618	3,946	72	303
Sporting goods stores and bicycle shops	9	23	549	2,538	21,057	9,032	79	113
Jewelry stores	21	25	1,225	3,118	6,869	8,032	58	123

A. Average population served per store is total U.S. population divided by the number of stores; population figures used were 1948—146.1 million, 1972—203.2 million.

B. Obtained by dividing total sales by number of stores. Sales are reported in $1,000.

Source: U.S. Department of Commerce, U.S. Census of Business, Retail Trade (Washington, D.C.: Government Printing Office, 1948 and 1972), various pages.

Table 5-3 An Example of the Data Provided by the *Editor & Publisher Market Guide*

Colorado Population Income, Household, Farm Products

Metro Areas Counties Cities	Population		Disposable Personal Income		Households		Farm Products (1974)		
	1970 U.S. Census	E&P Estimate Jan. 1, 1979	E&P '70 Estimate (add 000)	E&P '78 Estimate (add 000)	1979 Number of Households	E&P '78 Estimate Income per Household	Number of Farms	Value of Crops (add 000)	Value of Livestock (add 000)
State Totals	2,207,199	2,718,361	7,317,951	16,916,300	955,482	17,704	26,896	673,232	1,262,465
Standard Metropolitan Statistical Areas									
Colorado Springs, Colo.	239,288	311,418	661,114	1,759,651	107,777	16,327	697	3,901	9,538
Denver-Boulder, Colo.	1,237,208	1,509,046	4,391,991	10,043,269	530,358	18,937	2,477	59,807	47,658
Fort Collins, Colo.	89,900	130,140	271,833	875,025	47,294	18,502	1,074	16,627	39,467
Greeley, Colo.	89,297	116,157	247,664	817,114	39,569	20,650	3,177	108,218	466,612
Pueblo, Colo.	118,238	129,241	339,061	686,195	43,768	15,678	628	9,312	22,070
Counties, Cities									
Adams	185,789	237,408	475,465	1,273,939	71,432	17,834	861	27,571	27,077
Alamosa	11,422	12,684	21,351	64,413	4,298	14,987	328	11,276	2,587
Alamosa	6,985	7,243	12,757	35,936	2,344	15,331	*	*	*

Table 5-3 (cont)

Colorado Retail Sales—Census and Estimates

Metro Areas Counties Cities	Total Retail Sales			Number of Stores and 1978 Estimate of Sales ($1,000)								
	1972 U.S. Census ($1,000)	E&P 1977 Estimate ($1,000)	E&P 1978 Estimate ($1,000)	Lbr. Hdwr.		Gen. Mdse.		Food		Auto	
State Totals	5,869,039	9,366,127	10,058,812	1,166	758,156	578	1,342,091	1,964	1,951,572	1,445	2,155,143
Standard Metropolitan Statistical Areas											
Colorado Springs, Colo.	628,460	898,189	964,600	95	65,963	45	152,493	173	155,333	143	220,592
Denver-Boulder, Colo.	3,529,793	5,462,301	5,866,200	481	396,002	206	879,389	875	1,106,193	669	1,297,937
Fort Collins, Colo.	241,110	442,383	475,107	76	47,556	33	48,615	79	91,318	74	105,181
Greeley, Colo.	192,439	317,556	341,042	51	32,133	24	44,768	75	68,621	61	73,719
Pueblo, Colo.	270,633	446,441	479,449	44	39,239	27	74,786	130	104,149	88	102,473
Counties, Cities											
Adams	447,632	734,430	788,735	83	62,356	32	141,188	145	174,911	116	147,255
Alamosa	33,763	52,321	56,190	14	7,365	6	6,512	10	10,258	8	10,450
Alamosa	29,989	46,572	50,016	10	4,560	5	4,932	10	10,258	8	10,450

Metro Areas Counties Cities	Number of Stores and 1978 Estimate of Sales ($1,000)									
	Gasoline		Apparel		Furniture		Eat Drink		Drugs	
State Totals	3,170	760,873	1,365	373,449	1,520	466,042	4,384	914,000	588	280,111
Standard Metropolitan Statistical Areas										
Colorado Springs, Colo.	296	77,555	151	36,286	181	54,222	413	82,292	45	20,337
Denver-Boulder, Colo.	1,431	369,963	697	223,609	844	287,942	2,015	522,075	292	161,611
Fort Collins, Colo.	137	30,085	76	17,071	85	24,335	207	45,154	23	14,251
Greeley, Colo.	131	28,223	50	12,243	50	13,732	166	27,715	21	9,325
Pueblo, Colo.	154	35,467	54	20,248	60	23,058	257	34,740	29	14,607
Counties, Cities										
Adams	253	68,482	89	21,205	122	28,807	268	60,667	29	19,053
Alamosa	24	5,053	12	3,455	6	2,292	33	5,737	2	794
Alamosa	21	4,257	12	3,455	6	2,292	31	5,211	2	794

Source: *Editor & Publisher Market Guide*, 1978 Edition (New York: *Editor & Publisher*, 1978), pp. 77–80.

winter. Some communities, located in states such as Colorado, Wyoming and Michigan, have a large influx of tourists and summer residents who increase the potential number of customers for the summer months. Other communities, in Arizona, California, and Florida, obtain temporary population gains during the winter months. In some locations tourists and temporary residents may arrive at a fairly constant rate throughout the year. College and university towns benefit from the increased population of students during the September to June period. Whatever the seasonal pattern may be, the amount of business generated by these people must be added to the resident business potential to obtain a valid estimate of potential business for the general trade area.

Long-term trends in population growth must also be considered, because a store is expected to generate sales and profits far into the future. The U.S. population is expected to grow from 213.5 million in 1975 to 223 million in 1980 and to 245 million in 1990.[1] This represents a 15 percent growth over a fifteen-year period.

Not all areas will grow during the next ten years. Between 1950 and 1966 metropolitan dwellers increased from 56.1 percent to 67.3 percent of the U.S. population.[2] During the same period a large segment of the central-city population moved to the suburbs. Currently, slightly more than 45 percent of the metropolitan dwellers live in the central city and slightly fewer than 55 percent live in the suburbs.

The rate of population growth has not been equivalent for all areas of the United States. Population in the Pacific Coast area increased most rapidly during the 1960–1969 period. The south Atlantic, west south central, and mountain areas have also increased at a rapid rate during this period. These same areas also grew most rapidly from 1970–1975 (Table 5–4). Detailed state-by-state population increases and retail sales estimates are available from *Sales and Marketing Management.* An example of the data provided by *Sales and Marketing Management's Survey of Buying Power* is presented in Table 5–5.

Table 5-4 **Residential Population by Regions (in Millions, Including Armed Forces)**

	1970	1975 Est.	% Change
Northeast	11.8	12.1	.5
Mid Atlantic	37.2	37.2	less than .05
East North Central	40.3	40.9	.3
West North Central	16.3	16.6	.4
South Atlantic	30.8	33.7	1.8
East South Central	12.8	13.5	1.1
West South Central	19.3	20.8	1.5
Mountain	8.3	9.6	2.9
Pacific	26.6	28.2	1.2

Source: U.S. Department of Commerce, Bureau of the Census, *Statistical Abstract of the United States* (Washington, D.C.: Government Printing Office, 1976), p. 325.

Of course, some towns and cities within the same state will grow faster than others. The proximity to a large population center will encourage growth in the

Table 5-5 Summary of Data Available from Sales & Marketing Management

Metro Areas Counties Cities	Total Pop. Thousands	% of U.S.	Median Age of Pop.	Population—12/31/76 % of Population by Age Group				Households (Thousands)
				18-24 Years	25-34 Years	35-49 Years	50 and Over	
Anaheim—Santa Ana—								
Garden Grove	1,776.0	.8227	27.1	12.5	17.1	18.1	18.5	610.8
Orange	1,776.0	.8227	27.1	12.5	17.1	18.1	18.5	610.8
Anaheim*	203.5	.0943	27.1	14.4	16.1	19.1	18.2	72.7
Buena Park	62.9	.0291	24.8	11.6	16.7	19.7	13.3	19.2
Costa Mesa	79.3	.0367	27.4	14.0	17.3	17.0	19.9	29.0
Fullerton	97.0	.0449	27.5	14.7	15.0	18.7	20.1	34.3
Garden Grove*	119.9	.0555	26.1	11.9	17.2	18.9	15.7	38.9
Huntington Beach	158.8	.0736	26.2	10.4	21.4	18.1	13.1	51.5
La Habra	44.4	.0206	27.1	12.8	14.8	20.3	18.0	15.4
Newport Beach	65.1	.0302	32.8	14.6	15.8	19.5	27.0	28.3
Orange	87.8	.0407	26.8	11.9	16.8	18.7	17.4	29.2
Santa Ana*	185.3	.0858	26.0	13.8	17.4	15.1	19.3	63.3
Westminster	69.7	.0323	25.4	10.4	18.5	18.1	14.1	21.8
Suburban Total	1,267.3	.5871	27.4	12.1	17.1	18.3	18.7	435.9

Table 5–5 (cont)

Retail Sales by Store Group, 1976

Metro Areas Counties Cities	Total Retail Sales ($1000)	Food ($1000)	Eating and Drinking Places ($1000)	General Mdse. ($1000)	Furnit.- Furnish.- Appl. ($1000)	Auto- motive ($1000)	Drug ($1000)
Anaheim—Santa Ana— Garden Grove	6,379,478	1,258,666	714,665	950,363	374,124	1,190,150	171,356
Orange	6,379,478	1,258,666	714,665	950,363	374,124	1,190,150	171,356
Anaheim*	680,431	119,916	96,353	93,017	55,636	122,980	18,099
Buena Park	389,523	39,579	77,055	112,620	13,716	58,730	10,476
Costa Mesa	567,199	89,079	41,023	122,140	24,691	141,828	8,051
Fullerton	413,032	77,954	33,649	80,636	15,356	107,435	12,189
Garden Grove*	383,205	83,234	31,324	24,806	22,737	93,088	13,463
Huntington Beach	432,734	93,816	36,766	83,295	40,151	82,422	13,977
La Habra	195,989	42,733	16,047	31,755	8,622	45,935	5,294
Newport Beach	339,558	54,778	66,779	59,479	10,631	52,901	11,090
Orange	420,338	65,806	41,191	89,030	25,032	82,357	8,676
Santa Ana*	744,488	109,208	59,926	105,601	61,490	204,457	14,638
Westminster	287,132	68,502	16,928	21,844	16,237	100,071	7,994
Suburban Total	4,571,354	946,308	527,062	726,939	234,261	769,625	125,156

Table 5-5 (cont.)

| Metro Areas
Counties
Cities | Total EBI ($000) | Median Hsld. EBI | Effective Buying Income, 1976 | | | | Buying Power Index |
| | | | % of Hslds. by EBI Group
(A) $8,000-$9,999
(B) $10,000-$14,999
(C) $15,000-$24,999
(D) $25,000 & Over | | | | |
			A	B	C	D	
Anaheim—Santa Ana—							
Garden Grove	11,126,771	16,652	6.0	18.6	37.0	20.2	.9268
Orange	11,126,771	16,652	6.0	18.6	37.0	20.2	.9268
Anaheim*	1,245,431	15,775	6.5	20.9	37.8	15.8	.1026
Buena Park	345,464	16,534	5.4	22.2	43.3	15.7	.0382
Costa Mesa	452,593	14,550	7.4	20.6	33.9	14.3	.0523
Fullerton	670,780	17,169	5.8	18.1	33.5	25.3	.0562
Garden Grove*	657,454	16,211	5.5	21.7	42.4	14.3	.0564
Huntington Beach	997,998	18,016	4.7	17.0	42.3	22.2	.0763
La Habra	267,352	16,363	6.0	20.2	39.0	17.4	.0244
Newport Beach	685,010	19,170	5.4	14.6	25.2	36.2	.0505
Orange	518,420	16,573	5.8	18.0	38.6	18.5	.0492
Santa Ana*	925,391	13,347	8.9	22.9	31.8	10.5	.0903
Westminster	378,303	16,801	5.8	19.6	43.1	16.2	.0356
Suburban Total	8,298,495	17,379	5.6	17.3	37.0	22.9	.6775

Source: "1977 Survey of Buying Power," *Sales & Marketing Management* 119 (July 25, 1977): c-16 and c-29. © 1977 S&MM Survey of Buying Power.

nearby towns. The attractiveness of the city or town is enhanced by good schools and churches, health facilities, parking, shopping, and entertainment facilities. The town leaders' positive attitude toward attracting new industry is also a must if an area is to achieve its share of population growth.

An increased trading area may be obtained by sponsoring civic and merchant events, conventions, and the like that draw people from the fringe of the trading area into town. Improved public transportation and good highway and street systems can increase the size of the trading area by reducing the time required to reach the shopping area. As traffic becomes more congested, consumers tend to think more in terms of the additional driving time required to reach their destinations than in terms of the actual distance involved. Population changes and accessibility to population have a great influence upon retailing, since people tend to shop at the nearest, most convenient location.

The major chain retailers and franchisors have established a minimum population that an area must possess before they would consider locating an outlet in that area. The exact size of the minimum population requirement varies from firm to firm. Recent reports indicate that there is a lowering of the specified population on the part of some retailers. Apparently large retail organizations are beginning to realize the potential that smaller communities offer. One big advantage that many chains and franchise organizations have discovered is that competition from other chains or franchise outlets is absent in smaller communities. The result is they can capture a very large share of the market and do not have to divide it up with ten or fifteen closely competing franchise or chain outlets.

Kentucky Fried Chicken, which would not consider locating outlets in towns under 35,000 population ten years ago, now has over 890 outlets in towns of less than 10,000 population. In fact, one of their most successful outlets is located in Harlan, Kentucky, a town of 3,300 population (but the trade area consists of about 30,000 people).

Most of these national retailers use a scaled-down version of the urban outlets to serve these smaller communities. McDonald's Corporation, which would hardly look into the establishment of an outlet in a town of under 30,000 population five years ago, is now expanding into small towns with its Mini-Mac outlet that is smaller than its traditional outlets. Pillsbury Company's Burger King chain is also establishing forty- to fifty-seat restaurants (instead of the hundred seats usually placed in an urban outlet) to serve smaller towns. Pizza Hut Inc. has also done extremely well in towns of 5,000 to 10,000 people. The chain outlets benefit from the national advertising and from competing only with the local mom-and-pop operation which usually does not offer any special image appeal to the consumer.[3]

Even K Mart has discovered that it can conduct business profitably in a smaller town. From the inception of the K Mart program in 1962, the firm constructed its new stores in the path of growth around major metropolitan areas. The basic K Mart store that serviced these heavily populated communities ranged from 65,000 square feet to 96,000 square feet. In 1974 the company introduced a 40,000-square-foot store to serve smaller, more rural markets. These stores were opened to supplement their primary program of full size stores for medium size cities and major metropolitan markets.

The K Mart expansion has also recently moved into intra-urban sites located in high density areas where the population varies from 350,000 to 750,000 in a primary trade area. These locations are sometimes twice as costly to acquire as are the typical suburban locations. However, the intra-urban sites generally offer less retail competition than do the suburban sites.

These examples illustrate that the required population differs from one firm to another and even within the same firm according to the size of the outlet.

Income or Purchasing Power

Population influences the sales of all products and services, but it relates more directly to sales of products that are frequently purchased, such as groceries, than to seldom purchased durables (autos), semi-durables (clothing or small appliances), or services (insurance). Spending on all but frequently purchased goods is influenced by the level of disposable income, which is the money that families have available to them to spend. So population, while still important, may not be the dominant factor affecting sales.

As family income increases there are pronounced shifts in the relative demand for different categories of goods and services. Ernst Engel, in 1857, observed that although rising family income tended to be accompanied by increased spending in all product and service categories, the percentage spent on housing and household operations remained constant, and the percentage spent on health and savings tended to increase. These findings have been validated in budget studies.

The increases in income that have occurred in the United States since 1965 have resulted in a proportionately higher percentage of a person's income being spent for autos and parts, furniture and household equipment, other durable goods, gasoline and oil, and household operation services (Table 5–6).

Product lines that benefited least from the increase in disposable income included foods and beverages, clothing and shoes, and transportation services. Because of their low response to increases in disposable income, sales of these items may be more dependent upon population growth than upon increases in income. Thus, the demand for these products is not likely to increase as rapidly as sales of products that are favorably related to higher incomes.

There is no simple measure of income or purchasing power that can completely describe the consumer's ability to buy merchandise. The average family income and per capita income are provided in several sources, such as the *Editor & Publisher Market Guide* and *Sales and Marketing Management* (see Tables 5–3 and 5–5). The *buying power index* in Table 5–5 provides an approximate value for the ability of an area to purchase consumer goods. For example, Table 5–5 indicates that Anaheim, California, had a buying power index of .1026 in 1976. The projected buying power index for Newport Beach, California, was .0505. Thus the market potential in Anaheim is estimated to be approximately double the market potential in Newport Beach. This index is most applicable to mass market products (as contrasted with items not sold on the mass market) that are sold at "popular" prices. These index calculations provide a good estimate of the level of income available for spending, but they do not take into consideration the following factors:

Table 5-6 **Where Consumer Dollars Go**
(To eliminate the effects of inflation, the following figures are given in constant dollars; the Bureau of Labor Statistics chose the 1963 dollar as the base. The figures show per capita spending—that is, the average amount spent by every man, woman, and child in the U.S.)

Consumer spending	1965		1972		1980		1985	
	Per capita spending	% of total spent	Per capita spending	% of total spent	Per capita spending	% of total spent	Per capita spending	% of total spent
Taxes	$330.41	12.2%	$524.31	15.1%	$733.70	15.5%	$900.46	16.7%
Interest	56.61	2.1	72.78	2.1	119.73	2.5	139.55	2.6
Savings	143.07	5.3	183.38	5.3	275.92	5.8	304.87	5.7
Miscellaneous transfers	3.60	.1	3.83	.1	2.25	.1	1.71	—
Personal consumption:	(2,178.05)	(80.3)	(2,679.49)	(77.4)	(3,600.59)	(76.1)	(4,044.59)	(75.0)
Autos & parts	164.70	6.1	237.02	6.9	315.99	6.7	344.82	6.4
Furniture & household equipment	131.76	4.9	194.88	5.6	251.18	5.3	281.69	5.2
Other durable goods	41.69	1.4	60.34	1.7	89.57	1.9	103.92	1.9
Food & beverages	490.99	18.1	523.36	15.1	656.73	13.9	705.09	13.1
Clothing & shoes	174.47	6.4	211.16	6.1	257.03	5.4	269.67	5.0
Gasoline & oil	78.22	2.9	106.29	3.1	148.55	3.1	175.63	3.3
Other nondurable goods	210.49	7.8	257.60	7.4	363.70	7.7	412.66	7.6
Housing	321.67	11.9	400.29	11.6	560.86	11.9	658.71	12.2
Household operation services	131.76	4.8	170.47	4.9	235.42	5.0	273.96	5.1
Transportation services	69.47	2.6	79.48	2.3	104.43	2.2	113.79	2.1
Other services	362.83	13.4	438.60	12.7	617.13	13.0	704.65	13.1
Total (in 1963 dollars)	$2,711.74	100.0%	$3,463.79	100.0%	$4,732.19	100.0%	$5,391.18	100.0%

Source: Deborah Holmes, "Your Changing Consumers," *Jewelers' Circular Keystone* 143 (October 1977): 24–25.

1. *Distribution of income.* The distribution of income is important because average per capita income can be distorted by a few individuals with very high or very low incomes. More importantly, the dispersion of income can be estimated from the proportion of families that are homeowners, the average value of the single-unit dwellings, the number and make of automobiles registered in the area, and per capita retail sales.

2. *Stability of income.* Income is generally more stable in areas with diversified industries than in areas dominated by one industry. Of course, some areas that are dominated by one employer offer a strong but stable economy. Washington, D.C., and the small-town locations of large colleges and universities are examples of areas that usually have relatively strong but seasonally stable retail sales. Retail sales in areas dominated by employers whose sales are affected by seasonal or economic conditions are likely to fluctuate with the decline and expansion of these industries.

   The quality of the labor-management relationship also affects stability of income and hence retail purchases. Constant labor strife and periodic strikes may result in violent fluctuations in retail sales, and may also require merchants to overextend credit during strikes.

3. *Trend of income* in a particular area. For most retailers it is desirable to be located in areas where consumers' incomes are growing at a faster rate than the national average annual increase in income. However, some retailers prefer to appeal to the low-income market segment and thus locate stores in low-income areas offering a narrow merchandise assortment and high-risk credit terms.

Purchasing Habits of Potential Customers

Purchasing habits must be investigated to determine if the potential customers are likely to do their buying at the most accessible locations. If the majority of the people rely mostly upon mail-order purchasing or like to combine a shopping trip with a pleasure trip and travel many miles, it will take some additional advertising and promotional expenditures or price reductions to influence these consumers to change their buying habits. These differences in purchasing patterns may correspond to group differences in social class, age, race, nationality, or religion.

The basic industry upon which the town depends for the majority of its income influences the type of retail outlets that will be most successful in the area. Thus, retailers who are planning to expand into new areas must analyze the character and industrial base of the communities they have under consideration. Life style is also an important factor for retailers to consider when they locate a new outlet.

Better estimates of an area's sales are obtained if the prospective retailer is personally familiar with the buying habits, preferences, and prejudices of the people residing in the trading area. Familiarity with potential consumers' purchasing patterns will also make it easier for the prospective retailer to estimate the importance that consumers give to services and to wide and deep merchandise assortments. This knowledge is useful not only in the site selection process but also in decisions on what products and services the retailer will offer.

Legislative Restrictions

The legal environment influences the profitability, and may determine the existence or nonexistence, of any store. Local zoning ordinances limit the number of sites that are suitable for retailing. Municipal or state regulations relative to the hours of business may limit night and Sunday openings for many types of retail outlets. The decision on location is also influenced by the tax and license structure in the particular area. The relative level of sales tax charged in nearby areas is particularly important to retailers who sell shopping goods. For example, the difference between a 3 and a 6 percent sales tax on a $1,000 stereo system is $30. Such marked differences can influence consumer buying habits toward making purchases in the lower tax area.

Competition in the Area

The choice of a location is also influenced by the number, type, location, and floor space of competing stores. The competition should be evaluated to determine to what extent its merchandise and service mix meet the desires of the prospective consumers.

The trend toward scrambled merchandising—selling many unrelated lines in a single outlet—has made this evaluation more difficult. Today much of the competition for items that used to be sold in specialty stores is not derived from other specialty stores but from chain, department, discount, grocery, drug, or hardware stores. Thus, the study of competitors must be based on a realistic estimate of the share of the total market that can be obtained when one faces this vigorous competition.

Store Saturation

Preliminary estimates of the extent to which the competition has already obtained the retailing opportunities in the trade area can be obtained from several sources.

County Business Patterns, which is published annually by the U.S. Department of Commerce, uses a classification system called the Standard Industrial Classification (SIC) to classify most manufacturers, wholesalers, and retailers into designated categories for each geographical area. Using this information, one can determine the number of retailers doing business in the trade area. State sales tax revenue offices sometimes summarize and make public the number of retail outlets doing business in each county and also provide information on the volume of business obtained by each type of outlet (as defined by the SIC code system).

No matter which source is used, the SIC system of trade area appraisal has several weaknesses. It is difficult to identify the precise activities of a particular firm because some retail outlets sell wide assortments of merchandise. Then, too, the mere number of a specific type of store in an area does not give an evaluation of the aggressiveness of the outlets.

A more precise measurement tool, called an index of retail saturation, can be used to determine if the stores in a trade area supply consumer needs adequately or inadequately. When an area has too few stores to meet the needs of the consumer community satisfactorily, an *understored* condition exists. This situation presents the best retailing opportunity for new stores to satisfy consumer needs.

If an area is *overstored* it has more stores than are needed to satisfy consumer demand. This situation would probably result in a low return on investment for the retail outlets operating in the area. It would not represent an opportunity for a new store unless the new store could serve the consumer needs much more effectively than the current outlets. In such a case some of the current outlets would probably be driven out of business.

The *index of retail saturation* can be calculated by dividing estimated consumption by the ability of current retailers to satisfy consumer needs. In formula terms, that calculation could be obtained as follows:[4]

$$\text{Saturation Index} = \frac{(C)\ (RE)}{RF},$$

where C is the number of prospective consumers of the proposed product, RE is the average expenditure for the proposed product line for a selected period of time, and RF is a measurement of competing (and planned) retailing facilities in the trade area, measured in square feet of space devoted to the proposed lines of merchandise.

The use of this index may be illustrated by the following example. Saturation index calculations could be made for several different areas to indicate which area offers the most potential for a proposed supermarket. There are 50,000 consumers in area A. The average consumer in the area spends $12 per week in supermarkets. The six supermarkets serving area A have a total of 60,000 square feet of selling area. The index calculation is:

$$\text{Saturation Index} = \frac{(50,000)\ (\$12)}{60,000} = \frac{\$600,000}{60,000} = \$10$$

The $10 sales per square foot of selling area can be measured against the sales needed per square foot if the business is to just break even. The $10 calculated sales per square foot could also be compared with the index figure for other possible location areas. The highest index would indicate the area with the best potential. It does not indicate that the area will be a profitable location unless the highest index is higher than the break-even sales needed per square foot, and even then it does not guarantee success because the outlet must be well managed, competition may change, and so on.

This index of saturation is an excellent measure of potential sales (per square foot) because it uses both consumer demand and competitive supply to evaluate the trading area. However, the index does not reflect the quality of the competition in each trade area. Some areas may have more progressive merchandisers than others, and this difference may not appear in the square footage measurement of competitive strength used in the denominator of the formula. Thus, qualitative evaluation of competition should also be made to determine if and to what degree competitive strength differs from the assumed power made on the basis of square feet of selling space.

Retailers can develop other indices that can be used to evaluate competition. Their own experiences in the industry can determine which of these measures can yield a reliable assessment of the competitive environment. Other factors that can be used in this evaluation of the level of retail saturation in an area are:

- The number of persons living in the area divided by the number of competing retail outlets in the area
- The population in the area divided by store front footage of competing outlets
- Annual category retail sales in the area relative to amount of competitor's advertising
- Counts of pedestrian and vehicular traffic going past competitor's location
- Number of salespeople on the floor of competitor outlets during a specified time period
- Number of checkout counters in use at competitive outlets during peak business hours
- Number of autos in competitor's parking lot during peak business hours
- Size and quality of competitor's inventory
- Assortment of competitor's merchandise
- Percentage of retail facilities that are vacant
- The appearance of a leading department store in a community

(Table 5–7 contains a listing of the top twenty department stores in the U.S. in order of sales volume.)

Type of Location Considerations
A retail outlet's type of location has a strong influence upon the size and shape of the trading area that the store is able to serve. The type of location also determines the degree to which a store is able to penetrate its market area.

Classification of Location Types
Locations may be either *free-standing* (no other retailing businesses are adjacent to the site) or *business-associated sites*. Most locations are business associated as a part of either a planned shopping center or an unplanned shopping district. Characteristics of both store location types are:

Table 5-7 **The Top Twenty Department Stores in 1976**

Company/Division	Affiliation	Stores	Sq. Ft.	Volume[A]
1. Macy's, New York	(RHM)	16	6,164	$520
2. Hudson's, Detroit	(D-H)	13	5,105	512.6
3. Broadway, Los Angeles	(CHH)	42	7,300	485
4. May Co. California	(May)	25	6,578	465
5. Abraham & Straus, Brooklyn	(Fed)	10	4,295	445
6. Bambergers, New Jersey	(RHM)	17	4,811	440
7. Marshall Field, Chicago	(Ind)	15	3,318	420
8. Korvettes Metro New York	(Arlen)	29	N.A.	415
9. Bloomingdales, New York	(Fed)	13	3,019	385
Alexander's, New York	(Ind)	10	N.A.	383
11. Bullock's, Los Angeles	(Fed)	17	3,647	365
12. Rich's, Atlanta	(Fed)	13	3,385	340
Jordan Marsh, Boston	(Allied)	11	3,323	340
14. Lord & Taylor, New York	(ADG)	22	3,410	325
15. Macy's California	(RHM)	13	3,184	310
16. Hecht-May, Baltimore-Washington	(May)	19	3,892	295
17. Dayton's, Minneapolis	(D-H)	12	3,184	284.8
Goldblatt's, Chicago	(Ind)	45	4,749	285
Foley's, Houston	(Fed)	8	2,494	285
20. Lazarus, Columbus	(Fed)	11	3,149	265

A. Sales volumes not rounded off to 0 or not ending in 5 are actual reported figures; all others are estimated. Sales volume and Sq. Ft. figures are in millions.
Affiliation Code: RHM, Macy's; D-H, Dayton-Hudson; CHH, Carter, Hawley, Hale; Fed, Federated; Ind, Independent; ADG, Associated Dry Goods.
Source: Edward S. Dubbs, "The Top 100," *Stores* 59 (July, 1977): 22–23. Reprinted from *Stores* Magazine; © National Retail Merchants Association, 1976.

1. Free-standing
    a. Neighborhood—an isolated retail outlet which serves the needs of a small portion of the town
    b. Highway—an isolated outlet located on a highway
2. Business-associated
    a. Unplanned
        1] Downtown—the traditional commercial core of the town. It may contain department, variety, apparel, and food stores plus many offices and service shops.
        2] Edge of downtown—the area located at the edge of the downtown area.
        3] Neighborhood business district—neighborhoods are small parts of a town that are usually defined by social, economic, or geographic boundaries. A neighborhood business district contains small stores with nothing larger than a supermarket or variety store.
        4] Secondary business district—a small-scale downtown area usually bounded by major street intersections. It must contain at least a junior or general

merchandise department store and a variety store and some smaller retail and service shops.

5] Highway business string—an elongated area which contains several retail businesses. Extensions of the string down perpendicular streets are very shallow.[5]

b. *Planned shopping center*—location, size, type of tenants, and parking space are the result of conscious planning by the developers. The expansion of this type of retailing has been continuing. Retail shopping center sales have expanded from about 20 percent of the total retail sales in 1964 to more than 35 percent of all current retail sales in 1977 (Figure 5–1). The three types of planned shopping centers are:

1] *Neighborhood shopping centers*—oriented toward convenience shopping, so they contain nothing larger than supermarkets, variety stores, or small department stores. Total (gross area) store space in the center ranges from 25,000 to 75,000 square feet. The supermarket or the drug store is the leading tenant in a neighborhood shopping center. This type of center generally serves about 10,000 people. A typical neighborhood center uses about six acres of land.

2] *Community shopping centers*—can serve both the convenience and shopping goods needs of a city and a few of its suburbs through its larger junior department store, smaller branch stores and specialty shops. The community shopping center offers wider style assortments, wider price ranges, and more stores designed to attract more impulse sales than stores located in the neighborhood shopping center. Total store space in a community shopping center usually ranges from 75,000 square feet to 300,000 square feet. With an average size of 150,000 square feet, a typical site requires about twenty acres of land to serve a population of 20,000 to 100,000.

3] *Regional shopping centers*—larger centers that contain over 300,000 square feet of gross store area. The average size is about 400,000 square feet of gross floor space. At least forty acres are required for a regional shopping center, but some large centers use more than one hundred acres for their buildings, parking areas, and landscaping. Regional centers feature at least one full-line department store and a wide range of department, variety, apparel, and miscellaneous stores. The smaller tenants are selected to offer a range of complementary goods and services formerly found only in the downtown area. Many regional centers are now featuring an enclosed mall for year-round shopping comfort. This type is designed not only to shut out the weather but also to provide psychological integration. Such climate-controlled malls give the impression of one giant store with individual shops. As a result, it often serves an even larger trade area than other regional centers.

A few new shopping centers are conceived as integral parts of new developments and are becoming the hubs of community social activities. The centers may include as many as five department stores, many smaller stores and services, plus hotels, apartment houses, office buildings, cul-

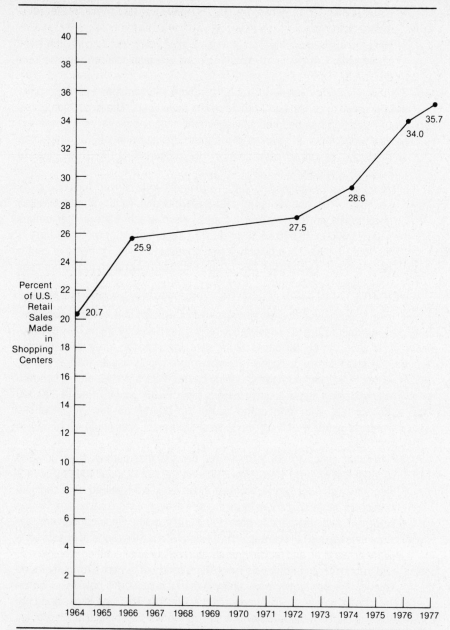

Figure 5-1 **Percentage of U.S. Retail Sales Made in
Shopping Centers, 1964–1972**

Figure created from data suggested by International Council of Shopping Centers.

tural centers, churches, and theaters. This type of center is also made
more attractive by using fountains, waterfalls, and landscaping. The size
of such centers is also becoming larger.

The expanded form of a regional shopping center integrates all of the retail and commercial functions plus activities in the areas of entertainment, health, shopping, eating, and education. These larger regional shopping cities are growing in importance, although only a few of the 12,000 U.S. shopping centers could currently be classified as shopping city centers. Such large centers have an added impact beyond their numerical importance, because large city centers outdraw smaller centers and can pull shoppers from much longer distances.

The trading area differs for each of these location types and even for each store in the center. Store size and operating procedures differ markedly from one company to another, so it is impossible to make accurate statements about trading areas for all companies. The experiences of two eastern companies provide an example of the drawing power of each location type for a supermarket (Table 5–8).[6]

Table 5-8 **Comparison of Trading Areas for a Supermarket Situated in Different Location Types**

Location Type	Primary Trading Area Size (Radial Dimension)	% of Total Sales 0–1 Mile Area
Neighborhood free-standing	½–¾ mile	65–70
Central business district	½–¾ "	70–75
Neighborhood business district	¾–1 "	60–65
Secondary business district	¾–1 "	60–65
Highway business string	1–1¼ miles	60–65
Highway free-standing	1–2 "	55–60
Edge of downtown	1½–2 "	40–45
Community shopping center	1½–2 "	50–55
Regional shopping center	1½–2½ "	35–40

Source: Bernard Kane, Jr., *A Systematic Guide to Supermarket Location Analysis* (New York: Fairchild Publications, 1966), p. 91. Reprinted by permission.

Shopping Center Location Considerations

The shopping center's characteristics attract customers who like the convenience, parking facilities, and variety offered by the wide assortment of stores located in the center. Some large shopping centers also provide social drawing power. Teenagers, particularly, are drawn to these centers on Saturday, not to shop, but to socialize. Some centers sponsor community activities such as dog shows, flower shows, and art and other special exhibits to increase their appeal to all age groups. Merchants who are deciding if they should locate in a center must weigh these positive characteristics against the higher rental costs in such centers and the limitations placed upon them as center tenants. The shopping center tenant must pay its prorated share of all joint center promotion efforts. The shopping center retailer must also keep store hours, light windows, and place signs in accordance with center regulations.

Developers and owners of shopping centers want to attract a wide assortment of successful retailers. Their initial selections are likely to include one or two prestige merchants (usually large chain stores or large department stores) as their *lead tenants* (retailers who provide major consumer attraction). Then at least one day-time restaurant and other complementary types of stores (usually small, independent retailers) are selected so that the center achieves an appealing *tenant mix* (the combination of all outlets operating from a shopping center) and offers a varied array of merchandise. The developer needs leases from companies with strong credit ratings to be able to obtain his financing prior to construction, and most lenders favor tenant rosters that include the best of the national chains. However, the average developer also prefers to devote at least 40 percent of its store space to specialty or other shops on short-term leases.[7] This provides the developer with some protection against inflation because many specialty shops pay a percentage of their sales as rental. Big chains usually will not agree to share a percentage of their sales with a developer. Specialty shops also carry a wide merchandise assortment, which can be adjusted to draw additional customer traffic. Also, an overbalance of major chain stores can be detrimental to small merchants' sales because of their rather complete merchandise assortments.

The retailer who is considering locating in a shopping center has several major items to investigate.[8] First, an objective trading area analysis (including an evaluation of competitive outlets analysis) must be performed. Second, an analysis of the merchandising characteristics of the stores must be conducted. The selection of stores should be sufficient to meet the needs of the area's customers. The arrangement of the stores should give the retailer's store at least an equal chance of obtaining passerby pedestrian traffic. Ideally, every retailer would like to be located between the stores with the greatest customer pull. Third, total rent should be evaluated in making the decision, and this includes the maintenance of common areas, the dues paid to the center's merchants' association, and the minimum lease guarantees—typically 5 to 7 percent of gross sales.

The retailer must evaluate these costs with the additional profits he believes he can obtain by locating in a center. He would choose the center location if he could reasonably project that the added profits would be greater than the added costs.

A fairly comprehensive list of the factors that should be investigated by a retailer who is considering a shopping center location is presented in Exhibit 5–1.

Summary

Considerable care must be used to select and review the general area where a retailer could locate a store. The population must be sufficient to support a new store that carries the proposed merchandise assortment. Thus, competition must also be evaluated to determine if an area has too few stores to meet the needs of the community's consumers satisfactorily.

If the current or projected population is not large enough to support an additional store, a new or proposed store will have to rely upon other elements of the marketing mix (such as low price, heavy promotion and advertising outlays, better service,

Exhibit 5-1 **Factors to Consider when
Evaluating Shopping Center Locations**

1. Who is the shopping center developer?
2. How long has he been in the business of developing real estate?
3. What are his financial resources?
4. With whom has he arranged for the financing of the center?
5. What is his reputation for integrity?
6. Who performed the economic analysis? Does the report cover both favorable and unfavorable factors?
7. What experience has the economic consultant had?
8. Has an architectural firm been retained to plan the center?
9. Has the architect designed other centers? Have they been successful from a retailing standpoint?
10. Who will build the center? The developer? An experienced contractor? An inexperienced contractor?
11. Has the developer had experience with other centers?
12. What is, or will be, the quality of management for the center?
13. Will the management have merchandising and promotion experience? (Some developers are large retailers rather than real estate operators.)
14. What percent of the leases have been signed? Are they on a contingent basis?
15. Has every facet of the lease been carefully studied?
16. Is the ratio of parking area to selling area 3 to 1 or more?
17. Has sufficient space (400 feet) been assigned to each car?
18. Is the parking space designed so that the shopper does not walk more than 300 to 350 feet from the farthest spot to the store?
19. What is the angle of parking space? (Ninety degrees provides the best capacity and circulation.)
20. What is the planned or actual car turnover? (3.3 cars per parking space per day is the average.)
21. Is the number of total spaces adequate for the planned business volume? (Too many spaces make the center look dead; too few openly invite competition around the center.)
22. Does the parking scheme distribute the cars so as to favor no one area?
23. Is there an adquate number of ingress/egress roads in proper relationship with the arrangement of parking spaces?
24. For the larger centers, a ring road is preferable. Is this the case?
25. Is the site large enough for the type of center?
26. Is the size sufficiently dominant to forestall the construction of similar shopping centers nearby?
27. Is the center of regular shape? If not, does the location of the buildings minimize the disadvantage of the site's shape?
28. Is the site sufficiently deep? (A depth of at least 400 feet is preferred; if less, the center may look like a strip development.)
29. Is the site level? Is it on well-drained land?
30. Can the center be seen from a distance?
31. Are any structures, such as a service station, located in the parking area? (If so, do they impede the site's visibility?)
32. Is the site a complete unit? (A road should not pass through the site.)
33. Are the buildings set far enough back on the site that the entire area may be seen?
34. Are all the stores readily accessible to each other, with none having an advantage?

Source: J.F. Mertes, "Site Opportunites for the Small Retailer," *Journal of Retailing* 39 (Fall 1963): 44. Reprinted by permission.

a larger merchandise assortment, and so forth) to drive current competition out of business. This could result in continual low profit margins, even if the new entry is successful in eliminating an established outlet.

The income level of the people living in the area will also influence retail sales. Retailers who stock shopping goods such as radios, TVs, sporting goods, and other items that are extremely sensitive to changes in income must place relatively more emphasis upon the area's income level than retailers who carry merchandise that does not appear to respond much to income changes. Other factors that must be considered are the purchasing habits of potential consumers, the legal environment, and the progressiveness of the community in attracting customers.

Type of location must also be evaluated, because stores located in shopping centers may have a much different trading area from stores that are located downtown or in neighborhood business districts. The trend is toward extremely large shopping centers that draw customers from a large trading area for entertainment, health, education, eating, and shopping purposes.

Each retailer must make an independent judgment, weighing all the variables, and then select the type of location that will provide the firm with the best possible chance of success.

Questions

1. Why is population an important factor affecting sales? For which types of merchandise is it most important? Discuss.

2. What factors do buying power index calculations fail to take into consideration?

3. Why does the legal environment influence profitability and determine the existence or nonexistence of any store?

4. Describe the three major types of planned shopping centers.

5. What are the major items that the retailer who is considering locating in a shopping center has to investigate?

6. What strategies are available to retailers who find themselves in an overstored area? Would you expect an understored situation to continue in the long run? Why?

7. Suggest several reasons why retail shopping center sales have expanded since 1965. Would you expect this trend to continue? If so, for how long? Why? What types of shopping centers will expand fastest in the future? Why?

8. Since lead tenants are considered so important in drawing customers to a shopping center, why would a shopping center developer want to devote at least 40 percent of his floor space to specialty shops?

9. If you were offered very low-cost financing to open a retail store in Watts, Harlem, or some similar inner-city ghetto area, how would you decide exactly where to locate and what to sell? Develop a complete retailing mix for whatever type of establishment you would suggest and give your reasons. What major problems would you anticipate in the first year of operation?

10. Some cities and states (Boulder, Colorado, and the state of Oregon, for example) have made deliberate attempts to limit population and/or economic growth. Considering the retailing industry as a whole, what are the implications of these limits? What line of merchandise and what retailing mix would you suggest for a potential retailer in these areas?

1. Projection Series II from Table 1–1.

2. *Economic and Demographic Projections for States and Metropolitan Areas,* Regional Projection Series (Washington, D.C.: National Planning Association, Center for Economic Projections, 1966), Report 68-R-1, p. 3.

3. "Fast-Food Chains Deserve a Break Today, So They Are Moving into Smaller Towns," *The Wall Street Journal,* 21 April 1976, p. 36.

4. B. J. LaLonde, "New Frontiers in Store Location," *Supermarket Merchandising,* February 1963, p. 110.

5. This classification was obtained from J. Ross McKeever, *Factors in Considering a Shopping Center Location* (Washington, D.C.: Small Business Administration), Aids No. 143, p. 3.

6. Ibid., pp. 6–7.

7. "Shopping Centers Grow into Shopping Cities," *Business Week,* 4 September 1971, p. 37.

8. John Mertes, *Site Evaluation for Small Retailers* (Washington, D.C.: Small Business Administration, 1966), pp. 1–4.

Case Study

Bi Right Agriservice Case

Bi Right Agriservice Incorporated is considering establishing an outlet in a rural town which has a population of 300 and includes a trading area population of 1,000 located on 150 farms. The average farm size is 640 acres. The proposed agricenter would include a service station and a chemical/fertilizer facility. Bi Right would be the only service station in town, with the nearest competition being ten miles away. Two other distributors already located in the town would be competing for the agrifertilizer and chemical market.

Market research indicates that the farmers spend $125 per acre per year for gasoline, diesel and oil products and $60 per acre per year on agrifertilizer and chemicals.

Discussion Questions

1. Forecast annual sales and profit levels for the proposed Bi Right installation for the first three years of business.

2. State your assumptions and any additional sources of information/data you have used.

Case Study

Asel Art Center

Asel Art Center is a quality art supply store located in Dallas, Texas. The store is situated in an area of town well known for its proximity to advertising agencies, professional artists, architects, and a community of art students and other creative or would-be creative types.

After five years of successful, profitable operation, the management of Asel believes it is time to consider opening another store. The president of Asel, Mr. Bill Cicherski, has stated a preference for the nearby cities of Fort Worth or Arlington. Since capital is limited it is necessary to select the best one.

Both cities are located west of Dallas and neither presently has a store of the caliber of Asel Art Center. Each of the cities has attractive features including a major university.

Prior to becoming the owner of Asel, Cicherski served as vice-president for finance for a large corporation. In this role he became quite familiar with the use of research to aid in decision making.

As a result, consideration was given to employing a random questionnaire to be administered to respondents in each of the proposed market areas. It was found that art supply customers represent such a statistically small percentage of the general population that a random sample survey would be extremely expensive.

An alternate plan under consideration was to place an in-house questionnaire in the Dallas store to be completed by customers. A profile of these customers would be compiled and compared to available demographic profiles of Fort Worth and Arlington residents.

As the plan was being discussed, someone pointed out that the real buyer, such as a well-known designer, might seldom or never visit the store. Instead, he or she would be likely to send a secretary or other person to make the actual purchase.

It was also felt that secondary data concerning the market potential in the two proposed markets might be available. As a result, the national trade association for the art supply industry was contacted. The executive director of this association stated that 90 percent of the members were not public companies and that no sales figures for any area were available.

Consequently, several long distance calls were made to manufacturers of art supplies requesting data concerning sales and sales potential in the two markets. Finally, the representative for one of the manufacturers stated that his company had conducted several marketing research studies over the past four years but he could only reveal limited parts of these studies.

As an example, he stated that the U.S. art supply market had been increasing at about 20 percent per year. He further estimated that the total market volume for art supplies in the Dallas-Fort Worth area was about $5,000,000 per year. This was a projection from the rule of thumb that paper products comprise 25 percent of all art supplies and the sales of paper products were known.

In looking over the location of other art supply stores, it was found that these stores generally clustered around art related businesses such as ad agencies.

After much consideration, it was decided to go ahead with the in-store survey during the month of October.

The results of this survey showed that the Asel customer was predominantly male, between the ages of twenty-five and thirty-four, with an annual household income of $15,000 to $24,999. Artists were the largest group by occupation.

It was also found that the purchase of art supplies is a planned shopping experience as opposed to impulse shopping.

The Asel customers showed a high degree of loyalty to the store judging by the fact that their last purchase had also been there. Most customers drove less than fifteen minutes to purchase at Asel's, and most were found to spend more than $75.00 annually for art supplies.

Although these findings were interesting, Cicherski believed that now was the time to utilize other information. He felt this should include traffic flow count and projections, area population, existing location of competitors, and existing zoning restrictions.

The Fort Worth Market Area

Population

In 1970, U.S. census figures showed Fort Worth to have a population of 393,455. Estimates of future growth compiled by the Forth Worth City Planning Department utilized four methods, namely the Dwelling Unit method, the Death Rate method, the Straight Line method, and the Migration method (for a detailed explanation of these methods, see Appendix H). An unweighted averaging of these methods results in population estimates for the years 1971–1975 as follows:

1971	1972	1973	1974	1975
399,402	402,129	405,067	407,495	409,412

While population projections for the incorporated city of Fort Worth are not available, Fort Worth City planning figures show an 18 percent projected population increase in Tarrant County between the years 1975 and 1980.

Commercial and Industrial Expansion

Nonresidential construction in Fort Worth has been steadily rising at a rate of approximately 10 percent per year over the past five years. This estimate is based on nonresidential construction permits issued in Fort Worth over that period.

Income Distribution

The mean income for families residing in Fort Worth according to the 1970 census of population and housing figures was $10,971 per year.

Consumer Shopping Habits

The Fort Worth market area yields over $3 billion annually in purchasing power. Effective buying income for the incorporated portion of Fort Worth was approximately $1.7 billion.

In 1973 a survey was conducted by the Fort Worth Chamber of Commerce of the adult Tarrant County residents to provide a base of information meeting the following stated objectives: (1) to assist local businessmen in evaluating an expansion program, (2) to assist parties unfamiliar with the Fort Worth area in evaluating a business or residential investment, and (3) to update the demographic data of the decennial census. Procedures used included the breaking of Tarrant County into twenty-four mini-market sections and conducting a stratified area probability sample.

Of particular interest was the yearly family income average by mini-market. Of the twenty-four surveyed, only three falling within the incorporated limits of Fort Worth had an average family income exceeding $15,000. Of those three, only one had an average annual family income exceeding $20,000, that being mini-market area 6 with an average annual family income of $26,294. This mini-market area surrounds Texas Christian University and is located approximately five minutes' driving time to the southwest of the Fort Worth central business district.

Arterial Access

Major arterial access to the central business district is provided by the West Freeway, the South Freeway, the Fort-Worth-Dallas Turnpike from the east, the Riverside Freeway from the northeast, and the North Freeway. Average twenty-four hour traffic flow counts in 1973 were 83,300, 74,700, 53,300, 46,800 and 77,800, respectively, at a distance of approximately three miles from the central business district.

Texas Christian University

Texas Christian University is located approximately four miles southwest of the Fort Worth central business district and has a total student enrollment of 5,847. Students in art-related majors totaled 132 in the fall of 1974.

The Arlington Market Area

Population

In 1970 U.S. census figures showed Arlington as having a population of 90,643. City Planning Department population estimates showed population to be 124,000 in

January of 1975 with growth projection estimates of 8 percent per year. These figures far exceed the national average and are attributable in part to the growth of the University of Texas at Arlington, the Southwest Industrial District, and the newly opened Dallas-Fort Worth Regional Airport.

Commercial and Industrial Expansion

Nonresidential construction in Arlington has been steadily on the increase with year-end figures showing an increase of 11 percent over the calendar year 1973. This substantial increase has been to a great extent the result of the rapid growth of the Great Southwest Industrial District in the northeast sector of the city.

Income Distribution

The mean income for families residing in Arlington according to 1970 census of population and housing figures was $12,617 per year.

Consumer Shopping Habits

While no formal studies exist for the Arlington market as an entity, effective buying income estimates based on total population, average family incomes, and available statistics on national averages, indicate a buying power of approximately $0.8 billion for calendar year 1974.

Arterial Access

Major arterial access to the central business district of Arlington is provided predominantly by Highway 80 for east-west flows and Highways 157 and 360 for flow from the north. Specific twenty-four-hour counts conducted in the spring of 1973 resulted in the following figures: Highway 80 from the west, 24,680, and from the east, 22,780. Highway 157 was 24,150, and Highway 360 was 28,650. These counts were conducted at points approximately three miles from the central business district.

The Dallas-Fort Worth Turnpike crosses the northern section of Arlington from east to west, but since the bulk of traffic is through traffic, counts on that artery were not considered significant for purposes of this study. Pioneer Parkway, Highway 303, crosses the southern portion of Arlington from east to west and when completed will link Dallas and Fort Worth with an eight-lane partial access freeway.

University of Texas at Arlington

The University of Texas at Arlington is located a few blocks southwest of the downtown business district of Arlington and has a total student enrollment of 14,603. The Departments of Architecture and Art had a combined enrollment of 1,202 in the fall of 1974. This latter figure represents the largest art related student body in the Dallas-Fort Worth metroplex area.

Discussion Questions

1. What conclusions do you draw regarding market potential from the data presented in the case and from consulting secondary sources?

2. What other information do you need before making a decision on the opening of the new store? How would you get this information?

3. What are your recommendations to Cicherski?

Chapter 6

Factors in Retail Site Evaluation

1. To understand the techniques retailers use to define the size and shape of an outlet's trading area.

2. To be able to estimate the population within a store's trading area and the dollar value of potential merchandise purchases originating in that area.

3. To be able to discuss the factors that influence the share of the purchases that an outlet can obtain.

4. To learn how the sales volume of a proposed store can be estimated.

5. To be able to list the advantages and disadvantages of buying or leasing retail land and buildings.

store's trading area
trading area overlays
credit record analysis
license plate analysis
customer interview
percentage of income method of sales forecasting

percentage of retail sales dollar method of sales forecasting
per capita method of sales forecasting
market share
compatability of nearby business
generative business

shared business
suscipient business
market share to selling space share ratio
payback period
storing land
economic value

The selection of the specific site must be made after the general trade area has been evaluated. The discussion in this chapter will concentrate on this process, which is critical to the successful operation of a retail business.

Although no standard evaluation procedure is used by all retail firms, the selection of a specific location within the chosen trading area can be determined by considering the location principles discussed in this chapter.

Defining the Trading Area

A *store's trading area* is that geographical area in which about 70 percent of the store's customers reside.

Measuring the trade boundaries for existing retailing facilities is much easier than estimating the trade area for proposed stores. However, studies of the trading area for similar existing stores can provide an excellent measure of the probable trading area for a proposed store. Chain retailers who must use more than one outlet to reach most of a city's population utilize *trading area overlays* to determine how well their stores are serving the consumers (Figure 6–1). Each store's trading area is plotted on a transparent plastic sheet and placed over a city map to spot geographical areas from which the chain is not drawing customers. A new store that is located in such an area could be a profitable addition to the chain's current list of outlets.

Trading area analysis also allows the firm to prevent trading area overlap, which results in higher retailing costs by having an excessive number of small, higher-cost, lower-volume outlets. In this case, the less profitable stores may be eliminated by building larger stores with more complete merchandise assortments which better serve most of the customers. This type of trade area analysis offers more benefits to chain retailers whose outlets have a relatively small trading area. Grocery stores are examples of stores whose trade areas are relatively small.

The hypothetical trade area analysis in Figure 6–1 contains the trade areas for the two chain A stores, numbered 1 and 2 on the map. The trading area for each store would be drawn independently so that about 80 percent of each store's customers reside within the outlined trade area designated for that store. This analysis indicates that the two chain A stores are not drawing customers from the extreme west side of the city (from the area surrounding competitor store number 7) or from the south central part of the city in the area surrounding competitor stores 4, 5, and 6. Chain A would be able to expand its sales if it would locate a new store in each of these areas. However, this is only the preliminary step in retail site evaluation. It must be determined if either of the new stores could generate enough sales to operate on a profitable basis.

The following techniques can be used to measure the boundaries of the trading area for retail outlets.

Store Credit Record Analysis

The observational technique of store *credit record analysis* consists of examining store credit records for data on the residences of the store consumers. It is relatively

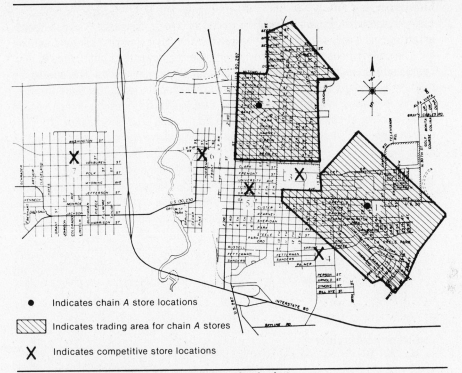

Figure 6–1 **Example of Using Trade Area Analysis to Identify Store Coverage**

inexpensive and can produce acceptable results if the credit customers' store patronage patterns do not differ from the store-selection habits of non-credit-using customers. The use of credit may vary among different consumer groups residing in an area, and in these cases the addresses of cash customers must be obtained if the trade area is to be accurately defined. Addresses of cash customers may be obtained by analyzing the addresses on checks written by cash customers. Addresses of cash customers may also be obtained from delivery tickets or cash sales slips. After a representative sampling of the store's customers has been made, the addresses of the clientele are plotted on an area map with dots or pins.

The trading area is then determined and area boundaries are defined. The intensity of a store's penetration within its trading area usually diminishes with increased distance, measured in travel time, from the store. The entire trading area can then be divided into primary, secondary, and fringe trading areas. All three areas should be defined in statistical and geographical terms. The primary trade area is usually determined on a population basis. For example, the area could be defined so that 55 to 70 percent of the customers reside within its boundaries. The secondary trade area could contain about 70 to 90 percent of the customers, and the fringe area, which will probably be widely dispersed, will contain the remaining customers. A similar analysis can be made by using telephone numbers, obtained when making reservations, cashing checks and so forth.

License Plate Analysis

License plate analysis, another observational technique, consists of inconspicuously recording the license numbers of cars in the store's or shopping center's parking lot. The county treasurer's office or some other appropriate county office is then contacted to learn the addresses of the owners of the automobiles. The addresses of these customers are then plotted on an area map to define the trade area.

This is a fairly inexpensive technique that yields, as does the credit record analysis, a list of customer names. These names can also be used for other research purposes, such as determining store image, improving store service, and so forth.

The person who records the license numbers should be certain that the person is a customer and not a store clerk or a patron of a different store in the same area. This may be done if the recorder watches the entrance and exit doors and records only the license numbers of persons passing through these doors during business hours.

Another precaution is that license numbers should not be collected during times when an atypical representation of consumers might be chosen. For example, large conventions, sporting events, or special sales could temporarily overstate the actual trading area.

Customer Interview

Interviews with people residing in an area can also be used to identify the trading area. These *customer interviews* can be conducted by mail questionnaire, personal interview in the respondent's home, or telephone. Cross-reference books provide listings of telephone numbers by address, so that persons in any selected area may be interviewed. These data collection techniques are discussed in detail in Chapter 17.

In addition, a short questionnaire may be placed in customers' shopping bags. A high percentage of the customers will return these questionnaires if the return postage is prepaid and if there is some incentive to return them. A contest or offer of a small prize is usually a sufficient stimulus to induce a good return rate of 60 to 70 percent of the customers receiving the questionnaire. This approach allows the store to obtain additional information on demographic characteristics such as age, family size, educational background, and the like.

The chief disadvantge is that the sample selected in this manner may not be representative of all customers. The middle-income customer is likely to be over-represented among those who respond to the questionnaire. In general, higher-income customers do not like to take the time to complete and return questionnaires. Lower-class customers are sometimes afraid to cooperate because of fear that a hidden commitment is involved or because of fear of revealing their lower level of formal education. The extent to which these types of biases occur should be determined carefully by examining the response rate. Last, many shoppers do not inspect the bags at home but simply remove the merchandise and discard the bags.

Household shopping surveys are also used to estimate trade areas for proposed outlets. They can provide detailed insight into consumer purchasing patterns. However, caution must be used when analyzing the results, since about 30 percent of all people will say yes to anything.[1]

A study of the proposed outlet's trading area is important because it reveals information about the consumer groups from which management of the outlet will select its target market. It also allows retail management to make a more careful analysis of the market segments toward which the outlet will direct its merchandising efforts. This should allow the firm's management to satisfy the demands of its consumers better.

It is necessary to analyze two other trading area characteristics, size and shape, to ensure that a realistic trade area is used in the planning process.

Trade Area Size

The size of the trading area must be related to the size of the proposed outlet. Other things being equal, a larger store will attract consumers from a larger trade area than will a smaller store.

The size of the urban area in which the store will be located also affects the size of the trading area. Larger populations attract a greater number of the same type of stores in the same general area. The clustering of competitive outlets results in a larger trade area for the retail cluster. It also diminishes the share of business that the store can obtain from the trading area.

In addition, a higher income level for the population surrounding the outlet results in a larger sized trading area. The higher income people tend to be more mobile and travel longer distances in order to shop in areas of greater merchandise depth and assortment. The advent of higher gasoline prices has recently placed even more emphasis upon the ability and willingness of consumers to drive past convenient shopping to get to an outlet offering more depth, assortment, or some other appeal. Further gasoline price increases or a limited supply of gasoline could rapidly alter the plans of the management of a proposed outlet which is counting on these people for a portion of their target market.

Finally, the size of the trading area is affected by the degree of ease of entering and exiting from the outlet. The more accessible the site, the larger is the size of the outlet's trade area. Natural or artificial barriers that impede the movement of traffic to the site can greatly restrict the size of the trading area.

Trade Area Shape

Theoretically, if consumers want to minimize driving time and if there are no barriers to traffic, the trade area around each shopping outlet would be a circle. The radius of the circle would reflect the optimum travel time for the consumer. The outlet would sell its products outward in all directions from its location to a point where the consumers are indifferent as to whether they shop at this outlet or at some other competitive outlet located outside the trade circle.

However, in the real world the shape of a trade area is influenced by more than distance. The trade area is shaped by other factors such as variations in land formations, the nature of transportation routes, political boundaries, and the power of competing retail facilities. As a result the shape of store trading areas is typically elongated in the direction of consumer movement, which may parallel a superhighway or a mass transit route. Certainly the existence of good roads and mass transit facilities will greatly affect the size and shape of the trade area.

Determining the Total Population of the Trading Area

The total population residing in the primary trading area may be estimated by taking a personal survey of the area and counting all the dwellings. If the proposed site is located within a standard metropolitan area, the U.S. Bureau of the Census provides detailed population and demographic data by census tract. Municipal agencies are usually able to provide an estimate of the number of water hookups in an area, which gives a rough estimate of the number of families residing within an area. Local utilities (power, gas, telephone) might be able to provide a more reliable estimate of the number of families residing within an area, because each family is more likely to be billed separately for these items than for water and sewage.

Determining Per Capita Product Line Purchases in the Trading Area

Per capita purchases are usually available from trade sources or from publications such as *Sales Management's Survey of Buying Power, Editor & Publisher Market Guide,* and other secondary sources. The latest *Census of Business* provides data on sales made by various types of retail outlets in standard metropolitan areas. The annual total sales made by different types of retailers may also be available from the state department of revenue. Whatever secondary source is used, the total sales may be divided by population to obtain an estimate of per capita expenditures on the proposed service or line of merchandise.

Consumer surveys or "diary" studies may be used to estimate per capita expenditures if the data are not available from secondary sources. (A diary study consists of a sample of typical consumers who record all their purchases for a week or month in a diary, which is then returned to the researcher for analysis.) A crisscross directory can be used to select the sample of "typical consumers" residing within a specified area, and the selection of an area can be based upon differences in consumer income, age, education, and the like.

The crisscross directory, which is usually available from a city office or public utility company, lists all the active addresses in an area. It also provides the names of the persons residing at each address. (A diary study is a fairly expensive method unless purchases of several product lines are observed simultaneously, allowing the cost to be shared by several retailers.)

The chief difficulty associated with consumer surveys that rely on querying consumers on past purchases is the inability of respondents to recall all the purchases they made during the previous month. Thus, the best estimates of purchases are sometimes made when the respondents are asked to recall last week's purchases with the aid of a prepared list of possible purchases. The short time period and the memory-enhancing list are especially important if consumers are asked to recall purchases of lower-price items. Of course expenditures on major items, such as autos, furniture, and appliances, are remembered for a much longer period of time.

Determining Total Product Line Purchases Made in the Trading Area

Total purchases can be obtained simply by multiplying the population by per capita consumption of the product line. This step answers the question, "If we obtain all the business available in this trading area, how large would our sales volume be?" The remainder of the volume estimation analysis has to determine how much of the total business can be obtained by the proposed outlet.

Frequently, the trade area may consist of an entire town or county. If so, secondary sources such as the *Editor & Publisher Market Guide* or *Sales and Marketing Management's Survey of Buying Power* provide current estimates of total retail sales as well as sales in the five or six major retail categories. In addition, state sales tax agencies generally have a breakdown of retail sales into many different categories. Thus, one may be able to obtain an estimate of the total product line purchases made in the trading area directly from these sources.

Other calculations may be required if the exact product line sales for the trade area are not available from these sources.

The *percentage* of income method estimates category sales in the trade area by using the percentage of current income spent on the particular merchandise category. In formula format the calculation procedure is:

$$\begin{array}{c}\text{\$ Spent Annually on Specified}\\\text{Merchandise Category}\end{array} = \begin{array}{c}\text{\$ Total Annual}\\\text{Personal Income}\\\text{in Area}\end{array} \times \begin{array}{c}\text{\% of Annual Personal}\\\text{Income Spent in the}\\\text{Specified Merchandise}\\\text{Category}\end{array}$$

The secondary sources, *Editor & Publisher Market Guide* and *Sales and Marketing Management's Survey of Buying Power* provide the current estimate of annual personal income by county and town. The percentage of annual personal income spent in different retail merchandise categories is presented in Table 6–1.

To illustrate how this method can be used to estimate sales, suppose one wanted to locate a hardware outlet which would serve the entire town of Greeley, Colorado. Table 5–3 indicates the estimated 1978 personal income for people living in the town of Greeley to be $817,114,000. Data in Table 6–1 indicates that on the average 0.4 percent of personal income is spent in hardware stores. Thus, one can estimate that if national average conditions hold for this area, annual sales can be computed for Greeley as: $817,114,000 $\times$ .004 = $3,268,456. Of course, this calculation yields just a rough estimate of category retail sales in an area. It does represent an initial forecast that can be adjusted or refined to better reflect the deviation of local conditions from the national average.

The *percentage of retail sales dollar method* of estimating category retail sales in the trade area follows a similar logic. The calculation procedure is:

$$\begin{array}{c}\text{\$ Spent Annually in}\\\text{Specified Merchandise}\\\text{Category}\end{array} = \begin{array}{c}\text{\$ Total Annual Retail}\\\text{Sales in the Area}\end{array} \times \begin{array}{c}\text{\% of Annual Retail Sales}\\\text{for the Specified}\\\text{Merchandise Category}\end{array}$$

Secondary sources such as *Editor & Publisher Market Guide, Sales and Marketing Management's Survey of Buying Power,* and state sales tax collection records provide the current estimates of annual retail sales in the area. The percentage of retail sales for different retail merchandise outlets is presented in Table 6–1.

Thus, hardware outlets serving the entire town of Greeley, Colorado, could forecast 1978 sales in Greeley by multiplying the total retail sales for the town, $341,042,000 from Table 5–3 times 0.9% from Table 6–1 equals $3,069,378.

A third approach to forecasting category retail for a trade area is to use the *per capita sales method*. The calculation is:

$$\begin{array}{c}\text{\$ Spent Annually in}\\\text{Specified Merchandise}\\\text{Category}\end{array} = \begin{array}{c}\text{\$ Annual Per Capita}\\\text{Expenditure in}\\\text{Specified Category}\end{array} \times \begin{array}{c}\text{Number of People}\\\text{Residing in Trade Area}\end{array}$$

The sources used in the percentage of income and percentage of retail sales approaches can be used to provide the current estimate of population in the trade area. The annual per capita dollar sales for different merchandise categories is presented in Table 6–1. For example, annual per capita expenditures in hardware stores was $19 in 1972. If per capita hardware sales have increased in proportion to the inflation in consumer prices they increased by 56 percent from 1972 to 1978 to $30 per capita.

Thus, the per capita method would indicate that annual hardware store sales in Greeley can be computed by multiplying 116,157 people (Table 5–3) times $30, resulting in $3,484,710.

Frequently the estimates obtained by using the percentage of income method, the percentage of retail sales dollar, and the per capita methods are quite close.

Table 6-1 **Percentages and Expenditure
Associated with Different Merchandise Categories**[A]

Type of Retail Outlet	% of Personal Income Spent in Category	% of Annual Retail Sales by Category	Annual $ per Capita Expenditures in Category
Retail trade total	51.0	100.0	2,259
Lumber & other building dealers	1.5	2.9	67
Paint, glass & wallpaper stores	0.2	0.3	7
Hardware stores	0.4	0.9	19
Department stores	5.7	11.1	251
Variety stores	0.8	1.6	36
Grocery stores	10.4	20.3	459
Retail bakeries	0.2	0.4	8
Automotive dealers	10.0	19.6	443
Auto & home supply stores	0.8	1.6	37
Gasoline service stations	3.7	7.3	166
Apparel & accessory stores	2.7	5.4	122
Women's clothing, specialty stores and furriers	1.4	2.0	46
Men's & boys' clothing & furnishings	0.6	1.2	27
Family clothing stores	0.5	1.0	24
Shoe stores	0.4	0.9	19
Furniture, home furnishings and equipment stores (total)	2.5	4.9	111
Furniture stores	0.7	2.3	51
Home furnishings stores	0.2	0.8	18
Household appliance stores	0.3	0.8	19
Radio, TV, & music stores	0.3	1.0	23
Eating & drinking places (total)	2.6	8.0	182
Eating places	2.1	6.6	150
Drinking places (alcoholic)	0.6	1.4	32
Drug stores	1.2	3.4	77
Liquor stores	0.7	2.2	49
Florists	0.1	0.3	8
Cigar stores & stands	0.4	0.1	2
Sporting goods stores & bicycle shops	0.1	0.6	13
Book stores	0.5	0.2	4
Stationery stores	0.4	0.2	4
Jewelry stores	0.2	0.7	15
Hobby, toy, & game shops	0.4	0.2	4
Camera & photo supply stores	0.4	0.2	4

A. Personal income for 1972 is estimated to be $900,379 million according to 1972 *Editor & Publisher Market Guide*. Retail sales were obtained from U.S. Department of Commerce, Bureau of the Census, *1972 Census of Business, Retail Trade* (Washington, D.C.: Government Printing Office, 1972).

If so, one may be more confident that the estimate is relatively accurate. Other times the three methods give widely divergent estimates. If this happens, the basic information going into each method should be reinvestigated to determine if it is accurate. If all of the input data appears to be reasonable, then the three estimates can be averaged to provide a single estimate. The range between the smallest and largest sales estimates can be used to establish the range of the possible sales volume. In the Greeley hardware example, the $3,069,378 estimate from the percent of retail sales approach is the lowest estimate and the $3,484,710 estimate obtained from the per capita method is the highest. The average of the three estimates is $3,274,181. This average might be the best estimate to use because it takes population, income, and other retail sales into consideration at one time. However, the most conservative estimate is the lowest of the three values or $3,069,378. Prospective retailers frequently overestimate the size of the market and their share of it. Use of the lowest figure will provide a little cushion and not allow would-be retailers to get carried away with their emotions.

Both the volume of total sales and sales by type of outlet obtainable in a shopping center can be determined by the following analysis:

1. A priori establishment of a tentative trade area for analysis. 2. Creation of a conceptual image of the completed shopping center in order to determine the strength of attraction which would be exerted by the envisaged facilities. 3. Determination of the gross personal consumption expenditures of the residents of this area through population tabulation, income analysis, and consumer expenditure studies. 4. Study of consumer movements, characteristics, and attitudes—both within and outside of competitive centers—to determine the probability of patronage from various segments of the subject trade area. 5. Derivation of quantitative sales expectancies and spatial requirements for specific retail facilities within the subject center.[2]

Determining the Share of Total Trading Area Purchases

The *market share* (the percent of category sales obtained by the store) that a new firm will be able to obtain is based upon many factors. Frequently prospective owners of independent outlets merely judge how well competitive stores are doing and then evaluate how well their proposed entry can fare against these competitors. If it is believed that the new outlet will be able to attract a normal portion of the market, then the firm's market share will be:

$$\text{New Firm's \% Market Share} = \frac{1}{\text{Total No. of Similar Outlets in Trading Area}} \times 100$$

Usually this figure is adjusted to account for the many other factors that influence the consumer's decision on where to shop. A prospective merchant may ask wholesale suppliers for their best judgement. Chain or franchise firms often prepare their market share estimates by comparing the planned store with other company outlets of a comparable size and type in cities of about the same population size, social class, and competitive environment. Skilled management is required to adjust the share estimates for any observed differences between the situation facing the proposed outlet and the supposedly similar existing outlets. Frequently these judgments focus upon the accessibility to the site itself.

Evaluation of Site Accessibility for Residents of the Trading Area

Passing foot and car traffic can be counted to determine how accessible the site is to a potential customer. A foot and car traffic count (which shows the number of passersby during a given period) can be made several times at the proposed location and at successfully operating stores. The comparative passerby traffic count at successfully established stores and proposed new sites provides a relative measure of accessibility. Passing foot and car traffic both offer customer potential that a good promotional merchandising effort can turn into business.

The minimum traffic count needed to indicate that the site has substantial potential will depend upon what type of retail or service outlet is being proposed. Outlets which depend upon shared or suscipient business will require a higher traffic count than outlets which depend upon generative business. Passing traffic must also be evaluated on a qualitative basis. Daily commuters going to and from work are much less valuable than passing pedestrian traffic.

Ease of entrance to and exit from the site must also be evaluated. Passing auto traffic offers no potential if it cannot enter the retailer's location with a minimum degree of accident risk and with little effort and time.

Evaluation of the Compatibility of Nearby Businesses

Compatibility of nearby businesses occurs when two adjacent businesses have a larger sales volume together than they would have if they were located in separate areas. Compatibility may be caused by the two firms selling complementary product lines or services. For example, a prescribing doctor's office and a pharmacy offer complementary services. Compatibility also occurs when firms sell competitive goods of different styles, lines, and prices. A drug store and a supermarket, for example, may benefit by being located next to one another, even though they carry many of the same product lines.

Generative business, which is produced by the store itself through an effective promotion and merchandising effort, can be calculated for each segment of the trading area. Retail outlets that must generate all of their own business should be located in the most accessible location, commensurate with cost.

Shared business, which is secured by a retailer as the result of the generative pulling power of nearby retailers, can also be isolated. This business is represented by customers who are in the area primarily because they want to visit a neighboring store or service agency. Much of the prescription business of a drug store located near prescribing doctors' offices will be a shared business.

Suscipient business comes from people whose principal purpose for being near the retail outlet is *not* because the store or its neighbors attracted them; thus a newsstand at a commuter railroad station or an airport does mostly suscipient business. It does not generate any of its own business but merely offers a service to people who are at the location for another purpose—transportation to another destination. Some downtown stores specifically serve people working in the area. Because these stores do not attract people directly from their homes, the accessibility requirements can be so specific that they can be satisfied only by an outlet located within walking distance of the work area.

The volume of business done by most retailers and service suppliers is composed of all three types of business; thus the evaluation of a site's accessibility must take all three business types into account. Estimates of the amount of business that is believed to be available from each source can later serve as a checkpoint to determine if a store is realizing its full potential.

Compatibility has contributed to the success of the planned shopping center and to well-designed downtown and suburban shopping areas. Compatibility is important because a number of stores dealing in the same lines of shopping merchandise will frequently do more business if they are located near one another than if they are widely scattered. The clustering of stores increases the drawing power of the stores in the retail center. This is the reason for large department stores being located near one another in the downtown areas and for the trend toward more regional shopping centers having two or more department stores as their principal tenants instead of just one.

Generally, shopping goods stores require a location near other shopping goods stores, so they locate in planned shopping centers or in the downtown business district where the consumer can easily do a lot of comparison shopping (Table 6–2). However, shopping goods stores also carry some items that some consumers consider to be convenience goods. For these convenience goods it would be better to be located near the consumer but not too near the competitive outlets. The convenience goods store will also benefit from this strategy of locating near the consumer but away from the competitors (Table 6–2).

However, the convenience store also sells some goods which some consumers consider to be specialty goods. For these types of goods the store may have a much larger trading area because consumers will spend considerable time and effort searching for the outlet.

Because the consumer will search for the particular store, the specialty goods store can locate in a free-standing site which does not require foot traffic (Table 6–2).

In addition to business interchange, a group of negative factors can be used in measuring compatibility. These variables tend to reduce the business of nearby retailers. Interruptions in pedestrian traffic flow can reduce business interchange with adjacent stores. Interruptions may be caused by "dead" frontage spots which cause a shopper to lose interest in continuing to walk farther in the same direction.

Table 6-2 **Most Suitable Type of Location for Various Types of Stores**

Store Classification	Type of Merchandise Sold	Consumer Purchasing Behavior	Most Suitable Type of Location
Convenience store	Convenience goods	Consumer buys most readily available brand at most accessible store	Neighborhood business district near target market population, away from competition, and in heavy pedestrian traffic areas
Convenience store	Shopping goods	Consumer selects purchase from assortment carried by most accessible store	Neighborhood business district near target market population and away from competition
Convenience store	Specialty goods	Consumer purchases favorite brand from most accessible store carring the item in stock	Planned neighborhood shopping center or downtown central business district
Shopping store	Convenience goods	Consumer is indifferent to the brand of product but shops different stores to secure better buy	Neighborhood business district near target market population
Shopping store	Shopping goods	Consumer makes comparisons among both outlet and brand	Planned shopping center or downtown central business district near similar outlets
Shopping store	Specialty goods	Consumer has strong brand preference but shops a number of stores	Planned shopping center or downtown central business district near similar outlets
Specialty store	Convenience goods	Consumer prefers a specific store but is indifferent to the brand	Free-standing site—consumer preference for outlet is stronger than brand preference
Specialty store	Shopping goods	Consumer prefers a specific store but is uncertain as to which product he will buy	Free-standing site—consumers will search for outlet
Specialty store	Specialty goods	Consumer has preference for a particular store and for a specific brand	Highway, free-standing site—consumers will search for outlet

Source: Figure is based upon consumer goods classification concept developed by Louis P. Bucklin, "Retail Strategy and the Classification of Consumer Goods," *Journal of Marketing* 23 (January 1963): 50–55. Reprinted from *Journal of Marketing*, published by the American Marketing Association.

Driveways and other physical disruptions in the sidewalk and heavy vehicular or pedestrian cross traffic that tends to create congestion[3] also cause interruptions. Other items that interfere with traffic flow are associated with hazard, noise, unpleasant odors, unsightliness, or other inhibiting qualities. Nearby businesses whose customers require an extremely long parking period will also minimize traffic flow.

It is extremely important that the layout of the shopping area ensures that consumers pass the specialty outlets on their way to the chief drawing attractions, which usually are major department stores. In the layout of a regional shopping center in Figure 6–2 note that the focal or anchor spots are located at the outer extremities of the center. The convenience shopping-type stores (supermarket, drugstore, variety store, and so forth) are dispersed among the comparison shopper-type outlets such as the department store, clothing, shoe, jewelry stores. The major retail attractions in the convenience shopping area are the drugstore and supermarket.

Customer surveys have revealed that anchor stores have a relatively stronger customer drawing power (they attract consumers from farther geographical distance) than convenience stores such as supermarkets. Surveys have also indicated that half of the customers in the drawing stores also shop in one or more of the other stores.[4]

Evaluation of the Physical Characteristics of Location

The size, shape, and frontage of a building can increase its visibility and thereby have a significant influence upon drawing traffic into the store. Also, proper interior layout can stimulate impulse sales after potential customers have entered the store. (A detailed discussion of store layout is presented in Chapter 7.) Parking space must also be analyzed to determine if it is sufficient to provide customers with parking near enough to the store so that it will be more convenient to stop and shop than to go to the next trading area.

Modern shopping centers provide a minimum of about four times as much parking space as store floor space to ensure adequate nearby parking facilities. A lower ratio is usually found in downtown shopping locations, since shoppers are expected to park in some commercial facility and shop at several stores on foot. Observation of parking opportunities and shopping patterns can indicate if there is likely to be a parking problem near a new store.

Evaluation of Competition

Other things being equal, people will seldom pass by a store to get exactly the same product at a more distant location. Thus, the location of the new store relative to the population density of the trading area and to competitive locations has a very significant influence upon what share of business can be obtained by the new store. It is easier to stop potential consumers en route than to pull them away from their normal traffic patterns.

Prospective retailers can improve their position relative to competitors by selecting locations near most of the potential customers (or their normal traffic routes) but near as few competitive sites as possible. They may also be able to protect their locations in the future by gaining control or by designating the use of unoccupied sites for noncompetitive purposes through restrictive lease provisions.

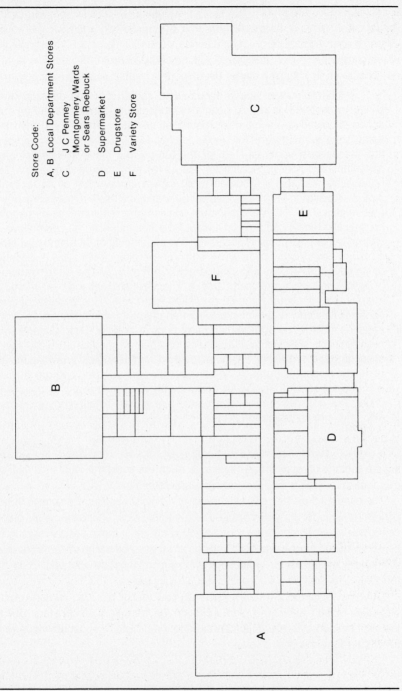

Store Code:

A, B Local Department Stores

C   J C Penney
      Montgomery Wards
      or Sears Roebuck

D   Supermarket

E   Drugstore

F   Variety Store

Figure 6-2 **Typical Layout of a Planned Shopping Center with Anchor Stores Located in Positions A, B, and C and Convenience Shopping-Type Stores Located in Positions D, E, and F**

A key factor to consider in selecting shopping center sites is the tenant mix, which is the combination of business firms that occupy selling space in the shopping center. If a large center is properly planned, its tenant mix should satisfy the needs of the consumers in the trading area with no duplication of offerings. The factors to be considered by shopping center developers in relation to the tenant mix include:

1. The total amount of space allocated to each major line of trade within a shopping center. This should bear a reasonable relationship to the amount of space allocated to every other major line of trade. These relationships are established after analysis of consumer needs in the trade area, competitive facilities existing or anticipated for the future, and the availability of tenants acceptable to financing institutions, the developer, and the community. 2. The relationship that space allocated to an individual merchant bears to the total space allocated to his specific line of trade and to closely related lines of trade. This relationship in a tenant mix must consider the requirements of the various prospective tenants and the limitations in accommodating all competitive merchants within the shopping center. 3. The exact location of each retail store in relation to every other retail store within a shopping center. This is closely tied to shopper convenience and shopper traffic patterns, and hence to the objective of optimizing sales for all merchants. 4. The minimum rent and the average rent, year by year, projected for each merchant. Rent projections, however, must also consider financing requirements, since tenants from whom high rents might be obtained may not be acceptable to financing institutions. Thus, the amount and proportion of retail space allocated to prospective tenants in relation to their financial standing must be balanced to optimize rent, without impairing the ability of the developer to borrow funds with which to construct and operate the center. 5. The retail sales projected for each line of trade and for each individual merchant. This provides a basis for projecting revenues. Total revenues, of course, also take into consideration projected average rentals.[5]

One method used to forecast a center's sales for each retail line is to multiply the square footage of retail space devoted to each line times the median annual sales per square foot for similar lines in comparable centers.

The center's projected sales for each retail line are useful when one is forecasting future sales for an outlet located in a center. Most shopping center planners conduct surveys of consumers' purchasing patterns for those people residing in the center's defined trading area. The findings are presented by the center's developers to financial institutions for projections upon which loans are obtained. Thus, these forecasts are likely to be optimistic but fairly reliable.

Conditions change, however, and the final tenant mix can deviate from the original or "ideal" tenant-mix plan. Although the number of competitors may vary, the total amount of space allocated to each major retail line usually departs relatively little from the original plan.

Estimation of Market Share

The amount of business that a store obtains from a given area can be divided by the total amount of business conducted in the area in the specified category. The result, multiplied by 100, equals the percentage share of market obtained by the store. The estimate of the market share must be made after all of the previously discussed factors have been evaluated. Subjective judgment and experience can then be used to adjust the share estimate.

The *ratio of market sales share to selling space share* can be used to estimate the market share that a new store can obtain, provided additional information is available from stores currently operating in other areas. If the new store is affiliated with a chain, or if it can obtain information from similar independent stores, this same ratio can be used. This ratio provides a measure that is most useful in forecasting shares for new stores.

The share of market sales volume is usually measured by dollar sales; the share of selling space is usually calculated on a square footage basis. The reliability of this ratio has been proved over years of research in the grocery industry.[6] If a store obtains a 25 percent share of market in an area and has a 40 percent share of the total selling space for the product line in the area, then the ratio of the market share to selling space share is 25/40, or 0.625. The average ratio for similar existing stores and the share of selling space to be occupied by the proposed store can be used to forecast the market share that a proposed store can obtain. Both figures can be inserted into the ratio formula to obtain this estimate of market share.

For example, if the average market share to selling space share ratio is 0.625 for similar stores and the proposed new store will occupy 20 percent of the selling space in the area, its estimated market share (X) would be $X/20 = 0.625/100$, or X equals 12.5 percent of the forecast market share. The estimated share projected from this ratio can then be adjusted to reflect the deviations from the average in regard to the quality of competition, the physical characteristics of the location, the compatibility of nearby businesses, and the accessibility of the site to the trading area.

Estimating the Sales Volume of the Proposed Store

The estimated sales volume that can be obtained by the new store can be found by multiplying its estimated market share by the total product line purchases made in the trading area.

Another method of estimating the sales volume that can be obtained by the new store is to multiply the number of square feet in the store times the average annual sales per square foot for that type of store. Average annual sales per square foot are presented in Table 6–3.

In calculation format this procedure becomes:

$$
\begin{array}{l}
\text{Estimate of Annual} \\
\text{Sales for Specific} \\
\text{Outlet}
\end{array}
=
\begin{array}{l}
\text{Number of Square Feet} \\
\text{in Specific Outlet}
\end{array}
\times
\begin{array}{l}
\text{Average Annual Sales} \\
\text{per Square Foot for} \\
\text{Outlets in This Specific} \\
\text{Merchandise Category}
\end{array}
$$

For example, suppose a new hardware outlet were to occupy 4000 square feet of selling space. The estimated annual sales for the outlet would be 4000 × $52 = $208,000. Thus, the new outlet would have to obtain annual sales of at least $208,000 to reach the sales per square foot sales level reached by an average hardware store. This value should then be compared to the other estimates of sales volume for the outlet. If it is smaller than other estimates, the chances for establishing a successful outlet are less than average. If the other sales estimates are larger than $208,000, then the outlet has a better than average chance of being successful.

Table 6-3 **Square Footage to Sales Relationships for Different Types of Outlets**

Type of Retail Outlet	Annual Dollar Sales per Square Foot of Selling Space	Selling Space as a Percent of Total Floor Space	Average Square Footage of Under-Roof Floor Space
Hardware stores	52	70	5,405
Department stores	100	67	98,682
Variety stores	44	73	12,297
Miscellaneous general merchandise stores	71	72	6,844
Grocery stores	165	71	5,971
Apparel & accessory stores	85	70	3,858
Furniture, home furnishings and equipment stores	52	73	6,864
Drug & proprietary stores	103	74	4,250

Source: U.S. Department of Commerce, *1972 Census of Retail Trade*, Volume 1 Summary and Subject Statistics (Washington, D.C.: Government Printing Office, 1972), p. 83.

The previous discussion has revealed that the site selection decision involves many factors which frequently interact with one another. Sales estimates for a specific site consume a considerable amount of time and money. Frequently, retail management wishes to evaluate many different sites in an area to determine which site offers the most retail potential. In this case the problem may become so complex and time consuming that the use of a computer may be required.

One such computer analysis is being used by Dunning Brothers, a firm specializing in commercial operations analysis.[7] This computer analysis is based upon the assumption that the consumer is attracted to each retail outlet in varying degrees depending on the travel time to each store. Travel time is computed for each quarter-mile square section. Then the percentage of the proposed outlet's share of the trade in that area is computed and an index describing potential sales is developed for that quarter-mile area. Every quarter-mile square is considered as a hypothetical store location. Each possible site is then rated according to its net trade area value. The net trade area value at any point is that portion of all surrounding buying power allocated to that particular site. The sites with the highest trade area values are those most advantageously located in the travel network serving the consumer field. Lower net trade area values indicate either a remoteness of customers and/or excessive existing store saturation (Figure 6–3).

The use of this and similar computer analyses to select the best available retail site is likely to increase in the future as increases in land and building costs make the location decision even more critical to the success or failure of the retail operation.

Determining Whether Estimated Volume Will Be Sufficient to Support a New Store

Costs must be examined and compared to expected profits to determine which proposed site will yield the most profit. Industry sources will usually provide estimates of the average rent expense for leased stores. For example, average rent expense for new supermarkets is about 1.5 percent of sales. If the estimated weekly sales volume is $32,000, then 32,000 times 0.015, or $480 per week, could be spent on the site if the store wanted to pay no more than average leasing rates for its facilities.

If the building and land price (or leasing) cost (not including equity buildup in land and buildings) is less than $480 per month, the proposed store should be more profitable than the average supermarket. If the cost exceeds $480, these extra costs must be overcome by reduction in other costs such as labor, and transportation. If these costs are not reduced, the profit margin will be below the industry average.

The *payback period*—the estimated period of time in which a project will generate cash equal to its cost—should also be calculated if the store owners are going to buy the land and building.[8] If the annual cash inflow is estimated to be received in equal annual amounts, the payback period (in years) equals the cost of the project divided by annual net income after taxes and depreciation. For example, if a retail building project costs $100,000 and is expected to yield an annual net income after taxes and depreciation of $10,000, the payback period would be $100,000 divided by $10,000, or ten years.

There is no common agreement on how many years it should take a building and land to pay for themselves from the revenues generated from the store. The selection of the appropriate payback period is influenced by the cost of obtaining money (interest rates) and alternative uses of the investor's money. Most realtor investors say that a building should receive 1 percent of its cost per month as a payment for its rental (or lease) value. The land should receive 0.5 percent of its appraised value as its monthly payment. This means that the building should pay for itself in 100 months, or 8 1/3 years.

In speculative types of retailing where market and environmental changes occur quite rapidly, the desired payback period might be much less—say five years. The higher the degree of uncertainty and the cost of obtaining money, the lower the desired payback period will be.

Of course the site evaluation analysis must also project the potential sales and

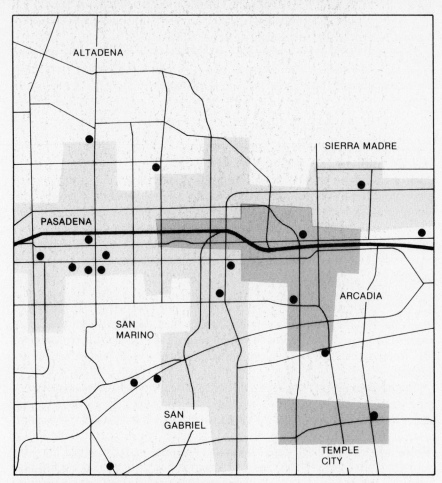

Above average (greater than $18,000,000)

Top 10% (greater than $23,000,000)

A Net Trade Area Value Map such as this simplified example rates every point on the map as a possible location for a new store. Data pertains to a business whose competitors are located at the black dots and whose customers are rated according to family income above $15,000. The net trade area value at any point is that portion of all the surrounding buying power allocated to a hypothetical new store located at that point after each family is divided among all competitors according to a proximity formula. High values would indicate a strategic advantage for a new site. Lower values indicate remoteness of customers and/or exessive existing service.

Figure 6-3 Illustration of the Use of a Computer Site Evaluation Program

Source: "Computer Analysis Aids Strategic Site Selection," *Stores* 58 (May 1976): pp. 25–27. Reprinted from *Stores* Magazine; © National Retail Merchants Association, 1976.

profits into the future. A growth area will be much more attractive than a declining area. A growing profit trend can legitimately be incorporated into the payback period analysis because, hopefully, the store will be generating profits over at least a five- to ten-year period. If the annual cash inflow generated by the building is not received in equal amounts, one may compile a list of cumulative cash gains expected to originate from the project until the year in which the running income total is equal to the amount of the expenditure.

Deciding to Buy, Lease, or Build

Another important aspect of the site selection problem is to determine if the firm should buy the property outright or if it should lease the facility. As noted earlier, some retailers prefer not to own property because of the high fixed cost involved and the uncertainty of future market potential. If the dollar return in inventory invest- ment is greater than the dollar invested in real estate, it is usually desirable to lease instead of purchase.

Leasing terms vary by location, type of store, and numerous other considera- tions. Supermarkets usually generate an annual sales volume of from $1 million to $3 million. Because of their low profit margin, supermarket rents are generally comparatively inexpensive on both a percentage of sales (1.5 percent) and square footage ($1.50 to $4) basis. Large, full-line department stores have a higher profit margin, but they also have a great deal of bargaining power. This usually results in a rent of 2.5 percent of gross sales.[9] Specialty stores, which have the highest markups and the least bargaining power, usually pay a higher percent of their gross sales as rent. A summary of rental rates for selected store categories is presented in Table 6–4.

Lease rates in a major midwest regional shopping center vary from a low annual cost of $1.17 per square foot for a major anchor department store to $60 per square foot per year for a small key-making outlet. Most of the tenants paid between $6 and $10 per square foot per year.

The rental rates also vary slightly from one area to another as indicated by the data contained in Table 6–5. These data show that the rental rates are slightly higher in the Los Angeles area than those found in either Chicago or Dallas.

The rental policy of shopping center developers is designed so that operating expenses (mostly maintenance, utilities, and upkeep) are only 15 to 18 percent of total gross rental income.[10]

Some land developers and some retailers are now using a philosophy of *storing land*. This involves the purchase of vacant land in the development path of a city or suburb on which low-cost business structures are erected. Taxes and interest payments can be made from the income generated by these buildings, and the buildings are constructed so that they can easily be torn down when the land becomes a desirable site for a major retail development.

Table 6-4 **National Percentage Lease Ranges for Selected Store Categories**

Store Category	1950	1960	1970	1976
Art shops	8-10	6-10	6-10	6-10
Auto accessories stores	4-8	2-5	3-5	3-6
Barber shops	10-12	8-10	6-10	5-10
Beauty shops	10-15	8-10	6-12	5-10
Books and stationery stores	8-11	5-11	4-10	5-8
Candy stores	8-12	5-8	6-10	6-12
Department stores	3-4	2-3	1.5-4	1.5-3.5
Discount department stores (over 75,000 sq. ft.)	NA[A]	1-2.5	1-2	1-2.5
Discount department stores (under 75,000 sq. ft.)	NA[A]	NA[A]	NA[A]	1-4
Drug stores—independent	6-8	3-6	3-8	2.5-6
Drug stores—chain	3-6	2.5-4.5	2.5-5	2.5-5
Drug stores—prescription (medical buildings)	8-12	5-10	5-10	5-10
Electrical appliance stores	4-7	2.5-5	3-6	3-6
Five and dime stores	4-6	3-6	3-6	3-5
Fabric (yard goods) stores	NA[A]	NA[A]	4-6	4-6
Florists	8-10	6-10	6-10	6-10
Furniture stores	4-8	3-7	3-8	3-6
Gas stations (costs per gallon sold)	1-1.5¢	1-1.5¢	1-2¢	1-2¢
Gift shops	7-9	5-9	6-10	6-10
Supermarkets	0-1.5	0.75-1.5	0.5-2.25	1-2
Convenience food stores	NA[A]	NA[A]	NA[A]	2-3.5
Hardware stores	5-8	3-6	3.5-6	4-6
Hosiery and knit goods stores	6-8	6-8	6-10	6-10
Jewelry stores	8-10	3-8	4-10	4-10
Luggage/leather goods stores	7-10	5-9	5-10	5-10
Liquor and wine stores	6-8	3-8	4-6	2-6
Men's clothing stores	6-8	4-8	4-8	4-8
Men's furnishings (haberdashery) stores	6-10	5-10	4-10	5-8
Motion-picture theaters	14-25	8-18	8-15	7-15
Radio, TV, and hi-fi stores	NA[A]	NA[A]	4-8	3-8
Record shops	NA[A]	NA[A]	5-7	5-7
Restaurants	6-8	5-7	3-8	5-9
Restaurants—liquor	6-10	6-8	4-10	6-10
Sporting goods stores	6-8	5-8	4-8	3.5-8
Women's ready-to-wear stores—chain	5-8	2.5-6	4-8	3-6
Women's ready-to-wear stores—independent	7-9	4-8	4-10	4-8
Women's furnishings/ accessories stores	NA[A]	4-10	5-10	5-8
Women's shoe stores	6-8	4-7	5-8	5-7

A. NA=not available.

Source: Nathan Schloss, "Inflation-Proofing Retail Investments with Percentage Leases," *Real Estate Review* 7 (Winter 1978): 37. Reprinted by permission.

This practice is based on the belief that development land values will rise faster than interest costs and taxes. Site selection that is based upon projected population

Table 6-5 **Percentage Lease Ranges in Selected Market Areas for Selected Store Categories (1976)**

Store Category	National	Chicago	Dallas	Los Angeles
Hosiery and knit goods stores	6-10	6-8	6-7	7-10
Luggage/leather goods stores	5-10	6-8	5-7	7-10
Radios, TV, hi-fi stores	3-8	4-5	5-6	5-8
Women's furnishings/ accessories stores	5-8	6-7	4.5-6.5	5-7

Source: Nathan Schloss, "Inflation-Proofing Retail Investments with Percentage Leases," *Real Estate Review* 7 (Winter 1978): 38. Reprinted by permission.

movements involves the additional risks associated with imperfect foresight. It also involves a high fixed cost. However, retailers should plan ahead so that consumers can be served near their places of residence. Storing land can be a part of expansion planning, since it can guarantee a location in areas where real estate is expected to become difficult to acquire.

Generally, developers have only a small percentage of equity in a shopping center or large retail building. Lending institutions usually mortgage up to 75 percent of the *economic value* (the value of the project based upon future estimated earnings) of a shopping center. The economic value of a well-planned center will usually be 25 to 33 percent higher than total building costs.

For example, the developers of Willowbrook Center in New Jersey were able to build their $23 million center by using only $500,000 as their own cash equity.[11] The other $22.5 million came from an insurance company that made a twenty-nine year loan at 7½ percent interest. An estimated net economic value of nearly $32 million was calculated by capitalizing on an estimated annual net profit of $2.7 million at the going interest rate of 8½ percent. The insurance company loaned about 70 percent of the estimated economic value ($32 million), but the loan ($22.5 million) amounted to nearly 98 percent of the total project cost ($23 million) in this case.

Unless individual stores develop their own centers or build their own large stores, they will not be able to obtain such low equity financing. Instead, they will have to pay rental fees similar to those in Table 6–4.

Despite the availability of low equity financing, retail developers are finding that storing land is appealing because of increasing costs for land, construction, and money. For example, land could be purchased for $20,000 an acre in the metropolitan New York area in 1966, whereas similar land cost from $40,000 to $80,000 an acre in 1971.[12] Construction costs in the New York area for the shell of a shopping center, exclusive of department stores, increased from about $10 per square foot in 1966 to about $17.50 in 1971. The interest costs in the area also increased substantially, from about 8 percent in 1966 to about 10 percent in 1971. Of course increasing construction and financing costs could not be avoided by storing land; however, the increase in land costs and some interest costs can be avoided if the land-storing policy is used.

Such factors as the financial condition of the company, the profitability of the business, and the degree of growth orientation in company philosophy determine the proper investment that should be made in buildings and real estate. Thus, each retailer must make commitments based upon his or her financial and marketing situation at the time a site is available.

Summary

The evaluation of a specific site requires a detailed study of the current or proposed outlet's trading area. The size and shape of the store's trading area must first be determined. This can be done by studying store sales records, conducting a license plate study, or interviewing consumers.

This trade area is then studied intensively to reveal its population level and characteristics, purchasing power, competitive outlets, accessibility to consumers, and compatibility with other business firms. An estimate of the total retail business potential for the site is then made. This is usually accomplished by using the percentage of income method, the percentage of retail sales dollar method, and the per capita sales method to provide a range of sales estimates for the specified category in the defined trade area. Then a realistic estimate of the firm's market share is made. These two factors (total category retail sales and the firm's market share) are then multiplied to give an estimate of the firm's expected sales at the site. Computer analysis is currently being used to evaluate sites and provide related sales estimates for each site. This data can be used to establish expansion priorities for a firm considering building several new stores in the near future. Finally, these same data can be used in the firm's critical decision to buy or lease a new building on a selected site.

Questions

1. Discuss the concept of trade area and describe how it is used.

2. How can you measure the current trading area for a grocery store? Discuss the usefulness of the method you describe.

3. Use the percentage of income method, the percentage of retail dollar method, and the per capita method to estimate the total variety store sales in Ft. Collins, Colorado. Use the data contained in Tables 6–1 and 5–3.

4. What are the factors that can be used in measuring retail compatibility?

5. Describe the differences between generative business, shared business, and suscipient business.

6. How can two adjacent stores selling goods competitively be considered compatible?

7. What is the value of the ratio of market share to selling space share? If a retailer estimates he must have 18 percent of the market to break even and the ratio is 0.5, what percent of the selling space must he have if all other variables are held constant? What other factors must be considered in reality?

8. If the average rent paid out in an area is 3 percent of sales and estimated annual sales are $1,600,000, how much monthly rent can a retailer with these sales expect to pay? If rent is expected to increase at 5 percent per year (that is 5 percent of the previous year's rent), what level of sales would be required for the first three years? (Assume all other variables to be held constant.)

9. What factors influence the payback period? What other factors must be considered in purchasing a store? Why should the payback period be shorter for high-risk locations?

10. How does "economic value" differ from building cost?

11. Describe the philosophy and practice of storing land.

Footnotes

1. David K. Hardin, president of Market Facts Inc., Chicago, Ill., as reported by Edwin Darby in the *Chicago Sun-Times,* 24 March 1971.

2. William Applebaum, *Shopping Center Strategy* (New York: International Council of Shopping Centers, 1970), p. 74.

3. Ibid., pp. 51–55, 65–68.

4. Ibid., pp. 135–136.

5. Ibid., pp. 111, 113.

6. Bernard Kane, Jr., A *Systematic Guide to Supermarket Location Analysis* (New York: Fairchild Publications, 1966), pp. 103–105.

7. "Computer Analysis Aids Strategic Site Selection," *Stores,* May 1976, pp. 25–27.

8. Joseph F. Bradley, *Administrative Financial Management,* 2d ed. (New York: Holt, Rinehart and Winston, 1969), pp. 140–141.

9. "Shopping Centers Grow into Shopping Cities," *Business Week,* 4 September 1971, p. 37.

10. Ibid.

11. Ibid.

12. Ibid.

Case Study

Self Serve Gas

Self Serve Gas, Incorporated, operates 200 self service gasoline stations in a ten-state area. One of its locations is being threatened by the completion of the Interstate Highway System.

The current site is located on the north side of a town of 20,000 people. It is situated on the only major two-lane highway that passes through the town. The new interstate highway will bypass the current Self Serve location by about one mile. The current site is fortunate to have direct access to one of four major exits off the Interstate. However, Joe Manuello, the vice president of marketing for Self Serve Gas, is worried that the Interstate traffic will not travel the extra mile to get gas at Self Serve. He is looking into another site on the south side of town. This site is only eight blocks off the major Interstate exit and is also located closer to the downtown area.

Self Serve Gas has been obtaining about one-half of its sales from the two-lane highway traffic for which it is ideally located. Its edge-of-town location makes it inconvenient for many local residents to trade at the current location. The current sales volume is good because the outlet can obtain the business of both local and highway consumers.

Discussion Questions

1. What alternative courses of action does Mr. Manuello have?

2. Evaluate the advantages and disadvantages of each alternative.

3. What should Manuello do? Why?

Case Study

Mid States Savings and Loan Association (B)

Follow-up of Mid States, Chapter 3

Ms. Gibson has decided that Mid States needs to establish a new drive-in branch facility outside of the downtown area. She has investigated two possible sites. One is in an area that is just beginning to develop on the northwest edge of town. The retail facilities in this area currently consist of a supermarket, a discount store, and two restaurants. A new high school is located two blocks away from the site. The residential area around the site will consist of townhouses and single family dwellings. About 20 percent of the county population resides within two miles of the site. The average daily traffic count past the site is 7000 autos.

The other location possibility is in an established area of the eastern part of town. The residential area consists of a mixture of new homes, new apartments, and older homes. A high school is located by this site, which is contained in a neighborhood shopping center. Stores located in the center include a supermarket, cafe, department store, a shoe store, women's clothing store, electronics store, fabric store, a theatre, and ten specialty outlets. Other retail outlets located near the site area include a K Mart and a supermarket-drug store combination.

A license plate survey showed that the shopping center drew about 70 percent of its city consumers from a two-mile radius of the site. It is estimated that about 52 percent of the county population of 70,000 resides within two miles of the shopping center. About 35 percent of the Mid States savings deposits came from people who live within this two miles of the site. The average daily traffic count past the shopping center is about 9000 autos.

Discussion Questions

1. Do you think either site will be a good location for a Mid States drive-in branch facility?

2. How would you evaluate the drawing power of the existing retail outlets that are located near each site?

3. How would you estimate the volume of savings deposits that the drive-in facility would obtain at each site?

Chapter 7

Attracting with Atmosphere

After the site has been selected the retail building must be constructed or remodeled and fixtures and equipment purchased and arranged so that customers may be attracted to the store, stimulated to make purchases, and served promptly with minimum cost. This chapter is devoted to a discussion of the factors that retailers should consider when they build, remodel, or rearrange their outlets.

Psychological Impact and Store Image

The image a store projects to its customers is one of the most important influences contributing to a retailer's success. It is also the most difficult variable to control, to measure, and, indeed, to define. If *store image* may be defined as "the aggregate stimulus value the company, store brand, or product has for a particular individual or group,"[1] it is obvious that a store's image may be seen somewhat differently by each person. Nevertheless, for a particular group of like customers or a market segment, a store's image may be fairly similar. A store such as Saks Fifth Avenue or Tiffany and Company may be thought of as ultraexpensive and out of reach by low-income persons, while more affluent individuals may think of them as stores with excellent quality products and service to match a sophisticated taste.

Another way of looking at image is to view it as the overall personality of the store. This personality is always present, regardless of whether or not it was planned by the management. Just as the personality of an individual attracts or repels certain types of people, so too does that of a store.

This is not to imply that a store's personality or image remains the same over time. It is often a shock for us to encounter a high school classmate several years after graduation and to witness the change in his or her personality. Some grow old before their time; others seem to develop a wit and charm they never had in school. For this reason it is not uncommon for old friends to discover at a class reunion that they no longer have much in common and that others, whom they scarcely knew, have become interesting and attractive individuals.

This analogy also holds true for retail stores. A store always has a personality, even if that personality reflects blandness, a lack of creativity, and general sterility. A store manager who feels that a store's image is a concern only for the supersophisticated, or who says, "I only worry about price and quality," is naive. Knowingly or unknowingly, he or she is developing an image for the store.

Consumers' patronage patterns differ from one type of retail outlet to another. Data contained in Table 7–1 reveal that consumers patronize a supermarket primarily because of its location and the low prices it offers. Consumers for women's clothing fashions were found to select their outlet on the basis of the best value for the money, the largest overall assortment, and the highest quality clothing (Table 7–2). Thus, management for each store must determine what image that individual outlet should project to the consuming public.

To provide the proper image, stores have to be remodeled to meet changing customer desires. Management can only change lights, fixtures, and other flexible

Table 7-1 Comparative Attribute Importance Data for Supermarkets: Share of Mentions Going to Each Response to the Question . . . "All Things Considered, What Is the Single Most Important Reason You Shop at (_____) for Most of Your Food Shopping?"

| | Cities | | | | | | |
| | North America | | | | Netherlands | | |
Reasons Given[A]	A	B	C	D	E	Tel	In-home
1. Location/convenience/easy to get to	34%[B]	35%	36%	34%	27%	23%	22%
2. Prices/low price	14	18	16	13	40	33	37
3. Large variety/well stocked/ assortment/everything you need	9	11	9	11	7	13	12
4. Meat quality/variety	11	6	8	7	5	0	0
5. Overall quality	9	3	5	5	1	6	5
6. Service/friendly/courteous/ fast checkout	4	6	7	6	5	7	5
7. Specials/sales, coupons/ stamps/weekly specials	7	5	6	7	3	2	1
8. Pleasant shopping environment	0	0	1	2	0	8	7
9. All others	12	16	12	15	12	8	11
Totals	100%	100%	100%	100%	100%	100%	100%
Sample Size (N)	(1000)	(1000)	(1000)	(1000)	(1000)	(1000)	(1000)

A. Question was asked in open-end form. Responses were recorded verbatim and later postcoded into the above categories.

B. In U.S. city "A," 34 percent of the total sample said location/convenience was the most important reason why they chose the store where they do most of their food spending.

Source: Stephan J. Arnold, M.A. Sylvia, and Douglas J. Tigert, "A Comparative Analysis of Determinant Attributes in Retail Store Selection," *Advances in Consumer Research, Proceedings for the Association for Consumer Research*, 1978, p. 665. Reprinted by permission.

elements for a certain period of time. Then they must remodel or they will lose sales. Store design itself is frequently found to be a fashion item that attracts consumers. For example, store remodelings stimulate sales by creating consumer interest. People who may not otherwise look into a particular window suddenly become sidewalk superintendents. Retail managers can tie many good promotions into the remodeling projects. Some stores have found that if they place the merchandise from areas being remodeled out on the selling floor in stacks of cartons, consumers will search through the inventory to find bargains. The temporary stacking of merchandise in cartons creates a "priced to go" impression even if markdowns are minimal.

A remodeled building provides an excellent opportunity for redefining the target market and creating a place the customers call "their store." The target market should be redefined in terms of such factors as income level, race, price consciousness for the products to be sold, geographical location, seasonality, age, and other important variables.

An example of a firm that used a remodeling program to better reach its rede-

Table 7-2 **Comparative Attribute Importance Data for Women's Clothing Fashions: Mean and Rank Scores on Store Characteristics for Likert Scales and Forced Choice Scales . . . "How Important is Each Specific Store Characteristic to You in Choosing a Store to Shop for Women's Fashions?"**

| | 5 Point Likert Scale | | | | 11 Point Forced Choice Scale | | | | | |
| | Netherlands (77) | | Canada (76) | | Netherlands (77) | | Canada | | | |
Store Characteristic	Mean	Rank	Mean	Rank	Mean	Rank	1976	1977	1976	1977
1. Gives best value for the money	4.5	1[A]	4.6[B]	1	3.9	2	2.5[C]	2.6	1	1
2. Has largest overall assortment/selection	4.4	3	3.9	2	4.4	4	4.5	4.1	2	2
3. Has the highest quality women's fashions	4.5	2	3.8	3	3.2	1	4.9	5.5	3	4
4. Has the most knowledgeable, helpful salesclerks	4.2	4	3.6	4	4.1	3	5.3	6.1	4	6
5. Best for current, up-to-date women's fashions	3.9	5	3.6	5	6.0	7	5.4	5.2	5	3
6. Easiest to get to from home	3.6	6	3.1	7	4.9	5	5.6	5.8	6	5
7. Best for conservative, everyday wear	3.5	8	3.5	6	6.4	8	6.0	6.5	7	7
8. Best for latest, most fashionable women's wear	3.5	7	3.0	8	6.9	9	7.2	6.9	9	8
9. Has the lowest prices	3.2	9	3.0	9	5.8	6	6.3	7.0	8	9
10. Has the best fashion advertising	2.6	10	2.4	11	9.2	11	8.8	8.8	11	11
11. Has the most exciting merchandise display	2.6	11	2.9	10	9.0	10	7.8	7.4	10	10

A. Rank scores involve examination of mean scores taken to third decimal place. For ease in reading, only first decimal is shown in the above table.

B. Five point Likert scale ranges from "very important" (score of 5) to "not important at all" (score1) with highest mean score ranking first.

C. Eleven point forced-choice scale ranges from "most important" (score 1) to "least important" (score 11) with the lowest mean score ranking first.

Source: Stephan J. Arnold, M.A. Sylvia, and Douglas J. Tigert, "A Comparative Analysis of Determinant Attributes in Retail Store Selection," *Advances in Consumer Research, Proceedings for the Association for Consumer Research*, (1978), p. 666. Reprinted by permission.

fined target market is the Mi Amigo chain of stores in Guatemala City, Guatemala. This chain began as a children's store but gradually added new merchandise lines and new stores. The new stores were located in different income areas ranging from high to low. The corporate logo, a stork carrying a baby, seemed dated and did not represent the stores.

When the two sons of the original owner accepted full management responsibility, a series of studies were begun. The young management team hired a marketing research firm to conduct image studies. They also carefully studied the sales contribution from each product line and each store. They reviewed the outside and inside appearance of each store and came to the conclusion that a dramatic change was needed.

An architect was hired and their stores were remodeled to resemble a circus or amusement park. A target market of children up to twelve years of age was selected. This meant designing an atmosphere that would appeal to both the mothers and the children.

The store became a setting that children enjoyed visiting and that said "We like babies and kids and want to please you."

A decision was made to turn the store in the low-income area into another type of store. Its logo was changed, salespeople were retrained, and even management thinking changed.

Store Image and Consumer Psychographics

The target market for a store is normally described in terms of **demographics** such as age, income, race, sex, and so forth. These are useful descriptions of the profile of a target market but they are incomplete. They are incomplete because two persons with identical demographic profiles may exhibit very different shopping habits and preferences.

In an attempt to describe the target market better, the concept of psychographics was developed. *Psychographics* attempts to describe life-style characteristics of the consumer that can be used by the retailer.

The management of Northpark Shopping Center in Dallas used psychographics to aid them and their retail merchants in the center with marketing planning. The center contained three major department stores—Neiman-Marcus, Titches, and Lord & Taylor. There was a question as to whether the three stores were attempting to share the same market segment or were appealing to different segments. Demographic results had failed to answer this question satisfactorily.

A psychographic study was then conducted among target group consumers to determine life-style characteristics. Sample characteristics studied included conservative or liberal attitudes, outdoor or indoor orientation, intellectual or nonintellectual orientation. The results showed psychographic differences for these stores as well as for other department stores not in the center.

In spite of the usefulness of psychographics, there are the following problems connected with its use.

1. Deciding upon which life-style characteristics to include

   It is often quite difficult to decide upon the type of psychographic characteristics that should be included. As an example, is a measurement of conservatism or a measurement of a person's interest in outdoor activities really meaningful to a retailer?

2. Deciding upon how to use results

   It is sometimes difficult for a retailer to know exactly how to use demographic statistics. The problem is compounded with psychographic data. For example, the management of a large service firm conducted a psychographic profile of its customers and found that they were more likely to drive sports cars than customers of competitive services. The management was then left wondering how to use this data.

Undoubtedly, psychographic information can be used by a creative advertising department or as a basis for store remodeling decisions. Use of psychographics often demands new habits of thinking on the part of management. An unresponsive management may dismiss the data as meaningless information.

Recall, for a moment, the notion of image and note that it is defined as the aggregate stimulus value the store has for an individual or group. It is apparent from this definition that image is a result of all our sensory reactions. Thus each reaction should be considered in the image-planning process.

Scent Considerations

Retail stores that sell food, flowers, perfumes, soaps, candles, and even automobiles need to be constantly aware of the effect that odor has upon overall image. Anyone who has passed a Karmel Korn store or a fresh roasted nut and coffee establishment in the heart of a city can attest to the value of smell. Fans that are placed to carry the aroma of these products to the sidewalk are not accidentally placed. Used-car dealers sometimes have been accused of spraying their near-new automobiles with a heavy spray to represent the odor of new cars in an attempt to change consumer images. Imagine the negative effect that stale cigar smoke would have in a dress shop, or even in a shoe store. New cars and new-car showrooms are expected to have a new-car smell. Strong disinfectants, greasy smells, and other foreign odors can adversely affect the image of many establishments.

Sound Considerations

The tinkling of Chinese wind chimes in an import store immediately sets the stage for image creation. Even the background noise of elevated trains, freight trains, or shopper congestion can add a vital ingredient to the image of a store. The "believability" of a freight salvage store may be enhanced if the sounds of switching trains and semi-trailer trucks are audible to shoppers.

Other stores depend upon the almost total absence of extraneous sounds. Many exclusive dress and fur shops eliminate unwanted sounds through heavy carpeting, multiple partitions, low ceilings, and the low-key, hushed tone of sales personnel. Yet only a short distance away, on the same shopping mall, other retail establishments such as teen shops depend upon loud noises, including recordings of the latest hit group.

It is a costly mistake for a retailer to overlook the effect of sounds on the success of the store. Appropriate background sounds or music convey the message, "Things are happening here. Stop, look, see what's going on." In fact, many stores deliberately start a retail day by eliminating the "dead store" silence when they turn on lively music. Activity generates customer interest.

Touch Considerations

We tend to say, "Let me see that, please," when we really mean, "Let me touch that, please." Many objects are meant to be touched, and can best be sold after they have been touched. Imagine the success an automobile dealer or furrier might have if no one were allowed to touch their products until after the purchase. Furs are irresistibly touchable. Toys are meant to be handled, books to be looked through, and cars to be sat in—with doors to slam and tires to kick.

As important as touch is, far too many retailers place artificial barriers in the path of the natural and desirable reaction of the customer to touch the merchandise. It is highly probable that the "Do Not Touch" or "Touch at Your Own Risk" signs in tourist and curio shops have caused lost sales far in excess of the breakage they have prevented. Small children cannot read these signs so they touch anyway, but shoppers—with dollars to spend—may be frightened away. The recent practice of covering books with cellophane or plastic may also be questioned, particularly if no sample books are provided.

Certainly there are places where touching must be prevented, as in art galleries featuring original oils, but in many other cases the touching of merchandise may be desirable and profitable. Displays and samples may be arranged in a store in a way that invites touch. In these cases only the samples may be soiled or damaged, and they can be inexpensively replaced.

Although the term *sensuous* is sometimes applied to a person, it is also applicable to some retail stores or sections within stores. The products sold within these stores appeal to our needs for love, affection, sex, and perhaps even religion. These stores should be designed to promote a feeling of sensuousness in the customer. The proper use of touch in these stores can add to the desired image. There's an old saying that sums up the discussion: Put the merchandise out where the customers can feel it and steal it so they will try it and buy it.

Sight Considerations

No one can deny the importance of sight. Yet thousands of retail stores each year are established without attention to sight. The visual impression that is imposed upon customers by signs, sidewalks, window displays, awnings, parking lots, and every nut and bolt of the building is of the utmost importance.

Visual merchandising is a combination of every factor that can affect the consumer's visual perception of the store. Moreover, visual merchandising is the utilization of every square inch of the building, inside and out, to sell the company and its products.

Visual merchandising is more than image building; it is the conscious recognition of the fact that a consumer is in one's store to buy goods and services. Therefore, each moment that a consumer is the guest of a retailer, he or she should be exposed to planned visual merchandising. The same retailers who spends hundreds of thousands of dollars a year on advertising, catalogs, and other material designed to bring the customer to them often neglect the importance of a total selling environment once the customer is in their store.

Because store layout usually concentrates on developing optimum traffic patterns, important areas are planned with total disregard for visual merchandising. Elevators and escalators are planned only for the function of hauling bodies from one floor to another. Yet in each case the customer is in a captive position for several seconds to several minutes. Why shouldn't this time and space be utilized to sell the products and services of the store? It would not be difficult to line the walls of the elevators with samples of carpet, wall paper, fabrics, or other goods sold in the store.

Many other store areas are traditionally treated as nonselling areas. These include the credit department, the employment and personnel department, and the rest rooms. Is it really too extreme to consider visual merchandising of toiletries, cosmetics, facial tissues, and other products in the rest rooms?

Today, companies such as Susan Crane Packaging are entering the field of visual merchandising. These companies manufacture and sell an integrated program to aid in visual merchandising. Such firms are able to provide supporting assistance with visuals from window dressing to tote bags. However, their effectiveness is limited by a store's commitment to visual merchandising as a concept and as a continuing program.

The appearance of the store can seldom be divorced from that of its neighbors. It might be impossible for a retailer of high-quality jewelry to convey such an image, regardless of the creativity in design, if his store is surrounded by discount record shops, fast-food drive-ins, and a pawnshop or two. It might be equally difficult for a low-margin retailer to establish an appropriate image in an area known for its appeal to the affluent carriage trade, which is conscious of good taste and proper style regardless of cost.

In most cases, errors in location and their effect upon image are not as extreme as those described in these examples. Exorbitantly high rents, zoning restrictions, shopping center restrictions, and common sense prevent such glaring errors. Nevertheless, errors are made. This can be easily proved simply by observing the variety of stores in one's area.

Small-town department and clothing stores sometimes feel compelled to try to be all things to all people. A department store in a small Michigan town was once observed to feature in its front window men's work overalls *and* women's formal dress. The end result of such image building is often a loss of customers to the nearest metropolitan shopping center.

Of course image impression through sight extends beyond the appearance and location of the building, equipment, and signs. The dress, personal grooming, and composition of the labor force are equally important. It is not enough to consider simply the sales force, since the appearance of delivery crew, credit personnel, and many others leaves strong impressions upon customers and potential customers. The fact that a particular store employs members of minority groups only as janitors and shipping clerks can be a strong negative factor for customers from these racial groups.

Employees' mode of dress is of particular importance in the case of high-quality merchandise, since the total image of the store can be lowered by even one employee. While the problem of dressing below the image of the store appears to be most common, the reverse situation can also be true. Stores that specialize in products such as feed, fertilizer, auto parts, and plumbing supplies generally expect their sales personnel to dress in work clothes for practical as well as image-building purposes. Individuals in these types of retail establishments often perform laborious and dirty tasks.

The wearing of a coat and tie may also place a barrier between the customer and the retailer, for it is not uncommon to find among middle-class consumers a distrust of those who wear a suit and tie. As retailers grow larger, they often hire salespeople and troubleshooters to call on their customers in the field, and when these persons are hired they sometimes assume that a coat and tie is the proper dress. This, however, is usually incorrect; they will be calling upon contractors, farmers, ranchers, and others who are seldom dressed in suits and ties and who often resent such attire in the sales representatives who call on them. Thus, the sight-image impression that customers hold of a retailer extends well beyond the confines of the retail store.

Image Control

The development and control of image creation cannot be planned for a store opening and then forgotten. It is an ongoing and everyday function of retail management. It requires a coordinated effort from all areas: promotional mix, personnel policy, pricing, location, and indeed every function of retailing.

In a very true sense, image creation and control is what retailing is all about. It has allowed retailers such as Saks Fifth Avenue, Tiffany's, Neiman-Marcus, and other firms that are known for their quality and high prices to grow in the face of discount houses and other mass merchandisers.

Land Utilization Considerations

The increased price of energy has resulted in rapidly increasing building costs. This, in turn, is creating pressure for more concentrated designs. These designs limit open space and encourage the building of more multi-level buildings that occupy less land space.

Choice pieces of land are valued at a high rate; therefore the retailer must decide carefully how much space should be allocated to the building and how much to parking and other open, landscaped space. Although the cost of providing a one-car parking space may amount to $2,000 in downtown areas and about $50 in suburban shopping centers, consumers may demand the convenience associated with the availability of a nearby parking space.

The amount of land required for a parking area varies according to the type of retail outlet. Shopping centers usually provide four square feet of parking space for every square foot of selling space. Outlets that cater to consumers who spend only a short amount of time in the store can provide less parking space. However, stores such as supermarkets, whose customers typically spend about twenty minutes per store visit, must provide parking space if a large volume of consumers is to be served.

Outlets that wish to create a more prestigious image will probably need to allocate more space to open, landscaped areas, fountains, and so forth, than will discount or bargain-image retailers (see Exhibit 7–1).

Exhibit 7–1 **Shopping Center Focal Point**
This multilevel mall serves as a focal point for a shopping center. Such a focal point and the open-space surroundings create a prestigious image for all of the stores in the center.
Source: Reprinted by permission of Joshua Freiwald, Photographer.

Building Exteriors

High interest rates, rising construction costs, new construction materials and techniques, and rising crime rates have caused numerous changes in the type of buildings used as retail outlets. Retailers have attemped to reduce building costs by using more multistory outlets, some of which are windowless, at least in the upper-floor levels (Exhibit 7–2). The absence of windows also improves security and reduces heating and air conditioning costs.

The storefront should convey the impression that the outlet is permanent, stable, and progressive. It should also clearly identify the store. Customer entrances should be wide enough to prevent consumer congestion and inviting enough to attract walk-in trade. Curtains of warm or cold air may serve as doors during store hours, and this increased ease of entering may attract some consumers who might otherwise hesitate to enter through a revolving or regular door (Exhibit 7–3).

Despite their cost, display windows continue to be used to attract consumers into stores. In fact, many stores use an open or all-glass store front through which the consumer can see even the store's interior displays (Exhibit 7–4). The visual storefront allows the consumer to view most of the store's merchandise offering at a glance. Other stores may use a closed-background show window display, which lets the consumer see only the specially prepared window display and shuts off the interior view of the store completely (Exhibit 7–5). This practice allows merchants

Exhibit 7-2 **Example of a Windowless Exterior**
*Such a design provides an attractive appearance and reduces air
conditioning and heating costs.*
Source: Reprinted by permission of Smitty's.

to focus consumer attention on displays which can convey either a quality or a
popular-price image.

Higher building and land costs and effective display techniques have caused
more retailers to use inexpensive out-of-door merchandise displays. These displays
may be erected in the parking lot or in a specially designated space that is incorporated into the building and landscape design plans. The displays are generally crude
in construction, so care should be taken that they do not detract from the permanent
exterior appearance. The merchandise that is sold from these exterior displays is
usually bulky, seasonal merchandise, such as lawn and garden-care products in the
spring, boats in the summer, Christmas trees in December, and so on.

Building Interiors

The interior of a building must be attractive to the consumer. This may be accomplished by providing good lighting, colorful walls, attractive floors, colorful displays,
and ceilings of a proper height and by arranging store fixtures and equipment in a
manner that will accommodate the anticipated consumer traffic.

The appearance of an outlet's interior and its effectiveness in servicing custom-

Exhibit 7–3 **Illustration of Doorless Design**
Source: Reprinted by permission of Pigeons, Inc.

ers in an efficient manner are strongly influenced by the fixtures and equipment it uses in its retail operations. Fixtures are usually defined to mean any durable good that the retailer uses to display, store, protect, or sell merchandise. Items included as fixtures are: shelves, counters, cases, display cabinets, racks, tables, and freezers. Equipment is any durable good used in or outside the store to facilitate both retail selling and nonselling activities. Equipment items are: cash registers, delivery trucks, elevators, escalators, and air conditioning units.

Fixtures and equipment should be selected that will be most consistent with the expectations of the store's target market and the degree (self-service vs. full service) of the outlet's service offering. The fixtures and equipment should blend in with the interior environment and not divert the consumer's attention away from the merchandise. The fixtures and equipment selected should be appropriate for the type of merchandise handled so as to provide protection from spoilage or theft but still display the merchandise in the most attractive manner possible. The trend in the selection of fixtures and equipment is to use as much portability and flexibility as possible. Finally, fixtures and equipment should be selected upon the basis of the item's cost and its expected maintenance cost.

One type of equipment that deserves special mention is the equipment that is used to move consumers from one floor to another floor. Few people realize how large a problem it is to move 250,000 people efficiently over eight floors on a daily basis. Yet this is what most large department stores must do.

Exhibit 7-4 **Illustration of an Open Store Front**
*The mirrors are arranged so the consumer can view the store's interior
displays by looking straight ahead or view window displays by viewing
the front from an angle.*
Source: Reprinted by permission of Bullock's Northern California.

Stationary stairways are frequently found to be adequate to handle the consumer traffic that goes up or down one floor from the main floor. Elevators and escalators must be used if the store consists of more than three floors. Elevators are usually more advantageous than escalators in smaller stores because only one or two elevators may be required. The space required for two elevators is considerably less than the space required for one escalator. In addition, the installation cost is lower for two elevators than for one escalator.

Escalators are considered a must for large, multilevel stores. The escalator offers: (1) a reduction of crowding and congestion, (2) fast transportation between floors, (3) a low use of power, (4) the use of less space when many elevators would be required to move people, and (5) a maximum view of the merchandise as consumers pass slowly by or over the selling area. Despite all of these advantages, larger stores also provide a minimal elevator installation to satisfy consumers who prefer not to use an escalator or who want to move up or down several floors at a time.

The color of a store's interior can enhance the store's appearance and emphasize its individuality. Color and design patterns can be used to direct consumers to specific areas and to put them in a buying mood. The effect that different colors have upon consumers is discussed in detail in Chapter 14, where it is noted that a different color scheme is likely to be most appropriate for each department, or perhaps even for each merchandise line. The men's section of Neiman-Marcus reflects a man's

Exhibit 7–5 **Illustration of Closed-Background Window Display Featuring Quality Image**

color preference, with a combination of deep blue and oak wood. Only a few feet away, the children's section offers a contrast in light pastels and designs that incorporate movement. Even different floor tile designs can be used to differentiate departments.

Every retail facility must be properly lighted to direct or attract the consumer's attention to the desired areas of the building. Lighting can be an effective sales tool if it is used to highlight different types of merchandise. A qualified lighting engineer can provide suggestions on the use of colored lights, as well as on the physical arrangement of lighting fixtures. Lighting can also be used to increase employee productivity by properly illuminating the checkout, storage, receiving, and other work areas.

Consumer buying decisions are the result of seeing. The shopper's eye is attracted to the brightest thing in its field of vision, so the lighting on a display should be between two and five times stronger than the light in the room. The brightest light can be used to draw attention to special retail displays that may occupy different locations from time to time. This gives consumers something new to look at and enhances shoppers' interest. However, strong light alone will not induce consumers to buy. Lighting must also have the quality and color which brings out the best features of the merchandise.

Effective lighting catches the consumer's eye and encourages the consumer to examine and buy the merchandise that is featured to its best advantage.

Retail managers must realize that the purpose of lighting is to bring attention to the merchandise. The amount of light must be varied to attract attention, pull shoppers to the desired areas of the store, and create the desired impression. Colored lamps and soft lighting can be used to create a buying mood that will encourage the consumers to "see" that living room set in their home. Lighting tips for specific types of merchandise are presented in Exhibit 7–6.

Exhibit 7–6 Lighting Tips for Specific Merchandise

1. Use large area lighting fixtures plus incandescent downlighting to avoid heavy shadows when displaying major appliances and furniture.

2. Use general diffuse lighting, accented with point-type spotlights to emphasize the beauty of china, glass, home accessories, and giftware.

3. Bring out the sparkle and luster of hardware, toys, auto accessories, highly polished silver, and other metalware by using a blend of general light and concentrated light sources—spotlights.

4. Use concentrated beams of high brightness incandescent sources to add brilliant highlights to jewelry, gold and silver, or cut-glass.

5. Highlight the colors, patterns and textures of rugs, carpets, upholstery, heavy drapes, and bedspreads by using oblique directional lighting plus general low intensity overhead lighting.

6. Heighten the appeal of men's wear by using a cool blend of fluorescent and incandescent—with fluorescent predominating.

7. Highlight women's wear—especially the bright, cheerful colors and patterns—by using Natural White fluorescents blended with tungsten-halogen.

8. Bring out the tempting colors of meats, fruits, and vegetables by using fluorescent lamps rich in red energy, including the deluxe cool white type. Cool reflector incandescent lamps may also be used for direct type lighting.

Source: Charles B. Elliott, "Pointers on Display Lighting," *Small Marketers Aids No. 125*, Washington, D.C., November 1972, p. 5.

Interior Layout

The *layout* of a retail store refers to the plan that designates the specific location and arrangement of equipment, fixtures, merchandise, aisles, and checkout facilities. Store layout automatically and instantly invites or repels a customer the moment the customer looks through the window or passes through an entry. This may be the most crucial moment in consumer shopping behavior, particularly in modern shopping center malls where dozens of stores stand one against the other.

There is only one universal law in layout that applies to all retail stores: each store must have a distinctive layout. Plan it with the store's clientele in mind and make certain it reflects the desired image and personality of the store.

Retailers have discovered that it is impossible to design a general layout that works for all types of retail stores in all areas. A certain degree of uniformity is possible within a single chain or a single industry, but strict adherence to a generalized model even within a single chain usually leads to disaster. The layout that is best suited for a store in Skokie, Illinois, may be completely out of character in Honolulu.

There is a basic conflict in all mass merchandising layouts for which a compromise must be reached. The customer wants a layout that does not cause undue inconvenience, or take added time, or tend to hinder shopping. The retailer wants a plan that exposes the shopper to the maximum amount of merchandise.

In the case of existing stores, *in-store traffic pattern analyses* should be conducted before remodeling to determine the natural flow of customers. In such studies, the percentage of consumers who pass or buy from each merchandise area is recorded by interviewers, who plot the paths of a sample of consumers on a floor plan similar to the one in Figure 7–1. Retailers believe that those merchandise lines which have high passing or buying percentages should be dispersed about the store so that consumers are exposed to more merchandise lines.

A scientific study of this nature usually is not available to new retailers, but observation of the patterns followed by shoppers in similar and competing stores is possible and desirable. Although the layout requirements facing retailers tend to vary, there are basic and common considerations.

Planning Layouts with Customers in Mind

Various social, age, and race segments exhibit different shopping habits and have individualized needs. Thus, the store's layout must be designed to meet the needs of the customers in its target market. For example, elderly people may prefer not to use an escalator or a curved, underground parking ramp, so a department store that caters to this group of people would have to use more elevators and more above ground parking facilities.

Promoting a Buying Mood

It is important to establish a buying mood. This is the sum total of what layout is all about. The most creative designs and the best research are valueless unless an effective environment for buying can be created.

Using a Simple Layout

In general, the more simple and natural the layout, the more likelihood of success. Consumers object to being treated like mice in a laboratory maze. They express

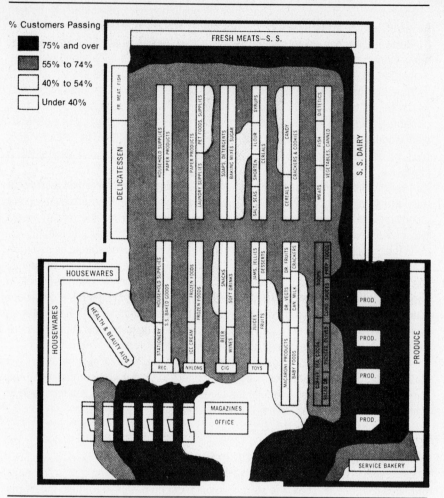

% Customers Passing

■ 75% and over

▨ 55% to 74%

□ 40% to 54%

□ Under 40%

Figure 7-1 **Percent of Consumers Passing by Different Sections of a Supermarket**

Source: "Colonial Study," *Progressive Grocer* (1964), p. C 90. Reprinted from *Progressive Grocer*, 1964, with permission.

their objections in a silent but forceful manner: they do not return to the store! Have a well-defined entrance to the sales area. Again, this goes hand in hand with a simple layout (Exhibit 7–7).

Using Color, Design, and Lighting

Design patterns and color combinations should be planned on the layout so that they can effectively direct the attention of consumers to a particular location in subtle and attractive ways. Color and lighting can be used to create the effect of a separate

Exhibit 7-7 Illustration of a Well-Defined Entrance to the Sales Area
Note the room divider and departmental sign. Different floor patterns can also be used to direct consumer traffic.

Source: Reprinted by permission of Mercantile Stores Company.

department without using permanent walls or fixtures. Built-in fixtures and permanent walls are difficult to change if remodeling becomes necessary.[2] An illustration of the use of portable designs and fixtures is presented in Exhibit 7–8.

Lighting should also be planned as part of the layout. Lights are not simply fixtures that provide illumination; they create moods and atmospheres. Only certain types of lighting are appropriate for particular retail stores. Neglect of this results in consumer fatigue, improper reflection, and shadows on merchandise. Additionally, the shade of fluorescent lights must be considered, particularly in apparel shops. In artificial light a beautiful blue sweater may appear to be purple. Lighting, in both quantity and quality, is of paramount importance.

Planning Definite Themes

The layout and decor should not be simply brought together in a haphazard fashion. A definite theme is more effective. A central theme, such as a North Woods, Mexican, or Hawaiian setting, helps give the store a personality and helps set the pace for departments within the store.

There are mixed feelings as to whether the theme of the store should follow the general theme of the shopping center. In general, if acceptance of the shopping center theme will tend to make the store another me-too retailer, it is wise to select something else. In many cases a slight variation from the central theme can achieve the desired results without a "sore thumb" effect. An overall North Woods shopping center theme might be varied by using a ghost town or Alpine village theme. Such a change is distinctive, yet it complements the overall theme.

Exhibit 7-8 **Illustration of the Use of Flexible Fixtures**
Source: Reprinted courtesy of Foxmoor, division of the Melville Corporation.

Avoiding Natural Shoplifting Areas

A layout can be designed to minimize shoplifting. Secluded areas or areas that do not lend themselves to observation by store personnel are open invitations to shoplifters. Store fixtures and related displays should be kept low so that maximum customer visibility is maintained.

Capitalizing on the Flow of Traffic

The entire display layout should be neither too random nor overly rigid. Two major patterns are used in planning store layouts that follow the natural flow of traffic. The *grid pattern* routes consumer traffic in a manner similar to that of the rectangular street plan of a city (Figure 7-2) and creates a series of aisles similar to those found in most supermarkets, where customers' movements are directed by the aisles and fixtures. A warehouse image may also be created by the grid layout pattern unless colorful walls and fixtures are used to enhance its appearance.

The grid layout is designed to promote retailing efficiency, since it maximizes the use of selling space and simplifies security. As noted in Figure 7-2, customers are practically forced to pass by the bakery, produce, meat, dairy, and frozen food departments. This is a major characteristic of a grid layout in a mass merchandise outlet. In such cases the grid design pulls the maximum number of customers past the sides and back of the store. In department and specialty stores, the grid pattern is usually designed to draw consumer traffic down the main central aisles. In these cases high demand merchandise is placed near the sides of the building to draw consumer traffic to these otherwise slow-moving areas.

The *free-flow pattern* allows consumers to form their own traffic patterns and browse within the outlet. It is a more casual pattern, since right angles are eliminated (Figure 7–3). It is most appropriate for shopping goods and specialty stores, in which the customer wishes to compare and evaluate products in a relaxed atmosphere. Less merchandise and fewer fixtures can be placed per square foot of space in the free-flow pattern than in the grid pattern; however, the more favorable consumer impression generated by the free-flow pattern offsets the higher display costs in stores where relaxed shopping is important.

Rising space costs have forced even the most exclusive department stores to discontinue using free-flow arrangements on their prime first floor selling space. Thus, one currently finds the grid layout being used on the main floors of multilevel department and specialty stores. These same stores may use the free-flow arrangement in other areas where the space cost is less and where it is important to maximize consumer convenience and allow the consumer to browse and make impulse purchases in a more relaxed atmosphere.

Supermarkets and other outlets where customers make frequent repurchases of the same items can use the grid pattern more effectively. In these stores consumers follow the same traffic pattern regularly and become familiar with the location of the various products. The customers want to make their purchases with a minimum amount of time and effort, and the grid pattern layout is both efficient in displaying products and convenient for consumers with these shopping motives.

Most stores use some combination of these two basic layout patterns to display various types of merchandise better and to serve the different target market customers. The "shoppe" or *boutique concept* utilizes the free-flow pattern within a department that sells related merchandise. In effect, these boutiques become small specialty stores within a large store.

Thus, the boutique arrangement brings complete offerings together in one department instead of having the merchandise displayed in many separate departments. This allows the shopper with a particular interest to shop in one location for a complete assortment of related merchandise. For example, a ski boutique in a department store will feature not only skis, ski boots, and ski poles but also warmup boots, sweaters, pants, goggles, gloves, socks and other appropriate clothing.

Even slight modifications to the traditional grid layout, such as the forty-five degree entrance shown in Figure 7– 4, can be used to offer more consumer exposure to merchandise that depends upon heavy consumer traffic.

Grouping Merchandise

Assemble together items of merchandise that carry a natural association. Hammers and nails, syrup and pancake mixes are examples. A close examination of merchandise may reveal some previously unthought-of related items and chances for extra sales. Studies by *Progressive Grocer* have demonstrated that sales were nearly

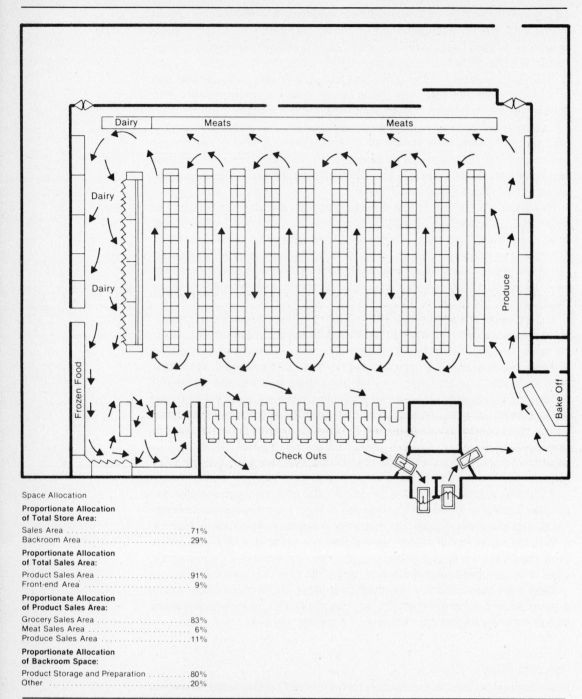

Space Allocation

**Proportionate Allocation
of Total Store Area:**

Sales Area 71%
Backroom Area 29%

**Proportionate Allocation
of Total Sales Area:**

Product Sales Area 91%
Front-end Area 9%

**Proportionate Allocation
of Product Sales Area:**

Grocery Sales Area 83%
Meat Sales Area 6%
Produce Sales Area .11%

**Proportionate Allocation
of Backroom Space:**

Product Storage and Preparation 80%
Other 20%

Figure 7-2 **Supermarket Design Using a Grid Layout**

Other space includes areas used for mezzanines, conference rooms, employees' lounges,
restrooms, compressor rooms, janitor closets, etc.

Features of this suggested supermarket layout are:

1. A right-hand single traffic pattern for customer shopping. Studies continue to show that this pattern minimizes shopping congestion, allows for a relatively smooth flow of traffic, and enhances maximum product exposure.

2. The attractive, high impulse bakery (including rolls, pies, cakes, cookies, doughnuts, etc.) and produce departments are located first and second respectively in the shopping pattern.

3. The attractive natural color, and freshness of the fresh fruits and vegetables, along with a good margin, help the produce department to attain either the first or second location in the shopping pattern.

4. The meat department is located across the back of the store. This location gives the department repeated exposures as the shopper travels the grocery aisles, encourages wider aisles in the meat area, and greater customer convenience.

5. The dairy department is located next, about as far from the entrance as possible, because nearly 80 percent of the shoppers will shop in this department. This location assures that the shopper will be exposed to a wide variety of other merchandise while making a dairy item purchase.

6. The frozen food department is placed near the end of the shopping pattern to minimize the chances of the product thawing with resulting quality depreciation. Placing it last also serves to eliminate some doubling back in the shopping pattern by customers as is presently the case in many stores.

7. As much as possible, the back room storage and preparation areas should be located so they are immediately back of, and supporting their respective sales display areas. All doorways for handling the receiving products should be at least five feet wide to accommodate materials handling equipment.

Source: Clyde R. Cunningam and Harold S. Ricker, "Supermarket Guidelines—Store Design and Layout," *Food Distribution Research Bulletin No. 1*, University of Missouri, 1973, pp. 29–32.

twice as great for pretzels and potato chips when these items were displayed near complementary products such as soft drinks, as when they were near noncomplementary items such as milk and cheese.[3]

Departmentalize when possible. Form sections of the store into departments such as shoes, men's clothes, bakery goods, and auto parts. Departmentalization personalizes the store and tends to reduce the feeling on the part of both consumers and store personnel that they are numbers in a vast wilderness of merchandise (Exhibit 7–7). Also, management planning and control are facilitated if operating expenses and receipts are maintained separately on a departmental basis. However, because of increased labor costs and computerized merchandise control, central "cash-wrap" stations on the floor are diminishing the importance of departmental considerations.

Two criteria can be used to group merchandise into departments. The generic or functional kind of merchandise (such as footwear, or health and beauty aids) is one criterion. The other involves using target market groups (economy-minded consumers might be served from a bargain basement).

The location of the various departments depends on such considerations as the size and shape of the building, the type of clientele, the nature of the merchandise, and the value of the floor space. In a single-floor outlet, the most valuable space is the area nearest the store entrance. This is the area with the heaviest consumer traffic. Floor space decreases in value as one moves from the entrance to the rear of the building. In a multifloor building, the space decreases in value as one moves up or down from the main floor.

Merchandise departments usually are located according to their sales-generating capacity relative to the value of the space occupied. Frequently-purchased items

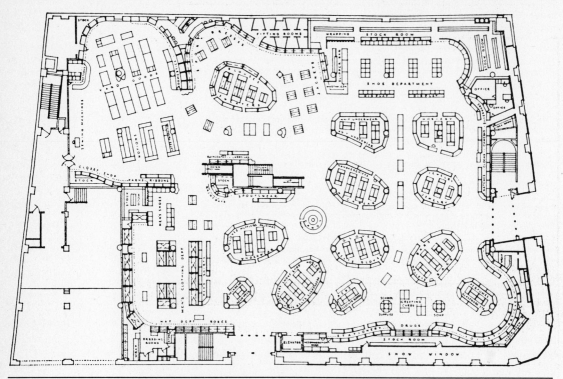

Figure 7-3 **Illustration of Free-Flow Layout Pattern
in a Department Store**

Source: William R. Davidson and Alton F. Doody, *Retailing Management*, 3rd ed. (New
York: The Ronald Press Company, 1966), p.168. Reprinted by permission of John Wiley &
Sons.

usually are given the most favored space allocations. However, the nature of the
merchandise also must be considered. Impulse items, high-rate replacement items,
and convenience goods, such as cigarettes, should be located in the heaviest traffic
areas because consumers will not search them out. Shopping goods, such as
furniture, and specialty goods, such as sporting goods, can be located in less heavily
traveled areas because they will pull traffic to the outer locations. Bulky merchandise, such as large appliances, or boats, generally are located in less heavy consumer traffic areas.

If possible, it is advisable to locate departments with different seasonal sales
patterns adjacent to each other. An exchange of selling space among adjacent
departments can provide a more efficient use of space if the departments have
different seasonal selling peaks.

A store that merchandises on many levels may display a portion of its offerings
on the main floor. Impulse items and a small sample of the type of merchandise that
a consumer can expect to see in the primary location are also usually displayed on
the main floor. This main-floor display can encourage consumers to make a trip to
the primary department location.

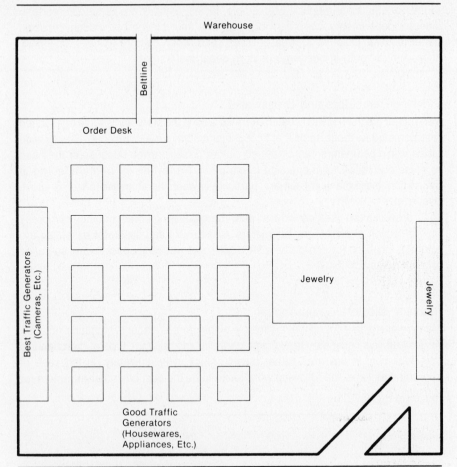

Figure 7–4 **Illustration of the Use of a
45-Degree Angle Entrance in a Grid Layout**
*Jewelcor, Inc., a New York–based operator of 14 catalog showrooms,
uses this forty-five degree angle entrance to gain immediate exposure to
its jewelry counters. The layout subtly forces customers to pass
high-profit displays in order to reach promotional items and the order
counter in any of its catalog showrooms.*
Source: "Catalog Plan Designed to Direct Traffic," *Chain Store Age*, March 1973, p. E34.
Reprinted by permission.

Department stores (retail stores that carry several lines of merchandise that are
organized into separate departments for the purpose of promotion, service, and
accounting control) provide an example of the most extreme use of departmentalization. Each department is set up almost as an individual store, with separate
merchandise and expense budgets, individual accounting statements, and inventory
control. Such departmentalizing frequently results in duplication of lines in the various departments of the store. This is done not only to reach different market
segments but also to promote in-store competition among the buyers and managers

of the various departments. For example, ladies' blouses are carried in fourteen different departments (basement blouses, first floor blouse bar, budget blouses, better blouses, junior sportswear, misses sportswear, couture blouses, collegiate shop, and so forth) in one large eastern department store.

Planning Perimeters and Crosswalks

Perimeters are the heaviest customer traffic area in the store and should be planned to accommodate those items that account for a store's major revenue. Unduly wide aisles within perimeters can create consumer dissatisfaction because of the need to cross continually from one side to the other. Narrow aisles create a feeling of claustrophobia in many consumers, particularly when merchandise is stored above eye level.

Crosswalks are often considered poor merchandising areas, but they can break up the canyon effect of long perimeters. Crosswalks and escalator exits also are effective locations for end-of-the-aisle displays of weekend specials and so-called impulse items (Exhibit 7–9).

Planning Midstore Sales Appeal

Many retailers have found that the middle of the store is a poor merchandising area. As a result, it is necessary to examine carefully and relist the type of merchandise that sells best in this area rather than to stock indiscriminately. In the case of supermarket items, the following were found to be the best customer attractors for a midstore location.[4]

Product Group	Percent of Total Store Traffic Attracted
Coffee	66
Cookies and crackers	65
Canned vegetables	62
Baking needs	60
Paper products	59
Canned soup	58
Laundry supplies	55
Cereal	55
Sugar	55
Salad dressing and oils	53

Designing "Eyeball" Merchandising

Studies and experience have demonstrated that merchandise displayed at eye level sells better than merchandise at either a very low or high level. *Eye-level merchandising* should be planned for a retailer's "bread and butter" lines. Retailers can locate brands and items within a merchandise category to maximize profitability. Per

Exhibit 7-9 **Illustration of Mobile Displays Near the Escalators**
*The two cubicles move up and down, providing maximum display
exposure to customers who are riding the escalators.*

unit margins, sales volume, and the sales sensitivity of each brand and/or item must be considered. Brands and/or items providing the highest profit contribution as calculated by margin times volume divided by space used should usually be given the eye-level shelf space.[5] An exception to this rule would be an item whose popularity is so strong that consumers will search for the item no matter what height level it occupies.

Shelves should not be more than fifty-four to sixty inches high, or they will block the view of consumers. And, of course, sales will suffer if the consumer cannot see the merchandise. In the case of mass merchandising displays, consideration should also be given to peripheral vision, since few consumers walk sideways down a shopping aisle.

Planning Return per Square, Linear, or Cubic Foot

Plan the *return per square foot* of selling space. A dollar return per some measurable unit of space is the most common measurement used by retailers to establish rental rates and to gauge merchandising success. (This concept is discussed in detail in Chapter 4). While it should always remain in the back of the retailer's mind, it should not be overemphasized in the planning of layout. For example, if a retailer finds that men's undershirts return more per square foot than any other product, should the store stock contain nothing but this item? Unless there is sufficient demand for a specialty retail store of this nature, the answer is obviously no. Yet if reliance upon return per measurable unit of space is the sole consideration, dangerous merchandising errors such as this can occur. Likewise, complete dependence upon other considerations involved in layout can result in stores that are works of art but have a very low dollar return.

Planning Locations of Sales-Supporting Areas

Plan the locations and space occupied by sales-supporting and sales-generating equipment. Multifloor outlets require stairways, elevators, or escalators to move customers from one floor to another. Stores that merchandise from the ground level, basement, and only one floor above the ground level can often provide only a stationary stairway. Larger stores must provide some more elaborate system. Customers do not like to wait for elevators or escalators or to climb steps; so adequate facilities must be provided if consumers are to be attracted to another floor.

Sales-supporting equipment and space must be arranged so that goods can be received, inspected, marked, and placed on the shelves with minimum effort. Mechanical handling equipment, communication devices, and other labor-saving equipment should be considered and incorporated into the store layout if economically feasible. The storage and work areas should be located in nonprime areas, but they should be easily accessible to the selling areas. These storage and work areas are generally located at the rear of single-floor outlets and not on the ground floor of multifloor outlets.

Higher retail land values and increased building costs have caused some retailers to reduce the amount of nonselling space in the retail outlet or to move the nonselling area to less valuable space, such as mezzanines.[6] Faster and more frequent delivery and labor-saving techniques, such as prepackaged and pre-marked merchandise that is ready for display when it arrives at the store, are being used to reduce the amount of space devoted to nonselling activities. Even so, from 25 to 50 percent of the total floor space in most stores is used for nonselling activities. These nonselling activities can be grouped into four categories: (1) those that must be located in some particular area of the store, such as receiving docks, (2) those that relate directly to certain departments, such as the kitchen adjoining the restaurant, (3) those that do not require any particular location, such as executive offices, and (4) those that involve direct customer contact, such as escalators, dressing rooms, and rest rooms.

It should be noted that only categories three and four allow for much flexibility as far as location is concerned. The nonselling activities described in category three offer the most flexibility. For this reason, executive activities are usually performed in the lowest-value areas, such as upper floors away from the consumer traffic.

The other area that would appear to offer some flexibility in layout involves those activities that involve direct consumer contact. The complex nature of each activity influences where the facilities are located and how they are operated. The following discussion points up factors to consider in planning these consumer contact centers.

Checkout Areas Plan the placement and size of checkout areas. There is no other single area in a store more important than the checkout counter. Once customers have decided upon their purchases, they want to make the purchase transaction as quickly as possible.

Most of the problems at the checkout counter can be controlled only by providing adequate checkout facilities and by careful scheduling of clerks, but the location can have important bearings on the efficiency of operation. If the checkout stand is designed so that incoming and outgoing customers mingle in traffic jams, customers will be dissatisfied, and there is a good chance that shoplifting will increase.

At best, a checkout counter necessitates a short wait. The checkout area should be planned with a layout that incorporates attractive impulse items (items bought on an unplanned basis) in point-of-purchase displays. One mass retailing chain has deliberately engineered a five-minute wait per customer by designing the checkout system to generate an average waiting line of three people. This retailer has determined the average time, and deviation from the average time, that each checkout activity (sorting, ringing up, and bagging) requires. The three-customer-average wait line was selected because it makes better use of the cashiers' time. In addition, the retailer may encourage impulse buying at the checkout stands by placing last-minute convenience items in the checkout area.

The wisdom of such a plan depends on how dissatisfied consumers become over the wait. The consumer is likely to react negatively when the line happens to be a little longer than planned. If this happens, the loss in patronage could easily amount to a loss in future profits that will exceed the savings in cashier wages and the extra margin generated by the impulse items purchased.

Dressing Rooms and Rest Rooms Incorporate dressing rooms and rest rooms in the plan. Unless they are incorporated in the original layout and overall theme, they tend to become conspicuous boxes and can easily detract from the overall purpose of creating a favorable buying mood. For security reasons, only one entrance should be provided to the dressing room. This entrance should not be located near a stockroom, stairwell, rest room, or outside exit.

The overall store theme should give the planner many ideas for creative design for the dressing room and rest room areas. In a circus theme, the dressing rooms might be identified and designed as the "magic show." These areas should be used to sell merchandise, but the dressing rooms in most stores are hardly designed to encourage purchases. It is difficult for the most expensive suit or dress to complement the wearer in a coffin-like upright rectangle complete with faded mirror and unpainted walls. A dirty, unkempt, barren rest room can suddenly reduce the image of any store to little more than that of a backwoods filling station.

The problem of rest room security is becoming increasingly serious. Rest rooms located in large, busy retail stores have been the scenes of assaults and robberies that have occurred during prime daytime hours. This has caused the management of some stores to use security guards in the rest rooms.

Planning Uses for Dead Areas

Regardless of the best planning, dead spaces are likely to occur within the store. Such areas as corners often become dead areas. These can be utilized for vending machines, a play area for children (complete with toys), or for other functions that attract customers and add directly or indirectly to sales.

Summary

Each retail outlet has an image. Retail management must discover what factors are the most important to the firm's target market customers. The store's entire merchandise and promotional offering and its physical appearance must be coordinated to achieve the image demanded by its target market customers. Stores that have a more distinctive image are more likely to appeal to a specific market segment.

Retail outlets are being remodeled more frequently to meet the changing needs of their customers. The remodeling may take the form of a major renovation or it may merely represent a facelift. Regardless of the extent of the change, it must be planned from the viewpoint of the consumers sensory reactions to scent, sound, touch, and sight. The image control process includes using land properly. Using a lot of open space and fountains creates a more prestigious image, but it also increases the cost for land. This increased cost must be passed on to the consumer. Attractive building exteriors are a good investment since they can increase the outlet's consumer traffic.

Interior fixtures and equipment must be selected to go along with the rest of the store, so they must be coordinated with the interior lighting and color scheme. The arrangement of the fixtures, merchandise, and equipment should be designed so that consumer exposure is maximized. The two major forms of store layouts are the grid pattern and the free-flow arrangement. Most mass merchandisers use the grid layout because it allows a maximum amount of merchandise to be displayed from a given floor space. Department stores are also using the grid layout on their main floor, but they may use a free-flow arrangement in other areas to increase consumer convenience and allow the consumer to browse and make impulse purchases in a more relaxed atmosphere.

Consumers must be able to locate merchandise with a minimum of effort. Retailers have established separate departments and boutiques to make this an easier task for consumers. Placing high demand and high margin merchandise at the consumer's eye level and in prime space areas also allows consumers to find the merchandise more easily and increases store profits.

Retailers should consult the Small Business Administration, industry trade associations, and similar stores in other locations when they begin to plan a layout. The entire physical project (including outside surroundings, parking lot, exterior building appearance, and interior layout and appearance) creates an overall store personality for consumers. Each consumer will perceive the store image differently, so the entire project should be designed to appeal to the store's selected target market group.

A list of items that the Small Business Administration believes must be planned into the proper retail image creation process is presented in Exhibit 7–10 on page 208.

Questions

1. At what eye level should you put goods designed to appeal to children?

2. Considering the general advisability of diversified merchandise, how would you account for the existence of stores that sell only ties or only shirts. Where are stores of this type usually found? What generalizations can you make about this type of retailing with regard to risk, target segment, marketing mix, location, and so forth?

3. What is *visual merchandising?*

4. State your opinion of the importance to retail stores of image creation and control.

5. Distinguish between the grid pattern and the free-form pattern of store layouts. In what types of stores is each pattern most useful? Why?

6. How is the concept of image related to the wheel of retailing?

7. What factors might cause a retailer to want to change an image? How would a retailer go about deciding whether it would be beneficial to do so?

8. In what types of retail establishments would you expect the sensuous approach to selling to be most effective? Can you make any generalizations about types of products and demand for those products which are sold by using a highly sensuous approach?

9. In what types of stores is the free-flow traffic pattern most useful? Why? In what types of stores is the grid pattern most useful? Why?

10. Considering as many variables as you have studied (location, layout, risk, retailing mix, and so forth), suggest a store design, given the following parameters: supermarket in a middle-class suburb; private bookstore in a college town; sporting goods store in a wealthy suburb.

Exhibit 7-10 **Checklist for Interior Arrangement and Display**

Layout

1. Are your fixtures low enough and signs so placed that the customer can get a bird's-eye view of the store and tell in what direction to go for wanted goods?
2. Do your aisle and counter arrangements tend to stimulate a circular traffic flow through the store?
3. Do your fixtures (and their arrangement), signs, lettering, and colors all create a coordinated and unified effect?
4. Before any supplier's fixtures are accepted, do you make sure they conform in color and design to what you already have?
5. Do you limit the use of hanging signs to special sale events?
6. Are your counters and aisle tables *not* overcrowded with merchandise?
7. Are your ledges and cashier/wrapping stations kept free of boxes, unneeded wrapping materials, personal effects, and odds and ends?
8. Do you keep trash bins out of sight?

Merchandise emphasis

1. Do your signs referring to specific goods tell the customer something significant about them, rather than simply naming the products and their prices?
2. For your advertised goods, do you have prominent signs, including tear sheets at the entrances, to inform and guide customers to their exact location in the store?
3. Do you prominently display both advertised and nonadvertised specials at the ends of counters as well as at the point of sale?
4. Are both your national and private brands highlighted in your arrangement and window display?
5. Wherever feasible, do you give the more colorful merchandise in your stock preference in display?
6. In the case of apparel and home furnishings, do the items that reflect your store's fashion sense or fashion leadership get special display attention at all times?
7. In locating merchandise in your store, do you always consider the productivity of space—vertical as well as horizontal?
8. Is your self-service merchandise arranged so as to attract the customer and assist her in selection by the means indicated below:
   a. Is each category grouped under a separate sign?
   b. Is the merchandise in each category arranged according to its most significant characteristic—whether color, style, size or price?
   c. In apparel categories, is the merchandise arranged by price lines or zones to assist the customer to make a selection quickly?
   d. Is horizontal space usually devoted to different items and styles within a category (vertical space being used for different sizes—smallest at the top, largest at the bottom)?
   e. Are impulse items interspersed with demand items and not placed across the aisle from them, where many customers will not see them?

Source: U.S. Small Business Administration, "Small Store Planning for Growth," *Small Business Management Series No. 33* (Washington, D.C.: Government Printing Office, 1966), pp. 98–99.

Footnotes

1. William J. E. Crissy, "Image: What Is It?" *MSU Business Topics* 19 (Winter 1971): 77–80.

2. "Kennedy's Uses Lights Instead of Walls," *Chain Store Age,* Executive's Ed., September 1971, pp. E46-E49.

3. *Consumer Dynamics in the Super Market* (New York: Progressive Grocer, n.d.), p. 2.

4. Ibid.

5. James F. Engel, David T. Kollat, and Roger D. Blackwell, *Consumer Behavior* (New York: Holt, Rinehart and Winston, 1968), p. 485.

6. "Double-Deck Saves SCOA Backroom," *Chain Store Age,* Executive's Ed., March 1970, p. E20.

Case Study

Wilson Supermarkets

The management of Wilson Supermarkets was concerned about the low level of sales in two of its newest stores in San Diego, the Corona Hills Store and the Martin Park Store. Both stores had been built within the last two years and both were producing fewer sales than had been projected.

A survey was conducted in an effort to determine the reasons for the poor performance of the stores.

A total of 4000 questionnaries were sent to households in the areas surrounding the two stores. A random sampling procedure had been used to select the households.

By the end of the survey, 900 questionnaries had been returned. This was felt to be a very good response rate.

The questionnaires were sorted into Corona Hills and Martin Park groups and the responses were analyzed.

Results

The respondents were analyzed according to the number of times they said they shopped in Wilson Supermarkets. These groups were called "Wilson shopped—the most" and "Wilson shopped—the least." The remainder of the respondents were called "all others."

Of the 425 responses from Corona Hills, 7 percent were "Wilson shopped most," 5.8 percent were "Wilson shopped least," and 87.2 percent were "all others."

Of the 481 responses from Martin Park, 11 percent were "Wilson shopped most," 9 percent were "Wilson shopped least," and 80 percent were "all others."

A set of 23 attributes for an ideal store were analyzed from the questionnaire concerning the consumer's perception of an ideal supermarket. The respondents indicated the degree of importance that each attribute would have by checking *most important, important, not major,* and *least important.*

The scores were tabulated, added, and divided by the number of responses for each attribute. The average ranged between one and three, with the lowest average indicating the highest degree of importance.

After the scores were tabulated, the twenty-three attributes were ranged according to their importance as perceived by the respondents.

ABOUT THE SUPERMARKET WHERE YOU SHOP THE MOST[A]

Place an X by the names of the stores you have shopped in during the last six months.

Cents-Able _____   Red Giant _____   Western _____

Oceanic _____   Alberts _____   Dollar Saver _____

Wilson _____

There are many things that you may like or dislike about the store where you shop the most. Indicate how you feel about them by placing an X in the figure that best describes your feeling about the question asked.

Factors	Like Very Much	Like Some	Does Not Matter	Dis-Like Some	Dislike Very Much
Store appearance?	_____	_____	_____	_____	_____
Store prices?	_____	_____	_____	_____	_____
Non-foods?	_____	_____	_____	_____	_____
Store location from where you live?	_____	_____	_____	_____	_____
Store arrangement?	_____	_____	_____	_____	_____
Store's own brand named goods?	_____	_____	_____	_____	_____
Store bakery?	_____	_____	_____	_____	_____
Produce (fruits and vegetables)?	_____	_____	_____	_____	_____
Store personnel?	_____	_____	_____	_____	_____
Services the store has?	_____	_____	_____	_____	_____
Meat poultry and fish?	_____	_____	_____	_____	_____

A. An identical set of questions was asked "About the supermarket where you shop the least."

WHAT CORONA HILLS SHOPPERS LIKED AND DISLIKED ABOUT WILSON

Factors	% Wilson Shopped Most			% Wilson Shopped Least			% Others Most Shopped		
	Like	No Diff	Dis-like	Like	No Diff	Dis-like	Like	No Diff	Dis-like
Location	87	7	6	67	4	29	96	2	2
Appearance	94	0	6	63	21	16	60	10	30
Prices	67	13	20	42	12	46	63	3	34
Personnel	93	3	4	63	17	20	90	5	5
Arrangement	94	6	0	76	12	12	87	4	9
Meat, Poultry, Fish	83	3	14	32	16	52	78	7	15
Produce	86	3	11	79	9	12	84	3	13
Private Label	57	23	20	37	32	31	69	15	16
Services	70	23	7	34	50	16	80	15	5
Store Bakery	12	72	16	50	40	10	59	32	9
Non-Foods	43	43	14	26	52	22	59	32	9

WHAT MARTIN PARK SHOPPERS LIKED AND DISLIKED ABOUT WILSON

Factors	% Wilson Shopped Most			% Wilson Shopped Least			% Others Most Shopped		
	Like	No Diff	Dis-like	Like	No Diff	Dis-like	Like	No Diff	Dis-like
Location	100	0	0	73	10	17	92	3	5
Appearance	95	5	0	95	5	0	83	5	12
Prices	69	0	31	50	5	45	58	4	38
Personnel	76	10	14	54	27	19	81	2	17
Arrangement	76	9	15	81	5	14	74	9	17
Meat, Poultry, Fish	74	9	18	68	9	23	79	2	19
Produce	83	0	17	77	9	14	73	11	16
Private Brand	60	17	23	50	14	36	73	11	16
Service	72	18	10	54	32	14	72	14	14
Non-Foods	47	50	3	32	64	4	58	28	14

WHAT CORONA HILLS SHOPPERS PREFERRED
IN COMPETITORS' STORES OVER WILSON

Factors	Wilson Average	Others Average	Preference	
			Wilson	Others
Location	1.765	1.665		+
Appearance	1.930	1.990	+	
Prices	2.67	3.10	+	
Personnel	2.06	2.065	+	
Arrangement	1.87	2.18	+	
Meat, Poultry, Fish	2.745	2.81	+	
Produce	2.06	2.135	+	
Private Label	2.755	2.885	+	
Services	2.37	2.27		+
Store Bakery	2.855	2.48		+
Non-Foods	2.76	2.41		+

Note: Lower average indicates greater consumer preference than higher average.

WHAT MARTIN PARK SHOPPERS PREFERED
IN COMPETITORS' STORES OVER WILSON

Factors	Wilson Average	Others Average	Preference	
			Wilson	Others
Location	1.69	1.88	+	
Appearance	1.74	2.26	+	
Prices	2.74	2.79	+	
Personnel	2.205	2.36	+	
Arrangement	1.95	2.05	+	
Meat, Poultry, Fish	2.3905	2.8105	+	
Produce	2.07	2.64	+	
Private Label	2.6905	2.4305		+
Services	2.2505	2.4705	+	
Non-Foods	2.53	2.4605		+

Note: Lower average indicates greater consumer preference than high average.

YOUR IDEAL SUPERMARKET

Here is a list of some of the things customers generally find important in a supermarket. If you were to describe your ideal supermarket check the space next to each item below that indicates its importance to you in an ideal supermarket. Check only one space for each item:

Factors	(1) Most Important	(2) Important, not major	(3) Least Important
Friendly atmosphere			
Rest rooms			
Store's brand name			
Snack bar			
New items			
Store hours			
Check cashing			
Checkout baggers			
Personnel at meat counter			
Low prices			
Trading stamps			
Nationally advertised brands			
Friendly store personnel			
Convenient parking			
Health & beauty aids			
Store cleanliness			
Wide selection of merchandise			
Advertised specials			
Wide, clear aisles			
Location of product			
High quality meat			
Store easy to get to			
Fresh produce			

THE IDEAL STORE, MARTIN PARK

Factors	Shop Wilson Most Rank	Shop Wilson Least Rank	Shop All Others Rank
Friendly atmosphere	14	10	16
Restrooms	19	22	20
Store's own brand name	20	20	21
Snack bar	23	23	23
New items	18	20	18
Store hours	17	16	15
Check cashing	15	10	10
Checkout baggers	16	7	8
Personnel at meat counter	11	10	17
Low prices	4	2	3
Trading stamps	22	19	22
Nationally advertised brands	9	1	11
Friendly store personnel	11	10	12
Convenient parking	10	5	9
Health & beauty aids	21	15	19
Store cleanliness	2	5	6
Wide selection of merchandise	7	17	4
Advertised specials	11	18	14
Wide, clear aisles	6	7	7
Location of product	4	10	13
High quality meat	7	4	2
Store easy to get to	3	7	5
Fresh produce	1	2	1

THE IDEAL STORE, CORONA HILLS

Factors	Shop Wilson Most	Shop Wilson Least	Shop All Others
	Rank	Rank	Rank
Friendly atomosphere	14	13	13
Restrooms	20	22	21
Store's own brand name	20	20	20
Snack bar	23	23	23
New items	18	18	18
Store hours	16	17	17
Check cashing	16	9	14
Checkout baggers	9	7	10
Personnel at meat counter	14	16	16
Low prices	3	5	6
Trading stamps	22	21	22
Nationally advertised brands	10	11	11
Friendly store personnel	11	8	12
Convenient parking	5	3	5
Health & beauty aids	19	19	19
Store cleanliness	1	1	1
Wide selection of merchandise	2	4	4
Advertised specials	12	14	9
Wide, clear aisles	8	12	8
Location of product	12	15	15
High quality meat	6	6	3
Store easy to get to	7	10	7
Fresh produce	4	2	2

Discussion Questions

1. What does the data contained in the tables mean to the Wilson Supermarkets?

2. What is Wilson's current image?

3. What should Wilson's image be?

4. What do you recommend that the management of Wilson's Supermarkets do? Explain.

Case Study

Bob's Men's Stores

The original Bob's store is located in Omaha and does approximately $1 million in sales volume per year.

The store carries medium-priced branded wearing apparel for men and boys. This line of merchandise is designed to appeal to the "young of all ages." These styles were described by a member of management as "traditional, but with a flair of what's-going-on." Way-out fashion boutique and formal men's attire are excluded from the product line.

Several new Bob's stores are scheduled in the company's expansion program in other metropolitan areas. These new stores are planned around the merchandising concept of selling men's wear to the wife or mother, along with the male consumer.

Mr. Robert O'Neill, executive president and owner, believes that it is difficult to motivate men to buy new wearing apparel and that women buy around 60 percent of men's clothes, especially accessories.

With this philosophy in mind, the advertising sales personnel and in-store decor were planned with women in mind.

Advertising would be pointed toward the wife or mother, and suggestions had been made about a series of "witty ads" such as "Bring your best friend's husband." A free bottle of perfume for women shoppers was also considered as an incentive.

Store location was also an important factor, and it was felt that new regional shopping centers would be the future sites.

With the large numbers of men's wear shops in existence, management was convinced that a new merchandising strategy was essential, and believed it had hit upon a sound approach.

Discussion Questions

1. Do you agree that most married men cannot be motivated to buy men's wear?

2. What do you think of the strategy being planned for new Bob's stores?

3. Would you advise the firm to seek out locations near women's wear shops?

4. What type of in-store decor and sales personnel would you suggest as most likely to appeal to women customers?

Chapter 8

Buying and Handling Merchandise

1. To be able to discuss the buying process and the organization needed to implement buying decisions.

2. To be able to describe a system for successfully buying profitable goods at market.

3. To understand the procedures used for evaluating merchandise.

4. To be able to assess the impact of vendors shifting the marketing functions of financing and inventory accumulation downward to retailers.

5. To understand the buyers' role in managing the transportation function for their retail store(s).

6. To know how a systems approach can be used to reduce loss through stock shrinkage, employee theft, and shoplifting.

Learning Goals

buying process	keystoning policy	handling process
economic order quantity	work the line	stock shortages
marketing middlemen	negotiation process	pilferage

Key Terms and Concepts

The buying process consists of four phases: search, evaluation, selection, and review. Search activities involve determining what to buy and from whom it should be purchased. Ideally, the retail merchant should formulate a merchandise plan that best reflects the needs of the firm's target market and then seek suppliers who can provide the products in a timely, profitable manner. Unfortunately, in the short run the real world of retailing does not conform to the ideal model of marketing theory. Usually the search process is implemented by entering the market with a basic outline of desired products, which is subsequently compared with what is currently available in the market. Some large retailers, such as Sears, Roebuck and Company can go directly to manufacturers and have products made to their exact specifications, thereby precisely implementing their merchandising plans. Small retailers may make suggestions to manufacturer's representatives that may result in ideal products being produced at some future date. However, for most retailers, the actual merchandise assortment represents a calculated compromise between ideal requirements, supplier substitutes and new innovative products selected to stimulate customer interest.

Evaluation activities involve the specific analysis of merchandise and vendor on the expected performance each is likely to yield in terms of quality and service. Naturally, the cost of the merchandise is also a prime consideration in the evaluation process, so alternatives are really evaluated on a benefit-to-cost basis.

The selection phase consists of the actual purchase of the merchandise from the chosen vendor after all available alternatives have been evaluated.

Review, the final phase of the buying process, involves the buyer's reappraisal of the activities in the previous three buying phases. This reappraisal is designed to identify trouble areas in the buying process so that mistakes are not repeated. The review process may also yield suggestions that can reduce the amount of time the buyer spends on the more menial and routine tasks, thereby allowing the buyer to spend more time on the important buying considerations.

Buying Merchandise

Buying merchandise is not an occupation for the timid or indecisive individual. Anyone who has difficulty making personal decisions probably has a limited future in retail management. Each decision situation will present certain alternatives that must be effectively evaluated in a short time frame and a choice or decision to be made expeditiously. Once the decision is made it must be implemented and the results evaluated. Anxiety or worry about past decisions is nonproductive and cannot be tolerated because it clouds present perceptions and impairs the quality of future decisions. Everyone makes mistakes; the effective buyer-manager recognizes mistakes, acknowledges them and learns from them.

Determining the Reorder Quantity for Staple Merchandise

Staple merchandise is considered to be any good that the retailer must always have on hand in appropriate quantities to meet customer demand. Usually the rate of sale of this type of merchandise is stable and thus quite predictable. Occasionally changes in the product or in competition or vendor relations require a major adjustment in the staple merchandise line, such as the introduction of stretch socks. This innovation revolutionized the sock market in a period of approximately three years. Given this length of time, most merchants were able to gradually shift their purchasing emphasis to the new line and ultimately clear out remaining stocks through selective price reductions.

Reorders of staple merchandise represent periodic replenishment of current stocks to maintain a balance in sizing or color assortment or price lining. The objective of this exercise is to balance opportunity costs associated with missing sales due to stock outs and the interest costs associated with carrying excessive inventory.

The reorder quantity is a function of the projected rate of sale for the goods (usually for one year), the length of time needed to replenish inventory stocks, the cost of reordering and the cost of carrying excessive inventory.

When one begins to calculate a staple reorder quantity, the retailer should review the past year's performance of the merchandise line with particular emphasis on the last six months' rate of sales by discrete categories. For example, a men's work clothes department manager might want to know the rate of sales of work uniform shirts by neck size and sleeve length in each price range. What were the projected sales during the period? What were the actual sales? How well did the manager anticipate demand? Were there any stock outs or totally depleted stocks during the period? If so, how many sales were missed? The answers to these questions will give the retailer better guidance as future demand estimates for the next selling period are corrected.

Each time an order is placed certain costs are incurred. Direct labor costs include counting the merchandise, preparing the order, and receiving, checking, marking, and placing the merchandise in appropriate locations for sale. Additional charges include computer time, mailing or telephone charges, and freight. If the firm places frequent small orders, the costs can rapidly reduce the overall profit margin.

Conversely, if the firm places large orders infrequently, it will incur large inventory costs. Such costs include spoilage or soiling of the goods, theft, insurance, rent of additional space, inventory taxes, and interest charges on the invested capital. These hidden charges often spell the difference between profit and loss in highly competitive merhandise lines, which carry low margins. Therefore the astute merchant attempts to optimize the relationship between ordering costs and inventory costs.

Assuming that the retailer has kept accurate, detailed records, the demand (D) for the goods can be determined along with the average order cost (OC) and the inventory costs (IC). The *economic order quantity* (EOQ) is that quantity of merchandise that achieves a balance between average order costs and inventory costs. The EOQ is determined by the formula:

$$EOQ = \frac{2\,(D)\,(OC)}{IC}$$

Even staple merchandise may experience unexpected surges in demand. Also, suppliers may be unable to make regular deliveries due to strikes, transportation breakdowns, unexpected bad weather or factory fires. Some retailers attempt to maintain a safety stock on hand to tide them over such situations. Figure 8–1 illustrates this concept. As the merchandise is sold, the stock level sinks toward the reorder point.

The reorder point is that point when the level of current inventory will just cover the anticipated demand during the replenishment period. When the merchandise reaches that level, an order for an economic order quantity should be executed. In the example one should note the "sawtooth" inventory pattern particularly in May when a wildcat transportation strike resulted in an unexpected one-week delay in delivery of the merchandise.

Most suppliers package merchandise in standard packings of a dozen to a box or a gross (144) to a carton to optimize their costs of operation. Alternately, transportation companies usually charge by the pound for shipments under 100 pounds but will give substantial discounts for shipments over 100 but less than 200 pounds. The result is that the retailer is often forced to buy more or less than the economic order quantity. The decision maker must exercise sound judgment and realize that the EOQ is just a decision tool, not a rule.

Transaction centers, when hooked to computer systems, can provide more current stock and sales data. Such systems also reduce the order placing cost and thereby make it economically possible to cut the reorder period. The computer system can also automatically prepare reorders and allow the buyer to *be* a buyer, not merely a reorder clerk.

Sufficient flexibility must be maintained, no matter what system is used, to allow the buyer to identify items quickly that are in a low or out-of-stock condition and to place rush orders to minimize out-of-stock occurrences.

Organizing for Buying

Every retailer, regardless of the size of the operation, must perform the buying process efficiently if the firm is going to remain competitive in the marketplace. The merchandise or service provided must be of the appropriate type, quality, and price demanded by the consumers. In addition, the firm's offerings must be available in quantities that will parallel consumer needs at the *time* that customers want to shop for such goods or services. The offering must also be placed in the store in a way that customers can easily locate it. Both the manager of a small independent outlet and the merchandise division of a large retail organization usually perform the job of buying and maintaining merchandise that will satisfy these consumer demands.

The merchandise division of the large independent store does more than buy merchandise. Usually it is also responsible for selling, planning, and control activities. Buyers are generally appointed for each major merchandise line, so they buy, direct sales, plan, and control their activities in view of consumer demand and profit opportunities. Divisional merchandise managers supervise the activities of these buyers so that all departments reflect the image that top retail management is striving to achieve. This organizational plan allows the division merchandise managers to devote the majority of their time to activities that plan and control the merchandise assortment. The execution of these plans is left largely to the buyers.

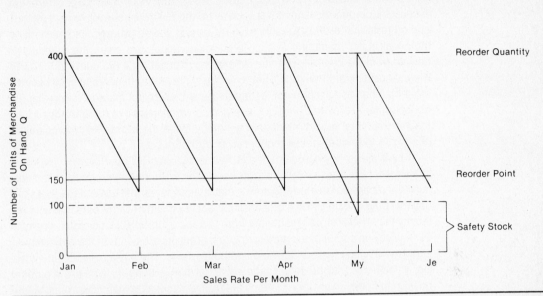

Figure 8-1 **Economic Order Quantity Model**

By contrast, responsibility for buying and selling is usually separated in the chain store organization. Central buyers usually establish an approved buying list that contains new and regular items that the central buyers believe will enhance the chain's merchandise assortment. These same central buyers also make the decision of removing items from the approved buying list when they believe the items are no longer contributing to the overall merchandise assortment. The negotiation of terms is also handled by the central buyers. Individual store managers are then generally responsible for actually placing orders for specific quantities of each item and presenting the merchandise appropriately to stimulate sales.

The central organization in some chain systems may perform all of the buying and reorder activities. In this case, the store managers are responsible only for proper merchandise presentation, servicing consumers, and other selling-related activities. Merchandise planning is then performed by merchandise controllers, each of whom supervises one or more central buyers. These merchandise controllers plan stock assortment requirements for the entire chain after appropriate sales forecasts have been made. The central buyer(s) orders the specific items in the quantities required by the entire chain. The incoming merchandise is then allocated to the individual store units by merchandise distributors.

Branch store operators may follow a different approach in the buying process. A branch organization usually tailors its merchandise/service assortment to reflect differences in local market conditions. Chain organizations are more likely to provide a standardized merchandise/service assortment to all geographical areas. Variations in merchandise/service assortments are usually required to meet differences in consumer preferences for items such as better-quality jewelry, clothing, furniture, and so forth that are fashionable, distinctive, and subject to regional peculiarities. Individual outlet managers in such branch operations are given the authority to deviate from the centrally devised purchasing plan because the demand for some merchandise differs from one area to another. The central buyers usually plan the initial merchandise assortment, establish the prices, select the new items that are added to the approved buying list, and decide which items are to be dropped from the list. Individual branch managers generally place the reorders in the quantities needed to meet the special requirements of that outlet.

A centralized buying committee is frequently used by both branch and chain store operations to allow regional representation in the buying process while maintaining the considerable buying power that is associated with volume purchases. A national buying committee may consist of approximately twenty persons, who are mostly the "better store" managers from various geographical locations. The centralized buying committee determines which products are good for the entire nation, and generally purchases the bread-and-butter items. The buying of specialty, fashion, or fad items may be done by the individual store managers, who are in a better position to know which specific items are likely to appeal to their customers. Allowing the individual store manager to buy specialty items that best reflect unique consumer differences can allow the store to set trends with its merchandise assortment. This kind of leadership can generate a progressive image that cannot be established with a buying organization that is not in tune with local consumer demand.

A disadvantage of the centralized buying committee is that an overestimated demand can quickly generate a massive overbought condition in some, if not all, geographical areas. Trading of inventory within the retail corporation is used to balance company inventory with consumer demand. The items that will not sell in one area or outlet frequently sell well in another (or even in a nearby outlet that serves a different type of consumer).

Centralized buying of some type usually is used despite the disadvantages cited. The discounts given for large-volume purchases are generally large enough to make it economically attractive. In addition, individual central buyers may believe that they must justify their existence by buying all items. Such buyers may hesitate to relinquish any outright buying functions to the individual outlet managers for fear of losing "political" power in the retail organization.

No matter what organizational system is used, sufficient flexibility must be maintained to allow the buyer to identify quickly new items that are being requested by consumers. Individual outlet managers can inform their district sales manager of the consumer requests. The district sales manager can then check with other outlet managers to determine if it is a common demand. The best ideas can then be passed on to the central buyer, who can check with other district sales managers to determine if the new item has appeal in other areas. If the item appears to have sufficient consumer demand, a manufacturer could be contacted to produce the item.

This "customer feedback" system can provide very useful new merchandise ideas for a retailer in fashion and other fast-changing merchandise lines. Use of the customer feedback system can result in a progressive or new merchandise image for retail outlets affiliated with such a retail organization. Smaller, independent retailers also have the opportunity to identify consumer needs. They have an additional advantage in being able to react to these needs without having to go through a large retail organization before the product can be ordered.

Resident Buying Offices Resident buying offices provide both independent and chain retailers with current marketing information that can enable the retail buyers to achieve higher stock turnover and better stock assortments. Both local and central retail buyers need a great deal of information, because a single buyer or store system cannot keep up with changes in (1) types of new products being offered, (2) offerings of the numerous suppliers, (3) business levels, and (4) consumer preferences for different types of goods. The resident buying office usually makes such information available to retail buyers. The resident buying office is also a source of training for the local store buyers. Resident offices may conduct training workshops, and their personnel may even shop with the retailer's local buyers when the latter come to the wholesale market. Some resident buying offices check on orders and even expedite deliveries on urgently needed merchandise. Resident buying offices may also provide assistance in planning promotional events.

The resident buying office may be either an independent office or a store-owned office. Independent offices can be either "salaried offices," which serve their clients on a contractual basis, or "merchandise brokers," who receive their payment (usually a 2- to 4-percent commission) from the vendor instead of the buyer. Hence local buyers can receive free buying assistance from merchandise brokers. However, the retail buyers should be aware that the merchandise broker is also trying to present, in the most favorable way, the products from which the commission is derived.

Store-owned offices may be "private offices," which are owned and operated by and for a single retailer, such as the Neiman-Marcus New York City office, which assists only buyers in all Neiman-Marcus stores. If several different retail groups own the resident buying office, it is called an "associated office." In this case the buying power and authority remains mostly with the individual buyers who use the service. The "syndicated office," on the other hand, represents the chain store system in the ownership group situation; so the syndicated office purchase recommendations are usually adopted by local personnel.

The wide range of services provided by all types of resident buying offices is very helpful to both large- and small-scale retailers. Therefore, retail buyers should at least investigate the possibility of using a resident buying office to assist them in their buying procedure.

Sources of Merchandise

The trend toward "scrambled merchandising" has complicated an already enormous problem for retail buyers. Merchandising many nonrelated merchandise lines requires that many different sources of supply be used to meet consumer demands. The magnitude of the problem of evaluating different sources of supply is readily apparent for any large-scale retailer who handles well over 10,000 different items. However, even small-scale retailers make an important decision when they select their suppliers.

There are three major sources of supply available to the retailers: middlemen, manufacturers or producers, and foreign exporters.

The different types of *marketing middlemen,* the product lines they normally carry, and the type of retail outlet for which they are especially well suited are described in Table 8–1. Middlemen provide many services that are valuable to small and medium-size retailers who cannot afford to hire specialists in many different areas. However, retailers are themselves getting into the wholesale business by using many different retail-wholesale combinations in which a group of retail outlets either owns the wholesale organization, as in the case of "cooperative chain" operations, or performs the wholesaling functions of assembling and collecting goods in chain distribution centers. Retailers also enter into group buying arrangements to perform some (if not all) of the functions normally performed by middlemen.

Retailers purchase their merchandise directly from manufacturers or producers for several reasons. First, manufacturers' salesmen can cooperate in training the retailers' salesmen to use proper selling and display techniques for the specific merchandise purchased.

Second, direct buying may reduce the time required for delivery of the merchandise because the shipments can be made directly to the outlets or sent prepackaged for each outlet to the chain's distribution center. This reduction in delivery time can be especially important for fad, fashion, or perishable items.

Third, retailers may buy direct because they can obtain lower net prices by not using the middleman. If some of the wholesalers' functions can be eliminated or absorbed by the retailer at a lower cost, direct buying offers an economic advantage.

Fourth, direct buying allows large retailers to purchase goods made according to their specifications. Consumer requests can be translated more easily into these specifications than in the case where the middleman is also involved in the communication process. Many large retailers, such as Sears, Roebuck and Company, now specify the design of nearly all the items they handle.

Some large retailers have purchased manufacturing companies that produce sizable amounts of the merchandise they handle. Of course, this guarantees control over merchandise quality. In addition, it allows the retailer to reap more profits from the trend toward private label merchandise. Distribution costs frequently can be reduced because the products are placed in the mass market without incurring heavy advertising or sales costs. Per unit manufacturing costs may be reduced because high-volume sales allow spreading the fixed cost invested in machines, administration, and so forth over the many units sold.

Foreign markets are becoming a more important source of merchandise supply as new trade agreements are made with nations such as Russia and China and as

Table 8-1 Characteristic Types of Middlemen Serving Retailers

Type of Middleman	Characteristics
Service (regular) wholesaler	Serves as the retailer's buying agent by assembling and collecting goods, storing goods, providing fast delivery, extending credit, and furnishing market information. These services appeal especially to small and medium-size retailers.
Limited function wholesaler	Charges less because he provides less service, since he generally does not grant credit or offer delivery service. Offers only fast-moving items; may do business only by mail.
Rack jobber	Supplies mainly non-good items to supermarkets, sets up displays, maintains merchandise assortment, and receives payment only on goods actually sold; thereby guarantees a pre-specified percent markup to the outlet.
Broker	Receives a commission to bring retail buyers and suppliers together; does not handle merchandise or take title to goods. Handles only a few lines—mainly grocery specialties, dry goods, fruits, vegetables, drugs, and hardware.
Commission agent	Similar to broker, except that he handles merchandise, although he does not take title to it; supplies mainly large retailers with dry goods, grocery specialties, and fruits and vegetables.
Manufacturer's agent (representative)	Renders services similar to those of a salesman; is restricted to a limited territory and by limited authority to negotiate price and terms of sale; sells only part of his client's output.
Selling agent	Similar to manufacturer's agent, except that a selling agent is responsible for disposing of entire output of his client.
Auctioneer	Product is placed on display and sold to highest bidder. Used mainly to sell livestock and fruits and vegetables to small restaurants, large chains, or other wholesalers.

other countries, such as Japan, become more familiar with U.S. consumer needs. Foreign goods purchased by retailers pass through importers, who send catalogs and/or salesmen to retailers. Most importers are located in the New York area, the Pacific Coast area, Canadian and Mexican border towns, and several large metropolitan areas.

Some large retailers send their own buyers to foreign countries to negotiate purchases. An alternative is to make purchases from foreign buyers through resident buying offices. If a large retail firm buys large quantities of foreign merchandise, it may establish its own buying offices in the major foreign supply areas.

Many retailers elect to use the resident buying offices or regular wholesalers as their main source of merchandise. This is particularly true for small retailers who may not have sufficient volume or cash resources to take advantage of volume or cash discounts offered by manufacturers or primary sources. The retailer can save time and effort and gain financing by using the services of a regular wholesaler, but not without added cost. When the wholesaler performs these marketing functions and services, the retailer sacrifices a portion of the trade discount offered by prime sources, which in turn increases the merchant's cost of goods. The cost of goods is further increased by more frequent shipments of smaller quantities, which increases freight charges and handling costs. All of these factors lead to the need for relatively higher unit markups and tend to make these retailers less price competitive. The decision to depend on any marketing middlemen as a regular source of supply should be made only after weighing the costs and benefits associated with the services offered.

The supplier decisions should be reviewed periodically, because competitive pressures and marketing dynamics may make certain sources more or less attractive over time. Most authorities agree that the retailer should spread the firm's purchases among suppliers if possible. Such action spreads the risk of being temporarily without merchandise during periods of peak demand or tight supply situations. This wise advice should be used judiciously, because any attempt to spread buying orders usually results in smaller quantities being ordered from each source, with attendant higher costs.

Last, the retailer should not change sources of supply capriciously. One may be tempted to switch the business to alternate sources in search of lower prices or better service, but the retailer-buyer must remember that the supplier represents the lifeline to continued existence. Without a regular supply of needed goods the retailer cannot stay in business. Such relationships are partially based on a feeling of reciprocity. When times are good, supplies are widely available and middlemen competition is intense. The retailer may pay a bit more in price or tolerate less intensive service in the expectation that in the future when the retailer has problems, such as restricted cash flow or unexpected demand for merchandise, the wholesaler will extend "earned courtesies" to help out a loyal "good" customer. Ultimately the retailer must decide how valuable this tentative, unstated relationship is in terms of dollars and cents or shipments promised but not delivered. In the long run, in any situation, change can be the pathway to improved performance, and if suppliers are not competitive the retailer must search for better product/service offerings.

Evaluating Merchandise

Retailers must constantly remind themselves that customers buy products and services that will yield some form of satisfaction. Regardless of the services offered by a marketing middleman, if the product does not live up to customer expectations the customer will not come back for further purchases. Therefore, successful retail buyers must be able to judge the quality of the merchandise to be certain their purchases will meet the needs of their customers. Hence, buyers need considerable knowledge about raw materials, manufacturing methods, workmanship, and current fashion trends. Merchandise may be evaluated by personally inspecting all of the goods purchased. However, this can be a time-consuming process when volume purchases are made, so a sampling procedure (evaluating only a portion of the merchandise to be purchased) can be used to reduce the time devoted to inspecting goods.

Merchandise is also frequently purchased on the basis of a description of the item. U.S. government grades or standard industry definitions allow the buyer to make purchases on the basis of a description because the goods must meet prescribed quality standards to bear the label issued by the government or industry. The grading system used for beef is an example. Grocery outlets generally inform the meat suppliers of their needs in terms of both quantity and quality for a specified date. The quality description is merely a statement of which U.S. Department of Agriculture grade(s) a store desires to buy. The meat suppliers then respond with a bid price on the stated quantity and quality. Generally, the supplier who quotes the lowest price obtains the business for that specific period.

Testing bureaus are also used to assist the buyer in making quality judgment. These bureaus may either be store-owned or independent commercial bureaus that charge a fee for evaluating goods. United States Testing Company of Hoboken, New Jersey, is an example of an independent commercial testing bureau.

Buying at Merchandise Markets

Regional merchandise showings are held in strategic locations throughout the nation. They provide excellent opportunities for small and medium-sized retail buyers to select their various lines and make their buying decisions based on their first-hand experience in comparing available goods. Usually these buying opportunities are referred to as regional shows or markets or marts. Periodically, either annually or semiannually, retail buyers gather at strategic regional centers in large auditoriums or in special showrooms with manufacturers' representatives and other middlemen to buy their merchandise for the coming selling season. A list of merchandise marts can be found in Appendix 8-A.

Most showings last three to five days in each location, usually over a weekend so small retailers can attend on Sundays while their stores are closed or when business is slow and they feel free to leave the store operation in capable hands for a few days. Admission is restricted to legitimate retailers who present business licenses or have permanent I.D. cards. The same merchandise offerings may be presented by middlemen in similar markets in fifteen different locations during a buying season. An example of such markets is the international dress, western apparel, and equipment show held annually in early January in Denver, Colorado. Thousands of buyers from all over the nation attend. The 1978 show included buyers from nineteen foreign countries. During this five-day show it is not uncommon for western boot manufacturers to write over $1 million (wholesale prices) worth of orders. The pace is fast and an unprepared buyer can easily be persuaded to buy more merchandise than the store will need during the forthcoming selling season.

The Prebuying Process

The merchandise manager and corporate retail management use dollars as the unit of measurement in planning. The buyer must convert merchandising plans from dollars into units of merchandise. Actually, the buyer may first plan the unit sales and the unit assortment and then convert the figures into dollars to check against the merchandise manager's dollar plan.

Buyers often develop a "trip buying plan," which indicates the specific quantity of each item they intend to buy on a forthcoming buying trip. Several different forms can be used to coordinate the buyers' purchases with the merchandise budget and the firm's open-to-buy quantity. Exhibit 8–1 shows a trip buying plan form.

Regardless of store size or the merchandise line carried the same prebuying process should be followed. For the sake of simplicity the discussion will focus on the activities that should be undertaken by a small retailer with one to five individual outlets carrying merchandise that has seasonal characteristics.

Complete, accurate, and appropriate merchandise records are the heart of any successful retail operation. They form the basis for sound buying decisions. Prior to buying any merchandise from a traveling salesman or attending a market, each retailer or buyer must systematically review the performance of past merchandise decisions from the previous comparable selling periods, such as "last spring sales." Admittedly such reviews take time and are sometimes psychologically painful, but the time will be well spent. Also, such critical analyses tend to preclude repeating buying errors of the past.

The process begins by taking inventory of the present merchandise on hand by type and vendor or seller. Any outstanding unfilled orders that have been invoiced or are likely to be shipped during the selling season are combined with the present inventory to create a total picture of the present and projected merchandise position in the store.

Forecasting the Firm's Future Sales

The next step is perhaps the most difficult and subjective step in the entire process —estimating the future selling season sales. How much will the store sell during the projected selling season? Past sales records may be helpful if one assumes the best predictor of the future is the immediate past. Unfortunately the competitive and economic environments in the last few years have been quite unstable, and retail sales have reflected this ebb and flow in consumer discretionary purchases. Competition seems to be constantly on the increase, and any future sales gains beyond those attributable to inflation must be aggressively earned by effective merchandising and tight cost control.

Each retailer must predict the level of economic activity for his or her selling region and what share of the retail dollars the firm can expect to attract. Usually this is expressed as a certain "percent of gain" over the previous year's business. This figure will be affected by new competition, changes in traffic patterns, amount of disposable income, and so forth. Once this gross dollar figure is determined, it must be broken down by merchandise line. Some merchandise lines, such as western denims, will sell better one year than western shirts, due to new fashion acceptance or product innovations. Alternately, women's western hand-tooled handbags may be down this year while leather shearling coats may be up. Each line must be closely examined to assess its promise for the coming selling season.

Once the merchandise manager or owner/buyer has allocated the total gross

Exhibit 8-1 Example of Trip Buying Plan Form

Department _____

Store _____

Date _____

Buying trip to _____

On order for next month delivery _____

Planned purchases next month _____

Estimated sales next month _____

Trip buying limit $ _____

Merchandise Code and Description	Units on Hand	Units on Order	Units Available for Sale	Forecast Sales until Delivery	Planned Stock at End of Month	Open to Buy This Month	Units Planned to Buy Now	Per Unit Cost	Planned Retail Price	Units Purchased	Dollar Amounts Purchases
(1)	(2)	(3)	(4) = (2) + (3)	(5)	(6)	(7)	(8)	(9)	(10)	(11)	(12)

Delivery date _____

Signed _____
(Buyer)

Approved _____
Merchandise Manager

sales dollars by merchandise category, the buyer must determine how much merchandise will be needed to generate the projected sales dollars. The number of buying dollars to be spent will be determined in part by the firm's markup policy. For simplicity, assume the firm has a keystoning policy of doubling its wholesale cost on all items purchased. This practice is not recommended as the optimum pricing strategy, but it is a common practice among retailers. Thus, if a merchandise line is projected to generate $50,000, the store must have $25,000 (at cost) of merchandise. Current inventory plus merchandise on order totals are subtracted from the total season's sales to create an open to buy figure to be allocated to future purchases.

Past Purchase Performance

At this point the buyer turns to past sales records, previous orders, or paid invoices of the relevant sales period and any buying notes made at the last year's market. Often buying notes and unfilled orders can be particularly useful in selecting suppliers. Often manufacturers will make up special samples of merchandise for regional sales presentations to test the product's appeal among buyers. If the product finds poor order support, the firm will not put the item into production and cancel any existing orders. Alternately, some items will be a hit and enjoy such success that the firm is unable to deliver the merchandise as promised. If the buyer has committed a significant amount of purchase dollars to such items in the past, it may have cost the store valuable sales dollars, because the money was committed but no merchandise was available to sell. Past experiences of nondelivery must be known before going to market and may become important negotiating points and/or may affect vendor choice and requested delivery dates for the coming season. If an item is especially attractive, the buyer might move up the delivery date to be sure the firm is not shut out if demands do exceed supply.

What sold well last year; where did it come from? How many did we sell? Did we reorder? If so, how many? More importantly, what didn't sell? Why? These vital questions can be examined by reviewing the invoices and inventory recapitulations if accurate records have been maintained. Most large retail stores place most of this information (vendor number, lot number, date and quantity received) on a detachable price ticket and collect and record them as each sale is made. Small firms do not have either the time or facilities to maintain such complete records. However, elementary efforts in this area will pay significant dividends when buying is undertaken. In any event, the buyer should go to market with the past invoices, separated by merchandise line, to serve as a guide to selecting both vendors and merchandise to implement the buying plan.

Buying Procedures at the Market

An early arrival at the market, prior to its official opening can be extremely beneficial in locating special promotional goods for the future selling season. Most manufacturers will set out samples of discontinued lines and cut the price to clear their stocks before the market officially opens. The buyer must be wary about overbuying such merchandise so that the bulk of the line will be purchased in new, fresh, current offerings. However, if an item has been a good seller and a few are needed to fill out a size run to be offered at a promotional price, such close-outs may represent good buys. Usually after the show begins these items are "put in the back room" if any remain and are only shown to special customers upon request. Additionally these items must be paid for upon receipt of the invoice.

Once at the market the prudent buyer should not make any spontaneous decisions without surveying the entire market and the individual offerings. Some buyers will spend the first two days getting a feeling of the range and price of the competitive offerings. What common themes are present? Is there an item or items that every vendor is selling? Who has the best quality for the best price? Can they deliver on schedule? Who offers the best terms on small and large quantities? Some buyers rely heavily on a salesperson they know personally and depend on that person's past experience and advice in making purchase decisions. Good salespersons will give sound advice on quantities and prices even if it means that the initial order is cut back or reduced. Salespersons know that if they load up the retailer they have made two sales, first and last, to that merchant/buyer. Future good will is always more valuable than immediate gain for the professional salesperson.

Narrowing the Alternatives for Price Lining

The buyer must constantly keep in mind that customer needs and satisfaction are paramount and that the choices that must be made should not be based on "what I like" or "I like this so I'll buy it." Admittedly, many of the buyer's personal choices will be consistent with the firm's customer group, but it is quite easy to slip over the line separating personal tastes and customer preferences.

Another point to keep in mind, particularly for those buyers who have a small store or a few outlets, is that the buyer will often not be selling on the merchandise floor. The buyer must depend on a few key full-time salespersons to be so enthusiastic about the new offering that they will personally accept it and suggest it to their customers. Often buyers will take one or two of the professional, full-time sales staff to market to get their opinions of the new merchandise as well as to acquaint them with the challenges of the buying process.

Working the Line

"Working the line" means to review past sales records and current stock positions systematically, to project sales estimates for the next sales period, and to determine the amount of "open-to-buy" for each merchandise line, all of which is stated in units and purchase dollars. Then, in consultation with the sales representative, the buyer reviews the current merchandise offerings. Past poor performers and discontinued items are deleted, new, interest-generating goods are added, and the staple line is reordered. The end product is an order stating the specific quantities being ordered by lot number and size, the price, all terms and conditions of sale, and specific shipping instructions.

When the buyer sits down to write and work the line, the sharp salesperson will usually offer to provide the buyer with copies of the relevant past orders. Together the buyer and salesperson briefly review the past purchases and analyze the line results in terms of both units and dollars purchased. Demonstrated winners or staple items are usually reviewed first in depth. Most of the time certain styles or renderings are offered year after year but in new fabrics, colors, or with slight changes in design. Such items form the core of the line and are usually bought in depth (large quantities).

Most of this merchandise comes in ranges, or standard assortments by the dozen or carton lots. The manufacturers know certain items in an assortment will sell better than others. However, when they are making up the samples, they cannot predict the "number of styles or sizes 1s or 2s," so they present what they think will be a balanced offering. Thus, the buyer is precluded from picking and choosing individual items. One either buys the range or passes up the merchandise. Some higher priced merchandise in all lines is a available " by each," and often these items are added by the buyer to provide assortment recognition of local color or style preferences.

After the major staples have been selected by size, color, or range, the buyer considers new items that will add spice to the line or increase the attractiveness of the offering. Usually these items are purchased on a highly subjective basis because there are no sales records available to guide decision making. At this point the buyer must exercise intuitive judgment or gut feeling as the new items are presented. Some new items may have been introduced or test marketed on a limited basis earlier, and the salesperson will have those results available to help guide the buyer. Caution is advised in using the salesperson's verbal reports because the representative may be tempted to puff up the results or employ the standing-room-only sales technique to increase the order. Usually the new items are sampled on a limited quantity basis, with subsequent reorders later in the season if the item enjoys early sales success.

Each item purchased, each line worked must fit into a nebulous but vital concept of store image. Each decision represents a piece of the jigsaw puzzle that will ultimately become a completed picture. The buyer must constantly be thinking about such tangential issues as how the merchandise will look on display, how many will be needed to fill up a counter, whether the colors can be fashion coordinated with other merchandise, and so forth. Also, one must keep in mind the need to reserve a pool of purchase dollars to buy new items from new suppliers not currently patronized.

New, Innovative, Unique, Attractive Items

Experienced buyers know that the large, major suppliers concentrate on accepted merchandise items with yearly touch-ups to create a fresh image on the old line. The new, innovative ideas and products are usually brought out by new, small, fledgling firms that may only have one good item out of ten new offerings. The astute buyer identifies that sleeper from the other nine items and places a sample order for early delivery with the intent of placing early reorders in depth if the product is a success. The buyer knows that such fad items move quickly in the market and that the small supplier will be unable to meet all the reorders during the current selling season if the product is highly successful. Early recognition of such new items is essential if the firm is to get in and out before the item is widely imitated and readily available from competitors. The secret to success lies in widely but selectively sampling the new items, taking early delivery, and closely monitoring the daily sales of these items. Again, mistakes will be made; but over time the risk turns into profit, creates customer interest, and establishes the store as a place where the action is.

Buying Negotiations

The climax of a successful buying effort occurs in the negotiation process. Regardless of the development and use of elegant economic buying models, retail buyers must realize that the negotiation of prices and terms of sales remains an exercise in the skillful use of relative economic power.

The negotiation process begins when the retail buyer has determined the type of merchandise needed and after a choice of suppliers appears to be acceptable. Price, of course, is one of the major elements to be negotiated. Table 8–2 contains a description of the various discounts that may be deducted from the vendor's list price to arrive at the net purchase price. Retail buyers should attempt to purchase the desired merchandise at the lowest net cost, but should not expect unreasonable discounts or price concessions from the supplier. It is important to develop the respect of the vendors, who can aid the buyer by providing services, advice, and speedy delivery of the merchandise. Thus a long-run relationship, based upon mutual respect for one another, is desirable.

Retail buyers must be familiar with the prices and discounts generally allowed on each item. However, the buyer should realize that the store's bargaining position for small-volume purchases is not as great as for large-volume purchases. As a result, the large retailer may be able to purchase goods from the same vendor at a lower net price. Although the Robinson-Patman Act places limitations on the price bargaining that large retailers may use, it does not prevent the buyer from negotiating for the lowest lawful price that sellers are willing to accept.[1]

Another negotiation issue is dating, which determines when cash discounts may be received and when payment is due if an interest penalty is to be avoided. The terminology for cash discounts under several frequently used future dating statements, such as 2/10-net 30 and 2/10 E.O.M., is explained in Table 8–2.

Future-dating negotiations take many forms. The invoice date can be used as the *base date,* so that any cash discount and billing statement refers to the number of days after the invoice date. However, several other kinds of future dating are commonly used. End-of-month (E.O.M.) dating allows for cash discount and full-payment period to begin on the first day of the following month instead of on the

Table 8-2 Characteristics of Price Discounts Given to Retailers

Type of Discount	Description
Quantity	Price reduction given from invoice price because purchases are made.
	Amount of discount must be justified by either a reduction in cost associated with handling a larger quantity or by meeting a competitior's equally low price if retail buyer is to avoid prosecution under Robinson-Patman Act.
Trade (functional)	Price reduction is based upon the marketing activities performed by the buyer. Discounts are deducted from list price in order stated, so a trade discount of 20, 10, 5 would be calculated as 20% off the list price, 10% off the balance, and 5% off the second balance, and the retailer would pay 100%—20% (=80%), —8% (=72%), —3.6% or 68.4% of the list price.
	Trade discounts may be given in addition to quantity discounts.
Seasonal	Price reduction given to encourage ordering during "off" seasons.
Advertising allowances	Price reduction made to retailers who promote a product or service for the supplier. Amount of allowance must be justified by being a reasonable payment for such promotions and by similar offerings made by the seller to competitive dealers if retailer is to avoid prosecution under Robinson-Patman Act.
Cash	Price reduction given if retailer pays his bills promptly.
	Cash discounts are usually stated as 2/10, net 30, which means that a 2% discount is given if payment is received within 10 days of the date of the invoice, and interest charges will not be added unless bill is not paid during the 30 day period.
	Other forms of cash discounts are: 2/10 (2% discount if paid within ten days, balance due in thirty days), 2/10—30 extra (2% discount is extended ten days to forty days), and 2/10 E.O.M. (2% discount runs for ten days after end of month in which purchase was made).
	Retailers should use cash discounts because they are profitable (even if money must be borrowed) and they promote vendor good will.

invoice date. For example, 2/10, n/30, E.O.M. on an invoice dated any day in June indicates that a 2 percent cash discount may be received until July 10. The full amount of the invoice is due by July 31. If no net period is indicated, the full amount is usually due at the end of the next calendar month (July 31 if the purchase was made any time during June).

Under *receipt of goods (R.O.G.) dating,* the period begins on the date that the goods are received by the retailer. Thus payment on merchandise received on June 10 with a 2/10, n/30, R.O.G. dating must be made on or before June 20 to obtain the 2 percent cash discount and by July 10 to avoid possible payment of interest.

Advance or *seasonal dating* specifies a date in the future when the terms become applicable. For example, an order placed July 20 and shipped on October 15 with a 2/10, n/30 as of November 1 dating would indicate that a 2 percent cash discount may be obtained if payment is made on or before November 11.

Future datings are advantageous from a retailer's point of view because they allow the firm to operate with a lower level of investment in merchandise. As a result, the retail buyer will benefit from, and negotiate for, the type of future dating that will delay the cash discount payment date as long as possible. Some suppliers will not accept future dating dealings but insist on immediate settlement. In this case the merchandise is sold on a C.O.D. (cash on delivery) basis and discounts must be taken and payment made when the goods are received. Cash-on-delivery shipments are not generally used unless the retailer has not established his credit standing with the particular vendor.

Retail buyers may also negotiate for an extra cash discount, called an *anticipation discount,* if the bill is paid before the expiration of the cash discount period. This extra discount is generally calculated on the basis of a prespecified annual percentage rate, which is determined by the going commercial loan rate. Anticipation payments are normally calculated on the number of days remaining until the end of the cash discount period.

For example, suppose an invoice for $5,000, issued with terms of 2/10–30 extra with a 9 percent prespecified anticipation rate, is paid in ten days. This invoice is anticipated thirty days (40 − 10) prior to the expiration of the cash discount period. In this case the buyer would be entitled to a 2 percent cash discount ($5,000 × .02), or $100, plus an anticipation reduction equal to 9 percent interest on the balance ($4,900) for 30/360 of a year (360 days), or $36.74.

Some retailers may obtain external financing from vendors who do not allow either cash or anticipation discounts and who do not charge interest on the unpaid balance after a stated number of days. Retailers, in this case, intentionally delay the payment of bills for thirty to sixty days beyond the due date. The amount of money owed to vendors is used by the retailer at no interest charge, but long-term vendor relationships are likely to suffer by using this *delayed payment* approach. Large retailers, however, may be sufficiently important and their overall credit rating good enough to force the supplier to allow them to be continually behind in making their payments. The supplier will also be forced to maintain good service and speedy merchandise delivery to these retailers or risk losing their business.

The delayed payment approach is not likely to be successful for smaller retailers. These firms, as individual accounts, do not represent a significant volume of business to the supplier. In addition, their credit rating is likely to decline rapidly if they attempt to use the delayed payment approach. Thus the supplier can reduce the level of service provided to the smaller retailers, or even cease to sell to them if they attempt to use the delayed payment approach.

Currently some firms have begun to factor or sell accounts receivable the day after the due date. The factor buys the accounts at a negotiated discount and then turns them over to collection agents. The collection agents attempt to get immediate, full payment of the account including a substantial collection fee. While such actions may be necessary for persistent slow paying accounts, this practice hardly seems justified in all cases. Factoring may increase cash flow and funds utilization, but it usually results in the long-term loss of some profitable business if applied without due consideration for the retailer's situation.

Transportation and physical handling considerations are still another set of items that need to be negotiated. Suppliers usually quote prices as:

1. *F.O.B.* (*free on board*) *factory,* which means the buyer pays all transportation costs from the supplier's delivery platform
2. *F.O.B. shipping point,* which means that the supplier bears the transportation charges to his local shipping point but the retailer pays all further transportation costs
3. *F.O.B. destination* (*or store*), which means that the seller pays the freight
4. *F.O.B. (freight allowed)* which means that title to the goods passes as soon as the freight agent picks up the merchandise at the plant or warehouse but the seller absorbs all freight charges

The F.O.B. point is critical because it determines the point of ownership transfer, the assumption of responsibility for freight charges, and any damage to the merchandise while in transit. For example, a furniture store might order a bedroom suite to be shipped F.O.B. destination, and after months of waiting it never arrives at the store. In this case, the retailer is not responsible for payment or freight follow-up because the ownership of the furniture has not passed to the firm.

Buyers must be knowledgeable about freight and handling costs to make comparisons of prices quoted on different transportation terms. Extra physical handling services may also be provided by some vendors. Vendors who sort and package merchandise separately for each store in a chain (or branch) retail system are able to reduce the handling costs for that chain or branch store system. These and other vendor-provided services, such as prompt delivery of merchandise are quickly reflected in the firm's net profit picture.

Unfortunately, in today's markets freight payment by the middleman or manufacturer is rapidly disappearing. Most retailers now have to pay all freight charges.

Retail buyers may also want to negotiate a guaranty against future price changes. If such a *price guaranty* is granted, the retail buyer can benefit as well as current buyers do if the supplier lowers his price after the order is placed. If the vendor raises his price after the order is placed, the buyer has the benefit of the originally stated price under the provisions of the price guaranty. Price guaranties are used frequently on orders for seasonal merchandise and for staple goods during periods of price uncertainty.

Current Negotiation Considerations

The retail buyer must negotiate cost/price, delivery dates, and credit terms. All three elements are significantly interrelated because they affect the cash flow and profitability of the firm. For example, if the merchandise is delivered early, with credit terms that dictate payment before demand and sales develop, the retailer will be forced to use precious capital or expensive borrowed funds to pay for the goods. This adds to the cost of the merchandise and must be recouped in larger markups.

In the last few years there has been a marked trend by manufacturers to shift the marketing functions of finance and inventory accumulation downward to the retailer. In the past it was a common practice for manufacturers to accept orders for "at once" or "when ready" delivery and offer dating as the sales generated a cash flow. Now most large firms offer a maximum dating of sixty days, and the more common offer is "net thirty days" with no cash discounts.

Additional pressure is being exerted by the manufacturers to take early or "at once" deliveries. Any order carrying a delayed shipping date carries the explicit condition that the order may not be filled. Thus, the retail buyer must weigh the consequences of having to borrow heavily at a high interest rate or risk not having adequate quantities of goods on the shelves and racks to sell.

Another problem associated with future order dating arises between large and small retail accounts. Informally, large manufacturers encourage their large accounts (volume buyers) to split their orders, placing some for "at once" and some for future deliveries. In this way manufacturers have firm orders and can give the large accounts assurance of steady periodic deliveries and a predictable cash flow. Any surplus production is then parceled out among the smaller volume buyers. In some cases, the smallest buyers do not receive any of their ordered merchandise until late in the selling season, and even then they may experience a large number of substitute nonordered items. If challenged, the manufacturers plead overselling and unexpected demand and note thay buyers were forewarned of the risk when they placed their orders.

Additional strains are being placed on small retailers' limited capital and plant as manufacturers shift the inventory storage function to the retailer. When merchandise is shipped early the retailer must rent additional storage space, hire more stockroom personnel to handle the flood of merchandise, and risk product deterioration while awaiting the major portion of the selling season. All these activities increase the financing requirements for the small merchant operating on limited invested capital.

During the negotiation process most alert buyers will reaffirm any prior return privileges agreements or attempt to gain such benefits. Usually these privileges are limited to defective merchandise that did not meet customer or buyer expectations. This return privilege is becoming increasingly important as retailers are asked by customers to assume their responsibilities under the Consumer Products Warranty and Guaranty Act. Usually manufacturers require that each retailer write for specific permission to return such goods for credit toward future purchases. Many retailers who have only a few such defective items simply prefer to charge them off (mark the item down to zero) and throw them away. Such decisions assume that the cost in clerical time and postage is not worth the credited amount. While this may be true, the retailer must realize that the entire cost of the item is lost and must be recovered from future profit margins on other products. Buyers should always seek and use such return privileges.

Credit Considerations When Buying

Astute retail buyers take time to prepare their credit plans as meticulously as they do their merchandise plans. If the firm is large enough to have a finance/controller department, the retail buyer should work out a detailed buying budget to assure prompt payment of invoices to receive any cash discounts that may be offered later at the market. If the firm does not have specialized functions, the buyer/manager should work closely with the firm's financial backers and commercial banks to assure that adequate funds are available when needed.

Before going to market the buyer must work out cash flow projections based on anticipated monthly sales and expenses. The buyer must constantly juggle the desire to have the new merchandise early to test customer acceptance with the stark realization that merchandise should not be received before it is needed. Usually the small retailer/buyer negotiates a loan large enough to cover the season's buying and operational needs. The specific details vary with the type of retail operation, the state of national and local business conditions, the local demands for loans, bank discount rates, and most importantly, the past repayment history of the retailer. The retailer will periodically draw funds against the loan balance as needed to pay the bills as they come due. In this way the interest charges may be minimized and the funds borrowed only as needed.

The next step is to accumulate supplier letters attesting to the firm's credit worthiness. Usually these come unsolicited if the firm pays its bills promptly and takes advantages of the available discounts. If the firm deems it useful, it might be helpful to establish a credit rating with Dun & Bradstreet, the national credit rating bureau for business firms. Armed with these credit references and a line of credit through the firm's checking account, the buyer is ready to go to the market and is not restricted to doing business only with past suppliers who know the firm's credit worthiness. The ability to open accounts with new suppliers on the spot is important when new, innovative goods are encountered. Some small manufacturers may be "cash short" or undercapitalized and request payment with the order. One should question such a shaky position because it might affect future delivery. The experienced retailer always carries a few spare checks for "instant opportunities."

Purchase Procedures

Once the details of merchandise assortment, terms, and delivery dates have been settled, the buyer must be sure the oral agreements are acccurately transcribed into specific orders. Most salespersons prefer to take the working sheets and transcribe them onto order forms during nonshow hours, usually late at night. The following day the buyers returns, verifies the order, signs it, and receives a copy. One should always get a copy of the final order so that any future "misunderstandings" between buyer and seller can be avoided and, more importantly, when the buyers return home, they can complete their merchandising, promotional, and financial plans and create the necessary budgets to translate purchases into profitable sales.

Some retail buyers complete a *purchase order* form when all the negotiations have been completed. This form may be supplied to its buyers by the retail firm itself (Exhibit 8–2 is an example of such a form) or a vendor's order form may be used. Large retail firms are likely to use their own standard form because information can be printed in one location and on as many copies as the firm needs to handle and control merchandise internally. These same forms are also used to give vendors shipping instructions. The written purchase order is issued by the purchasing department of the retail firm to the vendor. Upon acceptance by the vendor, it becomes a legal, binding contract.

Exhibit 8-2 **Example of Purchase Order Form**

Purchase Order

THIS SPACE FOR OFFICE USE

Customer Number	Credit Department
Pairs	
Entered	

PLEASE PRINT CLEARLY

Charge to

Owner

Street

City   State   Zip Code

Customer Order No.	Date Ordered
Shipping Instructions	

SINGLE PAIRS OR LESS THAN THREE PAIRS OF <u>ONE</u> STOCK NUMBER $1.50 PER PAIR EXTRA
ORDERS FOR ONE ACCOUNT NUMBER FOR TWELVE PAIRS OR MORE BY SAME SHIPPING METHOD TO ONE ADDRESS NO EXTRA CHARGE
ALL SIZES 12½, 13, 13½, 14, $1.50 PER PAIR EXTRA. SIZE 15 AND UP $2.50 PER PAIR EXTRA. STOCK <u>GOODS NET</u> – <u>NO DISCOUNT</u>.

This and each future order of the Purchaser must be specifically accepted in writing by the Seller to become binding. Acceptance of this or any other order will not constitute the Purchaser an agent of the Seller.

TERMS: Stock Goods NET 30 DAYS. F.O.B. FACTORY.

Stock Number	Width	5	5½	6	6½	7	7½	8	8½	9	9½	10	10½	11	11½	12	12½	13	13½	14	15	Total	Price
		5	5½	6	6½	7	7½	8	8½	9	9½	10	10½	11	11½	12	12½	13	13½	14	15	Total	Price
		5	5½	6	6½	7	7½	8	8½	9	9½	10	10½	11	11½	12	12½	13	13½	14	15	Total	Price

PLEASE CIRCLE ANY PAIRS ALREADY SOLD FOR WHICH CUSTOMERS ARE WAITING
PRICES SUBJECT TO CHANGE WITHOUT NOTICE

The vendor sends an *invoice* to the buyer after the vendor has recived the purchase order. The invoice is the itemized statement (or bill) containing the quantity, price, terms of sale, and other negotiated agreements on the merchandise being shipped. An example of an invoice form is presented in Exhibit 8–3.

Another step in the negotiation process involves the *transfer of title,* which usually occurs when the supplier releases the goods to a common carrier for delivery. If the goods are damaged in transit, the buyer's recourse is *generally*

Exhibit 8–3 **Example of Invoice Form**

NO.

DATE

YOUR
ORDER NO.

SOLD TO   SHIPPED TO

OUR ORDER NO.	SALESMAN	TERMS	F O.B.	DATE SHIPPED	SHIPPED VIA		
QUANTITY ORDERED	QUANTITY SHIPPED	STOCK NUMBER/DESCRIPTION			UNIT PRICE	UNIT	AMOUNT

against the transportation firm, not the vendor. But there are two variations from this procedure.

Goods may be bought on a *consignment* basis. In this case, title to the goods remains with the vendor until the goods are sold by the retailer. The supplier agrees to accept the return of any merchandise not sold; so the retailer does not take any risks caused by merchandise obsolescence or price declines. The retailer, however, is liable if the product is not properly cared for or is inadequately merchandised. Thus, retailers should carefully evaluate the consignment merchandise and the vendor. New items are frequently introduced on a consignment basis because the retailer does not like to invest in a product that may not sell well.

Goods may also be purchased on a *memorandum buying* basis, which is a special form of future dating. In this case, the title to the goods passes to the retailer, who assumes all ownership risks but reserves the right to return any unsold portion of the goods to the supplier without payment. The retailer assumes little risk and is free to price the merchandise at any level. Memorandum billing is used frequently when goods are introduced on an experimental or test market basis.

Order Cancellation

A final area for examination is the process of order cancellation. A buyer should not hesitate to cancel orders if projected sales levels do not materialize or goods are late in arriving. Such action, if taken promptly, preserves valuable capital to be spent in more important ways. If sales are down markedly, the firm does not want to continue receiving more markdowns with the subsequent loss of money. Alternatively, if the supplier cannot deliver the merchandise, it is important to take corrective action and scramble for any available merchandise from other suppliers. In both cases future contractual obligations are terminated and a revised merchandise plan must be devised.

In the first case, if the firm seriously overestimated the season's sales levels, then the buyer must go back through the outstanding orders and selectively prune the remaining orders. Mass cancellation of all orders will result in sure disaster, because the merchandise lines will be riddled with stock-outs in the best selling sizes, colors, and so forth. In order to stay in business and remain viable, the breadth of the assortment must be reduced through promotion and perhaps selective markdowns. Any resulting funds should be used to consolidate the assortment and reestablish some degree of merchandise depth. Fresh stock may temporarily revive customer interest and buy time for an orderly disposition of unsold seasonal merchandise.

In the second situation, missed sales are inevitable. The buyer must decide whether there is enough time to get merchandise and meet customer needs or lose the sales. The normal buyer reaction is to pick up the telephone and place orders for immediate delivery from distant suppliers or rush out to buy from local middlemen. Hopefully such action will maintain customer loyalty and patronage. Nine times out of ten, however, such action results in losses because customers have already gone elsewhere and bought the needed goods. The buyer is best advised to put the cancelled order dollars in the next season's merchandise that can be brought in to test early customer acceptance. In any event, those suppliers who consistently do not deliver as promised should be dropped from any further consideration.

Handling Merchandise

The *handling process* entails the additional activities that must take place after the merchandise is purchased to ensure that the goods are properly assembled and presented to retail customers. First, the goods must be shipped from the supplier to the retail outlets. Then the goods must be examined to determine if the shipment contains merchandise that corresponds to the prespecified quality and quantity stated on the purchase order. The merchandise is then marked, prepared for sale, and placed in the appropriate display area. However, close control activities are required to keep stock shortages, pilferage, and damaged goods to a minimum. The entire retail handling process must be planned to facilitate easy consumer pickup of merchandise or retail delivery to consumers. Finally, the merchandise that does not sell even after repeated sales promotion efforts may have to be disposed of by returning it to the supplier, by transferring or selling it to other retail outlets, or by throwing it away.

These activities will be discussed in more detail in the remainder of this chapter.

Moving Merchandise to the Store

Freight rate increases have tended to enhance the relative importance of activities that will allow merchandise to be moved to each retail outlet with minimum cost while maintaining a short delivery period. The activities involved in merchandise movement will be discussed under two topics: transportation and shipment consolidation.

Transportation Considerations

The retail manager or the retail traffic department of large retail organizations must select the desired carrier and routing of the incoming goods. The relative cost, the amount of time required to deliver goods, the care used in handling goods, the amount of packaging required for shipment, and the willingness and ability to deliver separate, small shipments to each outlet are major items that must be evaluated in making the routing and carrier decision. Cost may be the most important consideration for low-value, staple merchandise whose product life cycle is long and whose sales are fairly predictable. However, speed of delivery may be the dominant consideration for an order on out-of-stock or low-stock fashion merchandise.

Railroads and truck lines are the major carriers of full carload shipments of merchandise. Railroads usually offer the lowest freight rates on long hauls of more than 500 miles, but trucks provide more flexibility in getting merchandise directly to the retailer. The convenience of receiving merchandise by truck has made truck lines the major carrier of consumer merchandise. Piggybacking (hauling trailers on flat-bed rail cars) has reduced handling costs and speeded up delivery of railroad shipments, and is increasingly being used on intermediate and long-distance shipments.

Air freight offers the fastest method of delivery over long distances. For high-value, short-life merchandise (such as fashion or fad goods), the slightly higher rates can be justified. For example, a Denver department store receives twenty-four hour delivery via air on fashion clothing, which allows the store to offer a wider and more current merchandise assortment.

Retailers frequently encounter problems in transporting small shipments. Parcel post, air freight, United Parcel Service, and Bus Package Express represent alternative ways of shipping freight weighing less than fifty pounds. The three most attractive choices for shipments of merchandise weighing from 50 to 500 pounds are air freight, freight forwarders, and shipper associations (cooperatives).[2] (The latter two methods represent shipment consolidation techniques.)

Freight bills must be carefully audited to detect clerical errors and overcharges caused by classifying goods in the incorrect freight category, by using a higher tariff rate when a lower rate could be utilized, or by calculating the freight rate over a longer route than is needed to deliver the merchandise. Sizable savings can be obtained by audits conducted by a knowledgeable freight expert, since there are numerous special rates that can reduce the transportation costs considerably.

Prompt action should be taken when merchandise is delivered in a damaged condition or when the quantity of goods received does not agree with the quantity stated on the invoice. Retailers should make every attempt to determine who is responsible for the shortage and/or damage, the supplier or the carrier. Then the responsible party should be notified as soon as possible.

Shipment Consolidation

There are several methods that are frequently used to consolidate small shipments into large-volume shipments before the goods reach the individual outlet. Such consolidation is beneficial because a transportation cost reduction can be obtained by shipping large quantities, which may move on a carload rate basis. The manufacturers may provide a distribution center that receives different carload quantities of single products, stores these shipments, and sends large mixed-product shipments of ordered goods from the center to large retailers under carrier mixing privileges at truckload rates. Grocery product manufacturers, such as General Foods Corporation, have been using this type of distribution system effectively.

Consolidation may also be performed by commercial freight forwarders, which combine less than carload (L.T.C.) or truckload shipments from several manufacturers into full carload or truckload shipments.

Several independent commercial freight consolidation companies are expanding their services to include examination of merchandise for quantity and quality, marking merchandise with the stores' tickets, local distribution to retail outlets, maintenance of inventory control and sales data, and picking up merchandise returned by a store. These services can be especially helpful to the small retailer who cannot take advantage of quantity shipping rates or hire the expertise needed to analyze sales and inventory reports properly.

Numerous shippers' cooperative associations also perform consolidation services. These cooperatives, located in most major U.S. cities, consolidate the shipments, provide long-distance shipping, break down the shipments, and store the merchandise either in a local warehouse or at individual retail outlets.

Most large retail chain organizations have their own chain store distribution centers, which perform the same services as the other consolidation centers but may also check the merchandise, mark it, and provide inventory control services.

Managing Incoming Merchandise

Merchandise delivered to the retail outlet is unloaded at the store and moved to an area for unpacking. This procedure, commonly called receiving, involves certain inspection and recording activities. All merchandise containers should be inspected immediately upon delivery to determine if there is any apparent merchandise damage. If the receiving clerk finds no apparent damage, the individual usually signs the carrier's receipt. If damaged goods are detected, the word *damaged* is written on the receipt and is then signed. This will facilitate the filing of future damage claims by the retailer against the common carrier. Only the outside of the containers are examined at this point, unless there is noted fragile merchandise contained in the packages. If so, one should open the cartons and inspect the goods carefully for any damage. Nonfragile goods are then immediately moved from the freight dock into the receiving room, the containers are opened, and the contents are checked for damage. Such prompt attention to getting merchandise inside will reduce the opportunities for theft and accidental damage or deterioration.

Incoming shipments must be recorded to provide data on the time of arrival, apparent condition of the shipment, delivery charges, vendor's name and address, carrier's name and address, name of the person making the delivery, number of containers, weight of goods, amount and number of invoices, and the department for which goods were ordered. A typical receiving record is presented in Exhibit 8–4. Such records may be analyzed by computer to assist and support the preparation of damage claims and vendor payments. Retailers can avoid paying for goods not yet received by comparing invoices against the receiving records.

The checking process begins after the receiving records are completed. The

Exhibit 8-4 **A Receiving Record**

RECEIVED FROM__________ RECEIVING RECORD **122357**

ADDRESS__________ DATE___/___/___

OUR ORDER NO.__________

CARRIER__________ UPS____ AIR EXPRESS____ PARCEL POST____ OTHER____

FREIGHT BILL NO,__________ PREPAID__________ COLLECT CHARGES PAID__________

NUMBER OF PACKAGES	WEIGHT	CONDITION	DELIVERED TO	RETURNED GOODS ☐

	QUANTITY	STOCK NO.	DESCRIPTION
1.			
2.			
3.			
4.			
5.			
6.			
7.			
8.			
9.			
10.			
11.			
12.			

REMARKS__________

CHECKED WITH PURCHASE ORDER BY__________ CREDIT MEMO ISSUED BY__________

ORIGINAL COPY RECEIVED BY__________

goods are usually moved into a separate checking and marking room to facilitate the checking procedure. This checking process begins with a comparison of the invoice and the purchase order. This allows the checker to determine if the description and quality of goods billed agree with the order. The dating and discount information is also compared at this time.

The merchandise is then removed from the shipping containers and sorted into similar categories. It is then advisable to check the incoming merchandise against the invoice immediately to determine if the correct amount and quality of merchandise has been received. Sometimes invoices are not available on goods that are needed on the selling floor. In this case, the purchase order can be compared against the shipment to determine if there are any discrepancies in quantity or quality. Making this check immediately allows the merchandise to reach the consumer quickly, but, even more important, discrepancies between the checker's count and the invoice count can be rechecked very easily. This recheck is usually made by the checker's supervisor, or by the proprietor in the case of a small store.

Merchandise is then marked by using tags, price tickets, gummed stickers, automatic imprinting systems, handwriting, and hand stamping. The mark should be legible, neat, and as permanent as possible without damaging the goods. If a price ticket is used, other necessary data, such as the cost of the item (coded), date received, department number, and size and color of goods, can be placed on the price ticket to assist in the merchandise management process.

There are many different systems of merchandise marking. Some large retailers reduce marking expense and speed the within-store merchandise preparation time by having the vendors mark the goods prior to shipment. This practice, called source marking, involves a standard tag code and format, so retailers can easily use electronic data processing (EDP) equipment to improve the flow of sales and inventory information. Other retailers require the buyer to place retail prices upon the store's copy of the purchase order at the time the order is placed. This practice, called preretailing, forces the retail buyer to consider the retail price when the purchase is made. This discourages purchases of items which do not appear capable of being sold at the retail price needed to provide the desired markup. Preretailing facilitates the marking procedure because the marking clerk merely refers to the purchase order to obtain the appropriate retail price.

Many different forms of price tickets are used in retailing. Several automated systems use precoded tags that can be read by electronic devices.

Once the merchandise has been marked, it is ready to be moved to the selling floor. The retail buyer may give instructions on the purchase order indicating which department and area is to receive the merchandise. Otherwise the store manager of a chain store, the proprietor of a small retail store, or the department head may indicate where to move the goods. If the shelves are full, the merchandise may be placed temporarily in a reserve stockroom. (Generally, all of the store's shelf-stocking clerks are allowed in the stockroom to obtain goods as they are needed in the selling area. It is important to realize that merchandise in a reserve stockroom or in the checking or marking areas cannot be sold until it is displayed in the selling area; therefore these goods must be checked frequently and moved to the selling floor as quickly as possible.)

Several automated retail systems involve the linking of the transaction centers to central computer processing units either in the store or to one large regional buying center. One such system, the National Cash Register (NCR) 280 Retail System is widely used by J. C. Penney and Montgomery Ward in checkout and recording inventory data. The technology being applied is changing so rapidly that the interested reader would be well advised to consult the competing firms for current systems designs and supporting software quotations. Most of the major systems have entire packages that have been developed for, or can be adapted to, any retail need.

Reducing Stock Shortages, Pilferage, and Damaged Goods

Retailers encounter a continuous and growing problem in their efforts to reduce stock shortages. Theft of goods by employees, customers, shoplifters, and robbers has increased with the growth of self-service merchandise.

Reducing Internal Theft

Retail personnel offices have the task of screening applicants before they are hired. Retail personnel offices keep records on employees whom the organization has terminated because of theft. Most large retailers have a security department that works very closely with the personnel department to detect internal theft. Constant supervision of employees and informative, preventive communication programs presented to store employees must be used to combat internal theft.

Small retailers don't need to keep such detailed records on their employees who are terminated for theft, because the manager or proprietor is likely to know and recognize all employees personally. Large chain or branch retail organizations need to maintain detailed records, which contain fingerprints, photos, signatures, and so forth, to prevent a terminated employee from being rehired at a different outlet without the knowledge of the personnel office.

Reducing Shoplifting

Shoplifting is reduced by many different techniques. Mechanical gadgets, such as two-way or "anti-pilferage" mirrors, closed-circuit television, one-way-glass observation posts, and completely automated detection systems, are used to detect shoplifting activities. However, store employees must be motivated to keep a sharp watch for shoplifting. Frequent meetings of employee groups, such as an employees' security committee that sets up rules and policy for both retail employees and customers, encourage all employees to keep alert to the problem. Using plainclothes security floorwalkers has also increased the detection of shoplifters. Unidentified floorwalkers might make only occasional appearances, or they might be regular in their observation efforts. In any case, they are notified immediately when a known professional shoplifter enters the store and they are constantly at that person's side. Store employees also observe, from more distance, suspicious customers who loiter without buying, who carry a large purse or shopping bag, or who wear a topcoat in mild weather.

Detection and apprehension of shoplifters is only part of the process. Many stores evaluate a person who has been apprehended to determine if the case should be turned over to the law enforcement agencies or whether some other treatment (such as having him clean up the parking lot) should be used. Many local and state laws now allow the retailer more protection from false arrest charges. The courts now are taking a more serious view of shoplifting by placing larger monetary fines and/or imposing mandatory jail sentences on convicted shoplifters. Everyone —retailers, employees, and law enforcement officials—must work together to curb shoplifting by letting it be known that shoplifters will be prosecuted by courts that impose meaningful penalties.

The importance of the pilferage problem is illustrated by looking at it from an economic point of view. Retail net profit may only be 2 percent of gross sales volume, and pilferage may amount to 1 percent of sales volume. In this case, if pilferage can be reduced by 50 percent, net profit can be increased by 0.5 percent of sales, so net profit will increase by 0.5 divided by 2, or 25 percent (minus the additional cost needed to reduce pilferage). Hence the payoff generated by pilferage prevention systems is likely to be high.

Reducing Handling Errors

Employees are always going to make honest errors in marking goods, in counting inventory, in handling merchandise returns, in making change for customers, in record keeping, and so forth. Careful employee selection, training, and supervision can reduce the frequency of mistakes of this type. Internal auditing is being used increasingly by retailers to reduce the amount of shortages caused by both honest handling errors and employee theft. Less complex recording forms, less frequent label changes, and generally simple information-relaying systems can reduce the occurrence of honest errors. Systems need to be developed to ensure that employees understand why consistent marking, re-marking, recording, and accounting procedures are needed. The advocates of the widespread acceptance and use of the universal product code stress that such handling errors would be minimized if the system were used. Further research is needed in the area of proper application before one can verify these claims.

Taking Physical Inventory

An actual count of all the goods in each outlet is usually conducted once or twice a year to provide financial and inventory control information. The physical inventory results in a listing of the types, quantities, and values of all the items in the store. These data are then used to classify merchandise by any desirable grouping— department, merchandise category, SKU (Stock Keeping Unit), size, and so forth— so that the retail buyers can purchase merchandise intelligently and the amount of inventory overage or shortage can be determined.

The inventory-taking procedure must be carefully planned to provide accurate information. Several different approaches are used for taking the physical inventory, although it is usually valued only in retail prices. This allows retail management to measure the total value of merchandise on hand. The value can then be compared to the book or "perpetual" value to determine the amount of shortage or overage.

Frequently, the store manager will carefully inspect his stock prior to counting each item. Slow-moving and out-of-season items are featured in advertising citing price reductions by using a "pre-inventory clearance sale" theme. Sales of this type can reduce some of the work associated with inventory counting. Employees are then instructed in inventory taking and the importance of accuracy. Standardized inventory forms (obtainable from trade associations or office supply houses) usually are used to record the desired information in a uniform method (Exhibit 8–5).

Exhibit 8-5 **Example of Inventory Recording Form**

INVENTORY ______ 19 ______ Folio ______

Sheet No. ______ Department ______ Priced by ______

Called by ______ Location ______ Extended by ______

Entered by ______ Examined by ______

ITEM NO.	DESCRIPTION	√	QUANTITY	UNIT	PRICE	UNIT	EXTENSIONS

Some chain and branch retail organizations give no advance notice that an inventory is going to be taken. In this case an inventory crew arrives at the outlet unannounced and begins the stock recording procedure. Each person may go through the stock, calling out the description of the items and giving the number of units of each price. This verbal information may be recorded either by a tape recorder or by an assistant. The detailed analysis of the data provided by the inventory is then conducted at retail headquarters. The unexpected element of the inventory-recording procedure can reduce internal theft in large organizations by detecting theft earlier and keeping employees informed that they will be caught if they steal.

Department stores and other outlets that merchandise fashion goods communicate with the retail buyer and merchandise manager to check the accuracy of their perpetual or ongoing records against the count obtained by the physical inventory method. The perpetual inventory records, the unit control records, and other essential forms are then adjusted to reflect the findings of the physical inventory. All information is shipped to the controller's office after counting and recording the data on a standardized form or recording sheet. The controller's office prepares the necessary financial reports (discussed in Chapter 12) and makes historical inventory comparisons. It also determines turnover ratios and stock levels, and calculates the amount of stock shortages or overages by departments.

Merchandise Returns

Merchandise is frequently returned to suppliers because goods may not conform to specifications, or they may be defective, or incorrect items or quantities were shipped, or the terms of the sale are different from what was communicated in the original negotiation.

A full explanation of the reason for returning goods should precede or accompany the returned goods to maintain good vendor relations. Of course, the merchandise should be returned promptly after it has been discovered to be defective or unsatisfactory. Vendors usually do not expect to receive goods back simply because they do not sell. Changes in price and consumer preferences are part of the risks that the retail firm assumes once it has accepted title to the goods. Suppliers' relations are likely to be strained by practices whereby the store benefits entirely at the vendors' expense. For example, refunds may be obtained for some consignment merchandise simply by proving that the goods did not sell. Vendors are not likely to appreciate retailers who repackage such goods and sell them at a considerably reduced price, although they have already claimed the refund from the vendor.

Re-marking Merchandise

Re-marking of merchandise can result from price changes, lost or mutilated tickets, and customer merchandise returns. Most retailers have such merchandise re-marked by the same employees who performed the original marking of the goods. Whoever performs the re-marking process must use standardized ticketing and accounting procedures. Any new tickets must contain the same information that the original label provided. A complete lack of inventory control will result from any system that allows department or sales personnel to make their own tickets or to make price changes without informing the appropriate supervisors.

Consumer Pickup and Delivery

One of the most important links in merchandise handling is consumer pickup and delivery. Since these functions are a major part of retail customer service, a detailed discussion is presented in Chapter 15.

Summary

The previous discussion has examined the buying process in considerable detail. The general model that has been presented can be adapted to a wide range of retail situations. Large department stores, chain stores, and mass merchandisers have their own unique mode of operation, but the basic buying duties presented in the chapter must be accomplished if the firm is to obtain the best merchandise at the lowest costs. Particular attention was given to "market buying," which is a common practice for many small and medium retailers. Often the success or failure of the organization or store hangs on the quality of the decisions made in one to five days spent at the market. Buyers should always be alert for new and profitable products that fit into their assortment plans and complement their retail store image.

Merchandise handling, or back-room operational efficiency, is critical to maintaining a smooth flow of merchandise from the suppliers to the sales floor. Receiving departments must be aware and report any goods damaged in transit as well as matching invoices with packing slips to make sure the firm pays only for merchandise it receives. An old maxim notes that "merchandise doesn't sell in the stockroom or can't be sold if the sales staff can't find the items when floor stocks are exhausted." Thus it is important to move as much merchandise as possible to the selling floor and arrange the surplus stock so it can easily be found.

Last, most retailers are constantly being victimized by major losses of merchandise through sloppy markdown procedures, internal theft, and shoplifting. Unfortunately, the courts do not seem inclined to make this form of theft unprofitable, so the merchant's best defense seems to be to eliminate the opportunities by bolting everything down or putting it back in more secure showcases. Some large chains are sensitizing sales tags so that if the merchandise is not processed through a checkout line the tag sets off an alarm and the thief can be stopped.

Merchandise buying is a risky, challenging profession that is fast paced and very demanding. However, the rewards, both in money and personal satisfaction, are significant. Positive professionalism seems to be the road to success for many aspiring retail merchandisers.

Questions

1. Define the types and characteristics of middlemen serving retailers. Which one is most often used by small retailers? Why?

2. How can accurate, complete merchandise records aid buyers in performing their duties? Explain.

3. How should the buyer attempt to forecast a firm's seasonal sales? What variables must be considered? Why are they important?

4. What is meant by "keystoning" a product? Is this a good policy to follow in all situations? Explain.

5. What part should manufacturers' close-outs play in a retail store's merchandise program? Explain.

6. How can professional middlemen and manufacturers' representatives assist the buyer in making appropriate buying decisions?

7. How should a buyer balance the merchandise assortment to both present staple items and add spice with new items? Explain.

8. What additional problems are experienced when suppliers shorten dating terms and demand "at once" shipping privileges? Explain.

9. How does cash flow generated by retail sales affect the buying process? Discuss.

10. Under what conditions should buyers cancel orders? What are the probable consequences of such action?

11. What responsibilities does the buyer bear in handling the receipt and processing of the merchandise that has been purchased? Explain.

12. What advantages are to be gained by having the supplier preretail the merchandise? What are the disadvantages?

13. How can the retailer reduce shoplifting while using self-service fixtures? How does a retailer determine how much the firm is losing through theft?

14. Suppose a customer returns a defective radio to an electronics shop and is given a replacement. The manufacturer has a policy of no returns or repairs. How should the exchange be recorded so that the replacement will not be counted as a merchandise shortage?

Footnotes

1. Lawrence X. Tarpey, Sr., "Buyer Liability under the Robinson-Patman Act: A Current Appraisal," *Journal of Marketing* 36, (January 1972): 38–42.
2. David R. Gourley, "Transportation Alternatives for the Small Shipper," *Journal of Small Business Management* 9 (October 1971): 32–34.

Case Study

McBrayer Piano & Organ Co.

During the summer months, retail sales of pianos and organs show substantial decreases. It isn't until school opens that sales again show any sizeable increase. Unfortunately, overhead continues despite the slack sales.

This was the situation facing Mr. George McBrayer when he received a call from a potential customer on a hot July afternoon. The caller identified herself as Julie Walters, a friend of Ralph Preston, who had recently purchased a piano from Mr. McBrayer.

After a few minutes of conversation, the woman asked if credit was available through the McBrayer Piano and Organ Co. Rather than answer the question directly, Mr. McBrayer began asking the caller several questions.

He soon discovered that she did not have any of the major credit cards, such as Bankamericard, so could not make use of this source of credit. The woman went on to say that she was recently divorced and had not had time to build a line of credit.

Ms. Walters indicated that she had a good paying job and could meet the payments. She went on to say that she had no children and therefore could afford to purchase a luxury item like a piano. A further reason given for being able to afford a piano was that she lived in an apartment and didn't have the cost of house payments and maintenance.

Before the conversation ended, Ms. Walters asked if Mr. McBrayer thought it was worth her time to come in to see him. He replied that he felt it was but couldn't promise anything regarding credit at that time.

When the conversation ended, Mr. McBrayer called Ralph Preston and asked him about Ms. Walters. Ralph said that he was a good friend of her ex-husband and knew him much better than he knew Ms. Walters. He stated that her ex-husband was a real gentleman and a good businessman and that Ms. Walters was a fine woman about thirty years of age. He knew she had a good-sounding job and wanted a piano, but beyond that he couldn't even guess about her credit or ability and willingness to pay.

This certainly wasn't the first time that Mr. McBrayer had been faced with a problem of whether or not to extend credit to a customer. The McBrayer Piano & Organ Co. had been started in 1895 by his father. Mr. McBrayer had spent all his life in the company and felt he had seen all manner of customers pass through his doors.

The company remained a family business, with stores in Fort Worth, Dallas, and the Irving store run by Mr. McBrayer. Each of the stores continued to be managed by members of the McBrayer family.

Over the years McBrayer Piano & Organ had become one of the largest retailers in terms of volume of sales for the Kimball brand of pianos and organs.

In spite of his years of experience, Mr. McBrayer stated that today is one of the toughest times for extending credit in the history of the firm. In fact, it is now at a point where all the manufacturers of pianos and organs absolutely refuse to become involved in retail credit to customers. The Baldwin Company used to have a finance plan for customers but had to discontinue this program due to high costs and losses.

Thus, each piano retailer is forced to work out his own credit plan through major credit card companies, local banks, and finance companies.

Although the McBrayer Co. accepts credit cards, the primary finance plan is through local banks. The arrangement that McBrayer uses is to send credit applications from potential customers to any one of several local banks. The bank is then supposed to check out the applicant's credit information and tell Mr. McBrayer whether or not credit will be given. (See Exhibit 8–6.)

Unfortunately, all of these loans are on a recourse basis. This essentially means that if the customer fails to keep up the payments, the McBrayer Company is responsible. The banks also demand that a reserve deposit of 5 percent of the outstanding paper must be maintained by McBrayer in a separate account in the bank as insurance against nonpayment by customers.

This arrangement had generally been satisfactory, but in the last few years Mr. McBrayer had the sad experience of discovering that some of the banks were not screening the credit applicants as they should. This recently led to $20,000 in bad loans, which had to be covered by McBrayer Piano & Organ.

In theory, McBrayer can recover these losses by repossessing the piano or organ. In fact, things are not this way. Mr. McBrayer directly blames the wave of consumerism with its resulting laws for this. He feels that many of these were passed without consideration for the honest retailer, particularly smaller ones.

"It used to be we could knock on the door of a person who had failed to make payments and have a truck standing outside to collect the piano. Today we have to go to a lawyer and then the sheriff for a Writ of Sequestration. Then we have to store the piano for a set period of time and finally place it in an auction. This takes a long time and costs us at least $150 in fees, to say nothing of storage and miscellaneous costs."

Mr. McBrayer stated that many pianos simply disappear and cannot be found. People have left town and taken the piano with them. "We have one in Guatemala right now, and it's doubtful we'll ever see it or another payment."

The problem of recourse could be avoided by selling paper to a finance company rather than the local banks. The reason that Mr. McBrayer does not use a finance company is that he believes the costs are too high and may discourage sales. The local banks charge an annual rate of 8 percent "add-on" per year which is an annual rate of 14.55 percent on a three-year basis. By contrast, the more reputable finance companies charge between 10 to 12 percent add-on (the maximum allowed by law), which amounts to 18 percent on an annual basis at the 10 percent rate.

The 10 percent add-on rate also applies to Bankamericard and Master Charge.

It was also the opinion of Mr. McBrayer that when a retailer used a finance company rather than a bank it reflected poorly upon the image of the store. "It used to be that two men would shake hands and that was it. You had a deal and you were 99 percent certain that it would be a good one. Today things are completely different." Mr. McBrayer followed this statement by placing the blame on the changed moral climate in the nation and the increasing lack of responsibility on the part of people.

Over the years, Mr. McBrayer believes he has learned to judge people somewhat. In addition to the information given on the credit application (see Exhibit 8–6), he judges people by the way they act. A man who will not look him squarely in the eye is always suspect, although Mr. McBrayer admits this is not foolproof.

However, Mr. McBrayer believes that these instincts and means of judging a man do not necessarily apply when it comes to a woman. In the case of a divorced woman, he believes that it is important to look at the man she was married to.

"The problem with a divorced woman is that she may remarry and the new husband won't accept responsibility for her debts. All the things that Ms. Walters felt were good selling points in regard to her credit could be bad. First, she doesn't have children to tie her down. Second, she doesn't own a home and could skip town tomorrow. Third, she's only thirty and I understand fairly attractive. This means she stands a good chance of getting remarried. I know these things sound rather prejudiced, but they are facts that any good businessman had better consider."

"We have built a reputation for selling the best available merchandise and for helping people. Somebody has to help this woman establish credit, or she'll never get ahead. At the same time, we're not a charitable organization. We can use the sale at this time of the year, and I'm probably more likely to take a chance on her now than I would be in a few months when business is at a peak."

As Mr. McBrayer spoke he concluded by saying, "I just wish there was a better way to judge a credit applicant, particularly a women. We want to make this sale, but we sure don't want any credit problems with it."

Exhibit 8-6 **Sample Credit Application**

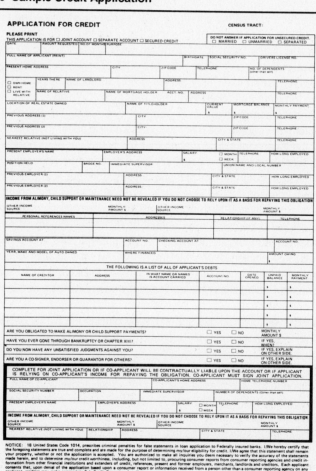

Discussion Questions

1. What else, if anything should Mr. McBrayer do to evaluate credit applications?

2. Can a woman be judged on the same credit standards as a man?

3. Check with several local independent retailers of consumer durables and see if their sales contracts are sold on a recourse or nonrecourse basis. Do you agree that the use of a finance company could lower the image of the store? What do local retailers you interviewed believe?

Appendix 8-1A

Centers of Merchandise Trade

Merchandise Marts

Atlanta
240 Peachtree Street, N.W.
Suite 2200
Atlanta, Georgia 30303
404-688-8994

California Mart
110 E. 9th St.
Los Angeles, Calif. 90015
213-620-0260

Chicago
Merchandise Mart Plaza, Rm. 830
Chicago, Illinois 60654
312-527-4141

Cleveland
420 Prospect Ave.
Cleveland, Ohio 44115
216-771-5566

Dallas Trade Mart
2100 Stemmons Freeway
Dallas, Texas 75207
214-748-6832

Dallas Apparel Mart
2300 Stemmons Freeway
Dallas, 75207
214-637-1970

Dallas Home Furnishings Mart
2000 Stemmons Freeway
Dallas, 75207
214-748-6832

Oak Lawn Plaza
1440 Oak Lawn Ave.
Dallas, 75207
214-631-0600

Kansas City, Missouri

K.City Trade Mart
250 Richards Rd.
K.City, Missouri 64116
816-842-5939

Los Angeles
712 South Olive St.
Los Angeles, Calif. 90014
213-622-7538

Los Angeles Home Furnishings Mart
1933 South Broadway
L. A. 90007
213-749-7911

Pacific Design Center
8687 Melrose Ave.
L. A. 90069
213-657-0800

Miami
777 N.W. 72nd Ave.
Miami, Florida 33126
305-261-2900

Minneapolis
(Midwest Merchandise Mart)
800 N. Washington Ave.
Minneapolis, Minn. 55401
612-339-8788

New York Merchandise Mart
Madison Ave. and 26th St.
N.Y., N.Y. 10010
212-889-6540

New York Gift Center
225 Fifth Ave., Rm. 123
N.Y., N.Y. 10010
212-MU5-6377

Adams Co. Real Estate, Management
11 East 26th St.
N.Y., N.Y.

San Francisco

Western Merchandise Mart
1355 Market St.
San Francisco, Calif. 94103
415-552-2311

The Icehouse
(showcase for home, commercial,
and institutional furnishings)
151 Union St.
San Francisco 94103
415-989-5796

The Showplace!
2 Kansas St.
San Francisco, 94103
415-864-1500

Seattle
1932 First Avenue
Seattle, Washington 98101
206-622-3860

Northwest Home Furnishings Mart
121 Boren Avenue North
Seattle 98109
206-623-1510

Other Centers of Merchandise Trade

American Furniture Mart
(American Mart Corp.)
666 Lake Shore Drive
Chicago, Illinois 60611
312-787-4100

Brack Shops
527 W. 7th St.
Los Angeles, Calif. 90014
213-629-1201

Brack Shops/East
649 Olive St.
Los Angeles, Calif. 90014
213-629-1201

International Trade Centers

Belgium

Brussels International Trade Mart
130 Avenue de Madrid Laan
B-1020 Brussels,
Belgium
02/478.49.89

France

Paris Mart
19 Rue Vignon
75008 Paris,
France
073-64-81

Centre International Textile
Maine Montparnasse,
3, rue de l'Arrivée,
75749 Paris, Cedex 45
France
538-52-00

Mexico

Mexico Mart
Izazago No. 89
Mexico City, Mexico
585-0709

Montreal

Place Bonaventure Inc.
P.O. Box 1000,
Place Bonaventure,
Montreal H5A, 1G1, Quebec
Canada
514-395-2233

Part Three

Operating Policies, Practices, and Controls

Chapter 9

Merchandise Management

Key Terms and Concepts

merchandise budget

annual sales forecast

seasonal sales forecast

monthly sales index

basic stock method of planning inventory

percentage deviation method of planning inventory

weeks' supply method of planning inventory

stock to sales ratio method of planning inventory

marginal analysis method of planning inventory

retail reductions

open-to-buy amounts

initial markup percentage

physical inventory

perpetual inventory

overage

shortage

universal product code (UPC)

stock turnover

net sales to inventory ratio

Merchandise management, one of the most critical areas in retailing, is defined in this book as the activities involved in balancing inventories to meet expected consumer demands. This process is depicted in Figure 9–1. The major merchandise policy decisions—those decisions relating to the question, "What products do we stock?" were discussed in Chapter 4. This chapter concentrates on the other major merchandising issues—how much to buy, when to buy, and merchandise planning. Several techniques (such as the merchandise budget and stock turnover analysis) that can be used by retail management and buyers to plan and control inventory levels will be presented in this chapter. These techniques can simplify many of the activities associated with merchandise planning and control by establishing routine procedures. A discussion of the remaining buying issues—how to buy, organizing for buying, sources of merchandise, buying negotiations, and legal considerations—was presented in Chapter 8.

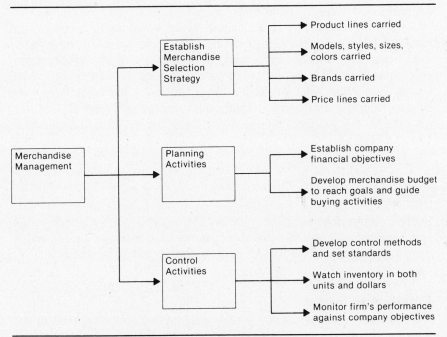

Figure 9–1 **The Merchandise Management Process**

Merchandise Planning

Retailers should recognize several factors that determine whether their merchandise plans are providing the optimum balance between inventory levels and potential sales.

Planning and control methods are simply aids to the buyer's judgment. Such planning and control methods provide data that must be analyzed and interpreted in light of the buyer's previous experience and knowledge. Frequent review of the planning and control techniques must be made to ensure that such tools provide realistic information. Planning and control procedures are usually designed to provide information that is realistic only under a specific set of assumptions about the environment. Retail situations change quite frequently, so the planning and control procedures must be reviewed to be certain they are the most practical means of providing the desired information.

Planning and control procedures are effective only when information is analyzed and translated into action. The merchandise control process involves taking steps to bring actual results closer to stated retail objectives. The trend to larger retail organizations, combined with the tendency for the consumer environment to change more rapidly than ever, has made the use of some type of control process essential. However, changes in consumer preferences also have necessitated flexibility in allowing individual store managers to adjust their merchandise assortment to reflect the needs of their specific trade area more quickly.

Small owner-operated retail outlets have fewer formal control problems than large chain retail outlets. However, even the small retailer can make profitable use of such tools as merchandise budgets and stock turnover analysis to simplify buying procedures and to meet the needs of potential customers. Even the smallest retailers need to plan their sales, stocks, purchases, reductions, and margins by reviewing past records and observing inventory levels on a periodic basis.

Basic Merchandise Information Procedures

Efficient merchandise management involves the use of the most detailed, accurate, and current information that is available. The merchandise budget is one management tool that can be used for both planning and controlling inventories.

Merchandise Budget

The *merchandise budget* can be used in planning and controlling sales efforts, markups, purchases, markdowns, and shortages. It usually consists of:

1. a forecast of sales for given periods
2. a plan for the stocks to be carried at the beginning of each period
3. planned retail reductions
4. planned purchase quantities
5. a planned profit margin

Such a budget enables the retailer to buy merchandise of the kind and in the quantity that better reflects the needs of potential customers. By identifying fast-moving and/or highly profitable items, it provides information that the retailer can use to plan promotional efforts more efficiently. The merchandise budget contains a record of both actual and predicted past sales, which can be used to evaluate the performance of both the budget procedure itself and the store's merchandise buyers.

The budget can be constructed on a weekly, monthly, quarterly, semiannual, or annual basis. However, the longer the time period covered by a budget, the more difficult it is to obtain accurate forecasts. Frequently, the budget is made for six months or one year in advance and is revised each month. A normal sequence in merchandise budgeting is presented below. Deviations from the sequence of activities are both appropriate and common if other, relevant information is available.

Step 1: Forecasting Sales

Either unit or dollar sales are forecast for each merchandise type for the specified time period. Past monthly (or weekly) sales performance should be recorded and analyzed to identify trends and seasonality patterns. The estimated sales volume is a critical element in the merchandise budget because an error in the estimated sales figures can cause a serious error in the projection of the firm's profitability.

Annual sales forecasts must consider such factors as past trends in store sales as well as local changes in (1) population, (2) income, (3) employment, (4) competition (both in number and in action), (5) consumer preferences, (6) the general price level charged by the store, and (7) any of the other internal elements used by the store to attract customers.

Annual sales forecasts may be made simply by estimating a "reasonable" change from last year's sales or by using more complicated statistical forecasting techniques, such as multiple regression analysis (which is discussed in Chapter 17). Several pre-written computer programs are available at reasonable cost, so a commercial service bureau, such as Statistical Tabulating Corporation, may be able to provide annual forecasts less expensively than the individual retailer can.

Seasonality of sales differs by the type of merchandise being sold; so *seasonal sales forecasts* must be made for each different merchandise category on a monthly, weekly, or sometimes even a daily basis (Figure 9–2). In some cases an entire selling period, such as Christmas or Easter, can be analyzed separately. Monthly sales indexes can be used to forecast monthly sales. Monthly sales can be forecast by dividing the estimated annual sales by twelve to obtain the *average* monthly sales estimate. Past monthly sales records can then be used to obtain a *monthly sales index* for each merchandise category. The monthly sales index is calculated by dividing each month's sales by an average month's sales and the result is multiplied by 100.

In formula format:

$$\text{A month's sales index} = \frac{\text{that month's sales}}{\text{an average month's sales}} \times 100$$

For example, suppose sales data for the past five years indicated average sales in January were $10,000, and the five-year annual average sales were $240,000. In

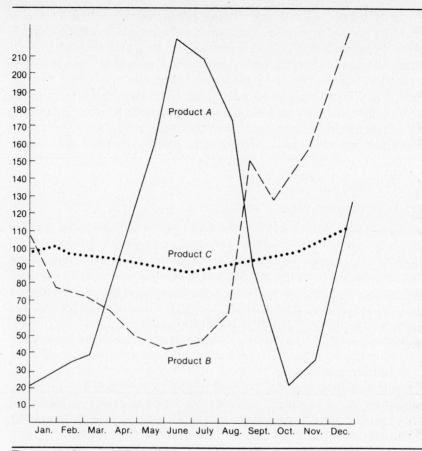

Figure 9-2 **Seasonal Sales Patterns**

this case the average previous monthly sales would be $240,000 divided by 12, or $20,000. The January sales index is ($10,000/$20,000) × 100, or 50.

Each monthy sales index is calculated in a similar manner, so an index of 100 represents sales made during an "average" month. The percentage that a monthly sales index deviates from 100 is the percentage deviation of that month's sales from the sales of the average month. In the above example, the 50 index for January indicates that January sales are 50 percent *below* average. An index of 110 for May would indicate that May sales are 10 percent *above* an average month's sales (because 110 is more than 100).

Once the value of the monthly sales index has been determined, it can be divided by 100 and the result multiplied by the average estimated monthly sales to provide an estimate of that month's sales for the upcoming year.

For example, suppose the forecast sales level for the upcoming year is $300,000 and the January sales index is 50. The forecast January sales is the estimated average monthly sales, or $300,000/12 = $25,000 × (50/100), or $12,500.

Even the best estimates must be revised to account for unanticipated developments, such as abnormally severe weather, epidemics, and so forth. However, the seasonal index approach can be used to make accurate sales forecasts by making comparisons against similar pay periods, holidays, etc. Of course, the occurrence of a holiday in a different week or month from year to year must be accounted for in making weekly or monthly forecasts. This adjustment in forecast sales may consist of simply adding and subtracting the normal value of that holiday occurring or not occurring during the specified period. For example, forecasts should reflect the fact that Easter occurs during one week one year and another week the following year.

Step 2: Planning Inventory Levels

Inventory levels should be planned to maintain the necessary depth and breadth in merchandise assortment that will meet expected customer needs. However, the investment in inventory should also be held low enough to allow a sufficiently high inventory turnover.

Several methods are frequently used to plan needed inventories. The *basic stock method* involves ordering sufficient stock to begin the month (or any other specified selling period) with an inventory that exceeds estimated monthly sales by some "basic stock amount." The basic stock amount is really a basic inventory level or safety stock below which the retailer would not like to fall (Exhibit 9–1).

Exhibit 9–1 Using the Basic Stock Method to Plan Inventory Levels

In this method planned sales for each month are added to a basic stock to obtain the stock on the first of each month. Thus, basic stock equals average stock for the season—average monthly sales for the season.

A. Calculation Formula:

Retail stock at the first of a month=Estimated sales for the month+(Average stock for the season−Average monthly sales for the season).

B. Example: Given data are:

Estimated sales for May=$35,000, average monthly stock for April, May and June=$40,000, and average monthly sales for the April, May and June quarter is $30,000.

Calculation: Stock needed on May 1=$35,000+($40,000−$30,000) or $45,000. In this example the basic stock is $40,000−$30,000 or $10,000.

The *percentage deviation* (*variation*) *method* involves ordering stocks so that the beginning monthly inventory fluctuates from the planned average stock by 50 percent of the sales fluctuations from the average monthly sales (Exhibit 9–2).

The percentage deviation method is usually used when an outlet's inventory turns over at least six times per year. Experience has shown that in stores that obtain a high inventory turnover, the change in inventory should generally be one-half of the planned increase or decrease in sales as provided by this method.

In fact, inventory turnover can be used in establishing the average stock level for

Exhibit 9-2 Using the Percentage Deviation Method to Plan Inventory Levels

In this method the stock is increased or decreased from the average stock desired by one-half the percentage variation in sales from average monthly sales.

A. Calculation Formula: Retail stock at the first of the month =

$$\text{Average stock} \times \tfrac{1}{2} \left(1 + \frac{\text{Sales for month}}{\text{Average monthly sales}}\right)$$

B. Example: Average monthly stock for year = 40,000, Estimated May sales of $35,000 and Average monthly sales for the year = 45,000

$$\text{Calculation: stock needed on May 1} = \$40,000 \times \tfrac{1}{2} \left(1 + \frac{\$35,000}{\$45,000}\right)$$

$$= \$35,555$$

---

any specified time period. For example, in Exhibit 9–1 the average monthly stock for April, May, and June is $40,000, which is equal to

$$\frac{\text{Sales for the season}}{\text{Estimated number of inventory turns}}.$$

Quarterly sales are $30,000 $\times$ 3 months = $90,000 and the store is estimated to obtain an annual inventory turnover of 9, or a quarterly turnover of 9/4, or 2.25. Thus the $40,000 average monthly stock was obtained by dividing $90,000 quarterly sales volume by the 2.25 quarterly stock turn.

Another technique, the *weeks' supply method,* consists of inventory being planned on the basis of a predetermined number of weeks' supply, with some stock turnover used as a goal (Exhibit 9–3).

Exhibit 9-3 Using the Weeks' Supply Method to Plan Inventory Levels

Based on planned turnover, the number of weeks' supply to be carried is determined and sales estimated for this number of weeks ahead.

A. Calculation Formula: Retail stock at first of the month=predetermined number of weeks' supply based on desired stockturn.

B. Example: Desired annual stockturn=10, Estimated sales for next 4 weeks=$35,000, Estimated sales for next 8 weeks=$65,000 and Estimated sales for next 12 weeks=$90,000. Stock needed on May 1=52 (number of weeks in a year)/10 (Desired annual stockturn)=5.2 weeks.
Stock needed on May 1=Sales estimate (Average weekly sales[A] $\times$ 5.2) for 5.2 weeks

$$=\frac{\$35,000+\$30,000/4}{5} \times 5.2$$

$$=\frac{\$42,500}{5} \times 5.2$$

$$=\$8,500 \times 5.2$$

$$=\$44,200$$

[A]Average weekly sales for the period is obtained by using the $35,000 for the first four weeks plus an average week taken from the second four weeks.

Thus, this method is used when sales and stocks are planned on a weekly basis instead of monthly as is the case with the other inventory planning methods. This method is used in planning stocks for staple merchandise, not fashion, fad, or general departmental inventories where sales may fluctuate widely. The reason the method is not usually used on nonstaple merchandise is that stock levels may become much too high when sales are considerably above average. This is caused by a rapid rise in planned stocks, which rise in proportion to expected increases in sales. Stocks also can become much too low when sales are considerably below average because there is no provision for a minimum basic stock when sales are low.

The *stock to sales ratio method* is also used to decide on inventory levels. (Exhibit 9–4). This method involves multiplying the estimated sales volume for the month by the planned beginning-of-the-month stock-sales ratio to obtain the amount of inventory to be carried at the beginning of the month. In formula form,

Estimated sales for the period $\times$ desired beginning-of-the-month stock-sales ratio = retail stock to be carried at the beginning of the month.

Exhibit 9–4 **Using the Stock to Sales Ratio Method to Plan Inventory Levels**

This method yields a planned ratio between the stock on hand on the first of any given month and the sales for that month.[A] This ratio is multiplied by the planned sales for that month.

A. Calculation Formula: Retail stock at first of the month=Estimated sales for the period $\times$ desired beginning of the month stock: sales ratio.

B. Example: Desired monthly stock: sales ratio=2.0 and Estimated sales for May=$35,000.

Calculations: Stock needed on May 1=$35,000 $\times$ 2.0=$70,000.

[A] The monthly stock: sales ratio= $\dfrac{\$ \text{Value of Inventory on Hand at Beginning of Month}}{\$ \text{Sales Expected for That Month}}$

Retailers can analyze their past stock-sales ratios or use the stock-sales ratios of similar retailers to determine the desired stock-sales ratio. Stock-sales ratios are available from several trade publications, such as *Departmental Merchandising and Operating Results of Department and Specialty Stores,* published by the National Retail Merchants' Association in New York.

Each of the four methods provides a different solution to the inventory problem. The stock level indicated by the basic stock method is usually larger than the inventory level given by the stock-sales ratio method. Each method has the major disadvantage of not considering such serious factors as net margin contribution, perishability, fashion influences or style obsolescence, lead time needed before a new order can be received, and the effect that an out-of-stock condition can have upon regular consumers' store preference patterns.

Determining Inventory Levels on Perishable and Fad Items A relatively simple method, termed *marginal analysis,* can be used to determine the quantity of goods that should be stocked. This method is appropriate for goods that are either perisha-ble (such as Christmas gift boxes of fresh fruits) or that are likely to become obsolete because of time (such as newspapers, magazines, or fad items). It can be used to examine the retail price, the wholesale cost, and the reduced price that can be obtained for perishable or out-of-date goods if they cannot be sold before they lose quality or become obsolete.[1] The marginal analysis method gives the retailer the minimum percentage chance he should have of selling the *additional* unit he adds to his inventory before he can profitably stock that unit.

Marginal analysis involves the calculation of *p*, which represents the minimum percent chance of selling at least an additional unit in order to justify the stocking of that unit. The value of *p* is found by using the formula

$$p = \frac{ML}{(MP + ML)} \times 100,$$

where ML is the marginal loss or the decrease in profit resulting from stocking an additional unit that is *not* sold at the retail price, and MP is the marginal profit or the increase in profit resulting from stocking an additional unit that *is* sold.

The use of marginal analysis can be illustrated in the following example. Suppose an item is purchased at wholesale for $4 per unit and is resold at retail for $10 per unit. If the product cannot be sold to a retail customer within a stated period of time, it can be sold to an industrial user for $1 per unit. The per unit profit obtained by stocking and selling the item is the marginal profit (MP), which is the retail price ($10) minus the wholesale cost ($4), or $6. The marginal loss (ML) is the per unit wholesale cost ($4) minus the reduced per unit price that the product can be sold for in the secondary market ($1), or $3. The calculation of *p* is [3/(6 + 3)] 100, or 33 percent. Thus a retailer would have to be at least 33 percent certain that he can sell the additional unit of stock before it will be profitable to purchase that additional unit. His previous sales records could be checked to determine at what stock quantity he is 33 percent sure of selling that additional unit.

For example, suppose the previous sales records follow the pattern in Table 9–1. The retailer would stock 16 units in this situation because he has a 39 percent chance of selling at least 16 units. It will not pay to stock the 17th unit because the percent chance of selling 17 or more units is 23 percent, which is less than the calculated 33 percent.

It is important to note that the retailer expects to sell about 15 units (the average weekly sale) but is stocking 16 units. He can justify stocking more units than he expects to sell because the per unit marginal profit ($6) exceeds the per unit marginal loss ($3). The retailer can afford to take more risk whenever marginal profit is greater than marginal loss. This is the case for items that carry a high markup on cost. The reverse also holds: if marginal profit is less than marginal loss, the retailer will want to stock less than he expects to sell if consumers do not become so dissatisfied with the outlet that they discontinue shopping in his store. If the marginal profit and marginal loss are equal, the retailer outlet would stock exactly what it expects to sell (the average sales) because the calculated *p* value is equal to 50 percent.

This marginal analysis approach can be incorporated into computer programs, which can rapidly indicate the proper inventory level for any item, provided its

Table 9-1 **Illustration of the Marginal Analysis
Approach to Determine Optimal Retail Inventory**

Level of Past Weekly Sales in Units	Number of Weeks When Sales Level Occurred[A]	Percent Chance of Sales Level Occurring[B]	Cumulative Percent Chance That Sales Will Be at This Level or Greater
10 or less	0	0	100
11	6	3	100
12	18	9	97
13	26	13	88
14	34	17	75
15	38	19	58
16	32	16	39
17	26	13	23
18	14	7	10
19	6	3	3
20 or more	0	0	0
Total	200	100	

Average weekly sales = 14.93

Median weekly sales = 15

[A] Weekly sales level may have to be analyzed as "adjusted weekly sales level," where a seasonality adjustment is used to increase the forecast accuracy for products whose demand fluctuates on a seasonal basis.
[B] Percent chance of sales level occurring is obtained by dividing total sales (200) into the frequency (6 for the 11-unit level) and multiplying the result by 100.

average sales and the variation in average sales are known.[2] This marginal approach is limited by the assumption that a customer will not become dissatisfied enough to refuse to trade with the retailer after that consumer finds an out-of-stock condition on a product he had intended to buy. This assumption is not too unrealistic in situations where close substitute items are available from the same store or where high buyer loyalty to the store has been developed.

Determining Inventory Levels on Staple Items Large retail outlets will reorder thousands of staple items regularly, so it is essential to develop a systematic method of reordering merchandise. Several kinds of data are needed to determine the appropriate stock level on staple items whose demand is not subject to wide fluctuations in preferences. The data needed are:

1. S = the level of sales expected before the next order can be received

2. DP = the delivery period, which is the amount of time estimated to elapse between the time an order is placed and the time the merchandise is delivered and prepared for sale by the retailer

3. R = The reserve or safety stock needed to take care of deviations from expected sales

4. I = The level of stock currently on hand

5. O = The amount of merchandise currently on order but not yet received

6. The store's policy with regard to inventory review and reorder periods (where "review period" refers to the frequency with which inventories are checked to determine stock levels and "reorder period" (RP) is the time interval that normally elapses between orders).

Retailers need to order enough stock to meet the expected purchases during the combined delivery (DP) and reorder periods (RP) plus an additional "safety stock" (R) which is carried to prevent an out-of-stock condition if actual sales should exceed expected sales. The safety stock level, R, may be determined by observing the sales fluctuations that have occurred in the past. A prespecified level of confidence can be used to correspond to the desired inventory condition. If a merchant desires to create an image of not being out of stock on staple items, he can set a goal for a safety stock that is intended to accomplish this result nearly all (say 97 percent) of the time.

If sales of a staple item were distributed as indicated in Table 9–1, this would mean that a safety stock of 4 units (19 minus 15, which is the average) would be needed. If 90 percent protection is considered adequate, the safety stock would be 3 (18 minus average sales of 15 units), assuming immediate delivery can be obtained.

The order level on a staple item (following the sales distribution given in Table 9–1) for a firm which every two weeks reorders an item that requires three weeks for delivery and preparation for retail sale could be determined by a similar analysis of the distribution of sales over a five-week period of time—three weeks for the normal delivery period (DP) and two weeks for the reorder period (RP). The usual minimum stock level would be the number of weeks (three) required for delivery and preparation times the average weekly sales, plus the desired safety stock. This is the point at which another order should be placed to prevent an out-of-stock condition before the newly ordered merchandise arrives.

The maximum amount of stock (M) that a store should have on hand in inventory and on order at any point in time is:

Maximum = (Reorder Period + Delivery Period) Rate of Sales + Reserve Stock

| M | RP | DP | S | R |

Suppose that an item is selling at the rate of seventy-five units per week, a thirty-unit reserve stock is desired, the delivery period is three weeks and the reorder period is two weeks. In this case the combined maximum number of units that the store should have on hand and on order is:

$$M = (RP + DP) S + R$$
$$= (2 + 3) 75 + 30$$
$$= (5) 75 + 30$$
$$= 375 + 30$$
$$= 405$$

Frequently, past sales information is not available on an item. Guidelines can be used to reveal the safety stock needed for these items and for items whose past sales have changed enough to make analysis of past sales records unreliable. Table 9–2 contains safety stock formulas that provide varying degrees of protection from running out of stock if average sales levels can be forecast with reasonable accuracy. The data in Table 9–2 indicate a general stocking rule that the level of safety stock relative to sales needed is usually lower on fast-moving merchandise than is the required safety stock on slow-moving items.

Table 9-2 **Safety Stock Levels Needed to Obtain Varying Degrees of Protection against Running Out of Stock**

| Approximate Safety Stock Level Needed to Obtain Stated Degree of Protection against Running Out of Stock If Expected Delivery and Reorder Period Sales Are: | | Retail Stock Policy: Approximate% Chance of Not Running Out of Stock | Safety Stock Level Needed to Obtain Stated Degree of Protection against Running Out of Stock | |
25	400			
12	46	99	2.3	$\sqrt{}$ Forecast Sales Level for Delivery and Reorder Periods
8	32	95	1.6	$\sqrt{}$ Forecast Sales Level for Delivery and Reorder Periods
5	20	80		$\sqrt{}$ Forecast Sales Level for Delivery and Reorder Periods

Note: This table is applicable to situations where average sales can be forecast with reasonable accuracy. In such cases, the Poisson probability distribution appears to describe variations in retail sales appropriately. See John W. Wingate, Elmer O. Schaller, and F. L. Miller, *Retail Merchandise Management* (Englewood Cliffs, N.J.: Prentice-Hall, 1972), pp. 342-343.

For example, the safety stock level of 12, when expected sales are 25, represents a safety stock of nearly 50 percent of expected sales to reach the 99 percent level of protection from running out of stock. When expected sales are 400, the safety stock required to provide 99 percent protection is 46 units, which is only 11.5 percent of the 400 units forecast to be sold.

The data presented in Table 9–2 can also be used to determine the level of the reserve stock = $ required to maintain a specified percentage protection against running out of stock. For example, data in Table 9–2 indicate that the retailer could use a retail stocking policy of being about 99 percent sure of not running out of stock on a staple item by calculating the value for R in the following formula:

$$R = 2.3\sqrt{(RP + DP)\ S}$$

Thus, if the weekly sales are estimated to be 75 units, the reorder period is two weeks and the delivery period is three weeks:

$$R = 2.3\sqrt{(2 + 3)\ 75}$$
$$= 2.3\sqrt{(5)\ (75)}$$

$$= 2.3\sqrt{375}$$
$$= 2.3 \ (19.4)$$
$$= 44.6 \text{ or } 47 \text{ units}$$

The same retailer could be about 95 percent sure of not running out of stock by calculating the value of R in the following formula:

$$R = 1.6\sqrt{(RP + DP) \ S}$$
$$= 1.6\sqrt{(2 + 3) \ 75}$$
$$= 1.6 \ (19.4)$$
$$= 31 \text{ units}$$

Or finally the retailer could be about 80 percent sure of not running out of stock by finding the value of R in:

$$R = \sqrt{(RP + DP) \ S}$$
$$= \sqrt{(2 + 3) \ 75}$$
$$= 19.4 \text{ units}$$

The above calculations illustrate a general rule in regard to establishing the reserve stock level on staple items; namely, if the retail policy is designed to be out of stock only one percent of the time, the required reserve stock will be 2.3 times the level of the reserve stock needed to be 80 percent sure that the item will be in stock.

Determining Inventory Levels on Fashion Items Fashion items such as apparel and home furnishings present the most complex and critical inventory problems because they are usually offered in many different styles, colors, sizes, materials, and so forth. The major characteristics of fashion goods are:

1. A short product life span
2. Relatively unpredictable sales level
3. Broad assortments, needed to create favorable store image
4. Extreme amount of consumer emphasis on style and color
5. Consumer purchases made on impulse basis or on subjective evaluation of the item and its close substitutes.

Additional safety stock must be carried on fashion items, not only because of their wide fluctuations in sales but also because of a need to provide a broader merchandise assortment for fashion customers. The formulas in Table 9–2 can be used to determine the safety stock needed for fashion goods, but another reserve amount, called the "basic assortment reserve," must also be carried.[3] The amount of the basic assortment reserve is based upon the buyer's judgment of the level needed to provide the basic merchandise assortment demanded by consumers. Thus the total reserve stock of fashion goods will be larger than the safety stock level required of staple items.

There is some degree of predictability that can be used to estimate sales of fashion items. Because each retail outlet caters to a certain target market, the average-price merchandise sold within a merchandise line is not likely to change drastically over a short period of time. Thus, an apparel merchandiser's total sales on all different price lines can be predicted with considerable accuracy. The distribution of sales by size is also fairly constant from year to year, as the distribution of human body sizes and shapes does not change suddenly for the population as a whole.

Seasonal patterns also exist in fashion merchandise, so monthly sales indexes can be used to forecast the sales distribution by color and type of material used. For example, black and white-colored clothing sells better during the summer months, pastel and light-background prints sell better in the spring, and green and rust are preferred in the fall.[4]

Step 3: Planning Retail Reductions

Retail reductions can occur because of (1) markdowns and (2) stock shortages. Markdowns are price reductions that are used to stimulate sales of overstocked items and discounts that are given to employees or other specific customer groups, such as cash customers. Stock shortages are caused by pilferage, shoplifting, damaged merchandise, and the like.

Both markdowns and shortages are inevitable in retail outlets despite the efforts made to prevent them. Thus, these items must be included in the merchandise budget. Markdowns reduce the value of retail inventory because the retail price is lowered on the same number of physical units. Shortages reduce both the value of the retail inventory and the number of physical units as well, because some portion of the physical stock is no longer available for sale.

Every effort should be made to minimize the value lost by markdowns and shortages. The discussions of markdowns in Chapter 10 indicate that good sales forecasting will reduce the volume of marked down items. (The effect that good management and control practices can have on reducing shortages was discussed in Chapter 8.) However, markdowns and shortages will occur in spite of even the most rigorous control methods. Therefore retailers should use their past experience, or that of similar stores, to provide an estimate of the value of the inventory loss. The reductions are usually estimated on a percentage-of-sales-dollar volume basis and entered as part of the store's merchandising budget.

Step 4: Planning Purchases

The quantity to purchase is easily obtained if (1) sales have been forecast, (2) desirable inventory levels have been determined, and (3) retail reductions have been planned. If these data are available, the following formula can be applied to an entire store, department, or merchandise line:

Planned purchase quantity = desired inventory at end of period
    + estimated sales + estimated reductions
    − inventory available at beginning of period.

The dollar amount of allowable purchases that the buyer can make during the remaining portion of the period under a merchandise budget system that establishes maximum inventory levels and planned purchasing figures is called the *open-to-buy amount*. Thus, the open-to-buy device assists the buyer in determining how much merchandise he is able to buy during the remainder of any merchandising period and still remain within the guidelines established in the merchandise budget.

Open-to-buy amounts are usually stated in retail-price dollars. The open-to-buy concept can be illustrated by an example of a buyer who is making purchases for the month of September. Suppose that the merchandise budget calls for a planned inventory of $20,000 on September 30, estimated September sales are $40,000, the beginning inventory on September 1 was $22,000, the planned markdowns and shortages are estimated at 10 percent of retail sales dollar volume, or $4,000, and the planned initial markup on cost is 30 percent. Also assume that during the first ten days of September net sales amount to $18,000, markdowns or shortages amount to $2,000, $12,000 worth of retail goods (valued at retail prices) are delivered, and goods already ordered during September are valued at $12,000. The open-to-buy amount may be calculated as illustrated in Table 9–3, which indicates that the buyer can still purchase goods costing $12,600 at wholesale prices during the remainder of September and remain within the merchandise budget.

The open-to-buy figure should not be a set quantity that cannot be exceeded. Consumer needs are the dominant consideration. If sales of a product line, depart-

Table 9–3 Illustration of Open-to-Buy Amount

Inventory Requirements		Available Inventory	
(a) Desired inventory level, September 30	$20,000	(e) Actual inventory, September 1	$22,000
(b) Estimated sales for remainder of September ($40,000–$18,000)	22,000	(f) Value of goods received during September 1–10	12,000
(c) Planned markdowns and shortages for remainder of September ($4,000–$2,000)	2,000	(g) Total inventory handled (e+f)	34,000
		Less deductions such as	
		(h) Markdowns and shortages during September 1–10	2,000
(d) Total Inventory Requirement (a+b+c)	$44,000	(i) Sales during September 1–10	18,000
		(j) Total Deductions (h+i)	20,000
		Plus	
		(k) Value of inventory already ordered for September delivery	12,000
		Equals	
		(l) Total Available Inventory (g+k–j)	$26,000

Total Inventory Requirement (item d or $44,000) minus Total Available Inventory (item l or $26,000) equals Open-to-Buy ($18,000) at Retail Prices. Open-to-Buy at Cost equals Open-to-Buy at Retail times [(100—markup percent)/100] or $18,000 [(100−30)/100] equals $12,600.

Note: All inventory, reductions, and sales are valued at retail prices.

ment, or store exceed the forecast, additional quantities should be ordered above those scheduled for purchase according to the merchandise budget. Thus, a buyer must have permission of the management to make occasional additional purchases of fast-moving goods whose demand has been underestimated. However, additional purchases of the same goods should not have to be made on a frequent basis. If this is the case, either the forecasting procedure is too conservative or the buyer is overbuying other goods that are not selling as well. Retail management should determine the causes of frequently overbought conditions and then take steps to prevent their recurrence.

Step 5: Planning Profit Margins

The *initial markup percentage* (the percentage of the retail price that is not spent for merchandise) should be adequate to cover expenses, reductions, and profits.[5] The initial markup percentage is usually planned on all the merchandise carried because detailed data on expenses and reductions are not available for each item.

The necessary markup percentage may be calculated by first forecasting the total sales for the store for the desired time period. Then expenses and price reductions needed to reach the sales goal can be estimated. And then a realistic profit goal can be established. These three components—expenses, reductions, and profits—are then added together and that sum is divided by the sum of sales plus reductions to give the required initial markup percentage needed to achieve the desired profit goals.

The calculation for initial markup percentage is:

$$\text{Required initial markup percent} = \frac{(\text{Expenses} + \text{profits} + \text{reductions})}{(\text{sales} + \text{reductions})}$$

For example, suppose planned sales are $500,000 annually, with estimated operating expenses of $100,000, reductions of $70,000, and a profit goal of $50,000. The initial markup percentage would be:

$$\text{Required initial markup percent} = \frac{(\$100,000 + \$50,000 + \$70,000)}{(\$500,000 + \$70,000)}$$

or 38.6 percent.

This same equation can also be used when expenses, reductions, and profits are planned in percentage terms instead of dollars. Sales simply become 100 percent in the equation in this case. The remaining figures are expressed as percentages converted to decimals. In the previous example, expenses were estimated to 20 percent of sales, the profit goal was 10 percent of sales, and reductions were estimated to amount to 14 percent of sales. Thus the required initial markup percentage would be:

$$\frac{(0.20 + 0.10 + 0.14)}{(1.00 + 0.14)} = 38.6 \text{ percent}$$

This equation can be used to determine what percentage markup a retailer must obtain on all his purchases if he is to cover all expected expenses, reductions, and markdowns and still make the desired planned profit. It should be reemphasized that this calculation yields the overall, or average, markup on all merchandise. The markup used on each item or in each department will deviate from this average markup depending upon consumer demand, competition, and so forth. However, the formula is a useful guide that shows the average markup needed to generate the desired profit level.

The retail buyer should strive to attain the planned markup goals. Expense percentages have been rising during recent years, and unless sales can be substantially increased by using lower prices, a higher initial markup is required to achieve the target net profit. Thus, the basic merchandise budgeting problem consists of accurately forecasting a realistic initial markup percentage that will yield the desired net profit margin.

Use of the Merchandise Budget

Retail management can use the merchandise budget to determine how efficiently the retail operation is being conducted and to locate possible sources of trouble before they become too serious. For example, management can use current and past merchandise budgets to see if the open-to-buy quantity is being frequently exceeded. If so, it can determine which departments have been guilty and identify who was responsible for the action. Merchandise budgets also allow management to check actual results against the planned figures. This will not only indicate which people are the most accurate planners, but it will also indicate which budgeted figures need to be revised. A form similar to the one presented in Exhibit 9–5 is frequently used to provide a summary of the data obtained by following the steps of the merchandise budget process.

The merchandise budget should be used as a management tool that improves the judgment of retail management, who review it at frequent intervals. Although the merchandise budget is a useful tool, its benefits must be weighed against its costs to ensure that the time and effort expended are worthwhile expenditures. The budgeting process should remain sufficiently flexible so that unique purchasing opportunities are not stifled and that changes in both the wholesale and retail marketplaces can be quickly identified and new estimates used in preparing a revised budget.

Merchandise Planning and Control Systems

Merchandise planning and control techniques are related to both overall merchandise values (dollars) and to measurable quantities of goods or services (units). Unit controls are needed because the retail firm's buyer and the retail customer make their purchases in units. Dollar controls are needed because overall store sales,

Exhibit 9-5 A Completed Six-Month Merchandise Budget

SIX-MONTH MERCHANDISE PLAN

STORE Downtown

DEPARTMENT Hardware

FROM January 1 19 __

TO June 30 19 __

Control Data	Last Year	This Year
% Initial Markup	45.0	43.5
% Reductions	10.0	8.0
% Maintained Markup	39.5	39.0
% Alteration Expense	1.5	1.0
% Cash Discount	2.0	2.0
% Gross Margin	40.0	40.0
% Operating Expense	35.0	35.0
% Net Profit	5.0	5.0
First Half Turnover	2.0	2.5

Planning and Authorization

Buyer _____

Merchandise Controller _____

Date Prepared _____

Date Authorized _____

	First Half / Last Half	Jan. / July	Feb. / Aug.	March / Sept.	April / Oct.	May / Nov.	June / Dec.	Total
Sales	Last Year	$ 42,315	$ 78,120	$ 65,100	$ 55,335	$ 52,080	$ 32,550	$325,500
	Plan	39,385	71,610	82,350	64,450	64,450	35,805	358,050
	Actual							
Retail E.O.M. +	Last Year	186,620	173,600	163,835	160,580	141,050	162,750	
	Plan	155,155	165,895	147,995	147,995	119,350	143,220	
	Actual							
Reductions +	Last Year	4,300	1,790	6,445	8,590	7,880	6,805	35,810
	Plan	5,728.80	1,718.64	4,296.60	7,161.00	7,447.44	2,291.52	28,644
	Actual							
Retail B.O.M. -	Last Year	150,815	186,620	173,600	163,835	160,580	141,050	
	Plan	122,930	155,155	165,895	147,995	147,995	119,350	
	Actual							
Retail Purchases =	Last Year	82,420	66,890	61,780	60,670	40,430	61,055	373,245
	Plan	77,338.80	84,068.64	68,746.60	71,611.00	43,252.44	61,966.52	406,984.00
	Actual							
Cost Purchases	Last Year	50,110	40,670	37,560	36,890	24,580	37,120	226,930
	Plan	43,696.42	47,498.78	38,841.83	40,460.22	24,437.62	35,011.08	229,945.95
	Actual							

expenses, and financial reports are stated in dollars as well as in the quantity of physical units. Dollar control is the usual basis for establishing initial merchandise control systems.

However, the retail buyer must look beyond dollar figures to determine which sizes, colors, styles, and price lines are selling. This information is contained (both in dollar and unit terms) in the store's daily sales slips or records. In small stores, the sales data are likely to be recorded on sales slips or booklets. In large stores, cash registers are frequently linked to electronic computer systems, which provide detailed information on inventories and sales for each item.

Sales and inventory information also is usually summarized and analyzed by classifying and categorizing the entire merchandise assortment into different subassortments, such as departments, merchandise lines, and so forth. Classification is needed in merchandise planning and control because it is easier to analyze smaller and similar types of products and services than the entire merchandise offering and then make inferences for the different merchandise lines. The split-total cash register, hooked up to a computer, is an efficient method of recording and analyzing data on large numbers of product categories. The categories may be defined by differences in color, price line, size, style, product content, and so forth, provided the appropriate key is pushed on the cash register. A more detailed discussion of the use of such systems will be presented in Chapter 12.

The main point for the current discussion is that stores using such systems obtain their classification totals at the end of the day as a by-product of their normal sales-registering procedure. These totals can easily be posted manually to merchandise control records from the cash register tape, or the computer can automatically print out the desired control records.

Dollar Planning and Control

Retail buyers plan and control dollar inventory values because they need to keep the stocks of each department or merchandise category in line with its sales. Proper dollar planning and control procedures allow the buyer to minimize both stock shortages and the markdown pricing that is required if the inventory is too large relative to sales. The dollar control process also allows the buyer to identify easily those merchandise items or lines that have the largest inventory investment and those that have the highest dollar sales.

Dollar control is initially concerned with determining the value of the firm's inventory at any point in time. Without the inventory valuation data, the buyer cannot plan or control any portion of the merchandise management process. Purchases, cost of goods sold, gross margins, and profit margins cannot be planned or determined until inventories are valued in dollar terms.

A periodic *physical inventory* count must be taken at least once a year to satisfy legal requirements. The counting of the actual physical inventory is a time-consuming process, so retailers use a technique called *perpetual inventory* to estimate inventory levels. The perpetual inventory results from recording the beginning inventory (counted at the start of the period), all purchases, and all sales in retail prices. The following formula is then used to estimate the retail value of the current inventory:

Retail value of current inventory = retail value of beginning inventory + retail value of purchases made during the period − retail value of sales made during the period.

The perpetual inventory method provides current, useful information, particularly if it involves the use of a computer-reported inventory system.

Reductions in inventory values resulting from pilferage, damaged merchandise, other forms of dishonesty, and price reductions do not appear on the perpetual inventory. Thus, despite the time required, retailers may decide to take a physical count more than once a year. Retailers of large items, such as automobiles, can afford to take physical counts quite frequently, compared to retailers of many small items, such as grocery stores that handle over 10,000 items at one time. Taking a physical inventory permits the buyer to determine the overage and shortage magnitudes by which the perpetual inventory deviates from the physical inventory.

Overage is the dollar amount by which the physical inventory value exceeds the perpetual inventory value. Such a discrepancy is usually caused by clerical error, such as overcharging customers on sale merchandise or marking merchandise higher than it is supposed to be marked. *Shortage* is the dollar amount by which the perpetual inventory value exceeds the physical inventory value. Such shortages can originate from both clerical error and retail reductions caused by markdowns and shrinkage.

The National Retail Merchants' Association has established electronic processing centers in New York and California to provide its member stores with a variety of reports for standard classification numbers.[6] Stores send in their sales, purchase, inventory, and markdown data and receive dollar and unit information on merchandise sold, received, and held in inventory, as well as stock to sales ratios and gross margin percentages for each category. A report is sent to the participating stores on a monthly basis. The opening inventory figures in each category are reported semiannually or annually by the stores as they take a new physical inventory. The inventory for the intervening months represents estimated inventories calculated by the computer. A report such as the one in Exhibit 9–6 can indicate merchandise categories in which inventories appear to be out of balance relative to sales. If the present percent inventory distribution is much higher for a category than its percent of sales distribution, the merchandise described in this category may be overstocked.

On the other hand, if the percent of sales distribution for a product category greatly exceeds its present percent of inventory distribution, the category would probably be understocked; so inventories could be built up in this product line. Of course the gross margin and profitability ratios would also have to be considered to ensure that the retail outlet was not overstocking a low-margin category.

A comparison of the perpetual and physical methods of obtaining merchandise data by merchandise classification indicates that when a computer is available, the perpetual inventory method can function accurately and at a lower cost to provide a more current source of data than the physical method. When the computer equipment is not available, the periodic physical inventory method can be used profitably in merchandise planning.

Unit Planning and Control

Unit merchandise control is used to maintain ideal merchandise assortments by recording and reporting quantities in inventory, on order, and the rate of sale of individual items. Unit control procedures are needed if the buyer is going to be able to (1) identify the items that are selling best, (2) invest properly in inventories, and (3) use good buying procedures, based upon the knowledge of what is needed and what has been selling well. Merchandise controls are valuable aids to the decision-making process the buyer must use in developing his purchasing strategy. Therefore unit control procedures should be designed to assist the buyer in his purchasing function.

Unit control involves the same general procedures as dollar control:

Exhibit 9-6 Retail Inventory Management Report

PAGE 01 OF 04 WEEK MONTH   WEEK 01 OF 04 WEEK MONTH   WEEK 10   SPRING 1977   DEPT   FASHION ACCESSORIES •   04/09/77

OPEN TO BUY

		SALES						STOCK				MARKDOWNS				LINE 1 ORDERS / LINE 2 COMB. STOCK. ORD. / LINE 3 OPEN TO BUY			
		CURR WEEK	% CHNG	MTD	% CHNG	APR	MAY	JUN	STD	% CHNG	CURR WEEK	APR	MAY	JUN	CURR WEEK	MTD %	STD %	STD % SLS	APR	MAY	JUN	FUTURE
TY NY	409.0		409.0								7,390				-.2	-.2	259.8	7.6	7,330			ORDER S&O OTB
TY NR	18.8	-100	18.8	-100	80.6	83.1	95.1	149.9	-100	-16.0 462.3	459.6	436.9	374.2	3.0	3.0	1.0 12.5	73.3 8.3	-16.0			ORDER S&O OTB
TY FM	41.4		41.4					302.3		718.1 726.8				2.5 3.0	2.5 3.0	16.0 20.5	5.3 6.4	718.1			ORDER S&O OTB
TY ST	54.6		54.6					385.8		781.2 866.6	735.6 844.5	668.4 725.5	580.0 612.0	12.0 5.1	12.0 5.1	22.1 21.0	5.7 5.9	781.2			ORDER S&O OTB
TY BC	77.1 74.3		77.1 74.3					546.7		989.0 1,024	1,067 1,006	953.2 889.6	862.4 806.9	4.5 15.4	4.5 15.4	24.0 31.4	4.4 5.3	989.0			ORDER S&O OTB
TY SH	69.6 54.1		69.6 54.1					496.6		951.0 923.8	874.3 896.0	786.8 777.8	715.1 748.8	3.3 1.7	3.3 1.7	26.7 28.9	5.4 6.3	951.0			ORDER S&O OTB
TY GC	68.4 54.1		68.4 54.1					471.3		1,063 963.7	871.0 948.6	778.2 918.3	712.1 832.8	-1.8 9.1	-1.8 9.1	15.0 30.0	3.2 6.9	1,063			ORDER S&O OTB
TY HP	70.1 54.8		70.1 54.8					501.6		983.3 982.6	957.2 977.2	853.2 847.3	774.7 771.4	12.7 .3	12.7 .3	27.4 14.6	5.5 3.1	983.3			ORDER S&O OTB
TY JT	-.1		-.1					-.1		1.2 -1.5	-1.5	-1.5	-1.6					1.2			ORDER S&O OTB
TY TC	57.5 63.1	-9	57.5 63.1	-9	254.2	291.0	283.8	503.5 520.5	-3	1,095	1,083	980.5	894.6	4.2	4.2	24.6	4.9	1,095			ORDER S&O OTB
TY WF	76.3 75.2	2	76.3 75.2	2	284.3	312.6	293.3	379.1 380.3	-3	1,394	1,052	923.6	845.4			.3	.1	1,394			ORDER S&O OTB
TY SC																					ORDER S&O OTB
TY CH																					ORDER S&O OTB
TY HA																					ORDER S&O OTB
TY JR																					ORDER S&O OTB
TY T	924.0 929.5 695.6	-1 33	924.0 929.5 695.6	-1 33	3,566 2,962	3,836 3,074	3,851 3,147	7,011 7,125 6,008	-3 17	15,29 12,58	13,90 12,56	12,65 11,39	11,84 10,76	37.1 38.7	37.1 38.7	416.8 368.1	5.9 6.1	22,58	989.7	405.9 1,774	
TY ES	790.1 791.2 695.6	14	790.1 791.2 695.6	14	3,027 2,962	3,232 3,074	3,274 3,147	6,129 6,118 6,008	-1	12,80 12,58	11,77 12,56	10,75 11,39	10,10 10,76	32.9 38.7	32.9 38.7	391.9 368.1	6.4 6.1				ORDER S&O OTB

COMBINED STOCK & ORDERS	MARKUP PERCENT	SEASON PLAN PERCENT	SELLING COST PCT	IMPORTS
TY 22.58	TW 51.5 MTD 51.5 STD 51.4	MU 51.4 MD 7.7 GM 51.2	TW 8.3 MTD 9.0 STD 9.6	TY 2,865
LY 13.65	LY 51.7 51.7 51.0	TY LY	TY 7.8 8.6 9.1	LY 2,743

WEEK 01 OF 04 WEEK MONTH   WEEK 10   SPRING 1977   DEPT   FASHION ACCESSORIES •

1. Implement some form of classification system.

2. Use either a perpetual or physical inventory system to provide unit inventory, order, and sales data.

3. Establish the ideal merchandise assortment to be carried and the unit levels of inventory needed to be stocked on each item.

Item inventory requirements are established only after considering such factors as the item's rate of sale, the amount of time required to receive the item after it has been ordered, the markup obtained on the item, the effect an out-of-stock condition has on the retail customers, and so forth. Naturally, high inventory levels must be maintained on the faster-moving items if supplies are to satisfy consumer demand. Inventory levels will also be higher for items that require longer delivery periods, because a store manager does not want to be out of stock on an item for a long period of time. Higher inventory levels should also be established for high markup items because lost sales, caused by an out-of-stock condition on such items decrease net profit considerably more than the same volume of lost sales on a low-margin item. A larger inventory level may be carried on unique items that the store stocks. If no close substitute products are sold by the store, other things being equal, management could justify a larger inventory on that item than on an item that is quite similar to several other items that are sold in the store.

Unit control systems are designed to minimize lost sales and consumer dissatisfaction caused by out-of-stock conditions and, at the same time, identify items or merchandise lines that are overstocked in relation to their consumer demand. In addition to periodic physical inventory counts and perpetual inventory methods, retail managers are also using unit control devices such as checklist systems, warehouse control systems, and requisition stock control.[7]

Cash register systems hooked to electronic computers are used to implement unit control procedures as well as cash control techniques. As the use of these types of systems spreads, the cost of implementing and using item control procedures will decrease. As a result, store managers will probably use even more unit control techniques as the basis for sounder merchandise management planning.

For example, COSMOS, a computer program, is used by a number of food chains to compute direct product profitability and projected rate of movement for individual items. The COSMOS program also calculates optimum selling space assignments, based on assigned-category space constraints and logistical considerations.[8] Chains that use COSMOS report that a significant profit improvement has been obtained by using the program. This may be attributable to (1) a reduction in out-of-stock conditions, (2) use of released surplus space for product line additions, or (3) increased sales obtained from products given more shelf space.

International Business Machines Corporation, through its Retail IMPACT system, has been able to use advanced computer inventory systems to solve basic retail inventory problems.[9] The Inventory Management Program and Control Techniques (referred to as IMPACT) program consists of two models: a sales forecasting system and a merchandise ordering model.

The Retail IMPACT forecast system is designed to yield the maximum return from each dollar invested in inventory. It does this by providing the maximum opportunity for reordering profitable items and the data for identifying and eliminating unprofitable merchandise rapidly.

IMPACT order models are used to identify the costs incurred in the ordering process. This allows management to analyze the IMPACT forecasts to determine when to buy and how much to buy. The system allows management to analyze each vendor's offerings to obtain the lowest total cost by considering factors such as the best economic lot size to order in view of each vendor's quantity discount structure and the desired level of safety stock required by the retailer.

The *Universal Product Code (UPC)* was developed in 1973 to reduce operating expenses in supermarkets. This process uses a laser checkout scanner that contains a light source to illuminate and automatically identify each premarked item as it passes through the checkout facility. The UPC symbol is a unique twelve-digit item identification number that is marked both in decimal characters and in a bar coded form that is read by the laser scanner. (Exhibit 9–7).

There were about 200 supermarkets using the UPC system in 1977. These stores maintained instantaneous inventory records because the system keeps track of each item's sales as well as its inventory level. This item movement data can be used by management to implement optimal inventory policies and use better shelf allocation procedures that reduce stockouts, level of inventory required, and ordering costs. The value of benefits can be substantial. For example, Mr. Joseph B. Danzansky, President of Giant Food Inc., in testimony before the Maryland Senate, indicated that their average store, which has sales of about $140,000 per week, could save about $2,745 per month by using the UPC system. The savings could be attained in six areas:

Front-end productivity is an evaluation of the computer-assisted checkout's impact on the dollar savings that could result from more quickly processing our customers through the checkout operation.

Price marking is an evaluation of the labor dollars that could be saved if Giant was no longer required to maintain prices on the items stocked in the store.

Routine reordering is an estimate of the dollar savings if store personnel no longer have to manually reorder stock items.

Register balancing includes all of the cashier functions that can be automated by computer-assisted checkouts. These have been translated into man-hour dollar savings.

Under-rings refer to those errors caused by the checker or by mismarking which are in favor of the customer.

Register replacement is the cost avoidance of having to buy conventional registers.

The most significant savings is in front-end labor, which accounts for 42 percent of the savings. Elimination of price marking accounts for 23 percent of the savings and register balance for 15 percent. Routine reordering accounts for 9 percent, under-rings for 8 percent and register replacement for 3 percent.[10]

The practice of marking all prices on the shelf but not marking the price on each individual merchandise item has been criticized by consumer groups. As a result, most of the supermarkets using the UPC system are still maintaining the price marking on each individual item even though the laser-computer system does not use this price mark. Some supermarkets do not want to give up the significant savings that can be obtained by eliminating the price marks on all individual items. Thus, consumer acceptance appears to be an important factor in on how the UPC system will be adopted and used. Steinbergs, a grocery chain in Montreal, has come up with a method of reducing consumer resistance to the lack of marking on each item. After three months of operating its IBM system with UPC symbols, the chain was able to eliminate price marking without encountering any resistance from customers. It offered grease pencils, which shoppers could use to do their own price

Exhibit 9-7 **UPC Product Code Symbol and Checkout Sales Receipt**

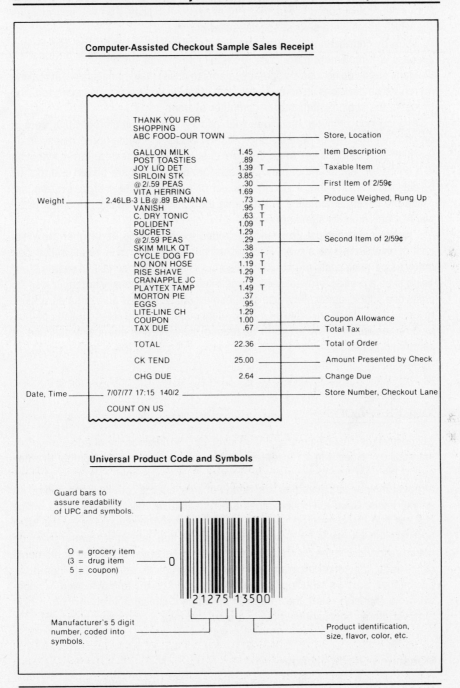

Computer-Assisted Checkout Sample Sales Receipt

THANK YOU FOR SHOPPING ABC FOOD-OUR TOWN			Store, Location
GALLON MILK	1.45		Item Description
POST TOASTIES	.89		
JOY LIQ DET	1.39	T	Taxable Item
SIRLOIN STK	3.85		
@ 2/.59 PEAS	.30		First Item of 2/59¢
VITA HERRING	1.69		
2.46LB-3 LB @ .89 BANANA	.73		Produce Weighed, Rung Up
VANISH	.95	T	
C. DRY TONIC	.63	T	
POLIDENT	1.09	T	
SUCRETS	1.29		
@ 2/.59 PEAS	.29		Second Item of 2/59¢
SKIM MILK QT	.38		
CYCLE DOG FD	.39	T	
NO NON HOSE	1.19	T	
RISE SHAVE	1.29	T	
CRANAPPLE JC	.79		
PLAYTEX TAMP	1.49	T	
MORTON PIE	.37		
EGGS	.95		
LITE-LINE CH	1.29		
COUPON	1.00		Coupon Allowance
TAX DUE	.67		Total Tax
TOTAL	22.36		Total of Order
CK TEND	25.00		Amount Presented by Check
CHG DUE	2.64		Change Due
7/07/77 17:15 140/2			Store Number, Checkout Lane
COUNT ON US			

Weight ——— 2.46LB-3 LB @ .89 BANANA

Date, Time ——— 7/07/77 17:15 140/2

Universal Product Code and Symbols

Guard bars to assure readability of UPC and symbols.

O = grocery item
(3 = drug item
5 = coupon)

O

2 1275 13500

Manufacturer's 5 digit number, coded into symbols.

Product identification, size, flavor, color, etc.

marking. No one took the chain up on the offer. The chain also used suggestions from independent consumer panels. For example, it indicated on the printed sales slip which items were sold at special sales prices.

Thus, by considering consumers as well as advances in technology, outlets can successfully implement more complex retail information systems.

Many stores do not use computer systems to assist their management in making merchandise decisions. In some cases both machine and training costs are too high to justify the implementation of a computer system.

A good noncomputer technique that can be used to implement unit control procedures involves perforated price tickets. Under this system, the salesperson tears off part of the ticket when the item is sold and deposits the torn-off section in a container. At the end of the day these torn-off portions are sorted and totaled by classification on either a manual basis or by the use of a tag reader system that reads the tickets automatically, tabulates the data, and prepares a printed daily, weekly, and monthly summary report.

The more mechanical assistance provided by the system, the higher the initial cost of establishing the system. This higher installation cost must result in reduced manual operating costs or improved accuracy if the more mechanical systems are going to be a profitable investment. Large retail chains can usually spread the setup costs of a sophisticated electronic system over enough stores and/or sales volume to justify the installation. Smaller, independent outlets may be able to lease computer time, equipment, and so forth to reduce the cost and still justify the use of electronic systems.

Stock Turnover Considerations

Successful merchandise management involves the maintenance of adequate profit markups combined with an acceptable level of *stock turnover* (the number of times during the year that the average amount of inventory is sold). The rate of stock turnover may be calculated for any period of time, but it is usually computed on an annual basis. Good buying practices are reflected by high turnover rates, which indicate that the consumers are buying the merchandise purchased by the retail buyer. Relatively low stock turnover rates indicate that consumers' preferences do not correspond with the purchases made by the store buyer or that other elements of the retail marketing program are failing. A high stock turnover rate has other advantages, such as reducing the use of price markdowns to move stale or shopworn merchandise. Also, the return on investment capital is likely to rise in high turnover stores because fixed costs are spread over a high sales volume.

Measuring Stock Turnover

There are three commonly used ways for calculating stock turnover:

1. On the basis of dollars in retail prices

2. On the basis of dollars valued at cost to the retailer

3. On the basis of units.

These calculation methods can be illustrated by the example of a grocer who begins the year with 30 cases of brand X canned peaches, which he sells for $10 per case and buys for $8 per case. If we assume no stolen or damaged merchandise and that no price reductions were necessary, the net sales of brand X peaches for the first half of the year consist of 600 cases, or $6,000. The grocer paid $4,800 for the 600 cases purchased during the first half of the year and $5,400 for the 600 cases purchased during the last half of the year. At the end of the year the grocer had seventy cases on hand, but the per case wholesale cost had just been increased to $9 at mid year, and the grocer had raised the retail price to $11 per case on July 1. The firm sold 560 cases @ $11 during the last half of the year.

The annual stock turnover rate calculated by the three different techniques is:

1. On the basis of dollars valued at retail prices:

Opening inventory $ value at retail (30 cases @ $10) = $ 300
Closing inventory $ value at retail (70 cases @ $11) = $ 770
Average inventory $ value at retail (300 + 770)/2   = $ 535
Net sales in retail dollars   = $12,160
Annual stock turnover rate

$$= \frac{\text{Net sales in retail dollars}}{\text{Average inventory at retail}} = \frac{\$12,160}{\$535} = 22.7$$

2. On the basis of dollars valued at cost:

Opening inventory $ value at cost (30 cases @ $8)   = $ 240
Closing inventory $ value at cost (70 cases @ $9)   = $ 630
Average inventory $ value at cost ($240 + $630)/2   = $ 435
Cost of goods sold (630 cases @ $8,530 cases @ $9) = $9,810
Annual stock turnover rate

$$= \frac{\text{Cost of goods sold}}{\text{Average inventory at cost}} = \frac{\$9,810}{\$435} = 22.6$$

3. On the basis of units:

Opening inventory in units   =   30
Closing inventory in units   =   70
Average inventory in units = (30 + 70)/2 =   50
Annual net unit sales   = 560

$$\text{Annual stock turnover rate} = \frac{\text{Annual unit sales}}{\text{Average unit inventory}} = \frac{1160}{50} = 23.2$$

Capital turnover is a ratio that is used to measure the number of times the cost of the average inventory investment is converted into sales.[11] Its value is calculated as follows:

$$\text{Capital turnover} = \frac{\text{Dollar sales at retail prices during a specified period}}{\text{Average inventory dollar value at cost}}$$

Analysis of previous turnover ratios generated by a firm and comparison of these ratios with those of similar retail outlets provide a good basis for planning the inventory needed to meet consumer needs and still reduce inventory to a sufficiently low level that will generate a good profit. The stock turnover ratios should be interpreted with considerable caution. Management should be certain that both the sales and the average stock figures used in the stock turnover ratio calculation cover the same operating period and that both are quoted in the same dollar terms—either in retail price or cost of merchandise.

Another factor that can lead to incorrect analysis is the use of an atypical inventory level as the average inventory level in the calculation procedure. The average inventory must reflect the average inventory level for the period of time covered by the calculation. For example, seasonal items or merchandise lines that sell well only during summer months will show an abnormally high stock turnover ratio in an annual analysis that uses only the beginning-of-year and ending-of-year inventory levels to calculate average inventory level. This illustrates the necessity of conducting more frequent (monthly or quarterly) stock turnover analyses to obtain a more accurate performance measure.

The net sales to inventory ratios, where inventory is valued at cost, presented in Table 9–4, indicate that turnover varies according to the type of retail line offered. Several factors are usually responsible for fluctuations in turnover ratios. Frequent consumer purchases result in higher stock turnover rates, as reflected by the high turnover rate obtained in grocery stores versus the low rate experienced by farm equipment dealers and jewelry stores.

Stores that sell the same types of merchandise may experience lower stock turnover rates because the store is located in a small town or community where trade is limited. Such stores may have to maintain a fairly high level of inventory merely to provide an adequate merchandise assortment. In these cases, store management might not be able to increase sales enough to raise the stock turnover ratio significantly. On the other hand, stores in high customer traffic areas will probably show high stock turnover rates because the required inventory level needed to meet consumer needs is not likely to increase in proportion to the increase in sales volume.

Stock turnover rates can be increased by changes in merchandise policies, such as eliminating slow-selling items, handling fewer sizes, colors, and styles, devoting more shelf space to fast-selling items, and maintaining only minimal inventory on slow-selling brands. Of course, stock turnover can also be accelerated by reducing the retail price charged customers or by using more advertising and price reduction promotions. However, turnover rates must increase considerably as a result of a price reduction or a promotion campaign if profit margins are to be maintained.

Manufacturers and wholesalers can also assist the retailer in achieving higher stock turnover ratios by reducing the delivery period needed to reach the retail outlet. Use of new production and/or distribution techniques that will allow more flexibility in producing merchandise required to meet the specific and immediate needs of an individual retailer with regard to sizes, colors, and styles can allow that retailer to reduce his stock level and still meet consumer demands for a wide

Table 9-4 **Median Net Sales to Inventory Ratios**
for Selected Retail Outlets, 1976

Retail Line	Net Sales to Inventory Ratio[A]
Auto & home supply stores	5.8
Children and infants' wear stores	4.3
Clothing and furnishings, men's and boys'	4.4
Department stores	5.5
Discount stores	5.2
Discount stores, leased departments	4.6
Family clothing stores	3.8
Furniture stores	4.4
Gasoline service stations	12.2
Grocery stores	17.0
Hardware stores	4.3
Household appliance stores	5.0
Jewelry stores	2.7
Lumber and other building materials dealers	6.2
Motor vehicle dealers	7.3
Paint, glass and wallpaper stores	5.1
Shoe stores	3.9
Variety stores	4.0
Women's ready-to-wear stores	5.8

Source: "The Ratios of Retailing," reprinted with the special permission of *Dun's Review*, September 1977. Copyright, 1977, Dun & Bradstreet Publications Corporation.

[A]Net Sales to Inventory—The quotient obtained by dividing the annual net sales by the statement inventory. This quotient does not represent the actual physical turnover, which would be determined by reducing the annual net sales to the cost of goods sold and then dividing the resulting figure by the statement inventory.

selection of merchandise. The use of the laser beam to cut material at a very rapid rate is an example of a process that can benefit the retailer. Through the use of computers, conveyor belts, and so forth, material can be custom cut to meet the specifications of an individual clothing merchant. The considerable decrease in time required to deliver the items to the retailer allows both the manufacturer and the retailer to sell more merchandise by reducing out-of-stock conditions on items that catch on in the fashion world. Without this system, a large volume of the same item has to be ordered before the manufacturer can justify a rerun on the same fabric, color, style, size, and so forth.

Some manufacturers have also built shelf or free-standing displays which make better use of floor space and provide a clear view of the merchandise, arranged in an orderly manner. Other manufacturers provide merchandise guidelines that assist the retailer by setting up ideal stock levels in the pertinent category; they may also take inventory and offer to replace slow-selling items with fast-selling items. Small retailers may find such advice to be very worthwhile, providing the manufacturer and/or wholesaler does not try to overemphasize the importance of his products relative to those of other manufacturers or wholesalers.

Summary

Merchandise management consists of the activities involved in balancing inventories to meet consumer needs. The merchandising department usually supervises these activities.

The merchandise budget is frequently utilized to plan and control sales efforts, markups, purchases, markdowns, and shortages. It consists of:

1. A forecast of sales for given periods
2. A plan for the stocks to be carried at the beginning of each period
3. Planned retail/reductions
4. Planned purchase quantities
5. Planned profit margin

Merchandise planning and control techniques use both unit and dollar measures. Unit planning is needed because both the retail firm's buyer and the retail customer make their purchases in units. Dollar planning is required by the firm's accountants and financial planners, who work with overall sales dollars, expense dollars, and ratios between sales and expense dollars.

Electronic data processing equipment allows retailers to use more current retail inventory management reports and direct product profitability calculations (exemplified by the COSMOS and IMPACT systems) to increase profits.

The use of the Universal Product Code (UPC) and laser checkout scanners is increasing at a rapid pace. The main advantages of this system are that: (1) it increases the speed of processing customers through the checkout operation, (2) price marking on each individual package is no longer needed, (3) a routine reordering procedure can be established, (4) checkout cash registers can be balanced faster, and (5) fewer pricing errors are made at the checkout counter because the computer can remember prices better than people can.

The use of the UPC and laser scanner system appears to result in improved merchandise management. The system provides so much data so quickly that managers can soon identify problem areas in their inventory and adjust their purchasing plans to correct the situation.

Consumer reaction to the system has been somewhat mixed. Shoppers in stores that use no price marking on individual packages complain unless the sales receipt contains a sufficient description of the item along with its price. A majority of the customers prefer the faster checkout procedure and the more accurate price recording at the checkout counter.

1. Develop a plan for implementing the use of a merchandise budget in a new, independent men's wear store.

2. Discuss ways that the annual sales forecast can be made for an established retail firm.

3. A retailer expects the firm's sales to increase by 10 percent during this next year. Last year the firm's sales were $300,000. The monthly sales index for January is 65; for February the sales index is 75. Calculate the sales volume you expect this retailer to have during the January 1 to February 28 period.

4. A grocery retailer has reviewed the firm's sales records for the past five years. Average monthly sales are: January, $150,000; February, $140,000; March, $155,000; April, $160,000; May, $165,000; June, $175,000; July, $200,000; August, $210,000; September, $170,000; October, $165,000; November, $175,000; December, $180,000. Calculate monthly seasonal sales index figures for each month.

5. What are the advantages and disadvantages of using the various methods of planning inventory levels?

6. What average markup must a retailer use to obtain a profit of 10 percent of gross sales if the firm's sales are estimated to be $500,000, its operating expenses are expected to be $200,000, and its reductions are estimated to be $50,000?

7. What is the gross margin percent for the retailer in problem six?

8. How can small retailers use the open-to-buy amount to guide their purchase activities?

9. Which is the more common occurrence in retailing, a shortage or an overage? Explain why.

10. How can a retailer increase the firm's stock turnover? Should retail management always strive to get the maximum stock turnover that is possible?

11. ABC Retail Company estimates its February sales to be $70,000 and its average monthly sales for the first quarter to be $60,000. The average monthly stock for the first quarter is $80,000. Use the basic stock method to determine how much inventory the firm should have on hand on February 1. What is the dollar value of its basic stock?

12. The shoe department of a local department store has estimated its sales for next year to be $144,000. It estimates January sales to be $9,000. The firm wants to have an average monthly inventory of $10,000. Use the percentage deviation method to determine how much inventory the shoe department should have on hand on January 1.

13. Stock on hand on February 1 is $10,000 and the estimated sales for the next two months are as follows:

Estimated Sales

Feb. 1	$2,500
Feb. 8	1,850
Feb. 15	1,540
Feb. 22	2,460
March 1	1,650
March 8	1,970
March 15	2,320
March 22	1,840

Find the number of weeks' supply that the firm has on hand on February 1.

14. The following weekly sales estimates have been prepared for a supermarket:

Week beginning	Sales	Week beginning	Sales
February 1	$40,500	March 15	$48,300
8	45,000	22	55,000
15	42,500	April 4	44,200
22	36,400	11	48,400
March 1	52,300	18	46,300
8	50,100	25	41,200

Management of the supermarket desires to obtain an annual stock turnover of 16. Use the weeks' supply method to calculate the planned stock for February 1 and March 15.

15. A local retailer wants to hold the firm's inventory to a monthly stock to sales ratio of 3.0. Estimated sales are:

Month	Sales	Month	Sales
January	$15,600	July	$24,000
February	20,800	August	28,500
March	23,000	September	23,200
April	24,500	October	21,100
May	27,000	November	27,200
June	25,400	December	30,150

Use the stock to sales ratio method to determine how much inventory the firm should have on hand on January 1, April 1, July 1, and September 1. What annual stock turnover rate is this retailer expecting to achieve?

16. From the following figures find the open-to-buy amount for July.

Actual inventory, July 1 $40,000

Planned inventory on hand, August 1	45,000
Value of inventory on order for delivery in July	20,000
Estimated sales for July	35,000

17. A local retailer plans the following for the month of April: sales, $50,000; markdowns and shortages, $4,000; beginning-of-the-month stock, $120,000; ending-of-the-month stock, $100,000; and planned initial markup, 30 percent of retail. Find the open-to-buy amount for April in dollars of retail value and in dollars of cost to the retailer.

18. The manager of a certain department of a general merchandise store believes that its annual sales volume will be $1,200,000 next year. Estimated operating expenses are $240,000 and estimated reductions are $96,000. The manager would like to achieve a profit of $12,000 next year. What percent initial markup must be used to reach this profit goal?

19. What is the value of inventory on June 30 for a retailer who is in the following situation: retail value of purchases made by the retailer during the January 1 to June 30 period—$87,000; retail value of sales made to consumers during the January 1 to June 30 period—$95,000; retail value of the beginning-of-the-month inventory in January—$33,000?

20. A local retailer has obtained net sales of $45,000 during the first three months of this year. The average stock for the firm has been $60,000. What will the firm's annual stock turnover rate be if business continues at the rate it has been going during the three months?

21. A retailer obtained net sales for last year of $225,000. The retailer made purchases totaling $135,000 of cost to the firm during the year. A physical inventory was taken at the beginning of the year, again on July 1 and again at the end of the year. The inventory values for these periods are:

	Value of Inventory	
	in Retail Dollars	in Cost Dollars
Beginning of year	200,000	120,000
On July 1	220,000	130,000
End of year	180,000	110,000

What is the firm's stock turnover rate valued in retail prices? What is its stock turnover rate valued at cost?

Footnotes

1. Richard I. Levin and C. A. Kirkpatrick, *Quantitative Approaches to Management* (New York: McGraw Hill, 1965), pp. 96–111.

2. Ibid., pp. 106–111.

3. Ibid., p. 366.

4. Ibid., p. 359.

5. Reductions include price markdowns, discounts to employees, and stock shortages.

6. Retail Electronic Systems, 100 Park Avenue, Staten Island, N.Y. 10302.

7. J. L. Heskett, Robert M. Ivie, and Nicholas A. Glaskowsky, *Business Logistics: Management of Physical Supply and Distribution* (New York: Ronald Press, 1964), chap. 11.

8. Ronald C. Curhan, "Shelf Space Allocation and Profit Maximization in Mass Retailing," *Journal of Marketing* 37 (July 1973): 54–60.

9. Retail IMPACT—Inventory Management Program and Control Techniques Application Description, 6th ed. (White Plains, N.Y.: IBM Technical Publications Department, March, 1970).

10. Testimony by Mr. Joseph B. Danzansky, President of Giant Food Inc., before the Maryland Senate Economic Affairs Committee, March 17, 1976.

11. Capital turnover, as used here, measures only turnover in capital invested in merchandise inventory, not total capital used by the retailer.

Case Study

Johnson Mercantile Company

Ms. Ruth Miller is the new buyer for Johnson Mercantile Company, which is a general merchandise outlet.

Ms. Miller is beginning to make plans for her January 4th trip to the wholesalers' merchandise mart. She has just come from her January 2nd meeting with Mr. Johnson, who has told her that the firm would like to reduce the level of its January 1st inventory (which is worth $150,000 using retail prices) by 10 percent by June 30th. Last year, sales for the January 2nd to June 30th period were $600,000 in retail dollars. Mr. Johnson believes that sales will be ten percent higher this year than they were last year. He also said the store has averaged a markup of 30 percent during the past year and that markdowns and shortages averaged ten percent of retail sales.

Mr. Johnson has already ordered $100,000 worth of merchandise, which will arrive by the middle of January.

Discussion Questions

1. How do you recommend that Ms. Miller approach her job assignment of going to market to purchase some merchandise that will be sold during the January 2nd to June 30 period?

2. How much money do you recommend she can spend at the merchandise mart? Why?

Case Study

A. B. Adams Company

The A. B. Adams Company, a large national chain of general merchandise stores, delegates much authority and responsibility to individual store managers. Each store manager has considerable freedom to adapt merchandise offerings to meet local circumstances and to adjust operating procedures and methods to cope with special problems that they encounter. Store managers delegate as much authority and responsibility as possible to their assistants and department managers so that these people will develop as managers in accord with the company's general management philosophy.

A new and fairly large unit of the company is located in a planned suburban shopping center in a major metropolitan area. The operating results of the shoe department of this store have been a disappointment to the store manager during the past merchandising season.

Total sales volume for this store was about $3 million for the past year. The shoe department, which has consistently accounted for about 5 percent of total store sales, has been the source of 30 percent of the total amount of all markdowns. The annual rate of stock turnover for the shoe department is 2.5, compared with a store average of 5.4 and a range from 1 on slow-moving lines such as jewelry to over 10 on fast-moving lines such as some women's clothing items.

The shoe department currently handles men's work and dress shoes, children's shoes, women's casual shoes, and a very limited number of styles in women's dress shoes. Information about the shoe department's performance for the last year is summarized in the table on the following page.

With the exception of women's dress shoes, which offer an unusually high mark-down risk, the department manager feels that she has a large assortment of styles in each classification. Stock depth for each style has been limited, however, in an attempt to keep the total dollar inventory at a minimum level.

Purchase control for most departments in the store is made on the basis of each department manager's current inventory being the equivalent of the next two months of expected sales, and on having on order an additional amount equivalent to expected sales in the third month ahead. If the stock on hand plus stock on order exceeds estimated sales for three months, the department has no open-to-buy. In the shoe department, purchase control is made on the basis of having a seventy-five-day supply on hand and a thirty-day on order allowance. The greater on hand allowance is justified on the basis of the complex nature of size buying for shoes. The manager has felt the need for a seventy-five-day stock in order to keep all sizes on the shelf.

According to a recent national survey of a representative group of shoe stores and departments, about one half of all lost sales are due to being out of stock on the particular size at the time of potential purchase. This factor has been particularly

Classification	Percentage of Dept. Sales	Average Percent Initial Markup	Range of Retail Prices
Men's work shoes	30	35	$15–30
Men's dress shoes[A]	20	40	$20–40
Women's casual shoes	20	35	$10–25
Women's dress shoes	5	45	$20–40
Children's shoes[B]	25	40	$15–25
Total	100		

Classification	Number of Styles Stocked	Percentage Reductions Are of Category Sales Dollar Volume	Average Dollar Inventory
Men's work shoes	6	10	$ 8,000
Men's dress shoes[A]	16	20	$12,000
Women's casual shoes	10	20	$15,000
Women's dress shoes	4	25	$ 5,000
Children's shoes[B]	14	15	$20,000
Total	50		$60,000

[A]Includes boys' sizes, 4–7.
[B]Includes infants' shoes.

important in the case of general merchandise stores, owing to the limited capital available for stocking a wide variety of styles in depth.

The department manager buys or orders shoes from a classification catalog, which contains pictures of styles available, size information, retail price, markup, wholesale price, and a qualitative description.

The inventory in each shoe classification is counted at sporadic intervals to determine movement of merchandise by style numbers since the last count, and this information is used as the basis for buying.

Since the shoe department has been operated at a loss from the time of store opening, the store manager is most anxious to increase the sales volume, reduce markdown losses, increase the rate of turnover, and begin to operate the shoe department on a profitable basis.

Discussion Questions

1. Analyze the inventory turnover for each merchandise classification.

2. Analyze the profitability of each merchandise classification.

3. What steps do you recommend that the store manager take to accomplish the objectives of increasing shoe sales, reducing markdowns, and increasing turnover and profitability?

Case Study

Pérez Duty Free Stores

Sr. Ricardo Pérez was concerned about how to better utilize the display space in his duty-free stores in airports.

Every square inch of the space in his airport stores needed to be used to maximum advantage in sales display. The amount of available space he could rent in the airport was fixed. Sr. Pérez could not obtain additional square footage in the airport unless he merged with a competitor. None of his competitors was interested in selling.

Pérez Duty Free stores was located in the South American nation of Moronda. It was established with a single store in 1971 and now totalled six stores. Two of these were located on the highway at the border of neighboring countries.

The remaining four stores were located in the capital city of San Martin. Two of these were located in major hotels (Sheraton and La Romana). The other two were located in the airport.

The airport stores provided the greatest volume of sales to the company but were also the ones with the greatest space problems. These stores were located near the ticket counters of international airlines including Pan Am, KLM and Braniff.

The products displayed in the stores could not be sold directly to the customer. Instead, by law, they could be sold only to persons who were leaving the country. Passengers would select and pay for the merchandise they wanted in the store. Their orders would then be sent by messenger to the warehouse located upstairs in the airport. There, the order was filled and packaged in a plastic sack with handles or a cardboard carrying case.

It was then carried to the gate for passengers to receive just before they boarded the plane. A passenger would claim his merchandise at the gate by showing a sales receipt.

Each of the airport stores sold a wide product mix. The product mix groupings were cigarettes, liquor, perfume and hardware. The hardware line consisted of small television sets, pens, pencils, wall clocks, cigarette lighters, toys (Tonka and Gorgi), tennis rackets and balls, baseball mitts, ladies' handbags, cosmetics, sunglasses, jewelry, electronic calculators, and gift crystal.

The sales and markups for the product mix groups were:

	Sales as % of Total Product Mix	Markups
Cigarettes	10.6%	200–300%
Liquor	35.4%	200–300%
Perfume	23.3%	75–100%
Hardware	30.8%	30– 75%

The San Martin Airport also contained four other duty free stores. These carried competitive products and brands for the most popular items purchased by travelers, such as American cigarettes and well-known brands of scotch.

Sr. Pérez felt that this store carried a wider line of items than the competition.

Since the customer did not directly purchase the products, the entire duty free store could serve as a showroom without the necessity of storage space. The available showroom space was limited, and Sr. Pérez believed it was essential to limit his products to those with the highest margin and the most rapid turnover to maximize profits. In spite of this, Sr. Pérez felt he was forced to carry certain items that did not have a high turnover. These were items such as expensive European pens, Dupont and Cartier lighters, which sold for over $100.00 retail, Omega watches, and certain brands of expensive brandy and champagne.

These items were carried since Sr. Pérez felt that he needed them to help maintain an image of high quality for his store. He also believed that if he did not carry these items, a certain number of customers would go to a competitor's store to look for them.

The primary problem with keeping these items in stock was that they tied up considerable amounts of working capital. They also absorbed retail display space, warehouse space, and the time of the salespeople.

Substitute products were available and Sr. Pérez often wondered if he should sell them instead. As an example, the Omega watches generally started at retail prices above $100.00, whereas the Seiko brand began at a price of $35.00. The Seiko was considered to be a faster moving item but one with less prestige.

Experience had demonstrated that unless a product was well displayed in the store it would not sell. Sr. Pérez had tried an experiment to reduce the amount of products that had to be placed on display. Instead of showing three sizes of a brand of liquor he placed only one on display. The salespeople were trained to tell customers that the particular brand came in other sizes. There was also a price list on the counter that informed the customer of the other sizes.

The experiment showed that if the customer could not see the actual product on display, sales declined. What happened was that customers crowded in front of the store before their flights. The salespeople could not wait on each customer at the same time.

Many would look at the products on display; if they did not immediately see the size or brand they wanted, they would go to a competitor's store. They would not wait to ask the salesperson if the product was available.

Sr. Pérez felt he needed to do something to improve the usage of his display space. In the last five years, sales volume had almost tripled, but profits had not kept pace. In fact, during the last two years, total profits had actually declined.

Discussion Questions

1. How should Sr. Pérez analyze the problem of utilization of display space?

2. Do you believe Sr. Pérez needs expensive but slow-moving items such as Dupont and Cartier lighters to give his store a high quality image?

3. Who do you believe are the customers of duty free stores in an airport such as the one at San Martin?

4. Why do people purchase items in a duty free store? What kind of products are they seeking?

5. Is the salesperson in a duty free store primarily an order taker? Does the salesperson in a duty free store differ from one in a department store in terms of his or her role in influencing sales?

Chapter 10

Pricing for Profit

1. To learn how the concepts of break-even, markup, and elasticity are effectively used in establishing pricing strategies.

2. To understand how price levels are related to profit levels.

3. To become acquainted with the dynamic and psychological aspects of retail pricing.

4. To be aware of the complex legal environment that affects retail pricing activities.

Key Terms and Concepts

pricing strategy	markup percent of cost	private label pricing
return on investment goal	maintained markup	odd pricing
merchandise costs	retail reductions	markdown percentage
variable costs	markdowns	off retail percentage
fixed costs	gross margin	low-price leaders
break-even point volume	merchandise turnover	loss-leader pricing
markup dollars	price elasticity of demand coefficient	bait-leader pricing
markup on cost	price lining	off-season pricing
	demand curve	preticketing
	unit pricing	price ceiling

The heart of an effective retail operation is pricing the goods or services so that the customer sincerely believes that he or she has received fair value. This is accomplished by using an appropriate pricing strategy and is implemented through aggressive pricing tactics. This chapter examines the proper use of long-term pricing strategies, such as initial mark-ons and pricing elasticity, price lining, and the overall psychology of pricing. The chapter closes with an examination of such tactical pricing practices as markdowns and promotional pricing and, finally, the legal aspects of proper pricing.

Pricing Strategy

Pricing decisions are important because they can nullify the effect of intelligently conceived product, location, and communication programs. The retailer's *pricing strategy* is a form of market cultivation, but it is also a reflection of all the firm's actions. Pricing is symbolic of the kind of product strategy used by the retailer because the price tag conveys a mental image about product quality to the customer. Pricing may be used as a store location substitute in an effort to attract customers from greater distances.

Pricing strategy must be consistent with the retailer's communication appeal. Generally, a retailer who uses a low-price appeal must sacrifice some methods of demand stimulation, such as advertising. Rarely can large sums be spent on advertising and promotion if low price is the dominant appeal. Discount retailers may initially appear to be the exception. However, if advertising and promotion budgets are considered as a percentage of sales volume, most discounters spend relatively less on advertising than other retailers.

Price is the dominant factor that directly influences the retailer's profit or loss. Other things being equal, price can be lowered to increase sales. However, the increase in unit volume may not be sufficient to generate a higher level of profit. Thus, retailers must review price changes with regard to their effects upon both sales and profits. Many factors must be considered when one is determining the firm's retail pricing strategy (Exhibit 10–1).

The pricing objectives of a retail firm are frequently twofold—to obtain a specified rate of return on the money they have invested in the firm and secondly to retain or strengthen their position in the marketplace.

The percentage return on investment obtained by typical firms in various lines of retailing is presented in Chapter 12. The new, small independent retailer may use the average percent return for typical firms in the industry as the goals the firm wishes to reach. As the manager gains experience, he or she may alter this goal to better reflect local conditions. Large retail institutions develop an annual return on investment objective based upon past performance and general economic conditions. For example, Sears, Roebuck has been reported to aim for a 10 to 15 percent after tax return on investment.[1]

The overall company objective is frequently applied to individual stores that are members of the chain. The store managers who exceed the specified target are

Exhibit 10–1 **Factors to Be Considered When Determining the Retail Pricing Strategy**

Factors retailers can control

1. Pricing objectives of the firm—return on investment, share of market
2. Type of merchandise offered
3. The cost of goods sold
4. Business expenses
5. Firm organization structure

Factors retailers cannot control

1. Consumer demand
2. Competition
3. Federal, state, and local laws

Tools used to obtain pricing objectives

1. Markup formula
2. Price linings
3. Demand elasticity
4. Prestige pricings
5. Odd pricing
6. Multiple unit pricing
7. Markdowns
8. Leader pricing
9. Off-season pricing
10. Unit pricing

then awarded extra compensation. This system works most effectively if store management has the responsibility of setting prices and selecting merchandise.

Retail firms also use the share of the market concept to determine if they are losing, maintaining or increasing their position in the marketplace. For example, the Great Atlantic and Pacific Tea Company has set a goal of obtaining at least 20 percent of the grocery store sales in each of its sales districts.[2]

The goal of maintaining a *minimum market share* can conflict with a minimum rate of return on investment objective statement. The firm may find that it is necessary to reduce price (or increase promotion) so much that the firm becomes less profitable. Thus, the adoption of a high market share objective is frequently accompanied by that firm's intention to be the price leader in that line of merchandise. Price leaders are generally perceived by other retailers as being the outlets offering the customers merchandise at the lowest price in the area.

Some retailers, especially the small, independent outlets, have difficulty getting data on their share of the market. The first difficulty is defining the exact market category. Large retail chains sell many different kinds of merchandise. Thus, it is difficult to estimate what dollar sales are for each category. For example, a small specialty store may be selling women's wear which is sold in similar competing stores, in department stores, large chain outlets such as J. C. Penney, Montgomery Ward, and Sears, Roebuck and Co. It is just about impossible for the outlet to estimate accurately women's wear sales in these large stores. In this case, the outlet may be content to simply state its goal as 25 percent of women's wear sales in the nonchain and nondepartment stores.

Costs are another important factor that need to be considered in retail pricing (Figure 10–1). Retailers are concerned with three types of cost: cost of merchandise, variable costs, and fixed costs.

Merchandise costs consist of the price that the merchant pays for the goods and services that he or she buys for resale to the ultimate consumer. Merchandise costs are the starting point in computing the general level of the retailer's price. Although the retailer may consider external factors such as consumer demand, competitor's strength, and so forth, he or she must still cover all of the firm's merchandise cost if the firm is to be able to meet other expenses and stay in business.

Fixed costs occur whether the firm is opened or closed. Costs such as square footage space costs, insurance, equipment and facility depreciation, a minimum level of employee and owner manager salaries, lights, heat, utilities do not increase or decrease with changes in the store's sales volume.

Variable costs fluctuate widely with changes in the store's activities. These variable costs are the expenses that vary with the outlet's sales volume. Added sales may be obtained by using advertising, adding more personnel to serve the higher sales level, keeping the store open longer hours, thereby requiring more utility charges, labor costs, and paying a higher rental cost because the property owner has specified that a percent of the firm's retail sales be paid as rent.

For example a department store may purchase a coat for $64 and sell it for $100. The gross margin for this item, which is sold at its original markup, is $36. But $30 of this gross margin goes for variable operating expenses such as wages, salaries, commissions, repairs, maintenance, advertising, delivery costs, bad debt losses, administration, and legal expenses; and for the fixed costs of rent, utilities, insurance, taxes, license fees, interest, and depreciation. This leaves only $6 for profit.

The distinction between these three types of costs is important to the retailer who is making pricing decisions, because one of the tools he or she may use is the break-even volume. This technique uses past cost data. The cost of merchandise figure is subtracted from sales, giving management an estimate of gross margin (the difference between what a retailer pays for the product and the price at which he sells it to the consumer), which must cover all of the firm's operating expenses as well as provide a profit to the owner.

The *break-even volume* is the minimum sales volume needed to avoid incurring a loss. Mathematically, the break-even volume is calculated as follows:

$BEV = $FC/[(100% − %MC) − %VC] where

$BEV = break-even volume at which the firm neither makes a profit nor shows a loss

$FC = fixed cost in dollars

%MC = percent merchandise costs are of retail sales dollar volume

%VC = percent variable costs are of retail sales dollar volume

For example, suppose past retail records show that an establishment has incurred annual fixed costs (rent, utilities, a bare bones labor charge, depreciation, and so forth) of $100,000. The cost of merchandise has averaged 70 percent of retail dollar

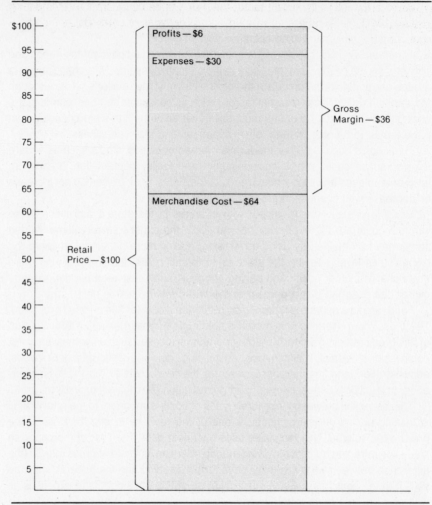

Figure 10-1 **Illustration of the Components of Retail Price**

sales during the past five years. Variable costs (advertising costs, added labor costs, and so forth) have amounted to 12 percent of retail dollar sales during the past five years. This firm's break-even quantity is found by substituting these values in the above formula as follows:

$$\$BEV = \$100,000/[(100\% - 70\%) - 12\%]$$
$$= \$100,000/[(30\%) - 12\%]$$
$$= \$100,000/[18\%]$$
$$= \$555,556$$

Thus, the firm would have to sell at least $555,556 a year to cover all costs (Figure 10–2). If it can obtain a larger sales volume, then it begins to make a profit of 18¢

on each dollar of sales over the break-even volume. For example, if the firm gets annual sales of $800,000 then its profit is ($800,000 − $555,556) × .18, or $244,444 × .18 = $44,000.

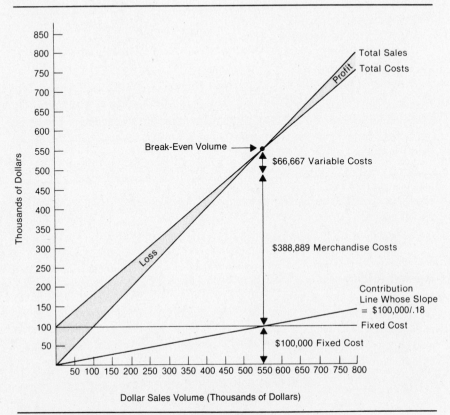

Figure 10-2 **Illustration of a Break-Even Chart**

If the firm cannot reach the break-even sales volume, it will incur a loss of 18¢ on each dollar below its break-even volume. For example, if the firm has annual sales of $400,000 then the loss would be ($555,556 − $400,000) × .18 = $155,556 × .18 = $28,000.

Managers of retail outlets can use many different ways (increase promotion, reduce prices, and so forth) to increase the firm's sales above the break-even volume. However, all of these actions also involve some additional cost. Management must then determine if the increased sales outweigh added costs.

Thus, the establishment of the firm's pricing policy must be based on this concept and attempts made to determine the optimum pricing strategy. Price changes can be used to influence the firm's sales volume. However, the price change also affects the firm's gross margin. For example, a 10 percent price reduction will increase store sales (say by 20 percent) but it will also increase the firm's break-even volume. In the previous example, the ten percent price reduction would affect the break-even calculation in the following manner: (1) The cost of merchandise has not changed, so it is still $70 of every $100 of the original sales. (2) However, because of the 10 percent price reduction, the same merchandise will now only bring in $90 to the retail firm. (3) The percentage merchandise cost is therefore increased to 70/90, or 78%. (4) The break-even calculation is changed to:

$$\$BEV = \$100,000/[(100\% - 78\%) - 12\%]$$
$$= \$100,000/[10\%]$$
$$= \$1,000,000.$$

Thus, the firm's break-even volume has nearly been doubled to $1 million from $555,556 just because it reduced prices by ten percent. Management should be reasonably certain that the firm's sales volume would be in excess of $1 million before it reduces prices by 10 percent.

As can be seen from the above example, the break-even volume estimates can play an important role in determining the pricing strategy of the retailer. This break-even concept should be considered when retail management establishes its markup pricing policies.

Markup Pricing

Most retail prices are determined by a cost-oriented markup. Markup is the difference between the cost of an item and its retail price. Cost, in this case, usually refers to the invoice cost of the merchandise, minus trade discounts, plus inbound freight paid by the retailer. Markup is generally expressed as a percent of the retail price. In formula form:

$$Markup\ percent = \frac{(retail\ price\ per\ unit) - (per\ unit\ cost)}{(retail\ price\ per\ unit)} \times 100.$$

If, for example, an item costs a retailer $50 but he retails it at $75, the markup percent is ($25/$75) × 100, or 33 1/3. Markup percent can also be calculated by using the following formula:

$$Markup\ percent = \frac{dollar\ markup}{dollar\ retail\ price} \times 100.$$

In the above example the dollar markup on the item is $75 − $50, or $25, so the markup percent = $25/$75 × 100 = 33 1/3 percent. Markup can also be defined by using the cost as a base. Markup on cost is calculated by dividing the margin by the cost to the retailer. In formula form,

$$Markup\ percent\ of\ cost = \frac{(retail\ price\ per\ unit - per\ unit\ cost)}{(per\ unit\ cost)} \times 100.$$

In this example the markup on cost percent would be $25/$50 $\times$ 100, or 50 percent. Markup percent of cost can also be calculated by using the formula:

$$\text{Markup percent of cost} = \frac{\text{dollar markup}}{\text{dollar cost}} \times 100.$$

In the above example dollar markup is $75 $-$ $50, or $25, and the dollar cost of the item is given as $50, so the markup percent of cost = $25/50 $\times$ 100, or 50 percent.

In this text the term "markup percent of cost" will always be differentiated from markup as a percent of price. In the real world the reader should always check to see which markup is being used. Many retailers have gone broke because they misunderstood the difference between markup on retail and markup on cost.

One important point should be stressed when considering markups using both cost and selling prices as bases. A markup percent based on the retail or selling price will always be smaller than an equivalent dollar margin based on the cost of an item. A conversion from a given markup percent on cost to an equivalent markup on retail can be made by using the following formula:

$$\text{Markup percent} = \frac{(\text{markup percent of cost})}{(100 + \text{markup percent of cost})} \times 100.$$

If the markup percent of cost is 20 percent, the comparable markup percent is equal to [20/(100 + 20)] $\times$ 100, or 16.7 percent. Table 10–1 contains equivalent markups, and may be used to convert markup percent into markup percent of cost. Markup percent of retail can be converted into markup percent of cost by using the formula:

$$\text{Markup percent of cost} = \frac{\text{markup percent of retail}}{(100 - \text{markup percent of retail})} \times 100.$$

If the markup percent of retail is 16.7 then the equivalent markup percent of cost = 16.7/(100 $-$ 16.7) $\times$ 100, or 20 percent.

Retailers frequently want to determine what price must be charged on an item to yield a desired markup. The following formula makes this conversion:

$$\text{Retail price} = \frac{(\text{cost in dollars})}{(100 - \text{desired markup percent})} \times 100.$$

Thus, if an item were purchased by the retailer for $10 and he wished to obtain a markup of 50 percent, the calculation would be:

$$\frac{\$10}{(100 - 50)} \times 100 = \$20.$$

Table 10-1 **Markup Table**

To use this table find the desired percentage in the left-hand column. Multiply the cost of the article by the corresponding percentage in the "markup percent of cost" column. The result, added to the cost, gives the correct selling price.

Markup Percent of Selling Price	Markup Percent of Cost	Markup Percent of Selling Price	Markup Percent of Cost	Markup Percent of Selling Price	Markup Percent of Cost
4.8	5.0	18.0	22.0	32.0	47.1
5.0	5.3	18.5	22.7	33.3	50.0
6.0	6.4	19.0	23.5	34.0	51.5
7.0	7.5	20.0	25.0	35.0	53.9
8.0	8.7	21.0	26.6	35.5	55.0
9.0	10.0	22.0	28.2	36.0	56.3
10.0	11.1	22.5	29.0	37.0	58.8
10.7	12.0	23.0	29.9	37.5	60.0
11.0	12.4	23.1	30.0	38.0	61.3
11.1	12.5	24.0	31.6	39.0	64.0
12.0	13.6	25.0	33.3	39.5	65.5
12.5	14.3	26.0	35.0	40.0	66.7
13.0	15.0	27.0	37.0	41.0	70.0
14.0	16.3	27.3	37.5	42.0	72.4
15.0	17.7	28.0	39.0	42.8	75.0
16.0	19.1	28.5	40.0	44.4	80.0
16.7	20.0	29.0	40.9	46.1	85.0
17.0	20.5	30.0	42.9	47.5	90.0
17.5	21.2	31.0	45.0	48.7	95.0
				50.0	100.0

Source: NCR Corporation, *Expenses in Retail Businesses* (Dayton: NCR Corporation, n.d.), p. 45. Reprinted by permission.

Initial Markup

In the above discussion we have referred to markup in a very general way, that is, the difference between the cost of an item and its selling price. It is now useful to distinguish carefully among three terms, initial markup, maintained markup, and gross margin, which are used to describe the difference between cost and retail price. The amount of markup on all items does not remain constant during the entire year. Some merchandise is always broken, damaged, or stolen. Other items are sold at reduced prices to employees and customers. Rarely will the first, full markup be realized. This first markup (the margin between cost and retail price) placed on merchandise is called the initial markup. The initial markup must be high enough to cover:

1. *Maintained markup* consisting of:
   a. Store operating expenses, including payrolls, advertising, taxes, supplies, services purchased, travel, communications, pensions, insurance, depreciation, professional services, donations, bad debts, equipment rental, real property rentals, and interest payments
      plus
   b. Alteration costs to goods sold
      plus
   c. Expected profit
      minus
   d. Vendor cash discounts
2. *Retail reductions* including:
   a. *markdowns,* which lower the original price to promote merchandise sales
   b. discounts to employees as a fringe benefit
   c. *shortages,* which are the difference between the amount of merchandise that should be on hand and the amount actually on hand (the difference may be due to merchandise being lost, stolen, damaged, or improperly counted, or due to improper handling of cash or charge transactions)

Thus, the initial markup measures what the retail manager hopes to retail the goods for. In percentage terms the initial markup can be calculated by using the following formula:

$$\text{Initial markup \%} = \frac{\text{maintained markup \% + reduction \%}}{\text{net sales \% + reduction \%}},$$

where maintained markup % = % store operating expense + % alteration costs
+ % profit − % vendor cash discounts

and reduction % = % markdown + % employee discounts + % shortages

To illustrate the use of this formula, suppose that there are no vendor cash discounts, expenses are estimated to be 33 percent, reductions are estimated to be 8 percent and profit is planned to equal 5 percent. Therefore:

$$\text{Initial markup percent} = \frac{33\% \text{ expenses} + 5\% \text{ profit} + 8\% \text{ reductions}}{100\% \text{ net sales} + 8\% \text{ reductions}}$$

$$= \frac{.38 + .08}{1.00 + .08} = \frac{.46}{1.08} = .425 \text{ or } 42.5\%$$

This formula can also be used with dollar figures as well as the percentages. For example, if the firm had sales of $100,000, no vendor cash discounts, expenses of $33,000, reductions of $8,000 and a planned profit of $5,000 the calculation would be:

$$\text{Initial markup percent} = \frac{\$33,000 \text{ expenses} + \$5,000 \text{ profit} + \$8,000 \text{ reductions}}{\$100,000 \text{ sales} + \$8,000 \text{ reductions}}$$

$$= \$43,000/\$108,000 = .425 \text{ or } 42.5\%$$

Maintained Markup

Maintained markup has already been defined as being store operating expense + alteration expense + profit − vendor cash discounts. The above calculation indicates that the initial markup percent is a very useful planning tool that can be used to ensure that maintained markup percentages exceed expenses by a preplanned percentage which represents profit to the firm.

Moving From Initial Markup Percent to Maintained Markup Percent

The relationship between initial markup percent and maintained markup percent can be used to determine what reduced price should be used to obtain a preplanned maintained markup percentage after a portion of merchandise has been sold at the initial markup. For example, suppose a retailer bought one hundred pairs of shoes at $14 a pair and sold eighty pairs at an initial markup of 33 1/3 percent of retail, or at $21 per pair. The retailer then wants to reduce the price on the remaining twenty pairs but wants to achieve the planned maintained markup percentage of thirty percent. The calculation procedure is:

1. Determine actual dollar cost of goods = number of units purchased × per unit purchase price

$$= 100 \times \$14$$

$$= \$1400$$

2. Determine dollar sales volume needed to obtain planned maintained markup percentage =

$$\frac{\text{actual cost of goods}}{(100\% - \text{planned maintained markup percent})} = \frac{\$1400}{(100\% - 30\%)} = \frac{\$1400}{70\%} = \$2000$$

3. Determine dollar sales volume obtained at initial markup percentage = Number of units sold at initial markup × initial price = 80 × $21 = $1680

4. Determine dollar sales volume still needed to achieve planned maintained markup percent = required dollar sales volume (obtained in step 2) minus dollar sales volume obtained at initial markup (step 3)
$$= \$2000 - \$1680 = \$320$$

5. Determine retail price for remaining units = dollar sales volume needed (step 4)/number of units left to sell = $320/20 = $16 per pair

Gross Margin

The previous discussion has indicated that maintained markup is the markup obtained after retail reductions have been subtracted from the initial markup. Thus maintained markup is really equal to net sales minus the gross cost of the merchandise. *Gross margin* is closely related to maintained markup in that gross margin = net sales − total merchandising costs. Thus, there are only two items (vendors' cash discounts and alteration expenses) that differ in the calculation of the gross margin and maintained markup figures. If a firm does not receive any cash discounts from its suppliers or make alterations on merchandise that is sold to its customers, then its maintained markup will equal its gross margin. This seldom occurs in the real world, since retailers rely on the cash discounts they receive on the merchandise they purchase from their suppliers to increase their profits. Most stores also find it necessary to incur some alteration expense, which is needed to convert some merchandise into a form that better satisfies consumer needs.

The conversion formula for finding gross margin is:

Gross margin = maintained markup + vendor cash discounts earned − alteration costs

The interdependence of gross margin and maintained markup is illustrated by slightly altering this formula to find maintained markup.

Maintained markup = gross margin − vendor cash discounts earned + alteration costs

The following example can be used to illustrate the relationship between initial markup, maintained markup and gross margin. Store X expects to obtain sales of $500,000 next year. Its operating expenses have been equal to 15 percent of sales, its combined value of employee discounts and markdowns have been equal to 7 percent of sales, its shortages have been equal to 3 percent of sales, and alteration costs have been equal to 1 percent of sales. Store management does not believe these cost relationships will change for the next year. The store has been receiving a 2 percent of retail sales vendor cash discount and expects this to continue next year. Store management desires to earn a 5 percent profit on sales for the next year.

Thus, maintained markup percent = 15% store operating expense + 1% alteration expense + 5% planned profit − 2% vendor cash discounts = 19%,

and initial markup $= \dfrac{\text{maintained markup} + \text{reductions}}{\text{net sales} + \text{reductions}}$

$$= \frac{19\% + (3\% \text{ shortages} + 7\% \text{ markdowns} + 3\% \text{ discounts})}{100\% + (3\% \text{ shortages} + 7\% \text{ markdowns} + 3\% \text{ discounts})}$$

$$= \frac{32\%}{113\%}$$

$$= 28.3\%$$

and gross margin = maintained markup + vendor cash discounts − alteration costs

$$= 19\% + 2\% - 1\%$$

$$= 20\%$$

Advantages of Markup Pricing

Retailers use markup pricing because it is a convenient method of pricing the very large number of items they stock. The retailer generally cannot afford to spend the time and effort to determine the best price to charge on every item, although few retailers use the same markup for all of their goods. In fact, some retailers use different markup percentages for each merchandise department and key each item's markup percentage into checkout facilities, thereby identifying sales by department and maintaining a perpetual inventory in the process.

Retail merchants also use markup percentages as a negotiation tool and as a control and planning device.[3] The retailer can gain significant benefits by using markup as a commitment to a specific minimum markup policy of X percent on all lines stocked in the store. The success of the commitment will depend upon the ability of the buyer to communicate this commitment to the supplier. A rigid markup schedule, if used by a retail outlet that dominates the trade in a locality, can help counteract the advantages otherwise held by a powerful supplier. Particular note should be made that such practices set only the minimum markup and still leave the retailer the option of increasing the markup.

Retail management can also use markup as a control and planning tool if it controls the level of markup required in each department. Markup pressures could induce department merchandise buyers to make purchases at the lowest possible price or to discover new products that yield more than the minimum markup. Management pressure for a minimum markup could also help top retail management protect the firm against a continually low sale-price policy that might injure the long-run image of a store selling high-quality merchandise. However, retail management should also realize that rigid adherence to a high markup percentage will not necessarily maximize store profits. At a lower markup, sales volume may increase enough to generate more profits than the firm obtained when a higher markup was used.

Factors Affecting Markup

The rate of markup percentage is influenced by many factors, including rate of turnover, product cost, branding policies, and the degree of retail competition.

Generally, the retail markup varies inversely with merchandise turnover.[4] A higher markup is usually placed on products that sell less frequently. Slow-moving products generally occupy the same amount of selling space and require the same investment as fast-selling items. Thus a higher margin is required on slow-moving items if these items are going to contribute an equivalent share to the retailer's profits.

This can be demonstrated by calculating the margin needed to return an equivalent profit on both fast- and slow-selling items. An item's gross margin can be determined by multiplying its per unit margin by its turnover. Suppose two products, A and B, both cost the retailer $500 and require about the same amount of shelf space, sales time, and investment. Suppose, further, that the retailer desires to obtain $1,000 annual gross profit margin from each product. The annual merchandise turnover is estimated to be 20 for product A and 4 for B. The per unit margins needed if each product is to contribute $1,000 gross margin can be calculated by using the following formula:

Annual gross margin = per unit margin $\times$ annual turnover.

The calculations for product A are:

$1,000 = (required per unit margin) $\times$ 20, or $\dfrac{\$1,000}{20}$;

so per unit margin is $50.

For product B:

$1,000 = (required per unit margin) $\times$ 4, or $\dfrac{\$1,000}{4}$;

so per unit margin is $250.

Therefore, to obtain an equivalent $1,000 gross margin, the per unit margin would have to be $50 on fast-moving item A, compared to $250 on slow-moving item B. The gross margin percent required would be (50 / 550) (100), or 9 percent for A, and (250 / 750) (100), or 33 percent for B.

The markup percent needed to obtain an equivalent $1,000 gross margin can also be calculated. For example, if total retail reductions (markdowns, discounts, shrinkage, pilferage, etc.) are estimated to be 5 percent of sales, the following formula can be used to determine the required initial markup percent:

Initial markup percent = $\dfrac{\text{(gross margin + retail reductions)}}{\text{(100\% + retail reductions)}}$

The calculations for product A are:

Initial markup percent = $\dfrac{(9\% + 5\%)}{(100\% + 5\%)}$,

or 13 percent.

For Product B:

Initial markup percent = $\dfrac{(33\% + 5\%)}{(100\% + 5\%)}$,

or 36 percent.

In this example, an initial markup of 13 percent is required to yield a gross margin of 9 percent on A. The initial markup of 36 percent would result in a gross margin of 33 percent for B.

In summary, per unit gross margin, gross margin percent, and markup percent must all be higher on the slow-moving item B if the item is going to generate the same annual gross profit margin as the fast-selling (high turnover) item A.

Higher-price items normally carry a lower markup percent than lower-price items. A study, conducted by Holden, indicates that this relationship holds at the retail level.[5] Consumers are likely to notice similar percentage price differences on higher-priced items, so competitive pressure may partially explain the lower markup percent on higher-priced items. For example, a 10 percent price difference (amounting to 3 cents) between two stores on a 30 cent item is less likely to be noticed by customers than a 10 percent difference (amounting to $600) on a new car selling for $6,000. Customers are likely to spend more time making purchase decisions (and to make more comparisons on prices and quality) on major items than on lower-price items that are purchased infrequently.

Branding policies also affect the level of markup. Higher markups are usually applied to private label brand items, which a retail chain prices below the price for similar national brand items.[6] Higher markups can be applied to private label items because their acquisition, distribution, advertising, and promotion costs are usually lower than comparable costs for national branded items. Thus the private label items are usually priced lower than national brand items, but still provide the retailer with a product line that has a higher markup percent.

Retailers may change their regular markup policy to meet a competitor's price, but few retailers meet all prices of all competitors. However, most stores compare merchandise and prices in competing stores. Thus the degree of retail competition in an area determines the markup level charged by its stores.

Other things being equal, more stores and more aggressive competition tend to produce lower markups. Larger stores generally use a slightly lower markup (and hence receive a slightly lower gross margin percent) on their merchandise than similar smaller stores.[7] Average gross margin percent data for forty types of retail outlets are presented in Table 10–2.

Price Elasticity and Markup

Most of the factors that influence markup are considered in the calculation of the *price elasticity of demand coefficient,* hereafter referred to as E_d. The value of E_d indicates the percentage change in sales per 1 percent change in price, other things being held constant. The value of E_d, if known, can be used as a guide to determine the markup for an item, group of items, or even a department in a store.

The price elasticity of the demand coefficient, E_d, may be calculated by using the formula:

$$E_d = \frac{(Q_1 - Q_2)/(Q_1 + Q_2)}{(P_1 - P_2)/(P_1 + P_2)};$$

where Q_1 is the quantity sold when the price is P_1, and Q_2 is the quantity sold when the price is P_2. The value of the calculated coefficient is nearly always negative because of the inverse relationship between price and quantity (an increase in price generally causes a decrease in the number of units sold).

The calculated value of the coefficient indicates if the price elasticity of demand is inelastic, elastic, or of unitary elasticity. If the calculated coefficient, E_d, has an absolute value of less than 1.0, the demand is said to be inelastic.[8] The price increase (to the higher of the two prices—P_1 and P_2) will increase both total revenue (sales dollars) and profit if the demand is inelastic. If demand is found to be inelastic, then a new, higher price level should be tested in the next time period to determine if demand is still inelastic at a higher price level. Any calculated inelastic E_d indicates that prices must be increased even further to maximize profit. Thus, retail markups can be higher on products that have few substitutes, as indicated by an inelastic E_d. Stocking exclusive brands, obtaining a regional dealer franchise, and keeping the store open when other stores are closed are several ways of reducing the competition from substitute products or retail outlets.

Unitary elasticity is indicated when the calculated value of E_d is $- 1.0$. Unitary elasticity maximizes total revenue but not profits. Thus a price increase to the higher of the prices P_1 and P_2 would reduce total gross receipts, but would increase profit unless production and marketing costs are zero or there is a large difference between P_1 and P_2.

An *elastic demand* occurs when the percentage change in quantity is relatively greater than the percentage change in price. In this case, the calculated value of E_d has an absolute value greater than 1.0. A price decrease in the elastic section of the demand curve will result in an increase in the total revenue. Profit at the lower price may be either increased or decreased, depending upon margin and product marketing costs. One must analyze the costs and total revenue obtained under the two price levels before one can determine the effect a price change will have on profit in the elastic section of the demand curve. A very elastic E_d indicates that there are many close substitutes for the product, so the markup must be low to allow the retailer to remain competitive.

Retail markups should vary inversely with the price elasticity of demand if profits are to be maximized. High-profit stores have been found to price competitively on readily identifiable items with a high turnover rate and "known" prices.[9] However, the high-profit stores also have used higher margins on less important merchandise. Thus they could charge relatively high average prices but still give the appearance of competitiveness. In this same study, stores receiving lower profits tended to charge a higher price on items with a fast turnover and to charge a lower price on items with a low turnover. This pricing strategy can give the consumer the incorrect impression that the store charges high average prices.

Estimating Price Elasticity
Estimates of retail price elasticity of demand usually are based upon the experience of the retailer or upon representative markups charged by competitors or quoted

Table 10-2 **Gross Profit Margin Percent for Different Types of Retail Outlets, 1976**

Type of Retailer	Median Gross Margin Percentage for All Sizes of Firms, Year Ending 1976[A]
Family clothing	40.0
Furs	43.0
Infants' clothing	39.1
Men's and boys' clothing	37.1
Shoes	38.9
Women's ready-to-wear	40.6
Books and stationery	34.2
Office supplies and equipment	34.2
Building materials	25.3
Hardware	30.9
Heating and plumbing equipment	26.6
Lumber	24.1
Paint, glass, and wall paper	30.0
Cameras and photographic supplies	25.9
Department stores	30.2
Dry goods and general merchandise	34.2
Drugs	30.5
Farm equipment	21.2
Farm and garden supply	22.2

by trade associations. There is no guarantee that any of these approaches will provide a reliable estimate of price elasticity for a specific product category sold by a specific store. Years of experience can provide the retailer with an approximate estimate of E_d, but it is a costly and time-consuming process. Several research techniques can be used to reduce the cost of making serious long-term pricing errors by analyzing sales data.

One way to measure price elasticity at the retail level is to change price and observe what happens to sales. However, care must be taken when interpreting the resulting sales since other factors, such as advertising, competitive actions, or seasonal fluctuations, may distort the sales data. A retailer should be able to control his advertising and promotion, or at least know that a promotion is planned, so that he can select a product line and time period when little abnormal promotional activity will be going on. Of course, retailers are not able to control competitive promotions. However, sales data obtained during weeks of abnormally heavy competitive promotion can be deleted from the analysis.

The effect that seasonal fluctuations have upon sales can be eliminated by comparing the weekly sales of a product during price changes with its weekly sales during previous years (Table 10–3). Other factors, such as shelf space devoted to the test products, sales personnel attention, shelf inventory on the test products, and so forth, also influence sales and should be controlled.

Table 10-2 **(cont.)**

Type of Retailer	Median Gross Margin Percentage for All Sizes of Firms, Year Ending 1976[A]
Cut flowers and growing plants	36.9
Dairy product—milk dealers	26.8
Groceries and meats	20.7
Restaurants	43.3
Floor coverings	25.0
Furniture	37.9
Household appliances	27.3
Radios, TV, and record players	29.4
Jewelry	43.8
Liquor	23.9
Luggage and gifts	38.5
Autos—new and used	14.9
Gasoline service stations	12.2
Mobile homes	20.1
Tire, battery, and accessories	31.1
Musical instruments and supplies	33.7
Sporting goods	31.9
Vending machine operators, merchandise	31.5

[A]Disclaimer statement: Robert Morris Associates cannot emphasize too strongly that their composite figures for each industry may not be representative of that entire industry (except by coincidence) for the following reasons: (1) Only member banks submit data, and only the most recent data are accepted. Thus selection is not made by any random or statistically reliable method. (2) The included companies differ as to product lines, methods of operation, and demographics, but they are categorized by their primary product line only. (3) The size and variation of the sample can cause a disproportionate influence on the composite.

Source: Annual Statement Studies, the Robert Morris Associates, the National Association of Bank Loan and Credit Officers, Philadelphia National Bank Building, Philadelphia, Pennsylvania, 1977 Edition, pp.137–159. Copyright © 1977 by Robert Morris Associates.

If a chain has several stores in similar areas, it can use several different experimental designs to obtain an estimate of price elasticity. A Latin square design statistical procedure may be applied. It involves the use of the same number of time periods, store groups, and price levels (Table 10–4). Products priced at each level appear in each store group and in each time period. Data obtained from the Latin square design and subjected to an analysis of variance statistical test allow price effects to be separated from sales variation caused by store groups, time, and other random elements.[10] The chief disadvantage of the Latin square design is that the price labels must be changed every time period. This is not only a costly process, but each time period must allow the consumer to follow a normal purchasing pattern on the product(s) whose price is being changed. If the time is too short, the sales estimate obtained at low prices will be inflated because the consumer stocks up at bargain prices. This pattern does not represent long-run behavior.

A less costly store testing procedure for retailers is the before-and-after design. This method uses several matched groups of stores. Sales are measured in each

Table 10-3 **Determining Price Elasticity for a Product Line (or Department) by Changing Prices in 1974 and Comparing Sales with Previous Sales Levels**

				Sales in Units	
Product Line (or Department)	Week of	Price Level	1974	1970–1973 Average	Index or Percent 1974 Sales Are of 1970–73 Average
Meat	May 1	No change	1,210	1,100	Plus 10
	May 8	No change	1,080	1,000	Plus 8
	May 15	No change	1,120	1,000	Plus 12
	May 22	No change	990	900	Plus 10
Pre-price change average			1,100	1,000	Plus 10
	May 22	Lowered by 10%	1,500	1,100	Plus 36
	May 29	Lowered by 10%	1,536	1,200	Plus 28
	June 5	Lowered by 10%	1,703	1,300	Plus 31
	June 12	Lowered by 10%	1,501	1,200	Plus 25
Post-price change average			1,560	1,200	Plus 30

Calculation of $E_d = \dfrac{\text{Percentage change in quantity}}{\text{Percent change in price}}$

$S_o\ E_d = \dfrac{\text{(Post-price change average index sales)} \\ \text{minus (Pre-price change average index sales)}}{\text{Percentage change in price}}$

Or $E_d = \dfrac{\text{(Plus 30) minus (plus 10)}}{\text{(Minus 10)}} = \dfrac{\text{(Plus 20)}}{\text{(Minus 10)}},$ or -2.0

Table 10-4 **Example Illustrating the Use of the Latin Square Design to Estimate Price Elasticity**

	First Six-Week Period	Second Six-Week Period	Third Six-Week Period
Store Group A (10 Stores)	Product (s) Price 79¢	Product (s) Price 99¢	Product (s) Price 119¢
Store Group B (10 Stores)	Product (s) Price 99¢	Product (s) Price 119¢	Product (s) Price 79¢
Store Group C (10 Stores)	Product (s) Price 119¢	Product (s) Price 79¢	Product (s) Price 99¢

group during a pre-test (base) period. Then price changes are made in all but one group (called the "control group") of stores (Table 10–5). Test product sales in each store are then recorded as a share of each store's total sales. The effects of the price change are measured by comparing the shares obtained by each group of stores.

Any estimation procedure is costly and time consuming, so retailers are likely to estimate the values of E_d for only their most important products.

Table 10-5 **Example Illustrating the Use of the Before-and-After Design to Estimate Price Elasticity**

Four Weeks Pre-Test Period	Twelve Weeks Test Period
	Store Group A—10 Stores Product (s) Price—79¢
Product (s) Priced at Regular Price—99¢—in All Stores	Store Group B—10 Stores Product (s) Price—99¢ (Control Group)
	Store Group C—10 Stores Product (s) Price—119¢

Price Lining

Price lining involves the search for merchandise that can be sold at previously determined retail price levels. It is contrary to markup pricing, which involves the purchase of merchandise and adding a markup to arrive at the retail price. Price lining results in selling merchandise at only a few (generally three to five) price levels. For example, men's sport coats could be separated into $69, $59, $49, $39, and $29 classes.

The retailer who uses price lining implicitly assumes that his merchandise follows a *demand curve* (a schedule that indicates the quantity of an item that can be sold at many different price levels) similar to the one presented in Figure 10-3. That is, the retailer believes that sales are not increased by making a *permanent* price reduction from $69 until the amount of the price reduction reaches $59. At that point sales increase from quantity A to quantity B. A further reduction of ten dollars is needed to increase sales. This decrease to $49 results in sales of quantity C.

Price lining is said to offer an advantage to the consumer. It reduces the number of product classes and thereby simplifies comparison shopping. If the consumer's decision-making process is simplified, sales might be increased on both the main item (men's sport coats) and on complementary items (ties, shoes, slacks, belts, socks).

Retail price lining simplifies buying, accounting, and pricing procedures for the retailer because it reduces the number of price levels. Price lining makes it easier for the retail salesmen to convince the customers they should purchase the highest-quality line they can afford. The limited number of price lines can easily be associated with different levels of quality by the consumer. The different price classes may also provide convenient steps for making a price markdown if the merchandise does

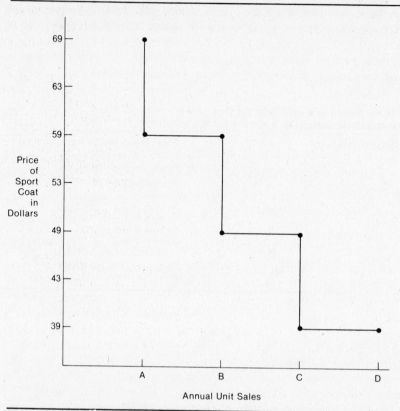

Figure 10-3 **Demand Curve for Men's Sport Coats as Perceived by a User of Price Lining**

not sell. Care must be taken to ensure that the consumer actually perceives that the price has been reduced.

For example, men's sport coats that have been priced at $59 could simply be moved into the $49 line without advertising the price reduction. Price lining would make this more convenient. However, the advertising of a price decrease might be communicated more easily if the price were *not* reduced to exactly the level of the next price line ($49 in the case of a $59 sport coat). The full reduction to the next price level might confuse potential customers, who might think that the store is merely trying to advertise the $49 line and sell it at the regular price. Pricing the coat at $53 and/or careful advertisement writing could reduce this confusion.

Merchandise handling and sales training become easier when price lining is used. Stock checkers, markers and sales personnel prefer to work with the fewer different levels of price because it is easier to identify, classify, and mark the goods and to charge customers for their purchases.

Price lining also gives the retailer more merchandise depth and breadth with less stock because it forces the buyer to concentrate the merchandise into definite price categories. For example, the stocking of 200 units divided among ten price levels would give little breadth or depth at any price. However, the 200 units carried at only four price levels would provide about 50 units in each price line, and this would more than double the selection within each price line.

The merchandise buyer may also encounter problems associated with price lining. Products must not only be selected on the basis of style, color, quality, price, etc., but they must also fit into the previously determined price lines. Price lines must be upgraded continually to reflect increases in wholesale purchase prices and increasing preferences by consumers for items possessing more quality. If the price lines are not upgraded by introducing a "new" top line and/or abandoning the lowest price line, markups will decline or quality must be reduced as wholesale prices increase.

Price lining is widely used despite the difficulties associated with it. However, the principles established in the discussion on markup pricing should be used to establish the price lines that best meet consumer needs. Usually, retailers survey competitive outlets to determine in which price lines they are strong and in which lines they are weak. They then carry the price lines that are not being well supplied by competitors or at least determine why the competitors are not emphasizing that line. Alternatively the retailer may battle the competitors head on by emphasizing the same price lines that competitors are carrying in a full assortment. This policy requires that the retailer offer unique merchandise so the firm can capture a large share of that market and/or that the sales potential in that market be sufficiently large to be profitable.

Consumer Knowledge of Retail Prices

Reliable knowledge about consumers' price awareness is needed if an appropriate pricing strategy is to be established. If consumers do not know the price of any products, the price elasticity of demand is likely to be more inelastic, since they are not aware that identical or close substitute items are available at different prices in other outlets. High markups would maximize profits in this case.

If consumers have a great deal of knowledge about prices on many products, the price elasticity is likely to be elastic, since consumers are aware of the existence of substitute products. Relatively low markups would result in maximum profits for those products.

Consumers' knowledge of prices is more likely to fall somewhere between the two extremes. They may know only the prices of a small number of frequently purchased items. In such cases it is even more important to determine which items' prices are known by consumers. These items could be priced lower to give a low-price or discount image. The items whose prices are well known are also items that would respond best to advertised, temporary price reductions.

Studies of consumers' knowledge of prices must be conducted separately for each type of retail outlet. Published results from such studies are very limited. A study of consumers' awareness of fifty-nine highly competitive and frequently advertised grocery items revealed that 71 percent of the consumers were unable to estimate within 5 percent of the actual price.[11] The responses—from about 2,000 customers—were obtained by placing unpriced products on tables in the store and asking the consumers what prices the products sold for. This study revealed that consumers were not aware of highly competitive and frequently advertised products. They were probably less aware of the prices of other items sold in a supermarket. Consumer awareness can change over time and distance, so there is a need to conduct similar studies every two to three years.

Unit Pricing

Unit pricing is a system that displays both the price per standard unit of weight or measure as well as the common per package price. This allows the consumer to compare the cost of several items in terms of content volume per dollar spent, for example, ten cents per ounce. It is most widely used when several competing brands of the same kind of product are sold in many different package sizes. The two prices, per package and the price per standard unit, are usually given on tags or stickers that appear on the shelves below the merchandise.

Unit pricing is a legal requirement for some types of stores in some states. Usually the requirement for the use of unit pricing has been confined to food, health and beauty aids, and related products in large stores such as supermarkets.

Private Label Pricing

The use of unit pricing grew out of a desire to better inform customers of comparative purchasing values. Chain stores usually have benefited by using this system as it shows customers that the per unit price of their private label products is lower than the store's prices on national brand products. Private label merchandise consists of items that are promoted under the retailer's own brand names, for example, Safeway's Townhouse, Sears' Kenmore, J. C. Penney's Towncraft, and Wards' Signature.

Most private label convenience items sell at lower prices than comparable brands because consumers will generally select the well-advertised national brand if prices are the same. Thus, the retailer must price his own brands lower to generate volume sales. In addition, these low prices placed on the firm's private label merchandise helps build an overall fair-price image among its customers. Finally, private label merchandise usually costs the retailer less to purchase than would a comparable national brand item. Thus, the retailer can mark up the purchase price by a greater percentage margin than he obtains for the national brands and still sell it to the consumer for a lower price. This can be done because of savings in transportation, advertising, distribution, and so forth.

Psychology of Retail Pricing

Markup pricing and/or price lining strategies can be used to establish a general price level. However, attention must be given to the psychological aspects of price when the specific price is established.

Odd pricing, which uses prices like 39 cents and $4.95 rather than the nearly equivalent even prices of 40 cents and $5, is frequently practiced. A study of all products advertised by supermarkets in newspapers in twenty-three metropolitan areas revealed that 57 percent of all advertised prices ended in 9.[12] Another 15 percent of the prices ended in 5.

The practice of using odd pricing probably began as a safeguard against petty theft.[13] Even-price items tend to be paid for with the exact amount of cash, and the clerk can then serve other customers before ringing up a sale. This provides an opportunity for pocketing a portion of the proceeds. If every shopper demands a receipt, this type of theft can be prevented; but there are always a few customers— small children, for example—who don't obtain a sales slip. When odd prices are used, the customer is likely not to have the exact amount of cash, so the clerk must make change from the cash register. Some of the advantages of odd pricing have been lost by the universal adoption of local sales taxes, which tend to create similar change situations.

The retailer who uses odd retail price endings implicitly assumes that his merchandise follows a demand curve similar to the one presented in Figure 10–4. That is, the retailer believes that sales are larger when the price ends in an odd number than when it ends in the next lowest number. In Figure 10–4 the sales at 59¢ are greater than the sales at 58¢ and greater at 57¢ than at 56¢, etc.

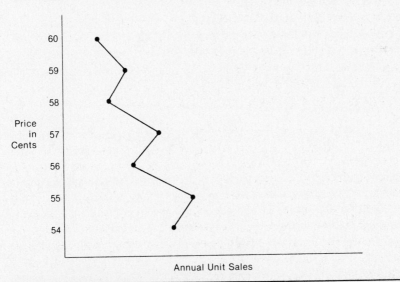

Annual Unit Sales

Figure 10–4 **Demand Curve for Merchandise as Perceived by a User of Odd Retail Price Endings**

The actual impact of odd retail price endings on sales and profits is not determined in the published marketing literature. Experimentation is needed to determine if odd prices really promote sales. If they do not promote sales, they could be abandoned because they are "sticky" prices that could hinder profit-maximizing pricing decisions.

Multiple-unit prices are also used in selling frequently purchased items. The "two for 50¢" or "five for $1" multiple prices convey the impression of potential savings to the consumer. Generally, the multiple price ends in 9 (two for 39 cents), so the consumer saves 1 cent by buying two items simultaneously instead of one unit at 20 cents on two different trips. The savings may be sufficient to persuade the customer to buy a larger quantity. However, the psychological aspect of buying a larger quantity may give the impression of additional savings.

There appear to be several different types of psychological reactions to price. A *quantum effect*[14] occurs when a certain price is the maximum price that consumers will pay for any quantity of a product. For example, a product may not sell well at $1.05, but a package containing only four-fifths as much, clearly labeled as to quantity content, will sell well at 98 cents. In this case, $1 is a quantum point from the consumer viewpoint. This quantum psychological reaction may partially explain the popularity of using odd prices, which are established just below the quantum point.

Consumers may also develop some idea of a fair price for many items. This results in a "best" price that will actually generate more sales than either a lower or higher price. A major retail chain discovered that a common hardware item sold better at $1.09 than it did at either 89 cents or $1.29.[15] Consumers apparently considered the 89 cents price too low to be attached to a quality item. The $1.09 price apparently reflected the image of a quality product to consumers.

Frequently, consumers think they can judge the cost of production. In this case their fair price standard is based upon the allowance of a modest profit, but no more. A lower markup usually must be charged when most consumers can accurately evaluate the production cost of an item.

Dynamic and Tactical Aspects of Pricing

Retail pricing strategies function as planned only when they are implemented effectively. Many decisions have to be made during these implementation efforts. These tactical decisions are concerned with day-to-day decisions that should be made within the guidelines established when the pricing strategy was determined. Tactical decisions are therefore the short-run decisions needed to carry out the basic pricing policy.

Many day-to-day pricing decisions are either passive responses to cost squeezes or estimated adaptations to what seem to be competitive requirements of the market. Many different price tactics can be utilized to make these day-to-day decisions more profitable. Familiarity with the different kinds of tactical price movements provides the background necessary if the retailer is going to expand or hold profitable markets.

Markdowns

Markdowns consist of a decrease from the original price of an item. The *markdown percentage* is usually stated as a percentage of the reduced selling price. In formula form,

$$\text{Markdown percentage} = \frac{\begin{array}{c}\text{(per unit original retail price)} \\ - \text{ (per unit reduced retail price)}\end{array}}{\text{per unit reduced price}} \times 100.$$

For example, the markdown percentage on a sport coat originally selling at $49 but reduced to $40 would be ($9 / $40) × 100, or 22½ percent.

The amount of the price reduction may also be calculated to reflect an *off retail percentage*. The off retail percentage is the reduction stated as a percentage of the original selling price—or ($9/$49) × 100 = 18.4 percent in the sport coat example.

There are many reasons that a retailer uses markdown pricing (Exhibit 10–2).

Exhibit 10–2 Reasons For Retailers Using Markdowns

Buying errors—Inappropriate sizes, colors, style, quantities

Timing errors—Merchandise delivery delayed, out-of-season, out-of-style, failure to spot slow sellers early, maintaining full assortments late in season

Selling and promotion errors—Rude sales practices, neglect to show some items, high pressure selling

Pricing errors—Initial markups too high

Deliberately planned—Assist in sales promotion to build image of meeting or beating competition

---

One objective of markdown pricing is to convert surplus merchandise into cash that can be reinvested in faster-moving merchandise or in some other demand-stimulating activity. Some markdowns are caused by an oversupply of merchandise, which must be sold to reduce the store's inventory level. Oversupply may result from errors in purchasing merchandise, which can be "overbought" by an overly enthusiastic purchasing agent. Overbuying of an item can arise because of overly optimistic sales forecasting or because of an inappropriate merchandise assortment which does not meet consumers' needs or likes. Thus overbuying is likely to occur with any merchandise that goes out of fashion (or never becomes stylish) because of preferences for different styles, color, size, etc.

Poor timing in the arrival of merchandise can also result in the oversupply of merchandise. This is especially true of seasonal merchandise, which consumers buy only once a year to meet a specific need. If the store's supply has not arrived at the time of peak consumer demand, sales are likely to be lost. Anti-freeze and winter overshoes are examples of products that are likely to be purchased over a short period of time.

Markdowns may also be necessary when the correct quantity and quality merchandise is purchased, but the selling and/or promotion efforts are deficient. Selling errors can originate from poor department management, a weak sales force, or a poor promotion program. Poor management may be revealed by a failure to interpret sales records early enough to spot items that are not selling well. Some retailers are now using computer systems to provide reliable inventory and sales data quickly. The sales force may contribute to the overstock problem by not exposing all of the products in the category, so that some items are unexposed until it is too late to sell them at regular prices.

Markdowns are required even in cases where proper purchasing and selling procedures are used. Odds and ends merchandise gradually accumulates over time, so most retailers use markdowns to unload the least desirable merchandise from their shelves.

Many markdowns are deliberately planned price reductions, designed to assist in sales promotion and in generating an image of meeting competition.

"Leader prices" are relatively low (or negative) markups on items that attract customers to the store, where, hopefully, they will also purchase other, regular-priced merchandise. Leader prices contribute little, if any, per unit profit, but may make substantial contributions to total dollar profits by generating added sales of products at regular prices. Leader items must be recognized as good values by customers, since their principal aim is to draw customer traffic. Good leader items are products whose normal price is known by most potential customers. A good leader item is usually purchased frequently by a large number of consumers.

The use of price leaders for a limited, specified time as a promotional device appears to create less disturbance among competition than general price reductions. General price reductions are likely to initiate a price war because they offer the threat of a permanent price cut. Leader prices are more acceptable to competition because the prices are viewed as only temporary reductions and hence are considered part of the normal pricing routine.

Leader prices are generally used on high-frequency purchase products, and a good price leader is:

1. Well known, widely used, and appealing to many customers
2. Priced low enough so that many people can buy it
3. Not so low in price that price cuts will generate no interest
4. Not generally bought in large quantities and stored
5. Likely to have a high price elasticity of demand
6. Not in close competition with other products in the retailer's merchandise assortment.[16]

Types of Markdown
Leader prices can be classified by the degree of markdown and the purpose of the promotion.

Low-Price Leaders Low-price leaders are products whose prices represent bargain prices. Low-price leader items are not priced below the actual cost to the retailer but merely represent a reduced markup percentage. The low-price leader does not violate the intent of most unfair trade practices acts, which usually prohibit sales of merchandise at less than cost when the intent is to injure competition. Often, large chains are able to make "special purchases" of seasonal merchandise at reduced costs, which serve as excellent low-price traffic generators.

Loss-Leader Pricing Loss-leader pricing involves sales of an item at a price below the actual cost to the retailer. The objective of loss-leader pricing is to attract customers to the store. A good merchandising program can then be used to stimulate consumers to make additional purchases of other regular-price items. The profit obtained from sales of the regular-price items must overcome the loss incurred on the loss-leader items. Proper placement of loss-leader merchandise within a department can encourage such additional purchases. Thus, loss-leader pricing is really a form of promotion, because loss-leader pricing costs the retailer money in the same manner as additional advertising.

The legality of loss-leader pricing must be established before it is used by retailers. Most states have passed laws prohibiting sales below cost and/or laws that establish a minimum markup if the intent of the pricing practice is to injure or extinguish competition. Exceptions are usually provided for specific merchandise which is sold for (1) clearance or close out, (2) charitable purposes, (3) liquidation of a business, or (4) liquidation of perishable, seasonal, or damaged goods.[17]

Bait-Leader Pricing Bait-leader pricing involves the use of an advertised price on an item that is not intended to be sold. It represents a very low price on a well-known item, which is found by the customer to be relatively unattractive after he arrives at the store. Bait-leader pricing could involve the advertising of a very low price on a relatively low quality (or small) item that is not likely to be purchased by a large percentage of the potential customers. After the consumer arrives at the store, the sales clerk uses persuasion to upgrade the consumer's purchase (at unreduced prices) to a better quality than was originally advertised. For example, USDA standard-grade beef may be advertised at 79 cents per pound, but the sales clerk would suggest that the good, choice, or prime grades are better-quality meats and would be better accepted by other family members.

Another version of bait-leader pricing involves the advertisement of some central component item (for example, a new-model car) at an extremely low price. However, the price is quoted on only a portion of the total merchandise that is likely to be purchased. Accessory items are sold at the regular price, so the total "package" purchase price may not be lower than competitive prices. Accessory items may take the form of both supplementary and complementary items.

The use of bait-leader pricing could also involve advertising an item that is in very short supply at a very low price and telling the customers who rush to the store that the last unit of the advertised item has just been sold. However, this practice has been made illegal and is policed by the Federal Trade Commission (hereafter referred to as the FTC). The FTC watches over deceptive acts by firms that do a substantial share of their business in interstate commerce. All firms may be required to make good on all offers made in advertisements, according to current legislation.

The FTC publishes guides for business people who want clarification of the legality of related practices. Examples are *Guides against Deceptive Pricing, Guides against Bait Advertising,* and *Guides against Deceptive Advertising of Guarantees.*

Firms should exercise care when any of the leader-pricing techniques are used. Low-price leaders and some forms of loss-leader and bait-leader pricing may be legal pricing practices, but they may strengthen customer support for the consumer movement. However, long-run businesses must be based upon providing consumer satisfaction. A poor post-purchase feeling, generated by a consumer belief of having "been taken," will not promote future patronage. Thus, leader pricing must be used in a way that will not offend or mislead consumers. The low-price leader and the loss-leader are not likely to offend consumers if the featured items are always available for purchase in quantity and quality without special qualifications (coupon clipping, etc.). The consumer movement is here, and—like it or not—the trend is toward more consumer protection from deceptive pricing of all kinds.

Off-Season Pricing Off-season pricing is another form of markdown. Firms engaged in the more seasonal service or retail businesses (for example, travel, resort, and tourist service) use off-season and special group-pricing practices to reach a different market segment from their regular-season customer. The off-season business may be promoted at the partial expense of the regular-season business, but the increased business volume may result in lower year-round average costs that justify price reductions.

Retail firms use special advertisements, mailings, and reduced off-season prices to generate a more constant sales level than they would otherwise attain. The more constant sales level reduces cost by better use of the somewhat fixed level of personnel who are needed to operate a retail outlet.

Farm machinery retailers have been using off-season price reductions during the fall and winter months to provide a more reliable sales forecast, which results in a more constant work load over the year. Sales are also promoted by offering a cash discount and delaying the payment until spring (the normal purchase period), with little or no interest charges being assessed.

Timing of Markdowns

The appropriate time to mark down the price on merchandise depends on many factors. Stores catering to the same clientele on a frequent basis will want to mark down prices early on items that are not selling well. Stores relying on sales made to different transient customers may delay the price reductions and hope to make additional sales at regular prices.

Earlier markdowns are more likely to be taken on fashionable and/or perishable merchandise than on items that are not subject to sudden changes in fashion or spoilage. Taking early markdowns keeps a retailer's stock fresh and more in tune with the latest fashion preferences. Retailers may mark down a fashion item when its sales begin to decline if the outlet is estimated to be in an oversupplied condition. Seasonal items whose sales are dependent upon fashionability are usually reduced in price as soon as the rush of seasonal buying is completed and excess stock is estimated to be held in inventory. For example, ski equipment prices may be reduced in January, although sales are still made during February and March.

Staple goods prices are usually reduced if the supply is excessive or if the products have been on the shelf long enough that their appearance and/or quality are about to decline. Staple items whose demand fluctuates seasonally are usually marked down if the store does not have sufficient low-cost storage space to carry them until next year. An evaluation of the costs incurred in placing these items in inventory is needed before seasonal items are stored for nearly one year.

Fashion merchandise is not carried over, no matter how costly the markdown. If it did not sell now, it will not sell next year. Recognize the mistake, mark it down, take the bath, and get merchandise that will sell.

Some fashion retailers are even using automatic markdown policy. For example, all of the merchandise that remains unsold after twelve selling days in the basement store of William Filene's Sons Company of Boston is automatically marked down 25 percent. After eighteen days the unsold merchandise is repriced at 50 percent of its original price, and after twenty-four days the remaining merchandise is remarked at 25 percent of the original price.[18] This policy has developed a large and loyal customer group for the Filene basement. Most retailers prefer to use a more flexible plan of making markdowns. However, it is desirable to have some written markdown policy that has proven itself to be most appropriate for that particular store.

Mass merchandisers are also more likely to use earlier markdowns than are exclusive outlets. Exclusive shops prefer to delay price reductions to discourage bargain hunters (sometimes referred to as "cherry pickers") who select only markdown items and thereby detract from the stores' class appeal. If price lining is used, exclusive outlets can move slow-selling items into the next lower price line without advertising the price reductions. This practice is less likely to attract "cherry pickers," and could increase sales to their normal market segment.

Pricing for Special Sales

Pricing for special sales poses particular problems of pricing for the retail operator. The amount of the markdown is not easily determined. The markdown level must be sufficient to generate sales on items that were not selling well. Department stores have been found to reduce the retail price by about a third on the first markdown.[19] The retailer must consider the quality of the merchandise and its sales relative to other items sold in the store.

For example, a retail store carried two major price lines of women's hosiery; one line was priced at $1 and the other at $2. A special purchase was made on the $2 line at a cost of 65 cents. Sales were poor when the better line was offered as a special at $1 per pair. When they were marked up to $1.14 a pair and could be more easily differentiated from the lower-priced line, they sold quite well. The higher price represented a higher value to consumers, and this increased sales.[20] However, reactions of competitors, and of consumers who bought the merchandise at the regular price, also must be considered.

The retailer must evaluate the effect that advertising and sales effort have upon sales. Other things being equal, a large promotional effort can stimulate as many sales at a moderate markdown as a larger markdown promoted on a small scale.

The language used to advertise special sale items usually involves hoopla and sensational-type advertising. Words and phrases such as "incredible," "unbelievable," "fantastic," "free," "2 for 1 sale," "1¢ sale" are frequently used to describe promotional sales, but indiscriminate use of such terms has been overdone by too many retailers. The FTC has been increasing its regulation activity by forbidding the use of deliberately deceptive language in the promotion of price specials.

This increased level of regulatory activity, plus the consumer movement, are likely to result in a continual growth of informational advertisements. Such advertisements clearly state all the terms and conditions of the sale. The advertisements would answer such questions as, "What is the product? How can it be used? What does the price tag include and what is extra? Does it come fully assembled?" These important questions are being asked by both consumers and the government.

Pricing Restrictions

The retailer is not entirely free to set any price that he may believe will maximize sales and/or profits. Manufacturers or distributors of well-known, branded products can strongly influence retail prices if they threaten to withhold products from retail outlets that do not comply with the manufacturer's pricing suggestions. Manufacturers and distributors control much of the marketing effort of franchised dealers (retailers), who represent the manufacturer or distributor in the market. Franchising allows the manufacturer to restrict his product to a few outlets that he expects to price his products according to his suggestions.

In nonfranchising situations, manufacturers sometimes preticket their products with "suggested retail prices." The retailer does not have to sell the item at the supplier's suggested price, but it is inconvenient to reprice the merchandise. In some cases, the re-marking of "suggested retail price" items can lead to strained dealer-supplier relationships. Alternatively, reticketing to a lower price has been used by discount retailers to reinforce a low price image.

The structure (number and size) of the local retail competition can influence a retailer to stress other, nonprice sales stimulating devices. In some cases, smaller, less powerful retailers may simply price their goods according to the price used by the dominant firm. The prevalence of price leadership of this type certainly impairs the effectiveness of the individual's price setting policy, which should be designed to maximize long-run profits. In other instances, several retailers of equal power may recognize that a reduction in price by any one of them will result in a retaliatory price reduction by the others. Such firms would probably attempt to prevent price wars by emphasizing nonprice competition. Nonprice competition has two general benefits: it may be longer lasting and it is more difficult to imitate. For the retailer attempting to build a distinct store image, both benefits are important. However, low profits by any of the current retailers or the entry of a new competitor will usually disturb static pricing after a period of time.

A retailer's freedom to establish prices is also limited by governmental authority at many different levels—local, state, and national. States and the federal government limit a retailers' price-setting power by preventing the maintenance of high prices if retailers get together and make price-fixing agreements. Governmental authority can also impose minimum price levels that prevent a retailer from cutting prices too drastically.

Fair Trade Laws (Resale Price Maintenance)

Fair trade laws have been important retail issues in the past. However, federal action in December of 1975 practically eliminated the use of fair trade laws as a legal method of controlling retail prices in the United States. Actually the use of fair trade laws had declined to apply to a very small percentage of retail items anyway.

Since laws have a habit of reappearing, although sometimes under a different name, it is useful to understand what the fair trade laws were and who supported them.

In general, the use of retail price maintenance declined because of legal difficulties and a changed attitude on the part of manufacturers. Most manufacturers came to believe that the volume sales made by discount outlets offered more of a market opportunity than a market threat.

The major advocates of fair trade laws were small-scale independent merchants who preferred to compete on the basis of product selection and service instead of price. In general, the fair trade laws resulted in higher retail prices that the consumer had to pay for the fair-traded merchandise.[21] The trend toward consumerism brought pressure upon the government to take the fair trade laws off the books.

Resale price maintenance agreements allowed the seller of a brand name or trademark item to set a minimum price that the retailer must charge his customers. Of course, this reduced the retailer's price setting freedom. The Miller-Tydings Act (1937) and the McGuire Act (1952) allowed manufacturers to establish the resale prices of brand name merchandise in states whose legislatures had passed an act containing a "nonsigner" clause.

A nonsigner clause enabled a manufacturer who was engaged in interstate commerce to sign a resale price maintenance agreement with one retailer in a state on the retail price of a branded item and thereby bind all other retailers in that state to the price agreement. As a result of this legal authority, it was possible for a manufacturer of a branded good that was in competition with other goods to fix the retail price of the item within any of the states that had passed legislation containing a nonsigner clause.

Preticketing

Manufacturers still attempt to influence the retailer's price by suggesting specific prices for their items. They frequently even mark their suggested price on the good. This act of premarking the price on the merchandise is called *preticketing*.

However, manufacturers cannot legally force the retailer to use the preticketed price if the retailer owns the merchandise. Manufacturers must be reasonably certain that most of the retailers selling their products will follow their price recommendations before they use preticketing. This is because the Federal Trade Commission believes that a preticketed price is deceptive pricing if a substantial number of retailers sell the item for less than the preticketed price. Since some retailers believe that a reduction in price from a preticketed level offers proof to the consumer that the outlet is offering low prices, manufacturers have little assurance that prices will not be cut. Thus, they are likely to incur the wrath of the Federal Trade Commission. As a result the use of preticketing is on the decline.

Unfair Sales and Unfair Trade Practices Acts

Unfair sales and unfair trade practices acts establish a mandatory minimum price for all goods sold in states where unfair sales practices, unfair trade practices, minimum price, minimum markup, or sales-below-cost laws (known by some other name) are on the books. The unfair sales act in some states defines the minimum price as the cost of merchandise without the addition of markup. Other states require retailers to add at least a specified percent of their invoice cost of goods. Usually the minimum retailing costs exceed the specified legal minimum markup percentage. Thus, unfair sales acts normally prevent the practice of drastic price cutting. However, the unfair sales acts do not generally force an efficient retailer to raise his prices above a low price level, based upon his low cost of operation, low merchandise costs, and/or a low profit margin percentage on a large sales volume. This would not be true if the minimum specified legal markup is higher than the markup required for profitably marketing some items. In this case, the unfair sales act can result in consumers paying higher prices than they would pay if this type of act were not law.

There are about twenty-five states that use unfair sales acts to establish a minimum price on retail goods. These acts are usually supported by small-scale, independent retailers, and wholesalers who wish to prevent or inhibit the establishment of large-scale retailers. Minimum markup laws are designed to prevent predatory price cutting, which a large, powerful retailer could use to drive small retailers out of business. The large retailer may then increase his prices above the original price level as soon as the competition is eliminated.

Predatory pricing of this kind is most likely to occur in areas where the retail competition is already weak. To be successful, this type of predatory pricing would not only have to eliminate current retailers but also discourage potential competitors from establishing a new outlet in the area. New retailers are likely to move into the area if the original predator uses an abnormally high pricing policy after eliminating all competition.

Unfair sales practices acts are also supported because they curb the use of loss-leader pricing, which may deceive customers into patronizing the store with drastically reduced prices on only a few items to which the consumer is price sensitive.

Deceptive Pricing The FTC regulates deceptive pricing that may mislead the consumer into believing that he is getting a bargain.

Former-Price Comparisons Retailers can use former-price comparisons, which indicate that an item was formerly priced at a higher level but is now reduced to a new price level. To do so, however, they must be certain that the former price has been regularly used in sales during the recent course of business.[22]

Comparable-Price Comparisons Bargain advertising that offers a reduction from the price charged by other local retailers for either the identical or comparable merchandise is legitimate if the higher price is a genuine price, regularly charged by merchants in the local trade area.[23] Thus, the advertisement of brand X cameras, "Price Elsewhere $75; Our Price $50," is legitimate if the higher price is truly established and if brand X cameras are made available to the customers.

This type of price advertising has several advantages. The retailer does not have to establish the higher comparative price in his own store, so he may introduce the article to his customers at the lower price and maintain the lower price on a permanent basis or raise the price later. This type of comparative pricing also combines the pull of a brand name product with the lure of a bargain to generate additional sales.

Use of comparable merchandise pricing is allowed if it is made clear to the consumer that a comparison is being made with other merchandise of essentially similar quality that is regularly available in the local market area. The terms "comparable value $75" or "comparable retail $75" can be used if the comparable merchandise is "competing merchandise" of "like grade and quality." The FTC also permits the retailer to relate a bargain price to one being charged by him for other merchandise of like grade and quality. Thus a retailer may compare the price of his private label brand with a higher-priced nationally advertised brand that he also carries, provided the private label product is of the same quality or quantity as that of the national brand.

Under revised FTC guides, a retailer is permitted to rely on a "good-faith estimate" (possibly obtained by a market survey) of the higher price that he advertises. A retailer operating on a regional or nationwide scale need not investigate all prices throughout his market area if he determines the price at which substantial sales are made by principal retail outlets in representative communities. However, if such information is not available, the FTC advises that price-comparison claims not be made.[25]

Free Offers Offering and giving free goods is a very effective merchandising and advertising method for attracting customers. The word *free* usually refers to an offer involving something other than an unconditional gift the consumer can receive without doing something or paying something. The "free" offer usually is an offer to give something if the customer purchases other goods or services for a stated price. In reality, most of these offers are merely price reductions, which are legal if the word "free" is not used in a deceptive manner.

Practices that are condemned by the FTC are:

1. Failure to fully disclose the terms and conditions of the bargain offer "at the outset"

2. Increasing the usual and regular price of the article to be purchased

3. Reducing the quality of the article to be purchased

4. Reducing the quantity or size of the article to be purchased.[26]

All bargain offers that are based upon the purchase of other items are judged on the basis of these four recommendations. The designation of the offer as "free," "buy one, get one free," "two for one sale," "half-price sale," "1 cent sale" or "50 percent off" does not influence the fact that the offer will be judged according to its adherence to the four guidelines.

An unconditional gift is not in violation of the FTC Act if it is truly a gratuity. Examples of such gifts are product samples received in the mail or distributed door to door, balloons and lollipops given to children who shop with their parents at a retail outlet, and coupons that must be mailed to a place of business. The inclusion in a "mail in" offer of a request for a small sum to cover handling and mailing costs is legitimate if the amount is no more than the actual cost to the distributor.[27]

Cents-Off Pricing The FTC is also involved in ensuring honesty in "cents off" promotion pricing. Under current regulations, the manufacturer must print the amount of "cents off" on the label and the retailer must stamp the resulting price on the box. In addition, the store must post a shelf placard that contains the product's regular price in that store.[28] For example, a can of corn might be labeled "10 Cents Off Regular Price." The store would stamp the can lid with the resulting price—say 20 cents—and also post a shelf placard saying "Regular Price 30 cents."

Price Ceiling Regulations

All deceptive pricing, fair trade, and minimum markup laws restrict the pricing freedom of the retailers, but the other restrictions are associated with price freezes. During some of the various phases of 1971–1973, retailers' prices were both frozen at base period prices and controlled on the basis of customary percentage markups that were added to the cost of the merchandise or service. The absolute prices or the customary percentage markups were not allowed to exceed those prices or markups used during the various base periods.

Price ceiling regulations provide another illustration of the trend toward more legal restriction on a retailer's freedom to determine price levels. The additional time and effort required to comply with price freeze regulations result in extra cost. If similar profit margins are maintained, this added cost eventually must be passed on to the consumer through higher prices. Apparently, governmental officials believed that price increases would be greater if free pricing prevailed than under controlled pricing, which requires more record keeping and new placard-posting costs.

Effects of Price Restrictions upon Retailers

The main feature of our free-enterprise economy has been competitive pricing. A major unanswered question now is, "How much can distributors' pricing freedom be limited if they are still expected to provide for an easy transfer of goods, service, and manpower?" On one hand, fair trade and minimum markup laws may prevent a retailer from being too competitive on the price variable. On the other hand, price ceiling restrictions limit the upward movement of retail prices. Considerable time must be spent making sure that the prices and the communication of the price level to consumers are permissible according to the latest legal interpretation. These additional costs will eventually be passed on to consumers in the form of higher prices, unless profit margins are allowed to decline. The consumers are paying for more information, which will presumably allow them to make more intelligent purchasing decisions.

These pressures result in a preference, on the part of most retailers, to concentrate on nonprice competition instead of outright price competition. Thus, we are likely to see more examples of Professor Malcolm McNair's wheel of retailing. The new retail firms are likely to appear first as low-margin, low-price establishments, but they will gradually upgrade their facilities and services and thus join the majority retailers by shifting to nonprice competition. The retail environment is again appropriate for the entry of new low-price retailers. (One of the major elements of nonprice competition—promotion—will be discussed in chapters 13, 14, and 15.)

Summary

Generally, retailers use markup pricing because it is a convenient method of pricing the very large number of items they stock. Retailers cannot afford to spend the time and effort needed to determine the best price to charge on every item. However, few retailers use the same markup for all items. The markup percentage that is generally used varies inversely with merchandise turnover and the price of the item.

For maximum profits, retailer markups should also vary inversely with the value of the price elasticity of the demand coefficient. Estimates of retail elasticity of demand are usually based upon the experience of the retailer or upon representative markups charged by similar outlets.

Experimental techniques can also be used to obtain elasticity estimates. Retailers can use the estimates to identify items whose sales are greatly influenced by price. Lower markups can generally stimulate greater profits on these items, besides drawing additional consumers to the outlet. Retail managers can estimate the change in sales that is needed to make a general price level change profitable by calculating break-even volumes for each price level.

Consumers do not always perceive prices from an objective, mathematical viewpoint, so the general price level must be fine-tuned to be compatible with consumer psychology. Multiple-unit pricing and odd pricing are two pricing techniques that might satisfy consumer preferences for certain exact prices.

It is important to note the relationship that exists between initial markup, maintained markup and gross margin. Initial markup is the first markup placed on merchandise, so it must be high enough to cover the maintained markup (which consists of store operating expenses plus alteration expenses plus profits minus cash discounts given by vendors) plus all retail reductions (which include all markdowns, discounts given to employees, and all shortages). Thus, the initial markup exceeds the maintained markup by the amount of the actual retail reductions incurred by the retailer. Gross margin is equal to the maintained markup plus any cash discounts given to the retailer by vendors but minus the amount retailers spend for alteration costs.

Retailers use markdowns to stimulate purchases of items that (1) have not been selling well, (2) are overstocked or (3) will draw potential consumers into the store, where—hopefully—they will purchase other, regular price merchandise.

Firms should use only pricing techniques that provide long-run consumer satisfaction. A post-purchase feeling of having been taken will not promote long-run purchases.

A price markdown is not likely to offend customers if the featured items are always available for purchase in the same quantity and quality, and without the consumer's having to meet special qualifications that are not clearly defined in the retailer's advertisements or price labels.

Some retailers are pressured by minimum markup laws to maintain their prices at high levels. Price ceiling legislation can be imposed to limit the amount of price increases that can be made by retailers. So, despite the apparent price-conscious mood of consumers, these legal pressures could cause well-established retailers to continue to rely upon nonprice elements of the marketing mix (such as advertising, service, and so forth) to attract consumers.

Questions

1. Distinguish between markup pricing and price lining. What are their advantages and difficulties?

2. What is the difference between markup percent and markup percent of cost? How do you make the conversion?

3. Describe the difference between initial markup and maintained markup.

4. Describe the difference between maintained markup and gross margin.

5. Explain briefly the four factors influencing the rate of markup percentage used by retailers.

6. How can the retailers use the price elasticity of demand coefficient, E_d, as an indicator in pricing strategy?

7. What are the objectives of retailers who use markdown pricing?

8. Which of the leader pricing techniques is most likely to offend or mislead customers?

9. A furniture buyer has a planned initial markup for the fall season (August 1 to January 31) of 43.5 percent. But on October 1, his figures in round numbers are as follows:

	Cost	Retail
Inventory, August 1	$285,000	$500,000
Inventory, October 1	250,000	440,000
Purchases, August 1 to October 1	200,000	325,000
Transportation charges	2,000	
Additional markups		1,000

The low markup on the purchases is due to August and September sales for which the furniture was closely priced. The planned purchase figure for the rest of the season, October 1 to January 31, is $400,000 at cost. What average markup should the buyer obtain on his purchases during the period October 1 to February 1 to get back his planned markup by the end of the season?

10. A book buyer makes the following purchases:

	Unit Cost	Markup on Cost	Markup on Retail	Unit Retail
6 books	$1.00	25%	—	—
8 books	—	30	—	$2.00
4 books	—	—	24%	3.00
5 books	1.75	—	32	—
10 books	1.25	—	—	2.00
12 books	—	44	—	5.00
10 books	5.00	—	34	—

(a) Fill in the blank spaces in the table.

(b) Find the cost, markup in dollars, and the retail of the purchases as a whole.

(c) Find the percentage of markup on cost and on retail for the purchases as a whole.

11. A retailer prices a coat so that the dollar markup amounts to $80. This is 60 percent of retail. What did the coat cost and what is the retail price?

12. A retail buyer informs one of his competitors that he was able to obtain a markup of 100 percent on cost for a certain line of merchandise. Since the competitor has always expressed his markup as a percent of retail, he wishes to know what the equivalent markup on retail would be.

13. The retail price is $60; the cost markup is 30 percent. What is the cost?

14. Determine the cost and retail price on an item that you have purchased and which will carry a markup of $70, or 30 percent markup as a percent of retail price. The nearest retail price will be:

15. What should the initial markup percent be in a store that has the following planned figures: expenses, $10,000; profit, $2,500; sales, $50,000; markdowns, $500; stock shortages, $250?

16. A ladies' wear buyer is able to purchase a line of ladies' dresses which will retail at $50 each. The manufacturer has offered these items to the buyer at a cost of $25 each. What is the markup percent on retail that the buyer will achieve on this item?

17. An item has been marked down to $40 from its original price of $50. What is (a) the markdown percentage and (b) the off-retail percentage?

18. A store has been able to purchase a color television set for $400 from a manufacturer. The retailer wishes to place a 30 percent markup at retail on the item and has asked you to determine the retail price. What price will allow a 40 percent markup as a percent of retail price?

19. A markup of 38 percent retail is equivalent to what markup percent on the cost base?

20. A pair of shoes costs a retailer $15.00. If a markup of 40 percent on cost is desired, what will the retail price be?

21. A retail buyer calculates his markup on the basis of the cost price of the item. A vendor has informed the buyer that he will obtain a markup of 20 percent of retail on a certain line of items. Find the equivalent markup percent on cost for the buyer.

22. A shirt costs a retailer $7.00. If a markup of 50 percent of retail is required, what must the retail price be?

23. Suppose you purchase a line of ladies' dresses to retail at $90. Since the manufacturer has offered these dresses to you at a cost of $60 each, find the markup percent of cost that you hope to obtain.

24. A sporting goods store has purchased a number of golf club sets at a cost of $50 and wishes to place a markup of 40 percent of cost on the sets. Determine what the retail price of these golf clubs will be.

25. How much will a men's wear buyer have to pay for a suit that will retail at $100 and carry a markup of 40 percent on retail?

26. The markdown percentage for a suit originally selling at $100 but whose price is reduced to $60 is:

Footnotes

1. A. D. H. Kaplan et. al., *Pricing in Big Business* (Washington, D.C.: The Brookings Institution, 1958), p. 188.

2. Ibid., p. 182.

3. Roger Dickinson, "Markup in Department Store Management," *Journal of Marketing* 31 (January 1967): 32–34.

4. Turnover is usually measured by dividing total sales by the average level of inventory valued at selling prices.

5. Bob R. Holden, *The Structure of a Retail Market and the Market Behavior of Retail Units* (Englewood Cliffs, N.J.: Prentice-Hall, 1960), p. 72.

6. Private label brands are brand names that are owned by a wholesaler or retailer.

7. *Annual Statement Studies* (Philadelphia: Robert Morris Associates, 1970), pp. 98–119.

8. The "absolute" value indicates that any value of E_d from 0 to minus 0.99 falls in the inelastic section of the demand curve. The demand curve indicates the quantity of an item that will be purchased, other things being equal, at various price levels during a particular time period. In graphic form, the demand curve generally appears as a downward-sloping curve.

A more detailed explanation of the elasticity concept can be found in Richard H. Leftwich, *Introduction to Microeconomics* (New York: Holt, Rinehart and Winston, 1970), pp. 62–68.

9. Holden, *Structure of a Retail Market,* p. 72.

10. Seymour Banks, *Experimentation in Marketing* (New York: McGraw-Hill, 1965), Chap. 5.

11. *Colonial Study* (New York: Progressive Grocer, 1962), p. C105.

12. Dik Warren Twedt, "Does the '9 Fixation' in Retail Pricing Really Promote Sales?" *Journal of Marketing* 25 (October 1965): 54–55.

13. Ibid., p. 55

14. Chester R. Wasson, *Managerial Economics* (New York: Appleton-Century-Crofts, 1966), p. 222.

15. Ibid., p. 223.

16. Roland S. Vaile, E. T. Grether, and Reavis Cox, *Marketing in the American Economy* (New York: Ronald Press, 1952), p. 447.

17. Marshall C. Howard, *Legal Aspects of Marketing* (New York: McGraw-Hill, 1964), pp. 44–45.

18. "Filene's Basement, the 9th Wonder," *Women's Wear Daily,* June 14, 1973, pp. 1 and 11, and "The Boston Supershoppers," *Time,* December 26, 1969, p. 27.

19. Richard M. Cyert and James G. March, A *Behavioral Theory of the Firm* (Englewood Cliffs, N.J.: Prentice-Hall, 1963), pp. 139–140.

20. Oswald Knauth, "Considerations in the Selling of Retail Prices," *Journal of Marketing* 14 (July 1949): 8.

21. Jerome C. Darnell, "The Impact of Quality Stabilization," *Journal of Marketing Research,* 2, 3 (August 1965): 274–282.

22. Earl W. Kintner, A *Primer on the Law of Deceptive Practices* (New York: Macmillan, 1971), p. 157.

23. Ibid., pp. 161–162.

24. Ibid.

25. Ibid.

26. Ibid, p. 171.

27. Ibid., p. 187

28. "Cents Off Rules Demanded," *Laramie* (Wyoming) *Boomerang,* November 26, 1971, p. 1.

Case Study

Jane's Boutique

Ms. Jane Abrams has been operating a women's wear specialty shop for the past year. The outlet is located in a college town of 30,000 permanent residents and 10,000 college students. The nearest large competing town is 100 miles away from Jane's site. Although the first year has had its difficulties, Ms. Abrams has finally gotten the firm into a profit-making situation during the last quarter of 1977.

Recently Ms. Abrams has received some complaints from a group of female students enrolled in a local college. Jane is really concerned that this criticism might cause her to lose sales next year. The complaints have settled solely on Jane's prices, which the students claim are too high.

Jane has achieved a 40 percent gross margin during her first year of business. She did this by using a 45 percent initial markup on every item. She surveyed the prices that local competitors charge and found that her prices are nearly identical to those of competition. When confronted with this information the students still persisted that her prices were too high and that, in fact, all of the local merchants were charging too much for their merchandise. Jane replied that she would see if she could drop prices.

A meeting with her accountant revealed that her estimated costs for 1978 are as follows:

Rent	$8,000
Utilities	1,200
Depreciation on fixtures and equipment	500
Wages for one full-time helper	6,000
Wages for part-time help	3,000
Insurance cost	500
Advertising	1,600
Supplies	400
Value of Jane's time spent in the store	9,000

First year sales for the boutique were $84,000 and its net profit was $3400. Jane hopes to increase sales to $100,000 and obtain $5,000 profit in 1978. She thinks she will be able to reach her sales goal by reducing her prices by an average of five percent, but she is not sure what effect this price reduction would have upon profits.

Discussion Questions

1. If Jane reduces her prices by an average of five percent and sales go to $100,000 what would her profit be?

2. How much must sales increase to make it worthwhile for Jane to reduce prices by five percent?

3. Do you think most of Jane's consumers will notice the price change?

4. Do you think the price change will influence Jane's customers to buy more of their clothing at Jane's?

5. How do you think the competitive outlets will react to the price reduction?

6. What should Jane do? Why?

Brown's Hardware

Joe Brown is the owner operator of Brown's Hardware store. Mr. Brown is in his late thirties and has owned the store for the past five years. He had worked in the store for five years before he bought it, so he has about ten years experience in the hardware business.

Recently Joe has noticed that several discount outlets have been advertising reduced prices on many of the items that he carries. Joe has visited these stores several times and found that: (1) they are frequently out of stock on the items that are advertised at very low prices, and (2) their prices on the nonadvertised items are actually higher than the price Joe regularly has on these items.

Joe is concerned that his regular customers are buying a considerable volume of competing merchandise from these discount houses.

Discussion Questions

1. What can Joe do to find out if he is right in believing that the discount houses are capturing a significant portion of his market?

2. If the discount houses are beginning to capture some of Joe's market, do you recommend that Joe reduce his prices? Discuss.

3. What other actions should Joe take?

4. Are the discount houses using illegal advertising and pricing methods?

Chapter 11

Management of Human Resources

Learning Goals

1. To develop a working definition and an appreciation for the wide diversity of people problems associated with human resource management in the retail industry.

2. To recognize the relationship between organizational objectives, philosophies, organization structure, job design, and employee motivation and satisfaction.

3. To be able to list the specific personnel functions and their interrelationships.

4. To be aware of governmental influence and intervention into the management of human resources in retail institutions.

5. To be able to discuss employment opportunities for selected retail professionals in the 1980s.

Key Terms and Concepts

personnel process

organizational philosophy

authority, delegation and job design

job description and supervision

recruitment, selection, and placement

direction and supervision

performance appraisal

training

management development

compensation components

One of the least understood aspects of retail management is the effective utilization of the human resource. Without doubt, labor is the largest single contributor to a retailer's variable cost. A retailer can adhere rigidly to well-planned merchandise budgets, hold markdowns to a minimum, closely scrutinize transportation costs, and control shrinkage—and still suffer continuing poor performance due to inadequate manpower planning and utilization.

At the outset of this discussion it is critically important to realize that the total image and lasting perception of any retail establishment is strongly affected by the person-to-person relationship between the retail salesperson and the customer. This interaction should begin when the customer enters the store and usually terminates at the transaction center. Thus, the quality of this experience strongly affects the future customer's perception of the firm's mass media efforts as well as store patronage. Effective retailers know that the viability of the firm lies in relative satisfaction of customer needs at all levels in the firm, from the stockroom through the administrative offices to the salesfloor and occasionally to post-purchase adjustments. Every employee's best effort is required to provide customer satisfaction profitably.

Human Resource Role in Retailing

Today retail management is faced with unprecedented challenges in the effective utilization of the firm's human resources. The problems begin when one tries to establish appropriate organizational goals that reflect society's changed perception of what is demanded from the business community. Such goals as full employment; equal rights for minorities, women, and the handicapped; increased corporate taxation, consumerism, occupational health and safety standards; and labor reform all compete with the profit motive for priority consideration by management.

Individual employee considerations emerge as the firm sets about designing jobs that provide entry-level challenge and motivation and lead to future career occupations that are stimulating and rewarding. Today's employees have been exposed to more education in the liberal tradition and expect considerable personal consideration and participation in the organization's decision-making process, which often requires job redesign.

Increased federal legislation, related court decisions, and resulting regulations have significantly increased the business community's level of responsibility in its dealings with employees. Personal equity, privacy, and compensation systems seem to be the main concerns of current employees.

The retailing industry is particularly affected because of its intense use of labor in the delivery of its product or service. Not surprisingly, research shows that retail managers spend approximately 80 percent of their time on people-related problems. Thus, the effective retail manager must be a human relations specialist as well as an excellent marketer.

Obviously, the text cannot provide a complete course in effective personnel management in one chapter, much less develop skill in interpersonal relations. The task is to highlight major areas of current concern and trust that the readers will be stimulated to take additional courses or expand their knowledge in this complex and dynamic field.

The Personnel Process

The personnel process involves the sytematic linking of the personnel functions into an integrated system of policies, procedures and rules that govern employee behavior while on the job. The personnel functions include organizational planning and job design; employment planning; recruiting, selection, and placement; performance appraisal, training, and career development; compensation administration; and collective bargaining. All of these functions are implemented on a day-to-day basis through appropriate decision making and supervision.

Retail managers may experience a wide variety of personnel responsibilities, depending on the amount of functional specialization in their organizations. For example, a small entrepreneur-retailer may carry the entire responsibility for the performance of the personnel functions. On the other hand, a department manager in a large retail chain may be charged only with implementing personnel decisions made by a representative of a personnel department. In any case, the manager should be aware of the entire personnel process. Alternately, each supervisor serves as the immediate representative for the staff, and in that capacity serves as the one who relates its needs to higher management and, conversely, interprets company policy for employees. In this dual capacity the supervisor is the keystone of any effective personnel program.

Organization Philosophy, Structure and Policies

Every organization is founded on a set of implied or specific principles that reflect a philosophy of doing business. This *organizational philosophy* provides an overall perspective of why the firm was formed and how it plans to operate to reach its ultimate objectives: survival and growth. Such statements of philosophy are often incorporated into policy statements that serve as guides for the firm's personnel when making decisions and assist in informing the client system of customers, suppliers, government, and so forth, of the firm's predispositions toward them and their interface relations. Such slogans as "satisfaction guaranteed or your money back," "we live by the Golden Rule," or "a fair day's work for a fair day's pay" give capsule views of various philosophies that firms have adopted and translated into policy statements.

Organizational philosophies are translated into organization structures that are designed to meet the firm's unique needs. Firms may be organized by function, such as store operation, merchandising promotion, finance, personnel, and so forth; or by client, such as retail and wholesale sales of electronic parts; or by product or service, such as large chain department stores that include men's wear, home furnishings, and tires, batteries, and accessories combined with automotive repair. Usually one refers to this division of labor as departmentation, which allows the firms to concentrate related activities in one area or under one authority to best serve its client group.

Employment Planning

Employment planning attempts to determine systematically the future demand for human resources in the organization. The need for human resources is a derived demand; that is, employment is a function of the level of sales activity for the retail firm. The employment planning process is implemented by forecasting total aggregate demand, industry demand, and the retail firm's future demand for goods and services. Once the firm's sales forecast is determined, the number of employees needed can be derived along with a list of needed skills.

A firm's manpower needs are composed of those people to be hired for new positions and those to be replaced due to retirements, deaths, "quits," and firings. These latter elements comprise the replacement component that must be recruited, selected, and trained to fill job vacancies during the current planning period. Once these aggregate requirements have been estimated, the manager must identify specific persons who are ready for promotion and those who are promotable when given more time and appropriate training. Also, specific terminations must be determined and the timing of such managerial action must be established.

When these planned personnel changes have been identified and categorized, the manager must consider and plan for store growth and/or decline and determine what effects such changes will have on the quality and quantity of the human resource required. All too often, overly optimistic managers anticipate constant store growth and are caught off-guard when temporary retrenchment is required. Accurate forecasting of the economic and competitive environment permits and encourages the manager to eliminate selectively the marginal producers in the department rather than take the crisis action of indiscriminate layoffs. Through such judicious pruning the entire human resource can be adapted to changing situations.

Obviously, such a detailed analysis is not within the scope of small retail organizations but is a necessity in large organizations for continued personal and organizational growth.

Authority, Delegation, and Job Design

All internal organizational functions revolve around the concept of authority and responsibility. Briefly, authority is the right to command and is derived by management from the owners' right to use private property as they see fit ". . . as long as it does not endanger public health and safety." This constitutionally guaranteed right is exercised through the use of contracts or promises between two parties to do certain things in return for some financial consideration. Thus employees accept orders or the authority, within certain limits, of the management in return for financial compensation.

The act of delegating the right to command gives management the authority to create an organizational structure by designing jobs based on work simplification principles. For example, activities to be performed by one person are grouped together to form jobs. Similar jobs are grouped together, usually based on the type of technology employed, to form departments or work groups. Job descriptions and specifications are drawn up to state clearly what an incumbent employee is expected to do and what necessary skills, abilities, and education are needed to perform the job successfully. Thus, when an individual is employed, that person is charged with the responsibility of doing the job appropriately and following the policies, procedures, and rules of the employing organization.

Job Evaluation: What Constitutes a Job?

The second phase in human resource management begins with a successful attempt to achieve some degree of congruency between the skill needs of a job and a person's ability to perform those tasks. Thus, as technology and competitive conditions change, commensurate adjustments will have to be made in job clusters. Resulting task reassignments may require job alteration and certain jobs may have to be eliminated. Constant vigilance in this area will result in more efficient operations.

Two points must be emphasized concerning job formulation. First, the quantity of activities and the quality of performance involved in any job will significantly affect the later staffing and compensation processes. Specifically, the more activites that must be performed or the higher the quality of performance, the more one narrows the range of appropriate human resources. For example, an electronic repair shop in a small town ideally may require the services of an electronic technician to repair television sets, stereo equipment, citizen band radios, and pocket calculators. Unfortunately, servicing all these products probably requires an inventory of test equipment and spare parts as well as a level of skill that is beyond the resources of the shop. Therefore, the shop may limit its on-site repair service to TVs and stereos that the local repair person can handle and offer factory service for C.B.s and calculators. Job formation should strike a balance between creating jobs that anyone can perform, and hence are likely to be boring and dissatisfying, and jobs that are so unique that only one person in 10,000 could perform them adequately.

The specific job tasks to be accomplished are found in the job descriptions, while the specific skill and related attributes of a successful job performer are found in the job specifications. Many small firms do not formalize each job in this manner because the employees are in daily contact with each other and can make informal adjustments in the performance of assigned tasks to see that the jobs get done. Also, the owner-manager is present to give instructions and supervise the individual, which allows greater individual flexibility in the order and method of accomplishing the needed tasks.

Second, a job should have "elastic activities"; that is, the job should be expandable or contractable as a function of the person performing the assigned activities or it should be variable with the seasonality of sales volume. Admittedly, there are a certain minimum number of activities to be performed and a level of quality of performance that any incumbent must meet, but as the job holder learns the job there should be opportunities for continuing challenge or job enlargement. It should be noted that not all individuals want to grow and develop in a job. They may simply want to perform the assigned activities at a minimum level of performance and seek their personal satisfaction elsewhere. There should be a place for both "upward mobiles" and "maintainers" in any retail organization.

Job Evaluation in an Ongoing Organization

Most retail students will not have the opportunity to form their own retail firms but, rather, will enter an organization with the jobs already established. Job evaluation in this situation entails determining what activities each individual is performing and whether these tasks are appropriate for the current situation. Such investigations usually disclose needless duplication of effort, overlapping responsibilities, and a host of inefficiencies that creep into any system over time if constant vigilance is not maintained.

The process of job evaluation involves reporting all the activities performed by a person holding a job or position. Such data may be gathered by a self-report based on a diary of daily activities or by a trained observer's recording both the activities performed and the amount of time spent in the performance of each activity. Daily activity schedules are condensed after some appropriate period, such as a week's observations, and the recurring activities are filtered out. An intensive review of these activities should be made to identify appropriate and inappropriate activities and what changes in the job can be affected. The adjusted routine thus becomes the job description.

Job Description

The job description becomes a checklist of activities that must be performed by anyone occupying a particular position or job. More importantly, the job description serves as a guide for any new employee or promoted job holder by specifically detailing what he or she must do to meet the minimum performance levels of the job. It is important to stress that a job description should not be construed as a limiting classification; it is simply a compliance-level statement of minimum activity performance. While a job description may be biased by self-reporting in favor of the job holder, every effort must be made not to include personal biases in the job specifications.

Job Specifications

Job specifications state the specific personal attributes, abilities, knowledge, and skills necessary to perform a job satisfactorily. Under the provisions of the Equal Rights Act of 1964 (amended in 1972), management may be called upon to prove that job specifications are based solely on ability to perform the assigned tasks and in no way are associated with the race, age, creed, color, sex, religion, or national origin of the job seeker. Many firms in the past have attempted to use minimum educational levels, such as a high school or college diploma, as a screening device to reduce their selection effort. Recently some firms have been called upon by the Equal Employment Opportunity Commission to defend such discriminating criteria and prove their relationship to successful performance of the associated jobs. Failure to establish such task performance-personal ability relationships may result in costly back pay to applicants who were unlawfully denied employment or advancement within the firm. Job descriptions must be based on demonstrated ability to perform the jobs successfully.

Recruitment

"Where do you find good people?" This is the essence of the recruitment process. In the past, most organizations had three alternative strategies from which to choose: (1) actively go into the various labor markets and search for talent, (2) passively accept "walk ins" or those individuals who presented themselves for employment, or (3) combine the first two strategies.

Recently, due to the "new social awareness," large retail organizations have been encouraged to recruit potential employees throughout their metropolitan and local areas. Disadvantaged or underrepresented groups are being extended employment opportunities, special upgrading programs are being offered, and additional efforts are being made to bring all segments of the population into the employment mainstream of mass merchandising. "Can do" ability and associated self-confidence should be sought wherever it exists—ghetto, public employment agency, community college, or university.

A Changing Personnel Mix

Unfortunately one must recognize that a three-level caste system prevails in large scale retailing. At the lowest level one finds retail sales personnel and supportive stock room and janitorial staffs. The second level includes entry level managerial trainees and successful, upwardly mobile salespersons who have demonstrated personal initiative, self-confidence and the ability to excel. The third level includes the store managers, corporate management and professional staffs. The entry into the last category is usually accomplished through in-firm promotions with occasional importation of specialized talent to meet changing environmental needs. For example, when J. C. Penney decided to enter the tires, batteries, and accessories market they recruited top automotive merchandising talent from Montgomery Ward. Such actions are not too common but not unusual either.

Entry level positions into the managerial training programs, contrary to common belief, include a wide range of specializations. Besides the traditional career role models of store management and buyer, large retail firms are recruiting individuals with college degrees in civil engineering and physical distribution for jobs in materials management to design and manage warehouses and handle related traffic problems; persons majoring in accounting, computer science, and finance to staff the control function of the firms; and persons with degrees in human relations and personnel administration for managing the human resources of the organization. No longer is mass merchandising the sole province of merchandise graduates.

The changing recruitment process represents a healthy realization on the part of retail employers that they should attempt to match potential personal abilities and levels of aspiration and achievement with realistic job and career tracks. Not every management trainee will become a store manager or a member of the executive staff. Selection procedures and self-awareness cannot assure such finite discriminatory decisions at this point in the development of testing and evaluative techniques. While some individual profile screening is possible at the present time, much more research and development is needed to refine the person-to-job matching process.

More importantly, the retail recruitment process should seek individuals who could be called "maintainers." They learn the merchandise, the needs of their customers, and the strengths and weaknesses of their staff, and turn their attention to "playing the game" or "tuning the system" to find and provide better retail products and services for "their customers." Each day holds a series of new challenges, even though they repeatedly perform the same set of activities. The personal attributes for a successful career in this kind of retail activity are markedly different from those necessary for a career that revolves around a constantly changing job, job environment, or client system. The overt recognition of such retail career differences in searching for human resources makes the following selection process potentially more effective.

Selection

Selection is the most crucial phase of the personnel process. By definition, the selection process is the exercise of discriminating among potential employees. Discrimination is not inherently bad; it is a fact of life. The basis for choice, or discrimination, is the point at issue. By law, such choice must be made on ability and nothing else.

Aside from the legal issues, selection serves an important function for potential employees that is often overlooked. All firms have a responsibility to match the requirements of the job with the abilities of the applicant. Specific quantifiable skills such as elementary mathematical manipulations or manual dexterity can be relatively easily assessed by valid, reliable tests. However when one attempts to measure a person's ability to interact with others or exercise personal judgment, the measurement task becomes much more complex. Additionally, personnel departments are increasingly being charged with assessing each potential employee's initial capacity for personal growth and development in a long term career path with the organization. Through use of the latest bias-free psychological techniques, those persons can be identified who have a chance for a successful, personally rewarding work experience in retailing. This assessment should not be considered a guarantee of success but rather an identification of personal potential for success.

Applicants who have negotiated "successive hurdle" selective screenings, including interviewing and testing, are usually employed subject to any appropriate union agreement or state laws, such as basic health requirements for food retailers and the like.[1]

An alternate method of selection is "multiple correlation."[2] Instead of rejecting applicants at each evaluation point, the final hiring decision is reached after all the information—including the application form, the interview results, and the reference checks—is complete and any subsequent interviews or evaluation mechanisms have been executed. Some personnel specialists feel that this process is fairer to potential employees, even though such a process admittedly is more time consuming and costly. As the penalties for the use of improper selection systems become well known, more employers may begin to use the "whole person" selection process.

In many large retail firms the personnel specialists who are in charge of the selection process make the decision to hire an individual into the firm, but often the employee's specific placement is yet to be determined. Where does the person begin his or her employment, at what time, in what department, for whom? The placement or orientation process is the critical link in employee acculturation into the firm's environment and assimilation into the work group. The new employee, particularly in a large organization, must become acquainted with the firm's operating policies and procedures, be introduced to his or her superior and all members of the peer work group, and be apprised of the merchandise in the assigned area. It is a good practice to designate an experienced employee to show the new member the ropes, which will facilitate that person's acceptance by the work group as a member of the team.

The employee's personal satisfaction and effective task performance will be highly affected by the initial acceptance or rejection by the relevant work group. Therefore the placement and orientation process deserves the same attention to detail as the recruitment and selection procedures.

Direction and Supervision of the Human Resource: Getting the Job Done Effectively

"Direction in the form of leading, motivating, teaching, guiding, developing, praising, and criticizing is the catalyst which really jells the enterprise."[3] The manager-supervisor is the vital link between that abstraction called "the company" and the staff. Each supervisor is the facilitator, supporter-critic, father confessor, represent-er-negotiator with the "higher powers" for all of the employees.

Effective supervision puts a heavy burden of responsibility on the manager to be "fair but firm" and "consistent but considerate." Supervision is much more than just giving orders and seeing that they are carried out. Supervision is a dynamic, never-ending personal interaction between the supervisor and each worker-colleague, not only on a formal job basis but also on an informal human basis.

Many managers who have been exposed to "human relations" feel that the supervising pattern should be based on sympathetic understanding of individual needs and problems. Unfortunately, this position only breeds individual dependence and, ultimately, a hostile backlash of animosity from the affected employees.

Effective supervision is based on empathetic, problem-oriented, problem-solving behavior. Sympathy simply reinforces negative attitudes that perpetuate an individual's problem. It is the supervisor's responsibility to guide a person in the direction of improvement and development, but one cannot make an individual improve unless the rewards of change outweigh the benefits derived from the current behavior.

Effective supervision stresses positive motivation, enthusiasm for living, and a positive attitude bordering on optimism. "Can't do" has no place in effective supervision. The supervisor must change an ability that is based on a "can do" individual attitude to one of "will do." The appropriate catalyst is proper motivation and rewards.

Unfortunately, many department managers do not have the delegated power to vary rewards among individuals to encourage their personal growth and development. The rewards given by the personnel department are based on cost-of-living adjustments, longevity, or other nonproduction-related criteria. This limitation, combined with numerous other responsibilities, makes the department manager or assistant buyer's job of motivating the staff difficult.

Effective Supervision

Supervision and leadership are not necessarily the same phenomenon, although the terms have been frequently used synonymously. Ideally, one would like to have the leader also be the supervisor, but this is quite rare in practice. An effective supervisor is familiar with behavioral research and is aware of the problems associated with the position.

A supervisor-manager is an individual who has authority over organizational resources and some degree of responsibility for utilizing these resources for the profitable transfer of goods and services. Concurrent with these duties each supervisor is responsible for employee need satisfaction. A supervisor's authority comes from the stockholders (or owners) down through the managerial chain, and when an individual accepts employment in an organization each person implies consent to this authority. The employee and the employer form two contracts: a legal agreement to comply for a certain period in return for a package of compensation and a psychological contract that assumes equity and fairness to the employee and loyalty and best effort to the employer.[4] Thus, the supervisor is charged with more duties and responsibilities than just getting the job done or the task accomplished. The manager must realize that each individual is unique and varies in both ability and needs, yet all people have their own perception of what constitutes "fair and equitable" treatment for themselves and others. The astute supervisor soon learns that equitable treatment does not mean equal treatment for all. Each individual expects personal consideration of his or her own situation within some nebulous framework of fairness for others. The relevent "others" represent the individual's peer group as well as the informal groups always found in any organization. These informal groups form to meet the social and ego needs of the individual members. No matter how well the formal organization performs its duties, the informal organization will be present.

At this point the potential for a supervisor-informal leader confrontation comes into play. As long as the supervisor-manager can provide the associates with personal need satisfaction, including higher-level need satisfaction, the leader and the informal group will be latent and inactive. However, if the supervisor, through ineptness or by higher managerial edict, is unable to fulfill employee expectations, an informal leader may come forth, galvanize the employees into social solidarity, and challenge the supervisor for effective control of the group.

Usually, this type of situation is found where subordinates have little job mobility or considerable tenure within an organization. In the retailing field, these individuals may be found in career or professional groups of sales personnel that represent the full-time corps of the sales organization. This problem may not be as potentially great in retailing as in manufacturing because of the former's high turnover in part-time employees. However, if the problem arises, it can be just as dysfunctional in retailing as elsewhere.

In summary, the supervision of employees is a complex task requiring genuine concern for the growth, development, and general well-being of "your people." Leadership should precede supervision, relying on the latter only when all else fails. The effective supervisor, at all levels, translates abstract plans, policies, and procedures into reality through directing, coordinating, and supporting the "doers"—the goal-achieving, motivated employees.

People make things happen when the leader connects "can do" to "will do" and to "job well done."

Performance Appraisal

Performance appraisal is the process of comparing the current or recent performance of an individual with predetermined performance standards set forth in the job description. The conclusions drawn from this comparative process can be used in several fundamentally different ways, although the most common usage is for merit increases in wage and salary administration. Periodic performance appraisals can also be used to identify individuals who are ready for promotion, or, conversely, it can point out those individuals in need of further training or motivation in their current job.

Many attempts have been made to soften the image and impact of the evaluative process, but no matter how the activity is performed, the process is a potentially threatening situation for the employee. The managerial philosophy vis-à-vis its employees becomes extremely critical in determining how employees view and participate in the evaluative process. Most experts agree that performance appraisals should be made quarterly. The first and third evaluations should be directed primarily at identifying employee deficiencies and creating a systematic supportive program for improvement. These evaluations should review the behavior of the past six months in relation to mutually established, quantifiable goals. Such programs are oriented toward developing the individual's potential and helping that individual meet some of the personal higher-order needs for achievement. These reviews should be mutual, collaborative sessions between the individual and the immediate superior, such as described in the management-by-objective approach.[5]

The second and fourth evaluations should be conducted for compensation considerations by the superior, and the results should be conveyed to the employee with supporting rationale. Such evaluations should be based on some form of written record, such as production reports, a critical incidents diary, or other appropriate records of behavior.

Once the factual data are collected, the comparison process can be undertaken. Such techniques as the forced distribution method, graphic rating-scale method, paired comparison method, or the forced choice-rating method can be used to overcome some degree of supervisor bias such as the "halo effect," "recency effect," and "central tendency effect."[6] In each evaluative situation the supervisor's emphasis must be objectively focused on the person's performance of the assigned and understood tasks. The employee can be expected to perform only the tasks that are contained in the job description and mutually agreed upon. Thus the importance of continually updating job descriptions to keep pace with the ever-changing job situation cannot be overemphasized.

A supplemental approach to performance appraisal has been developed and used more frequently in the last few years. In order to increase personal objectivity, peer ratings, subordinate ratings, group or committee ratings, and field-review methods have been selectively used.[7] The results of these evaluations can be compared with supervisory evaluations and any obvious discrepancies resolved.

Regardless of the combination of evaluative processes used, it is important to remember that the direct application of a generalized technique requires some specific modifications to deal with situations in a particular organization. In short, the appraisal system must be tested for validity and reliability. This is not only a good management practice but almost a necessity in future evaluations that may be subject to a court test by the Equal Employment Opportunity Commission (brought by an aggrieved employee or by the commission itself). Again, discrimination must take place, but only on the basis of ability.

Appraisal Interview

The appraisal process is not completed until the supervisor-manager discusses the results with the individual being evaluated, and they jointly plan for the individual's personal development. Although the concept of mutuality is critical to any behavioral change, it is important to note that not all appraisals result in negative or bad observations. For example, if the performance appraisal reveals that a department manager has met the quarterly sales goal, the person should be congratulated and encouraged to apply this winning game plan to the next period, along with any needed modifications.

When communicating with the employee about the individual's appraisal results, it is very important for the supervisor-manager to concentrate on problem identification and the generation of alternative solutions and to avoid any remarks that may be damaging to the employee's ego. Such supervisory thinking as "You're a lousy sales person'' has no place in constructive performance appraisal. If the employee is not measuring up to agreed-upon standards, what is the reason for this failure? Poor health, personal indifference due to lack of motivation, or inappropriate rewards—any of these could be a contributory cause.

Find the cause, devise a plan of action to remedy the situation, and set specific time/money milestones to check progress. Behavioral change occurs slowly, and an effective supervisor should channel job-related behavior for the mutual benefit of the individual and the organization.

Training and Development

Training and development programs vary widely in their scope and complexity. Some firms prefer to recruit trained, motivated employees, to utilize premium compensation packages to retain such individuals, and to leave personal development to each person's initiative and mode of learning, whether it be experience, night school, or other learning situations. On the other end of the spectrum, some organizations have in-house training and development programs specifically tailored for that retail firm and directed toward an individual's lifetime career development within the organization's many activities.

Regardless of the degree of a retailer's commitment to training and development programs, one fact is paramount: when such programs are properly designed, they will greatly facilitate a firm's adaptation to its environment. The benefits to the company are evident. Management must constantly recall that in order to change an organization one must first change the behavior of its people. People adapt, and organizations survive or perish on the basis of the appropriateness of their human adaptation.

Training

Many people in the retail industry tend to use the terms *training* and *development* interchangeably, which generates considerable confusion. Training and/or retraining refers to the acquisition of "basic skills and knowledge required in carrying out various specialized parts of the overall task of the enterprise."[8] Such skills as basic transaction center procedure, posting invoices, constructing advertising layouts, or operating a pin-ticket machine all constitute basic skills needed in the operation of some retail operations. Obviously, whenever a procedural change is introduced to increase efficiency or the amount of the average customer sale, the affected employees need to be informed and given an opportunity to practice the new selling technique. Experience has demonstrated that simply telling people about a new technique is not enough; they must practice it until they can demonstrate an acceptable level of performance. For example, one may conduct a training session on suggestive selling that actually requires the trainees to practice the art of selecting and selling related merchandise to fellow trainees. The use of such role-playing techniques and similar simulations has a demonstrated record of improving productivity.

Training methods vary from firm to firm, but the most common include on-the-job training (OJT), conferences or discussion, classroom training, programmed instruction, and education-employer cooperative programs. Most management trainees begin their retailing careers in merchandising by choosing between store management and buying. In small to medium-sized operations this distinction is less clear and is clearly demonstrated by the firm's use of an informal, short, on-the-job training program. Initial assignments usually entail working on the sales floor learning basic selling techniques, transaction center operation, charge account procedures and stock control policies.[9] Larger stores represented by department and chain stores employ training directors to implement their highly developed programs, which include orientation and instruction in basic skills needed to perform effectively in a retail organization. Once the trainee completes this general overview training, the individual either is selected for specialized training in store operation or in buying. Store operations training involves rotational assignments, in line capacities, in all phases of the firm's store operations (see Exhibit 11–1). Once the training period is completed, the management candidate is assigned to supervise a departmental sales staff, which primarily involves scheduling hours and handling employee problems. Over a period of time the trainee gradually assumes merchandising duties associated with the department, determining what items sell, when to order, and how to display the merchandise effectively. All these activities must be performed within the framework of an optimum profit objective.[10]

Buyer trainees usually have a shorter formal orientation period. The new buyer trainee usually completes the general overview segments in a matter of weeks and goes on to on-the-job experience in central buying offices located in New York, Dallas, Chicago, or on the West Coast.[11] During this training period one learns, under the direct supervision of a senior buyer, how and what to buy, merchandise presentation, which includes display, publicity and ad preparation, and most important of all, money management. "Budgets, monetary planning, basic accounting, profit responsibility and financial planning become second nature to a buyer trainee."[12]

Once the buyer training period has been successfully negotiated, the individual usually is assigned as an assistant or junior buyer in charge of one or two small departments. The principal portion of this position includes meeting frequently with department managers, store managers, and the corporate staff to select items, plan promotions and handle any vendor problems that might arise.[13] The ultimate objective, which is shared with store management trainees, is to translate merchandise into dollars and cents regardless of personal likes or dislikes.[14]

Advancement to Merchandise Manager

A few highly successful buyers may be promoted to the line position of merchandise managers. In this position a merchandise manager plans and coordinates the buying and selling activities for large stores. They allocate the various budget monies for buying, advertising, staffing and so forth to buyers to implement their merchandising

Exhibit 11-1 Rotational Assignments in Store Management Training

Basic Sales
softlines, hardlines

**Department Manager or
Assistant Department Manager**

Catalog Sales
catalog operations,
mailing,
ordering systems,
delivery

Data Processing
systems and methods,
programming techniques,
computerized terminals

Receiving & Shipping
receiving dock,
marking room,
warehouse and shipping
areas

Operations
security
protection,
store maintenance

**Auditing, Accounting, &
Finance**
auditing and accounting
procedures, sales reports,
financial planning,
financial control

Installation
procedures involved
in installing merchandise
(kitchens or aluminum
siding, for example)

Customer Service
refunds, repairs,
sales check routing,
delivery,
customer complaints

Personnel
recruitment, interviewing, hiring,
training, employee records,
labor relations, salary
administration, benefits,
personnel scheduling

Display
product display planning,
creative techniques,
store interior decoration

Merchandise Control
inventory control,
ordering procedures,
buying systems,
merchandise ranking

Advertising & Publicity
advertising planning, copy, art,
merchandise promotion,
clearance sales,
relations with
advertising agencies
and trade journals

Credit Sales
credit authorizations,
credit sales promotions,
credit reports

Source: Pamphlet "Have You Considered Retail Management?" Catalyst Career Options Series
for Undergraduate Women (New York: Catalyst, 1976), p. 14. Reprinted by permission.

decisions. They periodically review their merchandise plans to insure a balance in the emphasis and profitability of the store, particularly in establishing price lines.

In addition to their merchandising activities, most merchandise managers are responsible for final hiring decisions, sales promotion plans and their execution, and are usually responsible for creating and maintaining enthusiasm among the sales staff. Last, some merchandise managers actively participate in the actual negotiations with manufacturers' representatives while serving as the final arbiter of customer complaints.

In 1974, over 110,000 buyers and merchandise managers were employed in retail firms, primarily in clothing and general department stores. Interestingly, about 40 percent of these positions are held by women. Starting salaries for newly hired buyers with a college education in 1974 ranged from $8,300 to $9,000, with some experienced graduates starting at $12,000. Incremental wage increases every six months are quite common during the first two years. While more current data is not available, there is some evidence to suggest that these starting salaries have increased to $9,000 to $12,000 per year in 1977.[15]

Successful merchandise managers are often partially compensated with a bonus in addition to their regular salary, which varies with the type of store and merchandise sold. Often the bonus is a fixed percentage of the store's net profit. In 1974, some merchandise managers in single-store companies with sales of $5 to $15 million earned an average of $24,000. In contrast, merchandise managers for large discount stores and other mass merchandising firms with sales of $40 to $400 million earned $36,000 during the same period.

In a separate study conducted in 1975 covering fifty department stores with a cross section of 421 executives at all levels of the organizations, the salary ranged from $36,000 to $80,000 for presidents of stores doing $5 to $50 million in sales to over $225,000 for the same position in stores doing over $500 million sales annually. Top merchandising executives enjoyed salaries ranging from $30,000 to $182,000 during the same period.[16] Without doubt buyers and merchandise managers for these larger organizations are the highest paid in this segment of the industry and they earn every penny of it. Some go on to become chief executive officers in the same or competing firms.

One innovative change in the traditional career ladder for chain stores seems to be taking place on a limited scale. Sears, Roebuck and Co. has abandoned the traditional buyer organization and formed nine merchandising groups from approximately fifty buying departments.[17] This move was taken to recentralize and coordinate the entire merchandising operation and to improve profitability, particularly for special advertising fund allocations. Such profit center approaches may reduce the degree of autonomy that future buyers will have, but instead of acting independently they will now act as a unified team. The ramifications of such a radical change have yet to be assessed. All the major mass merchandiser competitors are watching this bold move with great interest.

Management Development

Management development, which has a broader scope than training, is directed toward the improvement of an individual's knowledge, skills, attitudes, perceptions, and personal characteristics in current and future managerial positions. Management development is increasingly extended not only to management trainees but to managers at all levels to improve their ability to cope with interpersonal relations. Interpersonal relations in retailing have become more important in recent years as more specialization has been required to keep pace with evolving markets. Cooperation and collaboration spell success, whereas individualism in large retail organizations is a relic of the past.

Management development may take the form of project or committee assignments, staff meetings, or simply coaching in an on-the-job assignment. Many professional associations and consulting firms offer management development courses both on and off the company's premises. Such development activities may take the form of in-basket exercises, management games, role-playing situations, sensitivity training, or professional reading. Regardless of the mode of instruction, the objective is the same: to increase the individual's ability to cope with a wide variety of situations by recognizing personal biases and to become better able to see the "real world" more objectively.

In summary, training and development are an expensive, never-ending price that an organization must pay as part of its costs of remaining competitive. Without some realistic program of constructive innovation, a retail firm's days on the economic scene are numbered.

Compensation: Pay and Fringe Benefits

"How much should I pay 'em?" This question, for many, sums up the compensation situation. Today the actual hourly or monthly wage represents an increasingly smaller portion of the total compensation cost. In addition to the federal minimum wage or the union-negotiated wage or the salary determined in the labor market, the retail manager must consider:

1. Incentive sales programs
2. Federally required social security payments
3. Unemployment insurance and workmen's compensation payments
4. Fringe benefits of life, health, and accident insurance
5. Retirement plans
6. Supplemental unemployment benefits
7. Paid vacations, holidays, and sick leave
8. Time paid but not worked, such as coffee breaks, lunch periods, time off for deaths in the family, and voting
9. Costs of maintaining employee records
10. Merchandise discounts to employees.

Some retail organizations offer profit-sharing plans for certain qualified career professional personnel and the executive staff. The question is not "How much should I pay 'em" but "What set of rewards is appropriate for the sales associate, stockroom employee, or department manager?"

A new concept of "cafeteria compensation" is being introduced on the American business scene.[18] Under this concept the employer determines the total compensation cost per employee within certain classifications, then subtracts the amount of legally liable charges for governmental programs, and allows the individual to determine how the rest of the compensation money will be allocated among the remaining alternative compensation components. For example, a young person without responsibilities may choose maximum wages, minimum life insurance coverage, moderate health insurance protection, and maximum paid time off. A person in the late fifties may choose minimum life insurance coverage, moderate wages, and maximum health protection. Although admittedly still in the experimental stage, this new concept of compensation shows promise of dealing with individual needs realistically and may therefore improve employee motivation and productivity.

Viewing the compensation question from a broader perspective than day-to-day individual compensation issues, retail executives have come to the realization that they are well advised to compensate their human resources at a premium level and hence indirectly avoid the threat of unionization. As noted earlier, it has been shown that employees take collective action when they perceive that they are not being treated equitably. Consequently, if the employees are currently receiving total compensation benefits that are greater than a union can deliver through the process of collective bargaining, the employees are reluctant to join in union activity. Thus many managers see this alternative as beneficial to both the employees and the firm over the long term. Whether this strategy will continue to be successful in the future remains to be seen.

Union-Management Relations

A complete discussion of industrial relations is beyond the scope of this text. It is important, however, to note some philosophical and legal aspects of union-management relations. From a philosophical point of view, a retail manager can view a union as a threat in a situation in which what one party gains, the other loses—the win-lose concept. The union movement is from such a viewpoint the adversary to be resisted by all legal means.

An alternative perspective is that a union can be a constructive partner in the resolution of common or complementary interests.[19] Operating under this premise, one is not out to increase one's share of the economic rewards at the cost of the other party; rather, each partner is vitally interested in increasing the absolute amount of economic reward possible. History has emphasized the win-lose strategy, while the international economic scene suggests that national unions and retail management may find it more appropriate to act as partners to maintain or increase this nation's competitiveness in the world marketplace.

A more particular concern to the retailer is the day-to-day relationship with the employees and the interpretation of a union contract. No matter how carefully the words of a labor agreement are chosen, no matter how well the negotiating representatives agree with each other on points in the contract, the provisions of the contract will be interpreted differently by both sides. If the supervisor and a union employee disagree, and that disagreement cannot be resolved by the union representative (the shop steward) and the supervisor's superior, the dispute becomes a formal grievance and must be settled by formal, agreed-upon procedures. Once grievance procedures are initiated, the supervisor-manager has lost control of the situation and must abide by the decision reached behind closed doors in a formal hearing. It becomes quite clear that when a retail firm becomes unionized the absolute formal authority of a supervisor-manager is markedly reduced, which means the superior cannot rely on an autocratic supervisory style to supervise the department effectively. Consultation and participation with employees in decision making, in a limited sense, becomes a practical necessity if the supervisor is going to be successful.

Another important implication of unionization is that the supervisor-manager loses considerable discretion in the use of the firm's reward and punishment mechanisms. In order to encourage, motivate, and channel the subordinates' behavior, the supervisor must rely on informal methods of leadership such as persuasion, influence, and negotiation relationships. Often a supervisor's management style may be dictated by company policy toward union employees, such as "following the book," "dealing at arm's length," and so forth. In that case, if a supervisor assumes an independent supervisory style, he or she risks higher management's wrath. Increasingly, the first line supervisor is the man in the middle.

Some Observations on Current Sales Force Personnel Practices

Generalizations about situations are always dangerous because one tends to overlook specific examples. With this qualification in mind it should be noted that a large gulf exists between "what ought to be" and "what is" in the practice of personnel management in the retail industry.

One study in particular documents this discrepancy in relation to the current sales staff personnel practices in department stores. Burstiner notes, "... it is evident that the perceived worth of today's salesperson among our mass retailing institutions, like the American dollar, has undergone considerable devaluation."[20] Without doubt the emphasis on personal selling, as noted earlier, has suffered for the following reasons:

1. A widely shared view among some retailers that the only people currently entering retailing are those who have no other employment opportunities. Entry level sales personnel are thought to be the dregs of the labor pool and are treated accordingly with minimal consideration.

2. When retailers examine the profit and loss statements they are constantly reminded that retailing is a labor intensive industry and remain convinced that they cannot pay more than the prevailing hourly wage and maintain profitability.

3. Given the first two convictions, retailers conclude that they are relatively powerless to deal with the high rate of employee turnover.

4. Management staffs have been convinced that personal selling is of marginal value because of the effectiveness of nationwide preselling by mass media, specifically advertising.

5. The rapid development and use of modern packaging technology and fixture redesign has led to widespread acceptance, by both retail management and the consuming public, of self-service. Sales staff are not needed to sell these products.

6. A perceived customer demand for instant gratification has led to extending store hours. In turn, in order to get coverage, retail employers have had to employ more persons to just ring up sales and stock shelves during slow periods.

7. As stores proliferate and hours are extended, more retailers seem to compete among themselves for the services of persons in the same limited, marginal labor pool. Disciplinary action or firing is perceived by the employees as "no big deal" because they can find similar employment in a relatively short time elsewhere.

8. If all the preceeding observations are true, then one cannot blame retailers for

assuming sales training would be of marginal value; hence they are unwilling to invest in any significant employee training or development.[21]

In the department stores surveyed most sales personnel are employed from "walk-in" or "write-in" candidates. Some are hired through employee recommendations, advertising, school systems, and employment agencies. About 72 percent of the stores surveyed used application forms as screening devices. About one-third of the stores did not have any educational prerequisites, another one-third required some secondary education, and only one-fourth wanted a high school diploma before employing the individual. Only six stores out of the fifty-eight responding required "some retail experience," while the remaining fifty-two did not have any prior experience requirement.

The firms spend a bare minimum on the selection process, which is consistent with the earlier conclusions. Only one interview was used to make an employment decision in 41% of the stores, while 56 percent conduct two interviews. The typical first interview lasted less than ten minutes with some lasting as long as twenty minutes. During the interview 70 percent of the reporting firms used nondirected interview techniques, which allow for little validity or reliability in making an employment choice.[22] The two most often cited reasons for not hiring (knock-out factors) were "poor communicative ability" (82.8 percent) and "job hopping" (70.7 percent). One might note that these two factors are only tangentially job-related criteria but again quite consistent with the earlier stereotyped perception of retail sales personnel.[23]

Once hired, only 56 percent of the new employees were exposed to any classroom training. Those fortunate enough to have this opportunity spent a median length of 12.5 hours prior to being placed on the sales floor. Half of this time (six hours) was spent on transaction (cash register) policies and systems. The emphasis on the "ring it up right" orientation was more evident when only one hour was spent on "customer knowledge" and the "art of selling."[24] In deference to rapidly changing transaction recording technology, 65 percent of the firms did give "refresher" courses after the initial training period.

Compensation took the form of straight salary (75 percent of the stores) with no store reporting straight commission plans. Surprisingly, about one-sixth reported using a combination salary and commission plan.[25]

When the study was completed in 1975, the hourly wages ranged from a low of $2.00 per hour to $2.76 or more. About two-thirds of the stores were at or below the minimum wage for that period. Almost all stores provided fringe benefits of paid vacations and paid holidays. Three-quarters of the firms had group insurance, but only two-thirds provided major medical plans. The lack of long-term employment relationships is evident in the fact that only 47 percent of the firms offered any form of pension plan to their sales employees.[26]

Admittedly a sample of fifty-eight department stores' personnel policies towards floor salespersons does not constitute enough information to be considered as a representative sample for the retailing universe. However, based on our collective experiences, either as customers or retail employees, the previous scenario seems all too familiar elsewhere in retailing. As Burstiner concludes, ". . . personnel management appears characterized not only by a notable lack of enthusiasm or vitality but also a deplorable absence of imagination."[27]

On a more positive note the fast food chains seem to be on the cutting edge in implementing innovative retail personnel practices. Initially, when Ray Kroc began McDonald's and Colonel Sanders launched Kentucky Fried Chicken, they applied available technology to create standardized fast food factories. Each product was similarly engineered so that the technology employed plus strict control procedures defied human improvisation, leaving training time to concentrate on customer relations. Later in their evolutionary development, even the bill calculation was automatically computed using a sensor marking the order form. The clerk concentrated on being pleasant and cheerful, marking the right quantity in the right place on the form, and counting out the precalculated change to the customer.

Currently faced with rising personnel costs, the fast food chains are decreasing marginally productive store hours, increasing the use of ultramodern kitchen technology, and reducing turnover ratios. McDonald's has launched a nationwide effort to reduce its current crew turnover ratio of three times per year per restaurant by raising wages to make employment more attractive to homemakers, who are generally considered more stable employees.[28] Steak 'n Shake, Inc. is following McDonald's example and installing automatic transaction centers, which are expected to save $840,000 a year and almost offset the extra $1 million in higher wage costs. Hardee's is using the same approach by planning to tie its new transaction centers into a computer to trace the individual store patronage patterns so that the employee hours may be scheduled more effectively.[29]

Similar innovative problem-solving can be applied throughout the retail industry. Each retailer must examine his or her operation to determine how modern personnel practices may be combined with new technology to reduce personnel costs and improve customer services.

Retail Employment Opportunities: Future Trends & Challenges

The retail industry employed about 17 million people (not including an estimated 2 million who are self-employed or unpaid family members) in 1974. Unfortunately, an accurate picture of current retail employment is impossible to present because the latest census data is three years old and the retail classification system used omits a large part of the retail service market. Inadequate though it may be, one can examine retail employment opportunities in the past and project similar opportunities in the near future.

The largest retail employment segment (three out of five employees) is in white-collar positions (professional, managerial, clerical, and sales). Sales personnel account for about 20 percent of this industry group. About an equal number are employed as proprietors or managers. Clerical workers, which include cashiers in supermarkets and food stores, make up about 16 percent of the retail labor force. Blue collar workers, including craft workers, mechanics, operatives, gas station attendants, drivers, delivery workers, meat cutters, and material handlers account for one-fourth of the retail employees.

Future projections for the retail sector employment appear bright through the mid-1980s. One must reiterate that retail employment is really a derived demand; that is, the need for employees is based on increasing sales, which depend on economic growth and increased disposable income. Thus, the overall demand for retail employees will rise at about the same rate as retail sales increase. As noted earlier, the increasing use of labor-saving innovations such as transaction centers coupled with UPC readers and computers may limit the demand for clerical personnel. The substitution of capital for labor will reduce the need for lower level employees but will increase the need for highly trained professional personnel to design and interpret information for the firm.

Careers in Nontraditional Retailing

Typically retailing is considered by the layman to be restricted to the sale of products. However, the personal spending patterns of Americans have been undergoing significant changes during the last decade. As noted elsewhere, the consuming public is spending an increasing proportion of its disposable income on retail services, particularly medical services. Time and space limitations prohibit a detailed discussion of career opportunities in retail services, but some consideration must be given to this growing sector of the retail industry.

As noted by the U.S. Census Department, about 30 million people were employed in service industries in 1974.[30] Approximately 50 percent were employed by private industry on a wage and salary basis. One of the larger employers of retail service personnel is the banking industry.

Occupations in the Banking Industry

The consuming public may not be aware of it, but banks have been described as "department stores of finance" due to their wide variety of available services. The banking industry has made a conscious effort to alter its staid image and now actively markets banking service. Notable innovations have included revolving credit plans, charge cards, money management counseling, and electronic funds transfer. When viewed in this light the bank truly has become a retailer of financial services.[31]

In 1974 the banking industry employed approximately one million workers. The employees found jobs in 40,000 full service commercial banks and their branches and approximately 2,000 mutual savings banks and branches. About 66 percent of all commercial bank employees are employed in the 800 largest commercial banks, while less than 6 percent found employment in the 6,000 smallest banks.[32]

Employment Horizon for Banking

Employment possibilities are very favorable through the mid-1980s, rising faster than the average of all industries. While most of the openings will be for clerks, who presently constitute about 66 percent of the bank labor force, an increasing number of trainee jobs will open and eventually lead to officer positions.[33] The trainee slots will be restricted primarily to college graduates; however, lower level employees will have opportunities to bid for these positions by completing extensive industry sponsored training and development.

Bank officers perform much the same functions as merchandising, administrative, financial, and operations managers in retail department stores. Each banking unit also has its chief executive officer, usually the president of the bank, who has total responsibility for the operation of the bank. Similarly, the banks have well-organized officer training programs that last from six months to a year and involve job rotation. Entry into bank officer positions is strongly influenced by the size of the bank, experience, ability, and demonstrated leadership. Smaller banks have fewer top positions; hence promotion is noticeably slower than in larger banks.

Entry level trainees started at $730 to $930 per month in 1974.[34] Current comparable salaries range from $1000 to $1400 per month, with senior officers earning two to three times as much per month. Again, the size of the bank has a great deal to do with the level of compensation paid to its employees.

In summary, as the banking industry continues to expand its financial services, more emphasis will be placed on effectively merchandising these services to expand the profitability of each banking firm. Thus, while the general public may not be fully aware of its place in the retail industry, commercial banks are retailers of financial services.

Other possible retail service industries include insurance, hotel management, food, personal finance, protective services, real estate, and financial securities just to name a few. Each industry has its own unique characteristics and employment potential. Anyone interested in these specialized retailers is advised to consult career counselors for further detailed information.

Summary

This discussion has attempted to give a general overview of the management of human resources in retailing. Organizational philosophy significantly influences the practice of personnel activities in every organization. The degree of delegation of authority strongly affects the design of jobs and shapes job specifications for positions at all levels in the organizational structure. Current governmental enforcement of employment legislation is strongly restricting the freedom of organizations in their selection and promotion of the firm's employees as well as structuring their conditions of employment.

Personnel functions, in chronological order, include recruitment, selection, placement, performance appraisal, training and development, wage and salary administration, fringe benefit management, attending to the general occupational health and safety of employees, and constant effort to maintain and improve the firm's personnel system. This order of presentation represents a normal employment sequence, but in the real world of retailing the process is not this orderly. A manager may find that he is faced with a "no show" employee problem one minute and the next minute may have to switch his attention to a "suggestive" selling problem. This acknowledgment of the behavior required of a manager in the competitive situation need not be considered a hindrance as long as the manager remains consistent in decisions on personnel matters. This reinforces the need for a manager to formulate guiding personnel philosophies ahead of time, so that when crises arise adequate preparations have been made to cope with the situation.

Future employment opportunities for retail buyers and managers look bright through the mid-1980s subject to continued economic growth and development. The fast paced world of retailing will continue to provide an excellent arena for tackling the challenge and problems of human resource management.

Questions

1. Why should retail managers be concerned with human resource management when most stores are designed and merchandised for self-service operation?

2. What is the relationship between organizational philosophies and goals and the way employees are managed? Explain.

3. How can job design improve the productivity, morale, and profitability of retail employees?

4. Why should retail job descriptions have "elastic parameters"? Explain.

5. What responsibilities does Title VII of the Civil Rights Act of 1964 (amended in 1972) place on the personnel managers in retail firms employing fifteen or more persons? Explain.

6. If you want to become the president of a large retail chain, what educational requirements are necessary, and what entry level position would you apply for?

7. What must a supervisor or department manager do to change the employees' attitudes toward the job from "can do" to "will do"? Explain.

8. What are the significant differences between employee training and development?

9. Can a successful buyer trainee transfer to store operations? In other words, can career ladders be changed after a person enters one program or the other?

10. What personal characteristics or qualities tend to increase an individual's chances for success in retail buying? In store management?

11. What are the future employment prospects for retail buyers during the 1980s? What environmental variables might change the current predictions?

Footnotes

1. Herbert J. Chruden and Arthur W. Sherman, Jr., *Personnel Management,* 3d ed. (Cincinnati: South-Western Publishing Co., 1968), p. 161.

2. Ibid.

3. Arion Q. Sartain and Atlan W. Baker, *The Supervisor and His Job,* 2d ed. (New York: McGraw-Hill, 1972), p. 14.

4. Edgar H. Schein, *Organization Psychology* (Englewood Cliffs, N.J.: Prentice-Hall, 1965), p. 11.

5. George S. Odiorne, *Personnel Administration by Objectives* (Homewood, Ill.: Richard D. Irwin, 1971), p. 448.

6. Wendell French, *The Personnel Management Process,* 2d ed. (Boston: Houghton Mifflin, 1970), pp. 291–308.

7. Chruden and Sherman, *Personnel Management,* p. 277.

8. French, *The Personnel Management Process,* p. 481.

9. "Have You Considered Retail Management?" Catalyst Career Options Series for Undergraduate Women. New York Catalyst, 1976, p. 14. (Pamphlet.)

10. Ibid., p. 17.

11. Ibid., p. 15.

12. Ibid., p. 16.

13. Ibid., p. 17.

14. Ibid.

15. Ibid.

16. "Retail Executive Compensation," *Stores* (February 1976): 2.

17. Louis J. Haugh, "Media-emphasis Changes Appearing in Ad Strategies of Top U.S. Retailers," *Advertising Age* 46, (July 26, 1976): 56.

18. George W. Hettenhouse, "Compensation Cafeteria for Top Executives," *Harvard Business Review* 49, (September-October 1971): 113–119.

19. Richard E. Walton and Robert B. McKersie, *A Behavioral Theory of Labor Relations* (New York: McGraw-Hill, 1965), p. 4.

20. Irving Burstiner, "Current Personnel Practices in Department Stores," *Journal of Retailing* 51, (Winter 1975–1976): 3.

21. Ibid., p. 4.

22. Ibid., p. 6.

23. Ibid., p. 7.

24. Ibid., p. 11.

25. Ibid., p. 13.

26. Ibid.

27. Ibid., p. 14.

28. Paul Ingrassia, "Fast-Food Chains Act to Offset the Effects of Minimum-Pay Rise," *Wall Street Journal,* 22 December 1977, p. 1.

29. Ibid., p. 13.

30. U.S. Department of Labor, *Occupational Outlook Handbook, 1976–77 Edition,* Bureau of Labor Statistics Bulletin 1875 (Washington, D.C.: Government Printing Office, 1976), p. 722.

31. Ibid., p. 716.

32. Ibid.

33. Ibid.

34. Ibid., p. 113.

Case Study

Mr. Jones' Challenge

Mr. Jones is the manager of a large department in a suburban nonunion department store. When he assumed his present job a year ago, the department had a gross annual sales of $600,000, which he raised to $750,000. He supervised six full-time employees and twenty part-time persons. The firm had a strong history of paternal, personal interest in its employees and each week held a store meeting to inform all the full-time personnel of the store's plans and achievements.

During the last month, one of Mr. Jones's full-time "dependable" persons began to fall behind in her sales volume and her merchandise responsibilities, and her absenteeism escalated sharply. Mr. Jones covered for a while by assigning part-time employees to do Mrs. Smith's duties, but after a few weeks it was quite clear that some corrective action was needed.

Mr. Jones took Mrs. Smith aside one morning before the store opened and confronted her with the situation. Mrs. Smith apologized for her behavior but said she was the sole support of her invalid husband and three children. She had stayed home to take care of sick children or her husband, whose health continued to deteriorate. She said the problems at home had been resolved and she could again devote her attention and energies to her work. In the closing minutes of the interview Mrs. Smith did mention that money was a continuing problem in the houshould and any raise in salary would be greatly appreciated.

A few weeks went by with Mrs. Smith apparently regaining her former composure and performance. However, the burst of effort was short-lived, and within a month it became clear Mrs. Smith could no longer be depended on to do the job.

After consultation with the store manager, Mr. Kline, it was agreed that Mrs. Smith would be terminated the next day with two weeks' severance pay. Mr. Kline concluded the meeting by saying, "Well, Mr. Jones, it's up to you to get her out of the store without any fuss or legal complications. I'm sure you can handle the situation. It's good experience."

Discussion Questions

1. How should Mr. Jones handle the situation?

2. What impact will the firing of Mrs. Smith have on the rest of the full-time store employees?

3. What legal issues are involved?

4. Would your action be different if the store were unionized? Explain.

Case Study

Consumer Cooperative Incorporated Case

Consumer Cooperative Incorporated is an agribusiness firm with home offices located in Bloomfield. The firm distributes gasoline, diesel fuel, oil, tires, batteries, feed, fertilizer, and agricultural chemicals. The coop has a second store nearby in Livingood. This store carries the same line of products and includes livestock feed for the local farming community. Both Bloomfield and Livingood have populations of 400 people with an additional 600 rural customers located on 150 nearby farms in each surrounding area.

The Consumer Cooperative Inc. has been modestly successful, with annual sales of $625,000 from each store resulting in a net profit of 10 percent. Seventy percent of the profits are being returned to its members. One-half the dividend is being paid in cash and the other half is retained in the firm as equity capital and covered by additional stock certificates, which are issued to the members. The retained earnings should provide an adequate source of funding for future growth and expansion of the business.

CCI is controlled by a board of directors elected by the membership. Three members reside in or near Bloomfield and three live in or near Livingood. A special meeting of the board has been called to deal with recurring personnel problems. The board believes strongly that one person should be in charge of the operations of the firm. Following this policy, Mr. Smith was employed some years ago as the full-time manager. Currently he receives a salary of $17,000 per year. He operates out of the home office in Bloomfield. Much of the credit for the firm's continued success and profitability is directly due to Mr. Smith's ability and strong background in accounting and finance. However, Mr. Smith does have a difficult time getting along with employees. Over the last four years, he has terminated twelve employees. Last week he fired Mr. Jones, the long-time manager in the Livingood store. Mr. Jones, at sixty-two, was well liked by both the local customers and the board members. Mr. Jones had been with the company fifteen years and was earning a salary of $10,000 per year. Despite Mr. Jones' ability to build good customer and employee relations, he was not "much of a person for recordkeeping and detail." The last straw occurred last week when Mr. Jones did not get his sales tax and payroll deduction records in on time so that the appropriate state and federal reports could be filed. Now both agencies are seeking fines for late reporting.

This emergency session of the board of directors was made necessary because the people in Livingood have besieged their board members with telephone calls asking, "How can Mr. Smith, living in Bloomfield, fire our manager, Mr. Jones, here in Livingood? The turnover of employees has been bad in both places and Mr. Smith hired and fired all of them!"

Additional personnel information has been presented for the board's consideration. Currently, there are four full-time employees in Livingood and seven in Bloomfield, including Mr. Smith. No current full-time employee has been with the firm for more than two years. All eleven full-time employees earn about $7,500 per year and have no chance of advancement beyond possibly filling the vacancy created by Mr. Jones' dismissal. One stipulation of the employment agreement is that employees can be assigned or reassigned to either store without any prior notice. In the past, such abrupt reassignments have resulted in understaffing one store or the other for several days in succession.

Discussion Questions

1. What would you recommend to the Board of Directors that they do at the emergency meeting to resolve the problems?

2. Does the firm have any further responsibility or obligations to Mr. Jones after his termination?

Chapter 12

Obtaining and Conserving
Money through Control

1. To know the sources of funds for retailers.

2. To understand the basic accounting records that are used in retailing.

3. To be able to discuss how cash flow forecasting can be used to meet the firm's need for funds.

4. To learn the ways that financial and operating ratios can be used to increase the firm's profitability.

5. To be aware of the need to protect the firm's assets by using insurance.

Key Terms
and Concepts

short-term funds	first in-first out (FIFO)	collection period
floor-plan financing	last in-first out (LIFO)	net-sales-to-inventory ratio
factoring		net-profits-on-net-sales ratio
intermediate term credit	retail inventory method	return-on-investment (or asset) ratio
long-term credit	income statement	net-profits-on-tangible-net-worth-ratio
assets	cash flow forecast	
liabilities	operating ratios	insurance
owner's equity	financial ratios	
balance sheet	current ratio	
current assets	liquidity ratio	

Adequate capital is a basic requirement for all retail operations. It is impossible to operate a retail outlet successfully unless sufficient funds are available, because the need for money is present in all phases of retailing. This chapter discusses sources of funds and the control concepts used in accounting, inventory evaluation, and finance. The cash flow analysis and financial ratios used in retailing also are presented.

The amount of capital required should be estimated before making a commitment to purchase, lease, or build. The estimate must include a reasonable safety margin that allows for unexpected demands for money not included in the original, carefully prepared estimate. The type and size of the retail outlet determine the capital requirement. It may require as little as a few thousand dollars to establish a small, limited-line outlet in leased facilities, while several million dollars may be needed to establish a large, fully stocked, wide-merchandise-line outlet in store-owned facilities. The purchaser of an established retail outlet can estimate the capital requirements by using company records. The purchase price for the outlet can be added to the estimated costs needed for remodeling, inventory changes, living expenses, additional working capital, and contingencies until the outlet is opened for business. Then a cash flow analysis can be performed to estimate ongoing capital requirements.

Estimating capital requirements for a new firm's outlet is considerably more difficult. Cost information may be obtained from comparable retail outlets in other communities. Trade associations, the Small Business Administration, university research bureaus, and other business organizations frequently prepare publications that contain cost estimates. Careful estimation procedures should also be used to ensure that inflation and unforeseen contingencies have been accounted for in the final estimation. Fixture and equipment costs should also be estimated, by obtaining bids from at least two different logical suppliers.

Sources and Applications of Funds

The sources from which capital may be obtained can be evaluated after the estimated capital requirement is determined. Generally, the retailer's own capital is the most important source of retail funds. Financing may be difficult to obtain unless the owner's investment funds account for about half of the required funds.

Three different types of retail financing are required to ensure that adequate funds are available. Short-term credit consists of funds that are used mainly as operating capital for periods of less than one year. Intermediate term credit consists of loans needed to finance fixed assets, such as machines, fixtures, equipment, etc. These loans vary in length from one to ten years and are generally paid on a monthly basis. Long-term financing involves loans made primarily to purchase buildings and land. They are generally made for more than ten years.

Sources of Short-term Funds

Several sources are available for obtaining the *short-term funds* (funds that are loaned for a period of no more than one year). As discussed in Chapter 8, operating (short-term) capital may be obtained from vendors, who may make an inventory available on a thirty- , sixty- , or ninety-day credit basis. These terms may allow the retailers to turn inventories over once before the invoice is due. It must be recalled, however, that considerable cash discounts can be obtained by paying bills before they are due. Thus, firms may find it profitable not to use this source of funds unless it is a matter of financial necessity.

Commercial banks provide short-term loans that can be used for operating capital if the retailer can show (by a cash flow and/or net worth analysis) that the loan will be repaid within a specified period. Simple commercial loans, generally made for 30 to 120 days, are one of the most common methods of obtaining short-term financing. Commercial banks generally make these short-term loans for seasonal financing and/or the building up of retail inventories. These loans may be secured by requiring the retailer to pledge some type of assets as collateral, such as inventory, accounts receivable, or stock. If the bank believes it can rely upon the retailer's credit reputation, it can make an unsecured loan, which does not require a pledge based upon physical collateral but upon a signature, for a specified credit purpose.

Some of the information that banks use to evaluate a loan application is presented in Table 12–1.

Floor-plan financing is an example of bank financing that requires the retailer to use inventories as collateral. Floor-inventory financing is most commonly used by retailers who do not have sufficient working capital to purchase an adequate inventory for their marketing needs. To be eligible for a loan in this case, the inventory must have unit value high enough to permit separate and positive identification by serial number.

The procedures for handling floor-plan financing begin when the supplier delivers the merchandise and prepares a draft on the retailer's bank for the full cost of the merchandise. The bank then contacts the retailer to determine if the merchandise is acceptable and if he wants to pay for the merchandise. If payment is to be made, the bank usually debits the retailer's account with 10 percent of the value of the merchandise plus freight costs. The remaining 90 percent of the cost is due in ninety days, but financing can be obtained on up to three additional ninety-day periods, providing at least 10 percent of the balance is paid before each option is renewed. The bank sends the original payment made by the retailer, along with its check for the remaining 90 percent of the merchandise value, to the supplier. This payment is made as soon as the retailer indicates the merchandise has been accepted.

Banks that lend money under the floor-plan financing agreement usually inspect the inventory monthly on an unannounced basis. The retailers are also required to keep all merchandise insured. The interest rate charged on floor-plan financing is generally 1 to 2 percent above the prime interest rate.

Retailers can also sell their customers' notes (or installment promissory notes) to a commercial bank to obtain short-term funds. The bank then advances money to the retailer against the customer notes. Another alternative is to retain the retail customer notes and use them as collateral for obtaining short-term loans from other sources. The interest rate charged by banks will vary according to the going interest rate, the degree of risk associated with the retail firm involved, and the financial reputation of the borrower. The interest rate charged by commercial banks is usually lower than the savings the retail outlet could obtain by paying its bills promptly and getting a cash discount from its vendors. Not using vendor credit to the limit also provides a safety margin which could be used if unforeseen needs for funds occur.

Factoring offers yet another possibility for short-term financing. Factoring involves selling a retailer's accounts receivable to another party. If the accounts receivable are sold "without recourse," the buyer (or factor) assumes the loss resulting from any uncollected accounts. The relatively high commission—usually 1 to 3 percent of the total amount—is one disadvantage of this method of financing.

Sources of Intermediate-term Funds

Intermediate term credit, used to finance fixed assets (such as equipment, machines, fixtures, etc.), is generally granted for one to ten years. Such capital is needed as a means for small retailers to finance fixed assets that will depreciate over time. The primary difference between an intermediate term loan and a short-term loan is that a formal loan agreement is always needed. Many banks extend a *line of credit* to borrowers of intermediate term loans. The line of credit is a fixed amount, say $50,000, that a retail borrower can have outstanding at any one time. The retailer can borrow continually up to that specified amount on a permanent basis.

Frequently, suppliers of capital equipment that is required in retailing will lease their products to retailers. Equipment leasing can reduce the fixed-capital investment needed so that the retailer's funds can be used in other, hopefully better-yielding activities. Other liberalized trade credit techniques—such as lease with option to buy, buying equipment on installment terms, and so forth—are also frequently used to provide a source of intermediate retail capital.

Sources of Long-term Funds

Long-term loans can be used to construct a new building or to buy a store or warehouse. *Long-term credit* differs from intermediate credit in the type of security needed. The lender must have assurances that the retailer is stable and large enough to be in existence over a period of years. Mortgages make up the bulk of long-term debt owed by small retailers because they seldom have the resources for selling a bond issue. Small retailers frequently must invest their own savings in the firm to meet long-term credit needs.

Mortgage bankers and insurance companies may be used to finance real estate or construction capital requirements. Generally, these financial firms are interested only in financing large projects and hence are more likely to finance large retail

Table 12-1 **Information Needed by Banks to Analyze a Loan Application**

Statement Item	Additional Information Needed	Why Information Needed
Cash	Where is it deposited? Is any of it restricted or pledged?	To establish total banking relation-ships.
Accounts Receivable	How many are current? Are they collectable? How many should be written off?	Frequently used as bank collateral. Banks need to determine a realistic current value.
Inventory	How is it valued? How marketable is it? Is it excessive or partly obsolete?	Frequently used as collateral. Bank needs to know its value in the event of liquidation.
Notes Receivable	Why do they exist? Are they collectable? Could they be assigned to the bank?	Only financial institutions should routinely have notes as assets.
Due from Officers and Employees	What circumstances caused these loans to be made? Are they collectable? When will they be paid?	In excess these assets reflect poorly on management.
Due from Affiliated or Related Businesses Investments	What are the circumstances? Are they collectable? When will they be paid? What are they? Why were they made? How are they valued? How liquid? Could they be assigned to the bank as collateral?	Indicate a need for consolidated and consolidating statements. It is hard to support the credit needs of a customer who uses working capital to make speculative invest-ments.
Property and Equipment	How is it valued? Is it all supporting the needs of the business? Is it encumbered? If so, how much and with whom?	Bank may want to pay these off and secure a first lien position in support of its loan.
Leases and Leasehold Improvements	What are they? What are the terms? Are they assignable? Any value in liquidation?	Frequent source of off balance sheet accounting.
Notes Payable	What are the terms, rates and maturities? Will loan be used to retire all or part of these notes?	Can the customer service these and the proposed loans?
Trade Accounts Payable	Are trade payables being kept current?	The trade can force the customer into liquidation.
Other Current Payables	Insurance current? FICA? Income taxes when due? Payroll?	All are sources of potential trouble.
Term Debt	What assets offset the term debt? What are the current maturities? Can they be serviced on schedule?	Usually a significant part of the demand on a customer's cash flow.

outlets or entire shopping centers. Local savings and loan associations are good sources for long-term loans for small retailers who have a good credit reputation.

Other Financial Sources

The Small Business Administration (SBA), an agency of the federal government, provides short, intermediate, and long-term retail capital to small retailers. In addition to making cooperative loans with private lending firms and making direct loans to small retailers, the SBA also provides financial and management assistance. If borrowing appears to be the answer to a retail firm's problem, the SBA will help the retailer obtain a bank loan or will furnish part of the required capital itself, providing the bank cannot lend all of the money and SBA funds are available.

If the local bank cannot lend any of the money, the SBA will consider lending the entire amount as a direct government loan. In loaning money to small retail firms,

Table 12-1 **(cont.)**

Statement Item	Additional Information Needed	Why Information Needed
Contingent Liabilities	What liabilities (real or potential) are there that are not shown on the financial statements?	These can be a serious source of trouble to the customer and the bank.
Sales	How are sales recognized? Are sales made with recourse? Have the goods or services been delivered? How many returns are there?	To establish that sales are actual and not book entries.
Expenses	Are executive salaries adequate or excessive? Is depreciation in line with asset values? What are the trends in C & A expenses?	Executive salaries and unnecessary expense items can be major source of working capital drain.
Other Income	What is its source? Will it continue?	Can the bank rely on it as a source of repayment.
Other Expenses	Why do they exist? Will they continue in the future?	Can the customer meet these payments?
Income Taxes	Do these appear reasonable? When was the customer last audited by the IRA?	Always a source of potential trouble. The bank wants copies of recent tax returns.
Profits	What are the trends? How reliable? What margin is there? Sufficient to service all debt?	This is the bank's primary source of repayment on most loans.
Dividends or Withdrawals	What is the historical pattern? How much will probably be drawn this year?	The bank may want to control these by a loan agreement.

Source: First National Bank of Albuquerque. Table first appeared in Edmond E. Pace and Frank Collins, "Bankers-Accountants-Financial Statements: Their Relationship to Small Business Loan Decisions," *Journal of Small Business Management*, October 1976. Reprinted by permission.

the SBA is not in competition with private sources. The SBA steps in only when private financing cannot meet the needs of the small businessman. SBA loans vary in amount, from $500 to $500,000.

In addition to its general loan program, the SBA offers a small loan program which is designed to meet the needs of the very small or newly established retailer. The limited-loan participation plan is designed to help worthy firms that have only limited tangible collateral. Under this plan, private banks and the SBA cooperate in extending financing to the small retailer.

Another source of capital is the Small Business Investment Corporation, which is licensed and regulated by the SBA. It is designed to be a profit-making company, and may be either privately or publicly owned and operated. The SBIC is in business to furnish capital and consulting and advisory services to small businesses.

Numerous other federal loan sources are applicable to the small retailer in certain instances. A retailer who is a veteran could utilize the Veterans' Administration to acquire real estate, supplies, equipment, and working capital. Loans can also be obtained through the Bureau of Indian Affairs by Indians and Eskimos who have no other source of financing. Loans are also granted to citizens of other minority groups through the SBA.

A small retailer who has justifiable needs for additional capital, and a financial structure strong enough to offer reasonable assurance of success and repayment, should be able to obtain the necessary funds from one of the previously mentioned sources.

Accounting Systems

Sound recordkeeping and accounting practices are needed to conduct a successful retail business. The numbers and types of records needed depend upon management goals and needs. Small retailers may not need as much detailed data on each merchandise line or department as large retailers require. The small retailer or the branch manager may be able to observe sales and inventories on each line and make decisions (based upon merchandise movement) before any of the financial records are available. It is nevertheless advisable to use accounting records to confirm the observation and to ensure that the firm's profitability corresponds to expectations.

A well-designed system of accounting should provide a record of all transactions that can be used to prepare periodic financial statements and reports. Properly prepared financial records can provide measurements of profitability and retail performance. An effective accounting system must also provide a basis for business planning. Only after a retailer can determine "where he has been" can he determine "where he is going." Thus, complete and accurate financial records are needed and must be used to make retail decisions. Accounting records are also used to detect errors, theft, and fraud. Finally, retailers must have an accurate record of the availability and use of their assets because profits are maximized by making the most efficient use of these assets.

Several accounting terms and concepts make important contributions to the basic records used by retailers. An *asset* is anything of value owned by the retailer and a *liability* is anything owed by the retailer. Retail assets consist of land, buildings, equipment, furniture, fixtures, supplies, inventory, cash, and accounts receivable. Retail liabilities consist of accounts payable, notes payable, accrued wages, and accrued taxes.

The owner's investment or *equity* in the retail enterprise amounts to the difference between the total retail assets and total retail liabilities. All accounting systems are based on this concept: assets equal liabilities plus owner's equity.

Nearly all accounting records are based upon the double entry concept, which simply records the twofold effect every transaction has upon the equation, assets = liabilities + owner's equity. For example, assume that a retailer pays $1,000 in cash for merchandise that has just been delivered to his store. In this case the value of one asset (inventory) will be increased by $1,000, but the value of another asset (cash) is reduced by $1,000, the total asset value remains unchanged, and the equation remains in balance.

In accounting terminology, every transaction involves at least one debit entry in one or more accounts and at least one credit entry in other accounts, so that total debits always equal total credits.

Basic Retail Records

The financial record of a retail outlet begins when merchandise is purchased by the retailer and the information is recorded. Most retailers bring this information together by recording daily transactions in one or more journals, which provide a complete record of each transaction in chronological order. Many retailers transfer the journal-contained information to ledger accounts, which are records of the increases and decreases of each type of income, expense, asset, liability, or capital. Retailers use as many ledger accounts as they believe they need to classify their business activities.

Ledger accounts are used to organize the data from the journals so that the business transactions can be grouped. This grouping provides the information needed to prepare the two basic financial statements: the balance sheet and the income statement. Information contained in either the balance sheet or the income statement can be used to make nearly every analysis needed to measure the financial performance of the retail enterprise.

Balance Sheet

The *balance sheet* shows the financial condition of the firm on a given date. This report is called the balance sheet because it represents the equation, assets = liabilities + owner's equity, and thus summarizes the various assets, liabilities, and owner's equity accounts. The balance sheet also contains information on the relationship between creditors' claims on the assets and the percent of the assets held in the form of owner's equity in the firm. A comparison of a current balance sheet with balance sheets for previous periods allows the proprietor conveniently to observe changes in the firm's financial condition. The balance sheet is a good summary report that eliminates the necessity of examining many detailed records.

Exhibit 12–1 is a typical balance sheet, together with brief explanations of the terms contained in a balance sheet. Most of the terms are described in sufficient detail in the exhibit so that they do not require further explanation. Those balance sheet concepts that require elaboration will now be discussed.

Current assets (cash, accounts receivable, inventories, and government securities) may be turned into cash quickly. *Retail inventories* comprise finished merchandise that is displayed in the store itself. Inventory values change as prices fluctuate, so retail inventories are usually valued at cost or current market price, whichever is lower. This method avoids overstatement of earnings and assets as a result of wholesale price increases.

The LIFO and FIFO methods are used to establish inventory values when a physical count of items is feasible. The *first in-first out* (*FIFO*) method assumes that the oldest items are sold before later-purchased items are sold. This method allows "inventory profits" (caused by increased merchandise prices at the wholesale level) to be included as income. Such inventory profits are not realized profits if the rising wholesale prices are followed by a price decline.

Another method of determining inventory evaluation is the *last in-first out* (*LIFO*) method. This method is designed to cushion the impact of rapid price changes by matching current costs against current revenues. Sales are costed on the basis of inventory purchased most recently (last in), while first-in inventory is regarded as unsold merchandise. The LIFO method results in the application of a higher unit cost to items sold and a lower unit cost to inventory still unsold during a period of rising prices.

Exhibit 12-1 **Typical Retail Balance Sheet**

Assets		**December 31, 1978**
Current Assets		
Cash	$ 9,150	
Accounts Receivable	5,300	
Merchandise on Hand	12,750	
Total Current Assets		$27,200
Fixed Assets		
Building, Equipment and Fixtures		$41,500
Total Assets		$68,700
Liabilities and Owners Equity		
Current Liabilities		
Accounts Payable	$ 3,170	
Current Maturity of Long-Term Debt	$ 1,000	
Total Current Liabilities		$ 4,170
Long-term Debt		
Notes Payable		$16,200
Total Liabilities		$20,370
A. Jones, Capital		$48,330
Total Liabilities and Owners Equity		$68,700

Many retail firms have switched to the use of the LIFO method recently as inflation has caused prices of merchandise to rise rapidly. When prices are rising, the LIFO method allows the firm to value the cost of merchandise sold higher than it can be valued under the FIFO method. This results in a lower profit on the firm's income statement, which allows the firm to pay less income taxes. (Exhibit 12-2) Internal Revenue Service regulations do not allow a retailer to make frequent switches from one inventory valuation method to another. Thus, the most current regulations must be consulted before a firm changes its method of inventory evaluation.

The *retail inventory method* of estimating cost valuation of inventory is used when a physical count is not feasible. This method is used in many chain stores to gain better control over store managers by charging goods to stores both at cost and retail prices. The retail method of inventory evaluation provides a procedure for determining the cost value of a closing inventory stated in retail price value. This method requires that both inventory and purchase figures be recorded and charged to each department in both retail prices and at cost. Complete records are maintained (in retail prices) on all additions to and reductions from stock. The markup percentage is determined, allowing one to calculate the cost percentage on the total merchandise handled. The closing retail book inventory (the retail value of the merchandise on hand in the closing inventory) is calculated from the records. The cost percentage is then applied to the retail book inventory and an annual physical inventory is taken (in retail prices) to check the accuracy of the method.

Exhibit 12-2 An Illustration of the Effect of FIFO and LIFO Inventory Evaluation Methods on Retailer's Cost of Merchandise

Situation
Beginning inventory—10,000 units with a $1 per unit purchase cost
Purchases made during the year—10,000 units with a $1.20 per unit purchase cost
Sales–15,000 units at $2 per unit

Calculation of Cost of Goods Sold

A. Using the first in-first out method of inventory evaluation:

10,000 units @ $1 (the per unit cost of the beginning inventory) plus	= $10,000
5,000 units @ $1.20 (the per unit cost of merchandise purchased during the year)	= $ 6,000
Equals the Total Cost of Goods Sold	= $16,000

B. Using the last in-first out method of inventory evaluation: 10,000 units

@ $1.20 (the per unit cost of merchandise purchased during the year) plus	= $12,000
5,000 units @ $1 (the per unit cost of beginning inventory)	= $ 5,000
Equals the Total Cost of Goods Sold	= $17,000

The closing physical inventory (in retail prices) can be converted to a cost valuation by using the following formula: cost value of inventory = retail value of inventory $\times$ cost percentage.

An example of the use of the retail method of valuing ending inventory is given in Exhibit 12–3. The retailer depicted in this figure began the period with merchandise worth $30,000 in retail prices and $20,000 in actual costs to the firm. Purchases of goods cost the retailer $35,000 during the period, but these goods had a retail value of $51,000. The firm had made additional markups (markups made in addition to normal, initial markups) of $2,100 during the period. These additional markups were a result of a higher than normal price being placed on some goods that had become recognized as having outstanding qualities or being very difficult to obtain.

The retail values for the opening inventory, net purchases and additional markups were added together to obtain the retail value of the goods available for sale ($83,100). The combined cost values for opening inventory and net purchases ($55,000) was then divided by the retail value of goods available for sale to give the cost percent (66.2 percent).

The firm made net retail sales of $59,900 during the period. It also had reductions of $3,500, so total sales and reductions amounted to $63,400. The retailer had $83,100 worth of goods available for sale during the period, so once its sales and reductions were deducted, its ending inventory was valued at $19,700 in retail prices. The ending inventory value at cost was then found by multiplying the ending value at retail times the cost percent (66.2%) to equal $13,041.

It should be noted that when a store using the retail method makes additional markups and markdowns it must keep a record of them. These data are then used to calculate its cost ratio and to estimate its ending cost valuation of inventory as shown in Exhibit 12–3.

Exhibit 12-3 **An Illustration of the Use of the
Retail Method of Determine the Valuation of Inventory**

Goods Available	At Cost	At Retail
Opening inventory	$20,000	$30,000
plus		
Net purchases	$35,000	$51,000
plus		
Additional markups		$ 2,100
equals		
Goods Available for Sale	$55,000	$83,100
Cost Percent (ratio of cost to retail)		
$55,000 / $83,100 equals 66.2%		
Net Sales at retail		$59,900
plus		
Reductions (markdowns and cash discounts)		$ 3,500
equals		
Total Sales and Reductions		$63,400
Ending Inventory at Retail		$19,700
($83,100 minus $63,400)		
Ending Inventory at Cost		$13,041
($19,700 times 66.2%)		

One should also note that markups enter into the calculation of the cost percent but markdowns do not. This results in an intentionally conservative figure for ending inventory.

Reasons for Using the Retail Method

The retail inventory method is widely used in chain stores, department stores, departmentized specialty stores, and in many independent stores.

The widespread use of the retail method is due to several factors. The retail method enables the retailer to determine the results of the operations at frequent intervals without the cost of making a physical count of goods. This is essential under the highly competitive conditions of today. Second, because of price lines, preretailing, and buying methods, retailers today are thinking more in terms of selling prices rather than cost prices. Third, the retail system of accounting provides an effective but simple method of controlling merchandise departmentally in terms of retail prices. Fourth, it allows one to take a physical inventory more quickly and less expensively than under the cost method because it is not necessary to assign cost to each item. Fifth, it enables the retailer to take the inventory on a staggered basis; inventories can be taken in different departments at different times, and the figures adjusted to the general closing of the books. Sixth, it furnishes information on shortages and thus directs attention to measures by which they may be reduced. Seventh, through the book inventory figure, it provides an equitable basis upon which to base insurance coverage and settle claims; and finally, it furnishes a sound, workable basis for the dollar control of merchandise.

Fixed assets, with the exception of land, have a limited useful life, so the process of depreciation assigns a portion of the assets' cost as expense for each accounting period. The depreciation is subtracted from fixed asset values so that the asset value is stated at the amount of unexpired cost. It is important to note that the depreciated amount is not a cash expenditure of money but merely a decrease in the value of company-owned assets.

Liabilities, which are on the other side of the assets-equal-liabilities-plus-owners'-equity equation, may be divided into two classes of debt. Current liabilities are amounts due and payable within one year. Long-term debt does not have to be paid until at least one year has elapsed.

Current liabilities include:

• Accounts payable are money that is owed to vendors and other unpaid costs that are incurred in operating a retail business

• Accrued liabilities are items such as unpaid wages, salaries, and commissions that have accumulated but are not yet due for payment

• Current maturity of long-term debt is the amount of long-term debt due within the upcoming year

• Federal income and other taxes are all accrued taxes

• Dividends payable are dividends declared by the board of directors but not yet paid

Company capital comprises *all* sums (including preferred stock and common stock and retained earnings) used in the business. The retail enterprise may have raised funds through the sale of long-term debt (mortgage bonds or debentures) or by selling ownership in the company by issuing common and/or preferred stock. The amount included in the long-term debt caption is the amount of the principal due at maturity less any amount that is payable in less than one year.

Income Statement

The *income statement* gives the retail manager a summary of income and expenses over a period of time. Income statements are usually prepared monthly, quarterly, semiannually, and annually. Comparison of a current income statement with the corresponding statement for the previous year allows the proprietor to observe trends in income, expenses, and profits. In most retail operations, sales records are generally broken down by major departments. Such divisions more accurately show the response of sales and profits to changes in the retail mix. These breakdowns also allow the manager to continually identify the performance of each department. Exhibit 12–4 is a typical annual income statement.

Retailers need to observe more detailed monthly income statements to deter-

Exhibit 12–4 **Typical Retail Income Statement**

Revenue	December 31, 1978	
Gross Sales	$99,300	
Less: Sales returns and allowances	930	
Net Sales		$98,370
Cost of Goods Sold		
Merchandise inventory, January 1, 1978	$ 9,700	
Merchandise purchases	46,320	
Goods Available for Sale	$56,020	
Less: Merchandise inventory, December 31, 1978	10,050	
Cost Of Goods Sold		$45,970
Gross Profit (net sales − cost of goods sold)		$52,400
Operating Expenses		
Rent expenses	$ 4,800	
Advertising expenses	$ 1,650	
Salaries expense	$15,230	
Payroll tax expense	$ 1,060	
Utilities expense	$ 2,710	
Total Operating Expenses		$25,450
Net income (gross profit − total operating expense)		$26,950

mine if any significant sales or cost changes are occurring. Table 12–2 is an example of a monthly income statement that allows one to make comparisons with the same month last year and with the year-to-date performance. The performance of the XYZ store in June of 1978 and for the first six months of 1978 appears to be an improvement over corresponding periods in 1977. Not only have sales increased in 1978 but operating and net profits also have increased. The increase in net profits occurred despite a slight reduction in gross margin percentage. Better utilization of employees and the spreading of the fixed costs (such as rent, insurance, depreciation, taxes) over a larger sales volume allowed the store to reduce its total expenses on a percent-of-sales basis.

Other Retail Records

Retailers should also keep a detailed record of accounts receivable so customer billing can be handled accurately and good customer relations maintained. In addition, these records can be used to provide the detailed information needed to evaluate the firm's credit and collection policy. For example, the number and names of customers who are slow payers can easily be identified by examining the accounts receivable records.

Detailed information on accounts payable can help protect the financial reputation of the retail firm. Organized accounts payable records allow retailers to identify

Table 12-2 Income Statement for Month of June, 1977 and 1978, XYZ Store

| | This Month | | | | Year to Date | | | |
| | For This Year | | For Last Year | | For This Year | | For Last Year | |
Item	$	% of Sales $	$	% of Sales $	$	% of Sales $	$	% of Sales $
Net sales	102,900	100.0	90,300	100.0	610,800	100.0	570,000	100.0
Less cost of goods sold:								
Beginning inventory	70,000	68.0	60,000	66.4	70,000	11.5	60,000	10.5
Merchandise purchases	70,000	68.0	70,000	77.5	410,000	67.1	390,000	68.4
Merchandise available for sales	140,000	136.1	130,000	144.0	480,000	78.6	450,000	78.9
Less ending inventory	70,000	68.0	70,000	77.5	70,000	11.5	70,000	12.3
Cost of goods sold	70,000	68.0	60,000	66.4	410,000	67.1	380,000	66.7
Gross margin	32,900	32.0	30,300	33.6	200,800	32.9	190,000	33.3
Less expenses:								
Salaries, wages, commissions	10,290	10.0	9,560	10.6	60,800	10.0	59,600	10.5
Rent	3,087	3.0	3,000	3.3	18,522	3.0	18,000	3.2
Utilities	515	0.5	510	0.6	3,118	0.5	3,120	0.5
Repairs and maintenance	3,087	3.0	3,100	3.4	15,200	2.5	14,700	2.6
Delivery expense	515	0.5	450	0.5	3,200	0.5	2,700	0.5
Supplies	515	0.5	510	0.6	3,150	0.5	3,020	0.5
Advertising	2,058	2.0	2,100	2.3	12,210	2.0	12,080	2.1
Depreciation	2,675	2.6	2,675	3.0	16,050	2.6	16,050	2.8
Bad debts	410	0.4	500	0.6	2,530	0.4	2,410	0.4
Taxes and licenses	1,545	1.5	1,500	1.7	9,210	1.5	9,020	1.6
Insurance	1,030	1.0	1,010	1.1	6,180	1.0	6,060	1.1
Interest	1,030	1.0	950	1.1	6,210	1.0	5,940	1.0
Other expenses	3,084	3.0	3,060	3.4	18,010	2.9	18,080	3.2
Total expenses	29,841	29.0	28,925	32.0	174,390	28.6	170,780	30.0
Operating profit (loss)	3,059	3.0	1,375	1.6	26,410	4.3	19,220	3.3
Other income	2,058	2.0	2,015	2.2	10,100	1.7	9,700	1.7
Net profit (loss)	5,117	5.0	3,390	3.8	36,510	6.0	28,920	5.0

due accounts as well as invoices that allow cash discounts if payment is made promptly.

Most retailers also maintain separate and more detailed inventory records, which are essential to the control and security of retail stocks. Inventory records also provide the data needed for making buying decisions and for effective merchandise management.

Detailed sales records may be used to provide a basis for the compensation of retail sales personnel. These sales records may also provide information useful in marketing research activities, such as determining trading areas, identifying market targets, and the like.

Finally, accurate and detailed tax records must be maintained. These records should contain all the information needed to fill out the various tax forms requested by all levels of government.

Separate departmental records may be maintained on a monthly basis to allow retail management to identify changes in operating performance in each area. A monthly departmental operating statement, similar to that for the total store in Table 12-2, can be used to identify performance changes within each department. Expense records on such items as salaries, wages, and supplies can be maintained on a departmental basis. Other expenses must be allocated to the various departments on the basis of time, space, or capital requirements for each department. For example, total store rent could be allocated to each department on the basis of square footage occupied by that department. Cost accountants can provide valuable assistance in the allocation of these expenses to each department.

Operating a Retail Accounting System

The development and use of accounting records are essential because they allow retail managers to carry out more effective planning and control. Appropriate accounting records can reveal errors, employee fraud, and waste and can identify other sales and expense areas that may require changes if retail performance is to be improved.

Retail firms need a good accounting system to safeguard business assets and prevent errors. The accounting records must be accurately and honestly maintained for each of the many transactions that occur each day in a retail organization. A system of checks and balances should be used so no employee will have complete control of any business transaction. Cashiers or account collectors who handle cash should not maintain the accounting books. Where possible, record analyses and reports should be the responsibility of at least two people. Cash register tapes should be used to double check the amount of cash received by the cashier. Employee earnings and purchase expenditures should be computed by one person and then rechecked for accuracy and honesty by another individual.

The typical store manager is deeply involved in the operations of his business. Frequently he believes he would accomplish more by spending his time doing tasks within the store instead of sitting at a desk analyzing accounting records. If this is the case, he should consider using part-time outside accountants and financial consultants who can help develop and operate an effective program.

Frequent meetings with outside accountants may involve a comparison of performance in the previous month with that of a year ago, and then with the preceding month. Major performance deviations and current and future plans should be discussed. Regular discussions of this type allow many retailers to avoid making serious business errors.

A list of questions that small retailers should ask their accountants on an annual basis is presented in Exhibit 12–5.

Exhibit 12–5 Questions Small Retailers Should Ask Their Outside Accountants on an Annual Basis

1. Are the firm's cash assets being properly protected?
   –Are receipts deposited in total daily?
   –Do different people handle accounts receivable and accounts payable?

2. Are the firm's fixed assets being properly protected?
   –What depreciation methods should be used to minimize taxes?
   –Is the investment tax credit being used to reduce taxes?

3. Have the firm's payroll tax returns and deposits been made on time?
   –Have the federal withholding funds been deposited in a federal depository bank on at least a monthly basis?
   –Have state and federal quarterly information reports been filed?

4. Have the firm's estimated income tax deposits been made on time?

5. Are all the necessary records required by the various state, federal, and local authorities available?
   –What is the statute of limitations for each type of record?

6. Have all required state annual reports been filed?
   –If the firm is incorporated, has an annual corporate report been made to the state?
   –Do other states in which the firm conducts business require an annual report?

7. Is the firm using the best legal form of organization?
   –Can the business be divided into several separate taxable entities such as a corporation, a partnership, a sole proprietorship, or subchapter S corporation to reduce taxes?
   –What will such a change cost in time and dollars?
   –What new reports are required if the change is made?

8. Are present accounting systems appropriate for the current size of the firm?
   –Can minicomputers, a UPC system, and time sharing computer systems be used to reduce costs and increase timeliness and accuracy of data?
   –Are there any new accounting information systems available that would improve the firm's operating efficiency?

Large retail organizations are likely to maintain their own accounting department, which performs nearly all of the firm's accounting services (except the independent audit). The functions of this internal accounting department are the same as those of an outside accounting service. The same honest, objective appraisals must be made to reduce errors, fraud, and waste.

Both internal and outside accounting systems are likely to make increased use of electronic data processing equipment. Such equipment speeds the processing of sales and expense data. Thus information is available for managerial review faster than under the manual system. In addition, electronic systems are able to make detailed calculations on ratios and percentages that are essential for more effective retail management.

Financial Planning

Financial management in a retail firm involves two objectives. First, an adequate flow of cash must be provided to meet current liabilities as they come due. Second, the retail firm must operate as profitably as possible in the long run.

Cash Flow Forecast

Cash flow forecast may be used to develop a plan that will ensure that adequate cash is available to pay bills as they come due. Retail cash receipts and cash disbursements fluctuate independently of each other. Thus, during certain periods of the year, cash inflows (sales receipts) exceed cash outflows and a surplus is created in cash. During other seasons of the year, cash outflows exceed sales revenue. In this case additional cash is needed to prevent a deficit, unless a surplus has been accumulating in the cash account.

Effective cash flow management involves an analysis of the timing of cash receipts and disbursements to identify the periods when the working capital may be inadequate or excessive in terms of meeting current liabilities. Maintaining excessive amounts of surplus cash (as non-working dollars) violates the profit objective. These excessive cash reserves involve an *opportunity cost* equal to the amount they would bring if they were used in some other way, either within the retail store (advertising, reducing the amount of a mortgage, fixture improvements, and so forth) or outside the retail store (investment in interest-bearing notes, and so forth).

An inadequate cash level is also detrimental to the profit maximizing objective. Inadequate working capital may result in insufficient advertising, inventories, and the like, resulting in consumer dissatisfaction and a loss in retail sales. It may also force the retailer to pass up trade discounts or even cause a loss in the credit standing of the firm.

Cash flow analysis expresses future retail income and expenditures on a dollar basis, so it is simply a prediction of future cash flows based on an expected sales volume. The cash flow records the movement of cash into retail inventories, receivables, and back into cash. This analysis reveals future needs for short-term funds by indicating when cash inflows will exceed outflows and vice versa. A cash flow analysis is vitally important to a retailer since it identifies what the firm can do to reach its objective of maintaining adequate (but not excessive) cash balances.

The first step in a cash flow forecast is to establish the period covered by the plan. The analysis may be prepared on a monthly (or even weekly) basis to project the cash condition for the next six months or next year of business. The procedure is simply to record expected cash inflows and outflows and add (or subtract) the expected amount of the net increase (or decrease) to (or from) the original cash balance to obtain the expected cash balance at the end of the period.

The second step is the estimation of sales. Sales forecasting techniques are described in Chapters 9 and 17; however, it is important to note that both internal factors (such as changes in promotion, price policy, and productive personnel) and external factors (such as changes in competition, economic conditions, seasonality patterns, and consumer preferences) affect a retailer's sales level. Thus, sales estimating procedures must use these variables to forecast sales volume accurately.

One cannot overemphasize the importance of sales forecasting. The accuracy of the entire cash flow analysis is highly dependent upon the accuracy of the sales forecast. Hence, every effort should be made to develop an accurate forecasting method. This usually requires a great deal of experience and good judgment. Historical data on past sales are usually analyzed to determine trends and seasonal sales patterns. Fortunately, it is usually easier to forecast sales for a store or group of stores than for an item or a specific merchandise line. Seasonal patterns on total store sales are not likely to change rapidly. Although the composition of the sales may change rapidly, the total volume is not likely to fluctuate widely unless the relative competitive position of the retail outlet(s) changes or unless the total industry sales are changing rapidly.

The third step entails anticipation of future cash inflows derived from the estimated sales level. The credit policy used by the firm will determine how closely cash inflows relate to sales, and this relationship should be identical if retail sales are made on a strictly cash basis. Of course, the handling of credit sales will also affect this cash-inflow-to-sales relationship. If most or all of the sales are made on a bank credit card basis such as Master Charge, or VISA, the retailer will be reimbursed almost immediately after the handling charge (usually 2 to 6 percent of sales) has been deducted. Factoring of accounts receivable will accomplish the same result, namely, a close relationship of cash inflow to sales volume. Historical records, combined with an analysis of the firm's retail credit policy, can generally yield a highly reliable estimate of the relationship between sales volume and cash inflow.

The fourth step is an analysis of the expected cash outflow for the previously specified time period(s). Historical purchase and expenditure records, employee payroll data, contracts, negotiated purchase agreements, and other commitments can be analyzed to obtain an estimate of upcoming expenditures.

The fifth step involves the comparison of the estimated cash inflow against the estimated outflow to determine the net cash gain or loss for the period. This consists merely of subtracting the expected outflow (determined in step 4) from the expected inflow (determined in step 3) to obtain the net change in the cash balance.

Cash flow analysis also provides, in the sixth step, an estimated cash balance for the end of the specified period(s). The expected cash balance is obtained by adding the net gain (or subtracting the net loss) for the period—as calculated in step 5—to the cash balance at the beginning of the period.

These six steps, which constitute the cash flow forecast, provide all the information necessary to plan a retailer's needs for short-term capital. Table 12–3 is an example of a cash flow forecast for a retail firm. Additions to working capital are required when the expected cash balance reaches a prespecified minimum level. The additions to short-term funds may come from either internal or external sources.

The main internal sources of funds are the liquidation of inventories and short-term investments, cash sales, and a turnover of accounts receivable. Retail credit policies are not likely to be changed frequently simply to provide extra cash during a short-term period of cash deficiency. Consumers become committed to established retail credit policies and are likely to switch retailers if an outlet continually changes its credit rules. Promotions can be used to increase cash sales during periods when cash shortages are likely to exist; however, retail management must consider the overall effect such promotions may have upon future sales, store image, and so forth. Thus, the stimulation of cash sales is not likely to be used as a solution to a short-term deficit cash balance problem.

Liquidation of short-term investments is frequently made to generate needed cash. Indeed, some money is sometimes put into liquid short-term investments not only to obtain a return on the money but also to provide a safety margin in case cash is needed internally at a later date.

External sources of funds (banks, trade credit, and so forth) are required if internal sources cannot provide sufficient cash.

Ratio Analysis

Retailers not only attempt to meet current liabilities as their bills come due but also attempt to operate as profitably as possible. Thus retailers must have a way to measure the profitability and operating efficiency of their enterprises. Examination of selected ratios and relationships derived from data in the firm's balance sheet and income statement can provide helpful appraisals of the current and past performance of that firm. External financial sources, moreover, frequently require these data before they will grant loans to a firm.

A number of different ratios and relationships can be used by the retailer to measure the past and current performance of his firm. Ratios are generally compared both on a historical basis and against the industrial standards considered to be normal for that type of retailing. Several different standards are available from various trade sources and such sources as the Small Business Administration, the U.S. Department of Commerce, Dun & Bradstreet, National Cash Register, Robert Morris Associates, etc. The inexperienced retailer must rely heavily upon the standards developed by these sources. An experienced retailer is more likely to establish his own standards and make historical comparisons on each ratio.

Operating Ratios

Retail *operating ratios* express relationships among the items in the income statement to provide an evaluation of the firm's operating performance. Operating ratios yield a detailed understanding of the retail expenses involved in generating sales. These ratios can be used as tools to lower costs and improve efficiency within the retail firm.

A detailed breakdown of expenses is usually required to calculate the important operating ratios for a retailer. The operating ratios are calculated by dividing each item in a detailed income statement by the retailer's net sales figure and multiplying

Table 12-3 Example of Cash Flow Forecast

	January Budget	February Budget	March Budget
Expected cash receipts			
Cash sales	$12,000	$13,000	$20,000
Collections on accounts receivable	10,000	10,000	10,000
Other income	300	300	300
Total cash receipts	22,300	23,300	30,300
Expected cash payments			
Raw materials, merchandise, and supplies	14,000	16,000	20,000
Payroll	2,500	2,500	3,000
Other expenses (including maintenance)	500	500	600
Advertising	300	300	500
Selling expense	1,200	1,200	1,200
Administrative expense (including salary of owner-manager)	1,500	1,500	1,500
New store facilities and equipment	2,500	1,000	1,000
Other payments (taxes, including estimated income tax; repayment of loans; interest; etc.)	300	300	500
Total cash payments	22,800	23,300	28,300
Expected cash balance at beginning of month	1,000	1,000	1,000
Cash increase or decrease	−500	0	2,000
Expected cash balance at end of month	500	1,000	3,000
Desired working cash balance	1,000	1,000	1,000
Loans needed	500	0	0
Total amount of cash borrowed[A]	500	500	0
Loan repayment due	0	0	0
Cash available for owners, dividends, etc.	0	0	1,500

[A]Assuming no debt on Jan. 1 and that surplus cash is used for loan repayment.

the result by 100. This procedure allows the ratios to relate each expense or income item to net sales by expressing each item on a percentage of net sales basis. These percentage figures are then studied to provide suggestions that will improve retail operating efficiency. Some retailers calculate and analyze some operating ratios each week on a department-by-department basis, which provides excellent control. Knowledge of current gross operating profit margins, inventory levels, and expense ratios can allow the retailer to spot a weakness before it gets to be a serious problem. Up-to-date ratio analysis can also let the retailer quickly determine the effects of changes in the retailing mix.

Thus a comparative analysis of operating ratio values over a period of time can be used to identify the cost of sales and expense trends. The year-to-year comparisions of expenses as a percent of net sales provide an important measurement of a firm's performance. Relatively small changes in the value of an operating ratio should be brought to the attention of the firm's top management. The operating ratios that are normally used to measure a retailer's performance are listed and explained in Table 12–4. Of course, retailers like to observe declining values for the cost of goods sold and operating expense ratios described in the figure. On the other hand, they also like to observe increasing values for their net sales as a percentage of gross sales, gross profit, operating profit, and for both net income ratios.

Table 12–4 **Operating Ratios Frequently Used to Measure Retailers' Operating Efficiency**

Ratio	Characteristics
1. Gross sales as % of net sales	Measures percent shrinkage occuring from returns, allowances, cash discounts.
2. Cost of goods sold as % of net sales	Cost of goods sold may be defined to be beginning inventory valued at cost plus net purchases less ending inventory valued at cost to provide a ratio that measures the relative importance of inventory cost to net sales volume.
3. Gross profit as % of net sales	Gross profit may be defined to be the net sales minus cost of goods sold as defined in item 2; this ratio will measure the relative performance of the firm before selling, general, administrative and interest expenses are deducted.
4. Operating expenses as % of net sales	Ratios may be calculated for each of the expense accounts (wages, supplies, maintenance, advertising, administrative salaries, bad debts, utilities, insurance, rent taxes, depreciation) as well as an overall operating expense ratio. Expenses are often grouped into controllable or uncontrollable categories to provide a measure of the relative flexibility of the firm. Watch year-to-year changes.
5. Operating profit as % of net sales	Operating profit is gross profit minus total operating expenses (listed in item 4); so ratio is pretax profit margin as % of net sales.
6. Net income before income taxes as % of net sales	Net income is operating profit minus the amount needed to meet interest payment on debt.
7. Net income after income taxes as % of net sales	Measure of after-tax profitability of retail firm stated as % of net sales.

New retailers can use average industry ratios to make an annual expense forecast. An example of the expenses encountered by automobile parts outlets is presented in Table 12–5. Similar expense estimates for other types of retailers are available from trade associations.

Table 12–5 **Expenses Encountered by Automotive Parts Outlets (Including Machine Shop Operations)**

	Average of All Reporting	Up to $150,000	$150,000– $250,000	Over $250,000
Total Sales	100.00%	100.00%	100.00%	100.00%
Total Cost of Goods Sold	66.02	65.99	66.22	65.97
Gross Profit	33.98	34.01	33.78	34.03
Expenses—				
Managers' Salaries (or Owners' Withdrawals)	4.70	7.92	6.03	3.92
Salesmens' Salaries Wages, Commissions	1.49	.46	.83	1.80
All Other Salaries & Wages	11.36	6.88	9.62	12.43
Total Wages, Salaries and Commissions	17.55	15.26	16.48	18.15
Advertising and Sales	.71	.75	.73	.71
Bad Debts	.28	.21	.29	.29
Car Expense—Sales	.10	.05	.09	.11
Car & Truck Expense	.83	.94	.88	.80
Depreciation	.53	.47	.49	.54
Freight, Express & Parcel Post, Postage	.34	.55	.38	.30
Insurance	1.05	1.14	1.06	1.03
Heat, Light & Water	.51	.71	.56	.47
Rent (or Equivalent)	1.44	1.83	1.58	1.35
Office & Store Supplies	.66	.72	.67	.65
Taxes (All except Income)	1.75	1.58	1.59	1.81
Telephone & Telegraph	.67	.85	.73	.64
Miscellaneous	1.62	1.83	1.67	1.57
Total Expense	28.04	26.89	27.20	28.42
Operating Income	5.94	7.12	6.58	5.61
Other Income	1.21	1.08	1.10	1.26
Other Expense	(.90)	(.96)	(.73)	(.94)
Net Profit (before Income Tax)	6.25	7.24	6.95	5.93

Source: "Consolidated NAPA Jobber Operating Statements for 1973," National Automotive Parts Association, Suite 1129, Parklane Towers West, Dearborn, Michigan 48126. Reprinted by permission.

Financial Ratios

A *financial ratio* may be used to express the relationship between two items on the firm's balance sheet or between one item on the income statement and one item on the balance sheet. These ratios can be analyzed to provide a basis for making comparisons on the historical performance of the firm. The financial ratios can also be used to make comparisons with similar retail operations and can thereby identify areas of relative financial weakness and strength. Thus, financial ratio analysis provides guides for spotting trends toward better or poorer performance.

Average financial ratio values for numerous types of retail businesses are presented in Table 12–6. Several ratios are used to measure a firm's liquidity. The *current ratio* indicates the ability of the firm to meet its current obligations and still maintain a safety margin to allow for possible shrinkage in the value of its inventories and accounts receivable.[1] The current ratio (ratio 1 in Table 12–6) is expressed in mathematical terms as: current ratio = current assets ÷ current liabilities.

High-volume, high-turnover outlets that handle merchandise whose demand is relatively stable do not require as much safety margin as low-volume, slow-turnover outlets that handle merchandise whose demand fluctuates widely. Thus, chain grocery stories may have a current ratio of slightly less than 2:1 and still be very able to meet their current obligations. Less stable types of retail business generally attempt to maintain at least a 2:1 relationship, although an extremely high current ratio merely indicates that excess cash is lying idle or that excessive inventories are being maintained.

The *liquidity ratio,* or "acid test," is calculated as (cash + marketable securities + accounts receivable) / current liabilities. This ratio also measures a retail organization's ability to meet its current obligations, but it is a more severe test because it concentrates on strictly liquid assets whose value is not likely to change radically. Inventories are not included in the numerator of the equation, so the liquidity ratio really evaluates the chance that a firm could pay its current obligations with readily convertible funds on hand. A liquidity ratio of less than 1:1 is a warning signal that a retail business would have to sell from inventory to meet current liabilities if the firm were pressured into paying its bills and could not borrow additional funds.

Several other ratios can be used to appraise the turnover relationships in retailing. The *collection period* (accounts receivable divided by average daily sales), which is ratio 7 in Table 12–6, is a rough measure of the overall quality of accounts receivable and of the credit policies used by the retailer. The collection period calculation can be compared to both the retailer's credit terms and to competitors' experience to determine if a collection problem exists.

A frequently used rule of thumb states that "the collection period should be no more than one-third greater than the net selling terms."[2] According to this rule, the collection period should not exceed 40 days for a retailer with selling terms of a 2 percent discount in 10 days, net 30 days. For retailers selling on an installment basis, "the collection period of the installment accounts, based on net sales after deducting the aggregate down payments, should be no more than 1/3 greater than ½ the average selling terms. If the average selling terms are 18 equal monthly installments, for example, ½ those terms would be 9 months, and 1/3 increase would give a standard of 12 months."[3] These rules of thumb have been designed to allow flexibility for a normal volume of slow but generally good accounts.

The *net-sales-to-inventory ratio* (number 8 in Table 12–6) expresses a rough measure of the frequency with which the average level of inventory investment was "turned over" on an annual basis. The inventory should be valued in retail dollars if net sales are used. A higher turnover rate indicates that the business has managed to operate with a relatively small inventory investment, which indicates that the inventory is relatively current and contains little unusable stock. A high turnover ratio could also mean that inadequate inventories are being maintained. The latter could have a detrimental effect upon long-term profits if consumers are increasingly dissatisfied with out-of-stock conditions and if it is easy for them to buy these items at competing outlets.

Retail profitability may be examined in relation to sales volume or in relation to the investment required. There are several profit margin ratios that are used to describe the relationship of profits to sales volume. The *net-profits-on-net-sales ratio* (ratio 2 in Table 12–6) merely expresses net retail dollar profits as a percentage of net retail sales dollars, or equals (net profit dollars / net sales dollars) $\times$ 100. This ratio is an indicator of the relative efficiency of the retail operation over time.

A more critical test of retail efficiency and profitability is provided by the *return-on-investment (or asset) ratio.* A high profit percentage on sales may be obtained on a relatively low sales volume. The result will be a low profit percentage on retail investment.

The *net-profits-on-tangible-net-worth ratio* (ratio 3 in Table 12–6) is one measure of return on investment that expresses net profit dollars as a percentage of tangible net worth. This ratio measures the return to the owners of the business after all taxes and interest have been paid. Hence it can be used to evaluate the earning power of the ownership investment in the retail enterprise.

The return-on-investment ratio is also used to describe profitability relative to investment in assets. This ratio is calculated as (net profit / total assets) $\times$ 100. This measure relates net profits to the firm's total assets (inventory, accounts receivable, cash, and fixed assets).

Return-on-Investment (Asset) Analysis

The return-on-assets analysis allows retail management to analyze most of the data in the previously discussed ratios in such a way that the firm's profitability can be determined. The return-on-assets chart in Figure 12–1 allows the retailer to establish goals in each segment in the chart. The top portion of the chart is used to determine net profit as a percentage of sales (ratio 2 in Table 12–6). The lower part is used to calculate asset turnover (ratio 5 in Table 12–6). The return-on-assets percentage is merely asset turnover times net profit percentage, so it equals the product of these two ratios. Since space has been provided for income taxes, the final return-on-assets percentage is an after-tax figure.

Retailers can improve their profitability by influencing the values of most of the factors in the return-on-assets chart. Cost of goods might be decreased by improved buying procedures. Expenses might be decreased by using better sales training. Sales might be increased by using better displays, improved promotion, and a better merchandise mix. Other income may be increased by taking advantages of cash discounts, placing excess cash in revenue-generating (but liquid)

Table 12-6 Median Values of Financial Ratios for Selected Retail Businesses

Line of Business (and Number of Concerns Reporting)	Current Assets to Current Debt	Net Profits on Net Sales	Net Profits on Tangible Net Worth	Net Profits on Net Working Capital	Net Sales to Tangible Net Worth	Net Sales to Net Working Capital	Collection Period	Net Sales to Inventory	Fixed Assets to Tangible Net Worth	Current Debt to Tangible Net Worth	Total Debt to Tangible Net Worth	Inventory to Net Working Capital	Current Debt to Inventory	Funded Debts to Net Working Capital
	Times	Percent	Percent	Percent	Times	Times	Days	Times	Percent	Percent	Percent	Percent	Percent	Percent
5531 Auto & Home Supply Stores (53)	1.79	1.41	8.21	11.27	4.54	6.39	**	5.8	27.6	105.0	166.2	123.0	95.3	53.0
5641 Children's & Infants' Wear Stores (41)	2.66	2.45	9.06	11.35	4.95	5.14	**	4.3	21.7	61.0	103.6	113.0	51.0	41.7
5611 Clothing & Furnishings Men's & Boys' (223)	2.75	2.21	7.14	8.26	3.49	4.19	**	4.4	16.5	47.5	88.1	92.4	61.8	28.1
5311 Department Stores (338)	2.71	1.59	6.25	7.71	4.10	4.97	**	5.5	22.9	40.4	73.1	77.4	52.1	25.2
Discount Stores (125)	2.26	1.40	10.89	12.84	6.31	6.77	**	5.2	14.7	61.5	98.3	127.9	55.8	27.2
Discount Stores, Leased Departments (24)	2.66	2.62	9.53	9.72	4.47	5.08	**	4.6	19.7	55.1	90.1	126.2	53.1	24.8
5651 Family Clothing Stores (103)	2.84	2.39	6.67	8.51	3.16	3.92	**	3.8	16.5	44.1	76.3	102.0	57.1	28.8
5712 Furniture Stores (159)	3.27	2.30	7.21	7.34	2.62	2.85	78	4.4	12.0	47.8	87.6	66.3	69.2	23.4
5541 Gasoline Service Stations (80)	1.81	3.19	15.07	40.97	3.76	10.65	**	12.2	36.4	44.9	72.6	69.3	119.2	45.8
5411 Grocery Stores (136)	1.68	0.93	11.77	26.71	11.64	24.34	**	17.0	73.1	67.7	101.7	150.6	100.3	64.1
5251 Hardware Stores (89)	3.09	3.23	10.83	14.99	2.61	3.66	**	4.3	18.3	34.3	69.5	80.2	58.5	28.2
5722 Household Appliance Stores (87)	2.40	1.75	8.40	9.96	4.25	4.84	27	5.0	14.4	61.0	133.8	95.0	75.7	32.7
5944 Jewelry Stores (93)	3.50	4.19	7.28	8.43	2.09	2.28	**	2.7	9.6	34.4	79.8	89.4	55.8	27.5
5211 Lumber & Other Bldg. Mtls. Dealers (159)	2.78	2.53	8.60	11.36	3.61	4.44	49	6.2	24.4	48.9	92.3	75.7	78.5	32.9
5399 Miscellaneous General Mdse. Stores (103)	2.43	2.06	9.80	13.79	4.75	5.60	**	4.7	25.0	45.3	99.2	103.6	55.7	38.2

Table 12-6 (cont.)

Line of Business (and Number of Concerns Reporting)	Current Assets to Current Debt	Net Profits on Net Sales	Net Profits on Tangible Net Worth	Net Profits on Net Working Capital	Net Sales to Tangible Net Worth	Net Sales to Net Working Capital	Collection Period	Net Sales to Inventory	Fixed Assets to Tangible Net Worth	Current Debt to Tangible Net Worth	Total Debt to Tangible Net Worth	Inventory to Net Working Capital	Current Debt to Inventory	Funded Debts to Net Working Capital
	Times	Percent	Percent	Percent	Times	Times	Days	Times	Percent	Percent	Percent	Percent	Percent	Percent
5511 Motor Vehicle Dealers (74)	1.57	1.04	11.44	15.50	9.89	14.11	**	7.3	21.7	124.3	180.6	196.3	87.7	23.6
5231 Paint & Glass & Wallpaper Stores (33)	3.51	3.53	10.73	14.33	3.18	4.35	**	5.1	25.9	34.5	76.6	89.7	57.2	28.9
5732 Radio & Television Stores (63)	1.96	3.25	21.74	26.16	5.43	6.21	**	5.3	23.0	74.3	165.5	116.8	78.7	33.0
5261 Retail & Wholesale Nurseries, Lawn, Garden and Farm Supplies (60)	2.05	3.58	15.77	26.27	4.16	7.49	**	7.7	30.7	52.1	77.0	87.6	111.5	28.8
5661 Shoe Stores (97)	2.61	1.61	6.09	7.04	3.71	4.52	**	3.9	17.1	53.4	106.8	123.1	55.0	31.1
5331 Variety Stores (65)	3.50	2.41	9.69	11.28	3.63	4.21	**	4.0	19.1	30.00	71.6	107.1	37.2	36.3
5621 Women's Ready-to-Wear Stores (190)	2.76	2.37	7.83	9.77	3.40	4.12	**	5.8	18.7	45.9	82.8	75.1	76.8	33.3

Note: Definitions of Terms

Collection Period—The number of days that the total of trade accounts and notes receivable (including assigned accounts and discounted notes, if any), less reserves for bad debts, represents when compared with the annual net credit sales. Formula: divide the annual net credit sales by 365 days to obtain the average credit sales per day. Then divide the total of accounts and notes receivable (plus any discounted notes receivable) by the average credit sales per day to obtain the average collection period.

Current Assets—Total of cash, accounts and notes receivable—Total of cash, accounts and notes receivable for the sales of merchandise in regular trade quarters, less any reserves for bad debts, advances on merchandise, inventory less any reserves, listed securities when not in excess of market, state and municipal bonds not in excess of market, and United States government securities.

Current Debt—Total of all liabilities due within one year from statement date including current payments on serial notes, mortgages, debentures, or other funded debts. This item also includes current reserves, such as gross reserves for federal income and excess

profit taxes, reserves for contingencies set up for specific purposes but does not include reserves for depreciation.

Fixed Assets—The sum of the cost value of land and the depreciated book values of buildings, leasehold improvements, fixtures, furniture, machinery, tools and equipment.

Funded Debt—Mortgages, bonds, debentures, gold notes, serial notes, or other obligations with maturity of more than one year from the statement date.

Inventory—The sum of raw material, material in process, and finished merchandise. It does not include supplies.

Net Profits—Profit after full depreciation on buildings, machinery, equipment, furniture, and other assets of a fixed nature; after reserves for federal income and excess profit taxes; after reduction in the value of inventory to cost or market, whichever is lower; after charge-offs for bad debts; after miscellaneous reserves and adjustments; but before dividends or withdrawals.

Net Sales—The dollar volume of business transacted for 365 days net after deductions for returns, allowances, and discounts from gross sales.

Net Sales to Inventory—The quotient obtained by dividing the annual net sales by the statement inventory. This quotient does not represent the actual physical turnover, which would be determined by reducing the annual net sales to the cost of goods sold and then dividing the resulting figure by the statement inventory.

Net Working Capital—The excess of the current assets over the current debt.

Tangible Net Worth—The sum of all outstanding preferred or preference stocks (if any) and outstanding common stocks, surplus and undivided profits, less any intangible items in the assets, such as goodwill, trademarks, patents, copyrights, leaseholds, mailing list, treasury stock, organizational expenses, and underwriting discounts and expenses.

Turnover of New Working Capital—The quotient obtained by dividing annual net sales by net working capital.

Turnover of Tangible Net Worth—The quotient obtained by dividing annual net sales by tangible net worth.

Source: "Key Business Ratios," copyrighted by Dun & Bradstreet, Inc.

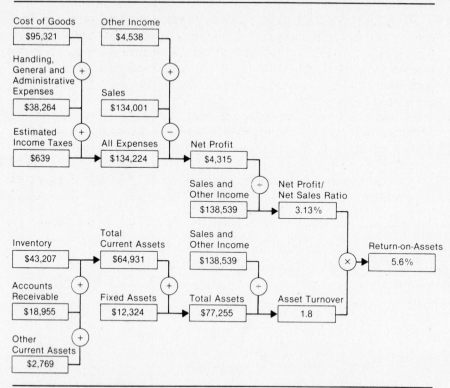

Figure 12-1 **Return-on-Assets Chart**

Source: Reprinted with special permission from the November 1970 issue of *Banking*, Journal of the American Bankers Association. Copyright 1970 by the American Bankers Association.

investments, and obtaining earnings from revolving credit programs. Managing these four factors properly can lead to an improvement in the profit-to-sales ratio.

The controllable factors in the bottom portion of the chart are inventory levels, accounts receivable levels, and other current assets. Inventory levels generally make up the largest portion of retail assets. Thus, every effort should be made to increase the net-sales-to-inventory ratio by eliminating nonessential stocks. If accounts receivable become too high, a retailer may want to reevaluate the credit policy to see if the finance charge could be raised or the due date shortened. Accounts receivable management was discussed earlier in this chapter, but it is important to note the role it plays in determining return on retail assets. Other current assets consist mostly of cash, so placing excess funds in liquid investments improves the situation for both other income and other current assets categories.

The chief benefit of using the return-on-asset approach is that it demonstrates the interdependence of these controllable factors. Reducing inventory and accounts receivable levels will certainly improve the asset turnover, but if sales are decreased because of the reductions in these assets, then the profit-to-sales ratio is also reduced. The result might be a decline in the return on assets instead of the desired increase.

These interrelationships make it possible to design a system of management control that can monitor the effect of changes in a retail firm's performance as expressed in the various components of the ratios. Retail management can use the ratio dependencies shown in Figure 12–1 to provide a series of charts that reveal performance trends. The reader may trace the effect that a change in any of the components will have upon the firm's return-on-asset calculation.

For example, the retailer described in Figure 12–1 may increase promotion by $5,000 per year. Suppose management estimates that the cost of goods sold, sales volume, and taxes will all increase by 20 percent as a result of the increase in advertising. If no other changes are anticipated, then the firm's new return-on-assets chart reveals that its return on assets has increased from 5.6 percent to 9.0 percent (Figure 12-2).

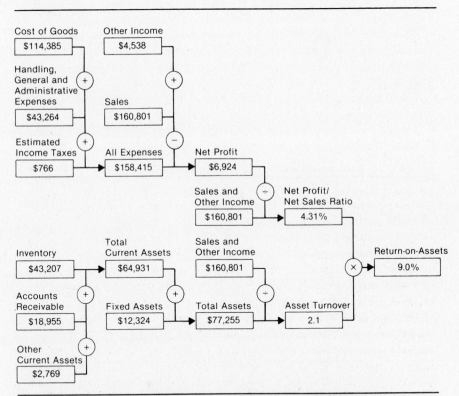

Figure 12–2 **Changes In Return-on-Assets Chart When Firm Increases Sales, Cost of Goods, and Taxes by 20 Percent as a Result of a $5,000 Increase in Promotion**

Thus, retailers can estimate the effect that changes in their retailing mix will have on any of the factors contained in the return-on-assets chart and trace through the chart the effect those changes will have on their return-on-assets percentage. Use of the return-on-assets chart in this manner can provide guidelines for making major changes in retail policies. This is illustrated in the previous example by the $5,000 increase in promotion, which led to a $2,609 increase in net profits although the action resulted in a $5,000 increase in the handling, general, and administrative expense category. The increase in net profits and increase in return on assets percentage indicate that this change should significantly benefit the firm.

Common Financial Mistakes

Retailers are involved in such a dynamic environment that they can easily get carried away with their emotions and concentrate nearly all of their effort on short-term problems. This leads to the implementation of a philosophy of "let the accountant worry about the firm's financial condition." It is true that accountants are a vital source of information. However, the outside public accounting firms and accounting departments of large retail organizations are not responsible for the retailer's profit situation. They do not receive either the rewards associated with a good profit nor the direct monetary loss suffered when a firm is not performing well.

Thus, retail management cannot rely entirely on accountants to place the firm in a sound financial condition. Hopefully, the procedures developed in this text will assist the retailer in developing good financial and merchandise planning and control policies.

There are some common types of mistakes that frequently cause retailers to suffer a decline in profits (Exhibit 12–6). In very extreme cases these mistakes result in a failure for the firm that finds itself unable to meet its financial obligations.

Exhibit 12–6 Common Financial Mistakes in Retail Firms

1. Lack of knowledge and use of proper accounting procedures.
2. Lack of knowledge and use of financial analysis.
3. Overly optimistic estimates of sales volume.
4. Lack of sufficient start-up capital.
5. Lack of working capital.
6. Overstating cash inflow.
7. Understating cash outflow.
8. Slow collection on accounts receivable.
9. Too many customer bad debts.
10. Improper inventory levels.
11. Inadequate productivity of retail space.

Most of these mistakes can be avoided with proper forewarning and the use of a good merchandise budget and the financial analysis techniques discussed in this chapter. An overly optimistic estimate of sales volume is a major problem for new retail firms that do not have past sales records to guide them. These firms can use the techniques presented in Chapters 5 and 6 to guide their estimates, but they must be realistic in terms of making the evaluations. Perhaps the best preventative action that can be taken is a two-year apprenticeship. Such employment experience with the best retailer in the aspiring retailer's specialization is a virtual requirement to get the feel of the business.

The lack of both start-up capital and working capital (generally defined as current assets minus current liabilities) can also be improved by working for a salary during these apprenticeship years and saving a portion of the salary for start-up capital. The pay-back situation can also be improved by obtaining a high percentage of long-term financing (as opposed to short-term loans) when the firm is started. After the firm is established, it is wise for the growing firm to reinvest a large proportion of its profits back into the firm. Irresponsible or ill-timed withdrawals should be avoided because they can seriously weaken the financial structure of the firm.

Even experienced retail management can overestimate cash inflow and underestimate cash outflow. It is just human nature to remember all the good and forget some of the bad. Thus, a consultation with last year's checkbook record of deposits and expenses can aid the memory process and provide a more realistic estimate of cash inflows and outflows.

The acceptance of bank credit cards such as Master Charge and VISA can eliminate the problem of slow collection on accounts receivable. Bank credit cards cost the retailer a percentage of the gross sales dollar, but they can increase sales as well as provide a nearly instant source of cash. They can also eliminate losses due to customer bad debts, since the banks assume the responsibility for collecting on the charge sales made on their cards.

Inventory levels are frequently too large to generate the profit level desired by retail management. In other cases the inventory level is so low it encourages customers to go to competitive outlets. Inventory planning requires careful thought on the effect different inventory levels will have upon sales and profit. The inventory planning methods presented in Chapter 9 and the return on asset model discussed in this chapter can be used to assist the manager in making more intelligent decisions on inventory levels.

Inadequate productivity of the retailer's selling space can also cause the firm's profit to decline. Constant monitoring of factors such as sales, gross margin, and net profits on the basis of per square foot of building area can reveal whether the firm is encountering problems in the use of its physical space.

Conclusions on Financial Analysis

The foregoing discussion acquaints the reader with the more important ratios and relationships that should be observed periodically. It is important to realize that rules of thumb and comparison of ratios with industry standards must be used with great caution. Each retail operation is unique, despite apparent similarities among competitive retailers.

Differences in accounting procedures can distort the comparative data. Thus, ratio analysis provides only guides, not precise measurements, that the retailer can use to analyze his or her performance.

Retailers are concerned with the most efficient use of money. The tools of financial analysis presented above provide a way to evaluate the firm's management policies. Problems in money management may involve leaks (such as overbuying inventory relative to consumer demand) in the flow of funds. Another type of money management activity involves decreasing the number of slow and bad accounts, which simply tie up excessive funds in receivables. Retail managers must also keep the firm in a liquid position so it is able to avoid late-payment charges and maintain a good credit standing. The ratios and the relationships discussed above should assist the manager in planning the need for funds and allow him or her to make more efficient and profitable use of the firm's resources.

Risk and Insurance

Retail firms operate under risk of loss from many sources. Retail managers must learn how to use the various kinds of insurance (a means of providing protection against a risk) to reduce the effects of these risks, because unexpected losses can mean the difference between growth and failure. Insurance plays a vital role in forestalling the damage that the unexpected can do to the retail firm. Remember, all of the work and money that is placed in a store can be destroyed in a matter of minutes by fire, lawsuit, flood, theft, and so forth.

Retail organizations lack funds for total coverage against all types of risks. The retail manager must develop a planned approach to risk management by identifying the most crucial areas that require coverage. Table 12–7 contains a list of the most common types of business risk and the types of insurance coverage available to retailers. Periodic reviews of the insurance program are needed to keep retail management abreast of changes in the type and size of risks that the firm faces. Replacement values of buildings, inventories, equipment, and so forth are increasing rapidly due to inflationary pressures. Thus, the coverage should reflect these higher values.

Once the risks have been recognized, retail managers can investigate the methods by which the costs of coverage can be reduced. The following considerations are important.

1. Determine which risks to insure against by estimating the amount of loss each peril could cause the firm.

2. Cover the largest loss exposure first, after considering premium costs and the funds available for protection. Be certain that coverage on all property and equipment is adequate to reflect its true current value. Conducting periodic, independent appraisals of property values can enhance the firm's ability to prove the amount of loss if a loss should occur.

3. Use as high a deductible coverage as the firm can afford to carry. This will result in a considerable decrease in premium cost.

4. Buy insurance in as large a unit as possible to reduce premium costs. "Package" policies are frequently very suitable for the coverage needed by retail organizations. It is best to conduct all of the firm's insurance with one good agent, because the account will then be large enough that the agent will be able to provide outstanding service. However, it is a good practice to have a competing agent

Table 12-7 **Types of Business Risk and Insurance Protection Available**

Type of Risk	Form of Protection
Loss of earning power	Business interruption insurance Profits insurance Rent insurance Life insurance on key personnel
Loss of property (destruction or damage)	Fire insurance Marine insurance Windstorm insurance Tornado insurance Explosion insurance Riot and insurrection insurance Automobile, fire, and collision insurance Aircraft insurance Property depreciation insurance
Theft or infidelity	Auto theft insurance Burglary, theft insurance Forgery insurance Fidelity insurance
Failure of others	Credit insurance Surety bonding Title insurance
Loss of property (legal liability)	Workmen's compensation insurance Employers' liability insurance Contractual liability Public liability insurance Advertiser's liability Automobile liability insurance Power plant insurance Elevator insurance Product liability insurance Sports liability insurance Physicians' insurance Aircraft insurance

Source: Reprinted from Harvey C. Krentzman, *Managing for Profits* (Washington, D.C.: Small Business Administration, 1968), p. 155.

examine the firm's insurance policies occasionally. Perhaps the competing agent will make suggestions that will provide better coverage and/or reduce the premium cost.

5. Be aware of the firm's previous experience. Such knowledge can be used to get lower insurance rates or as a basis for changing to another form of insurance. Doing everything possible to minimize losses is essential to accomplish a reduced loss experience.

6. Develop a plan to implement good risk and insurance management. First, a clear statement of insurance objectives is needed. Second, select an insurance agent who is aware (or can become aware) of the firm's exposure to loss. Third, establish insurance responsibility with one individual or group. Finally, keep complete records of all insurance policies, premiums paid, losses, and loss recoveries to get better coverage at lower costs in the future.

7. When a loss occurs, immediately notify your agent. This will reduce the period of time needed to recover the firm's monetary loss and establish the date on which the loss occurred.

Summary

The retailer's own capital is the most important source of funds for the firm. Large retailers issue stock that represents ownership in the company for the buyers of that stock. Independent retailers usually supply a portion of their own funds to the firm.

Outside sources of funds vary by the type of money that is required. The most common source of short-term funds is commercial banks. The Small Business Administration is commonly used as a source of long-term funds.

Retailers must use accounting records and control tools to evaluate their business activity. The balance sheet and income statement are the basic summary records that contain the data needed to chart the firm's financial performance.

Care must be taken in the interpretation of data obtained from these accounting records. For example, one must determine which method (LIFO, FIFO or the retail method) has been used to determine the cost of the merchandise inventory. Inflationary pressures are forcing more firms to switch to the use of the LIFO method, because LIFO allows the retailer to value the cost of merchandise sold at a higher value than it can be valued under the FIFO method. This results in a lower profit figure on the firm's income statement but also allows the firm to pay less in income taxes.

Retail financial planning involves two objectives: providing an adequate flow of cash to meet current liabilities as they come due and operating as profitably as possible in the long run.

Cash flow forecasting is used to plan monetary inflows and outflows so that adequate cash is available to pay bills.

It is very easy to forget past expenditures, so it is recommended that the preparer of a cash flow forecast consult last year's check stubs or income statement to improve the accuracy of the forecast.

Trends in the value of the firm's financial ratios and operating ratios can be used to evaluate its profitability and the direction the firm's profits are headed. They can also be used when preparing next year's budget.

The return-on-assets analysis is a useful method for tracing the interrelationships between the various financial ratios and for evaluating the desirability of making a change in the firm's retailing mix.

Questions

1. Trace through the effects of a change in retail policy for the firm presented in the original return-on-assets chart (Figure 12–1). The change consists of using a new supplier of merchandise. The new source of merchandise will allow the firm to

reduce the cost of merchandise by 10 percent. It is not anticipated that sales will decline because the merchandise obtained from the new supplier is identical to the current merchandise.

2. Use the original return on assets chart (Figure 12–1) to determine how much the firm's return-on-assets percentage will increase if it can use an improved method of inventory management to reduce the current level of inventory by 10 percent without incurring any change in sales. Assume the new method of merchandise management does not increase the level of the handling, general, and administrative expenses category. Would the change be worthwhile?

3. Using the same data given in question 2, what would the firm's return-on-assets percentage be if the new method of merchandise management cost the firm an additional $2,000 per year? Would the change benefit the firm enough to implement the new merchandise management system?

4. What are the best sources of short-term funds for an established retail outlet? Explain.

5. What are the best sources of long-term funds for a person who is going to start a new retail outlet? Explain.

6. How does the income statement differ from the balance sheet? How is each used by the retailer?

7. Under what conditions should a retailer use the LIFO method of inventory evaluation?

8. What are the advantages of using the retail method of inventory evaluation?

9. How long should a firm's collection period be before management becomes concerned? Explain.

10. Develop an insurance plan for a newly established women's wear firm that owns its own building and facilities.

Footnotes

1. Erich A. Helfert, *Techniques of Financial Analysis* (Homewood, Ill.: Richard D. Irwin, 1967), pp. 58–73.

2. *How to Control Accounts Receivable for Greater Profit* (New York: Dun & Bradstreet, 1966), p. 22.

3. Ibid.

Case Study

Cashis Department Store

Beth Graphus is the department manager of the shoe department for one of the Cashis Department Stores. She has the responsibility for generating a maximum long-run profit from the shoe department. In fact, her promotion to an assistant store manager depends upon how well she performs in the shoe department.

Beth is reviewing the performance of the shoe department for the past six months. Sales have been $140,000. The initial markup has averaged 40 percent. Markdowns have amounted to 7 percent of the retail sales. Stock shortages have been 1 percent of retail sales. The department has been able to receive cash discounts from the vendors of 2.5 percent of retail sales. Operating expense for the department has been 5 percent of sales. Other departmental expenses stated as a percent of retail sales are:

salespeople's salaries	7 percent
delivery expense	1.5 percent
other selling expense	3.0 percent
promotional expense	4.2 percent
occupancy expense	6.0 percent
administrative expense	7.7 percent

The income tax for the department has been 50 percent of the department's net profit.

The average inventory for the shoe department has been $46,000 during this six-month period. The department's accounts receivables are currently estimated to be $15,000. Cash on hand at the end of the period is $1,050. The shoe department has $17,500 invested in store fixtures, equipment and checkout facilities.

Ms. Graphus is rather pleased with the performance of the shoe department for this six-month period. However, the assistant store manager, Ms. Willowbee, has indicated that the performance of the shoe department is not as good as it should be.

Discussion Questions

1. What do you think of the performance of the shoe department?

2. How can Ms. Graphus demonstrate her worth to Ms. Willowbee?

3. How can Beth improve the performance of the shoe department during the next six months?

"I've Got a Good Business Here"

One day when you are in your local bank the commercial loan officer comes over and says, "Bill, you're a management consultant with a good reputation for bailing out small businesses. When you're finished come over and let's talk business." You feel flattered, but at the same time not sure what John has in mind.

The meeting is pleasant, challenging, and profitable. The bank would like to retain you to help out six of its small business loan clients and promises its financial support during the "recuperative period." The most pressing small business is a small fabric shop across the street run by a hard-working, dedicated woman, Mrs. Kelly, who bought the store last year. The bank loaned her some money to purchase the business but is now very concerned after receiving a copy of her first annual income statement last week. The store's solvency is in question.

You make an appointment to visit Mrs. Kelly the next day. Her shop is well laid out, has current, attractive merchandise, with several customers buying large quantities of material and notions. After the store is cleared, Mrs. Kelly comes to you and says, "Mr. Means, I'm so glad to meet you. I really need your help. I know fabrics and sewing, but I don't have much of a head for business. Where do we start?"

You compliment Mrs. Kelly on her store and apparent customer patronage. You suggest one place to start is a review of her financial and merchandise records. She leads the way to a small office in the back of the store, offers you a chair, and reaches in the right desk drawer and hands you a checkbook. "It's all right there in the checkbook. I pay my bills promptly so that I will not lose my good credit rating." When pressed for other records she produces bank deposit slips and current unpaid bills. "I've really got a nice business here. See, I've got two thousand dollars in the bank, even after taking out money from the cash register for my own salary," she proudly announces.

Discussion Questions

1. Is Mrs. Kelly's business in "good shape?"

2. How would you begin to assist Mrs. Kelly? What information do you need? What records should be established and maintained?

3. Monthly income statements have been prepared by Mrs. Kelly's accountant using only her cancelled checks and her bank deposit slips. Do these statements fairly present her true operating results? Is net income distorted by her practice of removing cash from the cash register for her own salary? How? Can you list some payments that represent expenses of future months as well as the current one?

4. Would a cash flow forecast be helpful to Mrs. Kelly?

5. What other documents or information would you advise the bank to require of any future small business retailer seeking a commercial loan?

Part Four

Promotion

Chapter 13

Advertising Strategy

Learning
Goals

1. To understand how the environment influences the development of a retailer's promotional strategy.

2. To be able to discuss the methods that are used to determine the size of the promotional budget.

3. To be aware of the factors that influence the scheduling of promotional expenditures over time.

4. To learn the methods that are used to allocate expenditures to the various promotional alternatives.

Key Terms
and Concepts

institutional
advertising

promotional mix

advertising

personal selling

sales promotion

publicity

self-analysis
or retail audit

marginal analysis

experimental approach

objective-and-task
approach

percentage-of-sales
approach

competitive parity
approach

return-on-investment
approach

promotional calendar

cooperative
advertising

selling process

cost-per-thousand-
potential customers
criterion

The discussion in this chapter is limited to the development of a retail promotional strategy. Promotional budget size, the scheduling of promotional expenditures over time, and the allocation of expenditures to the various promotional alternatives are the strategical promotional concepts covered in this presentation.

Retailers exert considerable effort to persuade prospective buyers that their merchandise or service offering is "right," that it is attractively priced, and that the circumstances surrounding its presentation will lead to purchase. It is the function of promotion to stimulate transactions by making a retailer's marketing inputs more attractive to potential customers who are currently engaged in the search process. Attracting consumers to a store by advertising is one function of this type of promotion. Another example involves a consumer who has visited a store in order to replenish his stock of groceries and personal care items and who encounters a display of toothpaste that reminds him that his supply of toothpaste is low.

Promotion may also generate an attitude among consumers that will be conducive to making future transactions. Institutional advertising is designed to accomplish this objective. Instead of calling for direct purchasing action, *institutional advertising* stresses (1) the variety and depth of the store's merchandise; (2) the wide range of services offered; (3) the general high quality and good value of its goods, services and sales personnel; (4) the convenience of the store's location; and (5) the contribution that the outlet makes to the community. This type of advertising recognizes that a consumer's purchase of larger, durable goods, such as furniture, may be the result of the cumulative effect of years of retail advertising. Even then, the advertising may not have been received directly by the purchasing consumer. Instead, he may have received the message from others, who passed the information along by word of mouth. Thus, retailers use institutional advertising to attempt to build up long-run good will for the store and to generate shopping loyalty among consumers. Because all retail advertisements should attempt to build long-run consumer good will, all retail advertisements can be viewed as being, to at least some degree, institutional advertisements.

Thus, promotion facilitates the flow of information from the retailer to the consumer concerning such bargaining issues as product features, price, service aspects, warranties, and so forth. A promotion program must make a retailer's goods and service offering meaningful to potential buyers. After all, consumers must see how products or services can be useful to them in achieving some personal or social goal before they will make the purchase.

In recent years the term *promotional mix* has been used to describe the combination of tools used to promote business firms, products, or services. The promotional vehicles available to retailers can be classified into advertising, personal selling, sales promotion, and publicity categories.[1] The promotional mix concept emphasizes the belief that each promotional vehicle persuades consumers more effectively if it is accompanied by some combination of the other methods. In other words, a retailer's promotional efforts are not likely to be effective if they are concentrated in advertising, personal selling, or any other single method. Instead, a combination of promotional methods is used because one method frequently complements another.

Before we proceed to a discussion of the promotional decisions facing a retail firm, it is essential to understand the definitions used to categorize the various promotional vehicles.

Advertising may be defined as:

... any paid form of nonpersonal presentation and promotion of ideas, goods, or services by an identified sponsor. It involves the use of such media as the following:

magazine and newspaper space

motion pictures

outdoor (posters, signs, skywriting, et cetera)

direct mail

novelties (calendars, blotters, et cetera)

radio and television

cards (car, bus, et cetera)

catalogs

directories and reference items

programs and menus

circulars

This list is intended to be illustrative, not inclusive. ... Advertising is generally but not necessarily carried on through mass media.[2]

Personal Selling involves:

... oral presentation in a conversation with one or more prospective purchasers for the purpose of making sales.[3]

Sales Promotion includes:

... those marketing activities, other than personal selling, advertising, and publicity, that stimulate consumer purchasing and dealer effectiveness, such as display, shows and exhibitions, demonstrations, and various non-recurrent selling efforts not in the ordinary routine.[4]

Publicity involves:

... non-personal stimulation of demand for a product, service, or business unit by planting commercially significant news about it in a published medium or obtaining favorable presentation of it upon radio, television, or stage that is not paid for by the sponsor.[5]

The combination and volume of the various promotional vehicles are problems that must be continually coordinated by retail management. Maximum returns from promotional efforts will not be achieved unless the purpose of the promotional mix is kept in focus constantly.

The promotional mix is used to achieve the overall corporate goals and objectives of the retail enterprise. Its purpose is not simply to serve as an outlet for creative talents, nor should it be viewed simply as a means to attract added customers for a "sale." If promotional goals and objectives have not been defined by management, the promotional efforts of the firm cannot be expected to serve at maximum efficiency or in a coordinated and meaningful pattern. They will, instead, tend to reflect either a "stone statue" or a "reed in the wind" position. On the one hand, promotional policies may become so rigid and unbending that it virtually takes a hurricane-force wind to change their direction. Or, like a reed in the wind, they may move in first one direction and then another at the slightest reason for change. Either position is damaging to the retailer and results in lost promotional opportunities and wasted dollars.

The retail firm's advertising objectives depend on the nature of the firm itself, the market opportunity represented by its potential customers, the overall retail store image desired by retail management, and the nature of the goods and service assortment offered by the retailer.

A sound promotional policy must consider the correct proportion of each element in the promotional mix in view of the objectives to be met. Retailers should have realistic and specific ideas concerning the image they want to project to the consumers. (The components of retail image were discussed in detail in Chapter 7.)

The first step involved in determining what image is best consists of an analysis of the outlet's target market consumers. Retailers need to identify their target market consumers by age, income, sex, family size, tastes, life style, place of residence, pay periods and so forth. Only after retailers have decided who their customers should be can they effectively decide what kind of image they are going to present in their promotional activities and how they can reach the target consumers.

The next step involved in determining the appropriate image for the individual retail firm consists of making a thorough *self-analysis*. This analysis might consist of a complete *retail audit,* which is discussed in Chapter 18, or a comparison with competitive retailers in terms of (1) price policy, (2) merchandise quality, (3) brands of merchandise offered, (4) employees' attitudes, (5) employees' appearance, (6) store layout, (7) store fixtures and display, (8) store windows, (9) customer services, (10) advertising layout, (11) advertised price level, and (12) type of clientele.[6]

The self-analysis, or retail audit, allows retail management to identify and remedy the things that appear to be inconsistent with the desired store image. The self-analysis also provides an analysis of the reasons why regular consumers continue to make purchases at that outlet. These same shopping motivations may then be featured in the retailer's general promotional effort.

A brief discussion of the promotional factors that influence the store image is required to illustrate how each factor can be used to create the desired image. The relative price level can reflect a bargain basement or discount impression by using a "we will not be undersold" pricing policy. At the other extreme, a "you get what you pay for" impression may be achieved by using a relatively high price policy, combined with relatively high quality merchandise.

Employee attitude and appearance are important factors in establishing a store image. Retailers who attempt to build a bargain basement or discount image may successfully use employees who have gruff attitudes and overworked appearances.[7] On the other hand, retailers who desire to maintain a quality merchandise image must employ helpful, neat-appearing personnel, because the personalities of the employees influence the consumer's perception of the personality of the store.[8]

The kind and quality of services offered influence the impression consumers get of the store. Few or no services suggests a bargain image. Offering many services, such as delivery, easy merchandise return, credit, carry-out service, and so forth, usually is associated with a prestige image.

Advertisements themselves can be prepared in such a way as to generate either a discount image or a high-quality, prestigious impression. Product display and advertising that are crowded and cluttered tend to make people think that the store is of the low-quality, bargain basement type. On the other hand, a clean, well-balanced advertisement, with considerable white space, can convey the opposite impression.[9] Cost considerations also enter into the layout decision, since more white space in an advertisement means less space for describing the products being sold.

A store's image is also influenced by its clientele. If the store's customers belong to one social group, the general population will tend to think that it is catering to that group. Thus, retail management must consider how the reputation of servicing its present customers will affect any new target market segment it may wish to cultivate.[10]

Promotional Expenditures

The volume of total advertising expenditures in the United States has closely paralleled the level of retail sales (Figure 13–1). Thus, total promotional expenditures as a percentage of the retail sales dollar have remained very constant during the 1960–1976 period.

Retailers can begin planning their promotional programs after they have determined what their message is and who should receive it. The planning generally begins with a determination of how much to spend on promotion, when to spend the promotional funds, what merchandise to promote, and which promotional vehicles to use.

Promotional Budgets

Advertising must be considered as a prime ingredient in the process of image building and control. This is true even when advertising is seldom or never used by a retailer. Retailers who can afford to commit promotional dollars to advertising but elect to spend little or none may pursue this strategy for any or all of the following reasons:

1. They feel that their ad would be lost in the mass of ads by other retailers in the mass media—principally newspapers.

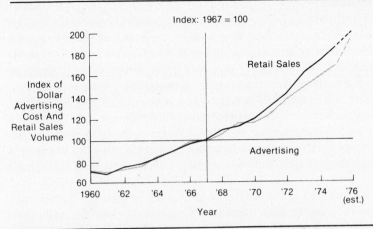

Index: 1967 = 100

Figure 13-1 **Growth in Advertising Outlays and Retail Sales**

Source: "Expenditures and Costs in Advertising," *Road Maps of Industry No. 1796* (New York: The Conference Board, December, 1976). Reprinted by permission.

2. They believe that their customers represent a different type of person, one who seeks out special values in particular quality, and may not even read the daily newspapers, listen to the radio, or watch much television.

3. They believe that their customers' shopping behavior is a result of their peer group association and that their shopping habits are directed by their social standing. It is felt that the customers are more apt to be affected by word of mouth and shopping patterns developed over years, or even generations, than by advertising.

4. They feel that their regular customers will be offended by advertising, since it might cheapen the store's image and place it in the class of all other retailers.

5. They are afraid that advertising might draw a different type of customer than their old customers and that this mixing of different social classes could cause their established clientele to shop elsewhere.

6. They believe the community they serve is so small that advertising is simply repeating things that people already know.

While any or all of these arguments may be valid for a particular retailer, they may prove to be dangerous myths in the long run. New generations within the old social class of dependable customers may change their shopping habits. They may become ardent television viewers. They may wish to break from tradition simply because they do not wish to follow exactly in the family footsteps. In addition, new social groups may emerge, armed with considerable purchasing power, and be "turned off" to the image and messages they receive from these retailers.

In addition, a policy of complete avoidance of advertising will cause retailers to overlook the growing segmentation of media. Thus, they may miss excellent opportunities to relate their message in specialized media directed specifically to their target market.

Marginal Analysis

Several different techniques are used by retail management to determine how much should be spent on retail promotion. Among them, *marginal analysis* considers the additional increment of return that is earned as an additional increment of expenditure. This method is appropriate for determining the impact of hiring additional salespeople (permanent or temporary), using additional promotional expenditures, extending credit, and so forth. Marginal analysis is accomplished by comparing the change in store profit that may be attributed directly to a change in the expense item being considered, other things being equal. In formula form, the marginal return ratio equals the change in store profits resulting from the addition of the last unit of input divided by the change in store expenses resulting from the addition of the last unit of input.

For example, increasing the number of permanent salespeople by one may increase store expenses by $520 per month. If this change alone increases store profits by $1,060, the marginal return ratio for the added salesperson is $1,060 / $520, or 2.04, and the store earns $2.04 per $1 of increased expenditure. A marginal return ratio of less than 1 indicates that the increased expenditure was not covered by the increased return. A ratio greater than 1 suggests there is money to be made through still greater expenditures. Promotional expenditures should be increased until the margin return ratio is "unity." In other words, retailers should continue to make additional promotional expenditures until the last marginal dollar spent generates one additional dollar of profit.

Use of the marginal analysis rule requires accurate estimates of the sales-to-promotional-expenditure relationship. The character or shape of the sales-response-to-promotion curve is likely to conform with the law of diminishing returns. This law indicates that as equal, additional promotional expenditures are added, while all other retail factors are held constant, the additional sales generated by each additional promotional expenditure will eventually be smaller than the sales response generated by the preceding unit. Thus the sales response function is likely to follow the pattern in Figure 13–2. Sales, in this figure, expand at an increasing rate up to point *A*, then at a decreasing rate up to point *B*, when additional promotional expenditures do not influence sales at all.

Experimental Approach

Retail management can experiment with different advertising expenditures, in the same way prices were changed in Chapter 10. Latin square and before-and-after designs can be used and sales comparisons can be made with previous sales levels, as already indicated. This *experimental approach* to estimating sales response to promotional expenditures are likely to yield satisfactory results for promotional—direct-action efforts. These efforts consist of promotion attempts to sell specific products or services by making a direct appeal to consumers to (1) come into the store and buy the product, (2) fill out a coupon and purchase the product by mail, or (3) purchase the product immediately by phoning the retail outlet.

Mail-order advertisers can measure the short-run effect of their advertising by keying their ads so that each customer can be attributed to a particular advertise-

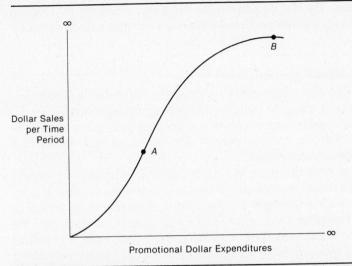

Figure 13-2 **Typical Response of General Sales to Promotional Expenditure**

ment. The short-run effect of changes in promotional—direct-action retail expenditures can be obtained by comparing the sales level in the days following the appearance of a given promotional campaign with the sales level in previous periods when different promotional expenditures were made.

Long-run-effect measurement may not be necessary for a retailer because most of the value of retail advertising is received within a few days.[11]

Long-run institutional advertising does not make a bid for direct consumer action. Instead, it uses the soft sell approach to stress the retailer's advantage in areas such as convenience of store location, the general high quality of merchandise, the wide range of goods and services offered, the friendliness and knowledgeability of personnel, and the like. Thus institutional advertising attempts to build good will and create a favorable image. The lag between expenditure and eventual sales stimulation makes it considerably more difficult to estimate the sales response to this long-run type of advertising than that of promotional—direct-action. For this reason, the objective-and-task approach may be used to evaluate the contribution of institutional advertising.

Objective-and-Task Approach

Under the *objective-and-task* approach, retail management defines the promotional objectives as specifically as possible. For example, an objective in institutional advertising may be to make 40 percent of the general population in the trading area aware of the fact that only XYZ Furniture Company carries brand X furniture. The tasks needed to be performed to achieve each objective are then listed, and management estimates the cost of performing these tasks. The promotional budget is then established by adding the costs of performing the necessary tasks for all of the objectives that are deemed worthy of pursuing on the basis of benefits derived from costs incurred. The method allows management to concentrate on achieving only those objectives that are most productive relative to their associated cost.

Percentage-of-Sales Approach

Many retailers use a *percentage-of-sales approach* to determine the level of promotional expenditures. Using this method, retailers budget their promotional expenditures at a specified percentage of current or anticipated dollar sales volume. For example, a retail firm may budget 2 percent of its forecasted sales of $1 million ($20,000) for promotional purposes.

This method of determining the level of promotional expenditures considers advertising to be a necessary cost, but it is difficult to support on the basis of logic. The percentage-of-sales technique lets the sales level determine the amount of money spent on promotion; however, the relationship should be reversed, since the level of promotion is supposed to influence sales. If promotion does not influence sales, there is no reason to make promotional expenditures. Using the volume of retail sales to determine the size of the promotional budget also ignores the marginal relationship of added promotional expenditures to added sales. The cost or worth of obtaining added sales is not considered under the percentage-of-sales approach. Nevertheless, the approach is widely used because many retailers are not able to estimate the sales-response-to-promotion relationship.

Competitive Parity Approach

The *competitive parity approach* involves establishing a promotional budget that will match competitors' outlays for promotion. Industry figures are frequently available to indicate the percentage of gross dollar sales volume that similar retailers use in their promotional efforts (Tables 13–1 and 13–2), and knowing the level of promotional expenditure that competitors are using is helpful in establishing the promotional budget. However, it should not be followed blindly, since it does not account for differences in location, reputation, opportunities, or company objectives. In addition, there is no reason to believe that the competition uses any logical method for determining promotional outlays.

Thus, the competitive parity approach can indicate only a starting point for determining the level of the budget. Changes in the budget can then be made and the resulting influence on sales observed to determine if promotional expenditures should be raised or lowered.

Return-on-Investment Approach

The *return-on-investment* approach is another method of determining the size of the promotional budget. This approach treats promotion primarily as a capital investment rather than a current expense. Determination of the amount of promotional spending then becomes a problem of capital expenditure budgeting, and the promotional budget must compete for funds with other kinds of internal investment on the

Table 13-1 **Percentage of Sales Dollars Spent on Advertising by the
Top Twenty-five Supermarkets in 1976**

Firm	Sales in Millions of Dollars	Expenditures on Advertising (Millions of Dollars)	Percentage of Sales Spent on Advertising
Safeway Stores Inc.	$10,442	110	1.1
Great Atlantic & Pacific	7,235	85	1.1
Kroger Co.	6,091	70	1.1
Winn-Dixie Stores Inc.	3,996	39	1.0
Lucky Stores Inc.	3,483	34	1.0
American Stores Co.	3,464	33	1.0
Jewel Cos. Inc.	2,981	36	1.2
Food Fair Stores Inc.	2,507	33	1.3
Southland Corp.	2,121	8	0.4
Grand Union Co.	1,622	24	1.5
Supermarkets General Corp.	1,612	24	1.5
Albertson's Inc.	1,490	14	1.0
Stop & Shop Cos.	1,474	26	1.8
Fisher Foods Inc.	1,442	15	1.0
Publix Super Markets	1,247	11	0.9
Dillon Cos.	1,148	11	1.0
First National Stores	991	10	1.0
Colonial Stores Inc.	975	12	1.3
Allied Supermarkets Inc.	901	9	1.0
Giant Food Inc.	895	12	1.4
Waldbaum Inc.	774	7	1.0
Fred Meyer Inc.	749	7	1.0
National Tea Co.	685	6	0.9
Von's Grocery Co.	640	9	1.4
Pueblo International Inc.	628	6	1.0

Source: Sales and advertising data obtained from "Here Are the 25 Top 1976
Supermarkets," *Advertising Age*, Nov. 21, 1977, pp. 42–55. Reprinted with permission from
the November, 1977 issue of *Advertising Age*. Copyright 1977 by Crain Communications Inc.

basis of prospective rate of return. Each piece of promotion affects current sales
and also builds good will to increase sales at a later date.

The relative importance of the two effects can vary tremendously, according to
the type of promotion used. At one end of the spectrum is institutional advertising
with its long-term orientation, which reflects an almost pure capital investment. At
the other end are promotional—direct-action efforts, such as advertising a special
sales event. This type of promotional expenditure usually represents only a small
portion of capital investment.

Isolating the portion of the promotional budget that can be considered a capital
expenditure and then estimating the rate of return that can be obtained on the capital
expenditure are difficult tasks, but not impossible.[12]

Table 13-2 **Percentage of Sales Dollars Spent on Advertising by the Top Twenty-five General Merchandisers in 1976**

Firm	Sales in Millions of Dollars	Expenditures on Advertising (in Millions of Dollars)	Percentage of Sales Dollar Spent on Advertising
Sears, Roebuck & Co.	14,950	543	3.6
K Mart Corp.	8,381	199	2.3
J.C. Penney Co.	8,353	204	2.4
F. W. Woolworth Co.	5,152	115	2.2
Federated Department Stores Inc.	4,446	160	3.6
Montgomery Ward & Co.	3,774	232	6.1
Rapid-American Corp.	2,346	15	0.6
May Department Stores Co.	2,119	121	5.7
Dayton Hudson Corp.	1,898	60	3.2
Allied Stores Corp.	1,797	96	5.3
R. H. Macy & Co. Inc.	1,660	114	6.9
Gamble—Skogmo Inc.	1,559	55	3.5
Associated Dry Goods Corp.	1,538	95	6.2
Carter Hawley Hale Stores Inc.	1,371	37	2.7
Zayre Corp.	1,160	29	2.5
Gimbel Brothers Inc.	978	28	2.9
Vornado Inc.	946	31	3.3
Mercantile Stores Co.	700	17	2.4
Korvettes	650	30	4.6
G.C. Murphy Co.	628	13	2.2
SCOA Industries Inc.	620	10	1.7
Marshall Field Co.	609	19	3.2
Rose's Stores Inc.	426	12	2.8
Cook United Co.	405	12	3.1
City Stores Co.	393	15	3.9

Source: Sales and advertising data obtained from "Top 25 Retailers in General Merchandising: 1976," *Advertising Age*, November 21, 1977, pp. 27–40. Reprinted with permission from the November, 1977 issue of *Advertising Age*. Copyright 1977 by Crain Communications Inc.

Concluding Remarks

The previous discussion has centered on the various methods used to determine the size of the retail promotional budget. Deciding how much to spend on promotion is a continual problem, because none of the approaches discussed is likely to yield an exact estimate of sales response to promotional efforts. Many factors, such as media effectiveness, the effectiveness of the promotional appeal, competitors' promotions, consumer attitudes, and so forth affect the sales-to-promotional-expenditures ratio. These factors are considered to be important to many retailers, who believe that either the percentage-of-sales or the competitive parity approach provides an acceptable way of determining the level of the promotional budget. These retailers believe that attempting to measure the response of sales to promotional expenditures requires too much time, expense, and mathematical proficiency.

There are several fundamental considerations no matter what method is used. The level of promotional expenditure will need to be higher for outlets that operate from less favorable locations. In addition, stores that operate in areas of exceptionally strong competition are likely to use higher promotional expenditures to combat the promotional efforts of the competitors. New and expanding retail firms must use larger promotional expenditures to make consumers aware of their existence and merchandise offering. Higher advertising expenditure may also be required by stores that continually stress low price in their campaigns.

The list could continue, but the point of this discussion is to indicate that each retailer operates under unique conditions. Thus, promotional expenditures must be tailored to fit the situation. If the promotional expenditure appears to be low, it might be raised a little at a time and the results observed to see if added sales contributed enough profit to more than cover the added promotional expense.

The essential steps used in planning and evaluating the retail promotional budget are summarized in Figure 13–3.

Scheduling Promotional Expenditures over Time

The timing of promotional expenditures over seasons, months, weeks, and days must be determined after the level of the promotional budget has been established. Some components of the promotional mix, such as personal sales, require fairly constant expenditures throughout the year. Certainly part-time salespeople can be added during the extremely busy sales periods, such as the Christmas season. Overtime payments can be paid to regular employees during these peak periods, but otherwise the level of expenditure for personal sales is likely to remain fairly constant.

It is much easier to change the level of retail spending for advertising and sales promotion, because advertising media and printing companies do not require a constant expenditure, as do store salespeople. Some media contracts contain cancelable clauses that may be used if it is necessary to reduce expenditures. Media options may be passed up to provide additional flexibility. Finally, a portion of the annual advertising and sales promotion budget is not contractually committed and hence can be shifted to a cash account if this is necessary to improve the short-run financial condition of the firm. On the other hand, when an unanticipated competitive threat develops, intensification of the advertising effort may be the easiest method of retaliation. Thus it may be argued that advertising and sales promotion are the most flexible retail marketing factors.

Despite the flexibility, retailers are likely to benefit more from spending smaller amounts of promotional money on a frequent basis than from spending a considerable amount on promotion for infrequent, special occasions. Consistency of the promotional effort reinforces the store's image in the minds of consumers. It also reminds consumers of the outlet's advantages and merchandise/service offerings.

This is not to say that the advertising and sales promotional budgets should be the same for all months of the year; it merely suggests that some minimal promo-

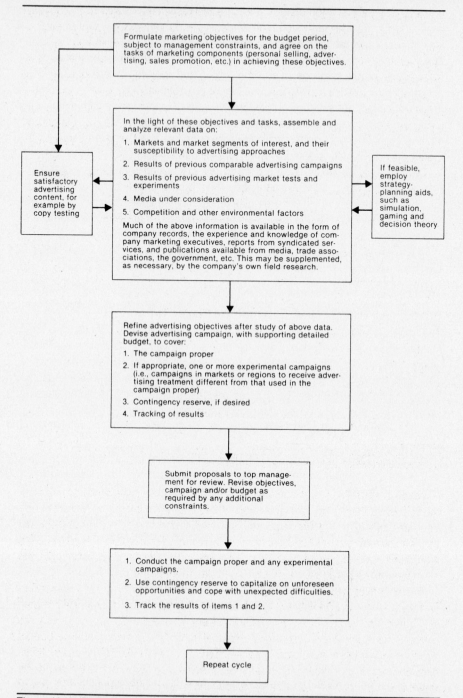

Figure 13-3 **Planning and Evaluating the Advertising Budget**

Source: *Some Guidelines for Advertising Budgeting* (New York: The Conference Board, Inc., 1972), p. 38. Reprinted by permission.

tional expenditure be made each month. The level of the total advertising and sales promotion budget will probably vary from month to month because of holiday, seasonal, and other special promotions, and it is a common practice for retailers to divide their monthly advertising and sales promotion expenditures into amounts that parallel expected sales patterns.[13] The actual promotional advertisements may be placed just before the expected peak in sales. For example, supermarkets spend a large percentage of their advertising budgets on Wednesday advertisements, which influence shopping on the high-volume days of Thursday, Friday, and Saturday. The same principle can be used to allocate promotional dollars during any period of time. Figure 13–4 illustrates the best division of a promotional budget over months of the year. In this case, promotional expenditures are higher just prior to periods for which higher sales estimates have been made.

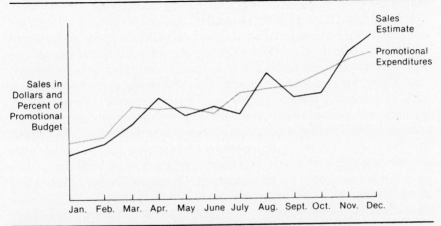

Figure 13–4 **Allocation of Promotional Expenditures over Time in Relation to Retail Sales Volume Estimates**

Allocating promotional expenditures in this manner allows the retail firm's communication to reach the consumers when they are beginning to make purchasing decisions. Heavier promotion can also be scheduled to reach the consumers when they will be able to react to the promotional activity. For example, response to an advertisement placed just prior to pay day may be considerably better than the response obtained from an advertisement placed just after pay day.

Promotional plans are generally made on a planning form, or *promotional calendar,* such as the ones in Exhibits 13–1 and 13–2. Such planning must be coordinated with merchandise planning, which is discussed in Chapter 9. Normally, retailers prepare the promotional budget, promotional calendar, and merchandise budget simultaneously because of their interrelatedness. The distribution of promotional expenditures during each month should be scheduled to take advantage of the payroll days of important area firms, days of the week in which sales and traffic are normally highest, national and local events, night openings, and seasonal merchandise sales patterns. These calendars can be used when one is planning future promotional expenditures, provided such factors as last year's sales figures, this year's sales figures, weather conditions, unusual competitor promotions, and so forth are recorded.

Allocating Promotional Expenditures to Departments and Merchandise Lines

Another important decision involves the determination of how much should be spent promoting each merchandise line and each department. One method of attacking this problem is simply to allocate promotional expenditures to the departments in proportion to their contributions to total sales. For example, if the hardware department is expected to generate 9 percent of the store's total sales volume next month, about 9 percent of next month's promotional budget is allocated for promotion of the hardware department. Another approach is to allocate promotional expenditures in proportion to the department's contribution to total profit.

Either approach is insensitive to the fact that promotion of some departments and merchandise lines creates more store traffic than others. Since the main purpose of promotion is to attract consumers to the store, the heavy traffic-generating departments should have a more than proportional share of the promotional budget. For example, many supermarkets allocate more than proportional advertising funds to the meat and produce departments. Since the same brands of canned, frozen, and packaged goods are available in most outlets, management believes that the perishable commodities give the outlets a unique chance to differentiate themselves from their competitors. Intensive promotion of the perishable items also is defensible on grounds that the consumer is likely to plan menus around the meat and produce items that are featured in the advertisements. Consumers are likely to purchase, at regular prices, the staple items that are used with the featured meat and produce items during their visit to the outlet. Other departments that frequently are believed to be heavy traffic generators are ready-to-wear apparel, furniture, and appliances.

Thus, the allocation of promotional expenditures to the various departments should promote the heavy traffic-generating departments by granting them a more than proportional allotment of the budget. Another consideration in the allocation process involves the relationship between each department's inventory level and its expected near-term sales. Some departments may require heavier promotional expenditure to clear overstocked merchandise because its selling season is nearly over or it is in danger of going out of style. New products and new or expanding departments may also require a more than proportionate share of the promotional budget to make consumers aware of their existence.

It is important to realize that specific merchandise lines and deparments benefit most from promotion during times when consumer demand is at its peak. Past sales patterns can be used to make allocations to departments in a way that will better balance departmental promotional expenditures with expected departmental sales. A special effort might be made to identify the best traffic pullers for each month. Promotion of these "hot items" attempts to match promotional expenditures with expected sales volume. The promotional campaign then tells customers that the store is offering those items that the consumer is seeking.

Thus, the retailer's promotional efforts should concentrate on the goods and/or

Exhibit 13–1 Worksheet for Preparing Monthly Promotional Budget

Month	Sales Volume						Promotional Expenditures					
	In Dollars			Percent of Total Annual Sales			In Dollars			Percent of Total Promotional Expenditures		
	Two Years Ago	Last Year	Estimate for This Year	Two Years Ago	Last Year	Estimate for This Year	Two Years Ago	Last Year	This Year	Two Years Ago	Last Year	This Year
January	—	—	—	—	—	—	—	—	—	—	—	—
February	—	—	—	—	—	—	—	—	—	—	—	—
March	—	—	—	—	—	—	—	—	—	—	—	—
April	—	—	—	—	—	—	—	—	—	—	—	—
May	—	—	—	—	—	—	—	—	—	—	—	—
June	—	—	—	—	—	—	—	—	—	—	—	—
July	—	—	—	—	—	—	—	—	—	—	—	—
August	—	—	—	—	—	—	—	—	—	—	—	—
September	—	—	—	—	—	—	—	—	—	—	—	—
October	—	—	—	—	—	—	—	—	—	—	—	—
November	—	—	—	—	—	—	—	—	—	—	—	—
December	—	—	—	—	—	—	—	—	—	—	—	—

Exhibit 13-2 Sample Promotional Calendar

Week of _____

Planned Promotional Expenditures: During Week _____
During Month _____

Sales Volume Data

	In Dollars				Percent of Annual Sales			
	Two Years Ago	Last Year	Esti-mate for This Year	Actual This Year	Two Years Ago	Last Year	Esti-mate for This Year	Actual This Year

Promotional Expenditures

Type of Promotion	Date Used	Merchandise or Theme Featured	In Dollars				Cost		Less Discounts and Co-op Funds Reimbursed	Percent of Total Promotional Expenditures				Actual Promotional Cost	
			Two Years Ago	Last Year	Esti-mate for This Year	Actual This Year	Last Year	This Year		Two Years Ago	Last Year	Esti-mate for This Year	Actual This Year	Last Year	This Year

(1) Advertising

Newspaper
Radio
Television
Outdoor
Direct Mail
Circulars
Other Advertising
(List Type Used)
Total Advertising

(2) Personal Selling

(3) Sales Promotion

Displays
Demonstrations
Other Sales Promotions
(List Type Used)
    Total Sales Promotion

(4) Publicity

    (List Type Used)

(5) Weekly Totals

Planned Promotional Expense for Week
Actual Promotional Expense for Week
Deviation from Promotional Expenditure Plan

services that most of its customers want. This results in attracting the maximum consumer traffic to the outlet.

Consumers' wants change over time. Therefore the promotion plan must be flexible to accommodate these variations in demand. At the beginning of a season most people are interested in the new goods or services, so the promotion should feature the latest fashion, style, or technology appropriate to the new season. When the season is nearly over, the promotions can feature special purchases or markdowns because consumers are looking for value and savings.

Another important consideration in deciding what items to promote involves the effect the promoted item will have upon the store's image. Is the promoted item consistent with the desired price and quality image? Is the promoted item likely to appeal to a desired group of consumers? Is there an adequate quantity on hand to meet anticipated consumer demand? These questions should be considered when items are selected and promotions are prepared.

Research has shown that a high-prestige store obtains more favorable results when its promotional efforts feature either highly prestigious brand names or no brand names at all. Consumer reactions are less favorable when it features low-prestige brand name merchandise.

Low-prestige stores featuring high-prestige brands produce the most believable advertisements. Consumers perceive they can get a good value for their money when these low-prestige stores advertise high-image brand names. When these stores advertise unknown brand names or low-prestige brand merchandise, the promotion takes on a negative image.

When a retail store has no established image in the consumer's perception, it can make its message more believable by featuring high-prestige brand name merchandise. Consumers also believe they get more value for their money when high-prestige brands are featured by these stores.[14]

The promoted items should also represent a good value from the consumer's point of view. It may not be the lowest priced, but by offering better quality, guarantees, service, advice, and so forth the consumer should see the total product/ service package as the best buy among the alternatives. Efficient use of this concept requires consumer knowledge of prices on different items. Price reduction advertising is likely to be more effective if it features an item whose price is known by most consumers. This simply makes the advertising more believable, since consumers can verify from their own experience that the price has been reduced.

Some retailers rely heavily upon manufacturers to assist them in their promotional efforts. These retailers advertise only those items whose manufacturing companies provide cooperative allowances. This practice, known as *cooperative advertising,* reduces the cost considerably, but it needs to be combined with advertisements on known traffic-pulling items to provide consistent results. Although the rate varies, the manufacturer most commonly pays 50 percent of the local advertising expenditure used to promote the specified items. (The contract usually states that any promotion must have the prior approval of the manufacturer.) These cooperative allowances let the retailer maintain a more consistent promotional effort over time. It also allows a retailer to use larger advertisements, thereby attracting more attention to the advertisements. Another benefit is the synergistic effect of national advertising and national brand names, which complement local promotional efforts and enhance the prestige of the local outlet. The manufacturers also benefit by paying lower local ad rates than if they advertised alone.

Cooperative advertising frequently features "in-ad couponing." "In-ad" coupons are authorized and paid for by the manufacturer; however, these coupons are distributed in the context of the retailer's own weekly newspaper ads. In-ad couponing has been successful in moving large amounts of merchandise. Retailers like these coupons because they can cooperate in the actual merchandising of the product, and because the redemption rate of coupons is increasing.[15] The need for more couponing stems from strong customer acceptance of coupons, which are used to reduce household expenditures. Departments that can take advantage of cooperative allowances are frequently promoted more heavily because of the reduced cost to the retailer.

Departmental managers may be asked to prepare their own promotional plan on the basis of their knowledge of monthly promotional requirements. The budget amount, the media usage, and the general theme may be worked out with the store manager, merchandise manager, or sales promotion director and may reflect the planning done on the promotional calendars. The decision as to which products and merchandise lines to promote within a department is likely to be made by the department head, who may be better informed on inventory levels, consumer preferences, seasonal patterns, and the like.

Allocating Expenditures to Promotional Alternatives

The allocation of expenditures to the various promotional alternatives is an ongoing process because both costs and audiences change over time. Advertising costs nearly doubled during the 1967 to 1977 period (Figure 13–5). Costs have risen most dramatically for television and least for radio advertising. Audiences also change over time, so retailers who stay with the same media expenditures will not be spending their promotional dollar in the most efficient manner.

Ideally, the promotional budget should be allocated among advertising, personal selling, sales promotion, and publicity in a manner that yields equivalent marginal profits on the last dollar spent in each of these four areas. To implement this principle, a retailer has to determine the dollar sales and profit response obtained by each promotional method. He or she then selects the alternatives that give the highest marginal return ratio, until all the ratios for all methods are equivalent at the value of 1.0. At this point the retailer is maximizing profits by using each type of promotion until the last expenditure is just covered by the increase in profits that it generated.

This reasoning simply involves the use of the marginal analysis approach to budgeting, discussed earlier in the chapter, for each individual type of promotion. The same reasoning can also be used when allocating expenditures within media by choosing the vehicles that generate the largest marginal profits per added dollar expenditure until marginal profits no longer cover marginal costs for each vehicle. This marginal analysis principle must be continually followed in making allocation decisions if unprofitable promotions are to be avoided. Measurement of the marginal

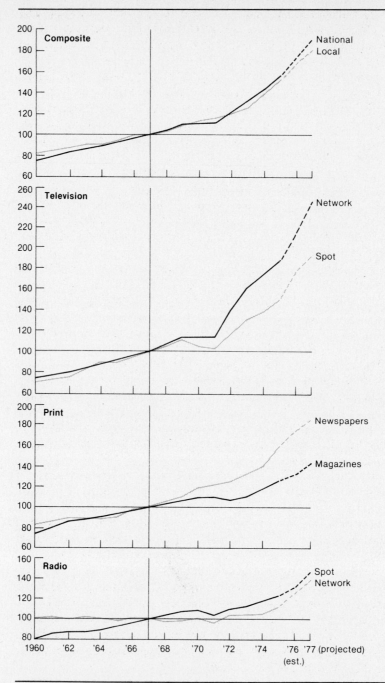

Figure 13-5 **Media Unit Cost Indexes**

Source: "Expenditures and Costs in Advertising," *Road Maps of Industry* No. 1796 (New York: The Conference Board, December 1976). Reprinted by permission.

sales and profit response to each alternative promotional vehicle is a complex and time-consuming procedure. Therefore the use of the marginal analysis principle is likely to consist of a managerial judgment as to whether the added benefits derived from the additional promotion exceed the added promotional costs.

The marginal effects of each vehicle depend upon the retailer's objectives, opportunities, and the constraints he or she faces. Different promotional mixes may be used successfully by similar retailing organizations, different tasks must be accomplished before sales can be generated, and each promotional tool differs in its ability to perform these tasks. The *selling process* may be considered to follow four steps: creating awareness; developing customer comprehension of the product/service offer; producing customer conviction that the offer is a good offer; and encouraging customer investigation that leads to purchase.[16]

Awareness is probably obtained most efficiently through publicity and advertising. For example, the opening of a new retail outlet or the handling of a new line of merchandise will probably require heavy advertising and publicity to make consumers aware of the change.

Developing customer comprehension of the product/service offer may require the use of a combination of all four types of promotion. The most effective techniques would probably vary from one retailer to another, depending upon the quality of the sales personnel used and the complexity of the product/service offering. Retailers who sell complex merchandise and services will have to place more reliance on salespersons to explain the advantages of their offering.

Personal selling is usually more effective in instilling consumer conviction of a good offer, especially for technical goods. However, extensive low-price advertising of national brand or private-label items may be the most efficient method of establishing conviction among a price-conscious segment of consumers.

Personal contact of some type is also influential in triggering the purchase act, even in self-service outlets where clerks may only provide information on merchandise location and availability.

The extent to which retailers should use each promotional vehicle depends on the target customer's reading, listening, watching, and shopping habits. The selected vehicles should reach the target customers at the lowest possible cost per potential customer. In addition, the vehicles' effectiveness for presenting the merchandise/service offering must be considered. The various media provide different opportunities for presenting demonstrations, conveying visual descriptions and impressions, providing explanations, and so forth.

The problem of allocation among various advertising media is complicated by the fact that they have overlapping audiences. Therefore it is difficult to determine which sales are attributable to each method. For this reason, allocation among promotional vehicles is usually based upon a judgment of the media believed to reach the largest number of target customers, as many times as possible, as steadily over time as possible, and with the minimum cost.

At this point the retail promotional planner begins to investigate specific alternatives in terms of which programs, newspapers, and so forth offer the best promotional purchase. The analysis will center on the characteristics of each vehicle, its coverage, the nature of its audience, and how these factors relate to the outlet's promotional objectives.

The *cost-per-thousand-potential-customers criterion* is frequently used to compare the effectiveness of the numerous vehicles in reaching the target market consumer. Under this approach, retail promotional planners calculate the cost per 1,000 potential customers reached by each vehicle. For example, suppose a retailer could reach 100,000 potential target market customers with a full-page newspaper advertisement costing $2,000. The cost per 1,000 target market consumers reached would be $2,000 divided by 100, or $20, because 100,000 target market customers are contacted with the $2,000 expenditure. The promotional planner would make similar calculations for each vehicle and rank them according to the lowest cost per thousand. Advertisements would be placed in those vehicles with the lowest cost per thousand target market homes reached. It is important to use the target market concept in making cost per thousand calculations because total readership, viewership, and/or listenership does not represent only potential consumers. The exposure value of each vehicle depends upon how closely the audience's characteristics match those of the target market. The cost per thousand in the target market calculation takes this into account.

The use of the cost per thousand in the target market concept requires the use of data containing detailed demographic and geographic breakdowns. Pulse Inc. and individual newspapers provide detailed newspaper readership information for 157 cities (Table 13–3). In addition, Standard Rate and Data Service publishes *Newspaper Rates and Data* and *Weekly Newspaper Rates and Data,* which provide six-month average summary circulation information. In the daily publication, circulation is divided into "city zone," "trading zone," and "other." In the weekly publication, circulation data are separated only into "paid" and "nonpaid." *Newspaper Circulation Analysis* breaks down the circulation of daily papers by county of distribution and makes a report for each county in which a newspaper achieves more than a 5 percent penetration of households.

Both Radio Advertising Bureau and Pulse Inc. provide detailed audience listenership data.[17] The *Nielsen Station Index* contains detailed viewer profiles for television audiences in over 200 markets.[18] Estimating the cost per thousand potential customers appears to be most appropriate when comparing two or more vehicles in the same medium (for example, several newspapers that claim to serve the trading area).

Estimating Relative Media Efficiency

The larger problem of determining allocation to each medium (for example, radio versus newspaper) is a more complex decision, involving considerations beyond the cost per thousand potential customers. The following factors, not considered in the cost per potential customer calculations, should be analyzed.

(1) Lead time, which is the length of time between submission of the finished advertisement to the medium and the time when the advertisement will appear. (2) Life of the advertisement, which is the length of time that a consumer will be exposed to an advertisement. (3) Intimacy, which describes the consumer's

degree of confidence in the medium which is being used. (4) Editorial climate, which refers to the degree that articles or programs are used to support the advertisements. (5) Repeat or multiple exposures to the advertisement, which is the number of times that a consumer may be exposed to the same advertisement. (6) Type of advertisement, which refers to product or promotional direct action advertising versus institutional advertising. (7) Competitor's use of the medium. (8) Availability or appropriateness of the medium.[19]

Analysis of all these factors and a review of the calculations of the cost per thousand potential consumers reached is time consuming, but the results can be rewarding.

Another measure of the relative efficiency of each advertising medium can be obtained by determining which media attract customers to the store.[20] This data can be obtained simply by asking each customer (or a random sample of customers if the number is large) how he or she happened to come into the store. A summary of their responses can be recorded for each type of advertising. Weekly records can be kept to indicate the number of people attracted to the store by each type of advertising. Sales slips can also contain sales volume for each consumer and can be totaled by category. The week's results can then be compared with costs, as indicated in Table 13–4. If the relative amount spent on each medium is not changed for several months, a retailer should have a fairly good estimate of how much it costs him to attract a customer by using each medium. Then expenditures can be changed on one medium for about a month and the results observed.

By carefully changing expenditures and analyzing the results, retailers are able to judge the relative efficiency of each medium. They may also be able to determine if there is a significant carryover of their advertising in each medium. Most retail advertising does not generate a significant carryover effect because sale or promotion—direct-action advertising is remembered for only a short time and does not generate a continual purchasing habit.

Both the cost-per-thousand-potential-customers approach and the analysis of relative media efficiency provide estimates that should be used with caution. These methods should be used to assist retailers in making allocations to the various promotional media and vehicles. They do not provide absolute answers on media effectiveness. It may take a considerable length of time to develop the skill needed to interpret the data. In addition, data provided by asking consumers why they came into the store may not reveal the true reasons. People are influenced by a combination of factors, but they tend to mention only the ones to which they have been most recently exposed. Despite these limitations, retailers can benefit by using all or portions of both techniques when they plan their promotional expenditures.

How Stores Spend Their Advertising Dollars

Newspapers have historically obtained the majority of the retailer's advertising dollar. However, there appears to be a shift toward a belief that some mix in the

Table 13-3 **Example of Newspaper Readership Data Available in a Market Area**

| | Market Composition for the Denver Standard Metropolitan Statistical Area | | Monday-Friday Newspaper Readership | | | |
| | | | Rocky Mountain News (AM) | | Denver Post (PM) | |
	Percent (Add Down)	Total Adults	Number	Percent	Number	Percent
Total Adults	100%	1,030,000	484,000	47	368,000	36
Adults by Age						
18–24	18	189,000	83,000	44	35,000	19
25–34	25	255,000	123,000	48	66,000	26
35–44	18	183,000	93,000	51	58,000	32
45–54	17	175,000	81,000	46	91,000	52
55–64	10	104,000	44,000	42	57,000	55
65 or Older	12	124,000	60,000	48	61,000	49
Adults by Household Income						
Under $5,000	10	101,000	39,000	39	23,000	23
$5,000–$9,999	18	188,000	80,000	43	41,000	22
$10,000–$14,999	21	213,000	96,000	45	70,000	33
$15,000–$19,999	14	143,000	76,000	53	53,000	37
$20,000–$24,999	16	171,000	82,000	48	75,000	44
$25,000 and Over	21	214,000	111,000	52	106,000	50
Adults by Education						
College Graduate or More	23	242,000	108,000	45	118,000	49
Some College	25	258,000	111,000	43	87,000	34
High School Graduate	33	337,000	167,000	50	115,000	34
Some High School or Less	18	187,000	92,000	49	47,000	25
Unreported	1	6,000	6,000		1,000	

media is desirable and a feeling that each medium is supportive to other media.

Home furnishings stores have shifted their advertising allocations in response to changing media costs and expected promotional benefits. The data presented in Table 13–5 breaks down the media preferences by store volume for 1972 and 1976. This breakdown allows retailers to compare their figures with those of other retailers in the same sales categories. Careful study of the data or percentage of dollar allocations as well as the percentage using each medium can lead to a most meaningful evaluation of how a retailer's advertising budget compares to the national average. For example, the relative spending on radio advertising has increased for all sizes of home furnishings stores.

The large national chains also make changes in their usage of the media (Table 13–6). Although Sears, Penney's and Ward's all use newspaper advertising as the predominant medium, they are increasingly using more inserts in newspapers. These inserts provide more control over the editorial content and allow economic

Table 13-3 **(Cont.)**

| | Market Composition for the Denver Standard Metropolitan Statistical Area | | Monday-Friday Newspaper Readership | | | |
| | | | Rocky Mountain News (AM) | | Denver Post (PM) | |
	Percent (Add Down)	Total Adults	Number	Percent	Number	Percent
Adults by Occupation of Chief Wage Earner						
Professional, Proprietor, Manager, Official	26	266,000	116,000	44	113,000	42
Clerical, Sales	18	189,000	107,000	57	69,000	37
Craftsman, Foreman	16	161,000	62,000	39	58,000	36
Service Worker, Operative, Farm Worker, Laborer, Armed Forces	18	185,000	99,000	54	43,000	23
Not Working (Retired, Etc.)	19	191,000	79,000	41	77,000	40
Unreported	3	38,000	21,000		8,000	
Adults by Size of Household						
1 or 2 Persons	49	509,000	216,000	42	196,000	39
3 or 4 Persons	34	350,000	174,000	50	121,000	35
5 or More Persons	17	171,000	94,000	55	51,000	30
Adults by Age of Youngest Child under 18 in Household						
Youngest Child under 2	8	77,000	34,000	44	17,000	22
Youngest Child 2–5	9	96,000	42,000	44	23,000	24
Youngest Child 6–11	12	122,000	55,000	45	37,000	30
Youngest Child 12–17	14	149,000	87,000	58	68,000	46
No Child under 18	57	584,000	264,000	45	223,000	38
Unreported	—	2,000	2,000		—	

Source: Reprinted by permission of the *Rocky Mountain News*.

production efficiencies because one run can be used in several different newspapers. Readership does not appear to be reduced, but a longer lead time may be required to prepare the insert.

The major gainer in the battle for these large chain retailers' advertising dollars appears to be television, which has overcome increases in cost to provide a complement to these firms' heavy newspaper advertising campaigns.

Advertising Ethics

The consumer movement has brought about the passage of laws which make false, misleading, and deceptive advertising illegal. While it is true that enforcement agencies cannot monitor the advertising of all retailers, it is equally true that consumers

Table 13-4 **Analysis of Relative Media Efficiency**

Media Category (1)	Number of Customers Attracted by Each Medium (2)	$ Purchases Made by Customers Attracted by Each Medium (3)	Advertising Expenditure in Medium (4)	Number of Customers Attracted per Advertising Dollar (5)=(2)/(4)	Sales per Advertising Dollar Expended (6)=(3)/(4)
Referred by friend	200	$1,000	—	—	—
Regular customer	400	1,600	—	—	—
Newspaper	150	500	50	3.0	$10.00
Radio	80	400	40	2.0	10.00
Television	50	250	100	0.5	2.50
Magazines	—	—	—	—	—
Yellow Pages	5	25	5	5.0	5.00
Special window displays	3	30	100	.03	0.30
Direct mail	—	—	—	—	—
Other	10	50	—	—	—
Total	898	$3,855	$295		

today demand not to be misled. Thus, retailers must prepare their promotional campaigns in such a way that consumers are not given misleading information.

Promotional claims must be established as true before the claim is made. These claims should be made available to consumers who request them. Retailers can create a good long-run image in the eyes of consumers by promoting factual information on health and safety matters and on performance comparisons for their merchandise and service. Since promotion is the most common way that the retailer can use to inform consumers of the benefits of the store's offerings, it is important that high ethical standards be maintained in the promotion program. Failure to do so will only undermine the consumer's confidence in the reliability of the outlet. Ultimately it will lead to a decline in sales as more and more consumers distrust the firm's offerings.

Summary

A retailer's promotional mix must be used to achieve the firm's unified goals. Thus, the promotional mix will depend upon the nature of the firm's merchandise/service offering, the needs of its target consumers, and the overall retail image desired by management. Promotion can generate either a quality image or a discount image, whichever is desired. Retailers can increase the believability of their advertisements by including highly prestigious brand items in their advertisements.

The level of promotional expenditures can be determined by using marginal analysis, experimentation, the objective-and-task approach, the percent-of-sales method, the competitive parity, or the return-on-investment techniques. Marginal

Table 13-5 How Retail Home Furnishings Stores Are Spending Their Advertising Dollars

1972 Advertising Budget Breakdown by Annual Volume of Stores

	Large (over $1 million)		Medium to Large ($500,000–$1 million)		Medium to Small (under $500,000)	
	% Using	% Budget[1]	% Using	% Budget[1]	% Using	% Budget[1]
Newspaper Space	93.8	63.4	100.0	61.3	100.0	65.1
Direct Mail, Stuffers, Handbills	81.3	8.9	75.0	8.4	58.4	5.0
Radio	68.8	6.8	93.8	11.4	70.6	11.2
Television	68.8	14.5	68.8	9.8	40.6	5.2
Classified Advertising	37.5	.7	31.3	1.4	36.6	3.5
Billboards	37.5	.4	25.0	1.8	14.5	.3
Display (Signs, etc.)	62.5	2.8	56.3	1.2	48.9	1.9
Other (Premiums, donations, etc.)	56.3	2.5	87.5	4.7	65.6	7.8

1976 Advertising Budget Breakdown by Annual Volume of Stores

	Large (over $1 million)		Medium to Large ($500,000 to $1 million)		Medium to Small (under $500,000)	
	% Using	% Budget[1]	% Using	% Budget[1]	% Using	% Budget[1]
Newspaper Space	100.0	69.5	96.4	57.3	100.0	55.0
Direct Mail, Stuffers, Handbills	14.3	2.9	17.9	4.8	21.1	8.0
Radio	88.1	10.9	92.9	20.3	73.7	13.9
Television	69.0	9.1	28.6	4.8	52.6	10.9
Classified Advertising	28.9	1.0	53.6	2.1	42.1	4.0
Billboards	16.7	.4	10.7	.2	21.1	.8
Display (Signs, etc.)	54.8	2.3	46.4	2.9	52.6	1.3
Other (Premiums, donations, etc.)	71.4	3.9	75.0	7.6	78.9	6.1

[1]Average per cent of annual advertising budget devoted to function

Source: "How Stores Are Spending Their Advertising Dollars," *Competitive Edge*, September 1977, p. 63. From *The Competitive Edge*, September, 1977, official publication of National Home Furnishings Assn. Reprinted by permission.

analysis and experimentation appear to offer the most logical approach to the problem, but both require considerable time, effort, and expertise. Thus, many retailers use either the percent-of-sales method or the competitive parity technique.

Supermarkets spend a fairly consistent 1 percent of their sales volume on advertising. General merchandise stores spend a considerably larger percent of their sales dollar on advertising, with the exact percentage varying from store to store. Advertising expenditures as a percent of sales for these general merchandisers usually varies from about 2 percent up to 7 percent.

The growth in retail advertising expenditures has been paralleling the growth in retail sales. Advertising costs in television and newspapers have increased dramatically since 1967, while costs for radio advertising have increased at a much slower rate. Although most retail advertising is conducted in newspapers, a trend is developing toward the increased use of radio and television. This shift in media is occurring because of the very rapid increase in the cost of advertising in newspapers

Table 13-6 **A Comparison of Sears, Penney, and Wards National/Local Advertising Expenditures for 1971 and 1975 (in Millions Of Dollars)**

	1971	% of Ad Budget	1975	% of Ad Budget
Sears				
Newspapers	$187	76.6	$229	69.8
Spot TV	19	7.8	20	6.1
Spot Radio	13	5.3	14	4.3
Magazines	10	4.1	7	2.1
Network TV	15	6.1	46	14.0
Network Radio	—	—	2	0.6
Total	$244		$328	
Penney				
Newspapers	$73	91.2	$121	86.3
Spot TV	4	5.0	7	5.0
Spot Radio	2	2.5	5	3.5
Magazines	1	1.2	0.4	0.2
Network TV	—	—	7	5.0
Network Radio	—	—	—	—
Total	$80		$140.4	
Ward				
Newspapers	$56	91.8	$104	85.2
Spot TV	3	4.9	15	12.3
Spot Radio	2	3.3	3	2.5
Magazines	N.R.	—	—	—
Network TV	—	—	—	—
Network Radio	—	—	—	—
Total	$61		$122	

Source: Louis T. Haugh, "Media-Emphasis Changes Appearing in Ad Strategies of Top U.S. Retailers," *Advertising Age*, 27 July 1976, p. 3. Reprinted with permission from the July, 1976 issue of *Advertising Age*. Copyright 1976 by Crain Communications Inc.

relative to radio. It is also due to the desire of retail managers to better complement their newspaper advertisements with television and radio promotions.

It is common for retailers to divide their promotional expenditures into amounts that parallel but precede expected sales patterns. This allows the firm to send more of its message to consumers when they are beginning to make their purchase decisions.

The cost-per-thousand-potential-customers approach is one method that can be used to guide expenditures to vehicles within any promotional medium. Other considerations, such as the permanence of the advertisement and the need for the merchandise to be displayed visually or demonstrated, also must be made when allocating expenditures among media.

In conclusion, promotion is an inexact science that is highly dependent on the situation, personal experience, and proper timing. Ultimately, each promotion program must be tailored to each retail unit in order to reflect the uniqueness of the outlet's target market.

Questions

1. Why would a retailer use institutional advertising? Is it a worthwhile expenditure of the firm's money?

2. What percent of a retailer's advertising budget do you think goes for institutional advertising? Is the percentage of the firm's advertising budget that is spent on institutional advertising higher for retailers or for manufacturers? Discuss.

3. What are the first steps a retailer should always take when the firm begins to develop its promotional strategy?

4. Which methods can a retailer use to determine the level of the firm's advertising budget? What are the advantages and disadvantages of each?

5. Why do so many retailers use the percentage-of-sales approach to determine the level of their promotional budget? Does it make sense to use this technique?

6. How can the promotional calendar be used by retailers?

7. What are the advantages and disadvantages of a retailer using cooperative advertising?

8. How can the four steps in the selling process be used by retailers in selecting the promotional tools that are most effective?

9. Why is the cost-per-thousand-potential-customers criterion a useful tool for retailers to use when they are selecting media? What are its disadvantages?

10. What are the advantages that a retailer gains by using the analysis-of-relative-media-efficiency concept to select advertising media? What are the disadvantages? Under what conditions should this method be used?

Footnotes

1. Jerome B. Kernan, William P. Dommermuth, and Montrose S. Sommers, *Promotion: An Introductory Analysis* (New York: McGraw-Hill, 1970), pp. 11–13.

2. Ralph S. Alexander et al., *Marketing Definitions: A Glossary of Marketing Terms* (Chicago: American Marketing Association, 1960), p. 9.

3. Ibid., p. 18.

4. Ibid., p. 20.

5. Ibid., p. 19.

6. Laurence W. Jacobs, *Advertising and Promotion for Retailing* (Glenview, Ill.: *Scott, Foresman,* 1972), pp. 6–15.

7. Ibid., p. 7.

8. Ibid.

9. Ibid., p. 10.

10. Ibid., p. 13.

11. Julian L. Simon, *The Management of Advertising* (Englewood Cliffs, N.J.: Prentice-Hall, 1971), pp. 14–15.

12. Joel Dean, "Does Advertising Belong in the Capital Budget?" *Journal of Marketing* 30 (October 1966): 15–21.

13. Jacobs, *Advertising and Promotion*, pp. 88–97.

14. James G. Barnes, "A Hierarchical Model of Source Effect in Retail Newspaper Advertising," *Advances in Consumer Research,* Proceedings from the Eighth Annual Conference of the Association for Consumer Research, Vol. V. (Ann Arbor: Association for Consumer Research, 1978), pp. 235–241.

15. *Editor and Publisher,* March 6, 1971.

16. Philip Kotler, *Marketing Management, Analysis, Planning, and Control* (Englewood Cliffs, N.J.: Prentice-Hall, 1967), p. 453.

17. The address of the Radio Advertising Bureau is 555 Madison Avenue, New York, N.Y. 10022.

18. The address of the A. C. Nielsen Company is 2101 Howard Street, Chicago, Ill. 60645

19. Jacobs, *Advertising and Promotion*, p. 128.

20. Ibid., pp. 132–133.

Case Study

Browne Real Estate & Insurance Company

John Browne is a recent college graduate who has established his own real estate insurance firm in Cheyenne, Wyoming. Besides Mr. Browne, the firm has two full-time salespeople and a secretary. John has been fairly well satisfied with the level of business that his firm has done during its first two years of business. However, he is concerned that the firm's promotional program is no different from any of the other real estate and insurance firms located in the area. Cheyenne has two daily local newspapers, three AM radio stations, one FM radio station, and a television station. Residents of the town also receive programming from numerous radio and television stations from the Denver metropolitan area.

Discussion Questions

1. How can Browne's differentiate its offerings from those of the other competitors?

2. How could Mr. Browne develop a promotional program that would accomplish the firm's objective of "being different"?

3. How should Mr. Browne establish a media mix that he can use to most effectively promote Browne Real Estate & Insurance Company?

4. How should Mr. Browne determine the amount of money the firm can spend on advertising? How should the promotional money be spent during the year?

Case Study

Southeast Grocery (A)

Southeast Grocery is owned and operated by Bill Greene. The firm has been in operation for five years. Last year, the firm sold $2 million worth of merchandise and obtained a net profit of one percent of its sales.

Bill has been using cooperative advertising as much as possible. As a rule, 80 percent of the items featured in the firm's newspaper advertisements are items that are advertised on a cooperative basis with manufacturers. The usual arrangement is for the manufacturer to pay for one-half of the advertising costs and for Mr. Greene to pay the other half. By using such a high percentage of cooperative advertising, Mr. Greene has been able to keep his annual advertising costs down to $8,000.

Mr. Greene has noticed that the Southeast advertisements do not feature the wide variety of merchandise that the advertisements placed by competitive supermarkets offer. He wonders if he has used too much cooperative advertising, since the current offers made by manufacturers limit the number of different items he can advertise.

Discussion Questions

1. What are the advantages of cooperative advertising for Southeast Grocery?

2. What are the disadvantages of cooperative advertising for Southeast Grocery?

3. What do you recommend that Mr. Greene do to improve his advertising?

Chapter 14

The Promotional Mix

Learning Goals

1. To be able to discuss the various features of print media and the advantages and disadvantages they offer to retailers.

2. To be aware of the various features, benefits, and shortcomings that broadcast media offer to retailers.

3. To be able to list the features, advantages, and disadvantages that position media offer retailers.

4. To understand how good print, broadcast, and position media advertisements are created and what they should contain.

Key Terms and Concepts

print media	broadcast media	point-of-purchase
direct mail	AIDCA process	promotions
coupons	white space	window displays
Yellow Pages	position media	specialty advertising

The discussion in Chapter 13 centered on the financial aspects to consider in developing a promotional strategy: level of expenditure, proper scheduling, in-store allocation, and appropriate media. Chapter 14 looks more closely at each promotional medium and focuses upon the considerations necessary to establish a promotional mix that will be consistent with the retailer's objectives and effective in reaching target market customers. The discussion of two other important elements in the promotional mix—personal selling and consumer services—is presented in Chapter 15.

Advertising

Perhaps the most difficult task in all marketing is the continuous problem of advertising faced by retailers. In most cases, stores are too small to purchase large amounts of advertising in any media. In addition, they usually serve a relatively small area, such as a suburb of 50,000 persons. There may not be a good local paper serving their trade area. Persons who live in the store's trading area subscribe to major newspapers and listen to the major radio stations. A small retailer usually cannot afford to buy time and space in these media, since that would mean paying for coverage in areas outside the firm's market perimeter.

Faced with these problems, retailers should be aware of the characteristics of each medium so that they can make appropriate promotional appeals and audience and cost comparisons.

Printed Media

Because they are durable, all *print media* vehicles (any vehicles that are printed on paper and distributed to the consumer's home) allow consumers more freedom in translating the meaning of advertisements into something that is meaningful to them personally. Consumers can read and look at the advertisement at their own pace. If necessary, they can reread the advertisement to understand its message more clearly. In general, print media, because of their durable nature:

(1) Provide greater opportunity for the consumer to translate the advertisement's message with more careful thought. (2) Allow for group participation in translating the advertisement's message. Members of a family can study a print advertisement together in a way that is not possible for radio or television advertisements. (3) Offer increased opportunity for consumers to make comparisons, by looking back and forth between pages, of the product-service offerings made by various retailers.[1]

The various kinds of print media possess different characteristics (Table 14–1). Therefore each will be discussed separately.

Newspapers

Although retailers may use all forms of mass media advertising, the primary promotional tool used by most retailers is the local newspaper and its supplements. The

Table 14-1 A Comparison of the Features of Major Print Media Used-by Retailers

Medium	Market Segment Reached	Type of Retailer Particularly Suited for	Advantages	Disadvantages
Daily newspaper published in metropolitan area	General population above age sixteen located in metropolitan area and its suburbs	Mass merchandisers serving entire metropolitan population area	1. Graphic potential can be used to illustrate merchandise 2. Advertisement is easy and inexpensive to prepare 3. Requires little lead time until advertisment appears	1. Competition for readership of advertisements is keen 2. Short life of advertisment 3. Waste circulation occurs because circulation covers wide area
Daily and weekly newspapers published in smaller towns	General population in immediate community	Local retailers of all types	Items 1, 2, and 3 above 4. Local indentification	Items 1 and 2 above 4. Limited coverage for national chains and mass merchandisers
Shopper handouts	Most households in immediate shopping area	Neighborhood retailers	Items 1 and 2 above 5. Written from a consumer viewpoint	Items 1 and 2 above 5. A give-away is not always read
Magazines	Special interest groups in metropolitan areas	Mail orders firms, specialty outlets and mass merchandisers	Items 1 and 2 above 6. Long life span for advertisement 7. Provides a loyal, special interest audience	Item 1 above 6. Waste circulation if special segmented group is not reached 7. High production costs in preparation of advertisment
Direct mail including coupons	Most segmented coverage since advertiser controls circulation	Mail order firms, new firms, catalog firms	Items 1, 3, and 4 above 8. Provides personalized approach 9. High percentage of personalized mail is read	Items 2 and 6 above
Yellow Pages	Active shoppers; brand loyal customers	Retailers of brand name merchandise, specialty retailers, service firms	Items 1, 2, 4, 6 10. High percentage readership 11. High percentage of purchase item	Items 1 and 3

local newspaper offers retailers the opportunity to reach a large percentage of their customers at a comparatively low cost with an extremely short lead-lag time between preparation of the ad and exposure to the customer. It also allows customers the opportunity to compare prices, shopping hours, and other differences between competitive retailers, if that is desired. Newspapers are sufficiently timely that retailers can tie their advertisements to current events, such as a forecast of the first freeze of the year.

Newspapers appeal to a broad range of customers, and local newspapers are perceived by the consumers as factual.[2] Newspaper advertisers regard newspaper advertising as being easily understood. It is believed that advertisements are read most closely by consumers who are in the process of making a purchase decision.[3] Another advantage of newspaper advertising is that the makeup of a typical advertisement requires less technical skill than the creation of advertisements for most other media.[4]

The short life of a newspaper is one of the disadvantages of newspaper advertising; consumers tend to spend only a little time reading each issue, and then they discard it. Another disadvantage for retailers who serve a small area is the wasted circulation resulting from the wide geographical distribution of the large city papers. Finally, the quality of reproduction in newspapers is generally low because they must be printed at high speed.

The type of newspaper can be selected for effectiveness in reaching the target market customer. The morning papers in most cities have a masculine image, with emphasis on sports and business. The advertisements in the morning paper frequently are read shortly before the consumer makes the purchase (later in the day).[5] The evening paper may be read more carefully, in a more relaxed environment, but is likely to be larger in size than typical morning papers. Sunday papers are read in an even more thorough manner, but are even larger in size than evening papers. The circulation is also expanded on Sundays, so that retailers may be able to place their advertisements in a specialized section of the paper. The disadvantages of the Sunday paper are the increased competition from rival retailers and the larger circulation, which may raise advertising costs. It is easy for an advertisement to become practically unavailable to the reader when the paper is very large and a particular location within it cannot be specified. This is the case when run-of-the-press rates are obtained.[6]

Specialized papers, with relatively small circulation, are increasing in popularity because they reduce waste circulation by aiming at a specific group of people. Such papers may limit circulation to only a small geographical area, or reach only a specific religious or occupational group. The cost per potential customer is frequently lower on specialized papers because wasted circulation is reduced.

Magazines
Magazine advertisements have a longer life and better-quality reproduction than newspapers. Consumers are likely to read and reread the copy at a leisurely pace and examine the pictures in more detail in magazine advertisements. This repeated exposure is a unique feature of magazine advertising. As such, magazines are well

suited for the creation of the desired store image or institutional type of advertising. Because different moods are created by the content of each magazine, advertisements can illustrate how the outlet or selected merchandise fits this consumer mood.

For example, city magazines are frequently used to promote entertainment facilities, restaurants, and so forth. Both the number and the circulation of local magazines have increased in urban areas. The largest local magazine is *New York.* Other large local magazines are *Philadelphia, Palm Springs Life, Texas Monthly* and *Chicago Magazine.* These magazines reach higher-income consumers who have the ability to make large purchases.

Despite these desirable characteristics, magazines are not used extensively by retailers because even specialized magazines are likely to have a high level of wasted circulation. Specialized magazines appeal to a specific group, but their per square inch advertising rates are usually higher than newspaper rates.[7] In addition, magazine editors require a much longer lead time for an advertisement to be included in a particular edition.

Direct Mail

Direct-mail promotion includes any literature that is sent to customers or prospective customers through either the U.S. or a private mail system. Although the cost of postage and handling has increased markedly in recent years, so too have the possibilities for using direct mail effectively. This may be attributed to the growth of credit sales, the increased use of the computer, and zip code mailing.

Direct mail can be used most effectively when the retailer is catering to a small, well-defined segment of the market. In this case the cost per potential customer reached may be lower with direct mail than with other media. The success of direct-mail advertising depends on the quality of the mailing list, which should be selective, so that all names should be potential customers for the product/service being offered. Mailing lists may be developed by a retailer from the records of his credit department. These can be further segmented, through the development of a computer program, to group customers on the basis of similar characteristics. Although the initial development of this system may be expensive, it allows a retailer to pinpoint the market and thus save on future promotions.

The use of zip code data and a crisscross directory, which contains names corresponding with the occupant of addresses grouped by area, enables the retailer to stratify mailings by income area and by areas of high social or ethnic concentration. Direct-mail promotion can then be employed, using a rifle method of hitting a target market rather than a shotgun approach.

Advances in printing have allowed the retailer a great deal of flexibility and much room for imagination. Samples of products (such as fabrics) have long been sent to prospective customers. Now it is also possible to appeal to the customer's sense of smell through direct mail. New perfumes and colognes may be introduced through a process that impregnates the scent in the direct-mail piece.

The nature of the sample must, however, be carefully considered in any direct-mail piece. A manufacturer of razor blades included a new blade in the evening edition of urban newspapers, only to get a rash of serious complaints by homeowners—children and dogs discovered the blades before the adults. It is a dangerous—and sometimes unlawful—practice to distribute samples of many products in a direct-mail campaign. Premium coupons, rather than the sample product itself, should be used for products such as razor blades, medicines, and other potentially dangerous products.

Another advantage of the direct-mail approach is that the advertisement does not compete directly for attention with other advertisements, since most mail is opened and at least scanned by the consumer. Thus, consumers may pay more attention to direct-mail advertisements than to other forms of advertisements. Retailers should nevertheless be aware that consumers frequently discard third class "occupant" mail without opening it. Personalized first class mail increases attention, but costs more than third class mail.[8]

Several different forms of direct-mail advertising are used by retailers. Personalized letters are designed to be similar in appearance to personal correspondence; and the more personalized the letter, the higher the readership—and the cost.[9] Cards are frequently sent out to introduce a sale; although the cost of mailing them is relatively inexpensive, they do not have a confidential or impressive appearance. Circulars, leaflets, and folders can be used to reach the audience at a low cost, but they suffer because they are not personalized. Catalogs and coupons are other forms of direct mail that, because of their importance, deserve a more detailed discussion.

The first things that probably come to mind when catalogs are mentioned are Sears and Montgomery Ward; yet the use of catalogs as a promotion and sales tool is by no means limited to the giants of retailing. Nor is it strictly limited to mass merchandise items. Thousands of firms rely heavily upon their catalogs for promotion and for direct sales. Moreover, the use of catalogs is increasing rather than declining, in spite of bigger and better shopping centers. Catalogs are usually quite expensive to produce and mail, but they have an extremely long life.

The expansion of catalog advertising is particularly noticeable in industries that sell specialized products to a particular market segment. The leisure industry is indicative of this increase. There has been a growth of specialty retailers selling items such as back-packing equipment and precut vacation homes.

Catalogs are also important promotional tools for carriage trade retailers, such as Neiman-Marcus. Customers look forward to viewing the Christmas catalog of Neiman-Marcus to discover what exotic new gifts are being offered for sale. These have included Egyptian mummy cases for him and her and his-and-her Chinese junks. Neiman-Marcus has been able to develop a suspense buildup in the introduction of these gifts, complete with all the secrecy that automobile manufacturers use with yearly model changes. At the correct moment, the catalogs are released and the press is informed of the his-and-her gifts for the coming Christmas. This promotional technique dramatically ties together the use of catalogs and publicity to enhance the overall image of Neiman-Marcus.

An entire mailing program could easily be a disaster if the tone of the catalog does not meet the image goals of the retailer. As a result, special attention is paid to layout, copy, color, and the overall esthetic appeal of the catalog. It is not simply a directory of products and prices, but a carefully planned promotional arm for the company. Unfortunately, the catalogs of many retailers are poorly planned and do not reflect an image consistent with that desired by the retailer. This is often true with small retailers who sell high-quality merchandise but feel they cannot afford the services of professionals in the design and layout of their catalogs. As a result, most of the planning is left to the sales manager and printer, who may only incidentally possess artistic talents.

Small retailers who are faced with this problem should give special thought to the possibility of selling their catalogs. Precut home manufacturers and many other retailers have demonstrated that consumers will pay over $1 for professionally designed catalogs. Such a program will enable a retailer to hire the services of professionals to produce a catalog consistent with the corporate image. The catalog must appear to be worth the charge. If it does not, customers will feel they have been taken and that the products sold by this retailer must also be overpriced. Retailers who sell their catalogs also believe that this policy results in a more careful reading of their information and a longer shelf life; that is, customers are reluctant to dispose of the catalog. They may also be more prone to show it to their friends than if it were acquired free.

Coupons

Coupons are a promotional tool that is widely used throughout the nation by manufacturers and retailers of supermarket items. *Coupons* are small cards or cutouts that are found in magazines, newspapers, direct-mail envelopes, and retail outlets. Coupons offer the consumer a savings on a particular product or service when they are redeemed at the cash register. They may be valued at as little as a few cents to as much as two items for the price of one.

Although coupons have been used for a variety of products, they are used predominately by manufacturers of branded products that are frequently repurchased, such as detergents, personal care products, and foods. Coupons are also a popular promotional tool for local retailers of services and prepared foods. Even the smallest pizza shop or beauty parlor generally can afford the costs of printing and distributing coupons door to door. Retailers and manufacturers have discovered that coupons are effective marketing tools when used in the following ways:

(1) In the introduction of a new or improved product; (2) Introducing a product into a new market; (3) In obtaining broader distribution of a product by using the coupon program as an inducement for more stores to carry the product; (4) Reducing excessive inventories of a product; (5) Equipping salesmen with an additional sales tool; (6) As a marketing research tool.[10]

The use of coupons as a marketing research tool is a side benefit that has been discovered and used by marketing executives. Since coupons can be coded by area, it is possible to derive such information as trading patterns, the effect of different types and values of coupons upon sales, generalized consumer profiles, and other important data.

It is obvious that a coupon is valuable as a promotional medium only if it is redeemed. In a study of coupons by the A. C. Nielsen Clearing House, five factors appeared to influence the redemption rate of coupons:

(1) Method used to distribute the coupon. The use of direct mail and inproduct coupons resulted in a higher redemption than magazines or newspapers.

(2) Size of the product class. As the rate of sale per $1000 increased, the redemption rate of coupons also increased.

(3) Rate of discount. The rate of discount relative to the price of the product also seemed to affect redemption rate. Although consumers may not know or calculate the exact percentage, they apparently recognize better discount values.

(4) Face value of the coupon. Consumers were influenced by high face values on the card, particularly when these reflected high discount values.

(5) Brand distribution. As can logically be expected, redemption rate increased as the distribution of the brand increased. Consumers can't buy a product if they can't find it.[11]

Although couponing can be an effective promotional tool for retailers and manufacturers, it is not without problems for both. Retailers often find it difficult or impossible to check purchases against coupon redemption. As a result, the manufacturer may redeem coupons for cash when in reality the product was never purchased. In addition, the sheer volume of coupons creates additional work and control problems for both parties.

In recent years a problem of counterfeiting has occurred in some areas. This is not a problem as long as the coupon is redeemed upon purchase of the specific product or service; it becomes a problem when coupons are redeemed for cash without proof of purchase.

The Yellow Pages

One of the best advertising media available to small retailers is the *Yellow Pages* of the local phone book. Because the vast majority of American homes now have a telephone, most retailers can be assured that their advertising message is present in their customers' homes. The only exception is in extremely low-income areas.

If a phone book serves an entire area of suburbs and city, the retailer may be forced to pay higher rates than desired, since the market area served by this medium is extensive. Nevertheless, the cost may still be worthwhile, and this method should not be automatically dismissed as an advertising possibility. Retailers in suburban areas are often faced with the question of placing an advertisement in the local phone book and another one in the larger metropolitan directory.

Retailers with limited lines may also use the Yellow Pages as either a catalog or a map. A map can be included in the firm's advertisement so that consumers can locate the outlet easily and determine if it is located in a nearby area. A scaffolding rental and sales company discovered the Yellow Pages worked well as a catalog. As the number of do-it-yourself homeowners increased, the company owner found that he and his staff were spending many hours on the phone trying to explain the different equipment to nonprofessionals. To correct this situation, illustrations of the major types of scaffolding were pictured in the Yellow Page ad. The owner and his staff were then able to ask a telephone customer to turn to the Yellow Pages and select the type of scaffold needed.[12]

Statistics by American Telephone and Telegraph Company have shown that during a twelve-month period 81 percent of the adult population twenty years old and older turned to the Yellow Pages to locate a product or service. Of the total references to the Yellow Pages, 84 percent were followed up with a telephone call, personal visit, or letter to the advertiser.[13] A more detailed analysis of a national study of Yellow Page usage is presented in Table 14–2.

Table 14–2 **National Consumer Usage of Yellow Pages**

		Adult Population	Users	% of Market	Total References	Average Reference per User	% Followed by Action
Sex	Men	65,427,000	53,328,000	81.5	1,977,492,000	37.0	83.4
	Women	72,349,000	59,238,000	81.8	1,937,439,000	32.7	85.9
Age	20–39	61,074,000	53,799,000	88.1	2,282,272,000	42.4	86.8
	40 & over	76,702,000	58,767,000	76.6	1,632,659,000	27.7	81.6
Household Income	Under $10,000	42,366,000	30,581,000	72.1	1,140,636,000	37.2	81.5
	$10,000–$14,999	33,273,000	26,024,000	78.2	892,993,000	34.3	86.3
	$15,000 & over	62,137,000	55,961,000	90.0	1,881,302,000	33.6	85.8
Household Size	1 or 2 persons	55,781,000	42,559,000	76.2	1,373,163,000	32.2	81.7
	3 or 4 persons	53,907,000	45,864,000	85.0	1,732,844,000	37.7	87.1
	5 or more persons	28,088,000	24,143,000	85.9	808,924,000	33.5	84.4
Residential Mobility	Moved within 2 years	40,630,000	35,450,000	87.3	1,476,312,000	41.6	86.1
	Has not moved	97,146,000	77,116,000	79.4	2,438,619,000	31.6	83.8
Home Ownership	Own	101,866,000	83,405,000	81.9	2,753,789,000	33.0	84.6
	Rent	35,910,000	29,161,000	81.2	1,161,142,000	39.8	84.9

Source: Data are based on a study conducted by Audits and Surveys Inc. in 1976. Copyright © American Telephone & Telegraph Company. Reproduced with the permission of AT&T.

Broadcast Media (Radio and Television)

Retailers use both radio and television advertising to relay their messages to consumers. The characteristics of both media are presented in Table 14–3. Both media reach a large number of people at a low cost, since nearly every home has at least one radio and one television set. But the amount of wasted circulation is also high for both media, unless the retailer is large enough to serve the entire broadcast area. If the retailer serves only a small segment of the population reached by the broadcasts, the waste circulation problem could be serious enough to make the use of broadcast media uneconomical. Some radio and television stations counteract this objection by scheduling programs that appeal to specific consumer groups. Retailers who cater to these groups can then advertise on these programs at a lower cost per potential customer simply because waste circulation has been reduced.

Table 14–3 A Comparison of the Features of Broadcast Media Used by Retailers

Medium	Market Segment Reached	Type of Retailer Particularly Suited for	Advantages	Disadvantages
Radio	Different programs reach distinct market segments	Retailers and service firms catering to a specific market segment and mass merchandisers catering to general audience at low cost	1. Requires very little lead time before advertisement is heard 2. Advertisment can be prepared easily and inexpensively 3. Advertisement can be altered quickly 4. Local identification on local radio stations 5. Can provide a loyal, special-interest audience 6. Personalities (D.J.s) provide believable advertisements 7. Low cost per minute of advertisment	1. Advertisements must be repeated to be of value 2. Wasted coverage for small retailers located in a metropolitan area 3. Message must be brief 4. Can cover too large a geographic area for small retailers 5. Absence of photos and illustrations
Television	General audience	Mass merchandisers and chain outlets; retailers of demonstratable merchandise	8. Low cost for mass merchandisers	Items 1, 2, 3, and 4 above 6. High cost of preparing good advertisements 7. High cost of television time

Another problem, shared by both radio and television, is that each medium presents many advertisements that are unrelated to the purpose for which the consumer is tuned to the medium. Television and radio audiences are normally in a mood for diversion, but unfortunately that mood usually has only a slight connection with the accompanying promotional message.[14] Despite the fact that consumers do not appear to give radio and television advertisements as much attention as they do to advertisements in print media, it appears that they remember a surprisingly large part of the former's commercial messages.[15] In general, the length of time that a television commercial is remembered is longer than that of a radio commercial, but shorter than that of a newspaper advertisement.[16]

One of the largest problems associated with radio and television advertising is that consumers frequently use these media as "background noise" and may not hear or see the presentations. A high level of creativity in advertisement writing and preparation and considerable repetition of these advertisements may be required to reach the consumer effectively.

Radio

Since radio is one of the most flexible media, a retailer can usually find a radio station, program, and broadcast time that will appeal to the target market. A retailer can broadcast the firm's message during any time period on any day of the week in such a way that the message is directed to specific audience segments. In addition, the composition of radio advertisements can be changed quickly. For example a Laramie, Wyoming, cafe changed the content of the firm's advertisement to include a reference to its convenient location for people who were stranded when the interstate highway was closed by a blizzard.

The commuting hours are generally the peak listening hours, and radio reaches most automobile drivers exceptionally well because they can simultaneously drive and listen to their preferred programs. Radio can become a companion to drivers and to people spending time at home reading or relaxing. As a result, radio's personalities frequently are perceived as personal friends by the listener. This intimate relationship is an advantage because these listeners place more trust in an endorsement when they believe they hear it from a friend.[17]

The per minute cost of advertising is much lower over radio than on television. A retailer can take advantage of this relatively low cost and combine it with an advertising schedule that is designed to reach the target market group in an effective promotional campaign (Exhibit 14–1).

Exhibit 14–1 How to Buy Radio Time

Radio is a selective medium that reaches different kinds of people through different kinds of programming. The following is a very quick outline of Radio buying to reach your best customers most effectively.

Station Programming Spectrum

In most every city and town you'll have a choice of Radio stations. In order to attract their own audiences, stations will program differently, so your choice of Radio stations may include:

- Middle-of-the-road stations
- News stations
- Conversation stations
- Country music stations
- Talk stations
- Contemporary stations
- Progressive rock stations
- Classical stations
- Ethnic stations
- Variety stations

And many variations of the above. From a programming point of view AM and FM stations are similar since these days FM stations have formats that include all of the above rather than just "good music" which used to be the case. All stations in your market should be considered on the basis of the kind of audience they deliver, the size of their audience and whether or not this audience will be interested in the merchandise you're selling.

How Time is Priced

The price you pay for commericals on stations is related to the size of your market, the number of people the station reaches, the kind (age, income, family size, etc.) of people reached and also the selling power of the station's on-air personnel. Radio stations can't expand the number of commercials they broadcast like newspapers can expand their ads—newspapers simply add more pages—because Radio stations limit the number of commercial minutes they broadcast each hour and the Radio day cannot be lengthened. This argues for planning Radio as far in advance as possible.

Source: Radio Advertising Bureau, Inc. Reprinted by permission.

Television

Television advertisement uses both sight and sound to take the retailer's appeal to the consumer. Indeed, its ability to show certain products that require demonstration may necessitate the use of television advertising. Because consumers spend many evening hours relaxing before a television set, advertisements reach these people when they are more susceptible to new ideas.[18]

Television also provides the flexibility needed if advertisements should be changed suddenly. For example, spot antifreeze advertisements can sometimes be inserted into a weather program when the retailer perceives a sudden change in temperature is coming.

The disadvantages of television include a high cost for advertising time and the relatively high cost required to prepare a good television advertisement. In addition, small retailers encounter much waste circulation because television does not generally offer as selective an appeal as radio. The total television audience in any area is also likely to be less segmented than the radio audience because there are fewer television stations. For these reasons, it is difficult for a small retailer to reach a target market through television.

Creating Print and Broadcast Advertisements

Although advertising creativity is not likely to be programmable, there are certain ideas that can be used by people who are responsible for preparing retail advertisements. First, the message must speak for the retailer in tone and content that match his or her objectives. Thus the retailer must:

(1) Identify his target market customers.

(2) Identify the reasons for advertising, be they stimulation of immediate purchases, changing of consumers' shopping habits, enhancing the store's image, informing consumers about the store's continued existence, the merchandise [and/or] service offerings, etc.

(3) Determine the unique selling features that are most likely to appeal to his target market group. Seeing things from the point of view of the target market customers can generate unique selling features. Talking to customers, and surveying consumers by the use of questionnaires can give retailers ideas on the desires of [their] target group.

(4) List the benefits that should be featured in his advertisements. Consumers want to know "what does this advertisement offer me?" Facts (such as a large number of automobiles on hand) mean little to the consumer until they are turned into benefits for him by emphasizing that he can choose from a large selection of automobiles.

(5) Develop the theme for the advertisement by taking the above factors into consideration.[19]

Converting the theme into an advertisement should follow the *AIDCA process*. This consists of attracting *attention,* stimulating *interest,* creating *desire, convincing* the consumer that the merchandise/service offering will provide the best solution to his problem, and, finally, suggesting that the consumer take *action.* The different ways of using print and radio advertising to take the consumer through the AIDCA process will now be discussed.

Print Media

Headlines are used to capture the reader's attention. On the average, five times as many people read the headline of an advertisement as read the body.[20] Therefore, if retailers do not "sell" a benefit in a short, simple headline, they waste 80 percent of their money. "Benefit headlines" are designed to answer the target consumer's question, "What does this advertisement offer me?" The good quality of the store's merchandise and service should be stressed relative to the most important consumer benefits that the merchandise and service provide.

Illustrations, if used, should reinforce headlines to capture the reader's attention. Usually photographs attract more readers, are more believable, and are better remembered than drawings.[21] Captions should be placed below a photograph because, in general, twice as many people read the captions as read the body of the advertisement.[22] More awareness can be obtained if each caption is considered to be a miniature advertisement containing brand names and benefits.

The headline and illustration should capture the *attention* and stimulate the *interest* of the readers. The text, or copy, is used to create the *desire* for the product or service and to *convince* the readers that the advertised merchandise/service offering is best in light of their needs.

Copywriting is truly a creative process, but several concepts may be helpful. First, the message should include the benefits that are likely to appeal to the target group. Second, the writing should be phrased in the type of language that is most familiar to the people in the target group. The arguments should be presented in terms to which target consumers can relate. Third, the benefits should be presented in simple words and short sentences that get the ideas across quickly and clearly. The creative element is involved in using words that arouse interest and encourage people to read an advertisement to its conclusion. Readership falls off rapidly during the first 50 words, but it drops off only slightly between 50 and 500 words if the copy is well written.[23] The decline in readership means that the most important ideas should be presented first in copy.

The layout of an advertisement involves visually fitting together the lead line, illustration, copy, and a signature or logotype, which may include the store name, location, store hours, and phone number. Whenever printed advertisements are used, special care should be given to the mechanics of producing the best layout for the money. For an advertisement of a given size, this involves careful consideration of the following details.[24]

Amount of White Space Retailers should consider the image that they want to project and allocate more *white space* (the lack of print in an advertisement) to expensive, quality merchandise if they wish to project a prestige image (Exhibit 14–2). If they wish to project a discount-price image, they will want to reduce the white space and use a more crowded, cluttered layout.

Exhibit 14–2 **Example of "Sale" Advertisment Conveying Prestige Image Using White Space**

MONTALDO'S
1632 California Street

Fall Clearance

Special Groupings

¼ to ⅓ off

Source: Montaldo's Denver. Reprinted by permission.

Placement Regular advertisers will find that newspapers are generally willing to place their ads on desired pages or sections. Retailers should give serious consideration to the correct area, even if a small premium is required to reserve space in this area. Many small retailers sell specialized products, such as women's wear, wigs, sporting goods, and pet supplies, that coincide well with such special areas as the sports or the women's section.

Print Style A retailer may wish to purchase a print type not carried by the local newspaper. This can be kept on stock at the newspaper and used only by the retailer. Although difference is desired, an extreme can actually work to the detriment of the retailer.

The Slogan A good slogan can aid in establishing an image and in repeating a message to the customer. It should contain the name of the firm and/or the merchandise or service offered. It should also have recall value; may arouse curiosity; and should serve as a focus point for the advertising policy of the firm.

Sponsor Identification A signature in the form of a logo or distinctive design can help improve identification. It does no good to advertise if the reader cannot remember later which store it was that was having the sale or confuses it with a competitor. Signature "cuts" may be purchased through engraving companies and stored with the local newspaper or printer.

Human Interest Illustration Illustration can add to the interest in the ad if well done. Newspapers carry a catalog of illustrations that may have applicability. A special illustration, to be used in a recurring theme, should be custom made and kept on file with the newspaper or printer.

Check the Advertisement Before Printing Each advertiser should check the advertisement to be certain that (1) the advertisement is easily recognizable, (2) a simple layout has been used, (3) a dominant element, such as a headline or illustration, has been used to present a benefit to the consumer, (4) the amount of white space is consistent with the store image, (5) the copy is complete, including the store name, (6) possibly related items are included in the advertisement, (7) wording is simple and excessive claims are not used, (8) the advertisement urges readers to buy now.

Mr. Sandman furniture galleries is an example of a retailer recognizing that innovation can be promoted through newspaper advertisements to create a desired image. The firm took a new approach to advertising modular furniture. "By introducing and continually promoting a new line of rugged and durable sleep-and-storage units, Mr. Sandman became synonymous with 'maximum living in minimum space.' "[25] The firm's advertising states, "We think ahead." This continual, innovative promotional approach converted the firm into the leader in their market.

Broadcast Media

Broadcast media present difficult creative problems because consumers must understand the message the first time. They cannot go back and reread the message as they can in print advertisements. Only a very short message can be communicated because the consumer's attention is not completely focused on the advertising presentation. Both television and radio commercials can suffer from wordiness. One-minute radio commercials should present between 120 and 150 words.[26]

There are different types of radio commercials.[27] A *straight announcement* involves an announcer's delivering the commercial without the use of music or any backup noise. The personality of a regular announcer is used to attempt to make the commercial more believable. Use of irrelevant celebrities, who are not connected with the offering, may only steal attention from the message.

A *dramatization* is a commercial playlet, which is a good attention getter but is also expensive to produce. Normally, a realistic consumer problem is posed and the sponsoring store eventually solves the problem in a believable way. The problem that is selected should be based upon some unique merchandise/service offering available at the store. A good *dialogue* commercial involves a realistic conversation between several announcers.

Good *jingle* or *singing commercials* and musical advertisements where the announcer reads the advertisement with a musical background are quite effective in gaining a listener's attention. However, they should be well done or they may irritate the listener and adversely affect the store's image. A checklist for writing radio copy is presented in Exhibit 14–3.

Exhibit 14-3 **Checklist for Writing Radio Copy**

Here are some suggestions to help you write effective Radio copy.

1. Write conversationally. Radio is a human being talking to another human being, not a novelist or poet writing to a reader.

2. Talk about benefits. Tell listeners what store or merchandise will do for them . . . fast. Here are some benefits: economy, health, good looks, current fashions, quality, etc.

3. Be direct and go straight to the point. Short sentences are better because they can be absorbed easily through the ears.

4. Repeat the store name, the price, the comparative, the benefits as many times as you can to register the points you want to make.

5. Know what you're writing about. Use fact sheets from manufacturers, national ads, actual experience to make the merchandise come alive on the air.

6. Try out your script before airing. Read the copy over or, better yet, have someone else read it or read it into a tape recorder. This way you'll hear if any phrases are stilted, hard to read or unbelievable.

Source: Radio Advertising Bureau, Inc. Reprinted by permission.

Television commercials use the same techniques as radio, but also allow the use of visual demonstrations. If they are honest and believable, these demonstrations are quite effective ways to communicate with customers. Animated and cartoon commercials can be used effectively to reach children. They are less persuasive than live commercials in reaching adults, who cannot identify with the character in the cartoon.[28]

Broadcast advertisements require the use of a natural, simple language that will appeal to the target group of consumers. The desired store image and its merchandise/service offering must then be turned into consumer benefits and presented in a short amount of time. Generally this means that the advertiser should try to communicate only one idea during a commercial. The more ideas presented, the less consumers remember about the content of the commercial. The name and address of the store should be repeated several times during the commercial. Musical jingles or spoken slogans that rhyme with the name of the store can be used to assist the memory of consumers. A strong windup, calling for consumer action, is also desirable.

Position Media

Position media include all types of signs, posters, programs, menus, directories, skywriting, and transportation advertising, such as the signs that appear on the back of taxicabs or inside public vehicles. The characteristics of billboard and transit advertising are presented in Table 14–4.

Table 14-4 A Comparison of the Features of Major Position Media Used by Retailers

Medium	Market Segment Reached	Type of Retailer Particularly Suited for	Advantages	Disadvantages
Billboard	Pedestrians, commuters, and motorists who pass by the specific location	Services, tourist attractions, amusements, retailers of brand name merchandise	1) Long life span for advertisement 2) High percentage of passersby read advertisemment 3) Humor can be used	1) High cost 2) cannot be changed quickly 3) Competition for readership may be keen 4) Limited to short message
Transit	Urban pedestrians, commuters, workers	Local retailers and service firms	Repetition of exposure to advertisement	Item 4 above 5) May provide limited audience unless advertisement moves around the city on the back of a bus or taxi

Signs Advertising by means of outdoor signs is more suitable for institutional image promotion than for product-direction-action promotion because it is difficult and expensive to change the message continually. Thus, position media are generally used to reinforce the messages presented in other media or other signs. The content of the former generally consists of no more than eight words, unless the sign is presented on the inside of a bus or train.[29] In the latter cases, the sign may contain up to fifteen words, since a consumer frequently has nothing better to do than read the advertisement.

It is becoming increasingly clear that decisions concerning outdoor signs are no longer strictly the province of the retailer. Legislation regulating outdoor signs is almost certain to increase in amount and severity. The more vociferous anti-sign groups argue that if all signs were removed, no single company would have an advantage. Unless this viewpoint gains more support, the argument will remain academic. In the meantime, retailers will continue to utilize signs.

In recent years, corporations have placed increasing importance upon their images and logos. Retailers of gasoline have been particularly concerned with the image portrayed through these signs. This reflects the fact that a logo must give quick and positive identification to the viewer and means that every aspect of such signs must be given careful consideration. The color, shape, size, and type of illustration also have taken on increased importance. For this reason, it is advisable to use the services of professional design firms. Although the design and planning of signs should be assigned to professionals, it is well for retailers to be aware of some of the considerations in design.

Color The role of color in our lives has taken on increased importance. As a result, many variables should be considered in the selection of colors.

Visibility is one major factor. Yellow can be seen from a greater distance than other colors when placed on painted or printed surfaces. Red and blue follow next in order of visibility from distances. Even though yellow exhibits greater visibility, it may not be selected because of other overriding considerations. Color combinations give maximum legibility and visibility in the following order.

1. Black on yellow
2. Black on orange
3. Orange on navy blue
4. Green on white
5. Scarlet red on white
6. Black on white
7. Navy blue on white
8. White on navy blue
9. Orange on black
10. White on black
11. White on bottle green
12. White on scarlet red
13. White on purple
14. Purple on white
15. Navy blue on yellow
16. Navy blue on orange
17. Yellow on black
18. Scarlet red on yellow
19. Yellow on navy blue
20. Purple on yellow

Symbolism and tradition also influence people. Certain colors traditionally have had specific images and meaning. Purple has long been associated with royalty, red with danger, green with safety, blue with first place, gold with richness, pastels with spring, and on and on. The symbols and traditions associated with colors are overlooked by retailers only at their loss.

Reference to the colors black and white and their symbolism can be extremely dangerous for today's retailer. White has long been used to designate cleanliness, virginity, goodness, wholesomeness, the "good guy," etc. Black has been associated with quite the opposite, and today the traditional use of black as a negative symbol is at best a risky undertaking. In an era of "Black is beautiful" and "Black Power," only the most "tuned out" will elect to represent the bad guy as the one in black.

Color may be used as a replacement for certain signs. The skillful use of colors in interior design can help to direct the consumer's eye to key spots within the store, thus avoiding the use of potentially objectionable signs. A chain of retail candy stores is credited with the use of color to eliminate the need for signs inside its phone booths to remind customers to keep conversations short. Since a person cannot remain long in a pure red environment, the insides of problem phone booths were painted red. This action was credited with the elimination of long phone conversations, and the store was able to remove its unsightly signs.[30]

Different colors have different sensory effects. Hues of brown and gold are appetite-stimulating colors and should be considered in connection with food products and areas of the store that sell these items. Yellow, orange, and red are generally classified as stimulating colors. Blue, green, and violet are sedative or "cold" colors. The stimulating or action colors may be used in an environment in which things are done quickly. Red is the most volatile, followed by orange and yellow. These colors cause farsightedness in large areas; they cause the colors to "come closer." Small rooms seem to close in psychologically when these colors are used.

Point-of-Purchase Promotions

Point-of-purchase promotions (P.O.P.) range from a simple counter display with a sign to free samples distributed by girls in bikinis accompanied by a brass band. Point-of-purchase advertising

> sells both by reminder and by impulse. When selling by reminder it utilizes the impact already made by other advertising media, serving as a link between them and the place where sales are made. When selling by impulse it also appeals independently. In either case, it is a potent instrument in clinching the sale. It asks for the order.[31]

Point-of-purchase promotions exist to strengthen overall retail promotional strategy. A great quantity of the point-of-purchase material available to retailers is furnished by the manufacturer. These displays may have been designed to tie in with a current promotional theme by the manufacturer, but may be completely out of place in the retail store. Retailers have both the right and the responsibility to reject any P.O.P. material they feel is damaging to the store's image. Unless P.O.P. material is planned around the habits, needs, problems, and fears of the retailer, it is almost assuredly headed for the trash can.

Even the best-planned and most creative P.O.P. display is destined for a short life. This is the very nature of P.O.P. material. Since the marketing and creative staffs of manufacturers and retailers continually create obsolescence in P.O.P. material, a precise classification is impossible. Retailers, are, however, beginning to demand more quality and longer lasting promotions from manufacturers. Retailers no longer want a last-one-week display, but expect a display to last six to eight weeks. This means the displays must be better constructed than previous displays. If this is done, retailers can use longer advertising periods to complement the P.O.P. display. Such a promotional program could feature common theme (for example, Hawaiian) displays of several different manufacturers. Consumers have been shown to spend more time in a store that offers a consistent theme on its P.O.P. material.[32]

Certain types of P.O.P. displays have emerged over time. These should not be considered totally independent classifications. Creative P.O.P. designers purposely blend one type with another to create hybrid displays.

Cut-Case Displays

The simplest type of P.O.P display is made from the shipping container. The carton is designed to be cut along dotted lines to form a display case. Cut-case displays have widest application in the mass merchandising field, particularly in food stores, variety stores, and discount houses. In addition, they are often used by liquor stores. Other retailers, including department stores, use these displays during heavy buying periods, such as Christmas.

This type of display is simple to assemble, and often comes with a "riser" card to be attached as a poster. Cut-case displays fit in nicely as end-of-aisle displays, and may be used to form temporary partitions to direct shopper traffic patterns. They are also used as displays near cash registers for so-called impulse items.

Dump-Bin Displays

As the name implies, dump bins are tubs, boxes, wire baskets, or any other container in which products are dumped in a random method. Although brands and varieties may be mixed, the dump bins furnished by manufacturers usually lend themselves to a particular brand. Dump bins are used in the same way as cut-case displays.

Mobile Displays

One definition of a mobile is a sign or figure that is generally suspended from the ceiling. It is widely used by supermarkets to direct customers to a specific brand. Another definition refers to any movable P.O.P. display.

Counter Displays

The checkout counter represents the last selling opportunity in the store and is an excellent location for impulse, or unplanned purchase, items. As a result, many manufacturers supply special racks or other display units specifically designed to be used at the counter. Items commonly sold at this counter range from penny mints in restaurants to expensive hosiery in women's style shops. Although items such as gum and cigarettes "sell themselves" in this manner, the sale of many others should be helped by suggestions from the cashier.

The old question, "Will there be anything else?" is practically useless as it is sure to be followed by the programmed response, "No, I don't think so." However, if a salesman suggests that a new pair of shoes needs the protection of wax or that a new pair of hose would complement the shoes, the chances for success are infinitely greater. This last-minute selling effort is made considerably easier by the careful placement of a counter display to remind both the salesman and the customer.

Permanent P.O.P. Displays

The term "permanent display" should not be taken literally. Unless the life of the retail store is extremely short, virtually no display is permanent. "Permanent" is used to express a relative measure, compared to many dump bins and other P.O.P. displays that exist only a few weeks. Most of the so-called permanent P.O.P. displays are furnished by manufacturers in an attempt to gain more shelf space. Over the years, three common types of P.O.P. units for displaying merchandise on a shelf have emerged. These are shelf dividers, shelf extenders, and spring loaders.

Shelf Dividers

This device usually sits on the shelf and contains notches into which the merchandise is placed. They are usually designed to display merchandise at an angle most appropriate for lateral vision.

Shelf Extenders

This is a small tray that is fastened to the shelf and extends beyond it to give additional shelf space.

Spring Loader

A spring loader is simply a special tray or double-deck tray with a spring attached to the rear. As items are loaded into this tray, they are continually held tight by the push of the spring from behind. This device is widely used as a counter display at the checkout stand.

Posters

Posters are undoubtedly the most common form of P.O.P. material used in retail stores. They can be printed on an infinite variety of material and sizes. They may take the form of a banner or, as it is sometimes called, streamer. The low cost and storewide applicability of posters ensure their popularity with retailers. Posters may also take the form of counter cards when mounted on a paperboard back. These are generally placed in store windows or on the counter.

Traditional rules for the design of posters have called for a clear style with easy-to-read numbers and letters, combined with an easy-to-understand message and illustration. It has also been felt traditionally that a poster should not attempt to relay more than a single message, such as "Fire Sale," "Vacation in Hawaii," "Fresh Peaches," or other simple messages.[33]

In recent years the growth of pop art, black-light posters, soul messages, and similar forms of expression has shown that traditional rules may be broken with success. This is not to say that overnight acceptance of such P.O.P. material is a wise policy for the retailer. However, if the retailer sells pop records, or clothing oriented to young customers, these posters may be absolute necessities.

Window Displays

Window displays, which represent the face of a store, must be viewed as a reflection of what is inside. For this reason, most large retail chains refuse to leave window dressing to chance. Instead, store managers are sent packaged store dressings complete with instructions and a photograph demonstrating how the window is to look. Manufacturers also realize the value of window displays, and may provide professionally created displays for a retailer's window.

Many retailers have found that they can create special buying moods by using a promotion aimed at a particular country or event. (Exhibit 14–4) For example, a week aimed at featuring the goods and services of Mexico can produce sales for Mexican goods, and may include a special section in which tours are sold. In cases such as this, the window display should feature a Mexican decor. The cost of such a program can be minimized by cooperation, or tie-in, promotion with other firms or organizations interested in promoting Mexico. Airline companies, national tourist promotion bureaus, and so forth, are usually anxious to supply material and labor to assist in window displays. These types of promotions can be used in slump buying periods to create new customer interest and to attract new customers to a store.

Retailers are often asked to display posters for neighborhood clubs, high schools, and other groups. Unless prior planning is given to these requests, a retailer can easily find his windows filled with a variety of signs that detract from the overall

Exhibit 14–4 **Use of an "Active Summer" Theme in a Window Display.** *This theme and type of display were used throughout the store.*

Source: Photo courtesy of May D&F.

appearance of the window and the store. Rather than either accept or reject all posters, a display policy can be used to the benefit of all.

Many retailers let it be known that their windows are available at certain times of the year at no cost to local groups. Schools, in particular, are encouraged to develop a window display for their homecoming, spring prom, or other events. These are particularly effective when a professional display person from the retail store helps coordinate the activity. Fall and winter sportswear may be featured along with the homecoming decorations. Spring formal wear can be arranged with posters and other information concerning the prom. These traditional displays generate a great deal of interest from sidewalk viewers and can have a strong appeal for teenage target markets. They also demonstrate the retailer's interest in community events.

Objectives of Window Displays

An effective window display has the following objectives:

1. To increase the drawing power of the store by attracting the attention of passing consumers
2. To achieve an attractive presentation of merchandise and services
3. To project a fashion or quality image

4. To convey a value or price image
5. To support other promotional activities of the firm
6. To show the consumer the selection of merchandise and services offered by the firm
7. To arouse the interest of consumers so that needs are suggested

Accomplishing the Objectives

The method of constructing window displays is based on (1) attracting the attention of consumers, (2) identifying with consumer needs, (3) conveying the appropriate message, and (4) providing an attractive presentation. It should be noted that the aesthetic aspect has been placed last. This is done deliberately to demonstrate that the window display must be a commercial means of communication with the future buyer, not merely a work of art.

Attracting Attention

The use of lighting, color and movement are the three methods of attracting the attention of passing consumers. A well-lighted window attracts attention. A brighter lighting intensity or the use of colored lights can add a great deal to the attention-getting power of a window display. For example, a specially placed spotlight can be used to emphasize the important areas of a display.

Color is another important factor in creating a unique atmosphere. Most consumers are sensitive to colors, so retailers can choose colors that are appropriate for the season. Blues, yellows, green and pink colors are used to reflect a spring theme and brown, tans and orange are colors used to create an image of fall.

Almost any form of movement also captures the attention of passersby. Animated displays, toys, or other types of moving devices can be used to attract attention.

Identifying With Consumer Needs

A well-designed window display must stimulate the consumer's interest by arousing the consumer's imagination. It must promote satisfactions that parallel the consumer's needs and not merely present goods for sale. Thus a good window display should serve as a mirror in which future customers can picture themselves. Naturally, consumer needs vary with the season. Thus, window display themes must also vary with the season. A seasonal theme should be developed from the viewpoint of personal situations that correspond with the seasons—return to school, graduation, gifts for Christmas, Mother's Day, Father's Day, Easter, and Mother-in-law Day. The reader may note that some holidays and special days have been created to encourage retail sales.

Conveying the Appropriate Message

A window display might include a written message to be better understood by consumers. A short text written in large type is frequently used to deliver a special message. For example, an office supply store may use a professional activities theme to guide its window display. The written message may read "For your profession: A calculator that works for you." The products displayed might be game type calculators for children, inexpensive calculators for younger students, scientific calculators for advanced students, financial calculators for business students and business people, printing calculators for accountants, and so forth.

A retailer can change window displays regularly and use them to show merchandise that is considered to be "the newest" to accomplish the objective of projecting a fashion or quality image. If the objective of the window display is to project a value or price image, the store's best buys can be prominently displayed in the window along with price tags that are clearly visible to the consumer.

Window displays can also be used to support other promotional activities of the firm. For example, the window display can feature both the merchandise and the store's latest newspaper advertisement.

The use of window displays can also convey the message of the selection of merchandise and services that the store offers. The window displays do this if a selective rotation of goods and services are features in the everchanging store windows.

Providing an Attractive Presentation

Attractive decorations can be used to communicate the sales message as well as be aesthetically pleasing. Window displays should contain suggestions instead of including all types of merchandise in the display. The most important objective of a window display is to encourage consumers to enter the store. A window display that conveys the impression that everything of interest is contained in the window leaves little incentive for the consumer to enter the store. It is therefore suggested that only a modest number of items be exhibited in the window. This recommendation is consistent with the belief that an uncluttered display helps to improve the presentation of merchandise and allows consumers to picture themselves using the product. The inclusion of too many items in a window simply creates the impression of confusion and disorganization.

The window display should appear to be balanced. Poorly balanced arrangements appear to be untidy and disorganized. Balance is obtained by placing items of equal size at equal distances from the center of the display.

Backgrounds for window displays may be full, partial or open. A full background, which blocks off the view of the store, can be used to provide an attractive setting for the display. The background should not be left bare but should hold signs, posters, decorative material, or display props. Merchandise can then be suspended from the background or leaned against it. A display positioned against a full background frequently generates more consumer attention because there are no in-store distractions present.

Partial backgrounds allow consumers to see inside the store. The goal is to get consumers to look at the display, then follow their impulse to join the in-store crowd.

The display is shown against the background of the store's interior in the open background display. This type of window display must blend in with the rest of the store. It does give the consumer an invitation to inspect interior displays and to join the in-store crowd.

Specialty Advertising

Specialty advertising consists of matchbooks, calendars, blotters, paper clamps, and other novelty items that are frequently used to keep the name of the retailer in front of consumers. This type of reminder advertising is best suited for outlets where consumers shop infrequently. The institutional message, of no more than five to ten words, should be used to communicate that the outlet is ready to meet consumer needs in specific merchandise-service areas.[34] This type of reminder message can usually indicate only who the retailer is, where his outlets are located, and what he sells. Short reminder messages of this type are usually supplemented with other forms of promotion which contain a more detailed message.

Specialties are generally more effective in keeping customers than in attracting new customers. These specialty items represent an invitation to continue to buy and a token of appreciation for the consumer's patronage. The effectiveness of a specialty item depends upon the attractiveness of the item to the consumer and upon its distribution. Items that are unusual but that can help solve small customer problems are likely to be used and valued more by the consumer. Because the message is presented each time the item is used, retailers should give items that will be used more often than those that are given away by their competitors. The items may also be associated with the business. For example, a gasoline service station may give away a free ice scraper imprinted with its name, address, telephone number, and store hours.

Matchbooks, calendars, pens, and pencils are the most frequently used specialties. Specially designed covers on book matches and calendars can increase the exposure of a retailer's advertisement by being used and displayed by consumers instead of being discarded. The effectiveness of such calendars, pens, and pencils is likely to depend on who receives them. A housewife will probably use these items because she is seldom oversupplied with them. Businesspeople probably receive many of these items from other sources and may not use them unless they possess some unique feature. A calendar, if displayed in a popular place of business consistent with the retailer's image, can be an effective but inexpensive type of advertising. The trick is to get the calendar displayed in other places of business that serve your target customers.

Theater Screen Advertising

Movie watchers are a fairly captive audience, so 40- to 60-second theater screen advertisements can be used to disseminate the retailer's message. The advertisement may consist of either slide or film presentations that are inserted between feature movies, news, and shorts. The rates are usually based on theater attendance. The retailer will want to consider how well the characteristics of the audience match those of the target market consumers before the firm commits itself to a long-run contract. Contracts are usually issued on a weekly basis, so a retailer may benefit by advertising only during those weeks when the featured movie appeals to the target market.

Sales Promotion

It should be recalled that sales promotions are different from advertising in that mass media are not used. Sales promotions include the use of premiums, such as stamps, free gifts, contests, and so forth. Sales promotions also include consumer services, such as packaging, alterations, wrapping, delivery, refunds and exchanges, and credit. The various types of sales promotion are designed to encourage the immediate sale of merchandise or service and to keep customers loyal to the store.

Premiums

The major appeal of premiums is that the customer believes he is getting something for nothing. Stamps and small gifts are thought of as being free. Even contests and sweepstakes give the consumer a chance to win something for nothing. Some of the more frequently used gifts include the following.

Giveaways or Traffic Builders

These are small items, such as a piece of candy or gum, a trash bag, and so forth, which are given away with each purchase.[35]

Referrals

"Thank you" gifts are given to customers who send their friends to your outlet.

New-Customer Gift

These are small, free gifts that are given to new customers the first time they enter the outlet.

Continuity Program

Given one at a time, matched glasses, chinaware, towels, and so forth, keep customers coming back to complete the set.

Trading Card

Customers can collect a free gift when their card is completely punched out—after making the necessary amount of purchases. If the free gift is some service—say a free car wash by an automatic machine—it can be a real benefit to the customer and still increase retail costs only slightly.

Trading Stamps and Games

Trading stamps and games, which are also used to promote retail sales, have been historically linked to supermarkets, service stations, and an assortment of small retailers, including a few small, independent department stores. These promotional techniques were never adopted in significant numbers by large department stores, discount houses, car dealers, furniture outlets, and many other types of retailers. There have been a few exceptions in almost every retail category, but they are the exception rather than the rule.

History shows that national diffusion occurred in the period 1951–1962 for trading stamps and in the period 1962–1966 for games. After these periods, the popularity and use of both methods declined.[36] The decline in the use of both promotional techniques may be traced to several developments.

1. The industry became saturated with both techniques. As a result, little or no competitive advantage was left.
2. Discount houses and other retailers who had not accepted stamps offered increasingly heavy competition to those with stamps. In fact, advertising campaigns were built around the fact that a particular store did not give stamps and thus offered consumers a savings.
3. In some areas, retailers were forced into stamp wars, in which a significant number of extra stamps were given for purchases.
4. The attitude of shoppers changed. People actually formed protest movements in certain areas against stamps, games, and other promotional techniques.
5. Stores that had dropped stamps and games reported initial losses, but then reported profit gains without giving stamps. Stamp companies charge the retailer between 1.5 and 3 percent of sales volume.[37] For many retailers, the expense associated with stamps is greater than their entire advertising expenditure. Recently some retailers have again started to use trading stamps and games to attract customers.

The history of these promotional techniques offers retailers several important lessons concerning these and other new promotional techniques that may occur in the future. These may be summarized as follows:

1. The use of promotional techniques that are readily available to other retailers cannot replace sound retailing/merchandising strategies and planning.
2. Consumer preferences and response to promotional techniques may shift in short periods of time, so that what was in vogue last year is the villain this year.

3. The first retailers to use new promotional techniques may easily capture larger market sales and gain greater profits in the short run; however, once the technique becomes widespread, they may easily be in a worse competitive condition than other, more powerful, retailers who adopt the same technique.

4. Dependency upon a promotional technique overlooks the fact that strong new retailers and retailing concepts may emerge while the older retailers are engaged in a competitive promotional battle.

5. It is evident that a particular market segment is attracted to stores that offer particular promotional techniques such as stamps and games. As a result, it may be possible for certain retailers, particularly independent stores and chains, to use these techniques as long as large competitors do not adopt the practices. This is particularly true after larger competitors have tried and discontinued the techniques.

Publicity

Unique approaches are required to get favorable publicity for retail outlets. Since the retailer does not have to pay for the coverage, the media programmers and writers must believe that the item appeals to the general population. Consumerism and ecological and minority-opportunity program campaigns may be used to bring the retailer's name before the public. No matter what the appeal is, a skilled writer and speaker is usually required to place the item in the media.[38]

Many retailers seem to feel that by hiring a specialist in publicity, or a P.R. director, they have satisfied the need to "do something" about publicity. Publicity extends well beyond placing free articles in newspapers. In fact, the values to be obtained extend beyond those of the promotional mix. They have a direct bearing upon employee morale, motivation, and education.

A large department store is faced with an abundance of publicity opportunities. Nearly every department will find there are clubs, fraternal organizations, and consumer groups that are interested in knowing more about their particular products. Art groups and garden clubs are examples of types of organizations with special interest in particular products. Yet all too often the only contact a retailer of garden supplies or art goods has with these groups consists of sending a $10 item to the yearly benefit auction.

The growing interest among American consumers in wines and specialty foods provides invaluable publicity opportunities. Retailers have found they can sponsor wine-tasting parties at a cost to the customer. These are excellent opportunities to educate the customer concerning wines—at cost—and at the same time subtly sell one's products. Retailers who sell baby goods might profit through infant-care sessions for expectant mothers. Auto supply stores might find a full house for a profitable evening on the need for high-quality motor lubricants.

We are an affluent nation—a nation of consumers—in which one of the most popular pastimes is shopping. In this environment, there is little reason to believe that consumers will not respond to well-planned informative sessions on the products retailers sell. The success of many retailers in this area has proved that the problem is not lack of consumer interest but, rather, lack of employee time to honor all the speaking opportunities they would receive.

Major Store or Group Promotions

Retail outlets that are located within close geographical boundaries may group together and organize an area retail promotion. Downtown merchants, especially those located in smaller towns, often use the Chamber of Commerce as the organization that plans the promotion by establishing the theme, coordinating the advertising and store hours, and so forth. Two of the more popular promotions take the format of a "Crazy Daze" where prizes are given to the retail clerks who wear the "best" costumes and prizes are given away to customers, and "Moonlight Madness" where the stores offer prizes and lower prices on merchandise during the late evening hours, 8 p.m.–11 p.m.

Shopping centers usually have a promotional director who plans and implements the major promotions for the center. The promotions are scheduled to coincide with peak sales periods such as the Easter, back-to-school, and Christmas seasons. The promotions may feature a circus, a clown, a carnival, or any other attention-attracting activity. Large department stores today have an executive who usually goes by the title of Director of Special Events. Neiman-Marcus has its world-renowned Fortnight promotion. Macy's has its Thanksgiving Day Parade. Better stores feature designer trunk showings, noon fashion shows in the tea room, bridal fashion shows, cooking schools, and so forth.

Summary

Selection of the media that will most effectively reach the retailer's target market consumers must include consideration of the characteristics of each medium. Retailers rely heavily upon printed media and radio for their promotional efforts. Some newspapers have the advantage of serving a specific geographical group of people, so they can be used to reach the local target market with minimal waste circulation. Direct mail, including catalog mailings, can be used to reach a specifically defined target group if a good mailing list is available. Coupons are frequently used to promote sales of special items that are designed to draw customers to the store. The Yellow Pages serve as reminder advertising and provide a listing to attract new customers. The chief advantage of Yellow Page advertising is the continuous exposure offered for a long-life period of one year.

Radio is one of the most flexible media in that many different stations offer many different programs at any time of day. Also, its per minute cost of advertising is relatively inexpensive. Thus retailers can use radio to reach their target market at a fairly low cost. Repeated radio advertisements may be required to be effective, however, since listenership changes nearly every hour and the message is presented for only a few seconds at a time. Television is a useful medium for large retailers who serve most, if not all, of the area reached by the television station.

Advertising by signs is more suitable for institutional image promotion than for product—direct-action promotion because it is expensive to change the message. Point-of-purchase (P.O.P.) promotions are used to create a buying mood after the consumer reaches the outlet.

Nearly all retailers use window displays to attract the attention of passing consumers and show them a limited selection of the type of merchandise and service offered by the firm. Retailers use lighting, color, and movement in their window displays to attract consumer attention.

Sales promotions use the appeal that the consumer believes he is getting something for nothing. The first retailers to use new promotional techniques can gain short-run sales increases until competitive outlets adopt similar techniques and a promotional war begins.

Individual retailers and groups of retailers are the sponsors of many major promotions that usually coincide with a peak sales season such as Easter, back-to-school, Christmas, and so forth. Downtown retailers usually organize such promotions through the local Chamber of Commerce. Most shopping centers provide a full-time promotional director to organize these promotions. The Director of Special Events in most large department stores organizes the store's promotional efforts.

Questions

1. What are the advantages and disadvantages that a small, independent retailer obtains from using newspaper advertising?

2. When should newspaper advertising be used by a retailer? When should it not be used?

3. What are the advantages that direct mail advertising offers to retailers? Under what conditions should direct mail advertising be used by retailers?

4. Why do most retailers advertise in the Yellow Pages? What percentage of its advertising budget would you recommend that a small, independent repair shop spend in the Yellow Pages? What percentage of its advertising budget would you recommend that a large supermarket that is affiliated with a large, national chain organization spend in the Yellow Pages?

5. What factors should one consider when creating a print advertisement?

6. What factors should one consider when creating a broadcast advertisement?

7. What are the advantages of radio as an advertising medium for retailers? What are the disadvantages? Under what circumstances should radio advertising be used by retailers?

8. What does television advertising have to offer retailers? Under what circumstances should it be used?

9. Develop a window display for a local apparel outlet. What factors do you have to consider when creating a window display?

10. Why do sales promotions appear to be most effective for the first retailer to use them?

Footnotes

1. Jerome B. Kernan, William P. Dommermuth, and Montrose S. Sommers, *Promotion: An Introductory Analysis* (New York: McGraw-Hill, 1970), pp. 11–13.

2. Ibid., p. 203.

3. Ibid.

4. Laurence W. Jacobs, *Advertising and Promotion for Retailing* (Glenview, Ill.: Scott, Foresman, 1972), pp. 6–15.

5. Ibid.

6. Ibid., p. 118.

7. Ibid., p. 124.

8. Ibid., p. 119.

9. Ibid., p. 120.

10. A. C. Nielsen, Jr., "The Impact of Retail Coupons," *Journal of Marketing,* October 1965, pp. 11–15.

11. Ibid.

12. *The Yellow Pages in Marketing and Advertising* (New York: American Telephone and Telegraph Co., 1970), p. 17.

13. Ibid.

14. Kernan et al., *Promotion,* p. 205.

15. Ibid., p. 207.

16. Jacobs, *Advertising and Promotion,* p. 123.

17. Ibid., p. 121.

18. Ibid., p. 123.

19. Ibid., p. 156.

20. David Ogilvy, *How to Create Advertising that Sells* (New York: Ogilvy and Mather Advertising Agency, n.d.), p. 1.

21. Ibid.

22. Ibid.

23. Ibid.

24. Adapted from Jacobs, *Advertising and Promotion,* p. 161; Carl W. Birchard, "Distinctive Advertising for Small Stores," *Journal of Retailing,* Spring 1964, pp. 23–29, 50; Harry W. Hepner, *Effective Advertising* (New York: McGraw-Hill, 1949), pp. 558–560.

25. Richard Elkman, "Positioning: Wave of the 70's," *The Competitive Edge,* October 1977, p. 90.

26. Jacobs, *Advertising and Promotion,* p. 174.

27. Ibid., p. 174.

28. Ogilvy, *How to Create Advertising that Sells,* p. 1.

29. Jacobs, *Advertising and Promotion,* p. 125.

30. Kurt H. Vahle, *The Importance of Color in Advertising* (New York: Direct Mail Advertising Association, n.d.) p. 3.

31. Association of National Advertisers, *Advertising at the Point of Purchase* (New York: McGraw-Hill, 1957), p. 1.

32. "Supermarket Panel Cites Growing Interest in P.O.P.," *Advertising Age,* 30 August 1972, p. 2.

33. Harvey Offenhartz, *Point of Purchase Design* (New York: Reinhold Book Corp., 1968), p. 111.

34. Jacobs, *Advertising and Promotion,* p. 126.

35. William C. Battle, "Attract—and Hold—Customers with Premiums," *Motor,* September 1967, pp. 80–81.

36. Fred C. Allvine, "The Future for Trading Stamps and Games," *Journal of Marketing* 33 (January 1969): 45–52.

37. Jacobs, *Advertising and Promotion,* p. 187.

38. A list of dos and don'ts that can guide the nonprofessional in preparing publicity releases is presented in Harold L. Jenkins, *Action Marketing for Savings Institutions* (Chicago: Savings Institutions Marketing Society of America, 1972), pp. 168–169.

Case Study

Southeast Grocery (B)

Mr. Greene, the owner-operator of Southeast Grocery described in Chapter 13, has decided that the firm does need to increase its promotional efforts. He is considering using trading stamps, games, continuity programs in which the consumer can purchase a small part of a complete set, such as a piece of silverware, for a specified dollar amount of purchases, and the giving of in-store coupons that can be used to purchase specified merchandise at much lower prices.

Discussion Questions

1. What are the advantages of using each of these promotional techniques?

2. What are the disadvantages of using each of these promotional techniques?

3. Which technique do you believe would be most effective for Southeast Grocery?

4. What are the nationwide trends regarding the use of each technique in the supermarket industry?

Southeast Grocery Company (C)

Mr. Greene has increased the efficiency of his promotional efforts. The firm's annual sales increased by twenty percent as a result of the more effective promotion.

Mr. Greene has become interested in using a Universal Product Code (UPC) and an Electronic Checkout System (ECS) similar to the system used by Midwest Supermarkets in Chapter 3. He believes that this system could increase the efficiency of the firm's merchandise management, reduce labor handling and transportation costs, and result in a faster and more accurate checkout process. Indeed, it appears that with all of these advantages Southeast Grocery should adapt the UPC-ECS system.

Discussion Questions

1. What are the chief benefits that the UPC-ECS system would provide Southeast in the area of merchandise management?

2. What are the estimated cost savings associated with the use of such a system by Southeast Grocery?

3. What are the disadvantages of Southeast Grocery's using such a system?

4. What do you recommend that Southeast Grocery do?

Chapter 15

Personal Selling
and Consumer Services

1. To understand the role professional salespeople play in retailing.

2. To be able to describe the appropriate orientation for retail sales staffs and define common job tasks.

3. To be able to discuss the retail selling environment, including the selling process, the training and evaluation of sales personnel and appropriate compensation systems.

4. To be aware of the profitability of merchandising customer services.

5. To understand the role of consumer credit in retail sales management.

6. To be able to identify the critical elements in a customer complaint system designed to provide customer satisfaction.

marketing concept

major elements of
a retail sale

selling process

stages of buying

trading up

straight salary

customer service
policies

consumer credit
legislation

Consumer Products
Warranty and
Guaranty Act of 1970

delivery service

This chapter focuses on the two elements in retailing that the consuming public most often finds unsatisfactory: the quality of personal selling and consumer services.

Personal Selling

Personal selling is the heart of all retailing. Advertising can attract consumers to the store, but the face-to-face communication that occurs in personal selling provides unique opportunities. As salespersons talk with customers they can read the customers' reactions and identify the individual consumer's needs. Salespeople then can tailor their message to meet the specific needs of that customer. The face-to-face communication also allows salespeople to provide information that will reduce consumers' uncertainties about the product/service offering. Only through personal selling can the customers receive individualized feedback from the retailer.

The Decline of the Selling Profession

Traditionally, personal salesmanship has been the final vital link in the distribution process. Drummers, peddlers, and traveling salesmen sold the industrial output of this nation from its birth. However, immediately following World War II and during the Korean conflict the demand for goods far exceeded the nation's capacity to produce the needed goods. Few salespersons were needed because merchandise was either rationed or allocated. However, in the late 1950s supply exceeded demand and a new method to stimulate consumer consumption was needed. A partial answer was found in the marketing concept.

The *marketing concept* suggests that profitable consumer consumption should begin with the determination of customer needs and be followed by the design of a package of goods and services that best meets those needs.

As an outgrowth of the application of the marketing concept, the mass media gained widespread acceptance both by consumers and producers as the most efficient means of moving merchandise. Significant research was undertaken in the applied behavioral sciences to determine why people purchased goods. Almost simultaneously the technologies of radio, television, and modern printing made great strides in providing excellent vehicles to present newly devised promotion strategies. "Preselling" and "self-service" were the bywords of the day. Mass media could sell anything to anyone given appropriate consumer research, product strategy, promotion design and enough money for implementation.

Some twenty years later there is a growing realization that a vital part of the marketing process is missing: personal salesmanship. It is quite true that many products, usually convenience items, can be presold by a combination of national branding and preselling via advertising. But not all products can be classified as convenience goods, nor can they be sold by mass merchandising techniques. Custom stereo systems require human interaction if the customer is to achieve the best sound reproduction available within a given budget constraint. If the purchaser wishes to listen to classical music, one set of components may render a "truer" sound than another. Such technical jargon as "watts per channel," "frequency response," "signal to noise ratio," "Dolby system," and many other terms become critical if the purchasers wish to get their money's worth.

In every sector of our retail system, products have become so complex that the average layman cannot make buying decisions independently. For a period of time the consumer relied on the old but not necessarily true maxim, "You get what you pay for." Price became the rule-of-thumb short-cut criterion for making purchase decisions. Unfortunately, some unscrupulous merchants noted this inclination and put high prices on products of inferior quality. Some people would argue that this practice is still in vogue.

Another semisuccessful technique for supplying buying information resulted in detailed package labeling. The federal government endorsed this action and together with industry convinced many consumers to read labels and do comparative shopping for the best buy.

Comparative shopping involves going to different stores and comparing similar products. Suppose you want a pair of jeans at a price you can afford. What characteristics must the jeans you purchase possess? Some criteria might include proper fit, weight of denim, regular or fashionable cut, zipper versus button closure, and relative price. Once the criteria are specified they must be put in order of importance. Which quality is most important? Usually the purchaser selects either price or fashion as the most important, followed by the other items, which represent personal preferences.

Next, the purchaser must limit his or her search pattern. With the cost of transportation increasing, one may want to minimize costs and time by making all purchases on one shopping trip to a regional shopping center where different stores will carry a broad assortment of goods on the shopping list. Once at the center, one simply goes from store to store noting the differences in merchandise based on the previously prepared criteria. Ideally, the purchase decision will be made easier by such objective preparation, but most of the time consumers are swayed by current stocks, availability of sizes and styles and where they can use a credit card. The retailer equivalent of this practice is called "shopping the competition." The criteria on products remain much the same; but additional factors of display, interior location, and fixturing become items of competitive interest. This latter practice should be carried out by every retailer regularly in order to be aware of what is going on in the market.

Not all products lend themselves to easy comparison. A growing consumer movement is actively advocating the purchase and use of generic pharmaceutical and food products. Generic products do not carry a brand name but are labeled with a list of ingredients. Usually these products sell for substantially less because they bear no advertising costs. Entire research laboratories and magazine empires were built by far-sighted business persons to test competitive products and report their findings. All of these actions, while laudable, are not enough to instill the degree of consumer confidence that a good salesperson can generate in face-to-face contacts.

Ethical Considerations:
Salesperson versus Con-Artist

At the outset of this discussion it is critically important to differentiate between salespersons and "hype-specialists." Unfortunately, few true salespersons are active in the current marketing system. A salesperson is an individual truly interested in matching consumer needs and product characteristics for optimal customer satisfaction, organizational profit, and personal gain in that order. Hype-specialists attempt to prey on the gullible and put their own self-interest ahead of their customer's satisfaction. They profit in the short run but must move often to work new territories as their reputation becomes widely known. In contrast, salespersons view the occupation as a career and attempt to establish a reputation for honesty and integrity that generates repeat business and a personal following.

Somewhere in the middleground one finds "cash register clerks" and "sackers." The former usually inhabit central cash-wrap stations and are trained to make a high volume of transactions in the shortest period of time. "Sackers" usually only handle cash transactions in express checkout lines and "sack" the merchandise. Management has not trained these clerks to sell or give more than rudimentary information. Such is in keeping with the self-service concept, which strives to keep personnel costs to a minimum. While a discussion of detailed sales training is beyond the scope of this book, it should be noted that an individual does not become a salesperson overnight. Various organizations, particularly house-to-house distributors, give intensive training in high-pressure selling techniques before the representative is placed in the field. In contrast, many of the life insurance firms spend considerable sums on training effective salespersons who take time to tailor their proposed insurance packages to the needs and goals of their clients. Other firms may hold periodic sales training sessions that stress both product knowledge and motivation. Perhaps the most important traits of any successful salesperson include acute perception of individual human behavior, personal positiveness that comes across as confidence rather than arrogance, and good health, which permits the long hours required in pursuit of sales. These traits will not make a salesperson, but they are beneficial attributes to be developed on the road to a profitable sales career.

In summary, salespersons are motivated to spend time and personal effort to either help the customer identify specific needs or present available merchandise/service offerings that will best meet the customer needs. Such efforts will entail considerable personal interaction, patience, and positive product presentations to achieve satisfactory merchandise/service matches. Occasionally, after a fair effort the salesperson must candidly admit that other products/services are better choices than he or she can offer and accept the loss of a sale. If this should occur, the salesperson should report these product/service deficiencies to top management so that adjustments in the marketing mix can be made and the offering restored to its competitive position. Thus, sales personnel provide a vital marketing service, feedback, so that the consumer will have greater choices in the future.

Retail Selling Environment

The major elements involved in a retail sale are the outlet and its policies, its merchandise, its promotion policies, its customers, and its salespeople. Salespeople need to be familiar with the store and its policies before they can offer the customer any reliable advice. First, the salesperson must know the types, price ranges, and quality of merchandise that the outlet has available. Second, the individual must know what services the store offers to its customers. A salesperson must be knowledgeable about the firm's delivery, credit, adjustment, and product/service offerings to serve the customers effectively. A working knowledge of the layout of the entire store is helpful in locating merchandise for consumers who have difficulty finding specific items.

The store's promotion policy should be another vital area of concern to the sales staff. The promotion mix concept should be understood by the sales organization so they know that advertising, sales promotion, and personal selling require coordinated teamwork to communicate with consumers successfully. The sales personnel should keep informed of the store's promotional activities by previewing and reading its advertisements, looking at its displays, and attending promotion meetings.

Useful merchandise information may be found by the salesperson on the label, tag, or package of the product and in wholesale or retail catalogs. Salespeople who represent manufacturers and wholesalers are excellent sources of information. Independent testing bureaus are another good informational source because their findings can be quoted to customers to enhance the credibility of the presentation.

The customer should be the focus of attention in every sale. The salesperson should realize that when a sale is to be made, the consumer must be pleased with the approach used and relatively satisfied with the outlet's merchandise and services if the sale is going to be of long-run benefit to the store. Thus, salespeople need to sell from the consumer viewpoint. To do this, the salesperson must be aware of consumer psychology and buying motives. Merchandise is purchased because it satisfies some consumer need for beauty, pride, romance, feeling important, comfort, convenience, durability, safety, health, or economy. Salespeople should attempt to identify each consumer's primary buying motives and determine what pleases or irritates that person.

Customers may be happily surprised when sales personnel have a thorough knowledge of the store's merchandise. The amount of information needed varies with the type of merchandise sold and the clientele served. High-priced products, such as automobiles, generally require the salesperson to be more knowledgeable. The salesperson should know the identity of the manufacturer, the ingredients or raw materials in the merchandise, its construction, color, size, model, and so forth. In addition, the salesperson should know what the product is used for, how it should be used, how it performs, and how much care and service it may require. Knowledgeable salespersons will acquire appropriate competitive product knowledge through their comparative shopping efforts so that they may answer customer objections and highlight their product's superior points.

The salesperson is the final element in the retail sale. The characteristics that are associated with successful retail salespeople may be discussed under five categories: objectivity, personal appearance, sociability, maturity, and mental alertness.[1]

Objectivity refers to the ability of salespeople to understand consumers from the individual consumer's point of view. By being objective, the salesperson can empathize with customers and then interpret their needs. Subjective salespersons are more concerned with forcing their own values and solutions on consumers than with solving the consumer's problems. Thus, subjective salespeople are not likely to be successful retail sales generators.

A good personal appearance is required to make a good initial impression on the consumer. The salesperson who is well groomed, poised, and uses correct speech and a pleasant tone of voice creates a good impression and gains the respect of consumers.

Sociability—the traits required to create an atmosphere in which consumers enjoy making purchases—include the enthusiasm displayed by salespeople and the ability to deal tactfully and courteously with consumers without offending them. Friendly retail salespeople make consumers feel welcome and greet them by name if possible. Salespeople who are confident about themselves give consumers the impression that they are receiving worthwhile opinions and suggestions.

Emotionally mature salespeople handle unpleasant situations smoothly because they are more understanding. They listen without judging and are better able to interpret the consumer's needs. Mature salespeople are also more dependable and industrious in being on the job and working hard to generate sales.

Mentally alert salespeople help make a sale by remembering customers and being knowledgeable about the features of the product/service offering that would best meet their demands and purchase capabilities. Salespersons must also use their imagination to interpret customers' needs in terms of the available merchandise/service opportunities. Retail salespeople must also be accurate in their handling of countless details and still remain courteous to all customers.

The Selling Process

After the salesperson has an understanding of the retail selling environment, he or she should consider the selling process. The selling process is a systematic series of steps needed to make a successful sale. These steps include: the approach, the sales presentation, handling objections, and the close.[2] Each segment of the process must be well planned and executed if the salesperson's time and efforts are to be rewarded with sales and satisfied customers.

Prospecting: Identifying Potential Customers

Retail salespersons must tailor their initial customer contact methods to suit the buying habits of their target market clients. "Big-ticket" items such as automobiles, home furnishings, and insurance require salespersons to "prospect," or find the majority of their clients outside of the confines of a store and persuade them to "invest" in new retail products. Names and addresses of potential prospects can be gained through the purchase or rental of magazine lists, automobile registrations or business, or entertainment and travel charge account lists. Additional names may be gathered by regularly checking school graduation lists, and engagement, wedding, and birth announcements in the local newspaper as well as by checking the public records of real estate transactions.

Additional prospect leads may be acquired through company advertising, promotional contests that require participants to register for a prize, and referrals from friends, acquaintances, and satisfied customers. Most of these prospects may have to be contacted off the premises, while others will present themselves by walking through the doors of the establishment. Regardless of the sales contact locale, each potential prospect must be systematically evaluated, or qualified, so that the limited time and energies of the salesperson may be used to its best advantage.

Qualifying Prospects What characterizes a good prospect? A good prospect must be reasonably easy to approach or contact, be aware of unmet personal needs or wants, have the ability to buy, have authority to buy without restrictions from important "others" such as wives, or husbands, be capable of legally contracting to buy, and be able to reasonably view the salesperson's products as satisfying his or her needs.[3]

As an illustration of how qualifying factors work, any male appearing alone in an automobile showroom wearing a wedding band is considered a marginal prospect for the immediate sale of a new car or truck. Research has shown that most automobile decisions in a family are a collaborative effort. The male may determine the brand and technical product attributes while the female may decide body style, exterior color, and interior decor, although these decision areas often shift from one partner to another. Thus, a married couple would constitute a better opportunity or prospect for a sale than the lone married male.

This information is gained usually by conversation over the telephone or in the establishment during the initial encounter between the salesperson and the potential customer. Salespersons who attempt to sell products that require considerable expense or decision time will usually qualify their clients before they initiate the first contact by checking with friends, business associates, and others to determine the target clients "ability to deal."

The Approach: Bridging the Gap between Salesperson and Client

Most in-store contacts require quick prospecting, qualification, and the choice of the proper approach. Usually people visit a store for one of two purposes: (1) to make a specific purchase or (2) to browse, "kill time," or "just shop." Experienced salespersons have learned to respond differently to a variety of initial customer requests. When customers ask to see a specific item, the product approach is used. The salesperson immediately moves to the merchandise requested and lets the product sell itself. One assumes that customers have clearly perceived their needs and are interested in making the purchase. The objective of the product approach is to get the item in the potential customer's hands so that he or she can feel the potential psychological value associated with possessing the item. When the customer is made aware of the psychological satisfaction and the physical utility of the item, the urge to purchase becomes almost irresistible.

Alternately, if the initial customer response is one of uncertainty, but general interest is expressed in a product line, the service approach is appropriate. The main objective of this approach is to focus the customer's need and direct attention to the firm's specific product that will best meet this need. Quite often this approach is used by saying to the customer, "May I help you?," "Do you need help?" or "What do you want?" Unfortunately each one of these opening questions can be answered with an emphatic negative, which terminates the sales contact. An alternate set of questions might be "What may I show you?" or "How may I help you?" The questions clearly convey the desire to be of service as well as eliciting information that may lead to the sales presentation.

The browsing customer represents a challenge because that individual is primarily spending leisure time and is only marginally interested in specific products. Suggestive selling leading to an impulse purchase will require the use of the customer-benefit approach.[4] As the customer wanders through the store, the salesperson should select some new, unique item that might appeal to the customer and direct his or her attention to the unique product benefits without mentioning price. This approach requires a low keyed, helpful, informative approach such as, "Have you seen the new _____?" Here, a no leads into a sales presentation and a sale because the benefits are undeniable.

In summary, a good approach should attract the potential customer's attention in an appropriate manner, encourage the potential buyer to focus attention on a specific need-satisfying product, and provide a direct entry into a sales presentation. A successful approach represents the first third of the path to a satisfying sale.

The Sales Presentation

The sales presentation is the "showcase of selling." The product's most beneficial attributes are stressed and the negative factors minimized. A successful sales presentation is based on a positive, enthusiastic attitude toward the product being displayed or demonstrated. The salesperson should invest his or her personal credibility in each sales presentation. Such an approach stresses factual information, personal experience, and customer satisfaction features. The sales presentation must convey to the potential customer the sincere conviction that the salesperson has the best product for the individual's needs.

The purchase decision is a complex phenomenon. One authority postulates that the buying decision is composed of five separate stages.[5] The first stage is usually characterized by the customer's overt recognition of a need or a problem that is important enough to require attention. This recognition leads to the implementation of a search process to find satisfaction.

In the pursuit of satisfaction the customer searches for products or services that will yield adequate satisfaction at an affordable price. In order to arrive at a satisfactory solution to their problems, customers seek information, advice, and personal assurances that products will meet their needs. As the search process begins the customer enters the second buying stage, which is typified by the statement, "I'm interested in hearing what you have to say about my problem."[6]

The salesperson's role consists of translating the merchandise/service features into individualized consumer benefits and advantages. The salesperson must be able to talk well and listen well in this consumer problem-solving approach. The sales presentation should be short enough to make shopping a pleasant but businesslike experience. Naturally, arguments should be avoided and the consumer's feeling of risk in buying reduced by assurances that the store is reliable, the brand is dependable, and the salesperson has a personal interest in seeing that the customer is properly served. It is the salesperson's job to make the customer feel important. The consumers must believe that they are *buying*, not *being sold*.

The salesperson should present merchandise that reflects what he or she perceives will satisfy the customer's needs. A request to see a certain item simplifies the interpretation process and the salesperson can immediately show the desired item. In most cases the consumer may be a little vague. If this is the case, the salesperson must present merchandise that seems to satisfy the consumer's desires. The first merchandise shown is usually medium-price items.

Then the salesperson must decide whether to attempt *trading up*. Trading up consists of selling either a better-quality item or a larger quantity than the consumer intended to buy. Frequently, better-quality merchandise will last longer and/or need less service and thus generate more long-run consumer satisfaction than the lower-quality item requested by the customer. To use trading-up selling, a salesperson must know the product line and be able to point out the benefits of buying better merchandise. The approach should not be misleading or dishonest but an objective evaluation of the item's future benefit for the customer.

When the store is out of stock on the item requested, the consumer should be informed of the unavailability of the item immediately. If the outlet has something in that line which will satisfy the consumer, that item should be presented to the consumer when the out-of-stock condition is determined. The requested product should not be criticized but the benefits of the in-stock item should be pointed out.

Demonstrating or showing merchandise involves several considerations. First, it is desirable to obtain consumer participation by asking the person to handle or operate it just as he or she would in normal use. Second, the way the salesperson handles the merchandise shows personal respect for the item. The demonstration should also show the advantages promised by the salesperson.

This stage concludes with the effective salesperson summarizing his or her case as convincingly as possible so that the potential buyer will arrive at the third stage of the buying process.

If the salesperson has a thorough knowledge of the product and its appropriate application and conveys these need-satisfying qualitities in an effective persuasive manner, the customer will become convinced that "I need this product."[7] The alert salesperson can sense this third stage by picking up such cues as facial expressions, voice inflections, and other body language signs. These same indicators can signal negative responses or objections to the product being presented. Every salesperson must be prepared to deal with customer objections.

Meeting Objections

Consumer uncertainty in areas of product, price, and time give rise to most buying resistance. Thus the salesperson is frequently dealing with a customer who is not completely certain that the product under consideration is the best buy for him.

Good salespeople learn to anticipate consumer objections and incorporate answers to the objections into the presentation of the merchandise. By presenting the most appropriate items from a consumer viewpoint, the salesperson reduces the amount of product objections. By pointing out all the benefits offered by the item, the salesperson reduces the importance of the price objections by emphasizing value instead of cost.

Time objections usually come in the form of a customer's saying, "I'll have to think it over." The salesperson might agree that some thought is desirable before making the purchase, and then point out that the store allows merchandise to be taken home on approval or on credit with a liberal return policy.

Frequently, time objections are used as excuses that are supposed to conceal the real reason the consumer does not want to make the purchase. Such excuses are more difficult to handle than real objections because they do not reflect the honest opinion of the customer. Thus the real objection is not defined so that the salesperson can meet it. Further questions may be asked in an attempt to identify the objection. If this fails, the salesperson should not argue with or belittle the customer's opinion.

The entire process of meeting objections should inspire consumer confidence in the quality of the merchandise and the knowledgeability of the salesperson. Additionally the completion of this phase will complete the second third of the road to a successful sale.

Closing the Sale

Closing the sale involves the last two stages of the buying process. The customer mentally says, "I want to buy this product now" and "I will buy this product now from this salesperson."[8]

Successfully meeting all of the customer's objections leads the customer to accept the product as appropriate, useful, and affordable, but does not guarantee a sale. The gentle art of persuasion must lead the customer skillfully to the implementative action of actual purchase. Mentally agreeing with persuasive arguments is a significantly different act involving a lesser degree of personal commitment than signing a check or a credit agreement or counting out the cash. Thus, closing or asking for the order is a complicated process in itself and must be considered an art that is developed after much experience.

All closing techniques rely on the assumption that all product-related objections have been answered and a sale will take place if the appropriate implementative actions are taken. Professor Buskirk proposes six different closing approaches to be used in differing situations. These assumptive closing approaches include: (1) the physical action, (2) closing on an objection, (3) SRO (standing room only), (4) closing on a minor point, (5) the inducement close, and (6) asking for the order.[9]

Briefly, the physical close simply requires the salesperson to put his or her body in motion to implement the sale, such as marking any needed clothing alterations so the merchandise will better fit the buyer. Closing on an objection is often used by car salespersons by having the customer sign an offer to purchase that is lower than the quoted price. Then the salesperson goes to the sales manager who usually agrees and accepts "the deal." This approach quickly separates the lookers from the buyers and saves the salesperson valuable sales time to devote to other customers.

The standing room only (SRO) close technique stresses the need for immediate action to secure the last item of a limited supply of the product. Urgency is stressed, with the implication that if the customer is not willing to accept the proposition the next person standing in line will be delighted to accept the offer. Admittedly this close seems to be used more as products become scarce. This is a risky close because the customer has the opportunity to say, "No, thank you." On the positive side, such a close does force an immediate decision.

The use of closing on a minor point approach is often appropriate when the customer has difficulty selecting between two equally favorable products that the salesperson has presented. Usually these closes take the form of a question such as, "Which color do you like best, the metallic brown or the blue model?" One should note that the question contains the implicit assumption of purchase and the only decision left to be made by the customer is which one will best meet his or her tastes or needs. Most importantly, such a question is not answerable with a simple no, which keeps the potential sale alive.

The inducement close is usually based on the "bargain" philosophy. Such concession closes usually are made by increasing the product's seeming value by throwing in, or offering something "free," or immediate delivery, which will appeal to the buyers' possession need. Such gestures of good will often result in significant sales at a considerable profit with minor cost or inconvenience to the salesperson or the employing firm.

The last and most direct close involves directly asking for the purchase or order.[10] This direct approach is the most risky but is often appreciated by time-conscious customers. Once they have been persuaded to purchase the item, the actual transaction is anticlimactic and a nuisance to be handled expeditiously. If a person starts reaching for a wallet, purse, or pen, the sale should be closed by asking for the order.

In summary, the selling process provides a mechanism to examine buyer-seller relationships. Each transaction is unique, but the negotiation process follows predictable buying stages. Salespersons must use all their skill and knowledge to be sure each stage is successfully negotiated. The end result should be personal satisfaction for the customer, a feeling of accomplishment for the salesperson, a profit for the firm, and the continued functioning of our complex marketing-distribution system.

Developing Customer Good Will

A sincere expression of gratitude for the purchase is required before the consumer departs. In addition to indicating it was a pleasure to serve each consumer, the customer might be sent away by name. Attempts should be made to follow up on major purchases to determine if the customer was really satisfied, and why or why not. Consumers should be thanked for their interest even though they may not have made a purchase. Such actions promote customer good will that has a long-lasting effect.

Telephone Selling

Telephone selling is used by retailers and service firms to generate additional business and smooth the work schedule of sales and service personnel. Service firms benefit by making a "reminder call" the day before an appointment is scheduled to assure a full schedule the next day. Reminder telephone calls made by firms selling merchandise or services that are purchased on a regular basis can stimulate additional sales from regular customers who should be ready to repurchase the item or service. For example, dentists can call regular customers after a proper interval has passed and the customer is ready to have teeth cleaned and checked. The appointments can be scheduled for hours and days when the dentist is least busy. The same type of reminder system can be used by auto service stations that know the proper interval for oil and lube jobs, tune ups, and seasonal changeovers for individual customers.

This process requires a detailed follow-up file of index cards that identify the consumer, the last date of purchase, and the type of item or service purchased. The solicitation is brief and friendly. The call should be made at a time when it is convenient for the consumer to talk. Housewives should not be called at hours when they may be preparing meals. Naturally, solicitations should be made from a telephone other than the one designated to receive the firm's incoming calls.

Personal Selling Outside the Store

Welcome Wagon, Howdy Pardner, and other organizations are engaged in acquainting newcomers with local retailers. These organizations send their representatives to the homes of new residents to give them free gifts from numerous local retailers. The cost of sending their representatives to consumers' homes is spread over all participating retailers. Providing free gift coupons to those consumers who are new in the trading area is a good way to introduce these people to a firm's location and its merchandise/service offering. It is important that the regular in-store clerks accept the gift coupons with a high degree of enthusiasm. A poor follow-through at the store level will negate any good will obtained by the initial contact.

Because store loyalties are frequently established soon after the newcomer has relocated, getting the consumer's attention during this crucial period can yield good results. Approximately 20 percent of the U.S. population moves during a year, so the size of this mobile market segment is substantial.

Successful sales can begin in a store and conclude in the home. Many large department and some chain stores employ salespersons as interior decorators or coordinators. They take various samples of carpeting, draperies, and paint to the home at convenient times to work out custom applications of ready-made merchandise. Limited custom fitting is also available on such items as draperies, slipcovers, and tile installations. In the future this kind of additional service, for home decoration in particular, should become more prevalent and profitable as the number of new household formations increases.

Evaluation of the Sales Staff

Every store should have a continual training program for both new and experienced salespeople. Sales records offer an overall indicator of salespeople's performance. Dollar volume of sales, units sold, number of completed transactions, and gross margin contribution can all be used to indicate the sales performance of employees and identify any need for specific training. In addition, the percentage of consumer contacts that resulted in purchases can be obtained by dividing the number of transactions by the number of customer contacts. A dollar per consumer contact figure can be calculated by dividing the dollar sales volume by the number of consumer contacts.

Regardless of the type of evaluation used, it is necessary that the evaluation procedure be based on job-related criteria and be thoroughly understood by each salesperson. It is also important that the method of evaluation be seen as objective and fair by all employees. This may be difficult because some retail salespeople do more than merely sell. They may provide customer service, handle complaints, accept merchandise returns, stock shelves, wrap merchandise, and perform other housekeeping duties.

Compensating Salespeople

Retail salespeople are usually paid a *straight salary,* which is either a prespecified monthly salary or a predetermined hourly wage. The straight salary approach allows the store manager to direct a salesperson's activities more closely, and includes more shelf stocking, price marking, and so forth. However, it may not provide much incentive for the salesperson to make sales.

The *straight commission* method of compensation rewards salespeople only on the basis of their sales volume. At the end of a pay period, an employee's sales are multiplied by the prespecified percentage commission rate to determine his or her earnings. This plan provides considerable incentive for salespersons because their earnings are solely dependent on making sales. The commission method also allows dollar selling expense to be more flexible from a retailer's point of view. Employee compensation is reduced when sales volume declines and increased when sales volume increases. The reduction in compensation during a period of slack sales is not desirable from the employee's point of view because income is uncertain. Thus the salesperson may ask to borrow from a drawing account against anticipated commissions. In addition, it is difficult to encourage a salesperson who is compensated on a straight commission basis to perform housekeeping duties that do not directly increase sales.

Combination salary and commission or bonus plans are frequently used for compensating salespeople. The bonus or commission, added to a straight salary, provides an incentive to make sales and still maintains control over employee activities. The bonus may be a cash bonus or a premium bonus of merchandise or a service—anything from clocks to a television set to an automobile. The premium bonus is an especially attractive incentive for higher-paid employees, who may be influenced by members of their family who want to use the premium. The cash bonus may be more appealing to lower-income employees, since their need to purchase necessities may be quite high.

Fringe benefits are another way to compensate employees. Employee discounts on in-store purchases, medical and life insurance, savings plans, and profit-sharing plans may all be used to better compensate the employee. The use of fringe benefits can increase employee morale and encourage store loyalty. Deferred profit-sharing and savings plans encourage good salespeople to remain with the retail organization.

In review, the authors feel that the art and skill of personal selling is woefully deficient in our retail institutions. A combination of forces have led to the present state of cash-wrap transaction specialists. While such depersonalization and the mechanical approach to sales transactions seems to reduce selling costs and increase the dollar per square foot of sales for presold products, many profitable dollars are to be made in rendering a personal selling service in narrow-line, big ticket, fashion-oriented, specialized stores. The consuming public who patronize these establishments will recognize professional salesmanship and reward the individual and store with personal referrals. A career in retail selling can be personally satisfying and economically rewarding if the aspiring candidate chooses the proper segment of the industry and plies the trade diligently.

Customer Services

Retailers should establish customer service policies and procedures under which services will be offered. These policies must reflect the fact that some services are required to meet those offered by the most competitive outlets. Often the type of merchandise carried influences the degree of service required in the offering. Bulky, high-value items that need to be installed and repaired by experts require more service than small, low-cost items that require little or no maintenance. Higher-quality merchandise is generally associated with higher prices and more service to appeal to the quality-oriented consumer group. On the other hand, bargain merchandise is usually sold with little service. Business hours such as late-morning openings, evening and limited Sunday hours are often required to blend with the customers' shopping patterns. Customers' life styles may dictate offering child-care facilities for shopping mothers, a package checkroom, personal shoppers, party counseling and catering services, entertainment ticket facilities, and travel bureaus and post offices on the premises.

The location of a store may dictate that it must provide services to meet the needs of its customers. For example, a furniture store that is located far from the residences of its target market may have to offer delivery services.

The retailer must choose the firm's service offering from the consumer's point of view and cast them within the parameters of certain federal government edicts, particularly in the areas of credit and warranty maintenance. In general, the inclusion of certain service components enhances the perceived utility of products and services and often becomes an integral part of a product purchase decision. Free coffee in a small consumer lounge area, clean rest rooms, free minor repairs, and so forth, cost little but generate considerable good will. Other services, such as offering maintenance contracts for major appliances, package and gift wrapping, delivery, credit, and merchandise refunds and exchanges represent larger monetary expenditures and thus require further discussion.

Credit

Consumer credit in retail stores is now almost an institution. Barring serious social or economic disturbances, such as a depression, it is almost a permanent retailing tool. Although credit sales have grown tremendously since World War II, they are not new to retailing but, instead, have changed in form and amount. Retailers have discovered that credit can be a powerful, double-edged merchandising-corporate sword that can be used both as a merchandising tool and a source of profit.

Advantages Of Using Credit

Customer convenience in paying for an item or service can be as important (or more important) a selling tool as advertising, personal selling, promotion, and so forth. Sometimes credit can be the major difference in influencing the decision to shop one store instead of a competitor's. More generous credit terms may make a prospective customer consider the retailer's total product more favorably.

The advantages of using in-house credit are:

1. A more personal relationship can be maintained with credit customers, who feel they are part of the firm.
2. Credit customers are likely to be more loyal than cash customers who tend to go where bargains are the greatest.
3. Credit customers tend to be more interested in quality and service than in price.
4. Good will is built up and maintained more easily when credit is used.
5. Goods can be exchanged and adjustments made with greater ease and, if necessary, goods can also be sent out on approval.
6. Credit account records provide valuable market information, which will allow the firm to:
   a. have a permanent mailing list for special sales promotions or research projects
   b. discover opportunities for suggesting the purchase of certain items considered appropriate in the light of previous purchases, buying habits, and so forth
   c. gather material concerning sales by department or by individual sales personnel, and
   d. detect any decline in purchases that might suggest a drifting away from the firm.
7. The firm's return on investment can increase if credit stimulates sales, because additional business can be secured and sometimes handled at practically no additional expense, thereby, reducing per unit costs.[11]

Whenever credit is extended by the retail outlet, it costs money. However, many retailers believe that credit extension is both necessary and attractive. Apparently, many target customers find immediate possession important enough to outweigh any extra costs.

Through the use of credit, individual retailers have demonstrated that demand for their products and services can be increased. In addition, total retail industry demand has increased through the use of credit. Whereas other promotional techniques, such as trading stamps, simply shift purchase patterns from one retailer to another, credit increases demand for goods and services in total.

Without credit, the demand for consumer durables such as refrigerators, boats, and automobiles would shrink markedly. The establishment of an installment credit department, General Motors Acceptance Corporation (GMAC), by General Motors played an important part in the tremendous marketing success of this firm.

Commercial bankers traditionally have been slow to finance new consumer durables, particularly when the payback period seemed long. However, this policy is changing rapidly, and the progressive banks and credit unions are broadening their loan portfolios and extending gradually lengthening maturities.

A sales program aimed at acquainting bankers with the merits of a new consumer durable should be a first-step, combination effort of retailers, the trade association, distributors, and manufacturers of these products. This is of particular importance to independent retailers who operate without the benefit of a credit plan backed by the manufacturer. Retailers of mobile homes, campers, sailboats, and snowmobiles are examples.

Disadvantages of Using Credit

An ill-conceived credit policy is responsible for an increasing number of business failures. Dun & Bradstreet has found that receivables difficulties rank first as fundamental cause of business failures.[12] Poor credit and collection practices have contributed a disproportionate share to the unchecked upsurge in receivables. Proper evaluation of the credit policy is essential if it is to be used in a profitable manner.

Some other disadvantages of using in-house credit are:

1. The firm's capital is tied up in merchandise bought by charge customers.
2. If the merchant has borrowed the extra money required when credit is granted, the interest is added to the cost.
3. Some losses from bad debts and customers with fraudulent intentions are bound to occur.
4. Credit customers feel more at liberty to abuse the privileges of returning goods and having goods sent out on approval.
5. Credit increases operation and overhead costs by adding to the expenses of investigation, bookkeeping, sending out statements and collecting payments.[13]

Deciding Whether to Offer In-House Credit

Credit can be used to stimulate sales, but the profitability of credit usage is influenced by:

1. How much sales are increased by using credit
2. How large the gross profit margin is on the goods being sold
3. How fast the money on credit sales is received by the retailer
4. The cost of financing this credit balance
5. The cost of maintaining the credit system
6. The loss incurred by bad debts[14]

One of the most significant factors that influences the decision to grant credit is the gross profit margin received on the store's merchandise. Other things being equal, the use of credit is more likely to be profitable if the profit margin is high. Thus, credit must stimulate sales considerably if credit usage is going to be profitable in retail outlets that have a low profit margin.

Naturally, proper handling of accounts receivable is required to keep consumers current on their payments and to reduce bad debts. (Accounts receivable records are discussed in more detail in Chapter 12.) Screening applicants for credit by checking with the local retail credit bureau can also reduce the incidence of bad debts and result in faster recovery of the retailer's money.

Other factors, such as the amount of capital available to the retailer, the use of credit by direct competitors, and the general consumer insistence that credit be granted also influence the retailer's decision of granting or not granting credit.

Kinds of Retail Credit

If the retailer decides to offer credit, the firm must evaluate the different types of credit available and choose the one that best meets its needs.

Bank credit plans, such as VISA and Master Charge, allow retail customers to use a credit account they have established with one of the financial institutions. Customers can charge purchases at any participating outlet. The billing, record-keeping, and collection activities are performed by the financial agency. This arrangement costs the retailer from 2 to 5 percent of the credit card sales volume. The exact rate depends upon the bargaining position of the retailer and the degree of competition between various bank credit card agencies. In return for this charge, a retailer transfers the work involved with offering credit and the responsibility for collecting unpaid bills to the financial institution. The retailer receives cash for bank credit card purchases when the charge slips are deposited in the participating bank.

The *thirty-day open account plan* is administered by the retailer who allows consumers to charge merchandise and pay the full amount within thirty days of the billing date. Interest is usually not charged unless a payment is not received when it is due.

The *revolving credit plan* divides the unpaid account balance into equal monthly payments, but approximately 1½ percent per month interest charge is made on the remaining balance if the account is not paid in full by the stated due date. Each customer has a credit limit that cannot be exceeded, but otherwise customers can charge and make payments to meet their needs, provided a minimal payment is made each month.

Deferred payment plans allow purchasers of large items to make equal monthly payments for the value of the merchandise, plus a carrying charge. Because the agreement involves only the particular item purchased, a separate agreement must be made on each item. Installment contracts, which are one type of deferred payment agreement, let the title to the goods stay with the retailer until the provisions of the contract have been fulfilled. Under installment contracts, payments are scheduled so that the remaining balance due is always less than the current market value of the depreciated merchandise.

Who Uses Credit

The use of credit is not limited to consumers from one social class or racial group. However, types of credit and the purposes of credit usage vary by class, and research on users of bank credit cards has demonstrated different use patterns among social classes.[15] Members of the lower classes were found to use their credit cards for installment purchases. Upper classes used theirs as a convenience tool in place of cash but not for installment loans.

Members of lower social classes also tend to look for stores that honor their cards. By comparison, upper-class members did not specifically seek out stores because they accept credit cards. Upper-class members did not feel their cards should be used to purchase most consumer durable goods. Members of this social class have more alternative sources of credit available to them, and also appear to be more conscious of interest charges then persons in lower classes.

There are also social class differences in attitude toward purchasing specific products by credit. Upper classes generally hold favorable attitudes toward using credit to purchase "luxury goods." Lower classes tend to restrict credit usage to durable and necessity goods.

The widespread acceptance and use of credit cards has generated considerable abuses and problems for both the retailer and the consumer. Under consumer and civil rights groups' unrelenting pressure, the federal government has been obliged to regulate consumer-retailer credit transactions and establish product liability responsibilities.

Consumer Credit Legislative Constraints

The entire area of consumer credit is undergoing considerable change as a direct result of the enactment of federal *consumer credit* legislation. As noted in detail in Chapter 2, the Equal Credit Opportunity Act and the Fair-Credit Billing Act of 1975 have placed far greater responsibilities on grantors of consumer credit. Without repeating the detailed discussion, suffice it to note that more and more department stores, chain stores, and mass merchandisers are finding that it is more profitable to discontinue their own credit operations and accept national bank credit cards. While not all stores have elected to make this decision, it appears only a matter of time, in light of increasing minimum wage costs, rising costs of capital to finance receivables, and strict enforcement of the federal acts, until most retailers will return to being merchants and leave the lending business to the banking industry, finance companies, and credit unions.

Consumer Products Warranty and Guaranty Act of 1970

Retailers have become increasingly involved in postpurchase performance of their goods since the passage of the Consumer Products Warranty and Guaranty Act. Specifically the act requires ". . . a supplier of a customer product or service actually costing more than $5 who decide to warranty or guaranty their products against defect or malfunction to follow certain guidelines such as:

1. The contents of such warranties and guaranties must be clearly and conspicuously disclosed . . .

2. A written warranty or guaranty on consumer products costing more than $5 must be designated either a "full" or "partial" warranty unless it is merely a general statement without limitation promising such blanket protection as customer satisfaction . . .

3. In order to designate a warranty a "full" warranty, the warrantor must assume certain duties, namely the duties to repair, or replace if repair is not possible or cannot be timely made, any malfunctioning or defective guaranteed consumer product, within a reasonable time, and without charge. There is no requirement that any supplier of a consumer product give a warranty or guaranty . . ."[16]

The critical point is that the full responsibility to fulfill any manufacturer's warranty or guaranty falls squarely on the retailer. The Federal Trade Commission has been given full authority to interpret, implement, and enforce the act as it deems appropriate. Their subsequent actions have forced many retailers to reassess their relationships with suppliers and the suppliers in turn have revised their warranty provisions to limit their liability under the act. Without going into further detail, retailers should be aware that they now bear a significantly larger burden of providing customer service under terms of manufacturer's warranties and guaranties than in the past.

Merchandising Maintenance and Repair: Service Contracts

Many large chain stores have found that it is profitable to be in the repair and home improvement business. Partially in response to the passage of the Consumer Products Warranty and Guaranty Act and in an effort to find additional sources of profitable merchandising, they have begun to actively promote their "service contract" product. Usually, as part of a closing approach for complicated, expensive appliances, salespersons are encouraged to suggest the purchase of a service contract that covers the product for one, two, or five years from the date of purchase.

Service contracts provide varying degrees of guaranteed product performance at a range of competitive prices. For example, a customer can purchase a service contract at the time of product purchase that will guarantee product replacement for a year for a nominal $20 to $25. As the contract life and replacement provisions are extended, the cost of the contract rises substantially up to a limit of five years. Thereafter, the useful life of the product is assumed to be realized and the customer assumes the full risk of repair or replacement.

Obviously the rates for service contracts have been carefully calculated and related to average product life so that the odds of having to pay off are stacked in favor of the retailer. However, many customers would prefer to have such guaranteed protection, which often includes in-home service, than be bothered with seeking out competent technicians and possibly be deprived of the use of that appliance while it is in the shop for repair. Accurate cost/profit data on this new service is not available, but increasingly more large retailers are experimenting with this and other customer services such as home decoration, insulation installation, fence construction, reroofing, and auto repair as another means of providing customer satisfaction in a profitable fashion.

Packaging and Gift Wrapping

A discussion of retail packaging cannot be confined to the product as it arrives from the manufacturer. In the long run, the retailer may have an important influence over the shape, size, color, and weight of the packaged product. However, in most cases the firm is relatively powerless to change the manufacturer's package. Thus, the primary responsibility for branded product packaging rests directly upon the manufacturer. It is critical for manufacturers to understand the problems and complexities of retailing so that their package designs can meet these needs.

There are, however, two areas of packaging over which certain retailers can exercise substantial control: gift packaging and bulk in-store packaging. The department store in particular has discovered a rich opportunity for increased profits, customer good will, and image building through the use of these services.

The practice of offering free gift-wrapping service for purchases can help create a favorable image of the store through the color and style of the package and may aid in establishing repeat sales or new customers. Nevertheless, this traditional approach to gift wrapping must be viewed as a cost center rather than profit generation. Many of the traditional gift wrapping centers also suffer from a lack of coordination as part of the store's total objective. They are simply areas of the store in which pretty wrappings are placed on merchandise.

Maximum benefits to a store can never be gained with this view of gift wrapping. Instead, gift wrapping must be viewed as a coordinated and integral part of the entire retailing system within a store. A coordinated and professional approach to gift wrapping can bring major rewards to retailers.

The package will become an integral part of the total image desired by a store. It can say much more than "I am a pretty package." By identifying the outlet tastefully on the wrapping, it can convey a store's total image of good taste, fashion, and styling—and to an audience far in excess of the buyer. Such packages will be seen by guests at showers, weddings, graduations, and dozens of other gift-giving occasions.

The package may be used as a part of the point-of-purchase display area. Wide lines of designs and materials are available to retailers from pre-designed package manufacturers. Retailers can now buy packages just as they do the merchandise to fill them. These are professional designs, which generally are sold to a retailer with the guarantee that the store will have exclusivity on this design within a particular market area. Yearly package designs are made, incorporating new trends and fashions. Professionally styled packages add to the point-of-purchase appeal of products and also help to differentiate departments or areas within departments.

The package itself can be sold at an excellent margin of profit. Thus, what was once a cost center can become one of profit, while corporate goals are enhanced.

Bulk, in-store packaging is of growing importance to the department store retailer who is facing a serious problem of maintaining a unique image. With the growth of shopping centers, many retailers have tended to become more alike in appearance. In addition, manufacturers have altered or eliminated their policies of brand exclusivity. Moreover, it must be admitted that competing brands have taken on an appearance of similarity. Brand names that at one time meant exclusivity and uniqueness now are simply competing brands.

Several leading department stores have discovered that a new and unique package can be created in the store by packaging several items together in a box, bag, tote bag, or other container. As an example, selected brands and scents of toiletries may be placed together in a unique box and sold as a single item. In this way the retailer is able to sell multiple products at one time, and in a container that is unique. To top this off, the retailer is also able to incorporate the price of the box with full markup into the total package price. The obvious problem in this is the selection of the right merchandise for the package at the right price.

Delivery

Offering delivery service to customers can be a competitive tool that can be used to create a unique image for the retailer. Many customers do not like to carry large packages while they are moving from one store to another. Urban customers who depend on public transportation and older or physically disabled consumers are likely to respond favorably to a retailer's delivery service. Therefore delivery service can be an important part of the retailing effort in reaching these market segments. Delivery service can also expand a retailer's sales if the delivery person is alert and can recognize additional consumer needs.

When delivery service is indicated, the firm must make two decisions: (1) will they charge for the service, and if so, what will the service cost, and (2) how will the firm implement the service decision, that is, will they own it, contract it out, or use a co-op system? Each option has associated advantages and disadvantages and all options will involve significant added cost of operation. The simplest mode of delivery for a small store is to put the merchandise in the owner's vehicle and make the delivery.

In many states this pragmatic approach may be technically illegal because the vehicle becomes a commercial carrier subject to commercial licensing and can only be operated by a person with a commercial license. If the private vehicle should be in an accident while being commercially operated, the litigation could become very expensive.

Once a firm outgrows the single vehicle delivery system, it usually turns to contracting for the service as needed. Perhaps the best known and most used contractors are the United Parcel Service (UPS) and the U.S. Postal System. The main advantage is that actual delivery costs are known and little managerial time is devoted to overseeing this facet of the operation. Disadvantages include loss of control over the quality of handling the merchandise will receive on the way to the customer; increased chance for theft, breakage, or loss of goods; and an increased opportunity for customer dissatisfaction as a result of untimely deliveries or discourteous, inconsiderate delivery people.

When contract delivery becomes unsatisfactory, many firms attempt to establish a cooperative arrangement to share costs while retaining control of the service. Specific legal agreements must be drawn up to assign certain responsibilities and costs, rent trucks, and hire delivery personnel. Usually this is a short term arrangement on the road to individual ownership of delivery fleets as the demands of each cooperating firm change.

When a large retail firm with multiple units or several branch stores offers delivery services, the firm must consider the costs of buying or leasing a commercial fleet of trucks; employing and training commercially licensed delivery people; planning timely, appropriate, and efficient delivery routes and schedules; and incurring the full cost of operation and maintenance of the fleet. Offsetting these costs are the advantages of convenient transfer of goods between stores; direct authority to control theft, loss, and damage of delivered merchandise, and direct expense control. Maximum utilization is needed if the optimum benefit is to be achieved. In any event, delivery costs can quickly exceed profit margins and what started out as perhaps a limited, free service becomes a pervasive and prohibitive expense. At this point retail firms usually either institute a competitive service charge for delivery services, which may not cover the entire cost but will make a sizable contribution to offset the incurred costs, or offer discounts for customer pick-up.

In the final analysis, if the decision to offer delivery services is made, the kind and geographical scope must be determined only after careful, thorough cost/benefit analysis and then there must be periodic reviews to determine if the costs truly represent a competitive advantage or disadvantage for the firm.

Parking Facilities

Plentiful, well-lighted, and well-maintained parking space costs retailers untold dollars. The original land and construction costs for a large shopping center parking area are significant. Careless patrons, vandals, and ordinary wear and tear take their toll, and periodically the area must be resurfaced and refixtured. This "free" service is often taken for granted and expected by the consuming public. In fact, some studies indicate that certain shopping centers have flourished partly as a result of readily available, convenient, noncongested parking facilities.

Downtown merchants are at a distinct competitive disadvantage because of limited, costly, inconvenient parking and general traffic congestion.

Parking space in some downtown areas may be so limited that retail firms may have to join together to purchase vacant buildings and convert them into parking facilities to encourage increased patronage. Alternately, when public transportation is available, downtown merchant associations may sponsor reduced fares during off-peak hours to encourage senior citizens and others to shop downtown. Even then these efforts have been negated by an increasing number of crimes and purse snatchings in which older citizens and women are primary targets. Increased police protection and urban renewal have been partial answers to these problems, but big city core retailers continue to labor under considerable disadvantages.

Procurement and Management of Leased-Space Customer Facilities

Often large department and chain stores find a need for a customer service that they do not feel is within their expertise nor one that they wish to develop, but it does offer a possible profit center if managed effectively. The classic example of such a venture is the leased-spaced optical department in most large Sears and Roebuck stores. The space is leased to an optician who provides the equipment and supplies for dispensing eyeglasses. Often the same vendor will provide the supportive staff during extended store hours to handle broken glasses or replacement orders that customers drop off during their regular shopping. Usually lease arrangements provide for Sears to receive a minimum space rental fee plus a percentage of the gross sales. In return the independent vendor gets high volume traffic, accepts Sears credit cards, and participates occasionally in the regular Sears promotion program. All three parties seem to benefit: the customer, the chain or department store, and the independent service operator.

Customer Consumerism

Retailers are becoming increasingly aware of the need to practice effective consumerism. Woodward and Lathrop demonstrated its concern for the customer by putting its furniture service center in its main downtown store just adjacent to the retail furniture department. It was staffed by fifteen employees who handled 96,000 customer complaints in one year alone.

Such customer service interests are not limited to department stores. A special section of one edition of *Sales Management* was devoted to customer service management. Such large firms as Honeywell, Otis Elevator, RCA, Maytag, International Harvester's Agricultural Equipment Division, Singer's Business Machines Division, B. F. Goodrich, and United Airlines all have instituted some form of formal organizational mechanism to handle customer complaints effectively.[17]

This rising interest in consumerism has led to the formation of the Society of Consumer Affairs Professionals (SOCAP) and the National Association of Service Managers (NASM) which, between them, have 1400 members spread across the nation. The officer ranks are filled with the Who's Who of industry, including top officers of Bell and Howell, Sears and Roebuck, Montgomery Ward, Firestone Tire and Rubber, and Coca-Cola.[18] The bulk of the memberships are made up of service managers for both large and small firms across America. Perhaps the essence of this movement was captured by Executive Director Marvin Lurie when he remarked, "There's a strong trend in every industry to make service executives responsible for managing [service departments as] profit centers . . ."[19] When viewed in this light, effective customer service and practical consumerism make good dollars and sense for all parties.

Customer Complaints

The way complaints are handled affects the store image and either serves as a way to gain loyal customers or negates any good will built up by various promotional activities. Thus, retailers should establish adjustment procedures that ensure that each dissatisfied customer receives understanding attention.

Complaints arise because of faulty merchandise, unsatisfactory installation or fit, delayed or incorrect delivery, damaged merchandise, errors in billing charge accounts, resentment with credit collection methods, and dissatisfaction with salespeople.[20]

Naturally, a store is obliged to make satisfactory adjustment when the consumer has a legitimate complaint based on any of these reasons. Even if the consumer has no legitimate complaint, complaining consumers nearly always are convinced that they should receive adjustment. Therefore it is better for a retailer to let the complaining consumer have all the time needed to explain the problem. The adjuster should not argue with the consumer but should suggest that some sort of adjustment can be made.

It is better to give generous adjustment to the customers than to irritate them. Customers who are dissatisfied with an adjustment generally inform their friends of their dissatisfaction, whereas satisfied customers recommend the store to their friends. If possible, many retailers try to satisfy customers with replacement items (which reduces the adjustment cost by the amount of the retail markup). However, the customer must be satisfied, so the adjuster should ask if the adjustment is fair.

Most consumers try to be fair if they believe the adjuster understands their problem and is trying to solve it. A few consumers, of course, are habitual complainers who can never be satisfied. Adjustment records can reveal the identity of such individuals, and they can be discouraged from trading at the outlet.

Retailers should keep good adjustment records, not only to identify habitual complainers but also to identify poor merchandise, poor delivery and credit procedures, poor performance in salespeople, and to show compliance with the law. For every reasonable complaining customer, there are likely to be numerous customers who encountered the same problem but simply chose to discontinue trading at that store as a silent protest.

Summary

Each retailer must devote considerable time and resources to personal selling and customer services. These two elements should be effectively integrated into a well-planned promotional mix that insures that a consistent message is communicated to customers.

Perhaps the major message contained in this chapter is that the effort put forth to do a good job of personal selling and the rendering of prompt, efficient customer service can put more dollars in the cash register and contribute profits to the "bottom line." When customer services cease to be viewed as a "free, menial, must-do-grudgingly task" and become an "opportunity to exploit a profitable product," retail employees and customers alike will see customer service as a product to be effectively merchandised and effectively consumed.

Questions

1. Many customers express the opinion that personal salesmanship and helpful customer service is a relic of the past. Should retail managers be concerned? Why or why not? Explain.

2. What role does face-to-face communication play in a successful sales program for retail stores?

3. The concept of self-service pervades large areas of retailing. Is there any need for personal salesmanship in retailing? Explain.

4. What are the major elements of a retail sale? What role do professional sales personnel play in the transaction process?

5. What are the five stages in buying? How can the sales staff use this information to improve their sales presentations?

6. What is the purpose of a selling approach? How can the different strategies be applied to advance a sale to a successful close?

7. How does a salesperson choose a proper closing strategy to improve the chances for a successful sale?

8. What impact has the Product Warranty and Guaranty Act had on retailers in regard to providing customer services?

9. Can customer services be profitably merchandised? If so, how? Explain.

10. What factors should a small retailer consider in deciding whether to accept bank credit cards or set up the store's own in-house credit operation? Should the firm extend credit both ways?

11. What impact has consumerism had on retail firms, particularly in the area of post-purchase service? Explain.

12. What major points must be considered when a retailer sets up a specific process for handling customer complaints? What should be the ultimate goal of such a program?

Footnotes

1. Karen R. Gillespie, "Revitalize Personal Selling in Your Store," *Small Marketers Aids Annual No.9* (Washington, D.C.: Small Business Administration, 1967), pp. 82–89.

2. Richard H. Buskirk, *Retail Selling: A Vital Approach* (San Francisco: Canfield Press, 1975), pp. 75–166.

3. Carlton A. Pederson and Milburn D. Wright, *Selling: Principles and Methods,* 6th ed. (Homewood, Il.: Richard D. Irwin, Inc., 1976), pp. 216–218.

4. Buskirk, *Retail Selling,* p. 75.

5. Ibid., pp. 69–73.

6. Ibid., p. 70.

7. Ibid., p. 71.

8. Ibid.

9. Ibid., pp. 160–165.

10. Ibid., p. 165.

11. John E. Payne, "What the Vice-President of Sales Wants from the Credit Department," *Credit and Financial Management* 69 (January 1967): 15–17; Pearce C. Kelley and Kenneth Lawyer, *How to Organize and Operate a Small Business* (Englewood Cliffs, N.J.: Prentice-Hall, 1961), pp. 491–521; and Wallace Reiff, "Capital Allocation in Credit Decision-Making," *Credit and Financial Management* 69 (September 1967): 20–23.

12. Merle Welshans, "Using Credit in Profit Making," *Credit and Financial Management* 69 (February 1967): 18–27.

13. Kelley and Lawyer, *How to Organize and Operate a Small Business,* pp. 491–521.

14. Raymond A. Marquardt and Anthony F. McGann, "Profit Analysis and the Firm's Credit Policy," *Business Ideas and Facts* 6 (Winter 1973): 12–18.

15. Lee H. Matheus and John W. Slocum, Jr., "Social Class and Commercial Bank Credit Card Usage," *Journal of Marketing* 33 (January 1969): 71–78.

16. U.S. Congress, Senate, *Consumer Products Warranty and Guaranty Act,* 91st Cong., 2nd Sess., 1970, Rept. 91–876, pp. 1–2.

17. "A Sales Tool For All Seasons," *Sales Management* 113 (February 17, 1975): 1–48.

18. Ibid., pp. 12, 36.

19. Ibid., p. 12.

20. Gerald D. Grosner, *Turning Complaints into Profits* (Washington, D.C.: Small Business Administration, 1959), p. 58.

Case Study

Murray's Hardware Store: A Case in Personal Selling and Store Image

Mr. Murray is a hard-working and gruff but impeccably honest hardware retailer in an upper middle-class suburb of a major metropolis. He grew up on New York's East Side in grinding poverty and has worked all his life to establish himself in his own store in the suburbs.

Murray's store is conveniently located on a very busy street in the center of town, directly across the street from the railroad station. He considers his location fortunate for two reasons. First of all, trains stop every few minutes during the rush hours and pick up or discharge hundreds of commuters going to and from the city. Many of these commuters pass Murray's store on their walk home; they do not drive to the station because it is too difficult to park there. Secondly, a major bus line, which passes in front of Murray's store, also carries commuter traffic, and stops directly in front of the store. The buses carry so much traffic that they often travel in pairs, or even three at a time. Consequently, the bus stop is three bus-lengths long. This ensures Murray and his neighbors good visibility from the street, because no cars can park in the bus stop.

Murray has always tried to promote a discount image while being careful to maintain an extensive inventory of hardware goods. Every item in the store is marked with two prices, and the higher one is crossed out. The lower price is sometimes competitive with the four other hardware stores in town. Murray's inventory is one of the most extensive in the area and his display shelves literally sag with merchandise. He handles every type of nut, bolt, washer, screw, and nail. He also handles all types of name brand hand tools, some power tools, paints, household goods, appliances, and garden hardware.

He carefully promotes his discount image by hanging signs in the window that say "Fantastic Savings," "Gigantic Sale," and so forth. He has done this even before the discount stores opened. In fact, he has used this technique so long that some of his signs have turned yellow.

Murray has two full-time employees and one part-time employee, all on straight salary. One of his full-time employees is a young man named Tony Novotny, who is also a hard worker but not as smart as Murray. Tony often sells goods off the floor, and he always points out to customers that the store is a member of a hardware co-op and that this is why it is able to mark down the goods. The customers show a general lack of enthusiasm about the "competitive" price they are getting.

Murray's other full-time employee is a bookkeeper, who often waits on trade when the store is busy. She is very talkative and vivacious and enjoys helping customers more than working on the books. She is generally untidy in looks, but Murray feels that her congeniality outweighs her often slovenly appearance. Her name is Julia Tuttle.

Murray's part-time employee is an 18-year-old college student who works 2½ hours each afternoon and all day on Saturday. He diligently takes inventory of the display shelves and restocks them every afternoon. He also notifies Murray or Tony if they are low on some item so they can reorder before running out. Thus, Murray is assured of a daily inventory check. The student also delivers merchandise to cash and credit customers daily, and he sweeps the floor before closing. Tony helps him deliver and install major appliances. The student also waits on trade when he has time and when customers are buying something he knows about and can find.

Murray buys most of his merchandise through the hardware co-op, but he also deals with hardware jobbers. Much of his business is done with Glib Hardware Wholesaling Company, and Murray's account is serviced by Harry Jacobs, vice-president and salesman. Harry has a reputation in the trade for being able to sell anything to anyone, but Murray has dealt with Harry for many years and cannot be taken in by him. Harry has dealt with Murray so long that he knows Murray's merchandise as well as anyone in the store, and since he visits several times a week, he often waits on customers when the store is busy. Everyone appreciates his help, and although he does not have his own cash register drawer, he appears to outsell everyone else on the floor.

Murray has recently started a new line of plumbing and electrical supplies. He has introduced these lines cautiously, by carrying only a few of the items needed by plumbers and electricians, but he and Tony know the business well enough that they can direct plumbers and electricians to other sources if they cannot supply what is needed. Since Tony worked for a plumber after he dropped out of high school and also wired his own garage, he was put in charge of the new departments. Murray had a shed constructed behind the store in which to keep long lengths of pipe and electrical conduits. If the alley is not too muddy, plumbers and electricians can pick up their supplies in back of the store, so that there is no need to carry these awkward pieces through the store. When it is wet, these pieces can be carried through the store and out the front door, if there are no buses at the curb.

Murray has recently been having trouble competing with the discount stores that have opened up in highway corridor locations. He has tried to compete by carrying low-price impulse items, using coupon sales, and advertising in suburban newspapers. These techniques have not been very successful and Murray is very disturbed. He often becomes belligerent when customers tell him they can get an item cheaper at a highway discount store, and he tells them to go there to buy it. He has other problems too. Tony is anxious to start his own hardware store, and Murray is afraid he will leave. Also, summer is coming and Murray's part-time helper is looking for full-time work for the summer.

As a retailing consultant, what would you suggest for Murray?

Case Study

Herman's Grocery, Inc.: A Case in Credit Management

Mr. Herman, owner-manager of Herman's Grocery, Inc., is evaluating his firm's credit policy. Herman's Grocery, Inc., is an independent outlet with annual sales of slightly over $1.5 million. The firm is one of two grocery outlets offering its own charge account system in a town of 25,000 residents. The other store, offering a similar plan, is on the other side of town.

Herman's trade area is concentrated in the surrounding neighborhood, but he draws 25 percent of his business from another neighborhood 25 blocks away. Herman operated another store in that neighborhood until it burned down nine months ago. Many of Herman's customers were then lost to competitive stores, but some remained loyal to Herman and drove to his remaining store. This store was built one year before his other store burned.

Herman operates his remaining store on a 21 percent gross margin. His net margin is 3 percent and his net sales to inventory ratio is 24. Credit sales now amount to 70 percent of Herman's total sales. Last year he lost $2,000 to bad debts. Last year's collection period varied from 33 to 36 days.

Herman is concerned about his bad debt loss, and he is also concerned about the high cost of maintaining credit records for each customer. He is considering dropping his credit plan entirely but does not know what effect this move would have on his customers. He does not know what his store's image is from his customers' point of view.

Discussion Questions

1. What alternatives should Mr. Herman consider?

2. Design a research project that will help Mr. Herman make the correct decision on his credit problem and at the same time reveal his store's image.

3. What methods can be used to reduce bad debt losses? List these methods, their relative costs, and their effects on total sales and make a recommendation.

Part Five

Retailing Services

Chapter 16

Consumer Service Firms

Learning Goals

1. To be aware of the size and growth of consumer expenditures for services.
2. To be able to discuss the different classifications of service firms.
3. To understand the peculiarities encountered in the marketing of services.

Key Terms and Concepts

service industry	contingency payment pricing	high price maintenance
rented goods service	fixed pricing	discount pricing
owned goods service	value pricing	flexible discriminatory pricing
nongoods service	loss leader pricing	price lining
repeat business	diversionary pricing	critical path analysis
cost pricing		

The field of retailing is much broader than simply selling goods to consumers; it includes the marketing of services as well. This might appear to be too broad a definition for retailing, until one takes a closer look at the type of services offered today. A great number, if not the majority, of these services are in direct competition with traditional retailing. This chapter discusses the peculiarities encountered in the *service industry* (an industry concerned with any work that is not connected with the manufacture or processing of a product or commodity or the wholesaling or retailing of a good).

The owner of a diaper service faces competition not only from other diaper service firms but also from retailers who sell disposable and nondisposable diapers. Innovations in retailing and in such retail products as low-cost disposable diapers may affect his business far more than any competitive efforts by other firms that offer a similar service.

When a homeowner needs a wheelbarrow, trailer, chain saw, plumber's snake, or a myriad other products, he can borrow, rent, or buy these items. If he elects to rent a tool, it is obvious that a retail sale has been lost for the moment. Thus, hardware stores, discount houses, department stores, plumbing supply outlets, and other retailers are in direct competition with the service industry. In addition, rental stores may also sell the product to the consumer. A customer who has enjoyed a successful day of cutting firewood with a rented chain saw may easily be in a receptive mood to purchase such a saw.

Many retailers have recognized the sales potential in the rental process and have added rental service to their line. It is common practice in many areas for paint stores to rent ladders, tarps, rollers, and other complementary equipment. Retailers with leisure-time-oriented products, such as motor bikes, canoes, and campers, have discovered substantial extra profits and sales potential in the rental business.

The service industry is not confined to a single market segment. It increasingly markets to all income and age groups and offers services from the day of birth through death. Weddings, bar mitzvahs, showers, and other special occasions are serviced by this industry, with goods and services ranging from rented chairs to thousand-dollar ice carvings. To serve people in sickness and in injury, wheelchairs, crutches, special hospital beds, and oxygen respirators are some of the products offered for rent.

The potential for the application of modern marketing and management techniques in the service industry is scarcely confined to running a better "mom and pop" type operation. This is an industry that has formed huge national and multinational organizations.

This is true even in industries traditionally thought of as strictly the province for small independents. Service Corporation International of Houston, an example of the opportunity in these areas, during a four-year period acquired 101 funeral homes and 36 cemeteries in twelve states, Washington, D.C., and six Canadian provinces, making it the largest in the industry. Yet, impressive as this growth is, it represents less than 3 percent of total industry revenues in an industry composed of 20,000 U.S. funeral service firms and 10,000 nonprofit cemeteries reporting approximately $3.5 billion in gross receipts.[1]

Growth of the Service Industry

The term *service industry* can be highly misleading, depending upon how the statistics are compiled. It is abundantly clear that a tremendous growth in the service industry sector has occurred in the last few decades. The United States is now described as the first service economy the world has ever seen, with over half the labor force involved in a service capacity. There have been estimates that this might reach 80 percent by 1990.[2]

It is a complex task to separate all the functions that can logically be classified as service retailing to form a dollar and cents value for the service industry. The fact is, however, that it is very large and obviously is growing. Consumer spending for services exceeded 45 percent of the typical American family's budget in 1976.[3] In the early fifties, services claimed about 35 percent of the consumer's expenditures. Although prices for services have risen faster than prices for goods, there has been a trend for consumers to buy more services from a wider assortment of service offerings.

About half of the total consumer expenditures for services goes into housing and the cost of operating the home (Table 16–1). Not only does this area account for the most important total service expenditure, it is also one of the fastest growing service areas (Table 16–2). Consumer expenditures for shelter and household operation services such as gas, electricity, telephone, and telegraph are increasing faster than increases in the consumer's income. This is illustrated by the income elasticity coefficient in excess of 1.0 in Table 16–2. The increased level of appliance ownership has resulted in increased power consumption. A large growth in the teenage population and emphasis upon color, style, and multiple connections are attributed to the rapid rise in telephone service.

Medical services accounted for about 17 percent of the consumer's service expenditures in 1976, but consumer spending for medical services also appears to be rising faster than the rise in consumer incomes. Other service areas that are growing most rapidly in the 1970s are airline travel, foreign travel, higher education, and intercity travel (Table 16–2).

Consumer dollar expenditures are influenced by rising prices, so they may not appear to be the best unit of measurement in the service industry. However, it is questionable how service productivity should be measured inasmuch as quantity measurements are generally inadequate. Trades (beauticians, barbers, repair firms, and so forth) depend upon the quality and uniqueness of their work, not upon the number of "look alikes" they can push out in one day. Nevertheless, as competition and chains of service firms grow, efforts to measure productivity and improve efficiency are bound to increase.

Classification of Consumer Service Firms

Although the service industry is highly fragmented, it can be grouped roughly into three main areas.[4]

Table 16-1 **Percentage of Consumer Expenditures for Services in the United States by Category, 1976**

Category	Percentage of Consumer Service Spending
Housing	36.6
Household operation	14.2
Transportation	7.8
Cleaning, laundering, and other services related to clothing, and watch and jewelry repairs	1.1
Barbershops, beauty shops, and baths	0.8
Medical care services	17.0
Services furnished without payment by financial intermediaries except life insurance carriers	4.3
Admissions to specified spectator amusements	1.2
Other	17.0
Total	100.0

Source: *Survey of Current Business* (Washington, D.C.: Government Printing Office), July, 1977, p. 30.

Rented goods service. As the name implies, these firms rent products—ranging from heavy-duty trucks to costumes for the Halloween dance. They may, however, engage in the sale of products at the same time.

Owned goods service. Firms in this category repair products, sell value (added to a product through custom work), or otherwise improve existing products. Upholstery shops, gunsmiths, antique clock repair shops, ski repair shops, and many others are examples of such firms. In almost every case they also sell products at retail, such as gun oil, upholstery sprays and cleaners, keys to wind clocks, ski wax and bindings, and thousands of other products.

Nongoods service. The primary product for firms in this group is *not* a product but a service. Beauty salons, funeral parlors, poodle barber shops, travel agencies, and insurance and financial institutions are a few examples.

The previous classification of retail services by rental goods, owned goods, and nongoods should not be interpreted as meaning that a retailer must be one or the other type. In practice, the retail mix of a firm (such as Sears) includes each of these areas, plus the regular merchandising services.

In recent years traditional retailers have expanded into a variety of services. This has generally been accomplished in the following ways:

1. Acquisition or establishment of service. Under this system the retailer acquires majority interest in the service company and then offers it as a part of the store's total merchandising mix. Insurance and finance companies have been among the major services established in this way.

Table 16-2 **Actual and Projected Annual Growth Rate for Consumer Service Expenditures, 1955-1980**

	Average Annual Percentage Growth Rate		
	Income Elasticity 1955-1970[1]	1955-1970	1970-1980 (Projected)
Disposable personal income	1.00	4.2	4.4
All expenditures	0.97	4.1	4.3
Non-durables	0.76	3.2	3.4
Durables	1.41	5.9	6.2
Services	1.04	4.4	4.6
Shelter	1.16	4.9	5.1
Household operation	1.06	4.4	4.7
Gas and electricity	1.27	5.3	5.6
Telephone and telegraph	1.69	7.1	7.5
Domestic services	−0.34	−1.4	−1.5
Transportation	0.56	2.4	2.5
Automotive services	0.69	2.9	3.0
Local travel	−0.64	−2.7	−2.8
Intercity travel	1.30	5.4	5.7
Airlines	2.68	11.3	11.8
Medical services	1.16	4.9	5.1
Physicians	0.97	4.1	4.3
Dentists	0.81	3.4	3.6
Personal care	0.76	3.2	3.4
Foreign travel	1.61	6.7	7.1
Higher education	1.55	6.5	6.8

[1]Percentage increase in consumer spending for the indicated services for each 1% rise in real disposable personal income.

Source: *The Conference Board Record*, May 1972, p. 51. Reprinted by permission.

2. Leased department. Travel agencies, optical service, and shoe repair represent services that are commonly sold through an independent service retailer who simply leases space from another retailer. In addition to paying the lease, the lessee may agree to share a percentage of the gross.

3. Tie-in agreement. In these cases the retailer may do no more than agree to provide a signed order to the vendor of services, who then reimburses the retailer with a commission. Banks and car dealers often have such arrangements for car loans. In other cases the retailer may sell the entire package of services under his name but, in actuality, perform nothing more than the selling and bill-collecting functions. The service vendor then performs the actual service.

The strength of tie-in agreements depends upon the amount of natural cohesion between the two parties. This is often referred to as reciprocity (you scratch my back—I'll scratch yours).

To be successful, each party must feel it is gaining more than it could if it were to act independently. This means that before a tie-in arrangement is offered to a second party, it must be clearly thought out. Each party must have certain strengths that the other party clearly perceives as necessary for the total success of the project.

The mix of retail and service firms can be illustrated by the acquisition of financial and insurance services by retailers. This move has placed retailers in direct competition with insurance companies, banks, credit unions, and personal finance companies. In turn, members of the financial service industry, such as Beneficial Finance and Household Finance Corporation, have responded by entering into retailing. With the exception of financial institutions that are specifically prohibited by charter or law from engaging in such vertical integration, there is every reason to believe that many more will do so. The possibility for large banks to establish huge national and international retailing chains is quite foreseeable.[5]

Commercial banks already perform a host of important services for retailers and retail customers, such as letters of credit, floor planning, factoring, credit cards, and installment lending, to mention only a few. The acquisition of a retail chain could provide a bank with a built-in market for its services and a retailer with an excellent source of consumer credit.

A further example of a traditional retailer moving into services is offered by Fred Meyer Supermarkets of Portland, Oregon. This firm opened savings and loan departments in its chain of supermarkets. The savings and loan departments appealed to small savers, a market that was not a prime target of traditional S and L associations. Fred Meyer applied grocery store promotion and merchandising techniques and found these techniques worked very well in marketing this service.[6]

Steps in the Marketing of Services

Service marketing can benefit from considering the following marketing activities.

Defining the Offering

An accurate generic definition of the service offering is required if a service firm is going to keep pace with or ahead of changes made by competitors and benefit from changes in consumer wants. Creative thinking can be rewarded with a tremendous growth in business volume. For example, some financial institutions are expanding their offering by providing one-stop services, including real estate development, investment management, credit card services, leasing services, safety deposit facilities, insurance coverage, savings facilities, travel scheduling, accounting services, and other money-related activities.

Defining the Target Market

Segmenting the broad generic definition into similar subgroups of people who have common characteristics and then identifying and meeting the needs of the most attractive segments can be a very profitable strategy to follow. An accurate definition of the needs of a market segment can allow the service firm to tailor its service offering and the marketing of that offering to best satisfy the consumers in that segment.[7]

The categorization of the population into different segments can be based not only on traditional demographic factors but also upon consumers' attitudes, activities, needs, and motivations. Indeed, in service marketing these four considerations may be the most profitable way to segment the market.

In addition to determining the market target groups, it is equally important for some service firms to determine which groups to avoid. Many professional service firms (such as market research firms, advertising agencies, lawyers, and so forth) are restrained from entering certain businesses because of possible conflicts of interests. For example, marketing research firms and advertising agencies usually refuse to handle two competing products simultaneously. In some cases it may be possible to set up separate task groups for each account and work on competitive accounts, but both competitors should be made aware of the situation and agree to it before the second competitive client is added to the list of clientele.

Planning Differentiated Service Offerings

Selling to different market segments usually requires a different marketing approach to reach each group effectively. Each segment of a market for a given service will not respond to the same approach. The presentation of the service must be geared to the needs of the target market segments. Service firms can provide a differential advantage in their service offering if any part of that offering creates a special value in the minds of their customers.

For example, the manager of an auto repair shop in a suburb might cater to commuters who catch the train to work in the city. The auto service firm could drive the customer to the station when he arrives in the morning and meet him at the evening train. Other extras, such as washing and cleaning the car at no extra charge, may be provided on repair jobs over a certain amount.

The development of companion service offerings frequently is based upon the desire to use all of the firm's resources at near-capacity levels.[8] Near-capacity utilization in retailing firms generally allows overhead costs to be spread over a larger number of sales units and therefore results in a per unit reduction in selling costs. Service firms have a more important advantage in operating at full capacity because their offerings are generally so perishable that they cannot be stored. There is no way to market the rental car that went unused yesterday, or the unused time that an interior decorator or barber spent waiting for customers to require his or her services. Thus, it is important to develop a service offering that can reverse the underutilization of capacity and recapture labor and capital costs as regularly and as completely as possible.

Identifying and Evaluating New Service Offerings

The generation of new ideas that may be included in the service offering is likely to originate with the consumer. Service firms benefit from a relatively short channel of communication that extends from the consumer through the service personnel (employees or agents of the service retailer) to the firm's management. Consumer problems can be translated into business opportunities if service personnel are impressed with the importance of reporting these consumer problems (as well as their recommendations for a solution) to the firm's management. A service firm's management can then screen out the better ideas, rank them in priority, and perform a business analysis of the best ideas. The business analysis would focus on sales projections, cost considerations, and evaluation of the company's resources (including managerial ability) to determine profitability and the availability of compatible equipment and knowledge. The effect the new offering will have upon the satisfaction of current clients is also important.

One difficulty associated with the development of new service offerings is that they are seldom patentable and only a few are proprietary. Thus, timing and resourcefulness are major ways that service firms can stay ahead of competitors. The need to search continually for new ideas and methods of better serving the consumer's desires is implied by the lack of protection provided by legal means. The progressive service firms must conduct continued service development programs if they are to keep ahead of the competitor who is simply copying old service offerings. The consequences of this competition through imitative action are evident by the ease of entry into many service industries and by the existence of many small service outlets.

Under the Lanham Act of 1946, the service industry has acquired the legal protection of "service marks," which are supposed to be the legal counterpart of the trademark.[9] The Lanham Act also made provisions for the legal use of the "certification mark" and the "collective mark" as service marks for the promotion of services. However, relatively few service outlets have used service marks to gain the advantages of market control, uniformity, and guarantee of quality that brand names appear to offer consumers. Perhaps future service marketing will make better use of the service mark to gain a competitive advantage over service-imitating competitors.

Packaging and Labeling

Except for very few cases—such as the wrapping that protects a piece of clothing on its return from the laundry or dry cleaners—services usually are not packaged or labeled in a manner that presents promotional possibilities.

Service Warranties

The provision of service warranties is another area in which service retailers can create a differentiated offering. The increasing importance of consumerism and the passage of new legislation must be recognized. Thus, the service retailer who offers a good warranty policy may obtain consumer good will and may benefit from the resulting publicity by acting before his competition does and before it is a legal requirement.

By 1970 the Uniform Commercial Code had replaced the Uniform Sales Act in every state except Louisiana.[10] Under the Uniform Commercial Code, service warranties are included as "express warranties." An express warranty arises as part of the bargaining process between buyer and seller. Case law since 1960 shows that service retailers create express warranties by their selling claims and their advertising. The growing number of warranty cases is influenced by class action possibilities against both the service firm and the manufacturer of the items being used and/or sold by the service firm.[11]

Thus, it is likely that warranties will become an important issue to service retailers, and courts are likely to see an increase in the number of cases involving service retailers. A service firm that recognizes this trend can take steps not only to avoid possible court action but to turn the warranty into a promotable item by including a unique and clear statement of warranty as part of its service offering.

Establishing warranty standards that are higher then those set by the industry can be illustrated by a policy of guarantees on parts and labor in a repair shop. If sixty days is standard in the industry, the service firm could establish a *ninety*-day warranty policy. The extra thirty days provides an indication of the firm's good intentions and conveys to the customers an impression of high performance standards in the services performed. Making an exception for a good customer who experiences difficulties several days after the guarantee has expired can also generate consumer good will.

Guarantees of performance, however, may be more difficult to substantiate for a service than for goods because for many services there is no acceptable method of measuring quality. The end result of service activity is frequently identifiable only in intangible terms. However, the performance of many services can be evaluated in tangible terms, such as speed, accuracy, frequency of service, and so forth. If it is possible to substantiate claims, service firms benefit by using these claims, because the buyer of services frequently may not feel comfortable in assessing the worth of a complex of activities that comprise the service offering. That is, the consumer frequently feels helpless because he is putting his fate in the hands of the service firm. Inclusion of a guarantee can reduce this feeling of uncertainty.

Many services (for example, medical, accounting, insurance, interior decorating, beauty shops) do not offer their skills and resources per se but really offer the consumer confidence, hope, or the reduction of uncertainty. In these cases the service firm promises the introduction of more certainty in an area in which customers feel unsure.

Displaying the industry code of ethics is one way to remind consumers of the quality service they can expect to receive from a service firm. However, merely displaying the code does little good unless service personnel live up to the code.

Reducing Consumer Uncertainty

It follows that the service firm will want to design a service offering that will minimize consumer uncertainty.[12]

Creating consumer awareness of the need for a service must be an objective of the firm's promotional effort. Frequently, the consumer will be aware that there is (or is likely to be) a problem. However, in many cases (making a will, obtaining a medical checkup, obtaining insurance, and so on) the consumer may not be aware of his need for the service. In these cases an awareness promotional campaign is essential for the industry or the individual firm.

Deciding what service is applicable for solving the consumer's problems is the next step. The successful performance of the service depends on a clear understanding of the customer's problems. Ideally, the potential service customer would approach the service firm with an objective description of the problem and request help in solving it. In reality, however, consumers infrequently take this approach. Thus, it is the job of the service firm to determine the consumer's problems by questioning him or her. If the subtle questioning results in an in-depth problem definition, the service offering can be tailored to meet the consumer's individual needs.

The consumer should be given an honest opinion, backed up by facts, on the worth of each purchase alternative. The objective is to gain customer confidence by giving an honest estimate. Even honest estimates are sometimes doubted by consumers, especially if the service outlet also sells new or replacement equipment. A consistent, honest approach, however, should win the trust of most consumers over the long run.

Selecting the employee who should render the service depends upon the person's demonstrable knowledge and skill in the claimed area of competence. Obviously demonstrable skill and knowledge will create consumer confidence. Many service retailers fail to recognize and acknowledge that they cannot do all things; that is, that there are limits to their skill and knowledge. In this case referrals to other people within the firm may be needed, or maybe it requires an honest admission that no one in the firm has the competence in that specialized area. Failure to admit incompetence in an area can cost a service firm longtime business if a customer loses confidence in the firm because of one bad experience.

However, admission of incompetence, if repeated several times, can point out new areas of expertise that could be included in the service offering.

How the service is performed is also important in establishing consumer confidence, and respecting the customer's time can gain consumer respect. People become distrustful of a service firm that always breaks promised service schedules, so every effort should be made to keep on schedule and not overcommit the service personnel. Service delays are sometimes unavoidable, and when this occurs the consumer should be informed that a repairman is going to be delayed. This allows the consumer to adjust his or her schedule. In the repair business, providing a replacement for the consumers to use while theirs is being repaired can lessen consumer aggravation when the service period is likely to be delayed.

Consumers also appreciate consideration and promptness in being informed when the estimated cost of service is changed because of unforeseen circumstances. In the repair business, the consumer may think that the revised cost is more than the item is worth and decide to purchase a new item.

Location

Location is another factor that the service firm can use to establish a differentiated service mix. For example, studies of consumer preference for airline service have shown that the most important reasons a consumer selects one airline over another are that the airline is going to the desired location at the desired time. Other factors, such as meal service, in-flight movies, stewardesses, magazine selection, and so forth are much less important.

The same is true of other retail services. It is not likely that a consumer will travel across town to a muffler shop, brake repair garage, shoe repair store, or laundromat if there is a comparable shop in the neighborhood, even if the nearby shop is not the favorite one.

The large car-rental agencies have been faced with stiff price competition from industry newcomers in recent years. Even so, they have been able to maintain their basic price policies because of their favorable image and the widespread availability of their rental counters. It is simply easier for an air traveling customer, particularly one on an expense account, to walk to the Hertz, Avis, or National counter than to call one of the competitive off-grounds firms and wait for a car to be delivered.

Studies have demonstrated the savings that can be realized by riding the bus rather than driving one's car to work. Yet, if an ample supply of gasoline is available, the real or imagined convenience of driving one's own car continues to win out over this service in most American cities. Motels must be located near a highway so that they are easily accessible to motorists. Laundry and cleaning firms must be conveniently available to their customers, even if the firm has to create the convenience by offering pickup and delivery service in the case of a poorly located firm. The list could go on and on, but it is generally true that location is an important consideration for all service firms that are visited personally by their customers. Unless very skilled personal expertise is involved, consumers are likely to patronize the service firm that requires the least effort to reach.

Services involving a considerable amount of personal skill (such as those of the medical doctor, lawyer, music instructor) and those service firms that are never visited by the customer can utilize relatively inconvenient locations. Examples of firms that are seldom visited by customers are window washing and television and radio repair services. These service firms can pay the lower rents generally associated with an inconvenient location and still satisfy their consumers' needs. The facilities do not have to be as elaborate for the seldom-visited service firms either, since the telephone is their primary method of communication with consumers.

Service firms requiring a customer visitation, on the other hand, depend upon a neat external appearance to draw the consumer inside. The interior must be neat, clean, and comfortable, and offer a pleasant atmosphere, especially if consumers have to wait for service. The layout, equipment, and furniture should convey an appropriate impression, being both attractive and functional. The land, building layout, equipment, and furniture should generate the desired image for the firm—in the same manner that goods retailers use these factors to project a store image.

Planning the Promotional Mix

Aside from packaging, the communication channels available to service firms are identical to those available to merchandise retailers. Many promotional methods are rejected by service retailers as being too brash and costly, without any real consideration given to their relationship to the firms' service offering and the habits of their target markets. This unnatural shrinking of alternatives can result in uncreative promotional campaigns. For example, it can allow a more progressive promoting firm to be the first to offer a premium gift to consumers who deposit $5,000 in the firm's savings account.

Some services can effectively use more promotional expenditures than others. Medical doctors, lawyers, and related professional service firms are restricted by their professional organizations in the type and amount of promotions they utilize. Besides advertising, personal selling, point-of-purchase promotions, and public relations, there are many types of sales promotion that service firms can use in making consumers aware of their offering and instilling consumer confidence in the quality of service offered. The main difficulty is selecting techniques that project the appropriate image.

Advertising

Service advertising differs from product advertising because it is more difficult (and sometimes impossible) to illustrate physically the use or benefits of a service. Thus, service advertising is likely to depend more on image appeals. The differences in the use of advertising media are strongly influenced by the size of the service firm and by accepted practice within each service industry. Small service firms may be content with a listing in the Yellow Pages, while large service firms (such as H & R Block) may rely heavily upon television advertising. Yellow Page advertising and select forms of specialty and direct-mail advertising for small service firms can mean the crucial difference between a sale or an empty cash drawer.

Sign Media

The mobility of many services, such as Greyhound, U-Haul Trailer, or a brightly colored Braniff jet, gives certain service industries an extremely important advertising tool. In a period of twenty-four hours a jet may be seen by thousands of potential customers in a number of states and nations. The airlines and car rental industries also have learned that their personnel can serve as subtle public relations and advertising media. It is small wonder that such industries carefully regulate the social activities of uniformed employees.

Point-of-Purchase Promotion

Point-of-purchase advertising is critical to many service firms. Unlike products, the point of purchase may be in the customer's home or office rather than a store. Nevertheless, there is a point of sale for all services, just as for any product.

The often overlooked business card can be an effective medium at the point of purchase. Business cards are retained by people, particularly businessmen, and since they are often held together with a rubber band or simply tossed into a desk drawer, it is important to give careful consideration to their design. Whenever possible, they should be distinctive and carry the service mark of the company.

It is equally important to plan carefully for the distribution of business cards and flyers in the service retail store. Service shops often fail to provide display racks or piles of cards and flyers for customers. Some service firms have found that a pleased customer will gladly distribute such items to his friends. Unless the retailer of goods has particularly distinctive merchandise or prices, it is unlikely he can share in this willingness of customers to cooperate gladly in advertising.

Word of Mouth

The success of a service retailer is probably much more dependent upon word-of-mouth advertising than goods retailing. "Bad mouthing" seems to be contagious. Airlines are particularly vulnerable to an infection of "bad mouthing," which sweeps through a population. While there is generally some substance to the bad imagery, it is apparent that a series of complex social and psychological variables is involved that causes both positive and negative image infection among a populace. The same phenomena witnessed in the sudden decline in popularity of an "in" restaurant or bar prevail throughout the service industry.

A high level of consumer satisfaction is the most crucial factor in obtaining good word-of-mouth advertising. Although much practical research is needed in this area, service retailers continually need to be aware of the "bad-mouth syndrome."[13]

Bumper Stickers

Bumper stickers can be used effectively to promote services, particularly if the sticker is designed to capture the curiosity of the reader. Service retailers of glamorous or "in" places and events are able to capitalize on the use of bumper stickers in a method that most retailers would never dare attempt. It is difficult to imagine parking lot attendants at a Sears store suddenly descending upon all cars in the lot with bumper stickers advertising the store. Yet this is precisely what happens at a variety of recreational-service areas, ranging from Reptile Gardens to the newest 40-acre amusement park. One of the few examples in goods retailing is the name plate of the dealer that is attached to the back of new automobiles and recreational vehicles.

Perhaps a consumer's psychological need is met through bumper stickers, or else there would be far more objection to their use. Bumper stickers may meet many of the same needs as college and fraternity window stickers and the travel decals that were popular during the '50s. They may say to others "I have visited unusual places" or "I am also a member of the group that enjoys 'in' things."

Other Specialty Advertising Forms

The service industry is particularly well suited to many forms of specialty advertising. A survey by the Specialty Advertising Association International showed that of the top ten groups of particular interest to specialty advertisers, seven were service-type industries.[14] Retail establishments such as camera and jewelry stores were given very low interest rankings by distributors of specialty advertising while banks and savings and loan associations ranked high.

The type of specialty item selected by a service retailer is only as good as the thought behind it and the application it has to the target market. In far too many cases a specialty gimmick has been used simply because it seemed clever and inexpensive. On the other hand, the success of Avis with its "We Try Harder" buttons in a variety of foreign languages is an example of the exposure that a good specialty item can give a service retailer.

Samples and Demonstrations

It is difficult for the service industry to give samples or demonstrations. How does a barber go about giving a sample of his service—by cutting only the front half of the head? Welcome Wagon and other greeting firms can distribute coupons that can be redeemed for a free haircut by newcomers to an area, but the alternatives are limited. Although free samples and demonstrations are normally not practical, special promotional cut rates can be given for services. This is true even in some regulated businesses, such as the airline industry. The introduction of the 747 was followed by low group rates for a half-hour ride in this plane. In many cases the revenue was donated to charity, and the ride became an effective demonstration or sample.

Promotion by Telephone

To many retailers the telephone is more of a hindrance to doing business than an aid. Many managers of supermarkets, discount houses, and other mass merchandising outlets believe that the telephone simply interrupts or intrudes on management and personnel time without adding to sales. This is scarcely the case with most service retailers, yet many treat the telephone as if it were a nuisance.

Generally, when a person calls a service retail establishment, he or she is genuinely interested in learning more about the retailer's service, and should be regarded as a potential customer. A call from a potential customer should be viewed as the near culmination of all the efforts a firm has expended in advertising, public relations, location selection, and total imagery. It is the firm's chance to invite the customer to use its services and may also be the moment to close the sale.

Thus, the telephone should be considered the "hot line" and should not be left to indiscriminate answering by anyone who may or may not be handy. Programs should be established for the purpose of training personnel in the correct use of the phone. Order blanks and writing material should be placed near the phone, and a follow-through system should be implemented. The airlines are leaders in this field and may be viewed as models. The Bell Telephone System should also be contacted for help, since it has trained experts in this field to assist firms, and provides free educational films as well.

Customer Contact and Personal Selling

A large portion, if not the majority, of service retailers are highly dependent upon direct consumer contact. This has been found to be true even in the case of services originally based on the concept of self-service. In some areas, the increasing rate of crimes of a personal nature, such as robbery and rape, plus vandalism, has created a need for attendants in, say, laundromats. Owners of these establishments have discovered that the attendant can do more than just police the place; the attendant can greet customers, instruct them in the use of machines, and provide additional revenue through personal ironing of clothes.

To be successful, a service retailer must place primary emphasis on customer contact. This should begin before the business doors are even opened. In the case of service businesses that serve a local area, a key to success can be door-to-door calling on customers—at the same time that the contractor or remodeler is working on the service building.

The message is simple. After an introduction, the service retailer tells the consumer about the service and what it can do for him, asks for his future business, and asks him to tell his friends. An inexpensive specialty gift item, with the retailer's name, address, and phone number imprinted on it, should be left with the potential customer. Customer contact then continues every minute of the service retailer's day.

There is rarely such a thing as too much customer contact. Unless the importance of this message is continually transmitted to all personnel, it will soon be forgotten. The teller at a savings and loan firm who shows displeasure at opening piggy banks and counting loose change is a very weak link in the service chain. Unreturned phone calls from customers, an empty, dirty pot at the free coffee table, and halfhearted welcomes to customers who bring in two-for-one or other promotional coupons are examples of the negatives in customer contact. Correct customer contact must be a continuous philosophy that permeates all levels of a service retailer's organization.

Relatively less emphasis can be placed on personal selling by service firms that make most of their sales to customers who have already decided to buy when they make their initial contact with the service firm.[15] Such a service firm can advertise to attract new customers and then concentrate on building repeat business by providing prompt, efficient service. Radio and television repair shops, for example, receive a telephone call requesting repair service. The customer does not need to be sold on the fact that he or she needs help. In this case the role of a service person may not include any selling, or it may be limited to a suggestion that the consumer upgrade the purchase by replacing more parts, which will provide a longer, more productive life.

On the other hand, extensive use of personal selling may be required of service firms that contact customers who are not committed to buying at the time of the original contact with the firm. Good personal selling techniques are required in this case. These techniques begin with an understanding of the customer's problem and end with an explanation of how the firm's service offerings can satisfy those needs.

Personal selling plays a different role in the marketing of services than it does in the selling of products. Retailers of goods generally place more reliance on tangible product benefits to consumers in their advertising and selling. Service firms are, of necessity, likely to turn to images that communicate the benefits to the purchaser.[16]

Build Repeat Business

The success of many service firms is dependent upon obtaining *repeat business,* in which consumers continually come back to the same facility to satisfy their needs. Repeat consumer business is based on satisfying the consumer with the service he has previously experienced. Satisfied consumers of services tend to show loyalty to the service firm and to return when they have a new problem that appears to fall within the area of the firm's expertise.

Established professional service firms such as doctors, lawyers, and accountants rely upon repeat business as the core, if not the entire source, of their business. In these cases, and in other service areas, additional business is fairly predictable and is forthcoming almost automatically, as long as a proper relationship is maintained with satisfied customers.[17]

Generating repeat sales from customers revolves mostly around the professional people who provide the services. Consumers become tied to personalities, particularly if they receive prompt, efficient service from the service person. The degree of loyalty may be affected by the amount of skill that the consumer perceives is required to solve his problems. For example, a consumer is likely to be more loyal to a doctor than to a barber. However, some customers change barber shops every time their favorite barber changes employment. Although no one is indispensable, these strong personal preferences must be recognized by service firms' management.

The importance of the service professional affects the firm's selling activity considerably. Technical service people are not as likely to want to develop selling techniques to the degree that good salespeople may consider essential for their profession. As a result, the selling of former service customers is likely to be less organized and systematic than in product retail outlets. Instead, service selling is more centered on opportunity selling, which consists of the technical service person's sensing an opportunity for future service and then communicating the benefits of using that service to his customer.

Undoubtedly, one of the best ways to build repeat business is to perform excellent service all of the time. A difficulty arises, however, because the customer is frequently unable to judge the quality of the service. Thus excellent service alone is not sufficient. It must be accompanied by an informal and discreet method of letting the customer become aware of the excellent service received.

Some scheduling of periodic contact is required if repeat business is to be maintained. As time passes from the date that the original service was performed, the less likely it is that the customer will return to the same service firm for future work.[18] Making periodic contact can remind the customer of the excellent service received, and it can also remind him or her that time has passed more rapidly than he or she thought. For example, by the use of a good card-filing system, dentists, doctors, and the like can identify customers who are due for their periodic checkup.

Opportunities for suggesting the benefits of some further service should also be utilized to build repeat business. An accountant who is making a regular audit might suggest a way of improving a firm's accounting practices or a way of making better managerial use of the data the firm already has. Many bowling firms help to build a permanent clientele by organizing and promoting bowling leagues, which use pressure from the team members to encourage each individual to be there at bowling time. Surely other service firms can use this competitive motivation to build repeat business.

Cooperative associations and chain organizations are also frequently used to build permanent patronage. For example, motels and restaurants benefit from association with one nationally advertised name. Generally the chain, franchise, or cooperative association establishes quality standards, inspects each establishment periodically, and extends the privilege of continued association only to those firms that meet the established standards. Their consumers, perceiving a more consistent type of service, tend to become loyal customers of the various associations' member firms. This consistent service concept is likely to grow in importance as people do more traveling and change their place of residence more frequently.

Customer relations—performing those activities that are designed to make the client personally attached to one of the firm's technical service people—is another method of stimulating repeat business. Providing special considerations, such as lunch, small gifts, and so forth are methods used to varying degrees in attempts to build consumer loyalty.

Credit

Credit also can be used effectively by service firms to generate business. Service firms have too long restricted the granting of credit because they sold intangible offerings that could not be repossessed if the consumer refused to pay his debt. The fact that unused capacity in service firms cannot be sold later makes the granting of credit attractive even if there are occasional losses due to bad debts. Compared to goods retailers, the service firm with excess capacity certainly has less to lose by granting credit and risking losses due to increases in accounts receivable.

The use of bank credit card plans has taken away most of the bad debt problem. The plans also make it easier and more economical for the service firm to make credit sales on small purchases.

In addition, surprising market segments can sometimes be discovered through research no more involved than examining company records. Many airlines found that their credit policies for unmarried young women were unduly restrictive. A policy of extending credit to married women or those over twenty-five did not take into account the number of gainfully employed career women. The number of people in this market segment is large, is growing, and is fully able to assume credit responsibility.

Planning Pricing Strategy

Developing good pricing strategies for service firms is an important activity. Most service firms use relatively little capital, so pricing and the use of time are the main factors used to generate profits. In addition, because of imperfect consumer knowledge about the quality of service performed, many services are less subject to the pressures and controls of the marketplace than goods retailers. As a result, these service firms have greater flexibility in their pricing activities.

Service firms can select many different pricing strategies, and the major alternatives will now be discussed.[19]

Cost Pricing

Cost pricing is a method of obtaining price by adding all of the chargeable costs. This method requires a reliable cost accounting system that identifies the costs and time used for each phase of the service. The allocatable costs are then assigned to each customer, and these costs are multiplied by a markup factor (2.5 is common for many professional service firms), which must cover profit, rent, utilities, insurance, taxes, and other nonallocatable fixed costs.

For example, a service firm performing a job that is estimated to cost $1,000 in wages and other allocatable costs would charge the customer $2,500 if the 2.5 markup factor is used. Only the value of service people's time used on this particular piece of work would be included in the $1,000 cost estimate. The time that these service people spend idle, in retraining, and so forth, would not be included in the allocatable costs, but would have to be recovered in the markup charge.

A major disadvantage of the cost pricing system is the difficulty of identifying and accurately allocating costs. For example, questions frequently arise on the ways to identify and allocate developmental costs, proposed costs, general administrative costs, and so forth. Good cost accounting systems can answer many of these questions, but all procedures are subject to the dedication of the management and service people. Cost pricing will not work unless everyone keeps records that indicate how much time is devoted to each activity and each service job. Frequently, because it is difficult to convince professional service people of this fact, many service firms cannot calculate the profit and loss contribution of individual types of services, individual jobs, customers, and so forth. Instead, they wonder why the overall profitability of the enterprise is low relative to what they think it should be.

Another disadvantage of the cost pricing method is that if costs are used as the sole basis for the establishment of price, there may be no incentive for controlling costs. However, competitive markets usually provide an indication, via decreased business, of when this is occurring.

Contingency Payment Pricing

Contingency payment pricing is the term used when the price for the service is quoted as contingent upon the accomplishment of the task. It is similar to the commission fee for a salesman, since no charge is made unless the task is performed. This method is used by real estate agencies, employment agencies, and similar organizations.

The contingency system offers a great deal of motivation to complete the work successfully. The difficulty arises in defining what constitutes successful performance of the task.

Fixed Pricing

A *fixed,* or *uniform price* is achieved by a controlling body such as a professional organization, or by governmental regulation, or by an informal agreement. Actually, this is a result of a pricing decision and not a method used to reach a decision. The service firm must abide by it, however, so its pricing strategy is predetermined by the controlling body. Transportation companies engaged in interstate commerce (moving companies, trucking firms, railroads, airlines) and beauty shops and barber shops are examples.

Value Pricing

Value pricing is based on the belief that buyers will respond to price in relation to the value that they associate with the service. One should recall that customers of most services have difficulty appraising the technical worth of the service offering because it is generally so intangible. The purchasing decision is likely to be based on the consumer's perception of the value of the service offering. Frequently, when consumers have difficulty appraising the worth of an offering, an association of poor quality is attached to discount prices. Thus value pricing may amount to a "what the market will bear" pricing policy, since the price is not based on cost but on the value the consumer attaches to the service.

Value pricing can be defended as fair despite the nonassociation of price with costs. Price, in this case, is associated with worth, so new ideas, new methods, and new knowledge that are valuable to the client are paid for in proportion to their value to the customer. Value pricing in small, local areas where there are no alternative sources of supply, or in cases of very essential services (such as brain surgery), may not be considered a just pricing policy by consumers.[20]

Planning Pricing Tactics

Service pricing strategy, no matter how it is determined, must guide shorter term (or tactical) decisions to establish the actual quoted price. The same tactical pricing techniques that are used to sell goods can be modified effectively to sell services. The application of some of the major pricing tactics to the service area will now be discussed.

Loss Leader Pricing

Loss leader pricing is a deliberate reduction in price to establish initial contact with a customer. It is frequently used by service firms such as auto service stations or dancing studios, which give price reductions as get-acquainted offers. One disadvantage of loss leader pricing is that a low price may tend to establish a price ceiling, above which the consumer may resist price increases if he knows he is getting the same service but paying a higher price.

Diversionary Pricing

Diversionary pricing is the practice of setting a low, basic price on selected services, which, hopefully, will develop a low price image for the entire firm. It is generally effective if prices are lowered on all service items on which consumers are price conscious. If these price-sensitive offerings cannot be identified, or if all of the firm's offerings are price sensitive, diversionary pricing will not be an effective pricing tactic.

High Price Maintenance

As the name implies, *high price maintenance* is the practice of establishing a price that is higher than the price offered by competitors. Both experience and marketing studies have demonstrated that some consumers tend to associate the price of the product or service with the quality.[21]

It is apparent that some service retailers follow this practice as a price policy. These seem to be the larger, more secure firms that have achieved a reputation and have carved out a particular market segment. Evidence of this was demonstrated in a study of the pest control industry on Long Island, New York. This study found that a small segment of this service industry was able to maintain higher prices. The study concluded that "they seem to be the major participants in the industry, able to hold out against the price threat of the low-price sellers."[22]

Discount Pricing

Discount pricing is a tactic that provides a price quotation that is subject to a discount on some predetermined basis, such as time schedule, volume of purchases over a stated time period, extent of commitment, and so forth. Discount pricing is widely used by leasing firms and many other service agencies. It provides an incentive for the consumer to remain loyal to the service firm because costs are reduced by purchasing all (or most) of the available services from one firm. The widespread use of discount pricing is explained by the fact that service firms are faced with a continuing problem because they are unable to inventory their particular service. If the goods inventory of a retailer does not sell, it can sometimes be returned to the vendor, or stored or placed on sale. This is not the case with a firm such as an airline or movie theater. Once the plane has left the ground, the empty seats are forever lost as revenue for that flight. As a result, service firms with this problem often turn to the practice of charging different customers different prices for only slightly different services.

Youth fares, tour packages, and Saturday afternoon matinees are examples of this type of pricing. Only rarely are these firms able to sell all their services without the aid of discount pricing. As a result, the concept of market segmentation is of paramount importance to firms in the service industry. It becomes a necessity to analyze market segments to determine new promotions and prices that might appeal to them. In the case of regulated and interstate firms, differentiated or discount pricing and promotion are automatically open to official debate and legal regulation.

Flexible, Discriminatory Pricing

Flexible pricing is the practice of charging customers different prices according to their perceived willingness to pay. This appears to be common practice in many sectors of the service industry, particularly in those where a custom price quote is needed for each job. The previously mentioned study of the pest control industry on Long Island, New York demonstrates the use of flexible pricing by that industry. It was found that 58 percent of the sample surveyed demonstrated that flexible pricing had been used. In other words, about 58 percent of the customers were charged different prices for the same work.[23]

The same study concluded that the best marketers in the pest control industry follow the following practices:

1. Set annual total project and sales volume goals
2. Keep a definite profit margin in mind when quoting jobs
3. Have good knowledge of costs
4. Review price schedules regularly
5. Try to secure higher, rather than lower or average prices
6. Tend to be flexible in pricing

An interesting conclusion of the pest control study was that ". . . The smallest firms appeared to be the poorest marketers and medium sized firms the best."[24]

Price Lining

Price lining is a tactic whereby prices are not varied, but the quality or extent of the service provided is adjusted to reflect changes in costs. This removes price as a major negotiating point, but the consumer may be able to perceive the change in the service offering and associate it with an inferior image of the firm in general. Leasing firms frequently use the price lining tactic when they make available, at different rental charges, different quality levels of the same item (garden rototillers with various size engines, for example).

The policy of price lining may sometimes be a questionable practice. A consumer may be quite willing to receive a lower horsepower rental tool but may expect a constant level of quality in regard to other services.

The repair sector of the service industry is an example. A study has shown that consumers are willing to pay disproportionately higher repair prices to have lower cost products repaired. In other words, they do not expect to receive lower quality repair service simply because the item such as a toaster costs less than a stove or refrigerator. They expect to have both repaired properly.[25] Owners of appliances seem to recognize that there is a basic cost for servicing their equipment regardless of the value of the product.

Procurement and
Inventory Control

Procurement in most service firms is generally limited to buying equipment and supplies. The inventory control problem, therefore, is not large unless the service handles physical items as part of its consumer service business. Control of the work in process can be very important for small repair shops, laundries, photography developers, and the like. Accurate control is mandatory in these firms if consumer satisfaction is to be obtained and a permanent clientele maintained. The inventory costs for these firms are not likely to be large, but they cannot risk the loss of business associated with a consumer whose possession has been lost.

There are a few service firms that encounter large inventory costs as part of doing business. Auto repair garages, radio and television repair shops, and so forth face the traditional retail problem of deciding how much inventory they can afford to keep on hand. In this case, the decision rules discussed in Chapter 9 can be used to evaluate inventory levels.

Service firms that require large amounts of inventory are in a better position to arrange financing than retailers who sell a product. The fact that a service firm retains possession of the merchandise rather than selling it can be advantageous in arranging financing for the procurement of inventory.

In addition to normal sources of financing, service firms have used two additional sources. These are (1) leasing corporations, and (2) investment plans for private investors.

Service firms have sometimes used the services of another member of the service industry, *leasing firms.* Today many enterprises find that the cost of purchasing new equipment is so great that purchasing is not possible. Consequently they lease the equipment they need from leasing companies.

A leasing company is a firm that specializes in leasing equipment of all kinds to industry and to public enterprises. A company such as National Equipment Leasing Corp. is an example. This firm is a division of Tiger Airlines.

National Equipment and other firms like it arrange for large amounts of financing from financial institutions. These companies then make arrangements with supplier companies such as Burroughs computers to lease this equipment to customers of the supplier. This relieves the supplier firm of the necessity of owning and establishing a leasing division.

The leasing company and the supplier often work in unison to make the leasing arrangements with the customers. National Equipment Leasing goes so far as to hire retired Burrough's salespeople to sell leasing services to new Burroughs accounts.

A wide variety of merchandise used by service retailers may be acquired by leasing corporations, ranging from the lease of a Boeing 747 to a store full of rental tuxedos for a Tuxedo rental firm.

Leasing corporations also provide service firms with the ability to upgrade models. In other words, if a product such as a computer becomes obsolete before the end of the lease, the leasee may acquire newer equipment from the leasor. In many cases, the service firm is also given the opportunity to purchase the equipment at the end of the lease.

Activities of leasing corporations are not limited to the United States. This can allow a service firm to enter international markets much earlier than if it had to purchase all inventory.

Private investment plans by service firms seem to be less common today than in the past. This is probably the result of the growth of leasing companies and wider availability of funds from financial institutions.

Nevertheless, private investment plans have served as the key to growth for service firms in the past and undoubtedly still can be useful devices for many service firms. Services that have used private investment plans include carnivals, railroads, and a well-known trailer rental firm.

Under such a plan the service firm offers investors an opportunity to share in the return from the use of the equipment (Examples: boxcars, a Ferris wheel or furniture trailer). Investors may be told that for a certain number of dollars they can purchase a number of trailers or a share in a Ferris wheel. The investor obviously has no personal need for half a Ferris Wheel or fifty trailers. Consequently, the investor leases this equipment to the service firm.

In turn, the service firm may give the investor a description of the equipment and will keep a tabulation of where the equipment is and how much it is earning. The investor then receives a check from the service firm based upon an agreed-to percentage of the income generated by the equipment.

This system has the built-in problem of administrative difficulty. Another inherent difficulty is that there is room for dishonesty on the part of the service firms.

Nevertheless, investors have been anxious to join such programs due to the high rate of return available.

This type of plan is probably more attractive to a service firm in the early years of its existence. It may later wish to phase out the investment program in an effort to retain a greater share of the earnings and to reduce administrative problems.

Before considering the use of a private investment plan, a service firm should hire the services of a competent lawyer. It is possible that a private investment plan could come under the jurisdiction of the Securities Exchange Commission.

Scheduling the Work Load

Work scheduling is of considerable importance in service firms because of the perishability of the unused labor and the consumer ill will generated by not meeting a deadline. Work-scheduling tasks, similar to those in manufacturing companies, are faced by most service firms. Labor costs comprise such a large percentage of total costs for most service firms that management must consider all possibilities to improve the work flow.

Use of such techniques as critical path analysis, control boards, and so forth can improve the overall labor performance by making better utilization of employee time.[26] *Critical path analysis,* which is simply a planning tool, provides a diagram that shows which jobs must be completed before other jobs can be started. It also uses estimated time requirements needed to perform each job so that they can be scheduled in an order that will minimize the time needed to complete the total job. This tool can be used to identify bottlenecks that limit the amount of work generated by a service firm.

Even small service firms can benefit from the type of thinking that critical path analysis requires. For example, parts can be ordered before they are needed so that they are available for use when needed by the service people. Repair and maintenance work can be done during idle time, so that equipment is in top shape and ready to operate at full speed during peak service hours. The list could continue indefinitely, but suffice it to say that proper planning, scheduling, and control procedures can result in increased profits for most service firms.

Summary

The marketing of services differs from merchandise marketing in that:

1. Repeat customer business is absolutely required.
2. The firm's offering cannot be stored, so it is even more important to operate at near-capacity levels.
3. It is more difficult for the consumer to measure the quality or worth of services offered.
4. Service firms are particularly vulnerable to the "bad-mouth syndrome" because it is difficult for consumers to judge the value of a service.

Thus, most of a service firm's marketing effort can be aimed at reducing consumer uncertainty. A consumer's confidence can be gained by analyzing his problem and providing an honest opinon, backed up by facts, on the worth of each alternative solution from the consumer's viewpoint. Competent employees should render the service, as demonstrable skill and knowledge will create consumer confidence. Warranties should reinforce the quality image.

Respecting the customer's time can gain his respect, since people become distrustful of a service firm that always breaks its promised service schedules. Some service delays are unavoidable, but the consumer should be informed that there is going to be a delay. Consumers also appreciate promptness in being informed when cost estimates are changed because of unforeseen circumstances.

Repeat business can be built upon satisfying the consumer so he or she comes back to the service outlet. Consumers frequently become tied to personalities and develop a loyalty to the person who is believed to deliver excellent quality and prompt and efficient service. Periodic contact can be made with consumers to remind them of the excellent service the consumer received and of the passage of time, i.e., that it is time once again to schedule a periodic checkup, oil change, etc.

Pricing strategy for services is based upon a number of things: cost plus a markup factor; the value that consumers perceive to be associated with the service; and some relationship to competitors price (such as the use of a high price maintenance policy or a discount policy).

Questions

1. How would you explain the trend toward vertical integration in the service industry?

2. Describe the steps you would use in marketing the following services.

    a. A travel agency in New York

    b. An insect extermination service in Des Moines

    c. A management consulting firm in Chicago

    d. A tourist guide service in Miami

    e. The only local computer service firm (the nearest competitor is 200 miles away)

3. Service firms often encounter negative publicity through the warranty litigation difficulties of some members of the industry. Can you suggest any methods by which a service firm with a clean record could benefit from this situation?

4. Very few members of the service industry have a worse reputation with the public than the automobile service firms. If you accepted a position as service manager for a typical auto dealer, how would you go about marketing your services?

5. What types of service firms would you expect to be sensitive to location, and why? Why would other types of service firms be less sensitive to location? Give examples of each (other than those cited in the text).

6. Discuss the ethics of taxing nonprofit organizations that compete with private service firms. Assume a position, state your opinion, and defend it in a logical manner, using sound business principles and your own code of ethics.

7. Independence and lack of tact are often considered to be admirable traits if they are accompanied by a high degree of technical competence. Discuss this phenomenon in terms of the market concept and the art of personal selling.

8. Discuss the advisability of physicians, lawyers, and dentists using bank cards to eliminate their bad debt problems.

9. Design a promotional mix for the following service firms:

    a. A small local flying service

    b. A print shop

    c. A real estate abstract service

    d. A professional photographer

    e. A psychological counseling service

10. Suggest a pricing strategy or combination of strategies for each of the retail firms in question 9.

11. Suggest at least two types of service firms that might find each of the various pricing tactics (loss leader pricing plan, and so forth) useful and explain why you think each tactic would be useful for the service firms you suggest.

Footnotes

1. Sam Weiner, "Monumental Undertaking," *Financial Trend* 18 (January 28–February 3, 1973): 7, 10, 12, 15.

2. E. B. Weiss, "Marketers: Don't Ignore Our Growing Service-Oriented Society," *Advertising Age,* 5 May 1969.

3. *Survey of Current Business,* U.S. Dept. of Commerce, July 1977, p. 30.

4. John M. Rathmell, "What Is Meant by Service?" *Journal of Marketing* 30 (October 1966): 32–36.

5. E. B. Weiss, "Will Retailing Be a New Bank Service?" *Advertising Age,* 4 September 1967, p. 60.

6. "Fred Meyer's Grocery S & Ls," *Business Week,* 24 January 1977, p. 76.

7. Richard P. Carr, Jr., "Developing a New Residential Market for Carpeting: Some Mistakes and Successes," *Journal of Marketing* 41 (July 1977): 101–102.

8. Robert C. Judd, "Similarities or Differences in Product and Service Retailing," *Journal of Retailing* 43 (Winter 1968): 2.

9. Ibid., p. 3.

10. Commerce Clearing House, *Products Liability Reporter* (Chicago: Commerce Clearing House, 1970), paragraph 1010.

11. Henningsen v. Bloomfield Motors, 32 N.J. 358, 161 A. 2d 69 (1960).

12. Warren J. Wittreich, "How to Buy/Sell Professional Services," *Harvard Business Review* 44 (March–April 1966): 127–138.

13. Johan Arndt, "Word of Mouth Advertising and Informal Communications," in Donald F. Cox, ed., *Risk Taking and Information Handling in Consumer Behavior* (Boston: Harvard University Graduate School of Business Administration, 1967), pp. 188–239.

14. George Z. Herpel and Richard A. Collins, *Specialty Advertising in Marketing* (Homewood, Ill.: Richard D. Irwin, 1972), pp. 181–182.

15. H. N. Broom and Justin G. Longenecker, *Small Business Management* (Cincinnati: South-Western Publishing Co., 1971), pp. 530–531.

16. Judd, "Similarities or Differences," p. 6.

17. Robert E. Sibson, *Managing Professional Service Enterprises* (New York: Pitman, 1971), p. 114.

18. Ibid., p. 115.

19. See also R. E. Sibson, *"A Service,"* in E. Marting, ed., *Creative Pricing* (New York: American Management Association, 1968), pp. 146–155.

20. Ibid, p. 103.

21. J. D. McConnell, "The Development of Brand Loyalty: An Experimental Study," *Journal of Marketing Research* 5 (February 1968): 13–19; J. D. McConnell, "The Price-Quality Relationship in an Experimental Setting," *Journal of Marketing Research* 5 (August 1968): 300–303; J. D. McConnell, "An Experimental Examination of the Price-Quality Relationship," *Journal of Business* 42 (October 1968): 331–334; and Martin L. Lansidsen, "The Relationship between Price and Perceived Quality: An Experimental Study," *Markeds Dommuniksjon* 2 (1973) Argang 10, 1–12.

22. Martin R. Scklissel, "Pricing in a Service Industry," *M.S.U. Business Topics* 25 (Spring 1977): 37–48.

23. Ibid.

24. Ibid., p. 48.

25. Adler Lee and James D. Hlavacek, "The Relationship between Price and Repair Service for Consumer Durables," *Journal of Marketing* 90 (April 1976): 80–82.

26. Philip Kotler, *Marketing Management, Analysis, and Control,* 2d ed. (Englewood Cliffs, N.J.: Prentice-Hall, 1972), pp. 412–418.

Case Study

First State Savings and Loan

First State Savings and Loan has its main office located in a growing town of 25,000 population. It is the only savings and loan facility in this town. The level of savings deposits placed in the main First State office are $35 million.

First State has recently established a new branch office in a coal mining town of 3,000 people. The increasing demand for energy is projected to cause more mining companies to locate in this area. Current employment in the area is completely dependent upon coal mining and the retail and public services that supply the needs of the local inhabitants. The population of this new area is expected to double in the next five years. The miners are well paid, with most earning more than $20,000 per year. The First State new branch office has been in operation for one year. It has attracted savings deposits of $220,000. Lending activity for construction of new housing has amounted to $2,130,000.

There is no other savings and loan facility in the area and only one bank.

First State management is not satisfied with the amount of savings that First State has attracted during this first year of business. They believe that some new promotional programs must be used to increase savings deposits at the new facility. They are presently spending $1,500 per year solely on local newspaper advertising. There is no purely local radio or television station serving the area since broadcast reception is obtained from a distant metropolitan area.

Discussion Questions

1. Is First State management correct in believing that savings deposits should be higher?

2. Develop a complete promotional program for First State.

3. What other factors could be causing the level of savings to be lower than management expects? What can be done to determine if a change should be made in one of these factors?

Case Study

ABC Cleaners

ABC dry cleaners is facing the problem of having to pay its three employees on a full-time basis for forty hours per week. Each employee is required to perform a specific skilled job, so ABC cannot fire or lay off any of these employees. Each employee is currently being paid $800 per month. However, because of an insufficient demand, ABC receives only enough business to keep the employees busy half of the time. The per unit cleaning cost (materials, chemicals, energy, and so forth) other than labor amount to 20 percent of the retail sales dollar that the customers pay to have their clothes dry cleaned.

ABC has conducted some research and found the following relationship between promotional expenditures and monthly sales. (ABC is currently using $100 per month for promotional purposes.)

Amount of Monthly Promotional Expenditures	$ Monthly Retail Sales for ABC
$100	$10,000
$200	$13,000
$300	$16,000
$400	$18,000
$500	$19,000
$600	$19,500
$700	$19,700
$800	$19,800
$900	$19,850
$1000	$19,900
$1100	$19,950
$1200	$19,975
$1300	$20,000

ABC owns its own building and equipment but is paying $1,000 per month to pay off its mortgage on these physical facilities. The owner of ABC is also the manager and she gives herself a monthly salary of $1,500. The ABC manager has a good tax shelter and will not pay any more taxes even if the income from ABC is doubled.

Discussion Questions

1. How much should ABC spend on promotion? Why?

2. What other alternatives does ABC have?

3. What do you recommend that ABC do? Why?

Part Six

Planning Future Growth

Chapter 17

Using Marketing Research to Reduce Retail Risks

Learning Goals

1. To understand the role that marketing research plays in the retail firm.

2. To be able to obtain the sources of secondary data that can be used to make managerial decisions in the retail industry.

3. To be able to discuss the methods of collecting primary data that can be used to make more intelligent managerial decisions.

4. To learn how to get more information from marketing research and data available from electronic scanner systems.

Key Terms and Concepts

retail market research	survey	semantic differential scale
primary data	personal interview	
secondary data	telephone interview	projective techniques
observation	mail questionnaire	simple random sampling
experimental research	Likert scale	

Retail market research is the process of systematically searching for, collecting, and analyzing information that can be used by the retailer in developing management strategies. The goal of retail research is to reduce the risks associated with the decision making process. Thus, it is similar to the concept of buying insurance. Retailers incur the cost of research because they want to minimize the potential losses that can occur because they were not well informed when they made a major decision.

Although research is usually used to solve problems it can also be used to examine what is currently being done. New and better ways of doing things can be developed as a result of such ongoing research involving the establishment of guidelines that automatically warn the retailer of possible trouble areas.

Only in recent years have retailers begun to recognize the importance of marketing research. The use of the marketing concept, which stresses the satisfaction of consumers at a profit, has increased the need for retailers to observe changing consumer demands. Marketing research can assist the retailer in observing consumers and making intelligent decisions. Retailers should have a basic understanding of research procedures so that they can contract for outside research studies, conduct the studies themselves, and understand the results better. This chapter concentrates on the use of marketing research in a retail environment.

Research can be beneficial to the retailer whenever a decision must be made. The question then becomes one of establishing priorities on the types of problems that are considered important enough to warrant the use of marketing research. The level of expenditure on research should be related to the importance of the decision. Decisions involving significant costs or serious consequences for the retailer are likely to benefit considerably from the added information provided by research.

On the other hand, decisions that do not involve much added cost or do not have serious implications for the retailer's present business may not require the use of much, if any, research. The expected payoff from new sales resulting from a change in the retailing mix must, however, be considered as important as the added cost involved in making the change. This "opportunity cost" is frequently overlooked by retailers who view the importance of the decision only from the "What will it cost me?" approach. They do not consider the "What will it make for me if the idea works?" concept.

Small and medium sized independent outlets are especially prone to view research from the cost approach instead of looking at both the benefit and the cost approaches. As a result they give away a prime competitive advantage to the large chain retail organization who employ well-qualified people to conduct their research activities.

The strategic areas of retailing such as location, merchandise policy, pricing policy, promotional allocations, and allocation or performance of sales personnel usually account for the most important decisions that a retailer makes. Consequently, they may account for most of the firm's research activity.

The retailer must start today to conceptualize the marketing plan philosophy as a way of running his business. The marketing plan concept should become a way of life for the retailer, enabling him to develop specific goals and objectives for guiding day-to-day operations. It matters little whether his is a multiple-store operation or a single-store outlet, the problems faced are basically the same: To attract more customers and to convince each customer to buy more of what the store has to sell.

In order to attract more customers and generate more sales, the retailer should begin his marketing planning activity by researching the following:

—What motivates present customers to buy at his store? What do they like or dislike about his store? How far do they drive to reach his store?

—Why do other consumers within his trading area not buy in his store? Are they aware of his store and the lines of merchandise he carries? What is his store's image in the minds of consumers?

—What are the strengths and weaknesses of his competition as identified by consumers in the market? How do consumers rate his store compared to his competition's, for quality of merchandise, selection, pricing, customer service, convenience, store operations, etc.?

—How well has he penetrated the market areas his store(s) serves? By what current definition? Pins in a map? Zip codes? Or, more specifically, census tracts?

Only after these questions have been answered through sound marketing research techniques can the retailer logically approach the marketing plan concept. The marketing plan which would then follow would include rational, attainable goals and the marketing strategies required to support the achievement of those goals.

Such marketing objectives can only be projected on the basis of a concise definition of current market positioning which properly identifies current problems and opportunities for the retailer. In today's challenging economic environment, the utilization of marketing research tools and sound marketing planning are critical. Now, more than ever![1]

Thus far we have seen that research is used to enable retail management to make informed decisions. This chapter will cover the steps in the research process itself.

Identifying the Central Problems and Opportunities

This phase consists of investigating the environment to determine just where the firm is going and how the competitive firms and consumer demands are changing. This type of research can reveal causes for changes that have occurred. Once these underlying causal factors are identified, they can reveal new opportunities for the firm. For example, some retailers noticed the trend toward increased suburban shopping patterns during the 1950s and 1960s and moved outlets to the suburbs. Other retailers were not aware of the shift to more suburban shopping and did not expand or relocate from their downtown sites. The result of their failure to recognize the change in the environment has been a significant loss in their share of the market, and in some cases they had to go out of business.

Determining Sources of Information

This step consists of a thorough search for all relevant information available from within the firm and from outside sources. If relatively little secondary information is available and little is known about the problem being investigated, then a special, uniquely designed research project may be the only way to obtain data that can be used to solve the firm's problems.

Primary Data

Primary data are pieces of information that are collected by the firm or its representatives by actively observing, experimenting, or surveying people. These data are called primary data because the retail firm must gather its own information or hire someone else to conduct a special study for that firm.

Secondary Data

Secondary data are the facts that currently exist within the firm or industry and existing facts collected from sources outside the firm or industry. Examples of secondary data are company data available from: sales records, customer return forms, merchandise budgets, promotional plans, inventory control records, invoices, warranty records, credit card sales, customer checks, financial records, and so forth. Secondary data is available from many different outside sources, such as the data available from industry trade associations. Appendix 17–A contains a listing of some of these retail trade associations. Trade associations can usually refer retailers to the major sources of information that have been collected for that type of business.

Retail trade journals also provide current information on industry trends. A listing of some retail trade journals is presented in Appendix 17–B.

Governmental sources are also important contributors of retail information. State sales tax records provide, on a city or county basis, the most current and accurate estimate of sales for each retail category. This can be used to calculate the individual firm's share of the market by simply dividing the individual firm's sales by the sales of all firms in the area. By observing the firm's share of the market on a quarterly basis, retail management can determine whether the firm is obtaining an increasing or decreasing share of the market. Such information allows management to evaluate the performance of the firm relative to competition. An increasing share indicates the firm is gaining on competition in the battle for the consumer's dollar expenditures. A decreasing share indicates that the firm is not keeping up with competition.

Other state offices such as the State Examiner's Office provide data on bank and savings and loan association deposits. Such data measures the attractiveness of the community. A rapid increase in deposits indicates the community is prospering and healthy. The implication is that retailers who do a good job in satisfying consumer demands will share in this increasing prosperity. A slow growth in financial deposits indicates that consumers are not going to be able to increase their spending on retail items.

A listing of governmental publications that supply retail information is presented in Appendix 17–B.

Local business firms are also good sources of retail information. The number of utility connections can provide an accurate and current estimate of town and country population. In some areas voter registration records can be used to provide population estimates for small areas within a county, city, or town.

Determining the Method of Obtaining Primary Information

The three basic methods of gathering primary data should be investigated to determine which is most appropriate for the praticular problem being investigated.

Observation

Personal observation techniques involve watching the consumer's actions in an inconspicuous manner. Thus, retail personnel observe consumer's actions to draw conclusions from what they see. Small, independent retailers especially use this method to keep abreast of changes in consumers' wants, and to evaluate their merchandise offering and performance of their personnel.

Some retailers use shopping services to evaluate their salespeople. The hired but unknown shopper comes into the store and pretends to be interested in some particular kind of merchandise. The hired shopper then asks questions about the goods and may even purchase them. The shopper, after leaving the store, evaluates the performance of the salesperson. Such an evaluation can be used by the retailer to suggest improvements in the salesperson's presentation.

Other observation studies involve the use of a traffic count. This technique consists of counting the numbers of passersby and noting certain characteristics of their behavior, for example whether they were on foot, in an auto, which direction they were going, whether they entered the store, or noticed a specific window display, and so forth.

An outside traffic count can be used to locate outlets that depend heavily upon foot or auto traffic. Sites with the heaviest pedestrian traffic are believed to be the best locations for stores selling convenience goods. Knowledge of the direction of the traffic flow outside the store can be used to determine the types of window displays and entrance facilities needed to provide a maximum inducement for the passing person to enter the store.

Traffic counts and direction of traffic flows inside the store can be used to maximize the exposure of departments that sell impulse goods and of all merchandise in general.

Experimentation

Experimental research is used when retailers want to study the cause and effect relationship between two or more elements in the retailing mix. For example, a retailer could change the number of shopping hours to see what effect it has upon sales and profits. Experimentation should be conducted under controlled conditions that hold the levels of all other factors constant and allow only the factor under investigation to be varied. This is a significant advantage of experimentation research over observation research, since observation does not involve the use of controlled conditions. Thus, a retailer can observe consumers' reactions to a change in store hours but unless the other factors are held constant, the retailer will not be able to determine if the change in sales was due to the change in store hours or to changes in some other factors.

The chief disadvantages of experimental research are the difficulties encountered in attempting to hold the factors constant. It is difficult to prevent changes in activity from competitors, the government, the climate, economic conditions, and so forth from affecting the results of the experiment. Careful research designs can overcome these difficulties but they do require the use of several months of time and the services of a well-qualified researcher.

Survey

Some of the information needed by retailers cannot be obtained by mere observation of consumer actions or by the use of experimental techniques. The *survey* method is the other major technique used by retailers. The three kinds of surveys are by personal interview, telephone, and mail. The choice between these three methods is influenced by the type of information requested in the questionnaire, the type of respondents, and the cost of using each alternative.

Personal Interview Method

The *personal interview* consists of the interviewer obtaining the information from respondents in face-to-face meetings. This type of interview allows the interviewer to obtain answers to a great number of questions. It also can be used to obtain more detailed information and can determine why consumers believe or act as they said they do. Thus it is used when open-ended projective techniques are needed to determine the consumer's attitudes.

Personal interviews generally result in a higher percentage of completed questionnaires than is the case for telephone interviewing or mail approach. This higher completion rate may cover a more representative group of respondents because many people will not respond to a mail survey and many people are not included in a sample from a telephone book.

On the other hand, more bias can creep into the interviewer's reporting of consumers' responses unless trained interviewers are used. Responses to personal questions may also be more biased if the personal interview is used, because the respondent may be more embarrassed.[2] The interviewer should be given a list of specific people or houses to contact; if not, a bias toward selecting the better-appearing houses will result. Also, interviewers can cheat by filling out a question-naire without making an interview.

These disadvantages of the personal interview technique can be reduced con-siderably by thoroughly training interviewers to recheck 10 to 20 percent of the responses and by using other good research methods. But the major disadvantage—substantially greater expense per completed interview—cannot be reduced by any significant degree.

Telephone Interview Method

Telephone interviewing is similar to personal interviewing except that communica-tion occurs over the telephone instead of in person. The interviewer can still probe, check conflicting statements, and use unstructured questions except, of course, those requiring responses to complex scaling techniques, drawings, or photo-graphs. The major advantages of telephone interviewing are the short time required to obtain the data and a relatively low cost of data collection. The questionnaire, however, may have to be a little shorter in a telephone interview than in a personal interview, since it is easier for the respondent to hang up the phone than throw the interviewer out of the house.[3] For personal questions, telephone interviewing may be better than personal interviewing because the respondent may talk more freely than in a face-to-face interview.

Telephone interviewing must be done when respondents will not be irritated by the call, but some evening re-calling is required to reach no-answer numbers of families where husband and wife both work. The same procedure is required for the personal interview, so there is no relative disadvantage to telephone interviewing because of the not-at-home problem.

Interviewer bias and cheating can also arise in telephone interviewing. However, if all interviews are made from a central location, the interviewer's technique can be controlled and checked with minimum effort.

The major difficulty in telephone surveys is drawing a representative sample of the target population. Unlisted numbers, families with a new telephone that is not yet listed, and families that do not have a telephone are excluded from the selection list and therefore are not represented in the sample unless random digit dialing can be used.

Mail Questionnaire Method

Mail questionnaires are given to the respondent through the mail, attached to products, placed in shopping bags, or placed in newspapers. Respondents gener-ally return the questionnaire by mail.

Mail questionnaires must usually be relatively short or the consumers will not send them back.[4] Also, fewer probing and in-depth questions can be asked in mail questionnaires than in the personal interview. In addition, respondents tend to give briefer answers to open-end questions in mail surveys than in personal or telephone interviews.[5]

Mail questionnaires reach nearly everyone, so the not-at-home problem is reduced and families where both husband and wife work are reached. In addition, the mail method can be economical in reaching a sample of people who are widely scattered over a geographic area. However, the cost per completed interview depends upon the return rate. Frequently only 10 to 20 percent of the people who receive questionnaires by mail return them.

Thus a sample bias may occur as only the people who are interested in the topic respond, and the undereducated consumers may hesitate to write responses to open-end questions or may not even return the questionnaire. Writing short, easy-to-answer questions on attractive questionnaire forms which are accompanied by a cover letter, an incentive premium, and a selfaddressed, pre-stamped return envelope, will increase the return rate and reduce some of this sample bias.

Robinson and Agisim report that by using these techniques and a good questionnaire construction it is possible to secure from 70 to 93 percent returns on mail surveys.[6] Their findings indicate that, with high-level returns, the differences between respondents and nonrespondents were due to chance and not to inherent variations in characteristics. They concluded that when returns reach the level of 80 percent, reliability can be given to the findings because nonrespondents would have little, if any, effect on the total.

The mail questionnaire approach has some disadvantages, however. First, the response to a mail survey is subject to a sequence bias in the questions asked: respondents can change their answers to early questions after they read the later questions. In addition, it is never quite certain whose response one is getting in a mail survey. The respondent can get aid in completing the questionnaire or even have someone else fill it out for him.

Collecting Data

There are two main tasks to be achieved in the data collection phase of a research project—deciding on the wording of the questionnaire if the survey method is used and determining what type of sampling plan is to be used.

Questionnaire Construction

Questionnaires are recording devices that are frequently used to learn consumer attitudes, knowledge, and behavior. Questionnaire design should begin with the definitions of the problems that are being researched. Any questionnaire must be short in length or respondents will not take the time to answer all the questions or return it. Oral interviews should not exceed thirty minutes.[7] The response rate is increased and respondent fatigue decreased with shorter interviews. It is desirable to limit self-administered questionnaires to an even shorter length. Thus it is important to determine what information is needed to satisfy the objectives of the research project before the questionnaire is written.

Generally, the researcher develops a list of topics that must be covered, and this list is then converted into questions. Each proposed question should be evaluated against the criterion, "What will be done with the information obtained from this question?" If the answer is "nothing," and the question does not contribute any information that can be used to satisfy the research objectives, it should be eliminated from the questionnaire.

Consumer attitude measurement studies generally involve a series of attitude scales consisting of attitude statements and questions that ask the consumer to express his degree of agreement or disagreement. Responses are then combined in a prespecified manner to yield an overall indication of consumer beliefs.[8]

Many different attitude scales and approaches are available in retail attitude research. The more frequently used techniques will now be discussed briefly.

Likert Method of Summated Ratings

Likert scales involve the use of a list of statements related to the attitude being investigated.[9] Each respondent is asked to indicate his degree of agreement or disagreement with each statement. Each degree of agreement or disagreement is assigned a numerical value in the following manner: strongly approve—5, approve—4, undecided—3, disapprove—2, and strongly disapprove—1. The respondent's total score is computed by adding his scores on all of the statements relevant to the attitude being investigated.

Likert scales enable a researcher to rank attitudes because an individual's final score can be interpreted only in relation to the scores of other respondents. In other words, Likert scales are ordinal measures only; they do not allow the researcher to measure the differences between attitudes.

Semantic Differential Scale

The frequently used *semantic differential scales* permit the development of descriptive profiles of consumer attitudes that facilitate the comparison of competitive stores.[10] This attitude-scaling technique consists of pairs of polar adjectives, with a seven-point scale separating the opposite descriptive terms.[11] Respondents are asked to select the point on each scale that best represents their attitude on the dimension in question. Usually an identical ordinal scale is used to obtain relative perceptions on several competitive stores. For example, the image of each of several competing stores might be measured on the characteristics in Exhibit 17–1.

The respondents are asked to rate several competitive stores on the same scales. The questionnaire is usually organized to measure consumer attitudes on one major dimension at a time—physical characteristics, conveniences, merchandise offering, prices, personnel, advertising, and so forth. The semantic differential is a relatively simple technique to use and analyze. Consumer perceptions of the stores can be compared easily by plotting on the original questionnaire the median response (one-half of the respondents' ratings are higher and one-half are lower than the median rating) on each scale for each store. The differences in store images usually become readily apparent when these comparisons are made.

The semantic differential has the advantage of being easily replicated, so trends in consumers' attitudes can be detected. A disadvantage is the neutral midpoint in the seven-point scale, which seems to attract many respondents who are reluctant to score a store unusually good or bad.[12] For this reason some researchers use even-number scales which force the respondent to take a position.

Projective Techniques

Several projective techniques are used to measure store image. All of these *projective techniques* use an indirect questioning procedure that leads the respondent to believe that he or she is answering in a way that will not reveal biases. These indirect approaches are used when customers appear to be unable or unwilling to specify their beliefs about some item.

Thematic apperception tests consist of presenting a series of pictures to the respondent, who is asked to tell a story about each picture. Questions such as, "What's happening in the picture? How did it come about? What will happen next?" are used to obtain the story. It is hoped that the respondent, in telling the story, will indirectly reveal the factors that motivate him or her.

The sentence completion approach consists of presenting respondents with a number of incomplete sentences. The respondents are then asked to complete the sentences with the first thought that comes to their minds. The respondent is usually given a limited amount of time to complete each question. The questions may be worded in either the first or the third person so that the respondent's inner feelings are better revealed.

The following questions have been used to identify components of store image: "When you think of *(store name),* what is the first thing that comes to your mind?" "What do you like *most* about shopping at *(store name)?*" "What do you like *least* about shopping at *(store name)?*" "What are the major reasons why you think other people shop at *(store name)?*"[13] Using the last three questions, Berry[14] identified twelve components of department store image (Exhibit 17–2.).

Proponents of unstructured, open-end questions believe that by allowing respondents to discuss only the concepts they remember, only the critical reinforcing image components are identified.[15] The semantic differential approach, on the other hand, forces responses on all image components listed in the questionnaire. Thus, the questionnaire should contain accompanying questions that allow respondents to evaluate the importance of the attribute as well as their impression of the store's relative rating on that attribute. For example, a questionnaire such as the one in Exhibit 17–3 could precede the rating questions in Exhibit 17–1. This would allow the researcher to identify the most important components of store image and then determine consumers' perceptions on the important attributes of each store.

Question Sequence

The introduction to the questionnaire should include a brief and very general statement of the objectives of the survey without identifying the retail sponsor. A guarantee must usually be made that the respondents' comments will remain confidential and will not be revealed except in group summaries.

The first question must gain respondents' interest and convince them that the

Exhibit 17–1 Example of the Use of the Semantic Differential in Obtaining a Store's Relative Rating on Different Characteristics

The following questions will permit you to express the level of your opinion for different characteristics about different stores. For example, if the store in question is extremely well known to you, then you would mark an X in the blank nearest "Well known generally" and below the word "Extremely;" i.e., the blank on the extreme left. If, however, you do not know the store, then you would mark an X in the blank at the far right, beside "Unknown generally" and underneath the word "Extremely."

Please rate the following items for (store name)

General Characteristics of the Store

	Extremely	Quite	Slightly	Neither One nor the Other	Slightly	Quite	Extremely	
Well known generally	—	—	—	—	—	—	—	Unknown generally
Small number of stores operated by company	—	—	—	—	—	—	—	Large number of stores operated by company
Long time in community	—	—	—	—	—	—	—	Short time in community
Open during convenient shopping hours	—	—	—	—	—	—	—	Closed during convenient shopping hours
Open during convenient shopping days	—	—	—	—	—	—	—	Closed during convenient shopping days

Physical characteristics of the Store

Dirty	—	—	—	—	—	—	—	Clean
Unattractive decor	—	—	—	—	—	—	—	Attractive decor
Easy to find items you want	—	—	—	—	—	—	—	Difficult to find items you want
Easy to move through store	—	—	—	—	—	—	—	Difficult to move through store
Fast checkout	—	—	—	—	—	—	—	Slow checkout

Convenience of Reaching the Store from Your Location

Nearby	—	—	—	—	—	—	—	Distant
Short time required to reach store	—	—	—	—	—	—	—	Long time required to reach store
Difficult drive	—	—	—	—	—	—	—	Easy drive
Difficult to find parking place	—	—	—	—	—	—	—	Easy to find parking place
Convenient to other stores I shop	—	—	—	—	—	—	—	Inconvenient to other stores I shop

Products Offered

Latest fashion or style is available	—	—	—	—	—	—	—	Latest fashion or style is not available
Wide selection of different kinds of products	—	—	—	—	—	—	—	Limited selection of different kinds of products
Fully stocked	—	—	—	—	—	—	—	Understocked

Undependable products	___	___	___	___	___	___	___	Dependable products
High quality	___	___	___	___	___	___	___	Low quality
Numerous brands	___	___	___	___	___	___	___	Few brands
Unknown brands	___	___	___	___	___	___	___	Well-known brands

Prices Charged by the Store

Low compared to other stores	___	___	___	___	___	___	___	High compared to other stores
Low values for money spent	___	___	___	___	___	___	___	High values for money spent
Large number of items specially priced	___	___	___	___	___	___	___	Small number of items specially priced

Store Personnel

Courteous	___	___	___	___	___	___	___	Discourteous
Cold	___	___	___	___	___	___	___	Friendly
Unhelpful	___	___	___	___	___	___	___	Helpful
Adequate number	___	___	___	___	___	___	___	Inadequate number
Knowledgeable about product and service offering	___	___	___	___	___	___	___	Not knowledgeable about product and service offering
Attractive appearance	___	___	___	___	___	___	___	Unattractive appearance
Acceptable sales pressure	___	___	___	___	___	___	___	Unacceptable sales pressure

Advertising by the Store

Uninformative	___	___	___	___	___	___	___	Informative
Unhelpful in planning	___	___	___	___	___	___	___	Helpful in planning purchases
Appealing	___	___	___	___	___	___	___	Unappealing
Believable	___	___	___	___	___	___	___	Misleading
Frequently seen by you	___	___	___	___	___	___	___	Infrequently seen by you

Your Friends and the Store

Unknown to your friends	___	___	___	___	___	___	___	Well known to your friends
Well liked by your friends	___	___	___	___	___	___	___	Disliked by your friends
Poorly recommended by your friends	___	___	___	___	___	___	___	Well recommended by your friends
Numerous friends shop there	___	___	___	___	___	___	___	Few friends shop there

Customer Services

Easy credit policy	___	___	___	___	___	___	___	Tight credit policy
Good layaway service	___	___	___	___	___	___	___	Poor layaway service
Good delivery service	___	___	___	___	___	___	___	Poor delivery service
Good product guarantees	___	___	___	___	___	___	___	Poor product guarantees
Prompt repair service	___	___	___	___	___	___	___	Slow repair service
Easy product-return policies	___	___	___	___	___	___	___	Tight product-return policy
Satisfies customer complaints	___	___	___	___	___	___	___	Does not satisfy customer complaints

Exhibit 17-2 Department Store Image Codes, Components, and Subcomponents Identified by Sentence Completion Approach

01 Price of Merchandise
a. Low prices
b. Fair or competitive prices
c. High or noncompetitive prices
d. Values, expect with specfic regard to premiums, such as stamps, or quality of merchandise

02 Quality of Merchandise
a. Good or poor quality of merchandise
b. Good or poor department(s), except with respect to assortment, fashion, etc.
c. Stock brand names

03 Assortment of Merchandise
a. Breadth of merchandise
b. Depth of merchandise
c. Carries a brand I like

04 Fashion of Merchandise

05 Sales Personnel
a. Attitude of sales personnel
b. Knowledgeability of sales personnel
c. Number of sales personnel
d. Good or poor service

06 Locational Convenience
a. Location from home
b. Location from work
c. Access
d. Good or poor location without reference to home or work

07 Other Convenience Factors
a. Parking
b. Hours store is open
c. Convenience with regard to other stores
d. Store layout with respect to convenience
e. Convenience (in general)

08 Services
a. Credit
b. Delivery
c. Restaurant facilities
d. Other services (gift consultants, layaway plans, baby strollers, escalators, etc.)

survey is interested in their views on a nonpersonal basis. The remaining questions must be arranged in a manner that is psychologically sound. Simpler questions should be asked first, but the writer must consider the influence that each question has upon succeeding questions. The questions are usually placed in a logical order that obtains responses in one general subject area before going to another topic. Questions for topics that are likely to cause difficulty (such as requests for personal or embarrassing information) are generally placed in the later sections of the questionnaire. The more involved the respondents are, the more difficult it is for them to discontinue an oral interview or throw away a mail questionnaire. For this reason, questionnaires usually conclude with a request for the necessary demographic information, such as classifications by age and income.

Exhibit 17-2 **(cont.)**

09 Sales Promotions
  a. Special sales, including quality or assortment of sales merchandise
  b. Stamps and other premiums
  c. Fashion shows and other special events

10 Advertising
  a. Style and quality of advertising
  b. Media and vehicles used
  c. Reliability of advertising

11 Store Atmosphere
  a. Layout of store without respect to convenience
  b. External and internal decor of the store
  c. Merchandise display
  d. Customer type
  e. Congestion
  f. Good for gifts, except with respect to quality, assortment, or fashion of merchandise
  g. "Prestige" store

12 Reputation on Adjustments
  a. Returns
  b. Exchanges
  c. Reputation for fairness

Source: Leonard L. Berry, "The Components of Department Store Image: A Theoretical and Empirical Analysis," *Journal of Retailing* 45 (Spring 1969): 19-20. Reprinted by permission.

Sampling

Seldom does a retailer have enough money to survey the entire population in his trading area. Therefore a sample of consumers is used to provide information about the population that the target consumers are supposed to represent. If the sample is selected properly and the survey is conducted appropriately, the sample should provide information that is representative of the data that would be found if the entire population were studied in a similar manner. Thus, sampling is used to reduce research costs.

It is especially important for retailers to define carefully the statistical population they want to study. This should be done in precise terms that describe the target market population in detail. The researcher must then devise a plan for selecting a sample of consumers from the defined population. This design must allow generalizations about the population being studied. Ideally, the composition of the sample should be such that it gives a proportional sampling by family size, economic group, city size, sex, nationality group, education level, and age group. In short, what is desired are samples that accurately reflect the characteristics of the market population to which the retailers merchandise their products and services.

Sampling Procedures

Simple random sampling is a method of choosing n people out of the defined statistical population (N) in such a way that every possible sample has an equal

Exhibit 17-3 Sample Questions That May Be Asked to Identify the Components of Store Image in a Semantic Differential Study

If you choose among several department stores, what factors would you consider important to the choice of shopping in a department store? Please score the importance of each of the following factors by circling the appropriate number. (For example, if the factor is one of your most important reasons for shopping in a department store, circle number 6; if it is of no importance, circle number 1, and so forth.)

	Most Important				Least Important	
General Characteristics of the Store						
Well-known store name	6	5	4	3	2	1
Small number of stores operated by company	6	5	4	3	2	1
Long time in community	6	5	4	3	2	1
Open during convenient shopping hours	6	5	4	3	2	1
Open during convenient shopping days	6	5	4	3	2	1
Physical Characteristics of the Store						
Clean	6	5	4	3	2	1
Attractive decor	6	5	4	3	2	1
Easy to find items you want	6	5	4	3	2	1
Easy to move through store	6	5	4	3	2	1
Fast checkout	6	5	4	3	2	1
Convenience of Reaching the Store from Your Location						
Nearby	6	5	4	3	2	1
Short time required to reach store	6	5	4	3	2	1
Easy drive	6	5	4	3	2	1
Easy to find parking place	6	5	4	3	2	1
Convenient to other stores I shop	6	5	4	3	2	1
Products Offered						
Availability of latest fashions and styles	6	5	4	3	2	1
Wide selection of different kinds of products	6	5	4	3	2	1
Fully stocked	6	5	4	3	2	1
Dependable products	6	5	4	3	2	1
High quality	6	5	4	3	2	1
Numerous brands	6	5	4	3	2	1
Known brands	6	5	4	3	2	1
Prices Charged by the Store						
Low compared to other stores	6	5	4	3	2	1
High values for money spent	6	5	4	3	2	1
Large number of items specially priced	6	5	4	3	2	1
Store Personnel						
Courteous	6	5	4	3	2	1
Friendly	6	5	4	3	2	1
Helpful	6	5	4	3	2	1

chance of being chosen.[16] Simple random samples may be selected by drawing numbers from a hat, by using a table of random numbers (which are found in most marketing research or statistics books), or by having a computer program develop a list of random numbers.

While it is desirable to have as representative a sample as possible, it is not always economically feasible to achieve a purely representative sample. Preliminary surveys and screening are added expenses that are probably justifiable only to a certain point. An added problem for many retailers is that it is difficult to identify the exact, relevant consumer population. Thus, the sample that is used in a particu-

Exhibit 17-3 **(cont.)**

Adequate number	6	5	4	3	2	1
Knowledgeable about product/service offering	6	5	4	3	2	1
Attractive appearance	6	5	4	3	2	1
Acceptable sales pressure	6	5	4	3	2	1
Advertising by the Store						
Informative	6	5	4	3	2	1
Helpful in planning purchases	6	5	4	3	2	1
Appealing	6	5	4	3	2	1
Believable	6	5	4	3	2	1
Frequently seen by you	6	5	4	3	2	1
Your Friends and the Store						
Well known to your friends	6	5	4	3	2	1
Well liked by your friends	6	5	4	3	2	1
Well recommended by your friends	6	5	4	3	2	1
Numerous friends shop there	6	5	4	3	2	1
Customer Services						
Easy credit terms	6	5	4	3	2	1
Good lawaway service	6	5	4	3	2	1
Good delivery service	6	5	4	3	2	1
Good product guarantees	6	5	4	3	2	1
Prompt repair service	6	5	4	3	2	1
Easy product-return policies	6	5	4	3	2	1
Satisfies customer complaints	6	5	4	3	2	1

lar test may be somewhat less than representative. In fact, many retailers use nonrandom sampling procedures such as convenience samples, which consist of surveying a group of people who happen to be at the place the study is taking place at the time the survey is being conducted, or quota samples, where the sample is chosen in a way that the proportion of people in the sample possessing a certain characteristic is approximately the same as it is for the people in the defined population. Under the quota sampling procedure, each interviewer is assigned a quota that specifies the characteristics (number of males, number of females, number of students, number of nonstudents, and so forth) of the people the interviewer is to survey.

The difficulty with using these nonrandom sampling techniques is that, because the people were not selected in a manner that guaranteed every person in the population an equal chance of being selected, no assessment of the degree of sampling error can be made. Thus, standard statistical tests cannot be used to analyze the data. This means the retailer must look at the data and interpret their meaning based upon a gut feel for their implications to the firm. Regardless of the method of sampling that is used, it should be remembered that the more representative the sample is of the entire population, the more valid the results will be.

Sample Size
Other things being equal, large samples yield more reliable results than small samples, unless the smaller sample is likely to be selected and interviewed more

carefully than the larger sample. On the other hand, the cost of conducting research increases as the size of the sample increases. Fortunately, relatively small samples, selected by the unbiased sampling procedures just discussed, will achieve satisfactory precision. In exploratory research, most information about attitudes and marketing processes can be obtained from a simple random sample of about one hundred people.[17] Motivation research studies designed to discover latent consumer attitudes have been conducted by obtaining about thirty interviews.[18]

The approximate degree of confidence that one can expect with varying sample sizes when the sample is selected by a simple random sampling procedure is presented in Table 17–1. This figure indicates that one can be about 95 percent confident that a reported sample of 50 percent does not differ from the true population percentage by more than approximately 4 percent if 500 completed responses are obtained. If one hundred completed responses are obtained, one is about 95 percent confident that the 50 percent estimate obtained from the sample is within 10 percent of the true population value.

Table 17–1 **Approximate Sampling Errors of Survey Findings**

Sampling errors of reported percentages: The chances are approximately ninety-five in one hundred that the reported sample value does not differ from the population value by more than the percentage points shown below.

Reported Percentages	Number of Interviews on Which the Percentage Is Based				
	500	300	200	100	50
From 35% to 65%	4%	6%	7%	10%	14%
Near 20% or 80%	4	5	6	8	11
Near 10% or 90%	3	3	4	6	—
Near 5% or 95%	2	3	3	4	—

Note: Standard error of a percent $\times$ 1.96 gives the figures in the body of the table, where standard error $= \sqrt{PQ/n}$. P equals the reported sample percentage, Q equals 100 minus P, and n equals the sample size. The calculation is made under the assumption that the sample is selected from a large population where the sampling procedure will yield that stated degree of accuracy over the selection of many different samples.

Putting Information to Work
(Analysis and Interpretation)

The information obtained from the research project must be organized, analyzed, and presented in a clear manner regardless of which techniques are used to gather data. Failure to summarize the findings properly and to draw managerial conclusions from the project frequently leads to a waste of time and money. Remember, the purpose of research is to provide information that can better assist the retail manager in the decision making process. Thus, the data obtained from a research project must help management solve its problems. If not it is worthless.

Getting More from Marketing Research

Although retailers are not expected to be experts in the field of research, it is wise to have a basic understanding of research procedures. This can prove to be very helpful when the retailer is contracting for research services or accepting the final results.

The costs of marketing research can be high. It is common for major studies to cost $10,000 or more. If a retailer were going to purchase $10,000 worth of merchandise from a vendor, he or she would, as a basic step, check the merchandise to see that it conformed with the purchase order. Unfortunately, such a basic step is too often overlooked by clients who purchase marketing research work.

There are several steps that a retailer can take to ensure the best purchase and use of research data.

1. Hire research employees who indicate a research orientation. In other words, hire professionals for your company's marketing research department—people who are truly interested in the field and have demonstrated their interest through their training, writing, and experience. In far too many cases the marketing research department is a short-run training ground for middle management. Personnel are moved there from a variety of areas regardless of training.

2. Know from whom you are buying research. The same qualities that apply to a lawyer are equally valid for researchers: experience, education, general background, success with other clients, and the individual's specialty. It is well known that not all lawyers are qualified to do patent work, and the same thing is true with many areas of marketing research. It is essential to determine the individual's or the firm's areas of specialty, but all too often the answer from the researcher is, "We can do anything!" Seldom is this correct.

   It is equally important to determine what other products or services the researcher is selling, such as advertising, public relations, or image work. It is questionable how objective such firms can be if the sale of other services rests upon the research results.

3. Who will do the actual research? Don't buy the old story, "We have qualified interviewers." In far too many cases these interviewers are part-time workers who may or may not have been given more than a five-minute set of instructions. All interviewers should be checked to be certain they are conducting the interviews completely and according to instructions.

4. Come to a firm price agreement. Research is not a blank-check operation and should not be treated as such.

5. Require a written proposal and record major design changes in writing. Don't even consider anything like this all-too-typical agreement: "Dear Bob, Thanks for lunch and the invitation to work with you in the study we discussed. We will proceed soon." In the first place, poor old Bob doesn't even know who should pay for the lunch, and in the second place he's buying trouble.

   A good proposal should contain detailed statements on six major elements.
   a. The problem. Often the researcher and the client do not agree on or under-

stand the basic problem. Unless there is agreement here, there can be nothing but chaos.

b. Objectives. These should state, "To determine ..."

c. Methodology. This statement does not have to be long and involved, but it should give the client a basic idea of the data collection method to be used, the sampling procedure, and the sample size.

d. Definition of terms. Terms such as "the Chicago market" should be clearly defined, since the client may be thinking of the Chicago phone district and the researcher may be thinking of the Loop.

e. Time schedule.

f. Cost.

6. Demand an interim report. This report doesn't have to be lengthy (it can be a letter), but it should give the client an idea of the progress to date and the expected time of completion, plus an indication of any unusual problems that have been discovered.

7. Inspect the test market. Make sure the test market is well set up. The only way to do this is to visit the area in person. It is not unusual to find that test markets have been established for the wrong retail outlets or shelf space.

8. Don't accept the word of experts as a substitute for objective research. This is especially true in international marketing research. Since income data and other statistics may be difficult to obtain in other countries, the researcher sometimes takes short cuts. The results from fifty government officials, ten bankers, and forty school teachers are not a substitute for a good sample of the potential users of a household product.

9. Examine the sampling technique from a logical standpoint. Do not worry about the hieroglyphics of statistics. The major questions are:

a. Is the size sufficient?

b. Who will be included in this sample?

c. Does the sample match the objectives?

10. Keep a diary of the outside environment. What important political, climatic, and social events took place during the time of the study that could easily affect the results?

11. Ask for a copy of the report before the presentation. Otherwise, the final presentation is simply a "dog and pony show." It is impossible for anyone to understand thoroughly the mass of results that will be thrown at one during a final, one-hour presentation. Come to that meeting prepared, by having read the report. The researcher will not like this and will do his or her best to avoid giving a prior copy of the report, but it is to your advantage to demand one.

12. Do not accept unfinished work. It is easy to give the client a huge bulk of data, but what do they mean? A retailer would not accept the work sheets of an accountant as the finished balance sheet, and the same is true for marketing research.

13. Make sure the report is readable; if it is not, reject it. The report must be written in a style that can be read by a layman and that lends itself to decision making.

If you cannot read it, chances are the president cannot either—and it will only gather dust and quickly grow useless.

14. Ask for clarification of details. The details of a balance sheet are questioned, and so should be the details of a research report.

15. Don't let statistics throw you. Keep asking the researcher, "What is the purpose of this test?" Ask until it is explained in a manner that an ordinary intelligent executive can understand. Basically, statistics serve these purposes:
    a. To determine sample size
    b. To test a hypothesis
    c. To forecast.

16. If necessary, ask the consultant to come back to explain the data further. If this was not agreed to in the original contract, pay extra.

17. Have the report checked and analyzed by others. If in-house capability exists, use it! If not, pay a small consulting fee to an outsider to evaluate the report.

18. Realize that the best research by the most qualified individual in the world is not 100 percent perfect. Any report can be picked apart in some area (trial lawyers long ago learned this). The point is not to be ridiculous about the depth of criticism but, instead, to look for gross errors and misinterpretation of data.

19. Apply common sense. Do not completely disregard gut feeling or forget past experiences.

Marketing research is an excellent aid in retail decision making when it is done well and used with thought. However, decision making is far too complex ever to let a research report replace all other considerations. In the final analysis, there is no substitute for sound management decision making by seasoned and knowledgeable executives who know how to use research as a useful tool.

Using Electronic Scanner Systems in Research

Electronic scanner systems have made it possible for retailers to obtain research data within a time period that has never before been possible. The following article features quotes and beliefs of Mr. Patrick Collins, president of Ralphs Grocery Company, which installed its first scanner systems in 1972.

"For the first time, the retailer and manufacturer can receive feedback on ads, promotions, etc., and determine what strategies have or haven't worked—and fast enough to do something about it. For the first time, we are looking at actual front-end sales data, by item, on an extremely timely basis; for us these previously unavailable data include 12,000 warehoused and direct delivery items.

"Over the past two years we have carefully evaluated the hard benefit areas in an attempt to fully justify the capital expenditure requirement of the scanning system. The results have been very encouraging. Front-end labor productivity has improved some 18 percent as the UPC (universal product code) marking level increases, allowing more items to be scanned.

"At the same time, we have seen grocery, dairy-deli, and liquor inventory shrinkage drop 25 percent where scanning has been installed. This reduction in shrink is a direct result of reduced cashier errors and retail price control from a central source."

Discussing the utility of the scanner-computer information, Collins told of a Ralphs test of a variety of prices for a house brand. Profitability of the house brand, it was learned, would be considerably improved at a different (and higher) price.

"We felt confident," he said, "that the private label gross profit percentage could be improved without a significant loss in volume."

"In the seven scan stores, the private entry label in one product category tested was priced at 83 cents and historically had achieved a 30 percent volume share," Collins said. In the test, stores were grouped according to demographics, market share, and unit volume.

One group of stores served as the control, and the price remained at 83 cents. In other groups of stores, prices of 89 cents, 93 cents and 95 cents were injected into the computer. After two weeks the control group showed unit volume off by 0.5 percent. (In part this was due to a 1.5-day out-of-stock condition at one store. Ability to discover an out-of-stock condition was not a test objective but proved to be an added benefit.)

In the second store grouping, where the price was 89 cents, unit volume share increased by almost 3 percent. In the third grouping, at 93 cents, unit volume share increased by 2 percent, and in the fourth grouping, at 95 cents, unit volume share fell by only 1 percent.

"When this phase of the test was concluded," Collins said, "we analyzed the results in terms of our warehouse activity as well as of sales dollars and profit contribution at each price level. Then we entered the selected price into all seven stores for four weeks; a positive trend held during that phase. This price test involved a product that moves almost 600,000 units per year in our stores, and I'm sure you can imagine the profit implications."

"Another major use of scanner-generated data," he said, "involves the evaluation of in-store displays." "Most of us feel confident that we know what sells best from what location," he said, "but do we know how a display affects other items in a category or the effects of a display on future sales of the product displayed?"

He cited three case histories of product displays, involving Treesweet grapefruit juice, Chicken of the Sea tuna, and Peter Pan peanut butter. In each case end displays were set up in the seven scan stores. The display period was two weeks, preceded and followed by four-week evaluation periods.

1. *Treesweet grapefruit juice.* In the display period the price was reduced 11 cents. Purchases per 1,000 shoppers increased to 25.7—up 786 percent. More significantly, when the product was returned to its original price and shelf location, purchasing dropped, but remained 369 percent higher than before the display period.

2. *Chicken of the Sea tuna.* This product was given case end display at its regular price, and sales increased 247 percent over the predisplay period. Even after the product went back to its usual shelf position, volume in the four-week post-display period remained 50 percent higher than before the test.

3. *Peter Pan peanut butter.* The display, with a 2-cents off deal, produced a 75 percent increase in product movement. After the display period, however, volume dropped to a level 25 percent lower than before the test. "Using existing techniques, but with item movement data available, we can measure precisely the impact of in-store displays," Collins said. "We have the ability to maximize today's profits without impacting those of tomorrow."

Turning to evaluation of advertising effectiveness, Collins gave three examples in which Ralphs achieved "an accurate assessment of the effectiveness of various ad strategies at significantly lower cost than experienced before."

1. In October, 1976, Clorox Co. used an ad in the *Los Angeles Times* for a bounce-back promotion on specially marked gallons of Clorox bleach; each package contained a form which, when returned to the company, was worth a free quart bottle.

2. In an ad in the *Los Angeles Times* in October, 1976, U.S. Borax offered a 20-cents off coupon on the purchase of New Liquid Borateem.

3. In December, 1976, Ralphs, in its regular Thursday ad in the *Los Angeles Times,* ran an in-ad 43-cent coupon with manufacturer support on Purex bleach.

"Both the Clorox bounce-back ad and the Borateem manufacturer's coupon caused some increase in product movement, but neither one approached the impact of the manufacturer-supported in-ad coupon which ran in the Ralphs ad. We recognize that the ads appeared under differing market conditions and that additional analysis is required to make quantitative decisions regarding ad effectiveness. It is not my intent to promote any form of promotional strategy, but rather to point out that scanner-generated item movement data facilitate fast and accurate assessments of promotional techniques."

Collins went on to point out advantages of checkout scanning in detecting inventory shrink, locating low-efficiency stores, and evaluating cashier performance. He also indicated that Ralphs is in the early stages of installing a store cash accounting system tied to the scanner-computer setup. He estimated that this system would save the chain $750,000 a year in bookkeeping costs.

"Other functions which may be improved through the use of the equipment," he said, "include (1) product mix and shelf allocation, (2) private label line extension and evaluation, (3) introduction information on new products, (4) improved labor scheduling techniques, (5) front-end configuration design, and (6) inventory control over problems such as overstock, out-of-stock, etc."

"It is virtually impossible to foresee all the benefits that will be made available by scan information over the next several years," Collins said, "nor to assess the marketing advantages associated with scanners. It is equally impossible now to totally quantify many of these 'soft' benefits with hard dollars."

Recalling a statement he made at a meeting earlier this year, to the effect that electronic checkouts are "probably the most important new development in the field of marketing research of the past decade," Collins said, "I find only two flaws in this statement. The first is the use of the word *probably,* and the second is the phrase *of the past decade."*

"I must say that for both the retailer and the manufacturer it is the *most* important new development and the *most* important research tool *ever* developed in marketing research."[19]

Summary

The expansion of retail organizations beyond a single location has increased the need for conducting research before making huge investments in land, buildings, and fixtures. The resulting growth in location and trade area research has provided the operational base from which other research activities have expanded.

Today, retail researchers are developing programs based on the firm's objectives. These programs assist the retailer in making improvements in the functions that propel the firm beyond its current levels of performance.

Research can be beneficial to the retailer whenever an important decision must be made. Priorities must be established and the level of research expenditures related to the financial consequences of the decision.

Retailers should be aware of the basic research procedures discussed in this chapter so they can spend their research dollar more wisely.

The following steps of the research process illustrate the sequence of a retailer's research efforts.

1. Identify the central problem and opportunities.
2. Determine the sources of information that are available from within the firm and from outside sources.
3. Determine which methods (observation, survey, or experimentation) will be used to obtain primary information.
4. Collect the data by using an appropriate questionnaire or some other suitable recording device.
5. Analyze and interpret the data carefully so the project findings can be put to use in the firm.

The use of electronic scanning systems by retailers has provided research data that have many implications for marketing and merchandising. Shrinkage can be reduced, front-end productivity increased, pricing decisions evaluated, private label merchandise evaluated, in-store displays analyzed, advertising effectiveness determined, shelf allocations evaluated, labor scheduling improved, and inventory can be controlled in a much more efficient manner when the electronic system is used as a research tool.

Questions

1. Who needs to use marketing research more, the small independent retailer or the large chain retailer? Who does use marketing research more, the small retailer or the chain retailer? Discuss.

2. Develop a list of secondary sources that you would search if you were going to open a new women's apparel shop.

3. What are the advantages and disadvantages of retailers using secondary data to assist them in making managerial decisions?

4. What are the advantages and disadvantages of retailers using primary data to assist them in making managerial decisions?

5. Under what conditions should a retailer use the observation method of collecting primary data? What are the advantages of using this method? What are the disadvantages?

6. Under what conditions should a retailer use the experimental method of collecting primary data? What are the advantages and disadvantages of using this technique?

7. When should a retailer use the survey method of collecting primary data? What are the advantages and disadvantages of using this method?

8. Discuss the merits and limitations of using (1) personal interviews, (2) telephone interviews, and (3) mail questionnaires to collect primary data.

9. Evaluate the effectiveness of using a semantic differential scale compared to unstructured, open-ended questions to determine the image that consumers have of a local department store.

10. Develop a complete research project that is designed to determine what people think of a local supermarket and determine why they do or do not shop at this market. Include (1) a listing of the secondary sources you would check before conducting any surveys, (2) a description of the method you would use to collect primary data, (3) a description of who will collect the data, (4) a sampling plan, (5) a copy of any forms that will be used to collect the primary data, (6) a summary of how the data would be analyzed, (7) a description of how the data could be used by the supermarket to increase its sales and profits, and (8) an estimate of what it would cost to conduct the project.

Footnotes

1. Walter G. Walker, "Marketing Research Is Important in Retailing, Now, More than Ever," *Marketing News,* 14 March 1975, p. 9

2. William F. O'Dell, "Personal Interviews or Mail Panels," *Journal of Marketing* 26 (October 1962): 34–39.

3. Glen H. Mitchell, *Telephone Interviewing* (Wooster: Ohio Agricultural Experiment Station, n.d.), p. 8.

4. Two studies that show that the return of mail questionnaires declined as the length of the questionnaires increased are Frank Stanton, "Notes on the Validity of Mail Questionnaire Returns," *Journal of Applied Psychology* 23 (February 1939): 95–104, and W. Mitchell, "Factors Affecting the Rate of Return on Mail Questionnaires," *Journal of American Statistical Association* 45 (1939): 683–692.

5. O'Dell, "Personal Interviews or Mail Panels," p. 36.

6. R. A. Robinson and Philip Agisim, "Making Mail Surveys More Reliable," *Journal of Marketing* 15 (April 1951): 415–424.

7. William J. Goode and Paul K. Hatt, *Methods in Social Research* (New York: McGraw-Hill, 1952), p. 134.

8. More complete discussions of the methodology used in attitude measurement studies are presented in A. N. Oppenheim, *Questionnaire Design and Attitude Measurement* (New York:

Basic Books, 1966), and M. E. Shaw and J. M. Wright, *Scales for the Measurement of Attitudes* (New York: McGraw-Hill, 1967).

9. R. A. Likert, "A Technique for the Measurement of Attitudes," *Archives of Psychology,* no. 140 (1932): 1–55.

10. C. E. Osgood, G. J. Suci, and P. H. Tannenbaum, *The Measurement of Meaning* (Urbana: University of Illinois Press, 1957), p. 138.

11. For a more complete discussion of the use of the semantic differential, see W. A. Mindak, "Fitting the Semantic Differential to the Marketing Problem," *Journal of Marketing* 25 (April 1961): 28–33; Ronald F. Kelley and Ronald Stephenson, "The Semantic Differential": An Information Source for Designing Retail Patronage Appeals," *Journal of Marketing* 31 (October 1967): 43–47; and Rollie Tillman, "The Semantic Measurement of Consumer Images of Retail Stores," *Southern Journal of Business* 12 (April 1967): 67–73.

12. James F. Engel, David T. Kollat, and Roger D. Blackwell, *Consumer Behavior* (New York: Holt, Rinehart and Winston, 1968), p. 456.

13. John H. Kunkel and Leonard L. Berry, "A Behavioral Conception of Retail Image," *Journal of Marketing* 32 (October 1968): 21–27; Leonard L. Berry, "The Components of Department Store Image: A Theoretical and Empirical Analysis," *Journal of Retailing* 45 (Spring 1969): 3–20.

14. Ibid., pp. 9–20.

15. Kunkel and Berry, "Behavioral Conception of Retail Image," p. 25.

16. William G. Cochran, *Sampling Techniques* (New York: John Wiley & Sons, 1953), p. 11.

17. Philip Kotler, *Marketing Management: Analysis, Planning and Control* (Englewood Cliffs, N.J.: Prentice-Hall, 1972), p. 324.

18. Ibid.

19. "Collins of Ralphs Says, 'Grocery Checkout Scanner Is Valued Research, Marketing Tool,'" *Marketing News,* 18 November 1977, pp. 1, 12. Reprinted from *Marketing News* published by the American Marketing Association.

Case Study

Goodwill Industries*

After reviewing annual sales figures Fred Sherman decided that the time had arrived for a marketing research study. Mr. Sherman was executive director of Goodwill Industries for Dallas, Texas. Although he had responsibility for all retail outlets of Goodwill in Dallas, he was particularly concerned with the level of sales performance at the Central store.

This store was located in a large, modern, one-story building, which also housed the central offices, processing plant, and rehabilitation training area for Goodwill Industries in Dallas. The building and grounds occupied more than one-half block in a predominately black area of the city. This area of Dallas consisted of factories and low income city housing projects. An area of town known as "Little Mexico" was located a mile to the west. It had received this name as a result of the large concentrations of Mexican-Americans and illegal immigrants living there.

---

*Reprinted with the cooperation of Goodwill Industries.

The retail store section of the Goodwill Industries building was surrounded by ample parking and was located on the corner of two busy streets. These were served by city bus and taxis.

The store had been designed to be functional yet clean and efficient. There were no frills in this store. The cement floor was not carpeted. The used book and gift item section was separated by simple partitions, but the rest of the store did not have partitions or other dividers.

The store was separated into three principal areas—clothing, furniture and appliances, and the book and gift section.

Most of the merchandise was used. It had been collected through the Goodwill collection boxes located in the metropolitan area. A part of the merchandise had also been donated by retail merchants who were unable to dispose of the goods otherwise.

The clothes had been washed and sorted according to sizes. Appliances and furniture had been reconditioned by Goodwill employees.

The Dallas store was part of the national Goodwill Industries. This was established as a nonprofit organization and had grown to a total of 850 retail stores throughout the U.S., with annual sales of over $85,000.000.

The stores were established for three purposes: (1) as a source of income to support the rehabilitation activities of Goodwill Industries, (2) as an outlet for products that had been cleaned and renovated by Goodwill employees, thus providing them with valuable training for employment by industry, (3) as a retail outlet offering low cost, useful items. The stores are open to the public, but their primary target market is lower income individuals.

After reviewing the sales figures, Mr. Sherman noted that sales had been increasing each year for the ten stores in the Dallas area. At the same time, the number of customers in the stores seemed to have declined.

Mr. Sherman was uncertain who these customers were. He felt that it was necessary to have information concerning the Goodwill customer to plan marketing-merchandising strategies.

Through his contacts at a local university, Mr. Sherman acquired the assistance of a team of graduate students in business administration to conduct a survey.

It was agreed that the purpose of the study was to perform a consumer profile survey of customers of the central store.

A questionnaire was designed, pretested and than administered in the store by the research team. Customers were selected on a random basis during different hours of the day and different days of the week.

The questionnaire and the results follow:

Total Number of respondents = 304

Factory Store Survey

1. **How long have you been coming to this store?**

   ☐ 6 Months or Less   ☐ 3 Years   ☐ 6 Years or More
   ☐ 1 Year   ☐ 4 Years   ☐ Don't Know
   ☐ 2 Years   ☐ 5 Years   ☐ First Time

Table I **Length of Factory Store Patronage**

Length of Time	Number of Responses	Percentage of Respondents
First Time	31	10.2
Less than One Year	68	22.3
Two to Three Years	65	21.4
Four to Five Years	42	13.8
Six Years or More	96	31.6
Other	2	0.7
	304	100.0

2. **How many times a year do you come here?**

_____ (write in response)

Table II **Frequency of Factory Store Patronage**

Times per year	Number of Responses	Percentage of Respondents
1–2	17	6.2
3–5	31	11.4
6–11	29	10.6
12–15	32	11.7
16–30	39	14.3
31–52	60	22.0
53–125	26	9.5
126–up	30	11.0
No Response	9	3.3
	273	100.0
Never before	31	

3. **How much money do you usually spend here?**

☐ Less than $5   ☐ $10 to $19.99   ☐ $50 and over
☐ $5 to $9.99   ☐ $20 to $49.99   ☐ Don't know

Table III **Amount of Money "Usually Spent" at Factory Store**

Amount	Number of Responses	Percentage of Respondents
No Answer	36	
Less than $5	60	22.4
$5 to $9.99	117	43.7
$10 to $19.99	64	23.9
$20 to $49.99	14	5.1
$50 and Over	1	0.4
Don't Know	12	4.5
	268	100.0

4. What do you usually look for here?
Check each that applies

☐ Clothing ☐ Books ☐ Other

☐ Furniture ☐ Shoes ☐ Nothing in Particular

Table IV Most Frequently Sought Items at Factory Store

Item	Number of Responses	Percentage of Respondents
Clothing	184	67.4
Furniture	95	34.8
Books	72	26.4
Shoes	68	24.9
Other	116	42.5
Nothing in Particular	33	12.1

Note: Totals exceed 100 percent due to multiple answers; 273 customers answered this question.

5. How did you get here today?

☐ Bus ☐ Someone Else's Car

☐ Walked ☐ Other

Table V Method of Transportation to Factory Store

Method of Transportation	Number of Responses	Percentage of Respondents
Own Car	245	80.6
Other's Car	32	10.5
Bus	19	6.3
Walked	7	2.3
Other	1	0.3
	304	100.0

6. Have you been to any of the following in the last year?

Salvation Army Store	_____	K Mart	_____
Sanger-Harris	_____	Target	_____
Garage Sales	_____	Penney's	_____
Salvage Stores	_____	Sears	_____
Disabled Veterans Store	_____	Gibson's	_____
Other Goodwill Branches	_____	Goodwill Only (Go to #12)	_____

Table VI **Other Stores Patronized by Factory Store Customers**

Store Name	Number of Responses	Percentage of Respondents
Salvation Army	118	38.8
Sanger-Harris	154	50.7
Garage Sales	153	50.3
Salvage Stores	87	28.6
Disabled American Veterans (DAV)	127	41.8
Other Goodwill Branches	125	41.1
K Mart	200	65.8
Target	121	39.8
Penney's	144	47.4
Sears	209	68.8
Gibson's	154	50.7

Note: Totals exceed 100 percent due to multiple answers; 304 persons answered this question.
Note Sanger-Harris is a chain of department stores selling a quality line of merchandise. Gibson's is a chain of discount stores.

7. **Other than Goodwill, what store would you most likely recommend to a new neighbor?**
_____ (write in response).

Table VII **Stores Recommended to a New Neighbor**

Store Recommended	Number of Responses	Percentage of Respondents
Salvation Army	16	5.3
Sanger-Harris	21	6.9
Garage Sales	3	1.0
Salvage Stores	3	1.0
Disabled American Veterans	22	7.2
K Mart	53	17.4
Target	9	3.0
Penney's	21	6.9
Sears	47	15.5
Gibson's	22	7.2
No Response	87	28.6
	304	100.0

8. **Compared to _____ (the answer to #7), how do you feel about prices here?**
☐ Much Higher
☐ A Little Higher
☐ OK; All Right with Me
☐ A Little Lower
☐ Much Lower
☐ Don't Know

Table VIII **Goodwill's Prices Compared to Recommended Store**

Goodwill's Prices	Number of Responses	Percentage of Respondents
Much Higher	24	8.9
A Little Higher	58	21.6
OK; All Right with Me	57	21.2
A Little Lower	46	17.1
Much Lower	65	24.1
Don't Know	19	7.1
	269	100.0
No answer	35	

Table IX **Price Attitude Related to Length of Patronage**

Goodwill's Prices	Length of Patronage			
	Less than One Year	2–3 Years	4–5 Years	6 or More Years
Much Higher	3	8	1	11
A Little Higher	11	15	10	21
OK; All Right with Me	11	17	9	14
A Little Lower	10	10	14	17
Much Lower	21	10	7	20
Don't Know	4	1	0	4

Table X **Demographic Profile of Customers Who Felt Goodwill's Prices Were Higher**

Age	Number	Income	Number	Sex	Number	Race	Number
19–24	5	Less than $5000	19	Male	18	White	41
25–34	22	$5000–$7999	17	Female	64	Black	25
35–44	21	$8000–$9999	9			Mexican-American	16
45–64	26	$10,000–$12,499	8				
65 and Over	6	$12,500–$14,999	5				
		$15,000–$24,999	11				
		$25,000 and Over	3				

Table XI Demographic Profile of Customers Who Felt Goodwill's Prices Were Lower

Age	Number	Income	Number	Sex	Number	Race	Number
19–24	7	Less than $5000	15	Male	19	White	65
25–34	39	$5000–$7999	23	Female	82	Black	25
35–44	30	$8000–$9999	16			Mexican-American	21
45–64	30	$10,000–12,499	18				
65 and Over	4	$12,500–$14,999	12				
		$15,000–$24,999	15				
		$25,000 and Over	5				

9. **What things are too high here?**
(Check each that applies)

☐ Clothing   ☐ Books   ☐ Other
☐ Furniture   ☐ Shoes   ☐ Don't Know

Table XII Items Considered "Too High" By Customers

Item	Number of Responses	Percentage of Respondents
No answer	147	
Clothing	55	35.0
Furniture	51	32.5
Books	5	3.2
Shoes	15	9.6
Other	22	14.0
Don't Know	9	5.7
	157	100.0

10. **Counting yourself, how many people live in your home?**

_____ (write in response)

Table XIII Number Of Residents Per Household

Number of Residents	Number of Responses	Percentage of Respondents
1–2	101	33.2
3–4	117	38.5
5–6	62	20.4
7–8	20	6.6
9–12	4	1.3
	304	100.0

11. **What letter matches your age group?**

☐ A (under 19)   ☐ C (25–34)   ☐ E (45–54)   ☐ G (65 or Older)

☐ B (19–24)   ☐ D (35–44)   ☐ F (55–64)   ☐ No Response

Table XIV **Basic Demographic Data: Age of Respondents**

Age	Number of Responses	Percentage of Respondents
Under 19	4	1.3
19–24	28	9.3
25–34	99	32.8
35–44	72	23.8
45–54	60	19.9
55–64	20	6.6
65 and Older	19	6.3
	302	100.0
No Answer	2	

12. **What letter matches your family income for the last year?**

☐ A (under $5000)   ☐ D ($10,000–$12,499)   ☐ G ($25,000 and Over)

☐ B ($5000–$7999)   ☐ E ($12,500–$14,999)   ☐ No Response

☐ C ($8000–$9999)   ☐ F ($15,000–$24,999)

Table XV **Basic Demographic Data: Income of Respondents**

Income	Number of Responses	Percentage of Respondents
Under $5000	61	22.1
$5000–$7999	62	22.5
$8000–$9999	37	13.4
$10,000–$12,499	45	16.3
$12,500–$14,999	25	9.1
$15,000–$24,999	35	12.7
$25,000 and Over	11	3.9
	276	100.0
No answer	28	

13. **Sex:** (Do not ask; observe)

☐ Male   ☐ Female

Table XVI **Basic Demographic Data: Sex of Respondents**

Sex	Number of Respondents	Percentage of Respondents
Male	80	26.3
Female	224	73.7
	304	100.0

14. **Race:** (Do not ask; observe)

☐ White   ☐ Black   ☐ Mexican-American   ☐ Other

Table XVII **Basic Demographic Data: Race of Respondents**

Race	Number of Respondents	Percentage of Respondents
White	170	55.9
Black	79	26.0
Mexican-American	55	18.1
	304	100.0

At the conclusion of the study, Mr. Sherman distributed copies to each of his subordinates and asked them to review the results carefully. He stated that the study would be carefully discussed at their next weekly meeting. In preparation for the meeting, Mr. Sherman asked that each individual be prepared to discuss (1) the general relevency of the study, (2) what changes in the retailing operation might be necessary in view of the results, (3) whether the same study should be expanded to all stores in the area, (4) what changes in the study format should be made if additional stores were surveyed, (5) whether or not consideration should be given to lowering prices as a result of the findings. The researchers had concluded that "The present pricing policy is not acceptable to a wide range of Goodwill customers. As a result, Goodwill needs to evaluate its current pricing policies, especially as regards clothing and furniture."

Discussion Question

How would you answer the questions raised by Mr. Sherman?

Case Study

Mid States Airline, Inc.*

It has been common practice within the airline industry for each airline to maintain and staff a city ticket office in each major market center. These sales offices are usually located near major hotels in the central business district. They are open Monday through Friday from 8:00 to 5:00.

The purpose of City Ticket Offices (CTOs) is to provide service for traveling professional business people.

Although a few tourists use the CTOs to plan trips and purchase tickets, the pleasure traveler is in the minority as a user of CTOs. Based on the general scuttlebutt in the airline industry, this condition seems to be true for nearly every airline.

The management of Mid States has been concerned about the substantial and continuously rising costs of maintaining CTOs. The costs of rental space for offices on the ground floor in the central business district of cities is extremely high.

In addition, several other conditions have arisen in recent years. First, the CTOs have been responsible for a smaller percentage of Mid States' sales each year. Second, major hotels are locating new buildings near airports and on the fringes of the city. Third, there does not seem to be a real need for a CTO other than for those travelers who feel they must have a ticket in their hands. Mid States Airline has been promoting the concepts of ticket-by-mail, using a travel agent, or calling the airline for reservations.

In evaluating the possibility of closing CTOs, Mid States feels that to justify the substantital overhead expense, a CTO would ideally:

1. Have sufficient sales to result in an adequate return on investment

2. Give Mid States substantial identity with the flying public

3. Provide convenience of location to the passenger, resulting in the passenger selecting Mid States rather than a competing airline.

The negatives associated with possibly closing CTO's seem to be:

1. Not all sales of the closed CTO may transfer to Mid States

2. The purchasing habits of the former CTO user might undergo changes negative to Mid States

3. A loss of identity for Mid States might occur.

*This case was made possible by an airline that prefers to remain anonymous. The purpose of this case is to serve as the basis for class discussion, rather than to illustrate either effective or ineffective handling of an administrative situation.

As a result of the question concerning the possible closing of CTOs, Mr. Tad Bennett, the Director of Market Planning for Mid States, decided to engage the services of a marketing research firm. The city of Omaha, Nebraska, was under consideration by the management of Mid States as a test site to determine the feasibility of closing CTOs.

Omaha was one of forty-two cities served by Mid States. The CTO in Omaha was in need of renovation and the lease was also due for renewal.

The lease price was sure to increase by at least 15 percent with a three-year commitment. In addition, almost $40,000 would be needed for remodeling. As a result, Omaha seemed like a very logical spot for research.

After a series of meetings the marketing research firm, Parker-Jones Research, Inc., brought a written proposal to Mid States' marketing director.

The proposal was approved by Mr. Bennett with the proviso that he and his staff could see and approve the questionnaire and sampling plan.

Approximately ten days later the marketing research firm provided Mr. Bennett with a copy of the questionnaire and the sampling plan for his approval.

A Proposal to Mid States Airline, Inc., by Parker-Jones Research, Inc.

I. Problem statement

Should Mid States discontinue operation of their city ticket offices?

Methodology

1. For the purposes of this study, two sample populations will be used.
   a. Users of the Mid States Airline city ticket office in Omaha, Nebraska
   b. General public in Douglas County, Nebraska
2. A questionnaire will be developed, pretested and submitted to Mid States for approval. The questionnaire will be distributed by Mid States city ticket office personnel who will give a brief explanation as to the purpose of the questionnaire to the city ticket office user.
3. The general public study will be conducted by telephone interviews.
4. Standard statistical techniques will be used to analyze the questionnaire responses.

II. The objectives of this report are to:

1. Determine to what extent Mid States ticket sales are gained as a result of Mid States maintaining city ticket offices
2. Determine what percentage of sales will transfer to Mid States subsequent to the closing of a Mid States city ticket office
3. Determine how the purchasing habits of the former Mid States city ticket office user would be affected subsequent to closing the Mid States city ticket office
4. Determine to what extent loss of identify caused by closing a Mid States city ticket office would affect sales
5. Determine the reasons that Mid States passengers purchase their tickets from a Mid States city ticket office
6. Determine why Mid States city ticket office users prefer to have tickets in their possession prior to date of departure

Telephone Interview Questionnaire

Hello . . . My name is _____. I represent the Parker-Jones Research Corp. . . . We are conducting a survey about airlines . . . We would appreciate your cooperation. It will take only a few minutes.

1. What airlines are you aware of that have offices other than at the airport that sell tickets to the public?

   (If none or Mid States not mentioned, terminate. Indicate airlines mentioned.)

2. Where are these offices located?

   (If Mid States location incorrect or not known, terminate.)

3. How many times have you flown on each of these airlines since New Year's Day?

   (Indicate response. If no travel on Mid States, terminate.)

4. Do you purchase your Mid States tickets at the ticket office mentioned?

   (If no, terminate.)

5. If this Mid States ticket office were no longer available to you, where would you most likely purchase your airline tickets?

   (Terminate)

   (Terminate survey) Thank you for your help and time.

Mid States Airline, Inc., Survey of Customer Ticketing Preferences

1. Including this trip, how many trips have you taken on M.S. since New Year's Day (1973)? Count a round trip as one trip.

   ( ) First trip   ( ) 2-4   ( ) 5-9   ( ) 10-14   ( ) 15-19   ( ) 20 or more trips

2. Please indicate with a check (√) the percentage of times you used each of the following methods for purchasing M.S. tickets:

	Business Travel Percentage of Times					Personal Travel Percentage of Times				
	0-20	21-40	41-60	61-80	81-100	0-20	21-40	41-60	61-80	81-100
At the Airport	( )	( )	( )	( )	( )	( )	( )	( )	( )	( )
At M.S. City Ticket Office	( )	( )	( )	( )	( )	( )	( )	( )	( )	( )
At the M.S. Drive-up Window	( )	( )	( )	( )	( )	( )	( )	( )	( )	( )
By Mail from M.S.	( )	( )	( )	( )	( )	( )	( )	( )	( )	( )
At My Place of Employment	( )	( )	( )	( )	( )	( )	( )	( )	( )	( )
From a Travel Agency	( )	( )	( )	( )	( )	( )	( )	( )	( )	( )
Other: Please Specify	( )	( )	( )	( )	( )	( )	( )	( )	( )	( )

3. Rank in order of importance (1=most important, 7=least important) where you would prefer to purchase your M.S. tickets for both business travel and personal travel.

Business Travel	Personal Travel	
_____	_____	By Mail from M.S.
_____	_____	At the M.S. Drive-up Window
_____	_____	From a Travel Agency
_____	_____	At My Place of Employment
_____	_____	At a M.S. City Ticket Office
_____	_____	At the Airport
_____	_____	Other: Please Specify _____

4. If your number one preference in question (3) were no longer available to you, where would you most likely purchase you tickets (check one only) for both business and personal travel.

Business Travel	Personal Travel	
_____	_____	By Mail from M.S.
_____	_____	At the M.S. Drive-up Window
_____	_____	From a Travel Agency
_____	_____	At My Place of Employment
_____	_____	At a M.S. City Ticket Office
_____	_____	At the Airport
_____	_____	From Another Airline
_____	_____	Other: Please Specify _____

5. How far in advance of your trip do you prefer to have your ticket?

_____Days   _____ No Preference   _____ Don't Know/Not Sure

And how important are the following reasons for having your M.S. ticket prior to your trip? (Please check(√) one for each category.)

	Very Important	Important	No Opinion	Un-important	Very Un-important
To Confirm Reservations	( )	( )	( )	( )	( )
Convenience	( )	( )	( )	( )	( )
Feeling of Security	( )	( )	( )	( )	( )
Avoid Confusion at Airport	( )	( )	( )	( )	( )

Other Reasons: Please Specify _____

6. How important are the following factors in determining whether or not to use a M.S. city ticket office for purchasing M.S. tickets? (Please check (√) one for each category.)

	Very Important	Important	No Opinion	Un-important	Very Un-important
Convenient to Home	( )	( )	( )	( )	( )
Convenient to Work	( )	( )	( )	( )	( )
Convenient to Shopping	( )	( )	( )	( )	( )
Ticket Can Easily Be Picked Up by Another Member of My Family	( )	( )	( )	( )	( )
Avoid Confusion at Airport	( )	( )	( )	( )	( )
Ease of Parking	( )	( )	( )	( )	( )
Quick Service	( )	( )	( )	( )	( )

Other Reasons: Please Specify _____

7. Please indicate which of the following best describes your occupation.
    ( ) Executive/Managerial   ( ) Housewife
    ( ) Professional/Technical   ( ) Student
    ( ) Salesman   ( ) Craftsman/Mechanic/Factory Worker
    ( ) Secretary/Clerk Office Worker ( ) Government (Except Military)
    ( ) Teacher/Professor   ( ) Military
    ( ) Other: ( ) Retired
        Please Specify _____
    What is your exact title? _____

8. What is your sex?
    ( ) Male   ( ) Female

9. Please indicate your age:
    ( ) Under 12 years   ( ) 30-39 years
    ( ) 12-17 years   ( ) 40-49 years
    ( ) 18-21 years   ( ) 50-59
    ( ) 22-29 years   ( ) 60 and over

10. Which of the following best describes your level of education?
    ( ) Grade School   ( ) Some College
    ( ) Some High School   ( ) College Graduate
    ( ) High School Graduate   ( ) Post Graduate

11. Please indicate the range of your approximate total annual family income:
    ( ) Under $7,499   ( ) $15,000-$19,999
    ( ) $7,500-$9,999   ( ) $20,000-$49,999
    ( ) $10,000-$14,999   ( ) $50,000 and over

12. Please indicate the city and state in which you live.

    _____   _____   _____
          City   State   Zip

Thank you for your cooperation. Your comments are welcomed.

Sampling Procedure to Be Used

Questionnaires for known CTO users—Questionnaires will be given to the sales personnel in the Omaha CTO of Mid States Airlines. These personnel will be instructed to hand a questionnaire to each customer during a two-week period. The questionnaire will contain a self-addressed and postage paid envelope.

A 90 percent confidence level with a 5 percent allowable error is expected.

Questionnaires from Douglas County residents—A telephone survey of residents of Douglas County, Nebraska, will be conducted. This will be a stratified random sample among individuals with a median income of $10,000 or higher.

Discussion Questions

1. Should Mid States Airline accept the research proposal by Parker-Jones Research, Inc.?

2. Can marketing research provide answers to the problem facing Mid States?

3. What functions does a city ticket office perform for an airline? Would the need for these functions disappear with the closing of city ticket offices?

4. How do airlines sell tickets besides through city ticket offices? What effect would closing the city ticket offices have upon these other outlets or intermediaries for passenger ticket sales?

Appendix 17-A

Some Retail Trade Associations That Are Sources of Secondary Retail Information

Food Marketing Institute, 303 East Ohio Street, Chicago, Ill.

International Fabricare Institute, Joilet, Ill.

American Booksellers Assn., 800 Second Ave., New York, N.Y.

American Retail Federation, 1616 H St., N.W., Washington, D.C.

Automotive Parts & Accessories Assn., 1730 K St., N.W., Washington, D.C.

Mass Retailing Institute, 570 Seventh Ave., New York, N.Y.

Menswear Retailers of America, 390 National Press Bldg., Washington, D.C.

National Appliance & Radio-TV Dealer's Association, 318 W. Randolph St., Chicago, Ill.

National Association of Retail Druggists, 1 E. Wacker Dr., Chicago, Ill.

National Association of Retail Grocers of the United States, 2000 Spring Rd., Oakbrook, Ill.

National Association of Variety Stores, 7646 W. Devon Ave., Chicago, Ill.

National Automotive Parts Associations, Suite 1129, Parkline Towers West, Dearborn, Mich.

National Home Furnishings Assn., 405 Merchandise Mart Plaza, Chicago, Ill.

National Lumber & Building Materials Assn., 1990 M St., N.W., Washington D.C.

National Office Products Association, 1500 Wilson Blvd., Suite 1200, Arlington, Va.

National Retail Hardware Assn., 964 N. Pennsylvania St., Indianapolis, Ind.

National Retail Merchants Assn., 100 W. 31st St., New York, N.Y.

National Shoe Retailers Assn., 200 Madison Ave., New York, N.Y.

National Sporting Goods Assn., 717 N. Michigan Ave., Chicago, Ill.

Retail Jewelers of America, Ten Rooney Circle, West Orange, N.J.

Appendix 17-B

Publications That Are
Sources of Secondary Retail Information

Retail Trade Publications

Appliances
Dealerscope, 115 Second Ave., Waltham, Mass.
Mart Magazine, Berkshire Common, Pittsfield, Mass.
Merchandising Week, 1 Astor Plaza, New York, N.Y.

Automotive
Auto Merchandising News, 1188 Main St., Fairfield, Conn.

Books
Publishers Weekly, 1180 Avenue of the Americas, New York, N.Y.

Children's
Earnshaw's Infants, Girls & Boyswear Review, 393 Seventh Ave., New York, N.Y.
Juvenile Merchandising, 370 Lexington Ave., New York, N.Y.

Curtains
Curtain, Drapery & Bedspread Magazine, 1115 Clifton, Ave., Clifton, N.J.

Druggists
Drug Topics, 550 Kinderkamack Rd., Oradell, N.J.

Fabrics

American Fabrics and Fashions, 24 E. 38th St., New York, N.Y.
Sew Business, 127 Avenue of the Americas, New York, N.Y.

Fashions

California Apparel News, 1016 S. Broadway Pl., Los Angeles, Cal.
Women's Wear Daily, Fairchild Publications, 7 E. 12th St., New York, N.Y.

Floor Covering

Floor Covering Weekly, 919 Third Ave., New York, N.Y.

Florists

Florist, 20900 Northwestern Highway, Southfield, Mich.

Furniture

Competitive Edge, 405 Merchandise Mart, Chicago, Ill.
Furniture News, P.O. Box 1569, Charlotte, N.C.

General Merchandise

Chain Store Age, Gen. Mds. Edition, 2 Park Ave., New York, N.Y.
The Discount Merchandiser, 641 Lexington Ave., New York, N.Y.
Volume Retail Merchandising, 109 Railside Rd., Suite 102, Don Mills, Ont.

Gifts

Gifts & Decorative Accessories, Geyer-McAllister Pub. Inc., 51 Madison Ave., New York, N.Y.

Groceries

Progressive Grocer, 708 Third Ave., New York, N.Y.
Supermarket News, 7 E. 12th St., New York, N.Y.
Thomas Grocery Register, 250 W. 34th St., New York, N.Y.

Hardware

Hardware Age, Chilton Co., Inc., Chilton Way, Radnor, Pa.
Hardware Merchandiser, 7300 N. Cicero Ave., Chicago, Ill.
Home & Auto, Harcourt Brace Jovanovich, Inc., 757 Third Ave., New York, N.Y.

Hosiery and Intimate Apparel

Body Fashions/Intimate Apparel, 757 Third Ave., New York, N.Y.
Hosiery and Underwear, 757 Third Ave., New York, N.Y.

Jewelry

Jewelers' Circular/Keystone, Chilton Way, Radnor, Pa.
Modern Jeweler, 15 W. 10th St., Kansas City, Mo.

Luggage

Luggage and Leather Goods, 80 Lincoln Ave., Stamford, Conn.

Management

Editor and Publisher Annual Market Guide 850 Third Avenue, New York, N.Y.
Department Store Economist, 48 E. 43rd St., New York, N.Y.
Sales and Marketing Management, 633 Third Ave. New York, N.Y.

Stores, 100 W. 31st St., New York, N.Y.
The Journal of Retailing, New York University, 202 Tisch Blvd., New York, N.Y.
Visual Merchandising, 407 Gilbert Ave., Cincinnati, Ohio

Men's

Daily News Record and Men's Wear, 7 E. 12th St., New York, N.Y.

Office Supplies

Office World News, 645 Stewart Ave., Garden City, N.Y.

Shoes

Footwear-News, 7 E. 12th St., New York, N.Y.
Shoe & Leather Journal, 1450 Don Mills Rd., Don Mills, Ont.

Sporting Goods

Sporting Goods Business, 1515 Broadway, New York, N.Y.
Sports Merchandiser, 1760 Peachtree Rd., N.W., Atlanta, Ga.

Toys

Playthings, 51 Madison Ave., New York, N.Y.
Toys, 757 Third Ave., New York, N.Y.

U.S. Government Publications

Bureau of the Census of the Department of Commerce

Business Cycle Developments
Census of Business
Census of Housing
Census of Population
County and City Data Book
Statistical Abstract of the United States

Other Publications of the Department of Commerce

Business Statistics
County Business Patterns
Survey of Current Business
U.S. Industrial Outlook

Bureau of Labor Statistics

Monthly Labor Review

Treasury Department

Statistics of Income

Chapter 18

The Retail Audit

Learning Goals

1. To understand how conducting a periodic retail audit prevents management from becoming entirely preoccupied with solving short-term, day-to-day problems.

2. To be able to discuss the concept of the horizontal retail audit.

3. To be aware of the vertical retail audit and to be able to show when it should be used.

4. To know the advantages and disadvantages of using an internal audit versus an external audit.

Key Terms and Concepts

financial audit	activity level audit	implementation (tactics)
retail audit	diagnosis	organization audit
inventory audit	prognosis	control
systems level retail audit	objectives	internal audit
	program	external audit

The retail audit involves more than a financial audit; the retail audit consists of a review of the major ingredients used in the effective retail management process and a financial audit discloses the retail performance of the firm in dollars. The financial audit is a formal examination of the results of past practices, but it does not reveal current management practices that may lead to financial difficulties. The inventory audit is another audit that is frequently used to verify that the firm possesses stock valued at a stated level of dollars. This audit is needed not only to prevent and detect employee theft but also to determine the extent of damage or out-of-date merchandise and record-keeping errors.

Nature of Retailing Audits

There is no universally established definition of the term *retail audit*. As used in this book, a *retail audit* consists of a broad analysis that includes a systematic evaluation of all retail procedures and practices. The primary purpose of the retail audit is to develop an independent judgment of the quality of the firm's effort to improve the future performance of its retail outlet(s). Retail management is always seeking improvements. Frequently retail managers are so involved in their day-to-day activities that they cannot determine if the activities are being performed in an optimum manner. The retail audit, with its fresh, overall, independent evaluation of the effort, can stimulate a retailer to make needed changes before inefficient procedures are reflected in a poor financial performance.

There are two basic types of retail audit: systems-level and activity-level audits. A systems-level audit consists of an examination of all the elements that the retailer uses to market his goods and/or services.[1] Particular emphasis is placed upon the relative importance of each of these elements. It is designed to develop a total evaluation of the retailer's marketing effort. The appraisal deals not so much with particular marketing activities as with their relationships with one another. Systems-level audits, however, do attempt to identify specific activities that appear to require closer investigation.[2]

The *activity-level* audit examines and evaluates in depth certain functional elements of the retail operation. It is a closer, more detailed investigation into one or more of the specific retailing activities.

Systems-Level (Horizontal) Retail Auditing

A comprehensive systems-level retail audit involves a periodic evaluation of both the basic framework used to generate retail activities and the performance of retail actions. The systems-level audit is comprehensive because it is an appraisal of all of the elements used in the retail effort, not merely an evaluation of the most problem-ridden activities. Confining the use of retail audits to occasions of company difficulties is likely to result in missed sales and/or lost cost-reduction opportunities. Successful retail organizations can benefit from retail auditing procedures by maintaining an objective view of changes occurring in both the outside marketing environment and the internal company operations.

Retail audits should be scheduled annually so that the retail audit is a regular part of the periodic review of the long-range company plan. The retail audit comprises the first two steps in the business planning process, and the latter begins with the retailer's diagnosis of the market situation and the factors believed to be responsible for it.

Diagnosis

The diagnosis phase attempts to determine where the retail firm is situated now and why it is situated there. Careful analysis of recent trends in company sales and market shares by territory, merchandise line, and other breakdowns can be used to identify the firm's current retail position. Image studies might be conducted to determine what consumers think of the retailer as a source of goods and services.

A more complete listing of questions to be answered during the diagnosis phase of the retail audit is presented in Exhibit 18–1.

Exhibit 18–1 **Questions to Be Answered during Diagnosis Phase of the Retail Audit**

A. Markets
1. Who are the firm's major markets?
2. What are the major market segments in each market?
3. What are the present and expected future size and the characteristics of each market segment?

B. Customers
4. How do the customers feel toward and perceive the firm?
5. How do customers make their purchase or adoption decisions?
6. What is the present and expected future state of customer needs and satisfaction?

C. Competitors
7. Who are the firm's major competitors?
8. What trends can be forseen in competition?

D. Macroenvironment
9. What are the main relevant developments with respect to demography, economy, technology, government, and culture that will affect the firm's situation?

Source: Questions are adapted from Philip Kotler, *Marketing for Nonprofit Organizations* (Englewood Cliffs, New Jersey: Prentice-Hall Inc.), p. 57. Reprinted by permission of Prentice-Hall, Inc., Englewood Cliffs, New Jersey.

Prognosis

A second step in the planning process, *prognosis,* involves an estimate of where the retailer is likely to go if the present policies are used in a marketplace that follows recent shopping trends. In other words, this step consists of determining where the retailer is headed; a prediction is made about the future. Naturally, all predictions will not be correct, but management that is aware of and uses recent trends in its forecasting is generally more accurate than management that does not believe in forecasting and hence assumes that nothing is going to change.

The systematic retail sales and profit prognosis consists of forecasting (1) industry sales, (2) company sales, (3) company revenues, costs, and profits, (4) investment required and, (5) rate of profit return on investment.[3]

Retail industry sales are usually forecast by using statistical demand analysis, which relates sales of the particular category to related factors such as employment, consumer income, and so forth.[4] The recent trends of the retailer's market share of retail sales for his merchandise category can be used to determine expected company sales.

The predictions made for the third item—company revenues, costs, and profits—involve the same process discussed in Chapter 12 as cash flow analysis. Costs are forecast by using past cost-to-sales relationships, and expected profit is simply the result of subtracting costs from sales.

The volume of needed investment (item 4) is based on the level of expenditure believed to be needed to sustain the present retail activities.

The last item (calculating the return on investment) reveals how profitable the retail operation is likely to be if things continue as they appear to be heading.

Objectives

The retail audit then turns to an evaluation of the firm's marketing and profit objectives. The *objectives* step consists of a determination of where the company should be headed in the future. A clear statement of the retailer's profit objectives is needed. For example, such a statement may establish a goal of obtaining an annual return on investment of X percent. However, explicit marketing objectives must also be established to satisfy consumers' needs at a profit. If this is not done, retail outlets and organizations can become obsolete quite rapidly as shopping patterns and preferences change.

Continuous changes in the retailer's marketing environment necessitate a clear statement of the definition of the firm's business. Objectives must define which consumers' needs are to be satisfied by the firm's retailing efforts. The objectives should identify those market segments that appear to offer the most long-range profit potential and those segments in which the retailer believes he or she has the competitive advantage. The marketing and competitive environment changes at an increasingly faster rate, so it is now easier to identify and enter a market niche by tuning in to these changes faster than competitors.

For example, a department store has used these concepts to clarify its marketing objectives. It recognized that the taste-making forces of American society have changed. The twenty-year-olds of the 1970s are the first generation reflecting the impact of growing up under the influence of a constant bombardment of television commercials and programs that emphasize that you should "live life with real gusto because you only have one chance." Thus, television's influence on the behavior of the young is probably more important than the traditional generators of values, namely, schools, churches, and parents. These factors, combined with the emphasis that all age groups placed on youth or on "looking young," were deemed to have an important impact upon the local clothing business.

The underlying desire in the United States is for consumers to buy goods and services that will make them appear to be at least ten years younger than they really are. The fashion-making forces have changed; no longer are fashions first adopted by upper-class Europeans and Americans then "trickling down" to adoption by the U.S. middle-class consumers to adoption by the U.S. lower class. Instead, the young "street people" have begun to generate fashion. Everybody else has followed this lead because of the basic desire to appear to be younger.

These rapid changes in the environment allowed the department store to enter a market niche that was not being captured by competitors, who were still selling essentially the conservative style of clothing that did not reflect the fashion consciousness of a growing segment of the market. The market was segmented not only on the basis of demographic characteristics such as age, sex, social class, and so forth, but also on the basis of psychographics of life style. The market segment that was fashion conscious was found to be growing and its preferences changing toward youth-generated styles. The department store adjusted its merchandise line to meet the needs of this market segment. It also promoted a whole new progressive retail image by generating a "making happiness happen" theme.

The image was carried over into non-clothing merchandise lines such as towels, bedding, and linens. In this case, the target customers were fashion-conscious people who were buying towels and bedding not merely for their functional uses but for their decorative purposes. Thus, the consumer was willing to pay much higher prices for goods that would match a color-decoration scheme. Additionally, the consumer was more likely to make more frequent repurchases of the item after growing tired of a particular decorative theme. Most of these goods would not wear out physically but they would be discarded early when they were no longer in style. Of course, more frequent consumer repurchases tend to generate additional sales and to build store loyalty if the consumer is satisfied with his or her purchase. The slowness of competitors to recognize these changes allowed the department store to establish itself as the leader in catering to this most profitable market segment.

Establishing retail objectives involves more than the selection of the generic marketing objectives (such as satisfying the clothing needs of a growing segment of fashion-conscious, local consumers, as illustrated in the above example). Retail objectives also involve the establishment of specific sales and profit target objectives. These targets should be set on a realistic basis that reflects an unbiased evaluation of the retail firm's capabilities.

Exhibit 18–2 contains a form that auditors can use to analyze the present condition of stated company policy for any retail firm. The form contains a description of three classifications on each item—outstanding, average, deficient. The auditor can objectively select the category that most accurately describes the situation in that specific retail firm. The auditor will be able to identify the areas requiring the most attention by reviewing all the category ratings for each area.

Exhibit 18-2 **Rating Form on Retail Policy**

Outstanding Condition	Average Condition	Deficient Condition
1. Company's policies and objectives clearly defined and understood by all.	1. Company's general policies not clearly defined nor understood	1. No general policy except to carry on company's tradition
2. All current and potential economic factors recognized in overall company planning.	2. Sporadic consideration of potential economic factors in company planning.	2. Planning done under impulse.
3. Aggressive participation in trade and business associations.	3. Interest in trade and business associations limited.	3. Trade and business associations regarded as a neccessary evil.
4. Company kept currently informed on federal, state and local regulations.	4. Government relationships determined by legal counsel but not passed along to company executives.	4. No policy on governmental matters. Local governmental office called when in doubt or in trouble.

Source: This form is a revised version of forms presented in Howard Ellsworth Sommer, *How to Analyze Your Own Business*, Management Aids No. 46, (Washington, D.C.: Small Business Administration, 1971).

Program

The efforts of retail auditors can then be focused upon the retailer's *program* that is used to achieve the objectives that have been established. The retailer's program consists of the decisions and policies on the level, allocation, and mix of the total marketing effort.

Initially the auditor wants to examine the level of resources the retailer is using in the marketing effort, because this level must be adequate to meet the firm's stated objectives. This involves an objective look at the total sales-generating budget to determine if the budget is large enough to allow the firm to accomplish its objectives. The evaluation might consist of an analysis of the relationship of sales volume to the level of the market budget. This analysis can reveal if past additions to the marketing budget resulted in increased sales and profits.

The auditor can also appraise the desirability of changing the balance among the retailer's marketing activities. A retail firm's marketing allocations can become unduly influenced by particularly strong functional area executives. An independent, objective appraisal of the retailer's marketing allocations may reveal an excessive use of advertising, personal selling, merchandise styling, price reductions, and the like. The more effective retail sales-generating programs offer a balance among all the available alternatives. It is not easy to identify when to shift money from one functional area to another, but analysis of past retail sales and expenditure data can guide this appraisal. Industry data can also be used to identify the functional areas that might be emphasized by the retailer. Larger emphasis upon a particular area, such as advertising, does not, however, indicate that the firm uses too much advertising relative to its other marketing efforts. The sales response may increase faster than the increased advertising expenditure for this particular retailer because the outlet is situated in a below average location.

Finally, retail auditors also examine how the marketing expenditure is allocated to various target market segments. The appraisal would evaluate the retailer's efforts vis-à-vis geographical areas, merchandise lines, and consumer segments. The task is essentially that of determining whether the current allocation generates maximum sales and profits for the given budget level. This is not an easy task, but an analysis of customer trading areas, consumer image, and purchase patterns can provide the basis for recommending an increase or reduction in marketing effort toward each target market segment.

Exhibit 18–3 contains three categories that describe a retail firm's efforts to evaluate its sales and merchandising activities.

Exhibit 18–3 **Form to Evaluate Retail Sales and Promotion Activities**

Outstanding Condition	Average Condition	Deficient Condition
1. Sound sales program based on known customer needs. Market research and analysis supported by good advertising and sales program.	1. Sales program based on past customer experience. Market potential not known. Advertising not selective.	1. Sales coverage incomplete. Knowledge of competition limited.
2. Sales budgets classified by products, customers, sales people, merchandise departments, geographic districts.	2. Sales total estimated but not budgeted by products to customers and geographic districts.	2. No sales budgets.
3. Sound pricing based on consumer demand and merchandise handling considerations.	3. Price structure rigid. Accurate product costs not used in setting sales prices.	3. Costs information not generally used in setting prices.
4. Profit or loss determined by sales people, customers' products, and geographic districts.	4. No attempt to analyze gross and net profit by sales people, products, customers.	4. No sales analyses.
5. Selective selling effort directed toward maximum profit possibilities.	5. Selling effort not directed toward best profit possibilities.	5. No selective selling program.
6. Trained sales people intelligently directed and compensated.	6. Sales people closely supervised but training program inadequate.	6. Sales people not well trained or supervised. Compensation not comparable to competitors'.
7. All sales records maintained currently.	7. Sales records not always maintained on a current basis.	7. No sales records beyond orders booked and sales billed.

Source: Form is revised version of forms in Howard Ellsworth Sommer, *How to Analyze Your Own Business*. Management Aids No. 46 (Washington, D.C.: Small Business Administration, 1971).

Implementation (Tactics)

Retail management may have designed an excellent program, but the firm's performance will depend upon *implementation,* or the proper execution of that program. Thus, the retail auditor focuses on both the *tactical means* and the *procedures* used to accomplish the objectives. An examination of the alternatives available for each *tactical decision* can reveal if the reasoning behind each decision was logical. The auditor has an advantage in examining these decisions after they have been made, since it is than possible to observe the consequences of each decision. (Hindsight is much better than foresight.) If such a historical examination is not periodically made by an auditor, it is not likely to be made at all. Regular retail management can (and usually does) become so occupied with the day-to-day operating procedures that it does not have time for periodic analyses of this type.

Tactical retail decisions are needed in many areas, including the following:

Selecting criteria used in hiring personnel

Selecting sales personnel compensation procedures

Selecting among different choices of vendors

Selecting among different modes of transportation to the warehouse and store

Selecting among different merchandise assortments

Selecting among different advertising media

Selecting among different promotional themes

Selecting among different amounts and kinds of price discounts

Selecting among different consumer credit plans

Selecting among different consumer services[5]

Retail auditors also want to examine the more important *procedures* used by the retailer to determine if improvements can be made. Procedures describe the way actions occur in the retail organization. Every retailer has numerous procedures regulating the flow of supplies, equipment, inventory, information, and personnel. Procedures, then, essentially identify who does what, when the action is performed, and how the action is performed. Special efforts must be made to determine if the most practical and most productive procedures are being used. The auditor must evaluate each procedure to determine if new technological advances (such as new computer capabilities or new management techniques) could increase retail efficiency.

Procedures that influence the retail performance include:

Developing current sales and cost information

Sales forecasting techniques

Determining current status of retail inventory

Routing of consumer product requests through the retail organization

Handling and expediting of customer orders

Handling and acting on new product and sales ideas

Training new salespeople

Preparation of marketing and promotional programs

Gathering information on competitors

Consumer checkout procedures

Consumer charging and billing procedures

Gathering information on attractiveness of current and proposed store locations

Developing control procedures to establish retail standards[6]

Exhibits 18–4 and 18–5 contain three category descriptions of both tactical means and procedures that a retailer can use to assess his efforts in personnel relations and merchandise assortment.

Exhibit 18–4 Form to Evaluate Retail Personnel Policies

Outstanding Condition	Average Condition	Deficient Condition
1. An executive, vested with adequate authority, formulates sound industrial relations policies and represents the company in labor negotiations.	1. Value of industrial relations realized, but authority and responsibility not clearly defined.	1. The industrial relations function is one of employment only, also coupled with other unrelated functions.
2. An industrial relations program minimizes labor turnover, builds employee morale and efficiency.	2. Industrial relations program not planned ahead, but ably administered; employee morale and efficiency average.	2. Little consideration given to industrial relations–employee turnover high.
3. Program for effective selecting, testing, placing, and training of all personnel.	3. Employee selection not developed beyond separate formulas used by office manager for clerical help and by employment manager for all other help.	3. No uniform procedure for applicant screening, placement, and training. Original interviewing left to each department head.
4. Salary and wage rates equitable and fair for each job classification from common labor to top management; established by sound job evaluation methods.	4. No job evaluation program. Wage rates increased under pressure. Top management and supervisory positions awarded largely on the basis of seniority.	4. Job rates fixed by personal opinion.
5. Incentive plans for all levels of employees, based on an equitable measurement of performance.	5. Incentive plans for some employees only.	5. No incentive plan.
6. Individual history and progress records for each employee; kept up to date for use as an inventory of qualifications.	6. Some records, but they are incomplete.	6. No records kept on individual employees beyond payroll requirements.

Source: Form is revised version of forms in Howard Ellsworth Sommer, *How to Analyze Your Own Business*. Management Aids No. 46 (Washington, D.C.: Small Business Administration, 1971).

Organization

The *organization audit* consists of an evaluation of the adequacy of retail management personnel both as a group and on an individual basis. An assessment of the

Exhibit 18-5 **Form to Evaluate Retail Merchandise Assortment**

Outstanding Condition	Average Condition	Deficient Condition
1. Continuous search for improved products; for the development of new products and markets.	1. Search effort spasmodic; objectives not definite.	1. No search for new products or markets.
2. Merchandise and service offerings thoroughly planned and highly organized under expert supervision with qualified personnel.	2. Merchandise search activities not well organized.	2. No personnel qualified to conduct merchandise search activities.
3. Close cooperation with merchandising and sales personnel to insure market acceptance.	3. The Company has a program for merchandise search, but these activities are not carried out in cooperation with other retail divisions.	3. Need for merchandise search ignored. No desire to add new products to assortment.

Source: Form is revised version of forms in Howard Ellsworth Sommer, *How to Analyze Your Own Business.* Management Aids No. 46 (Washington, D.C.: Small Business Administration, 1971).

way the retail organization functions is also needed to identify possible weaknesses in such areas as the lines of authority and responsibility and the communication channels used to relay consumers' desires to the appropriate retail decision maker.

A major factor contributing to business failure is a lack of experience on the part of key retail personnel. A successful retail firm must use the talent of people who have a knowledge of (1) buying, (2) products in demand by consumers, (3) how to attract customers, and (4) handling finances.

The amount of experience required is dependent upon the size and type of the retail operation. A complex retail organization, formal management practices, and established formal communications channels are required as different merchandise lines are offered and more outlets are opened. Single-unit operators especially should note the increased managerial effort required to open the second outlet. The business frequently runs smoothly until the new outlet is established; then the operator discovers that he can't communicate with the store employees unless he is continually present in the store.

The retail auditor cannot neglect any areas of the systems-level retail audit because all aspects affect retail performance. He must, however, place major emphasis upon the evaluation of retail objectives and programs. Establishment of effective retail objectives and programs provides the foundation for retail success. Poor store locations, merchandise lines, and store images cannot be overcome by making sudden changes in tactical or procedural areas. In other words, a retailer's strategy as reflected by objectives and programs is a long-run concept that cannot be changed in a short period of time. It takes time to locate and establish outlets on good retail sites or to establish the desired retail image in the minds of potential customers. Thus undetected errors made in establishing retailing strategy will have a severe effect on future performance for many years.

The consequences of poor tactical decisions and/or procedures will also adversely affect retail performance. However, they can usually be changed within a year after the mistake is recognized. The tendency for most people in retail management to spend most of their time dealing with problems of a tactical or procedural nature usually leads to identifying these problems more quickly than more strategical problems.

Control

Retail objectives, programs, tactics, procedures, and organizations are all based upon assumptions and expectations made by retail management. Rapid changes in the competitive environment and in customer preferences frequently go against management's assumptions and expectations. Thus, a control section must be incorporated into the retailer's audit. Retail *control* consists of monitoring the effectiveness of the retail plan and preparing several contingency plans that will shorten the retailer's reaction time to these kinds of changes.

The control section should establish performance standards that will be checked periodically to determine if the retailer's plan is leading to the achievement of its stated objectives. Exhibits 18–6 and 18–7 contain descriptions of control areas that are frequently used by retailers. First, good accounting procedures must be established to provide necessary data. Then standard costs and budgets can be established to indicate areas where the objectives are not being met. Finally, the financial condition of the firm must be analyzed periodically to detect any shortage of funds.

A listing of the major marketing questions that must be answered in the objectives, programs, implementation, and organization phases of the systems-level retail audit is presented in Exhibit 18–8.

Activity-Level (Vertical) Retail Auditing

The framework that can be used to conduct the system-level audit is also useful for auditing any specific activity. The coverage under an activity audit then consists of:

1. Determining and appraising retail management's *objectives* for that specific activity. The appraisal determines if the activity objectives are appropriate in terms of the firm's market targets, opportunities, and resources.
2. Determining if a satisfactory *program* is being used to achieve the activity's objectives. This consists of an evaluation of the level of the activity's total budget and the allocation of the money spent from the activity budget.
3. Determining the firm's *implementation* of the program in terms of making tactical decisions and using suitable retail procedures.
4. An appraisal of the departmental *organization* in terms of the distribution of authority and responsibility, the performance of the people who occupy the positions, and the intra- and interdepartmental communication process.

The activity-level audits are usually conducted when a problem appears to exist in any activity area. The problem may be uncovered by the systems-level audit or by

Exhibit 18-6 **Evaluation Form for Retail Accounting Procedures**

Outstanding Condition	Average Condition	Deficient Condition
1. Procedures, record forms, reports designed with a view to producing required information at lowest cost.	1. Accounting fairly comprehensive, accurate, prompt and well managed— some written procedures.	1. Accounting accurate from bookkeeping standpoint, but generally "old-fashioned" and incomplete.
2. Accounting data supplied promptly in a form best adapted to its use by management.	2. Accounting data not adequate in comparison with most modern control standards.	2. Accounting not highly regarded as a tool of management.
3. Modern accounting equipment used effectively in preparation of necessary information and reports.	3. Accounting machines used but not adaptable to modern methods.	3. Accounting equipment antiquated, cumbersome, and wasteful.
4. Cost system designed to reflect all variances between standard and actual costs.	4. Cost accounting fairly accurate but not organized to provide standard cost information.	4. No standard costs. Job costs inaccurate and uncontrolled.
5. Variances from standard performances supplied currently to management for corrective action.	5. Records and reports not best suited to control costs and expenses.	5. Cost information mostly estimated. Monthly profit and loss statements inaccurate.
6. Unnecessary accounting records eliminated— management control reports furnished as needed.	6. Many records, reports, and statistics maintained that are not useful as a tool of management.	6. Some records and reports prepared; have no practical advantage.
7. All control records and costs integrated with standard costs.	7. Records unrelated to control; therefore, of little assistance.	7. Production records required for suitable cost control not maintained.
8. All estimates for product pricing based on standard costs; loss of volume or profit is indicated.	8. Estimates not checked against actual cost.	8. Estimates determined by past performance and competition.
9. The effect that sales mixture and product selling prices have on the total company profits is known at all times.	9. No knowledge of the effect on total business profits of individual product or order pricing.	9. Profit or loss estimated monthly; verified and adjusted annually to inventory; no profit or loss known by product breakdown.

Source: Form is revised version of forms in Howard Ellsworth Sommer, *How to Analyze Your Own Business*. Management Aids No. 46 (Washington, D.C.: Small Business Administration, 1971).

management simply believing that something seems to be going wrong in a particular activity. A brief discussion of some of the points that may be analyzed in specific activity audits is now in order.

Customer Analysis

Identifying the retailer's most profitable customers is one of the most important things to determine in a retail market analysis. Not all customers generate profits

Exhibit 18-7 **Evaluation Form for Retail
Financial and Budgetary Control Procedures**

Outstanding Condition	Average Condition	Deficient Condition
Budgetary Control		
1. Budgetary control of all expenditures based on flexible performance standards equitably established by operating levels.	1. Budget structure rigid; ratios of expense to sales based on past performance, not on predetermined, flexible performance standards.	1. No attempt made to budget or forecast performance.
2. Sales budget by merchandise line, salesmen, customers and territories—based on market analyses.	2. Sales budget by merchandise line, salesmen, customers and territories—based on past sales performance only.	2. No sales budget. No quotas for salesmen. No program.
3. Knowledge and control of the effect of all selling price changes on budgeted amount of total net profits.	3. No centralized control of selling prices within limits of predetermined profit requirements.	3. No established pricing policy. Cost estimates ignored where considerable volume is involved. Effect of cutting prices to meet competition not projected in terms of lost profits.
4. Daily, weekly, or monthly reports on the performance of all departments controlled through: (a) standard or budgeted performance; and (b) variance form standard performance.	4. Divisional accounting reports periodically exhibited: (a) comparison of current with past periods; (b) no standards; therefore no comparison of actual results with what should have been accomplished.	4. No budgets; no broad long-term planning. Policies vacillating because not founded on complete comparative information and thorough analysis
Finance		
1. Forecast of working capital and cash requirements for planned business volume and profits level	1. No forecast of working capital or cash requirements. Funds not always obtained or employed.	1. Working capital and cash inadequate; credit policy lax. No forward planning.
2. Adequate reserves for replacement of obsolescent and depreciating assets— represented by earmarked liquid funds to the extent required.	2. Depreciation reserves conditioned on allowable deductions for tax purposes only; not properly planned from a capital asset replacement point of view.	2. Nominal reserves without due regard to actual value of assets; frequently used for purposes other than originally intended.
3. Dividend policy consistent with sound, long-term financial program.	3. No definite financial or dividend policy.	3. Financing dictated by immediate need for cash to meet pressing obligations.

Source: Form is revised version of forms in Howard Ellsworth Sommer, *How to Analyze Your Own Business*. Management Aids No. 46 (Washington, D.C.: Small Business Administration, 1971).

for the store they patronize, and retailers can use their resources in an inefficient way by catering to customers who buy only low-margin items on an infrequent basis but demand extra services. No retail outlet can be all things to all people, so the retail effort must be oriented to serve and satisfy profitable customers. Customers who do not pay their bills on time or who habitually return purchases add to the cost of conducting business. The low profit margins generally obtained in retailing may not be large enough to allow that kind of customer to be serviced at a profit. One way to determine if customers are paying their way is to estimate what it costs to serve different kinds of consumers and to sell different-size orders.

Exhibit 18–8 Major Marketing Questions to Be Answered during the Objectives, Program, Implementation, and Organization Phases of the Systems-level Retail Audit

A. Objectives
1. What are the firm's long-run and short-run overall objectives and marketing objectives?
2. Are the objectives stated in a clear rank order and in a form that permits planning and measurement of achievement?
3. Are the marketing objectives reasonable for the firm, given its competitive position, resources, and opportunities?

B. Program
1. What is the firm's core strategy for achieving its objectives, and is it likely to succeed?
2. Is the firm allocating enough resources (or too many) to accomplish the marketing tasks?
3. Are the marketing resources allocated optimally to the various markets, territories, stores, departments, and products of the firm?
4. Are the marketing resources allocated optimally to the major elements of the marketing mix; that is product quality, personal contact, promotion, and distribution?

C. Implementation
1. Does the firm develop an annual marketing plan? Is the planning procedure effective?
2. Does the firm implement control procedures (monthly, quarterly, and so forth) to insure that its annual plan objectives are being achieved?
3. Does the firm carry out periodic studies to determine the contribution and effectiveness of various marketing activities?
4. Does the firm have an adequate marketing information system to service the needs of managers for planning and controlling operations in various markets?

D. Organization
1. Does the firm have a high-level marketing officer to analyze, plan, and implement the marketing work of the firm?
2. Are the other persons directly involved in marketing activity able people? Is there a need for more training, incentives, supervision, or evaluation?
3. Are the marketing responsibilities optimally structured to serve the needs of different marketing activities, products, markets, and territories?
4. Do the firm's personnel understand and practice the marketing concept?

Source: Questions are adapted from Philip Kotler, *Marketing for Nonprofit Organization* (Englewood Cliffs, New Jersey: Prentice-Hall Inc., 1975), p. 69. Reprinted by permission of Prentice-Hall, Inc. Englewood Cliffs, New Jersey.

Retailers must be cautious in the way they identify unprofitable customers and in the way they treat them after they have been identified. Unprofitable consumers communicate with many potentially profitable customers. Bad word-of-mouth advertising can, of course, affect the purchase patterns of the profitable consumers.

No stores can serve everyone. The retail audit must determine if management has adequately defined the group(s) of customers (market targets) that the store is going to serve. The audit should reflect the fact that small stores are more effective in catering to distinct groups, such as customers who have special tastes or interests, local residents, business people working nearby, and so forth. Larger retail organizations may cater to several different market targets by using boutiques, subdividing large departments, establishing bargain basements, and so on.

Customer Relations

Customer relations revolve around the type of store image that management seeks to implant in the minds of customers. The retail audit must determine if a clear definition of the desired store image has been made. First, is store management aware of the store's special features—the special kinds of merchandise and services it offers? Are these special features communicated to both present and potential customers?

Many outlets suffer because store personnel fumble their roles after the customer has been attracted to the store. Stores that cannot match the merchandise assortments and low prices offered by mass merchandising competitors must gain their strength from the use of special services. Is quick delivery service, personal customer attention, and the ability to help solve specific customer problems, such as garden care, interior decorating, clothing selection, being used to attract and retain customers? If not, why not?

The retail audit should also determine if salespeople are treating each customer as an individual rather than as one of the crowd. Do they greet customers by name? Are salespeople helping consumers by listening to their problems and offering solutions? Have campaigns been conducted to encourage employees to be considerate of customers' viewpoints? As a competitive advantage, courtesy, especially at the cash register or checkout counter, is a powerful attraction. The customer gets the last impression of the store in the checkout process, and a friendly and interested employee can make certain that it is a good impression.

Is service being provided on the merchandise after it has been sold? In some cases this consists of merely returning goods to the factory for repair. In other cases it involves on-the-spot maintenance. In either case, the service should be provided quickly and courteously.

Is retailing management aware of the customer's need for convenience and shopping ease? A comfortable customer lounge can serve as both a meeting and a resting place. A "free" cup of coffee and other small extras can make a store a more enjoyable place to shop. Consumer convenience may also be provided by posting and maintaining regular store hours. This allows the consumer to depend on the store's being open and to adjust purchasing and consumption patterns to the store hours. The small cost involved in providing such services frequently yields large returns in repeat business.

Location

A good location is essential for the successful operation of any retail firm. One of the most frequent mistakes is made by retailers who want to minimize the monthly rental payment needed to obtain a good location. These retailers suffer because they will not pay enough rent to secure a good location that could generate volume sales. As a result, they have to spend more money to promote the store and still may not be able to attract convenience-oriented consumers.

The retail audit should determine if new outlets would increase the retailer's profits. If new outlets are being considered, is the firm's selection procedure an objective evaluation? The selection of a city or town that will contain the new outlet should be based upon characteristics such as population, area growth potential, consumer income and purchasing power, the purchasing habits of potential consumers, legislative restrictions, and competition. The index of retail saturation discussed in Chapter 5 may be used to measure the relative retail potential of an area.

Local trading area analysis of the most promising cities or towns can indicate if the firm's existing outlets are covering the market area that can be serviced profitably by the organization. New outlets may be required to serve areas in which few customers reside. This usually will be the case when each outlet's trading area is small, and when per outlet retailing costs do not decline rapidly as sales volume increases. Naturally, the firm should examine the characteristics of potential consumers residing in an area not currently being reached by the firm's existing retail outlets. A new outlet will not be warranted automatically unless the demographics and life styles of people residing in this untapped area are similar to those of the target market customers of the existing outlets. In untapped areas where residents' characteristics differ from those of current outlets, the firm could open a new outlet under a new name. Management may want to create a different store image that could better serve the needs of consumers in areas of sufficient size that will justify this additional expense. The location audit should include evaluations of the outlet's accessibility to residents of the trading area and its compatibility with nearby businesses. Exhibit 18–9 provides an illustration of the type of locational assistance that is available from commercial sources.

Outlet Layout

The retail audit should determine if the layout of the selling floor is planned for the convenience of the customer. This may be accomplished by providing a clear indication of the location of the different types of merchandise and by displaying related merchandise close together. Merchandise should be attractively displayed where customers can handle it (instead of having to ask a sales person to show it) so as to enhance sales and reduce clerical cost. Goods that the customer may not be specifically looking for, but is likely to buy if reminded of them by their visibility, should be displayed prominently. Impulse goods are usually displayed on sales counters near the store entrances and at other heavy traffic points. Interspersing impulse goods with demand items can also increase the chance that the consumer will see the impulse merchandise.

The audit should also evaluate the image that the layout projects to the store's customers. Is it consistent with the expectations of the outlet's target market?

Promotion

The retail audit may initially focus on the firm's promotional strategy. The general objectives of the retail promotion efforts are to:

1. Increase the competitive position of the outlet by obtaining a larger share of the retail business in the trade area
2. Encourage consumers residing outside the trade area to shop at the firm's retail outlet

Exhibit 18-9
**An Illustration of the Type of
Locational Assistance Available
from Commercial Sources.**

TELE/SITE

Trade Areas:
Any Size or Shape

Can You Afford To Be Left Behind?

We're a nation of movers. Yesterday's cow pasture is tomorrow's
sprawling city. Jobs, weather, boom or bust—all play a part in periodically reshuffling the landscape and dealing a new hand to decision-
makers in business and government.

Are you in a position to respond? Is the restaurant, department
store, day care center, or supermarket you're analyzing situated
where there's a population to support it now? A year from now?
Five years from now?

Let Urban Decision Systems' TELE/SITE service help you keep
in step with the changing demography of your trade or service areas.
How?

- By providing you with up-to-date information on population,
  households, income, consumer expenditure, and the latest available figures on age, sex, race, employment, education, and
  housing—to name just a few.
- By using the latest computer technology to produce inexpensive
  reports on your trade area—anywhere in the U.S.—and getting
  them to you quickly. (We send the reports on the next business
  day after your order.)

We're here to help keep you from getting lost in the shuffle. So open
up, read on, and give us a call.

TELE/SITE Requirements

Training	— 0
Staff	— 0
Special equipment	— 0
Your time	— **5** minutes to call us

**Do you keep getting
busy signals when you
call us?**

Now we have *two* phone numbers for
TELE/SITE callers
  (213) 826-6596 *and* **(213) 820-1581**
Urban Decision Systems office hours
are weekdays (except holidays) from
8:00 A.M. to 5:30 P.M. *Pacific* time

Rings

Bands

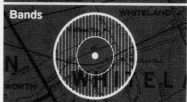

Sectors

Polygons

Travel Contours

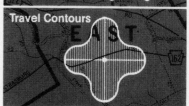

**Area Composed
of Counties**

Also:
Any combination of tracts, zip codes, SMSAs, ADIs, TSAs, or DMAs,
routes, corridors, and cuts

REPORTS

1 Area Profile
Our most popular demographic report. Over 150 key items drawn from the 1970 Census.

2 Household Equipment
Provides 1970 baseline information on the household equipment data in our consumer expenditure reports.

3 Updated Income
Up-to-date income, population, and household figures. Includes a breakdown of families by income. A valuable adjunct to the Area Profile report.

```
AREA PROFILE: 1970 CENSUS              URBAN DECISION SYSTEMS, INC.
ANYTOWN, USA                                             06/01/77
1.0 MILE RING


POPULATION    26213    AGG.INCOME   114.94M   FAMILY INCOME        %
                                               0-4.9T       433    6.6
BLACK          0.6%    HSHLD SIZE      3.5     5-7.9T       498    7.6
OTHER          1.2%    GRP QTRS/INST   2.0%    8-9.9T       523    8.0
SPAN AM        7.1%                            10-11.9T     751   11.5
                                               12-14.9T    1169   17.9
AGE              %     OCCUPATION        %     15-24.9T    2403   36.7
0-5      2276   8.7    PROF/TEC   2667  24.9   25-49.9T     705   10.8
6-13     4863  18.6    MGR/PROP   1539  14.4   50T+          64    1.0
14-17    2703  10.3    CLERICAL   1902  17.8   MEDIAN     $ 14740
18-20    1671   6.4    SALES      1096  10.2   AVERAGE    $ 16551
21-24    1373   5.2    WH/COL     7204  67.3
25-34    3061  11.7    CRAFTS     1147  10.7   SCHOOLING
35-44    3888  14.8    OPERTIVS    964   9.0   POP AGE 25+       13327
45-54    3908  14.9    SERVICE    1009   9.4   HIGH SCH ONLY     37.6%
55-64    1398   5.3    LABORER     367   3.4   ANY COLLEGE       41.5%
65+      1874   4.1    FARM WRK     15   0.1   MEDIAN SCH YRS    12.8
MEDIAN    25.2         BL/COL     3502  32.7   18-34 IN COLL     31.5%

SEX             LABOR FORCE  UNEMP  PART/R      AUTOMOBILES             %
MALE   12826 48.9%   7295    4.8%  79.1%       0            160    2.2
FEMALE 13387 51.1%   4044    7.0%  41.0%       1           2135   28.9
                                               2           3767   51.1
                 IN ARMED FORCES   0.2%        3+          1315   17.8

HOUSING UNITS    7614   HOUSING VALUE           RENT
OWNER OCC.      70.7%   0-14.9T      13   0.2   0-59          60    3.0
RENTER OCC.    26.2%   15-19.9T     164   3.1   60-99         87    4.4
VACANT          3.1%   20-24.9T     964  18.0   100-149      771   38.9
CONDOMINIUMS       0   25-34.9T    2359  44.1   150-199      759   38.3
MOBILE HOMES       2   35-49.9T    1431  26.8   200-299      287   14.5
TURNOVER        7.7%   50T+         414   7.7   300+          20    1.0
STABILITY      51.5%   MEDIAN    $ 31489        MEDIAN      $  154
                       AVERAGE   $ 33909        AVERAGE     $  159

UNITS/STRUCTURE     %
1         6065  79.7   ROOMS/UNIT         %     BUILT     OWNER RENTER
2           15   0.2   1-3         676  11.5    1965-70    6.9%  24.6%
3-4         23   0.3   4-5        2469  32.4    1960-64   31.2%  43.8%
5-49       880  11.6   6-7        3591  47.2    1950-59   56.9%  22.9%
50+        628   8.3   8+          677   8.9    <--1949    5.0%   9.6%
```

```
UPDATED INCOME: 1977                   URBAN DECISION SYSTEMS, INC.
ANYTOWN, USA                                             06/01/77
1.0 MILE RING


               1960      1970      1977    % CHANGE  % CHANGE
              CENSUS    CENSUS    (EST.)   1960-70   1970-77
POPULATION    16132     26213     26481      62.5      1.0
HOUSEHOLDS              7377      8853                 20.0

AGG.INCOME (M) $        114.94    169.44              47.4

AVE.HSHLD INCOME $      15295     18789               22.8
PER CAPITA INCOME $      4385      6399               45.9

                        1970               1977
FAMILY INCOME          CENSUS      %      (EST.)      %
LESS THAN $2000          165      2.5       179      2.6
$ 2000 - $ 2999           50      0.8        51      0.7
$ 3000 - $ 4999          218      3.3       150      2.2
$ 5000 - $ 6999          284      4.3       217      3.2
$ 7000 - $ 7999          215      3.3       127      1.9
$ 8000 - $ 9999          523      8.0       369      4.5
$10000 - $11999          751     11.5       462      5.9
$12000 - $14999         1169     17.9       796     11.6
$15000 - $19999         1744     26.6      1661     24.2
$20000 - $24999          659     10.1      1327     19.3
$25000 - $49999          705     10.8      1471     21.4
$50000 OR MORE            64      1.0       171      2.5

MEDIAN $                14740              18611
AVERAGE $               16551              21229
```

SOURCE: ESTIMATES BY URBAN DECISION SYSTEMS, INC.

```
HOUSEHOLD EQUIPMENT: 1970 CENSUS       URBAN DECISION SYSTEMS, INC.
ANYTOWN, USA                                             06/01/77
1.0 MILE RING


POPULATION     26213   UNITS WITH:       OWNER    %    RENTER   %
HOUSING UNITS   7614   AIR CONDITIONING  3820  70.9    1743  87.5
HOUSEHOLDS      7377   CENTRAL HEATING   4321  80.2     483  24.2
   OWNER       73.0%   1+ BATHROOMS      5082  94.4     767  38.5
   RENTER      27.0%                     TOTAL   %    1-FAMILY  %
                       BASEMENT           132   1.7      98   1.6
                       CONCRETE SLAB     4080  53.6    2704  44.6

HOUSEHOLDS WITH:  %
TV      7262  98.4   HEATING FUEL     %     COOKING FUEL       %
WASHER  5912  80.1   GAS        6503  86.2  GAS        4759  64.5
DRYER   5001  67.8   TANK GAS     39   0.5  TANK GAS     19   0.3
DISHWSH 4446  60.3   ELECTRIC    825  11.2  ELECTRIC   2599  35.2
FREEZER 2331  31.6   FUEL OIL      0   0.0  FUEL OIL      0   0.0
```

Pictured here are some of our most popular reports, including updated income and consumer expenditure. Other reports range from a single data item to over 2,000. Remember, too, that we can design a special report for you that you can order through the TELE/SITE service.

HOW TO ORDER

- Pick up your phone, dial (213) 826-6596
- We'll help you decide what kind of trade a list, and so on) and TELE/SITE Reports
- Tell us where your trade area is located

(213) 8:

Source: Courtesy of Urban Decision Systems, Inc., Los Angeles, California.

3. Stimulate consumers to increase the level of retail purchases

4. Create and maintain a favorable store image consistent with the quality of merchandise offered, the service provided, and the convenience of the location.

Thus, the audit must determine how successful the retailer has been in accomplishing these objectives.

Has the retailer determined what "message" should be communicated to the consumers? The message should be selected to accomplish objective 4 for the target market customers.

Other considerations that should be investigated in the retail audit of the promotion activity include an evaluation of the consistency of the promotional activity. Small amounts of advertising on a frequent basis are generally more effective in creating the desired image than large amounts of advertising on an infrequent basis. Constant reminders that the store carries certain merchandise lines, that new products are now available, that expert service and advice is available at the store, and that the store offers specific advantages in specific areas are required to reinforce the consumer's image of the store. Stores that rely upon strictly "sale-price reduction" advertising do little to attain a favorable quality and service image. The level of expenditure for promotional activities should be related to the expected sales level for the store. Promotional activity should be increased before the sales peak is expected to occur. Large advertising expenditures just prior to payday or normal shopping days are more likely to stimulate sales because consumers will have the ability to respond to the message.

Tactical considerations can also be made during an audit. For example, advertisement can be improved by retaining copies of the advertisements previously used and evaluating their effectiveness. Successful advertisements frequently contain products and/or appeals that can be featured again to repeat the former success. Cost of the advertisement, media usage, weather conditions, and unusual competitors' activities should be recorded and analyzed in the process of identifying the effective advertisements.

Pricing

The retail audit should determine if prices are established to provide as much markup as possible without losing a substantial sales volume. Have price levels been raised and lowered on different items over a period of time? This will allow the retailer to identify those items whose demand is highly dependent upon price. Setting a lower markup on those items responsive to price changes can bring enough added sales to yield a larger total profit. The reduction in price on these key items, however, may disturb the public image of the store. Maintaining or raising prices on items whose sales do not respond to price changes can result in higher profits, provided this action does not damage the store image projected to consumers. Higher markups should be obtained on items whose risk and handling costs are high and/or whose turnover rate is relatively low. These higher markups will offset the low markups that are taken on competitive merchandise.

Has the outlet established price lines that provide good merchandise assortments at the price levels demanded by its target market consumers? This practice can be a profitable pricing strategy.

Temporary price markdowns can be used to cater to customer groups that do not respond to regular prices. This can result in increased sales and may result in increased dollar margin.

However, the promotion must be truthful. The prices quoted in advertisements should reflect the store's intent to sell the merchandise at the stated price. Misleading promotions result in possible legal action and consumer ill will that, in the long run, far outweigh the temporary increase in store profits generated by the misleading promotions.

Buying

The retail audit may include an analysis to determine if the selection of merchandise assortments is meeting the needs of the retailer's target market consumers. Adequate stocking and quick reordering of new items that have been showing volume sales potential must be done to complement the buyer's original subjective judgment of consumers' needs. Can the firm that is being audited receive additional merchandise quickly? Why not? What can be done to improve speed of delivery?

Retail buyers should also be comparing new item offerings with the present merchandise assortment. Shelf space is not utilized efficiently if the new items are so similar that they merely represent a duplication of the current product offering.

Is central group buying being used advantageously on some items where individual store buyers cannot obtain style and price preferences? A central buying office may be able to act more quickly on new market offerings and developments, since it has a broader picture of lines that are coming in and going out of style.

Is a written buying plan being used to guide the selections of the retail buyer who attends a particular market or trade show? The buying plan should be based upon such factors as price line, type, material, size, and color, and should not be left to chance. It does not normally specify style numbers but may include the number of different styles that the retailer wants to carry.

The audit should also contain an evaluation of the way the retailer increases profits by taking advantage of available trade, quantity, seasonal, and cash discounts. Careful planning and proper timing of orders can result in substantial discounts not otherwise available. Transportation charges also can be reduced by proper planning. Placing orders too late for slower but cheaper delivery methods, ordering in uneconomical quantities (for example, ordering fifty-pound lots when the minimum charge is for one hundred pounds), permitting the use of unnecessarily heavy packing materials, and so forth result in excessive transportation costs. Procedures should be used to be certain that the order always specifies the method of transportation and the consolidator of the shipments.

Merchandise and Inventory Control

Merchandise control begins by checking the description and number of units of merchandise received against the description of the goods ordered. All orders must be followed to see that goods are shipped and received on time. Late delivery of ordered goods can result in consumer ill will and lost sales, which may necessitate price markdowns to eventually move the merchandise.

Organizing the store by departments allows retail management to determine the profitability of each merchandise group and the performance of employees. Department records should include information on gross sales, physical inventories, value of purchases, markdowns, direct department expenses, cash discounts, and other data needed to construct departmental operating statements. Sales, inventory, and purchase records must be kept by merchandise groups for each department if retailers want to balance inventories and purchases with sales. These records can be used to develop a model stock plan that can be used to maintain balance between breadth and depth of merchandise assortments. A unit plan can be developed to indicate the number of different items that should be carried in stock and the number of each variety that should be stocked to avoid out-of-stock conditions. The model variety can be broken down by price lines, types, materials, colors, and sizes.

A constant supply of staple and reorder items is essential if a retailer is going to maintain a steady stream of customers. Retailers should prepare a list of selected items that are deemed important enough to warrant particular efforts to almost never be out of stock. The item's rate of sale, its delivery period, the planned frequency of reorder, and the desired amount of safety stock can be considered to minimize the level of stock-outs on these key items.

A unit control system should be developed for nonstaple merchandise lines. This system may consist of a daily or weekly analysis of sales on nonstaple items, or it may involve keeping daily inventory records by computer hookup to the store's cash registers. These unit control records allow retail management to identify fast- and slow-selling items quickly. This quick identification allows the retailers to reorder the best-selling items promptly and in sufficient volume to minimize out-of-stock conditions. Slow-selling items are identified faster, so they may be promoted and sold at reduced prices, thereby reducing the inventory investment and shelf space allocated to slow-moving merchandise.

Additional planning is required on goods that have a short selling season. The introduction of short-lived seasonal or fad goods is likely to result in a loss unless careful preplanning is done in determining:

1. When the first orders are to be placed
2. When retail stocks are to be complete
3. The expected duration of the peak selling period
4. The start of the merchandise clearance sales
5. The date that the remainder of the merchandise should be completely sold out

Adequate safeguards must be used to minimize the theft, breakage, soiling, spoiling, and fading of merchandise if the retail firm is to operate profitably. Pilferage is rapidly becoming one of the greatest retailing problems. Detection and control systems must be established and implemented, or the level of stock shortage is likely to exceed the net profit level.

Periodic checks should be made to ensure that a sufficient level of insurance is carried to cover changes in the value of merchandise, real estate, buildings, and equipment. The coverage on public liability insurance should be evaluated at the same time. Inflation and greater awards on liability suits have caused many retailers to be underinsured when tragedy strikes.

A retail audit should contain an evaluation of the performance on these basic merchandise and inventory control factors.

Budgetary Control

Retail plans must be expressed in terms of a budget that establishes goals for sales, stocks, markups, and expenses. The audit should investigate the budgetary process used by the retailer. The budgetary period takes the form of both short-run and annual planning. The short-term budget must be prepared weekly or monthly to assure adequate control of current operations. The annual budget contains the expected cash flow for the upcoming year. It should include expected changes in costs and revenues resulting from implementing the retail plan.

Both kinds of budgets are more effective when the employees responsible for achieving the stated objectives have a chance to participate in the formulation of the goals. Previous company experience and published data on other firms engaged in a similar business provide a basis of comparison for determining the budget. The control process should also involve a comparison of actual company results against previous budget projections. Merchandising, promotion, and expense plans can then be adjusted as indicated by the deviation from the projections. Open-to-buy and open-to-spend controls are needed to keep purchases consistent with previous plans. These plans must be revised as changes in the competition and environment occur if the retailer is to remain responsive to changes in consumer purchasing patterns.

Retail Organization and Personnel Management

Retail firms should be organized so that each employee takes orders from and is under the direct supervision of only one person. This type of organization can avoid the conflicts of divided responsibility. The retail audit should determine if the functions and lines of authority have been established in writing, preferably on organization charts. This will assist all employees to understand their areas of responsibility and the relationship of their work to that of others in the retailing organization.

Written job specifications are essential in selecting, training, and evaluating personnel. The "management by objective" approach can be used effectively by insisting that employees set specific objectives for themselves. These objectives will guide their own activities and performance for the stated period of time. If the personal objectives that an employee first suggests seem inadequate, they may be upgraded by mutual consent. Once agreed upon, these objectives become the immediate supervisor's basis of evaluation.

The audit might also determine if top-level retail management is delegating as much authority as possible to those employees immediately responsible to it. The delegation of authority can free top management from using most of its time on unnecessary operating details. Top retail management and department managers can usually improve retail performance by allocating more of their time to planning, organization, coordination, supervision, and control activities.

Regular and consistent supervision of employees is more effective than sporadic criticism of poor performance. A retail audit will show whether this is being done.

Another factor that should be included in the activity audit in this area is the retailer's compensation policy. Wages and other forms of compensation must be competitive with wages paid by other firms. Wages must also be adjusted to the difficulties and responsibilities of each job. Most of the retail salesperson's earnings generally come from a base salary, which is supplemented with a commission on sales. The more reliance that is placed on commission, the more incentive the sales people have to make sales. Other incentive plans give consideration to employees' needs for recognition, security, reasonable hours, congenial working conditions, and opportunities for advancement. Commission and quota bonus plans usually provide incentives for salespeople, while seasonal bonus plans may provide more incentives for supervisors. Whatever pay plan is used, the pay policy (including overtime policy) should be clear to all employees.

Credit

A retail credit policy should be based on the costs of granting credit against the benefits obtained by granting credit. Bank credit card plans have advantages in that the store's cash is not tied up in accounts receivable. In addition, there are fewer problems in opening accounts and collecting overdue bills. Bank credit card plans, however, may weaken customer loyalty to the firm's outlets. The retailer's own credit card plan may encourage store loyalty because the card cannot be used in competing stores. If the retail firm uses its own credit plan, it must establish definite credit limits, explain the rules carefully to all applicants, and follow up promptly when customers do not make payments as agreed.

Periodic reviews should be made of the accounts receivable and revolving credit accounts to determine the collection period, the percentage of accounts that are current, overdue, and so forth. These regular reviews will be helpful when management sets up bad-debt reserves and establishes credit and collection policies. The firm's performance on bad debts, collection period, and so on can be compared with data for similar stores.

An audit of a retailer's credit policy should reflect these considerations.

Taxes and Legal Obligations

Important changes in tax and legal regulations occur frequently. The retail audit should determine if one specific individual or group is responsible for submitting the required taxes and various legal reports. Maintaining a calendar that shows when the various taxes and reports are due is a must as requirements and regulations become more numerous and more complex. Specialists in tax and other legal matters are required in order to keep up to date on the latest rulings. Laws on advertising, labeling, selling, and guarantee practices are changing rapidly, so periodic checks must be made to determine if the current practices satisfy the current laws and regulations. Wise retailers recognize legitimate consumer complaints. Through group action these retailers try to pass legislation that serves the consumer but does not add significant costs to the retailing effort.

Implementing a Retail Audit

The success of the retail audit depends upon who conducts the audit and when it is scheduled. The retail audit can be conducted either internally, by an individual or group of individuals who are permanent members of the retail organization, or externally by outside consultants. The *internal audit* has the advantage that the auditors are intimately familiar with the operation and, as a result, the cost is reduced considerably. However, an objective, unbiased audit is not likely from an internal audit. Each member of the retail organization is likely to suppress any shortcomings in his or her operation. Even those internal auditors who try to remain objective may take a more narrow view of the firm's opportunities and shortcomings than will outside or external auditors.

The advantages of the external audit are derived from the consultants' broad experience in many different areas. Retailers are able to benefit from the experience of others by not duplicating their mistakes. The external auditors are also likely to be more objective, since they have no self-interest to preserve. Finally, external auditors are more likely to concentrate on the execution of the audit, since internal auditors can concentrate on the audit only if they are not concerned with time-consuming, day-to-day operating details.

The major disadvantage of using an external auditor is that the consultant must spend a lot of time becoming familiar with the internal aspects of the firm before making an appraisal. This disadvantage is not great when the company enters a long-term relationship with a consulting organization, under which the consultants become familiar with the retailer's operations as they audit first one and then another of the company's operations on a fairly continuous basis. Their contribution can be enhanced even more if they work with an internal task force that provides information, studies the auditor's reports, and implements the important recommendations in the consultant's reports.

Annual systems-level audits should be scheduled so that they can provide input into the retailer's annual planning efforts. Activity-level audits should be scheduled as determined in the systems-level audit. An activity-level audit should be scheduled whenever the annual systems-level audit or retail performance reveals that an activity is in great need of reform or supervision.

Interpretation of the Retail Audit

It should not be concluded that positive findings in most of the areas covered by the systems-level and activity-level audits will assure the retail firm of a profitable future or that no further investigation is warranted. Even if the results of the audit seem to indicate that everything is well, it does not mean that management can afford to stop creating new approaches to reach the current or expanded target markets. The retail audit is only a tool that seeks to indicate information about the effectiveness of the organization. It can point out some crucial areas that warrant management's attention. When these weaknesses are revealed, the retail organization can rectify the situation sooner and more easily than if no systematic review process were used.

Financial audits and market research projects must be used in the retail audit to provide a truly creative approach to long-range retail planning. Creative changes should be made in an orderly manner by making only one change at a time so that its effectivenss can be measured. Continual changing of the entire program will generally allow management to evaluate only the success of the entire program, not each of the retail activities. When a reasonably successful plan has been developed, it is usually better to intensify it first and make only one major change at a time. All changes should be measured on a cost-versus-results basis. The evaluation then centers around the question, "Were the results worth the amount of time, talent, and money used to accomplish them?"

Summary

Periodic systems-level and necessary activity-level auditing keep management's efforts concentrated on identifying trends, establishing objectives and policies, and acquiring and analyzing the data needed for objective decision making. It causes management to become more alert to needed changes caused by shifts in consumer shopping patterns and shifts in the competitive or legal environment.

The systems-level retail audit begins with the retailer's *diagnosis* of the market situation and the factors believed to be responsible for it. This phase of the audit determines where the firm is situated now and why it is now in the situation. The second stage of the systems-level audit is the *prognosis* step, which involves an estimate of where the retailer is likely to go if present policies are continued. In step three, the systems-level audit then turns to an *evaluation* of the firm's marketing and profit objectives to determine where the firm should be headed in the future. The fourth step of a systems-level retail audit is the establishment of a *program* that is to be used to achieve the objectives that have been established in step three. The fifth step of a systems-level audit is the *implementation* of the program. Attention is focused upon both the tactical means and procedures that need to be used to properly execute the program. *Organization* matters are then evaluated in step six, in which the audit evaluates the adequacy of retail management personnel to identify possible weaknesses in such areas as the lines of authority and the communication channels used to relay consumers' desires to the decision maker. The final step of a systems-level audit is the establishment of *control* procedures, which involve the establishment of performance standards that are checked periodically to determine if the retailer's plan is leading to its stated objectives.

This same audit framework can be used to audit any specific activity. The activity-level audits are usually conducted when a problem appears to exist in any activity area such as consumer relations, location, layout, promotion, pricing, buying, merchandise management, inventory control, budgetary control, organizational structure, personnel management, credit, taxes, and legal areas.

Retail audits can be conducted internally by permanent members of the firm or externally by outside consultants. Permanent employees are likely to be more familiar with the business than are outside consultants. However, employees are also likely to be more biased and protective of their position than are outside consultants.

Questions

1. Today the "geriatric set" is larger in numbers than ever before in history and it shows no signs of becoming smaller. Yet we see a continued emphasis on "young living" in all forms of merchandising. Discuss the marketing and especially the retailing implications of this situation.

2. How does a retail audit differ from an accounting audit? Do you think the average CPA would make a good retail auditor?

3. How can a small retailer best identify the firm's target segment? Why is it necessary to do so?

4. Should location audits be part of every retail audit? Why or why not?

5. Would you expect a layout audit to be more useful in a variety store or in an appliance store? Why?

6. Constant price manipulations can be detrimental to customer relations, but these manipulations can provide data for calculating demand elasticities. How would you "balance" this situation?

7. How can a retailer decide when to start using private labels? How can he decide what volume of selling space to allocate to private label goods?

8. What is the use of spending time and money on inventory control? Why not just order large quantities of everything and use your time and money in the sales effort?

9. Retail managers often provide many benefits for their employees, and sometimes approach or even exceed unions' benefits. Union organizers accuse management of doing this just to prevent collective bargaining, and they refer to the practice as "paternalism." Do you think the union accusation is justified? Identify any possible ulterior motives on both sides. Is unionization in the best interest of the employees?

10. Distinguish between an internal and an external retail audit. Discuss the advantages and disadvantages of each.

11. How should a retailer decide on how often a retail audit should be performed? Be specific with regard to internal and external audits and what factors determine their frequency.

Footnotes

1. Richard D. Crips, "Auditing the Functional Elements of a Marketing Operation," *Analyzing and Improving Marketing Performance,* Report No. 32 (New York: American Management Association, 1959), pp. 16–17.

2. Philip Kotler, *Marketing Management, Analysis, Planning, and Control* (Englewood Cliffs, N.J.: Prentice-Hall, 1967), p. 595.

3. Ibid., pp. 155–162.

4. Ibid., pp. 114–120.

5. Ibid., p. 601.

6. Ibid., p. 161.

Case Study

Fabrica de Carretas Joaquin Chaverri*

The owners and managers of Fabrica de Carretas Joaquin Chaverri were discussing a report that had been given to them by Mark Hamlet, a retired retailing executive living in San Jose. No one in the company had requested the report; nor was there any charge for the work by Mr. Hamlet.

It was not unusual for a pensionado to visit the retail store and factory of Joaquin Chaverri. The pensionados would often bring with them guests who had come to Costa Rica.

The city of San Jose, Costa Rica, had become a popular retirement location for citizens of the United States and Canada. The mild climate, beautiful countryside, and agreeable culture of Costa Rica served as the primary attractions.

The factory-showroom of Joaquin Chaverri was only thirty to forty-five minutes from San Jose and it was a pleasant drive through the mountains to reach the little village of Sarchi.

Mark Hamlet had visited the facilities of Joaquin Chaverri several times and had

*This case was written by James C. Makens, Visiting Professor at INCAE, to serve as a basis of class discussion rather than as an example of effective or ineffective management. Copyright © by James C. Makens.

always shown a great deal of interest in the company. On several occasions he had talked with Arsenio Alpizar Chaverri and his brother concerning the business.

The report written by Mr. Hamlet came as a surprise. In mid July, Mark visited the store to buy a few handicraft items as gifts for friends back in the States. Before leaving he handed Arsenio a very professional-appearing report, which was typed and bound in a simulated leather binder. Mark explained that he had worked over thirty years for a large department store in Philadelphia. During the last six years before retiring he had reached a position as executive vice president. He went on to say that he had observed the operations of Joaquin Chaverri for the last eighteen months and felt they could make several improvements to increase efficiency and improve sales. As a result, he had written a report that might be of interest to the owners-managers. This report was being given free and Mark expected nothing in return. He explained that since leaving his executive position he felt the need to do something meaningful and had thoroughly enjoyed writing the report.

Mark went on to say that if the owners-managers felt they could use it they were free to do so. If not, they were equally free to dispose of the report in the next trash pickup.

The Company

The firm of Joaquin Chaverri had been in operation for over seventy years. It was started by Sr. Alpizar Frutoso Chaverri, the grandfather and granduncle of the present owners-managers.

In 1974 the employees of the firm were given the opportunity to purchase the company. As a result, seventeen of the thirty-five employees joined together and purchased the company. All of these seventeen people were related to each other. In fact, only five employees out of the thirty-five were not relatives.

After purchasing the company, the seventeen owners decided to establish a system in which each of the owners would receive equal pay despite his type of work. Those who worked in the factory received the same pay as those who worked in the retail sales area.

This equality of pay also extended to various positions. Although Arsenio Alpizar carried the title of sales manager, he received the same pay as one of the owners who might paint the carts or work on a lathe.

Arsenio also pointed out that titles did not mean much in this company and that they were primarily used to communicate with persons outside the company. He stated that if someone else wanted his title, he could have it with no hard feelings.

He stated that he served in the position of sales manager just because he enjoyed selling more than the other types of work he could do in the company.

Store and Product Line

During the settlement of Costa Rica, oxcarts served as important transportation vehicles. In fact, oxcarts were used throughout Central America and Mexico. It is not uncommon to see them in use even today.

For some reason, it became popular in Costa Rica for the owners to paint their oxcarts in bright colors. The historical accounts are not clear as to the exact origin of painted oxcarts but this custom developed into an art form unique to Costa Rica.

As oxcarts declined in importance as transportation vehicles, the art form persisted on smaller carts. These ranged in size from very small ones, which might be hung from a Christmas tree as decorations or used as toys, to larger ones, which could serve as movable liquor bars. According to Arsenio, the firm of Joaquin Chaverri was the original manufacturer of decorative oxcarts.

The bar-sized model was the one that seemed to be most widely promoted in tourist promotions concerning Costa Rica. It was large enough to hold eight bottles of liquor and a variety of glasses. The top of the cart was constructed in two pieces. Each could be used as a serving tray. The bar-sized oxcart was actually a very decorative and unusual piece of furniture on wheels. It was painted in designs that could best be described as similar to what one might see by viewing a child's kaleidoscope.

The oxcarts from Joaquin Chaverri were manufactured from a variety of woods. Those that were left in their natural color were produced from several hardwoods such as laurel. The intricate designs were painted over this wood and the carts were then varnished.

The other carts were first painted a base color such as white, black, blue, or orange and designs were then painted over the base color. These carts were made from cedar.

In some cases, the woods had to be allowed to age as much as one and a half years before they could be used in the manufacture of quality ox carts. Unfortunately, a few companies located in San Jose were reported to be using plywood instead of cedar or hardwoods. Since the plywood was painted, it was difficult for the average person to recognize the difference between a quality oxcart bar and those made from plywood.

In 1964 the firm produced only oxcarts, but then little by little began adding other products leading to the wide assortment of present products.

The store was situated next to an asphalt road. There was parking in front for approximately six cars or a tourist bus and two or three cars. There were two large picture windows in front and the front door was generally kept open.

After entering the store, a series of four display shelves could be seen in the center. Each shelf had four levels. These contained a variety of merchandise including wooden fruit, fruit bowls, wooden figurines, wooden carvings of birds, wooden chopping blocks, lamps, and an assortment of beautiful wooden bowls that might serve as candy dishes or simply decorative items.

Each of the four display shelves was topped with a tiled roof so that it gave the impression of a small building.

Several cement support posts divided the display shelves. These served as structural supports for the building but were also utilized as display areas. Round printed plaques and other decorative items were displayed on these posts.

To the left of the display shelves was an area that contained approximately fifteen of the large painted oxcarts. The wall on this side was covered with wooden carvings, such as huge wooden spoons. One section of this wall had shelves attached to it that held miniature copies of the painted oxcarts.

To the right of the center display shelves was a long glass counter with a wooden top. Behind this counter were more shelves holding miniature oxcarts, carvings and a variety of other souvenir products. The counter itself served as a display area for small items.

The walls behind the counter and over the entrance of the store contained a variety of hand paintings on canvas. These were primarily in a primitive art style and were not produced by the company. Instead, they were purchased from local artists.

In addition to the products already mentioned in this space, there was a rack of leather belts. Like the paintings, these were not produced in the store but were purchased from local craftsmen.

Immediately behind the central sales room was a series of wooden steps that led to a mezzanine room. This area was not well lighted; nor had any attempt been made to establish a merchandise display there. Instead, this area held pieces of wooden furniture. These ranged from inexpensive lawn-type wooden rocking chairs to a beautiful hand carved china closet. All items were for sale but the larger, more expensive ones did not bear price tags. If a customer was sufficiently interested, he had to ask what the price was.

The balcony overlooked the store and wooden walking canes were hung from the banister.

To the rear of the store and down three steps was the room in which the oxcarts were painted. This was open to the public, who were free to walk back and see the artists at work. Only the rare customer elected not to walk back and see the artists at work.

The area behind the store consisted of a sawmill, lumber yard and the factory in which the products were manufactured. Visitors were free to visit the factory, but there was no formal tour; nor was there a sign to direct them. Instead, a rough path led through large piles of logs and cut lumber to the factory.

Once inside the factory there was no preplanned visitor's touring area. Instead, visitors could walk in and look at the men at work. This did not seem to be a common occurrence, since many of the workers stopped work for a moment and seemed as curious about their visitors as the new observers were about them.

The store did not contain a lunch counter; nor did it sell soft drinks. A small pulperia[1] was located down the road about a hundred yards, and customers would sometimes walk there to buy a soft drink.

All of the canvas paintings had been marked up 30 percent over the price that Joaquin Chaverri paid for them. This margin did not apply for all products.

As an example, the glass show case near the cash register contained leather billfolds, which were also purchased from local craftsmen. These were purchased at a price of twenty-four Colones each and were sold for twenty-eight Colones each.

In general, the margin between cost and retail selling price was 15 percent for the oxcarts and 12 percent for the other products, but these were average markups.

---

[1] A pulperia is a small store. It is generally connected to the owner's home. Pulperias are small general stores and carry a number of products. There are thousands of these stores throughout Central America.

The retail prices for most of the products increased during the past few years, but in a few cases they actually declined.

An example of a product that declined in price was the miniature one-foot oxcart. In 1975 this sold for 185 Colones and in 1976 it sold for 175 Colones. The reason the price was reduced was that management felt it would sell better at the lower price and, in fact, Arsenio stated that more were sold at the new price than were sold the previous year.

The management of Joaquin Chaverri did not measure the stock turn of the merchandise. Products that did not seem to be selling well were replaced with others, but there was no specific time set aside to review this.

If an employee had an idea for a new product, a few would be made and tried in the store. If it sold, it would become a regular item. This same situation applied to the products that were not manufactured in the factory but were purchased from someone else. A formal committee to review new products did not exist.

The store was open each day including Sunday from 7 a.m. to 6 p.m. and did not close for lunch.

No credit cards were accepted since it was believed that the commission was too high. This could cause the retail price of the products to increase. Once in a while personal checks were accepted if it was felt the customer was reliable.

The store in Sarchi was the only one owned and operated by Joaquin Chaverri. Other sales outlets in nearby San Jose had not been sought. However, a few store owners did drive to Sarchi to buy products such as the oxcarts which they then resold in their stores such as gift shops. These people were charged the same price as any other customer.

This meant that a Joaquin Chaverri product would always be priced higher in any other store since the owner had to add a markup to the retail price.

Arsenio said that several times during the year foreign buyers asked about purchasing products in large volume. They almost never placed large orders since the policy of Joaquin Chaverri was to sell to all buyers at the same price regardless of volume.

Nevertheless in early 1976 an order was sold for about 60,000 Colones to a retail store in the U.S. Arsenio had not visited the U.S. buyer but he believed this buyer had stores in Miami and New York. He said that the order had not been repeated and had heard that the company had declared bankruptcy.

The feeling within Joaquin Chaverri had traditionally been that big sales were not desired. Big volume buyers always wanted discounts. In addition, it took just as much time to make products for big volume buyers as it did for the individual. In addition, big volume buyers normally wanted terms, and there were also problems with arranging for export.

A big volume sale could cause sales to be lost in the store because it tended to deplete inventory. Since the inventory and the products for sale in the store were one and the same thing, it simply meant fewer products for display and for sale in the store.

Each year sales had been increasing at the store and there did not seem to be any reason to do things that might disrupt that sales growth.

The owners of Joaquin Chaverri had agreed they wanted growth but were not willing to have growth if it meant heavy debt. There were plans to convert the balcony area into a showroom for the entire product line and to do away with furniture sales since they were slow movers and required a great deal of time to manufacture and sell.

The store could also be expanded by adding to the rear but there was no great excitement over quick expansion.

The Customer and Promotion

The greatest percentage of of the customers of Joaquin Chaverri were tourists. They came from many parts of the world, but Americans seemed to constitute the largest part of the tourists.

There was also a small local market but many of these were pensionados like Mr. Hamlet.

The company did not use any mass media advertising. In fact, the only advertising it used were the pocket exchange-rate tables printed on paper and the plastic bags in which the products were packaged.

These were white plastic bags in many sizes that bore a picture of a painted cart, the name of the company, the address and the telephone number. They were printed in four colors and were quite attractive.

When a customer purchased products, great care was taken to package the small ones separately from the large ones rather than package everything together. This required more sacks but provided greater protection for the products and also sent out more advertising from the store.

Many of the customers would arrive in tourist buses and sometimes in taxis. The store was one of the stops on the tourist tours offered by a San Jose sightseeing service.

Arsenio stated that none of the drivers were ever given a commission on sales to encourage them to bring customers. Once in a while they were given a few small handicraft items they admired as gifts.

The Instituto de Turismo encouraged tourists to visit Joaquin Chaverri, and Arsenio said this was done because the company was the oldest, made the best products, and sold them for less than competitors. He said it was not due to efforts on the part of the management to coerce those in the Instituto de Turismo.

When asked about competition, Arsenio very confidently replied that there really was none. He said it was true that another shop existed down the road about a kilometer but he stated this was smaller and did not have the quality products of Joaquin Chaverri. He also discounted the threat of competition from the factories near San Jose that manufactured oxcarts from plywood.

A woman tourist from the U.S. was overheard talking with a friend. She said that she had been in Europe and in Asia but had never seen such high quality products at such reasonable prices. When she left the store she had purchased a complete set of wooden salad bowls plus a miniature oxcart.

Arsenio smiled and said, "You see, this is the reason for our success and the reason we don't need expensive advertising."

The Hamlet Report

The report given to the owners of Joaquin Chaverri reflected an air of professionalism based upon years of experience in the business world.

It began by briefly reviewing the business practices of Joaquin Chaverri as observed by Mr. Hamlet and ended with a series of recommendations.

The recommendations were as follows:

1. A sales goal should be set for total sales to be met for next year. This should be divided into monthly and quarterly realistic goals that take into consideration possible seasonal variations. Regular meetings should be held to review whether or not these goals were met. If they were not met, corrective actions should be taken to meet the next goal.

2. A profit goal should be set as percentage of overall sales. This should also be divided into monthly and quarterly goals with review sessions by management.

3. A thorough review should be made of the sales of each product to determine whether or not it is contributing a sufficient profit margin and volume to assure that sales and profit goals will be attained. Products that do not appear likely to contribute the desired margin should be eliminated and replaced with others.

4. Profit margins should be increased on all products to cause them to conform more closely with established retailing practices for gift-type products. It is believed that quality gift type products are quite inelastic and can easily bear margins of 40 to 50 percent on the retail price.

5. The policy of charging all customers the same price should be changed. A schedule of prices should be developed that provides lower prices to volume buyers.

6. Active sales efforts should be made to sell Joaquin Chaverri products in as many retail outlets in San Jose as possible. These include gift shops in the airport and hotels. It also includes the major department stores in San Jose. This should be done to prevent competition from utilizing these sales outlets.

7. Organized plant tours of the factory should be developed. This is common practice in the glass factories of Mexico and in many other areas. It is felt this will substantially increase interest on the part of the tourist-buyer and insure that Joaquin Chaverri will continue to be included as a tourist stop on excursion tours.

8. Consideration should be given to opening a lunch counter featuring local Costa Rican foods. This would insure that each customer would remain longer in the store and would also add to overall profit.

9. Large volume sales should be actively sought among foreign buyers. It is recommended that department and gift stores with excellent reputations in the U.S. and Europe be sought as buyers. This would insure that sales would continue even if tourist trade to Costa Rica failed to increase or even declined. It is highly possible that signed orders from highly respected retailers such as The Federat-

ed Chain of Department Stores could be used as collateral at a San Jose bank. This would enable Joaquin Chaverri to modernize and expand the plant to meet the increased demand.

10. A sales incentive plan should be established to encourage members of Joaquin Chaverri to sell their products aggressively. This would require a revision of the existing policy in which each of the owners receives equal pay regardless of work task.

11. Consideration should be given to purchasing the competitor's retail store located one kilometer away. This store could be operated as a second outlet for Joaquin Chaverri. This would prevent the growth of a future competitor.

12. Advertising brochures should be sent to all travel agents who regularly send tour groups to Costa Rica. A letter should be sent to each inviting them to visit the store and factory during their next visit to Costa Rica. They should be told that a handsome gift will await them.

Discussion Questions

1. What should the owners of Joaquin Chaverri do with the Hamlet report?

2. How can a retail audit be used by the owners of Joaquin Chaverri to improve the firm's position?

3. Design a complete retail audit for the Joaquin Chaverri firm.

Case Study

Sears, Roebuck and Company—Its Maneuvers to Stay on Top*

Sears is the world's largest retailer of general merchandise with net sales of $17.2 billion in 1977. (Sales in Canada, Spain, and South America are not included in the $17.2 billion domestic total.) The company and its domestic subsidiaries employ an average of 460,000 people. Sears' salespeople move about $44 million of merchandise in an average day through some 3,800 selling locations situated in fifty states, Puerto Rico, and Central America.

---

*This case was written by Professor Steven J. Shaw of the University of South Carolina. It is published with the cooperation of Sears, Roebuck and Co.

Sears' headquarters and most of its buying offices are located in the Sears Tower in Chicago. Central buyers from these offices work with over 12,000 suppliers and negotiate on merchandise specifications, prices, and terms of purchase. Items approved for sale in Sears stores are itemized in a series of books called "merchandise lists."

The company has five territorial or regional offices located in Alhambra, California; Atlanta, Georgia; Dallas, Texas; St. Davids, Pennsylvania; and Skokie, Illinois. Each of these regional offices is headed by an executive vice-president.

Computers—The Heart of Sales Merchandising

The complete system includes 35,000 Singer electronic registers, more than 640 minicomputers, and 33 large IBM—370 main computers. Taken as a whole, the system helps cut credit losses and inventory shortages, speeds up checkout lines in the stores, assures an optimum product mix on shelves, and will handle numerous accounting and personnel records now processed manually.

Most important of all, the system provides instant national sales data for the company's central buyers in Chicago and furnishes a retail inventory management system to watchdog inventories for 41,800 merchandise departments in Sears stores throughout the country. Along with the company's 860 stores, the system also ties together more than 1,200 catalogue sales offices, warehouses, and business offices, plus 1,000 of Sears' largest suppliers.

The electronic system works as follows. The first step is receipt of the product from the warehouse or supplier. Assume the item is a coffee pot. An automatic ticketmaker produces a ticket that indicates the coffee pot's color, price, stock number, and clerk's department number. When a customer takes the coffee pot to the register, the clerk either keys the numbers into the register or uses the reading wand.

If the customer wants to pay with a credit card, the wand picks up a magnetic code and in less than one second clears the card through the store's minicomputer. That split second for wanding records the sales information for the entire inventory management system. The coffee pot data is stored in the minicomputer until nightfall when it is automatically transferred to one of the company's twenty-two regional data centers where big IBM computers process the information. There, the customer's credit account is charged, sales and tax figures are entered into the accounting department's records, and the salesclerk's commission record is credited to the payroll department.

Sales data also enter the coffee pot department's inventory management system. If the day's coffee pot sales lower the department's inventory below a predetermined point, the computer automatically prints a purchase order, which is sent by messenger to the department manager the next morning. If the manager decides to buy more coffee pots, the reorder goes to the supplier, who refills it.

At the same time the sales data is also channeled through the regional data center to a central data processing station in Sears' Chicago central headquarters, where national unit sale information is compiled.

From Decentralization to More Centralization

When the 1974 recession hit, Sears found itself in deep trouble. Stores were jammed with merchandise that would not move without drastic price cuts.

The company's greatest problem was what previously had been considered its greatest strength: decentralized operations, which put most merchandising decisions in the hands of the company's store managers and their regional supervisors —the people who presumably knew their local markets best.

The headquarters staff in Chicago could plan strategy and try to convince the managers to adopt it, but in the end it was up to the stores themselves to decide whether to go along with it.

The result was a lack of coordination. Prices and promotions varied from store to store in the same area and undermined regional advertising programs. Purchasing, too, had become fouled up. A buyer at the Chicago headquarters might make arrangements to purchase hundreds of thousands of record players, only to have a sizable portion of them rejected by store managers because the profit margin was thin. Store managers also tended to overbuy on special promotions on which Sears had obtained a cut-rate price from its suppliers. Then, after the sale ended, the managers would mark up the remaining inventory and sell it at the higher regular price. Thus, with a higher average markup a manager would improve his store's profitability and his own bonus.

With a sprawling network of 860 stores, 1,700 catalogue and telephone sales offices, 13 huge distribution centers, and 124 warehouses, something had to be done to improve cooperation between the autonomous store managers and central headquarters.

Chairman Wood had no choice but to move decisively toward more centralized control of Sears pricing, advertising, and promotion. Wood brought in McKinsey & Company to recommend organizational changes and Hay Associates, a Philadelphia-based consultant, to design a new compensation system for store managers.

McKinsey's reorganization, the first at Sears in thirty years, created an office of the chairman, consisting of Arthur Wood, chairman of the board; A. Dean Swift, president; James Button, senior executive vice president of merchandising; and a newcomer, Edward Telling, senior executive vice president of field operations. By bringing Telling into the decision-making group at corporate headquarters Sears was able to bring the field managers under closer control. With the creation of this policy-setting body, store managers lost much of their pricing authority, and nationwide retail promotions, for years a rarity, have become commonplace.

Sears curbed the tendencies of store managers to overbuy promotional merchandise by refusing to allow them to use their lower cost figures in computing profit for any sales after the scheduled special sale was over. Also, under the recommendation of Hay Associates, Sears began to encourage its store managers to think about sales rather than just profits. Specifically, Sears has begun to award bonuses to store managers on the basis of sales and profits rather than just profits. In addition, a particular store manager's bonus is not dependent only on the performance of his or her own store, but also on the performance of all the stores in the region.

A New Strategy of Pricing

During the 1974 and 1975 recession crisis, Sears found itself boxed in between the discounters on one hand and the fashion department stores on the other. Sears was being squeezed in the middle-price ranges. But since its recent centralization of decision-making authority at corporate headquarters, Sears was able to cut thousands of its prices and once again is competing vigorously with the discounters and bargain basement operations. Recently advertised savings include price cuts of 14 percent on color television sets, 15 percent on sewing machines, 16 percent on refrigerators, 21 percent on Craftsman power lawn mowers, 29 percent on Weatherbeater paint, 15 percent on hardwood dining room suites, 25 percent to 50 percent on fabrics, and 25 percent on shirts.

Sears price cutting, although widespread and more extensive than anything the retailer had done in recent years, is not across the board. The price cuts are designed to increase store traffic and sales. For example, in the company's national advertising of Kenmore washing machines, a low-priced, a medium-priced, and a high-priced unit are featured. The advertising emphasizes the many benefits the purchase a Kenmore might bring to the customer. These benefits might include the wide selection, a credit plan to suit every need, delivery and installation as part of the purchase price or optional for those who wanted to do it themselves, and nationwide availability of repair service. With a strategy of quality and prices for all incomes, Sears hopes to increase its market share by wooing away customers from the discount houses and the high-fashion department stores.

Selection of New Sites

Site selection for a new store, a new catalogue center, or the relocation of an existing unit is the responsibility of the Sears facilities planning department. With a sprawling network of 860 stores and 1,700 catalogue telephone sales offices throughout the country, there are few market areas where Sears does not have a retail outlet of some kind. But cities keep growing and most of this growth is farther and farther out in the suburbs. Consequently, every year the company finds itself opening new suburban units or relocating existing establishments in outlying areas that are more readily accessible to a majority of its customers who drive by automobile. In the smaller cities with a metropolitan population of under 300,000, the original Sears unit might be operating out of its second or third location. Almost all of Sears's larger stores are company-owned; smaller units are leased.

Counting both new suburban units and relocations of existing establishments, Sears opened a total of twenty-nine stores in 1976 and twenty-five in 1977. The table on the next page shows the number of new units and relocations broken down by size classification for 1977.

Generally, a medium-sized city or a metropolitan area of a large city has a number of attractive sites that local real estate developers offer to Sears. Before a decision can be reached in favor of a particular site, the company's real estate department has to evaluate the several areas and competing sites in terms of the following factors:

1. The size and composition of each area's population and the direction of future population growth
2. The number of low, middle, and high-income families in each of the areas as well as the expected growth of income among each of the income groups
3. The number and type of competing stores and their total sales
4. The overall adequacy of each available site. An ideal location must have enough space to house buildings and allow uncrowded parking during peak shopping hours and, should be easily accessible to motorists from all directions.
5. The price of the land at acceptable sites
6. The zoning laws in each area
7. The city's transportation grid
8. The city's transportation plans for the future. A new limited-access highway could isolate a site that otherwise would be ideal.

New Sears Establishments for 1977

	A-Size Hard and Soft Goods	B-Size Hard and Some Soft Goods	C-Size Hard Lines Only	Total
New Markets	5	3	1	9
Relocations	11	4	1	16
Total Opened	16	7	2	25

Sears, a Pioneer of Customer Services

Service to customers is all-important at Sears, and every store maintains a spacious service area for both its mechanical and electrical appliances. One of the company's policies most respected by customers is that of "satisfaction guaranteed or your money back." Sears mail-order division was the first retailer to introduce this customer-oriented approach back in the 1880s. And today every store manager strictly upholds this service policy. For example, all of Sears' Craftsman brand of tools except electronic ones carry a lifetime guarantee, and if a customer returns a hammer that breaks after twenty years of use, the store has to replace it.

Credit is another important service at Sears. The company was one of the first retailers to pioneer and develop different plans. It pushed credit when its leading competitor, the J. C. Penney Company, was sticking to a cash only policy, and today one out of every three Americans has a Sears credit card. In 1977 credit sales accounted for 54.3 percent of total sales.

Another service pioneered by Sears was night openings so that working customers could shop after work. The company also pioneered customer self-service and telephone shopping.

Product Development at Sears

Few customers are aware of the important role Sears plays in the improvement of existing products and the development of completely new ones. The company's merchandise development and testing laboratory was set up in 1911 and today employs more than 120 designers and engineers. The process of improving existing products frequently starts with market research. Sears uses all kinds of studies, primary and secondary: exploratory groups, concept tests, selling proposition screens, commercial testing, pre- and post-tests, campaign trading, brand trend analysis, and attitudinal studies.

For example, several years ago a consumer survey revealed that women customers twenty-five to forty years old had trouble purchasing slacks that fit them around the waist. Sears researchers studied the problem and came up with specifications for a new type of polyester pants that fit. These novel designs were proportioned by height, fitted with elastic waistbands and were made of fitted polyester that stretched easily and conformed to all figure types.

Next the prototypes were tested carefully for flaws by having a small sample of women with different figure types subject the new designs to heavy use and laundering. Once they were found to work satisfactorily, detailed specifications were drawn up and passed on to certain suppliers able to meet the new requirements.

Sometimes Sears laboratory researchers come up with their own ideas for product improvements. For instance, quite recently to help conserve energy Sears product developers came through with a new seventeen-cubic-foot frostless Coldspot refrigerator that requires 40 percent less electricity to operate.

Well in advance of recent government legislation calling for improved product safety, Sears product researchers had developed children's sleepwear and daytime apparel that was flame retardant. Also, Sears is now marketing flame retardant sleepwear for adults well in advance of any legislation or regulation requiring industry to do so.

One of product development's most noteworthy achievements is its recent success in the replacement battery business. After ten years of research and development Sears' DieHard has become the dominant top-of-the line battery on the market.

How was this success achieved? First, extensive consumer studies were launched to determine what qualities were most important to the purchasers of replacement batteries. Several consumer preferences were uncovered by these studies. Above all, customers wanted a durable, noncorrosive battery that would last as long as the car did. Also, consumers wanted a battery that would start their car quickly under all weather conditions. Finally, they wanted a battery that was maintenance-free—that is, one that would not require periodic additions of water.

Out of these consumer expectations, the conception of a DieHard battery was born. In 1966, Sears product designers went to work together with Globe-Union, a dependable supplier, in designing a replacement battery that would meet these tough consumer specifications. The first DieHards to come out on the market were so effective that J. C. Penney, K Mart and other leading retailers had to rush in with competitive makes. Developments and improvements continued over the past ten years and today Sears is way out in front of its competitors in the replacement battery business. Profits from the sale of DieHard batteries are only a fraction of the intangible benefits for corporate image, store traffic, and consumer perceptions of overall Sears product quality.

Discussion Questions

1. Could the policy of awarding bonuses to store managers on the basis of sales and profits rather than just profits boomerang in the sense that total corporate profits might be reduced?

2. Do you think that the Sears pricing policy of competing with K Mart and other discount houses is a sound one? Do you think that Sears can compete effectively for customers in all three income levels?

3. Evaluate the eight criteria Sears uses in area and site selection for its new stores.

4. What role has research and development played in Sears's rise to its number one position in retailing?

5. What are the advantages and disadvantages of going to work for a giant like Sears? If you would like to work for Sears, which area appeals to you most?

Case Study

W. T. Grant Company:
The Death of a Giant*

Founded in 1906, W. T. Grant, the seventy-year-old variety store chain, had 1,100 stores, 70,000 employees and was doing $2 billion in sales annually. The firm had compiled an enviable record. Except for a loss in 1932 at the height of this country's depression, the retailer had reported regular profits for the first sixty-seven years of its existence and had developed into one of the country's largest variety store chains. It had expanded into the suburbs and had tried to become a department store, selling furniture and major appliances on credit.

Then quite suddenly, for its fiscal year ending January 31, 1975, Grant reported the largest loss ever to hit a retailer, $177.3 million, even after it took a tax credit of more than $100 million. And a year and a few months later the company was liquidated out of existence.

History

The Grant Company was founded in 1906 on a $1,000 investment by its namesake, William T. Grant, who had been employed previously in the shoe department of a Boston department store. The first Grant store was set up in a corner of the Lynn, Massachusetts, Young Men's Christian Association building. And a window sign on opening day announced "A new kind of store—a department store with nothing over

---

*This case was written by Professor Steven J. Shaw of the University of South Carolina.

25 cents." The founder's merchandising idea was to fill the pricing niche between the then burgeoning "five-and-dimes" like Woolworth's and Kresge and the department stores whose wares at that time began at about fifty cents. Merchandise moved swiftly and profitably at twenty-five cents, since there were no size or fitting problems nor selling effort involved. With spartan surroundings and an emphasis on solid quality at bargain prices, the Grant chain expanded in New England initially and then moved into the mid-Atlantic states. Its customer base from the start was lower middle-class working people. By 1919 the chain grew to thirty-three stores. World War I inflation raised Grant's top price to $1, but it remained a working family's store with inexpensive ready-to-wear clothes and drygood staples as the backbone of its daily business.

The Great Depression was a period of further expansion and prosperity for Grant and other variety store chains, since consumers with reduced incomes turned to the lower-priced retailers. The severe depression deflation helped bring a wide variety of new goods under the top price, and Grant's now became a "junior" department store. The depression had lowered prices so drastically that Grant buyers were able to procure for the store such major items as all-silk slips, wool bathing suits, rayon bedspreads, and men's shoes and pants. This was in addition to such staple merchandise as goldfish, lipsticks, brass screws, art lamps, and brassieres.

By the mid 1930s, William T. Grant became chairman of the board and left day-to-day operations up to his managers. He remained at this post until 1966 when he retired at the age of ninety. For the Grant chain, the 1940s and 1950s were a period of nationwide expansion.

Removal of Price Ceilings and Movement to the Suburbs

During the 1940s Grant had removed ceiling prices on its merchandise and began slowly to introduce furniture and appliances into its stores. Also, during this decade the chain first started to open stores in the suburbs, shifting from its exclusive emphasis on in-town locations. However, in hindsight, the type of locations selected might have been one of the contributing reasons for Grant's later downfall. While realizing the need to locate stores nearer to its customers, management avoided the large regional centers, preferring small community or strip center locations. In 1963 management embarked on a rapid expansion program. During the next ten years, 612 new stores were opened, bringing the total to 1,188 with a payroll of 82,500 employees. But this rapid expansion was extremely costly and was financed mostly by external borrowing. Loans of $614 million from twenty-seven banks were necessary to launch the new stores.

Shift in Merchandise Emphasis

In 1968 under a new president, Richard W. Mayer, Grant shifted its merchandising emphasis from soft goods to hard goods. With an eye apparently on Sears and J. C. Penney, Grant tried to make the transition to a suburban department store at a time when aggressive discount stores like K Mart and Woolco were making the same move. The Grant stores began stocking refrigerators, television sets, air conditioners, and other big ticket appliance and furniture items. Usually these were produced by nationally known manufacturers such as Westinghouse and Fedders. But management insisted on removing the brand name and marketing these appliances under its own private label, Bradford. Unfortunately, the Bradford label was not well known to consumers. Shoppers were confused by the shift from soft goods to hard goods. They could identify with Grant neither as the retailer of variety soft goods it had been nor as the retailer of upgraded, higher priced hard goods it was trying to become.

Liberal Credit Terms

President Mayer who had moved up the corporate ladder through credit management went all out to induce customers to buy its big ticket items by offering liberal credit terms. Store employees were given bonuses for signing up new credit card customers. Credit applications were not carefully screened, and by January 1975, Grant's customers owed the company $600 million. Grant was now in the untenable financial position of having to borrow money to buy new merchandise while waiting for customers to pay their bills.

Merchandise Planning and Control

Inadequate merchandise inventory controls led to excessive accumulation of stock in many departments and out-of-stock conditions in others. Indiscriminate unplanned buying and lack of a sound markdown policy resulted in seasonal merchandise being left on the shelves long after the season had passed and consumers passed it by. By 1975 it was clear the company's problem was one of survival. Some suppliers began selling to Grant on a C.O.D. basis only. Others stopped shipments in mid-transit.

Final Efforts at Recovery

Under new management Grant petitioned for Chapter XI, a procedure under bankruptcy law that allows a firm to continue operating while formulating a plan to pay its debts. Robert H. Anderson, a highly successful ex-Sears executive, embarked on a program to close unprofitable stores and reduce excess inventory. He cut Grant down to 359 stores in the Northeastern United States with 24,000 employees. Under Anderson, Grant dropped its major appliance lines and returned to the merchandising of low-cost softgoods.

But these efforts came too late. In February 1976, creditors moved to have the company declared bankrupt, and the court so ruled. Robert Anderson, the chief executive officer, blamed suppliers for Grant's inability to make the recovery plan work. The merchandise didn't come in, he said, apparently because vendors were afraid of suffering further losses. With liabilities of $1.1 billion, the failure of W. T. Grant Company became the largest in retailing history.

Discussion Questions

1. Identify and discuss the principal reasons why Grant's failed.

2. Under what conditions should a retailer stick to marketing nationally advertised brands? What conditions are necessary for private branding to be successful?

3. Since Grant's was trying to transform itself into a merchandiser of expensive shopping and specialty goods, would location in regional shopping centers have been a sounder strategy?

4. Several years back a major West Coast aircraft manufacturer was saved from bankruptcy by means of a huge government loan and certain guaranties. Discuss the pros and cons of having the U.S. government move in and keep a giant like Grant's from going out of business.

Case Study

Tapp's Department Store: Exploration of Growth Opportunities*

The Tapp family, which operates a medium-sized downtown department store and two suburban units in Columbia, South Carolina, spent considerable time in 1976 and 1977 analyzing population growth trends in the outlying city areas. The situation was complicated by the fact that several shopping centers and many free standing stores were opening almost simultaneously. Without careful planning, overstoring could occur in one or more areas of the city. The family wanted to add another unit or two if the right locations could be found.

The parent Tapp unit opened in 1903 in downtown Columbia and grew with the city. The store building was enlarged from time to time. In 1939 operations were moved to new temporary quarters while the original structure was torn down and a new modern store was built. The new store was the first in the country to be built with all lights, sprinklers and air-conditioning recessed in the ceiling and walls. In 1951 the store was modernized again and enlarged by the addition of a fifth and sixth floor.

In 1961 a furniture annex was opened across the street along with parking for both stores. Also in the early 1960s, when the city of Columbia started to expand rapidly into the suburbs, a small branch called Tapp's Twig was set up in the Trenholm Plaza Shopping Center. The Twig unit prospered and was expanded several times, from the original 6,000 sq ft. store to the present 22,000 sq ft.

---

*This case was written by Professor Steven J. Shaw of South Carolina. It is published with the permission of Tapp's Department Store.

The store's biggest expansion occurred in 1970, when the family opened one of the three anchor department stores in the new air-conditioned and enclosed regional Dutch Square Shopping Center situated northwest of Columbia and next to a small cluster of stores called Boozer's Shopping Center. This regional center was the largest in South Carolina. The decision to locate here was not an easy one for the family, since the Tapp unit had to compete directly with two large chains. One of these competitors was J. B. White's, operated by the Mercantile Stores Chain, and the other was a Woolco discount store, operated by the F. W. Woolworth Company.

In 1968 and 1969, the family had retained the services of a New York consulting firm to help them with the location decision. After a careful market analysis of the surrounding areas, the firm had strongly recommended the opening of a full-scale store in the Dutch Square Center. The research findings indicated that the downtown store, which at the time had sales of $5,000,000, might very well lose up to 20 percent of its volume when the new regional center opened. If Tapp's did not take the space, another large competitor would. By being one of the three major units in the regional mall, Tapp's could probably more than offset the loss in downtown sales with a substantial share of the sales volume generated at the new location.

The consultant's analysis of market potential confirmed the estimates projected by the shopping center developer. Families residing within a twenty-mile radius of the Dutch Square Center would shop there regularly. Moreover, the consultant's report predicted that families living even further out would find the regional mall an easy place to reach, and these families might shop there frequently because of its strategic location at the intersection of two interstate highways. Interstates 20 and 26 formed a giant X that fanned out and connected distant parts of the state with Dutch Square.

On the basis of the consultant's optimistic forecast of potential, the Dutch Square store was opened in 1970 and operated successfully. The volume of the downtown store dropped as expected but the lost volume was more than offset by the sales generated at the Dutch Square location. Moreover, most of the stores at this regional shopping center were highly successful, since the population in nearby and far-out residential areas built up rapidly.

While the center was well planned and the stores were surrounded by two large parking lots, traffic congestion began to develop during peak shopping hours in 1975 and 1976, and parking became more difficult. A large part of the congestion was caused by the many other stores located in close proximity to the Dutch Square Center. Among these were K Mart and the large Sam Solomon catalog showroom.

With seventy-five years of retailing experience, the Tapp family could see threats to the continued profitability of both their Dutch Square store and the older downtown unit. Several smaller shopping centers and a number of free-standing stores had opened in various suburban areas of Columbia in 1976 and early 1977.

Moreover, a new giant Columbia Mall was to open in August of 1977 in the Northeast section of Columbia. This regional mall would be even larger than the Dutch Square Shopping center and would contain four large anchor stores and 145 specialty shops. This shopping center would be located within ten miles of Tapp's Dutch Square store and just six miles away from the downtown store.

Even more threatening was the fact that there were plans for a third regional mall just four miles away from Dutch Square along Interstate 26 North. When completed in about four years, the Harbison Mall would be comparable in size to the new Columbia Mall. The giant Harbison mall would certainly relieve the traffic congestion around the Dutch Square Shopping Center. But it could also take 20 to 40 percent of the sales volume away from the Dutch Square Stores.

Perhaps a loss of business could be avoided by setting up a Tapp branch store at the Harbison Shopping Center. When completed this center would serve some 7,500 middle- and low-income families in the adjacent Harbison community, and, of course, thousands of other families living further out.

One major expansion decision that the Tapp management had already committed itself to was the opening of another full-scale department store across town in East Columbia in the Woodhill Community Shopping center. This store would open in February of 1978. The other major tenant at this center was a Richway Discount store, which had already opened its door in early 1976. It was one of three large discount department stores already in operation in Columbia and owned by Rich's department store chain out of Atlanta, Georgia. About a quarter of a mile closer in to Columbia stood a large K Mart discount store, and this free-standing unit had already been operating profitably for a number of years. About half a mile beyond the Woodhill Shopping Center, a Woolco discount department store was already operating as the major tenant in the Landmark Community Shopping Center. And about a mile further out a community shopping center called Columbia East had sprung up during the past year. But this center had no major discount or full-service department store.

During the past two years Tapp management held frequent planning sessions to determine what expansion and perhaps even contraction strategies they should follow. The spread of population into Northeast and East Columbia and other areas presented new locational opportunities. But the situation was clouded by the rapid mushrooming of new centers and free standing stores. If this trend continued, metropolitan Columbia could end up with too many shopping centers in certain areas. Such overstoring had already occurred in several northern cities where developers had built centers without careful attention to what competing developers were doing.

Discussion Questions

1. How can the present drawing power of the Dutch Square Shopping Center be measured? What techniques could Tapp management or Dutch Square management use to determine the distances customers were traveling to the center?

2. List and describe briefly the growth and competitive factors Tapp management had to evaluate carefully before it could make its decision to open a new full-scale store in Woodhill Shopping Center in East Columbia.

3. With all the new shopping centers that have opened in the suburban areas of Columbia, the downtown merchants were losing sales, and several sites had become vacant. To counteract this exodus of customers to outlying shopping centers, the downtown merchants had launched a $1.5 million renovation. What various changes and improvements should be made in main street parking, street beautification, and traffic flow? Should the total renovation plan include any store improvements or arrangements for off-main-street parking? Would the construction of high-rise apartments for middle-income and low-income families within walking distance of the downtown stores help the situation any?

4. By early 1978, Tapp's will have three department stores and a Twig unit in operation. What operating expenses might be reduced for the whole company? Assume that Tapp's already has fully-trained managers who can assume the added responsibilities of running the new Woodhill unit.

5. Should Tapp's plan on opening a Twig unit in the forthcoming Harbison Mall that will be just four miles away from Dutch Square? Are there any alternatives that should be considered?

Glossary*

A

accessory items Merchandise that is coordinated with other larger items.

accordion theory A theory describing the tendency for the retail business to follow an alternating pattern in which general-line, wide assortment retailers are followed by specialized, narrow-line retailers.

accounting The method of recording all the transactions affecting the financial condition of a given business.

accounts payable A current **liability** that represents the amount owed to a creditor for merchandise or services purchased on an open account or short-term credit.

accounts receivable Money owed a business enterprise for merchandise bought without the giving of a note or other evidence of debt.

accrual system A method of apportioning expense and income for the period in which each is incurred, regardless of the date of payment or collection.

accrued interest payable Interest accumulated on an indebtedness that is not yet paid.

acid test ratio A ratio that indicates the ability of a business enterprise to meet its current obligations. The formula used to determine the ratio is as follows:

$$\frac{\text{Cash plus Receivables plus Marketable Securities}}{\text{Current Liabilities}}$$

Frequently, a 1:1 ratio is considered satisfactory.

activity level retail audit An evaluation of a specific activity in the retail effort. The activity may have been identified as a problem area during a **systems level retail audit.**

additional markup An increase in price above the original retail price. Thus, if one hundred articles, originally retailed at $1 each, are marked up to $1.09, the additional markup is $9 for the lot.

advance dating An arrangement in which the seller sets some specific date in the future when the terms become applicable. This date, which is some time after actual shipment, gives additional time in which payment may be made and during which the **cash discount** may be deducted, since the time for payment of the **invoice** is computed from the advance dating rather than from the invoice date. Example: For an order placed on April 10 and shipped on April 25, 1/10, n/30 as of June 1, the payment dates, in full or less discount, are calculated from June 1.

advertising A paid-for form of nonpersonal presentation of goods, services, or ideas to consumers made by an identified sponsor.

advertising agency An organization that prepares **copy** and **layout,** selects media, works on advertising strategy, and produces the advertisement.

advertising medium The vehicle by which the advertiser's message is carried to its audience. Advertising media are often classified as (1) print media and (2) broadcast media.

AIDCA process An acronym describing what an advertisement should accomplish: attract *attention,* stimulate *interest,* create *desire, convince* the consumer, and suggest that the individual take *action.*

allocated expenses Nondirect expenses for which good and appropriate bases of expense distribution exist, so that the

---

*Note: Terms within the definitions that are printed in bold-face type are themselves defined in the glossary.

assignment of expense represents a reasonable estimate of the true expense incurred by each department in a retailing organization.

allowances from vendors Rebates and credits granted by manufacturers and wholesalers on purchases made by the retailer.

annual sales forecast The estimated level of retail sales for the year.

anticipation An extra discount (usually 6 percent per year) allowed by vendors when a bill is paid before the expiration of the **cash discount** period.

asset Anything owned by an individual or a business that has commercial or exchange value. Assets may consist of specific property or claims against others.

automatic reorder The reordering of **staple merchandise** on the basis of a predetermined minimum quantity. When this minimum quantity is reached, a new order is automatically made.

B

backup stock Additional merchandise that is available in a warehouse or in a stock room. Backup stock is particularly important for runners or best-selling staples.

bad debts Bad debts are the amounts due on open accounts that have proved to be uncollectable.

bait-leader pricing Advertising a product at an extremely low price, then, when a customer wants to buy the item, refusing to sell it and using persuasive power to switch the customer to another, higher-priced item. Sometimes called bait-and-switch tactics.

balance sheet An itemized statement that lists the total assets and the total liabilities of a given business to portray its net worth at a given moment in time.

balanced stock A balanced assortment that makes the items customers want available throughout all price ranges in proportion to consumer demand.

bank credit card A bank card that entitles the holder to purchase merchandise or services at any place of business where the card is honored. The card-holder receives one monthly statement from the bank. Usually no service charge is assessed on merchandise purchases paid for within

twenty-five days of the statement rendering date. The bank immediately reimburses the merchant accepting the card and charges a monthly fee based on dollar volume.

bargain basement The downstairs division of a department store that emphasizes special values.

bargain store A store that stocks everything that can be sold in quantity at a below-market price. Distress merchandise and seconds are often stocked in huge quantities, but little attempt is made to maintain a **balanced stock** assortment.

base-point pricing The price to the buyer is the price of the product plus freight from a specified point, regardless of the buyer's of the seller's location.

basic assortment The smallest number of pieces within a merchandise group that will provide sufficient sizes, colors, style numbers, and so forth to satisfy customer demand.

basic stock The assortment plan of products to be kept continuously on hand for a defined period, usually at least one year. It includes a list of staple items to be carried in stock, reorder points, and reorder quantities. Nonstaple items can become basic when, for fashion or fad reasons, they enjoy intensified customer demand.

basic stock method A method of planning inventory levels by ordering enough stock to begin the sales period with an inventory that exceeds the estimated period sales by some basic inventory level.

billed cost Invoice cost of purchases less **trade** and **quantity discounts.**

bill of lading A receipt issued by a carrier for merchandise to be delivered to a person at some distant point.

bill of sale A formal legal document that conveys title to specific property from the seller to the buyer.

book inventory A statement of the amount of retail stock on hand according to a **perpetual inventory system.**

boutique A small shop selling fashions or fad items. It may be independent or located in a special area within a larger store.

branch store An outlet of a central store extended into another geographic area of the market.

brand A word, mark, symbol, or a combination of these that identifies the product or service offered by a seller.

break-even volume A retail sales volume that will provide just enough revenue to cover the direct expenses most likely to be incurred. It is the sales volume at which the store is expected to receive neither a profit nor a loss.

broadcast media Radio and television.

business associated site A retail location that is situated near other retail firms.

buying group (buying office, resident buying office) An organization representing a group of noncompeting stores, formed primarily for buying merchandise.

buying power index A relative measure of the effective buying power of a segment of the market, published annually by *Sales and Marketing Management's Survey of Buying Power.* It is an estimated value of the ability of an area to purchase consumer goods, especially mass merchandised products sold at popular prices. For example, if area A has a BPI of .06, its market potential is double that of area B, which has a BPI of .03.

buying process The search, evaluation, selection, and review activities that are carried out by the buyers for a retail firm.

C

capital investments The dollar amounts invested in capital or fixed assets or in long-term securities as contrasted with those funds invested in current assets or short-term securities.

capital turnover The ratio between **net sales** and the average inventory valued at cost. It is calculated as: net sales ÷ average inventory at cost.

careers in retailing The various fields of retailing that offer opportunities for lifetime employment.

carrier Any commercial railroad, trucking firm, airline, express company, bus line, steamship line, or river barge company that transports merchandise from a vendor to a purchaser.

carry outs Merchandise carried from the store by the customer.

cash discount A discount allowed by a vendor for paying the invoice within an agreed time. Example: 2/10 means that a

2 percent discount is allowed if the bill is paid within ten days of the date of the invoice.

cash flow forecast A projection of cash inflows and outflows. It is used to insure the expected cash balance at the end of a specified time period.

cash on delivery The buyer must make payment when the goods are delivered.

cash receipts report A form used by salespeople to list cash received from sale of merchandise at the end of each day's business.

CATV See **Community Antenna Television System.**

central business district The downtown area, which is composed of convenience stores that serve the downtown employees and **shopping goods** stores and specialty shops that attract consumers to the area.

centralized buying All buying done by a central merchandise staff, which may be located in corporate headquarters.

chain stores Two or more stores carrying similar merchandise that are owned by one company.

charge-a-plate The copyrighted name of the small identification plate that shows that a customer has a charge account with a specific firm.

Clayton Act An act that outlaws discrimination in prices, exclusive and tying contracts, intercorporate stockholdings, and interlocking directorates, whenever their effect "may be to substantially lessen competition or tend to create a monopoly."

C.O.D. See **cash on delivery.**

cognition The consumer's total belief system, which consists of the individual's values, ideas, and attitudes.

collection period A ratio that indicates the size of a firm's **accounts receivables** stated in the number of days it takes to obtain that volume of sales.

Community Antenna Television System A method whereby the signal received by an antenna can relay programs to subscribers through a cable.

community shopping center A planned shopping area consisting of twenty to forty stores, including at least one department store, and 75,000 to 300,000 square feet in store area that serves 20,000 to 100,000 people.

compatibility of nearby businesses The relationship that exists when two retailers, because of their proximity to each other, have a larger sales volume together than they would have if they were located in separate areas.

compatibility of products lines The degree to which merchandise lines are related to each other as opposed to unrelated (scrambled) merchandise.

compensating salespeople The package of commission, salary, bonus, and fringe benefits paid to salespeople.

compensation components The elements contained in an employee's total compensation package.

competitive parity approach A method of determining the level of a firm's advertising budget by matching competitors' outlays for **promotion.**

complementary items Goods or services that are companions and/or are consumed jointly, for example, shirts and ties, ham and eggs.

consignee The ultimate receiver of goods.

consignment purchases Goods owned by a **vendor** that are received by a retailer under an arrangement whereby the store has the right to return to the vendor any portion of the lot unsold within a specified period.

consignor The originator of a shipment.

consistent merchandise assortment Merchandise that is closely related in terms of consumer end use.

consolidated delivery Delivery service performed by an independent organization that accumulates and delivers packages from various stores.

conspicuous consumption The use of goods or services by a consumer for the purpose of creating a display that will impress others.

consumerism The activities that consumers use to exert their influence upon government, retailers, wholesalers, and producers.

Consumer Product Warranty and Guaranty Act of 1970 Legislation passed to protect the consumer against product defects and malfunctions.

contingency payment pricing A price quoted for a service that is contingent upon the accomplishment of the task.

control The final step in a retail audit, which consists of monitoring the effectiveness of the retail plan and preparing contingency plans to be used if acceptable progress is not being made.

convenience good Goods that the consumer desires to purchase with a minimum of effort. Purchase is usually made at the most convenient and accessible place.

cooperative advertising A way of advertising in which the manufacturer or wholesaler offers to pay some portion (most commonly 50 percent) of the cost that the retailer incurs in advertising the vendor's items in a local medium.

copy The verbal and visual elements that constitute a finished advertisement.

cost The price at which goods are purchased in the wholesale market, including the billed cost and the transportation cost. The billed cost is the amount charged by the seller before deducting **cash discounts.** Transportation cost is the amount charged the store for delivery of the goods.

cost (or market method) of inventory valuation Valuing an inventory at the cost price of the items involved or at their current market value, whichever is lower.

cost of merchandise sold The cost to the store of the merchandise that has been sold during a specific period.

cost per thousand potential customers The cost needed to reach one thousand potential customers who would be receiving a specific form of advertising. It is used in comparing the costs of alternative vehicles of advertising.

cost pricing A method of obtaining price by adding all of the chargeable costs together.

coupons Small cards or cutouts found in magazines, newspapers, direct-mail envelopes and retail outlets that customers can use to receive discounts or free merchandise.

credit record analysis An analysis of addresses from a firm's credit records to determine a store's **trading area.**

critical path analysis A planning tool that shows which jobs must be completed before other jobs can be started. It also analyzes time requirements needed to perform each job so that appropriate scheduling can minimize the time needed to complete the total job.

cues Stimuli within the individual and/or in the environment that influence the consumer's response. Cues are weaker than **drives.**

cumulative markon dollars The difference between the delivered cost of merchandise, including transportation costs, and the cumulative selling prices as originally set.

current ratio The ratio obtained by dividing current **assets** by current debt. A value greater than 2:1 indicates the ability of the firm to meet its current obligations and still maintain a safety margin.

customer interview A method of surveying customers to discover their attitudes and shopping habits.

customer service policies The strategy that a retail outlet uses with regard to customer services such as credit, delivery, gift wrapping, coffee lounge, and so forth.

cycle billing Correlating of alphabetical breakdowns to specific days of the month in billing customer's accounts so that billing for each consumer group occurs on the same day each month.

D

debit A debit entry in accounting records will increase the balance of an asset or expense account and decrease the balance of a liability account. All asset and expense accounts normally have debit balances and all liability, capital, and income accounts normally have credit balances.

delivery period The expected period of time occurring between ordering the merchandise and receiving it into stock.

delivery service A customer service offered by a retail outlet through which purchased items are handled and delivered to the place demanded by the consumer.

demand curve A schedule that indicates the quantity of an item that can be sold during a specified period at many different price levels.

demographic characteristics The distinguishing characteristics of a given population such as age, sex, income, educational background, occupation, et cetera.

departmentalizing Organizing related merchandise into a group and identifying the collection as a department.

department store A retail outlet that offers a large variety of goods under one roof. It has at least twenty-five employees and its merchandise includes apparel, appliances, home furnishings, and dry goods.

depreciation The loss in value of an asset as a result of the passage of time or use.

depth of merchandise assortment The number of items offered within each merchandise line. In a deep assortment many different items within the line are stocked.

diagnosis An investigation in a retail audit that attempts to determine what the firm's present position is and why it holds that position.

direction Supervisory activity that includes leading, motivating, teaching, guiding, developing, praising, and criticizing employees.

direct expenses Expenses incurred separately for the benefit of a specific department within a store. Direct expenses common to most departmentalized stores are selling payroll, salaries of buyer and assistants, promotional costs, and delivery charges. These four classes of direct expense usually total about 40 percent of the store's total expenses.

direct mail advertising Advertising that asks for and delivers the order by mail.

discount pricing A reduced pricing strategy used by retail outlets.

discount store A store that operates on a lower margin than conventional stores that sell the same type of merchandise.

discounts to employees and customers Retail reductions offered as a matter of policy to give a preferential price to certain favored groups.

discretionary expenditures Those purchases in which the consumer is not motivated by a compelling need and is not generally governed by habit and which entail some deliberation prior to purchase.

discretionary income The part of the consumer's income that involves a choice of spending or saving. Thus, it is considered to be that portion of income above an amount that is required to buy essential items.

diversionary pricing The practice of setting a low price on selected goods or services to develop a low price image for the entire offering of the firm.

dollar control The analysis and planning of sales and stocks in terms of dollar value.

drives Strong internal physiological or social stimuli that impel an individual to action.

drop ship A shipping method in which merchandise is shipped directly to a specific **branch store.** This procedure saves the time and expense of a vendor shipping to a central warehouse then having merchandise reshipped to the branch, but it is more expensive in terms of freight cost.

E

economic value of a retail facility The value of a retail project based upon its estimated future earning potential.

economic order quantity That quantity of merchandise that achieves a balance between average order costs and inventory costs.

EDP See **Electronic Data Processing.**

elasticity of demand The ratio of the percentage change in quantity sold to the percentage change in price.

Electronic Data Processing The science of converting data by electronic means to any desired form.

end-of-aisle Spaces fronting on the main traffic aisles. These locations are particularly important for displaying **impulse items.**

end-of-month (E.O.M.) dating Dating that requires the retailer to pay within a certain number of days from the end of the month during which the goods were shipped. When a bill is dated the twenty-sixth of the month or later, E.O.M. dating begins from the end of the following month. Example: 2/10 E.O.M. dating, when the invoice date is April 10, indicates required payment on May 10 (ten days from the end of April).

esteem needs Human needs for reputation, self-respect, prestige, success, and achievement.

expenditures Outlays made during an accounting period.

expense classification The grouping of expense accounts according to a standard plan.

expenses Costs of operating a business, other than the costs of merchandise, that are properly chargeable to a specified accounting period.

experimental approach The practice of holding other variables as constant as possible in order to determine the response that the firm gets by changing one element (advertising, price, and so forth) in its **retailing mix.**

external audit A retail audit conducted by people outside the firm.

extra dating The granting of a specified number of days in addition to the ordinary dating terms. Example: 2/10–30 extra means 2 percent may be deducted if the bill is paid in forty days from invoice date.

eye level merchandising The concept that merchandise displayed at eye level sells better than merchandise placed either higher or lower.

F

facing A shelf stock that is one unit wide extending to the top and back of the shelf in a display case.

factor A financing organization that specializes in lending money using **accounts receivable** or inventory as a pledge.

factoring The practice whereby a business sells the firm's **accounts receivable** to another party.

fair trade laws Laws that permit a manufacturer to establish, under certain conditions, a minimum resale price for his products.

family life cycle A concept that divides the population into different age groups, with each group representing a different stage in life.

fashion cycle A term describing the sales curve of fashion goods. A fashion cycle follows the same stages as the **product life cycle,** but the growth stage is very rapid and the decline stage is very sudden and severe.

fashion goods Items whose major appeal is a frequent change in design.

FIFO See **first in–first out method of inventory valuation.**

financial audit An investigation that discloses the performance of a firm in dollars.

financial ratios A series of ratios that are used to express the relationship between items on the firm's **balance sheet** or between item(s) on the **income statement** and item(s) on the balance sheet. These ratios are examined for trends and compared against industry averages to identify areas of financial strength and weakness.

financial statements The **income statement** and **balance sheet** are the firm's major financial statements.

first in–first out method of inventory valuation A method of determining the value of an inventory, when costs of individual items in the inventory are not identified, that assumes that goods sell in the same order in which they were received into stock. The goods in the inventory are assumed to be the newest goods purchased and are assigned the cost value of the newest goods.

fixed assets Those assets of a permanent nature required for the normal conduct of a business. Example: furniture and fixtures, land, buildings, and so forth.

fixed costs Those costs that the firm incurs whether it is open or closed for business.

fixed pricing A method of obtaining a price for an item by adding all of the chargeable costs together.

flexible, discriminatory pricing The practice of charging customers different prices according to their perceived willingness to pay.

floor plan financing A type of financing that supplies the capital to permit a retailer to acquire samples of the product or products to display for sale and that is liquidated when the sale is consummated.

F.O.B. See **free on board.**

franchising An agreement whereby an organization that has developed a successful retail product or service extends to others, for a fee, the right to engage in the business if they agree to follow the franchisor's established pattern of operations.

free-flow layout pattern A store layout that uses a series of circular or U-shaped patterns, which results in irregular, curving aisles and much open space.

free on board A shipping term that signifies that the vendor or shipper retains title and pays all charges to F.O.B. point.

free-standing A retail site that is not adjacent to other retailing businesses.

full line Stock of a given classification of goods that includes every variety of style, in every color, in every size, and in every material that a customer can reasonably expect to obtain at a given price.

functional discount A discount granted to buyers based upon the marketing activities performed by that buyer. A type of trade discount.

functional middleman An independent business that assists in transferring title to goods without taking title to the goods in the process.

functional needs Those consumer needs that are linked to the practical uses of an item or service.

G

general ledger The summary of all operating and control accounts in which the income and financial status of a business are reflected.

general merchandise stores Retail stores that handle a large number of lines of merchandise.

general trading area The entire city or county in which a retail outlet may be located.

generative business Those sales a retail outlet makes because of efforts of the store itself to attract consumers.

generic product Identifying the essential benefit that the buyer expects to get from a product or service; also, a nonbranded item sold at lower cost because of lower advertising and packaging costs.

gift certificate A certificate, suitably engraved, that can be used for the indicated cash value in a designated store.

grading Comparing goods with a previously established criterion as to the acceptability of certain aspects of the goods.

grid layout pattern A store **layout** where fixtures and aisles are arranged in a rectangular pattern.

gross cost of merchandise handled The sum of **opening inventory** plus purchases and additions billed at cost.

gross cost of merchandise sold The cost of merchandise sold without adjustments for alteration costs and **cash discounts** earned on purchases. It equals the closing inventory at cost subtracted from the total merchandise handled at cost.

gross margin The difference between net sales and the total cost of merchandise sold.

gross purchases (cost) The billed cost of merchandise purchased for resale during a given period, including special charges made by the sellers.

gross sales The sum of all prices charged customers during a given period for goods purchased by them, before subtracting deductions for returns from and allowances to customers. Gross sales include cash sales, open account credit sales, revolving credit sales, and installment sales.

group buying The action of individual stores consolidating their buying requirements into one group activity to gain bargaining power.

guarantee (guaranty) A statement by which the seller promises to do certain things should the item or service bought not perform as specified or prove to be defective in some way within a certain time after being put into use.

H

handling process The activities involved in moving goods from the vendor through the retail outlet.

hard goods A category of major appliances, including refrigerators, ranges, washing machines, dryers, hot water heaters, air conditioners, and so forth.

high price maintenance The practice of establishing a price that is higher than the price offered by competitors.

hold slip A form used to identify merchandise that a customer desires to purchase at a later time.

honor system A system in which employees record their own working time on time sheets.

horizontal integration The acquisition by one company of another company in the same or related lines of business and on the same level in the channel of distribution (the consumer being considered as the base).

house organ A publication for a store's employees.

housekeeping The action of presenting merchandise in a neat, attractive, and orderly manner. Includes physical maintenance (cleanliness) of the entire store.

hypermarket A combination warehouse, **discount store,** and supermarket that sells merchandise at below normal retail prices and stacks the goods up to twelve feet high.

I

implementation The fifth step in a retail audit, which focuses upon the tactical means and procedures used to accomplish the firm's **objectives.**

implied warranty Implicit assurance that the retailer and/or manufacturer will be responsible and accountable for the performance of an item or service sold to consumers.

impulse items Goods or services that are purchased on the spur of the moment and without prior planning.

in-store traffic pattern The pattern of consumer movements within a store. Analysis of traffic patterns provides information helpful in planning store layout and making merchandise arrangement decisions.

in transit Merchandise that has been shipped from the vendor but has not been received by the retailer.

income elasticity of demand The change in quantity demanded that may be expected to result from a one percent change in income, other factors remaining constant.

income statement The financial statement that contains the operating results during a specified period of time. The main elements of the income statement are the **net sales** revenue from which the **cost of goods sold** is deducted to give **gross margin,** which must cover operating expenses and net income to the firm.

inconsistent merchandise assortment A grouping of merchandise lines that are not related to one another in terms of consumer usage.

index of retail saturation A method used to aid retailers in choosing among the alternatives for the location of a new outlet by determining to what degree the number of stores in an area meet consumer demand.

inflation A situation in which prices are increasing throughout the economy.

initial markup percent The difference between the total merchandise handled at retail and the total merchandise handled at cost, expressed as a percent of the retail. Synonyms are cumulative initial markup percent, cumulative markon percent, and cumulative initial markon percent.

installment account A system of buying whereby the consumer makes a down payment and pays a specified amount, including a service charge, per month.

institutional advertising Advertising designed to build long-term good will for the advertiser rather than to stimulate immediate purchase of a product or service.

insurance A means of providing protection against a risk.

integrated marketing Using the firm's entire effort in a coordinated manner to build a desirable and consistent image in the minds of consumers.

integrated retailing A retail organization that also conducts business in some other level of the distribution channel such as warehousing, trucking, or manufacturing.

intensive distribution A type of distribution that gives the maximum exposure of goods to buyers in the market since it uses as many different types of retailers and retail locations as possible.

intermediate terms funds Borrowed funds that must be paid back during a one- to ten-year period.

interest The price paid for the use of borrowed money.

internal audit A **retail audit** conducted by full-time employees of the firm.

inventory audit Counting stock to verify that the firm possesses stock valued at a stated level of dollars.

inventory overage The value by which **physical inventory** exceeds **perpetual** (or book) **inventory.**

inventory, physical Determining how much merchandise on hand by actually counting the items.

inventory shortage The value by which **perpetual** (or book) **inventory** exceeds **physical inventory.**

inventory valuation A determination of the proper value of the inventory. The usual rule is "cost or market, whichever is lower." So, if an article in the inventory cost the store $100 but is now replaceable for $90, it is valued at $90. If

it is replaceable for $110, however, it is valued at $100.

invoice A bill prepared by a seller of goods or services given to the buyer. The invoice usually itemizes all articles included in the bill.

invoice cut-off Setting a specific time after which invoices received will not be included in the calculation of the inventory on hand. After this time, the merchandise corresponding to these invoices will not be included in the **physical inventory** count.

J

job description A statement of the duties, requirements and other features of the job. It is used for purposes of determining the rate of pay and advertising the position when it is vacant.

job evaluation A determination of the relative worth and importance of each position in a firm. A job evaluation program may be used to establish wages, determine promotion requirements, establish incentives, and so forth.

job specifications A statement that includes a description of the necessary skills, abilities, and education that are needed to perform the job.

jobber A wholesaler who buys from manufacturers and importers and sells the merchandise to retailers.

journal A book of original entry for a specialized type of entry such as cash disbursements, cash receipts, purchases, sales, and so forth.

K

keystoning policy The doubling of wholesale cost to arrive at a retail price for all items.

kickback A part of a fee, commission, or wage that is turned back to an individual in appreciation of the patronage or service rendered. It is an unethical practice because the funds are not paid back to the vending company but to the individual.

L

last in–first out method of inventory control A method of inventory evaluation used when physical counts can be obtained. It means that the price shown on the last incoming shipment of the particular item is the one that will be used for current valuations and cost. With fast moving items this should be close to market value.

law of retail gravitation A formula used for determining the interchange of retail trade between cities. It was formulated in 1931 by William J. Reilly and purports to tell at what distance between two cities a consumer would be indifferent to going to either city.

layaway A deferred payment purchase agreement in which merchandise is held by the store for the customer until it is completely paid for.

layout (1) A working drawing showing how an advertisement or publication is to look. (2) The arrangement of fixtures or departments in a store. (3) The arrangement of units in an office.

lead tenants The major attractions, such as department stores, that draw consumers to a shopping center.

lead time The time expected to elapse between the day of placing an order and the day of arrival of the goods.

learning The change in an individual's response tendencies as a result of the effects of his or her insights and experiences.

ledger A record of final entry in bookkeeping that contains all debits and credits from the journal. It refers both to individual records and to the whole group of ledger accounts.

leverage (1) The degree to which changes in sales volume affect profits as a result of **fixed costs.** For example, a relatively small increase in sales normally causes a relatively large increase in profits since many costs are fixed regardless of business volume. (2) The degree to which a retail firm uses debt instead of equity in its financing.

liability Money owed by a retailer to another person or firm.

license plate analysis Recording customers' license numbers and obtaining their addresses from county registration files (or from a published book) to determine a store's trading area.

life style The characteristic mode of living for a segment of or the whole of a society. It is concerned with those unique qualities that distinguish one group or culture from others.

LIFO See **last in–first out method of inventory valuation.**

Likert scale A survey tool that is used to obtain consumer opinions by asking respondents to indicate their degree of agreement or disagreement with each statement.

line of credit An agreement between a bank and a retailer whereby the bank agrees, over a future period, to lend the retailer funds up to an agreed maximum amount.

liquidity A term used to describe the solvency of a business. It has special reference to how readily assets can be converted into cash without loss.

liquidity ratio The ratio obtained by adding cash to marketable securities and accounts receivable and then dividing the sum by current **liabilities.** A value of less than 1:1 indicates the firm will have to sell some of its inventory to meet current liabilities.

list price The gross billed price, which is subject to a trade discount. In some cases, the list price is the retail price suggested by a manufacturer or vendor.

long-term funds Borrowed funds for which the repayment term for the entire principle is ten years or more.

loss-leader pricing Advertising and selling merchandise at or below cost to bring customers into the store.

low-price leaders Items that are priced at reduced markup percentage to attract customers.

M

mail questionnaire A means of obtaining information from consumers via the mails.

maintained markup The difference between **net sales** and the **gross cost of merchandise sold.** It is the margin on sales before making adjustments for **cash discounts** earned and alteration costs.

man hours The summation of all the productive hours worked by all employees in a work center during a given period.

management by objective A program that uses professional management techniques, merchandise, and economic trend indicators to keep ahead of competition. For example, these may be aimed at the goal of increasing sales per square foot—one of the key factors that measures earnings in retail business.

Management Information System A data processing system that is designed to furnish management and supervisory personnel with current information using computers or other organized data collection techniques.

manifest A shipping form used by carriers for consolidation purposes. It lists all pertinent information (consignor, consignee, commodity classification, number and weight of packages, and sometimes cost) used by carriers within a store and by stores in transfer operations from central warehouse to branches.

mannequin A clothing model representing the human form used in display windows and on ready-to-wear selling floors to display apparel.

manpower development A program directed toward the improvement of an individual's knowledge, skills, attitudes, perceptions, and personal characteristics in current and future management positions.

manufacturers' agent A middleman who sells a part of the output of client manufacturers in a specified territory.

manufacturer's representative A selling agent capable of giving informative talks to selling personnel.

marginal analysis A method of planning inventory levels, promotional expenditures, or changes in price by analyzing what effect the last unit that has been added has upon the firm's profits.

marginal cost The addition to total cost represented by the sale of one additional unit of product or service.

marginal return to space The addition to gross margin caused by the addition of one unit of shelf **facing** for a good. Profit maximization for the retailer occurs when marginal returns to space are the same for all items.

marginal revenue The addition to total revenue resulting from the sale of one additional unit of a good or service.

markdown A retail price reduction caused by a reduction in the value of the goods. Thus, if one hundred articles retailing at $1 each become slow-selling, and are reduced to 89 cents, the markdown is $11 for the lot.

markdown percentage The percentage that a reduction in price is of the reduced price.

market segmentation A process of identifying and categorizing consumers into mutually exclusive groups (segments) that have relatively homogeneous responses to controllable marketing variables.

market share One firm's proportion of the industry's total actual volume.

market share to selling space share ratio The ratio between an individual store's share of the market in an area and its share of total store selling space is calculated for present stores and is used to forecast sales for a new retail outlet.

marketing Those business associated activities that direct the flow of goods or services from the producer to the consumer.

marketing concept Focusing all company activity on what will best serve the consumer at a profit to the firm.

marketing functions Those activities that are performed to place goods and services in consumers' hands at the time, at the place, and in the form demanded by consumers.

marketing middleman services The services provided by vendors.

marketing specialists Those people who perform marketing functions for manufacturers, wholesalers, or retailers.

marketing mix The total complex of the firm's marketing effort. It includes pricing, promotion, product, and location. The central problem in planning the mix is to find that combination that will produce the maximum net income.

marketing research The systematic gathering, recording, and analyzing of information about problems relating to the marketing of goods and services.

marketing strategy A plan for marketing a product over a long period of time.

marking Placing the correct price tag on new merchandise.

markon The difference between cost price as billed (before deductions for **cash discount**) and retail price at which merchandise is originally offered.

markup The difference between the cost and the retail price of merchandise. In equation form: Markup = Retail − Cost. If an article is offered for sale at $100 and costs $65, the markup is $35. When the term *markup* is used in this book, it is (unless otherwise specified) the initial markup, which is the difference between the original retail price placed on purchases and the cost.

markup percent on cost The markup divided by the cost. In equation form, it is markup ÷ cost. If retail is $100, cost $65, and markup $35, the markup percent is $35 ÷ $65 = 53.8%. Markup percent on cost is higher than markup percent on retail. The generally accepted plan is to express markup on retail. Note: In all problems in this book, markup is expressed as a percentage of retail, unless it is specifically stated to be a percentage of cost.

markup percent on retail The markup divided by the retail. In equation form, it is markup ÷ retail. If retail is $100, cost $65, and markup $35, the markup percent is $35 ÷ $100 = 35%. The term *percent of retail* means the same as *percent on retail.*

mass merchandising The self-service store displaying and selling all kinds of merchandise. Displays tends to be massive; customers usually push wire carts to collect and carry their own selection of merchandise to cashier checkout counters.

maximizing space productivity Arrangement of selling fixtures and display of merchandise to produce increased sales volume per square foot of selling space.

maximum stock The amount of stock that should be on hand and on order just after a reorder is placed. As a formula,

Maximum = delivery period + safety factor + reorder period. These may be expressed in terms of **weeks' supply** or in terms of units of goods. Since the *minimum* equals the *delivery period* plus the *safety factor,* the *maximum* (in weeks' supply) may also be expressed as the *minimum* plus the *reorder period.*

media mix The planning, use, and coordination of advertising and promotional media, including: interior and exterior display, newspaper, direct mail, radio, TV, magazine, transit, and outdoor advertising.

media representatives The sales and/or service representatives from newspapers, radio, television, and other forms of advertising.

memorandum and consignment selling A marketing arrangement in which a vendor agrees to take back goods if they are not sold during a specific period of time.

merchandise budget A statement prepared by management containing planned commitments for all the components of the merchandise mix (sales, reductions, stocks, margins, and purchases) for a planning period (usually a season).

merchandise charge The extraneous costs, such as shipping charges, insurance, demurrage, and so forth, applied to cost of merchandise prior to markon.

merchandise classification A type of classification applied to a merchandise group within a department and controlled by dollar volume rather than by units.

merchandise control Maintaining accurate figures on purchases and sales of merchandise, either by dollar or by units, in such a way that the movement is monitored.

merchandise cost The billed cost of merchandise less any applicable trade or quantity discounts, plus inbound transportation costs if paid by the store.

merchandise manager The executive (sometimes called merchandising manager) in charge of a merchandising division of a store.

merchandise marts The buildings that house showrooms for manufacturers and importers where store buyers and merchandise managers can inspect many lines in a minimal amount of time.

merchandising The planning involved in marketing the right merchandise, at the right place, at the right time, in the right quantities, and at the right price.

merchandising division The division of the store that is responsible for planning stock assortments, for buying, and for **merchandise control.** It shares with the other divisions the responsibility for balancing the growth and profit factors.

middle management The secondary layer of divisional managers, that is, assistants.

middlemen Individuals, firms, or corporations that function between producers and ultimate consumers, assuming title to merchandise or assisting directly in its transfer.

minimum stock The amount of stock that a store plans to have on hand at the moment a reorder is placed. The minimum level should cover probable sales during the **delivery period** and allow for a safety factor.

MIS See **Management Information System.**

model stock A planned assortment of units of merchandise balanced to anticipate customer demand and resulting in the planned stock-turn.

multiple-unit pricing Pricing a number of like products together as a unit of one.

multiunit establishment One of two or more establishments in the same general kind of business that are operated by the same firm.

monthly sales index An index figure that is calculated in such a way that an average month's sales is 100. The percentage that a monthly sales index deviates from 100 is the percentage deviation of that month's sales from an average month. For example, an index of 120 for June indicates that June sales are 20 percent higher than an average month's sales.

mortgage An instrument of conveyance (generally of real estate) from a borrower, called the mortgagor, to the lender, called the mortgagee.

motivation The driving force behind consumer behavior and desires that initiate behavior.

N

national brand A brand name owned by a manufacturer.

negotiation process The final stage of the buying process during which price, terms, delivery dates, and so forth are determined.

neighborhood cluster A group of several stores in a residential district of a city composed mainly of **convenience goods** stores such as groceries, drugstores, and bakery goods stores, and service establishments such as dry cleaners and barber shops. Most patronage comes from residents of the area immediately surrounding the location.

neighborhood shopping center A group of ten to fifteen food, drug, sundry, and personal service stores situated on about six acres and serving about 10,000 people from under 75,000 square feet of selling space.

net alteration costs The difference between the cost the store incurs in performing the alterations and the amounts, if any, paid by the customers for this service. It is treated as an addition to the gross cost of merchandise sold.

net credit period The length of time for which mercantile credit is extended. For example, 2/10, net 30, provides a net credit period of thirty days.

net operating income (profit) Net sales less net cost of goods sold less operating expenses.

net profit on tangible net worth ratio A ratio that measures the firm's **return on investment.**

net profits on net sales ratio A ratio that expresses a firm's net dollar profits as a percentage of its net retail sales dollar volume.

net purchases. The cost of purchases plus freight in, less purchase returns, allowances, and **cash discounts** taken.

net sales The difference between the **gross sales** and **returns and allowances to customers** during a specified period.

net sales to net inventory ratio A measure of the firm's **turnover** of inventory.

net space yield concept A way of determining how retail selling space can be used in the most productive way with respect to handling costs, space costs, and margins.

net terms A condition of sale calling for the payment of the billed amount of the invoice at a specified date with no **cash discount** deduction. If the date is not specified, payment in three days from the date of invoice is generally considered acceptable.

net worth The **owner's equity** in the store computed as the difference between assets and liabilities.

never-out lists The key items listed separately from a **model stock** plan or **basic stock** list, or especially identified on the basic stock list by colored stars or other suitable means.

newspaper A print medium issued frequently (daily or weekly) and devoted mainly to reports of latest developments. It is a timely advertising medium for which audiences may be selected on a sharply geographic base or on the basis of demographics.

nongoods service The renting of goods as opposed to selling them.

nonprice competition Any competitive activity, such as promotion, that does not involve price manipulation.

nondiscretionary expenditures Consumer spending that represents contractual, necessary, and habitual expenditures.

nonfunctional needs Those consumer needs that are not linked to the practical use of an item or service but that are associated with the image of the item or service.

nonselling area Floor space other than the selling area used in the conduct of business in a retail outlet. It may include entrances, show windows, vertical transportation facilities, offices, boiler and engine rooms, alteration rooms and workrooms, repair shops, receiving and marking rooms, and stockrooms.

nonsigner clause A provision of the fair trade laws whereby all retailers had to agree to the terms of a resale price maintenance agreement if it was signed by a single retailer in a state operating under this provision.

nonstore retailing A form of retailing such as telephone shopping, door-to-door selling, and catalog buying, in which a consumer contact occurs ouside the confines of the retail store.

notes payable The name of a **ledger** account or **balance sheet** item showing the liabilities to banks, trade, and other creditors evidenced by promissory notes.

notions department The department in department stores, drug stores, variety stores, and discount stores that carries small sundries that are usually considered small-ticket necessities, such as ribbons and needles.

number of stock turns Stock **turnover** is calculated by dividing average inventory at retail into the **net sales** for the year. Average inventory is the sum of the retail inventories at the end of each month added to the initial **opening inventory** and divided by thirteen, the number of inventories used.

O

objectives The third step in a **retail audit,** which consists of a determination of where the firm should be headed in the future.

objective and task method A method of determining the level of a firm's

advertising budget by defining the promotional objectives as specifically as possible and then determining the costs associated with accomplishing each goal.

observation A way of obtaining information by watching consumers' actions.

occupancy expense An expense related to the use of property such as rent, heat, light, depreciation, upkeep, and general care of premises.

odd lot Broken lots or unbalanced assortments reduced in price for quick turnover.

odd pricing The use of uneven prices such as $9.95 rather than $10.00.

off retail percentage The **markdown** is calculated as a percentage of the original price. For example, an item originally retails for $100 and is marked down to $60; the off-retail percentage is 40 percent.

off-season pricing A form of **markdown** given during an otherwise low sales period.

on order Merchandise purchased but not yet received.

one-cent sale Selling two articles of a certain class at one cent more than the price of one.

100 percent location The retail site that has the greatest exposure to a retail store's **target market** customers.

one-price policy A policy in which at a given time all customers pay the same price for any given item of merchandise.

open code dating The date marked on perishable products to indicate the last day that the food can be sold in the store, stated in a code that can be understood by the customer.

open order An order placed without a price or delivery stipulation. It is sent to a market representative in a **resident buying office** without specifying a vendor.

open stock Additional and/or replacement pieces of merchandise, for example, china dinnerware, that are carried in bulk and kept in stock for several years.

opening inventory The value of the inventory on hand at the beginning of an accounting period.

open-to-buy The amount of merchandise that may be ordered for delivery during a control period. It is the difference between the planned purchases and the commitments already made for the period.

operating expenses Amounts disbursed or incurred in order to operate the business as distinct from outlays to finance the business.

operating ratios A series of ratios that express relationships among the various items in the firm's **income statement** These ratios are used to observe relative costs and improve the profitability of the firm.

operating statement A financial statement indicating the operating results for a given period. The format is to deduct the cost of sales from sales revenue, resulting in gross margin, which covers expenses and profit for the firm. See **income statement.**

ordinary dating The usual method of dating, as illustrated by such terms as 2/10, net 30. The two specified elements are the **cash discount** and the **net credit period.** The cash discount may be deducted if the bill is paid within the discount period (ten days); otherwise, the full amount is due at the end of the credit period (thirty days in the example given). Both the cash discount and the net credit periods are usually counted from the date of the invoice, which is usually also the date of shipment.

organization The sixth step of a **retail audit,** which evaluates the adequacy of retail management personnel.

organizational philosophy The set of principles upon which a firm is founded.

other income Income from sources other than the sale of merchandise. Such sources include, among others, **interest** and dividends received, carrying charges collected on **installment accounts,** and profits from the redeeming of securities.

outdoor advertising An **advertising medium** in which the message is not delivered to the audience, but rather, the units are placed in strategic locations where they can be seen by an audience on the move.

out of stock A lack of merchandise in a store.

overage The amount by which a **physical inventory** exceeds the figure generated by the **perpetual inventory system.**

overbought A condition in which a store buyer has become committed to

purchases in excess of the planned purchase allotment for a merchandising period.

overhead A synonym for fixed expenses.

overstored The condition that exists when an area has more stores than are needed to satisfy consumer demand.

owned goods service Service performed on existing products.

owner's equity The amount of money the owners of a business have invested in that firm.

P

partnership A relationship based upon an agreement between two or more persons who combine their resources and activities in a joint enterprise and share by specified agreement in the management and in the profits or losses.

payback period The estimated period of time in which a project will generate enough cash to equal its cost.

payroll expense percent The total payroll for the work center expressed as a percent of the total sales. When the work center services the store, the sales are the store sales, but where the selling department is regarded as a work center, the sales are the department sales.

per capita method A method of forecasting annual retail sales in which the annual dollar per capita expenditure in a specified merchandise category is multiplied by the number of people residing in the trade area.

perception. What the consumer "sees" as influenced by the individual's past experience, present attitudes, and inclinations.

percentage deviation method A method of planning inventory levels that involves ordering stocks so that the beginning inventory fluctuates from the planned average stock by 50 percent of the sales fluctuations from the average period sales.

percentage of income method A method of forecasting annual retail sales in which the total annual dollar personal income in an area is multiplied by the percentage of annual personal income spent in the specified merchandise category.

percentage of retail sales method A method of forecasting annual retail sales in which the total annual dollar retail sales in an area is multiplied by the percentage of annual retail sales obtained by the specified merchandise category.

percentage of sales approach A method of determining the level of a firm's advertising budget by establishing promotional expenditures at a prespecified percentage of the estimated sales volume.

performance appraisal The process of comparing the current performance of an individual with predetermined performance standards set forth in the **job description.**

periodic inventory method of classification control The determination of sales data within each merchandise classification from periodic counts of the inventory on hand.

perpetual inventory method of classification control The determination of sales data within each merchandise classification from periodic counts of the inventory on hand.

perpetual inventory system A method of keeping track of the inventory of a firm by continuous recording of the movement of items into and out of the firm.

personal interview A survey method in which the interviewer obtains information from respondents in face-to-face meetings.

personal selling Any activity that involves an oral presentation for the purpose of making a sale.

personnel process The process involving the systematic linking of the personnel functions into an integrated system of policies, procedures, and rules that govern employee behavior while on the job.

physical inventory The quantity or the value of merchandise on hand at a given time, as determined by an actual count.

physical inventory at cost The value of an inventory at aggregate **cost** prices.

physical inventory at retail The value of an inventory at aggregate retail prices.

physical inventory system of unit control A system of stock control whereby the stock is counted at periodic intervals and the unit sales are derived from the inventory and purchase data.

physiological needs The most basic type of human needs such as hunger, thirst, and sex.

pilferage Stealing in small quantities.

planned obsolescence Making changes in merchandise features for the sake of

increasing consumption, as in the practice of frequent model changes.

planned shopping center A concentration of a number of stores of different types developed as a unit.

point-of-purchase promotions Signs and displays at the final point of sale. These items are flexible as to permanence, format, position, and location.

position media Advertising media that include all types of signs, posters, programs, menus, directories, sky writing, and transportation advertising.

possession utility The characteristics of a good that make it possible to satisfy the human desire to have the right to use the item as needed.

preauthorizing The practice of obtaining credit authorization for charge-send transactions before allowing the package or merchandise to leave the department.

prebuying process The planning activities that precede the actual buying of goods by a buyer for a retail outlet.

premarking or preticketing The price marking of merchandise by the manufacturer.

prepackaging Merchandise packaging provided by the vendor for convenient display and for the take-with customer or for delivery by store.

prepay The payment of all shipping charges for the merchandise by the vendor, who rebills these charges to the purchaser on an invoice for the merchandise.

price elasticity of demand The change in quantity demanded that may be expected to result from a one per cent change in price, other factors remaining constant.

price leadership A method of retail price determination in which retailers set their prices according to the prices announced by a leading retailer.

price lining Buying goods to sell at a limited number of predetermined selling prices.

pricing strategy The development of a long-range plan to use price as a form of market cultivation.

primary data Data collected by the firm or its representatives by actively observing, experimenting, or surveying people.

printed media Any media printed on paper and distributed to consumers.

private brand A brand name owned by a middleman.

procurement The activities within a firm devoted to the buying function.

producers' cooperative marketing Type of cooperative marketing that primarily involves the sale of products of the membership.

product In a narrow sense, the physical thing marketed. In a broad sense, it consists of the satisfactions that may be derived from its use or consumption, including values added by **middlemen.**

product differentiation The situation in which two products of similar characteristics and end use are manufactured by different producers and acquire divergent images in the minds of consumer segments. This usually comes about through promotional activities.

product image How the consumer perceives the characteristics of a product.

product life cycle The stages through which products move while on the market—introduction, growth, maturity, and decline.

productivity The output of work on a per hour basis. It is found by dividing the work load by the number of hours required to handle the load.

prognosis The second step in a **retail audit,** which is an estimate of where the retailer is likely to go if present policies are used in a marketplace that follows current trends.

program The fourth step in a **retail audit,** which focuses upon the means of obtaining the firm's objectives.

projective techniques Indirect questioning procedures that lead the respondent to believe his or her biases will not be revealed.

promotion Any means used to stimulate sales or generate a favorable image in the minds of consumers.

promotional allowances An amount granted to the store by the seller of merchandise to cover all or part of the store's cost of advertising or otherwise promoting the sale of the merchandise to the consumer.

promotional calendar A calendar that contains the firm's promotional plans.

promotional mix The combination of all means used for promoting sales.

prorated expenses Joint expenses that cannot be charged directly to selling departments nor allocated to them on a basis that measures the service each has received. They are assigned to selling departments pro rata to dollar sales volume.

psychographics A concept that describes the life style characteristics of consumers.

public market A wholesale or retail market supervised or administered by a municipality, which rents space or stalls to dealers; also municipal market, community market.

public relations A planned program of policies and conduct designed to build confidence and increase understanding on the part of customers, suppliers, competitors, employees, stockholders, creditors, the local community, and the government.

public warehouse A storage facility that does not take title to the goods it handles. It may issue receipts, which can be used as security for loans.

publicity Public exposure, either favorable or unfavorable, for which a firm has not paid.

purchase order The written document issued by the purchasing department of a firm to a vendor to procure goods to fill a requirement.

purchasing agent The person authorized to acquire materials needed for operation and maintenance of a retail outlet.

purchasing manual A policy manual containing broad policy statements affecting the purchasing aspects of the entire firm. It may also be a procedures manual detailing how each activity is to be handled.

push money (PM) A bonus that salespeople receive on each sale made of specially designated merchandise.

Q

quantity discount A discount allowed when a given quantity is purchased. It is an inducement to buy a larger than average amount and may be deducted regardless of when the bill is paid.

quick assets Those assets that, in the ordinary course of business, will be converted into cash within a reasonably short period of time, usually one year.

quota A goal figure that salespeople are expected to achieve. If they sell more than their quota they may be paid a bonus.

R

rack jobber A limited-function wholesaler who receives payment only for actual goods sold.

radio An audio broadcast advertising medium whose coverage is geographic, with some stations appealing to specific ethnic or age groups. It provides reasonable flexibility to the advertiser but has two limitations: no possibility of later reference by the audience and no graphic portrayals.

random sampling A form of probability sampling in which each unit in the universe has an equal chance of being chosen.

receipt of goods dating Dating is computed, not from the date of the bill, but rather from the day the goods are received by the store.

receivables The **accounts receivable** owned by a business.

receiving The process of accepting new merchandise at a store.

receiving apron A form attached to a store's **purchase order** that contains information concerning the status of a vendor's shipment.

reference group Any group of people that is capable of influencing the behavior of an individual.

regional shopping center The largest type of shopping center, with several **department stores** providing the main drawing power for more than 300,000 square feet of selling space.

reinforcement The power of a favorable experience to generate a stronger motivation to repeat the action.

rented goods service The renting of goods as opposed to selling them.

reorder period The frequency planned for reordering a specific item.

repeat business Business generated by a consumer's returning to the same firm to purchase goods or services.

resident buying office An office established by a retailer or group of retailers to serve only that group by supplying them with information and buying assistance.

response The individual's reaction to all of the **cues.**

retail The price at which goods are offered for sale.

retail audit A self-analysis of a firm that is conducted periodically to determine the strengths and weaknesses of the firm in reaching its **target market** at a profit to the firm.

retail classification systems Methods of classifying retail firms from the viewpoint of: (1) merchandise offered, (2) number of outlets owned, (3) relative emphasis on price, and (4) number of surrounding stores.

retail deductions The retail value that is subtracted from total merchandise handled at retail during a given period. It consists of **net sales** plus retail reductions.

retail inventory method A method of determining the cost or market value of an inventory by listing and totaling the goods on hand at current retail prices and translating this retail value into cost.

retail life cycle A description of a retail firm's life from beginning to end. It is the same as the **product life cycle,** applied to a firm.

retail market research The process of systematically searching for, collecting, and analyzing information that can be used in developing retail strategies.

retail reductions The difference between the aggregate original retail value of merchandise disposed of during a period and **net sales.** It is the sum of **markdowns,** merchandise **shortages,** and **discounts to employees and customers.**

retail store cooperative A store owned and managed by a number of consumers. Patronage refunds are frequently determined by the proportion of business each participant buys of the total sales made by the store.

retailing The business activity that is concerned with selling goods to ultimate consumers.

retailing mix The variables (including product, price, promotion, place, operating policy, buying, and human resource considerations) that a retail store can combine in alternative ways to obtain a strategy for attracting its customers.

retained earnings The portion of a retailer's capital that is derived from earnings and has not been paid out in the form of dividends.

return on investment approach to advertising A method of determining the level of a firm's advertising budget obtained by viewing promotion as a capital investment rather than a current expense.

return on investment (ROI) or return on assets A concept used as a tool for deciding among alternative promotional plans.

return per square foot The amount of dollar contribution that is obtained from a square foot of selling space.

returns and allowances to customers The dollar total of goods returned to the store and of reductions in the price given to customers. It is deducted from **gross sales** to get **net sales.**

returns and allowances to vendor The dollar sum of purchased goods that is returned to the supplier and unplanned reductions in purchase price.

revolving credit A consumer credit plan that is commonly used for purchase of merchandise on a nonsecured basis.

R.O.G dating See **receipt of goods dating.**

run-of-paper (ROP) A term indicating that the position of an advertisement will be at the publisher's discretion.

run of schedule time (ROS) Time is allocated for an advertisement wherever in the schedule the radio or television station sees fit.

S

safety needs Consumer needs based on the desire for security, protection, and order.

safety stock A reserve for contingencies, especially for unforeseen increases in rate of sale. It may be expressed in terms of **weeks' supply** or as a specific quantity in units.

sales The dollar amounts received by the store in exchange for merchandise sold to customers during an accounting period.

sales clerk A person in a retail store who records the customers' purchases, is responsible for maintaining stock, and assists the customer in making a selection.

sales forecast An estimate of sales, in dollars or physical units, for a specified future period under a proposed marketing program and an assumed set of economic forces.

sales slip A slip of paper generated by a cash register showing the dollar and cents amount of purchase.

sales promotion Those marketing activities (besides **advertising, personal selling,** and **publicity**) that stimulate sales. These activities include displays, shows, and demonstrations.

scanning The process wherein the input into a checkout terminal is accomplished by passing a coded ticket over a "reader" or by having a "wand" pass over the ticket. Scanning may be done by a non-human-readable bar code called the **universal product code (UPC),** or by human-readable optical recognition characters.

scrambled merchandising A condition in retailing in which a store takes on merchandise to sell that is unrelated to the regular lines carried by the store.

seasonal dating A form of **advance dating** that is allowed on merchandise of a seasonal nature. It is granted by a manufacturer to induce early buying of seasonal goods so as to keep the plant occupied during slack seasons.

seasonal sales forecast The estimated level of retail sales for a specific period of the year.

secondary data Data that is gathered by others, rather than by the retailer himself.

secondary shopping district A well-developed cluster of stores outside the central business district, and generally found in larger cities. The sale of **convenience goods** predominates, but **shopping** and **specialty goods** are of considerable significance.

selective distribution The practice of limiting the outlets for one's product to those that will contribute most to profits and prestige.

self-actualization needs The final goal on Maslow's hierarchy of motives list. It consists of developing one's self to the fullest.

self-service A type of retail operation where the customer is exposed to merchandise that may be examined without sales assistance.

selling area That part of the sales floor devoted exlusively to selling.

selling process A procedure consisting of creating awareness of a need, developing customer comprehension of the firm's offering, providing the basis for customer conviction that the offer is a good offer, and encouraging customers to make a purchase.

semantic differential scale A technique used for measuring consumer responses. It employs a series of bipolar descriptive scales as a basis for evaluating respondents' ratings.

service area That part of the sales floor that is devoted to servicing the selling area.

service mark A mark used in the sale or advertising of **services** to identify those of a given firm and to distinguish them from those of others.

services Any work that is not connected with the manufacture, production, or processing of a product or commodity or the wholesaling or retailing of a good.

shared business That part of a retail outlet's sales that is obtained because of the generative pulling power of nearby retailers.

shoplifting The stealing of store's merchandise by customers.

shopping goods The type of item that the consumer usually wishes to purchase only after comparing quality, price, and style in a number of sources.

shopping the competition The practice of having store employees make price and product comparisons in competitive outlets.

short-term funds Borrowed funds that must be paid back in one year or less.

shortage The loss caused by **pilferage, shoplifting,** and damaged merchandise.

shrinkage The difference between actual stock on hand and the **book inventory.**

simple random sampling A method of choosing a number of people from a large population in such a way that every possible person has an equal chance of being chosen.

social class A group of people who are about equal to one another in prestige and community status. People within a social class regularly interact among members of their group and share the same general goals and philosophy of life.

social needs The consumer needs for affection and belonging.

soft goods Merchandise made of a textile base.

source marking The **preticketing** of merchandise by a source before shipment. It is very important in expediting the arrival of merchandise on a selling floor because the merchandise is not held up in receiving for price ticketing by store.

specialty advertising Advertising in which consumers are given an object (calendar, ball-point pen, key ring, ashtray, ruler, and so forth) with the firm name and possibly with other information printed on the item.

specialty goods The type of item that has such an attraction for a consumer that the consumer will go considerably out of the way to purchase it.

specialty stores Stores concentrating on a specific classification of merchandise, for example, jewelry, books, or men's clothing.

standard industrial classification system A classification system in which each industrial market segment is identified with a number for which statistics are collected by the government, thereby providing a great deal of information for the marketer.

standing order An arrangement with a vendor to make shipments periodically in specified quantities for a set period.

staple merchandise Goods that have a fairly active demand that continues over a period of years, and which the retailer finds it necessary to carry in stock continuously.

stock alterations The cost of altering and renovating goods in stock as distinct from goods ordered by customers.

stock book A record, usually maintained by the buyer, of purchases (made from orders) and of sales (obtained from stubs of price tickets).

stock control A broad term for various systems and methods used to control stock.

stock shortage All unexplained or unrecorded shrinkages in the value of merchandise available for sale.

stock-sales ratio The ratio between the retail stock at the first of the month and sales for that month.

stock to sales method A method of planning inventory levels that involves multiplying the estimated sales volume for a period by the planned beginning-of-the-month stock-sales ratio to obtain the desired beginning of the period inventory.

stock turn rate The number of stock-turns for a period of one year.

stock turnover The ratio between sales and average inventory. It is calculated in any one of the following ways: (1) Net sales ÷ average inventory at retail (2) Gross cost of goods sold ÷ average inventory at cost (3) Number of units sold ÷ average unit inventory.

store coupons A print medium sponsored by the store itself and indicating a "cents-off" or "free" deal by the store.

store image The overall personality of a store as viewed by consumers.

store layout The interior retail store arrangement of departments or groupings of merchandise.

store services Any service that is not directly related to the actual sale of a specific product within the store, such as **layaway,** gift wrapping, credit, delivery.

storing land The purchase of vacant land located in the development path of a city for possible future use.

straight salary compensation plan A compensation plan in which the retail employee is paid a set salary that does not vary with sales productivity.

stub The second part of the price ticket, which is removed by the salesperson at time of sale for unit merchandise control.

stub control A **perpetual inventory system** of **unit control** in which sales information is obtained from stubs of price tickets rather than from sales checks.

substitute items Goods or services that consumers perceive as being fairly similar.

supervision The act of overseeing and being responsible for employee performance.

survey Using personal interviews, the telephone, or direct mail to obtain consumer opinion.

suscipient business That part of a retail outlet's sales that is obtained from people whose principal purpose for being near the retail outlet is not because the store or its neighbors attracted them.

systems level retail audit A periodic evaluation of all the elements used in the retail effort.

systems selling The idea of selling the **total product concept.**

T

tangible assets Those **assets** that are of a physical and material nature such as cash, land, buildings, and so forth.

target market The particular segment of a total population that a particular retail store focuses all its merchandising expertise on to accomplish the profit objectives of the store.

telephone interview A survey technique in which the interviewer obtains information from respondents over the telephone.

television A broadcast medium that provides visual, aural, and motion communication possibilities.

terms of sale The terms agreed upon governing payment, invoice dating, and discounts.

testimonial An opinion given by the endorser of a product for the purpose of persuading others to use the product.

total cost of merchandise sold The **cost of merchandise sold** after adjustment for **net alteration costs** and **cash discounts** earned, when they exist.

total merchandise handled The sum of the beginning inventory plus purchases. It must be calculated at cost and, if the **retail inventory method** is used, at retail also.

total product concept The tangible item combined with the whole set of services that accompany it when it is sold to the consumer.

tracer A person in the receiving and marking area and traffic department who traces delayed or lost shipments of incoming merchandise and lost deliveries to customers.

trade discount A discount allowed only to certain classes of buyers, such as jobbers or other middlemen, and in some cases to retailers. Such discounts are deductible, no matter when the invoice is paid. It is synonymous with **functional discount.**

trademark Any word, name, symbol, device, or any combination of these adopted and used by a manufacturer or merchant to identify goods and distinguish them from those manufactured or sold by others. It is, thus, a **brand** name used on goods moving in the channels of trade.

trading area The surrounding area from which most of the store's trade is drawn.

trading area overlay A transparent plastic sheet on which a store's trading area is plotted. This sheet is then placed over a map to spot the geographical area for that store.

trading up A legitimate business activity in which a salesperson attempts to interest prospects or customers in goods of higher price that the salesperson feels can be shown to provide superior benefits.

traffic The number of persons who enter or pass by a store or a department within a store.

training The acquisition of basic skills and knowledge required in performing one's job.

transactions per square foot A figure obtained by dividing the number of gross transactions of sales checks for a department by the average number of square feet of selling space the department occupies.

tranfer in A purchase from another department or another unit of a chain or branch store system rather than from an outside vendor.

transfer out Value of merchandise conveyed to another department or unit of a **chain** or **branch store** system. It is not a sale in that it is not a source of profit.

transit advertising An advertising medium designed primarily to present the advertiser's message to an audience using public transportation or exposed to vehicles carrying passengers from one point to another.

turnover The total number of times, within a given period, that a stock of goods is sold and replaced.

U

understored The condition that exists when an area has too few stores to meet the needs of the consumer community.

unfair practices acts Laws that establish a floor below which the retail prices of goods may not legally be set. The floor is usually either invoice cost or invoice cost plus a certain modest percent.

unit billing A single statement of the total price, with the list of articles purchased posted on a detachable strip, which the store retains for adjustment purposes.

unit control The analysis and planning of sales and stocks in terms of pieces of merchandise.

unit pricing (1) The practice of pricing all items on a per unit basis. (2) The practice of pricing each item so that the price tag shows the price per unit of weight or volume in the package.

universal product code (UPC) A national, coordinated system of product identification by which a ten-digit number is assigned to every grocery product sold through retail grocery channels in the United States. The UPC is designed so that at the checkout counter an electronic scanner will read the symbol on the product and automatically transmit the information to a computer, which controls the cash register.

upgrading Increasing price lines by offering better quality and assortments in a specific classification of products.

V

value pricing The practice of pricing goods and services according to the value that consumers perceive to be attached to the item or service.

variable costs Operating expenses affected by changes in sales volume, increasing as sales increase and decreasing as sales decrease.

variety store A retail store offering a wide assortment and variety of articles that are mainly relatively low priced.

vendor The party who sells, or agrees to sell, an item or property to which he has title.

vertical integration The acquisition of a company operating at a different level in the channel distribution than the acquiring company (the consumer being considered as the base). It is backward if the acquired company is farther away from the consumer, forward if nearer to the consumer.

visual front An open storefront design that has no vision barrier between the interior and the exterior of the store.

visual merchandising Presenting merchandise to its best selling advantage and for maximum traffic exposure.

voluntary chain A group of stores organized by a wholesaler around a common interest in the goods or services the wholesaler can provide.

W

want-slip system The organized recording by sales clerks of merchandise asked for by customers but not in stock.

warehouse receipt A receipt given by a warehouse firm to the owner of goods that are deposited in the warehouse. These goods may not be withdrawn without surrendering the receipt, so this document can be used as collateral for obtaining loans from financial institutions.

warranty A synonym for **guarantee.**

weeks' supply method A method of planning inventory levels based on using a predetermined number of weeks' supply to achieve a desired stock turnover.

wheel of retailing An explanation of the evolution of retail institutions that is based on the premise that new types of retail firms first appear as low-margin, low-price establishments. They upgrade their facilities and services as time passes and thus require higher margins. Eventually they become high-cost, high-price retailers and are vulnerable to the next low-margin innovator.

white space Space not occupied by print or art in an advertisement.

wholesaler A business concerned with selling to those who buy for resale or industrial use.

width of merchandise offering The assortment factors necessary to meet the demands of the market and to meet competition.

will call Another name applied to **layaway.**

window displays A display in a store window that reflects what the store carries.

work the line To systematically review past sales records and current stock positions, and to project sales estimates for the next sales period in order to determine the amount **open-to-buy** for each merchandise line stated in units and purchase dollars. Then, in consultation with the sales representative, the buyer reviews the current merchandise offerings. Past poor performers and discontinued items are deleted; new, interest generating goods are added and the staple line is reordered. The end product is an order stating the specific quantities being ordered by lot number and size, the price, all **terms** and conditions **of sale,** and specific shipping instructions.

working capital The excess of current assets over current liabilities. It represents the capital immediately available for the continued operation of the business.

X, Y, Z

yellow pages The classified listing and advertising of business firms contained in a telephone book; a print advertising medium.

youth market Everyone under twenty-five years of age.

zone pricing The delivered cost based on factory price plus averaged freight rate for a section or territory to which goods are shipped. This yields the same delivered cost to all retailers located in the zone.

Index